An Historical
Atlas of
Oxfordshire

An Historical Atlas of Oxfordshire

edited by Kate Tiller
and Giles Darkes

OXFORDSHIRE RECORD SOCIETY
(ORS VOLUME 67)

First published in Great Britain 2010
by Oxfordshire Record Society
c/o The Hon Secretary,
Shaun Morley, Tithe Corner, 67 Hill Crescent,
Finstock, Chipping Norton, OX7 3BT

Reprinted with minor corrections 2011

Registered Charity No. 209808

Maps prepared by Angela Wilson of All Terrain Mapping (angela.atm@ntlworld.com)

Copyright © Oxfordshire Record Society and contributors 2010

All rights reserved. No part of this publication may be reproduced,
stored in a retrieval system, or transmitted, in any form or by any means,
electronic, mechanical, photocopying, recording or otherwise,
without the prior permission of the publishers.

British Library Cataloguing in Publication Data
A catalogue record for this book is available from the British Library

ISBN (paperback) 978 0 902509 63 4
ISBN (casebound) 978 0 902509 68 9

Designed and typeset by Simon Haviland
Printed and bound in Great Britain by Information Press, Eynsham, Oxford

Contents

Foreword *Tim Stevenson, Lord Lieutenant of Oxfordshire* — vii
Preface *William Whyte, General Editor, Oxfordshire Record Society* — viii
Introduction *Kate Tiller* — ix
List of Contributors — xi

Ecclesiastical Parishes *c.*1850 — 2–3
Civil Parishes 1933 — 4–5

1. Topography *Giles Darkes* — 6
2. Geology *Philip Powell* — 8
3. Prehistoric Oxfordshire *Gary Lock* — 10
4. Iron Age Oxfordshire *Alex Lang* — 14
5. Roman Oxfordshire *Paul Booth* — 16
6. Early Anglo-Saxon Settlement *Anne Dodd* — 18
7. Yarnton: Late Saxon Rural Settlement *Anne Dodd* — 20
8. Place-Name Patterns *Anne Cole* — 22
9. The Anglo-Saxon Minsters *John Blair* — 26
10. Communications and Urban Origins before 1066 *John Blair* — 28
11. Bampton: a Minster-Town *John Blair* — 30
12. Domesday Landholdings and Settlement *Mark Page* — 32
13. Domesday Landscape and Land Use *Mark Page* — 34
14. Castles and Moated Sites *James Bond* — 36
15. Medieval Towns, Markets and Fairs *Robert Peberdy* — 38
16. Medieval Wool and Cloth Trades *Robert Peberdy* — 40
17. The Development of Parishes *Elizabeth Gemmill* — 42
18. Vicarages and Appropriated Church Livings *Simon Townley* — 44
19. Religious Houses *James Bond* — 46
20. Medieval Forests and Parks *Stephen Mileson* — 48
21. Late Medieval Communications *Robert Peberdy* — 50
22. Wealth and Population in 1334 and 1524 *Simon Townley* — 52
23. Deserted and Shrunken Settlements *Stephen Mileson* — 56
24. Medieval Chantries and Hospitals *Diana Wood* — 58
25. University and College Properties before 1500 *Ralph Evans* — 62
26. Pottery and Potters *Maureen Mellor* — 64
27. Medieval Vernacular Buildings *David Clark* — 66
28. Medieval Watermills *James Bond* — 68
29. Oxford before 1800 *Alan Crossley* — 70
30. Agriculture and Farming Regions 1500–1700 *Mark Page* — 76
31. Early Modern Market Towns *Adrienne Rosen* — 78
32. The Dissolution of the Monasteries *Adrienne Rosen* — 80
33. Tudor Rebellions *Adrienne Rosen* — 82
34. Roman Catholic Recusants 1558–1800 *Mary Hodges* — 84
35. Early Protestant Nonconformity *Mary Clapinson* — 86

CONTENTS

36. Elites and Office-holders: mid 17th Century   *Vivienne Larminie*   88
37. Early Modern Shops and Shopkeepers   *Kate Tiller*   90
38. The Great Rebuilding   *Malcolm Airs*   92
39. Civil War 1642–1649   *Kate Tiller*   94
40. Country Houses 1500–1670   *Geoffrey Tyack*   96
41. Country Houses 1670–1815   *Geoffrey Tyack*   98
42. Schools in the 18th Century   *Geoffrey Stevenson*   100
43. Roads in the 18th and 19th Centuries   *Barrie Trinder*   102
44. Rivers and Canals   *Barrie Trinder*   104
45. Towns 1700–1900: Nodality, Growth and Decay   *James Bond*   106
46. Railways   *Barrie Trinder*   108
47. Agriculture 1750–1970   *Kate Tiller*   110
48. Parliamentary Enclosure 1758–1882   *Keith Parry*   114
49. Labouring Lives   *Kate Tiller*   116
50. Industrial Oxfordshire: the mid 19th Century   *Barrie Trinder*   118
51. Proto-Industries of 19th-Century Oxfordshire   *Barrie Trinder*   120
52. Brewing and Malting   *John Rhodes*   122
53. Country Houses 1815–1939   *Geoffrey Tyack*   124
54. Parliamentary Representation   *Philip Salmon*   126
55. Education in the 19th Century: Elementary Schools   *Kate Tiller*   128
56. Education in the 19th Century: the Private Sector   *Kate Tiller*   130
57. The Church of England in 1835   *Mark Smith*   132
58. Church and Chapel in 1851   *Kate Tiller*   134
59. Population Change 1801–1851   *James Nash*   136
60. Population Change 1851–1901   *James Nash*   138
61. Migration Patterns 1851–1901   *James Nash*   140
62. Friendly Societies   *Shaun Morley*   142
63. Poor Relief 1834–1948   *Chris Gilliam and Kate Tiller*   144
64. The Growth and Impact of Oxford after 1800   *Malcolm Graham*   146
65. The Motor Industry   *Malcolm Graham*   148
66. Local Government in the 19th and 20th Centuries   *Chris Gilliam*   150
67. Housing and Urban Renewal: Oxford 1918–1985   *Alan Crosby*   152
68. The Second World War   *Malcolm Graham*   154
69. The Cold War   *Trevor Rowley*   156
70. Town and Country Planning in the 20th Century   *Liam Tiller*   158
71. Education in the 20th Century   *William Whyte*   160
72. Religion in the 20th Century   *William Whyte*   162
73. Maternal and Infant Welfare in the 20th Century   *Angela Davis*   164
74. Tourism   *Mike Breakell*   166

Notes and Further Reading   168
Index   179

Foreword

One of the great pleasures of being Lord Lieutenant is the chance of getting to know Oxfordshire even better. From the rural calm of the Cotswolds, to the busy streets of Oxford; from ancient monuments to hi-tech companies: the 1600 square miles of the county encompass a huge variety of people and places. On every visit I make, I learn something new and discover something different.

Looking through *An Historical Atlas of Oxfordshire* is like taking a tour round the county with a remarkably knowledgeable friend. Every page yields some new insight or reveals a new fact. It is full of fascinating details. As a whole it suggests key patterns of change and continuity in the county. Having read it, I will never see Oxfordshire in quite the same light again. Certainly, I feel I now know it even better than I could ever have imagined before.

Anyone who loves Oxfordshire, and all those who have any connection with the county, owe Dr Kate Tiller and her contributors a real debt of gratitude. This has clearly been a labour of love – and it was work well worth doing. I should also like to pay tribute to the Oxfordshire Record Society, under whose auspices this atlas has been published.

As Lord Lieutenant, I am delighted to see that Oxfordshire – like so many of its neighbouring counties – now has an historical atlas of its own. I commend it to you.

TIM STEVENSON
Lord Lieutenant of Oxfordshire
President, Oxfordshire Record Society

Preface

On 24 January 1919, the *Oxford Chronicle* carried a report on the first meeting of a new society. Squeezed in between articles on the Bishop of Oxford's pointed enquiry 'WILL GERMANY REPENT?' and the novelist Hugh Walpole's views on the recent Russian Revolution, there came an account of the inaugural assembly of the Oxfordshire Record Society. Two days earlier, with the historian Ernest Barker in the chair, a gathering of the great and the good and the simply antiquarian had met in New College Library to create a body which would yield an 'output . . . so varied that all classes would get something of value and of use. There would be the generally intelligent reader, the technical, historical, and economic student, the teacher of history and geography in schools, including the elementary schools.' The Oxfordshire Record Society has been publishing ever since. Indeed, this is its sixty-seventh volume.

The Society has produced books on all manner of Oxfordshire history – from the medieval to the modern age. Recent volumes include *Oxfordshire Forests 1246–1609*, *The Court Books of New Woodstock 1607–1622* and *The Diocese Books of Samuel Wilberforce 1844–61*. Future volumes are planned to range from nineteenth-century friendly societies to collections of medieval deeds. Never before, however, have we published a book that attempts to cover the whole of the county's history. It is thus no exaggeration to say that the *Historical Atlas of Oxfordshire* is the most ambitious project ever undertaken by the society. Its achievement would not be possible without the generous financial support of the Greening Lamborn Trust and the Marc Fitch Fund. The expertise of Giles Darkes as cartographical editor, and the work of Simon Haviland in designing and preparing material for final publication, have also been vital in realising the project. The whole endeavour would be unimaginable without the energy, determination, and scholarship of the editor, Dr Kate Tiller. The Society – and all historians of Oxfordshire – will be forever in her debt

The publication of the *Atlas* coincides with the launch of a new website for the Society and a renewed effort to recruit members. If you, or anyone you know, share our interest in the history of the County and want to help us produce an 'output . . . so varied that all classes would get something of value and of use', then do please go to www.oxfordshire-record-society.org.uk. There, you will find more information about the Oxfordshire Record Society and an application form. The modest annual subscription will help us continue our work. Much has changed since 1919, but our commitment to scholarship – and to widening knowledge of the history of Oxfordshire – has not gone away. In future years we intend to do much more.

WILLIAM WHYTE
General Editor, Oxfordshire Record Society

Introduction

This is Oxfordshire's first historical atlas. It joins a well-established genre, a particular and uniquely useful form of county publication. The county historical atlas brings together current knowledge across a notably wide range of subjects. Its format, of short texts and specially prepared maps, distils information and interpretations in an unusually succinct way. It makes research findings accessible. Each entry has its separate message, but the sum of these parts, placed together, can spark questions, awareness and understanding across disciplines (archaeology, history, architecture, historical geography and landscape studies) and across periods. Bringing these perspectives together may point to issues and directions for further research. It helps put particular places into the context of county developments, and shows the county's experience in a wider setting. Thus the county historical atlas has much to offer its readers.

The first county to publish its historical atlas, with multiple contributors producing maps and short, explanatory texts, was Cheshire in 1958. Compiling such a volume is no trivial task, perhaps explaining the gap of 30 years before a second atlas, for Suffolk, appeared in 1988. Since then the momentum has grown, with coverage spreading (in the words of one reviewer) like a 'benign virus'. In 1998 it reached Oxfordshire's borders with publication of the Berkshire atlas, edited by Joan Dils. Several counties have gone to second and even third editions of their atlases. As the particular value of the county historical atlas has become clear so the absence of such a volume for Oxfordshire has become an obvious gap in publications on a county immensely rich in archaeological and historical research and activity. That is the gap we have set out to fill.

The Oxfordshire atlas covers the historic, pre-1974 county. (The Vale of White Horse is included in Berkshire's atlas of 1998.) Entries take the form of a text of up to 1,000 words together with a page with a newly drawn map or maps. A few topics bring together lengthy periods, or combine subjects. These are presented as double entries. All the maps have been prepared on the basis of one of three new base maps of the county: of relief, of ecclesiastical parishes *c.*1850 (providing a framework of historic boundaries before the most major modern changes) and of civil parishes in 1933. The two parish maps are reproduced on pages 2–5, for reference and to help readers wanting to locate in more detail information plotted for separate entries.

The map of ecclesiastical parishes also represents one of the unexpected gains of the Oxfordshire atlas project. It was easy to assume that existing maps would provide us with a complete and consistent picture of the county's ancient parishes, chapelries, townships, detached areas and extra-parochial places. This was not the case and so the map on pages 2–3 represents new work, based principally on Ordnance Survey books of reference, Kain and Oliver's national database of historic boundaries of England and Wales before 1850 (Economic and Social Data Service, University of Essex), the Victoria County History of Oxfordshire and F. A. Youngs, *Local Administrative Units of England*, vol. 1, *Southern England* (Royal Historical Society, 1979). I am grateful to Keith Parry for his painstaking research on these sources and for compiling a gazetteer of Oxfordshire places and the data for our published map.

Other features of the atlas are a section of Notes and Further Reading, underpinning the content of each entry, and providing pointers for readers wanting to find out more. There is a full index to the text, arranged by place, person and subject. This is designed, with the maps, to help readers in pursuit of references to particular places. It also points up some of the recurrent themes that have arisen, often across several entries.

No county is an island, but a county atlas can be in danger of making it look like one. With this in mind, the atlas entries deliberately begin with a wider topographical context, and with the one map in the volume that extends beyond the county 'island'. When defining Oxfordshire's identity it is clear that nothing could be further from an island from the county's creation as a shire in *c.*1007 to its reorganisation to include the Vale of White Horse in 1974. The unit established by the Mercian shiring of the 11th century lacked clear physical boundaries, with the exception of the River Thames in the south and west. Indeed it was historic Oxfordshire's character to share significant features with adjoining counties – the ironstone and limestone uplands of its north and west with Gloucestershire, Warwickshire and Northamptonshire, the clay vales of the centre, and the Chiltern hills and scarp with Berkshire and Buckinghamshire. Within its jurisdictional bounds the county was marked by internal variety rather than topographical unity. In some ways greater physical unity is apparent before 1007 and after 1974, when the new county took on greater physical coherence defined by the basin of the upper Thames and its enclosing uplands, and with Oxford centrally placed at a nodal point on the river system. In the archaeological, pre-1007 entries of the atlas the Thames appears as a gateway and a trading route as much as a barrier or political boundary. All of this may provoke reflection on Oxfordshire's regional as well as county identity. Charles Phythian-Adams has pointed to 'cultural provinces', frames of reference and identity which were culturally meaningful and geographically definable beyond a single county.* He links these to river systems and drainage areas, and finds them expressed over long historical periods in economic links, kin connections, dialects and vernacular architecture. In this pattern Oxfordshire is part of the Thames province, with Berkshire, Buckinghamshire, Hertfordshire, Middlesex and Surrey. Perhaps the overview provided by the atlas will help us reflect on Oxfordshire in both county and regional contexts, and take us beyond recent confusions, where weather forecast areas, central government regions and landscape historians have variously placed Oxfordshire in the midlands (east, west or south), the south-east, or central southern England.

* C. Phythian-Adams, *Societies, Culture and Kinship, 1580–1850: Cultural Provinces and English Local History* (1993), pp. 1–23.

INTRODUCTION

Many entries explain Oxfordshire's historical experience in context. For example, communications have been key at every period and to see the onward destinations of the main pre-Conquest routes through the county, or how local canals and waterways linked to an emerging national system *c.*1800, is essential to understanding what was happening in the county. Although the battle of Edgehill took place just over Oxfordshire's northern boundary it was vital to the county's experience of the Civil War. It would be misleading not to mention Harwell in an account of the Cold War and Oxford and Oxfordshire. So, always centring on Oxfordshire, it has been the editorial approach to allow occasional neighbouring features on to the maps where they are essential to the material presented.

The maps reveal many differences of experience between areas of the county. Some, like the four major farming zones of Oxfordshire, recur across the centuries and can be related to geology, soils and topography. However the texts show that geographical factors alone seldom determine the whole story. For example, the accounts of the varying pace of agricultural change or the importance of enclosure suggest other factors at work. With so many topics brought together it is possible to compare distributions, revealing some shared contrasts between the north and west of the county on the one hand and the south and east on the other. Why, for example, do 17th-century Nonconformists and 19th-century friendly societies flourish more in north and west Oxfordshire than in the south and east? How may this relate to underlying and long-term patterns of settlement and population, wealth and social structure? Many of these historical perspectives have been based on analysis of documentary sources covering the whole county. Data for archaeological and architectural topics typically has less full or even coverage, the mapped distributions inevitably reflecting finds, excavation and other field investigations to date. As discussed in several entries, the archaeological picture of Oxfordshire is particularly full for the Thames valley and its tributaries, where river gravels have preserved rich evidence, which have attracted intensive attention from archaeologists, including early aerial photography, and where gravel extraction and quarrying have thrown up some spectacular sites and finds. The atlas seeks to summarise evidence from all parts of the county, but it may also point to areas where future fieldwork could fill out and balance the picture.

I began by reflecting on the potential values of the county historical atlas. Now we have such a volume for Oxfordshire it is for the readers to test it in use. I look forward to reactions and perhaps, in due course, to considering updates, additional topics, more case studies (of which a few have been used so far) or other ideas for a second edition. For now it is important to acknowledge all those who have contributed to the present volume.

A project of this complexity would never have come to fruition without the help, talents and goodwill of many people. I am delighted to have the chance to thank them publicly. It has been both a pleasure and a challenge to bring together such a disparate and talented group of contributors. As one of them sympathetically commented, on receiving the improbable news that we were on schedule for publication, the parallel between trying to manage multiple authors and academics and herding cats is spot on. However, in the end it is the variety and range of the texts they have written and the maps they have specified that are the great strength of the volume. Maps were at the centre of the project and we have been immensely lucky to have Giles Darkes as cartographic editor. He has combined precision and imagination, patience and flexibility in great measure to produce large numbers of attractive and informative maps. He has contributed ideas and solutions that have greatly enhanced the atlas as it has developed over more than three years. Angela Wilson has played an invaluable part in creating the final versions for publication. Simon Haviland has done great work in developing the design of the volume, and has grappled with diverse presentations and technical complexities to prepare and see the book through the press. Simon Neal's extensive index will be a great help to readers in realising the full range of the volume.

Throughout the project Professor Robert Evans, Chairman, and the Council of the Oxfordshire Record Society have remained steadfast supporters of the concept of the atlas and have been its main financial supporters. The Greening Lamborn Trust and Marc Fitch Fund have made generous grants to support the publication. The General Editor of ORS, William Whyte, has joined me in final proofreading and has contributed two entries of his own. John Leighfield rapidly produced a fine copy of Saxton's 1574 map from his collection of historic maps of Oxfordshire and has kindly allowed us to use it on the book cover, alongside our own, early 21st-century maps.

This has been a collective effort from a large number of people. I thank them all, and hope that the result fills a gap in publications on Oxfordshire history and will prove a useful and continuing reference for those in the county and beyond.

KATE TILLER
Editor

List of Contributors

Malcolm Airs, MA, DPhil, FSA, FRHistS, IHBC
Director of the Centre for the Historic Environment, Kellogg College, University of Oxford

John Blair, MA, DPhil, FBA, FSA
Fellow and Praelector in History, The Queen's College, Oxford

James Bond, BA, FSA, MIFA
Freelance Landscape Archaeologist, based in Walton-in-Gordano, North Somerset

Paul Booth, BA, FSA, MIFA
Senior Project Manager, Oxford Archaeology

Mike Breakell BA, MS, MRTPI
Associate lecturer at Oxford and Oxford Brookes Universities

Mary Clapinson MA, FSA
Senior Research Fellow, St Hugh's College, Oxford

David Clark BSc, MSc, FSA, FSA Scot
Secretary, Oxfordshire Buildings Record

Ann Cole, MA, DPhil
Writer on place-names, and part-time Tutor, Department for Continuing Education, University of Oxford

Alan G. Crosby, MA, DPhil, FRHistS
Honorary Research Fellow at the Universities of Liverpool and Lancaster

Alan Crossley, MA, FSA
Former County Editor, Victoria County History of Oxford

Giles Darkes, BSc, MPhil, FRGS
Cartographic editor and lecturer in cartography

Angela Davis, BA, MSt, DPhil
British Academy Postdoctoral Fellow, Department of History, University of Warwick

Anne Dodd, BA, FSA
Head of Post-Excavation, Oxford Archaeology

Ralph Evans, BA
Former Assistant Editor, The History of the University of Oxford

Elizabeth Gemmill, BA, PhD
University Lecturer in Local History, Department for Continuing Education, University of Oxford

Chris Gilliam
Archivist, Oxfordshire Record Office

Malcolm Graham, MA, PhD, FSA, MCLIP
Former Head of Oxfordshire Studies, Oxfordshire County Council

Mary Hodges, BA, FSA
Former Principal Lecturer, Oxford Brookes University, and lecturer, Department for Continuing Education, University of Oxford

Alexander Lang, BA, MPhil, DPhil
St Edmund Hall, University of Oxford

Vivienne Larminie, PhD, FRHistS
Research Fellow, History of Parliament Trust

Gary Lock, BA (Hons), MA, PhD, MIFA, FSA
Professor of Archaeology, Department for Continuing Education and School of Archaeology, University of Oxford

LIST OF CONTRIBUTORS

Maureen Mellor, FSA
Part-time Tutor, Department for Continuing Education, University of Oxford, and Council member, Society for Medieval Archaeology

Stephen Mileson, DPhil, FRHistS
Assistant Editor, Victoria County History of Oxfordshire, and Lecturer at St Edmund Hall, Oxford

Shaun Morley, MSc
Freelance Local History Tutor and Honorary Secretary of Oxfordshire Record Society

James Nash, DPhil

Mark Page, BA, DPhil
Assistant Editor, Victoria County History of Oxfordshire

Keith Parry, BSc, MSc, PhD, MSc
Independent researcher, formerly research scientist and manager, Syngenta

Robert Peberdy, MA, PhD
Assistant Editor, Victoria County History of Oxfordshire

H. Philip Powell
Honorary Associate Curator, Oxford University Museum of Natural History

John Rhodes, MA, FSA
Freelance historian, Oxford

Adrienne Rosen, MA, DPhil
Departmental Lecturer in Local and Social History, Department for Continuing Education, University of Oxford

Trevor Rowley, MA, MLitt, FSA, MIFA
Emeritus Fellow of Kellogg College, Oxford

Philip Salmon, PhD, FRHistS
Editor, History of Parliament, www.histparl.ac.uk

Mark Smith, MA, DPhil, FRHistS
University Lecturer in Local and Social History, University of Oxford

Geoffrey Stevenson, MA
Former Principal Lecturer in Education, Oxford Polytechnic

Kate Tiller, MA, PhD, FSA, FRHistS, DL
Reader Emerita in English Local History, University of Oxford, a Fellow of Kellogg College, and Visiting Fellow, Centre for English Local History, University of Leicester

Liam Tiller, BSocSc (Geog)
Oxfordshire County Council's Chief Planning and Development Officer 1986–96

Simon Townley, MA, DPhil
County Editor, Victoria County History of Oxfordshire

Barrie Trinder, MA, PhD, FSA
Writer on social and industrial history

Geoffrey Tyack, MA, MLitt, PhD, FSA, FRHistS
Fellow of Kellogg College, Oxford, and Director, Stanford University Centre in Oxford

William Whyte, MA, MSt, DPhil, FRHistS
Fellow and Tutor in History, St John's College, Oxford

Diana Wood, BA, PhD, FRHistS
Part-time tutor and former Director of the Oxford Undergraduate Diploma in Local History, Department for Continuing Education, University of Oxford

An Historical Atlas of Oxfordshire

Ecclesiastical Parishes c.1850

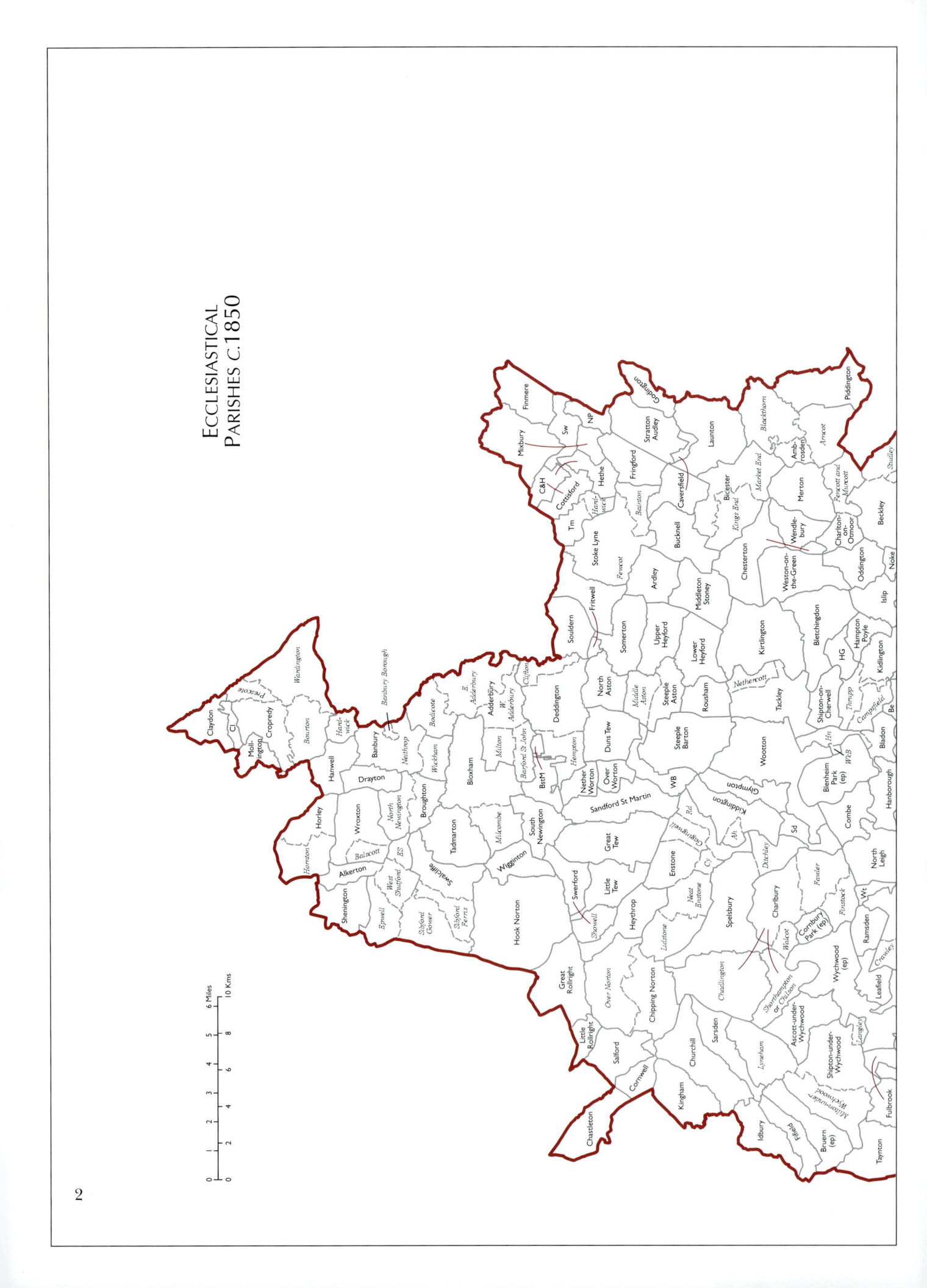

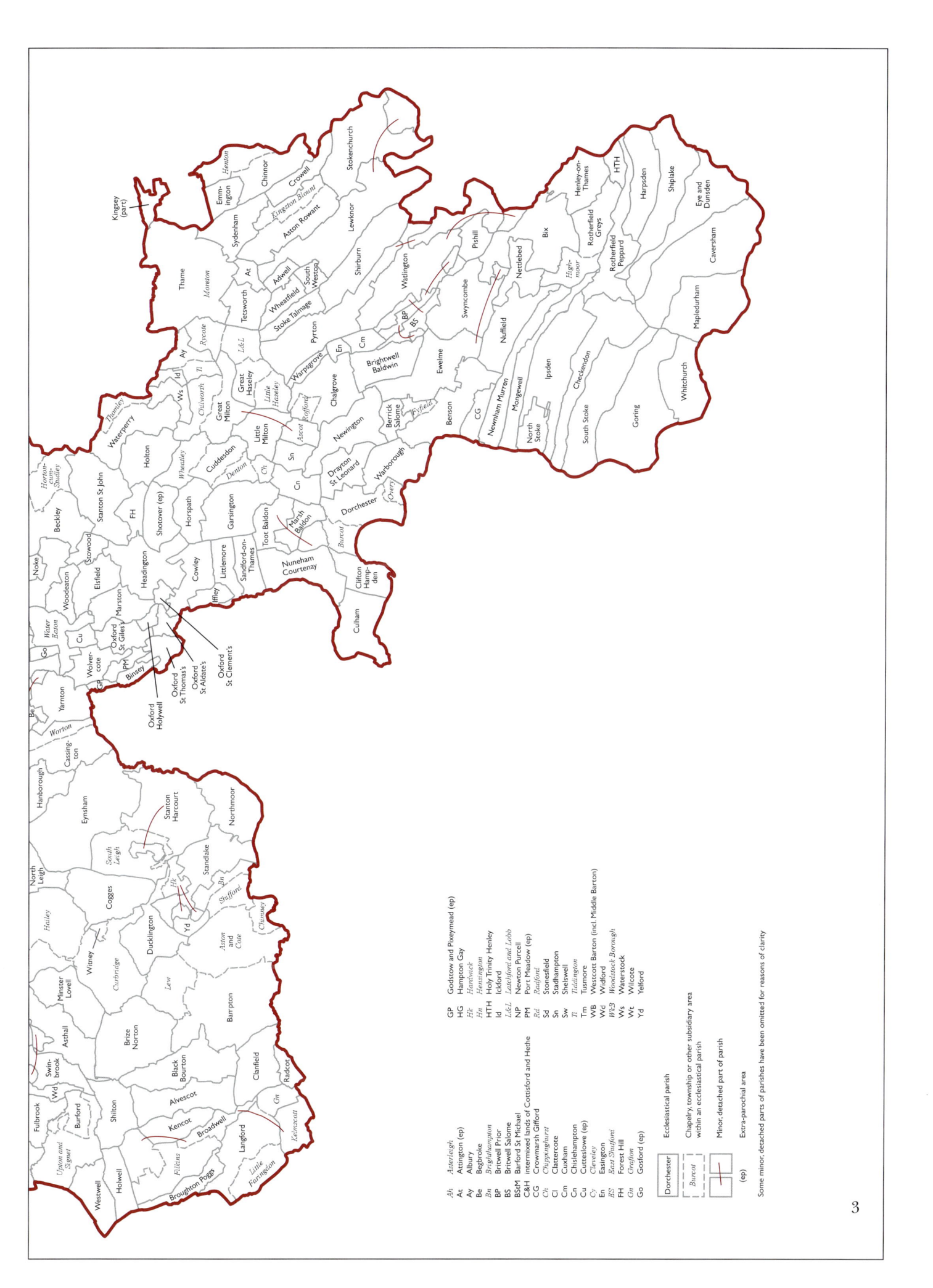

Ah	Asterleigh
At	Attington (ep)
Ay	Albury
Be	Begbroke
Bn	Brighthampton
BP	Britwell Prior
BS	Britwell Salome
BSM	Barford St Michael
C&H	intermixed lands of Cottisford and Hethe
CG	Crowmarsh Gifford
Ch	Chippinghurst
Cl	Clattercote
Cm	Cuxham
Cn	Chislehampton
Cu	Cutteslowe (ep)
Cy	Cleveley
En	Easington
ES	East Shefford
FH	Forest Hill
Gn	Grafton
Go	Gosford (ep)
GP	Godstow and Pixeymead (ep)
HG	Hampton Gay
Hk	Hardwick
Hn	Hensington
HTH	Holy Trinity Henley
Id	Ickford
L&L	Latchford and Lobb
NP	Newton Purcell
PM	Port Meadow (ep)
Rd	Radford
Sd	Stonesfield
Sn	Stadhampton
Sw	Shelswell
Tl	Tiddington
Tm	Tusmore
WB	Westcott Barton (incl. Middle Barton)
Wd	Widford
WcB	Woodstock Borough
Ws	Waterstock
Wt	Wilcote
Yd	Yelford

Legend:
- Dorchester — Ecclesiastical parish
- Burcot — Chapelry, township or other subsidiary area within an ecclesiastical parish
- Minor, detached part of parish
- (ep) — Extra-parochial area

Some minor, detached parts of parishes have been omitted for reasons of clarity

3

Civil Parishes 1933

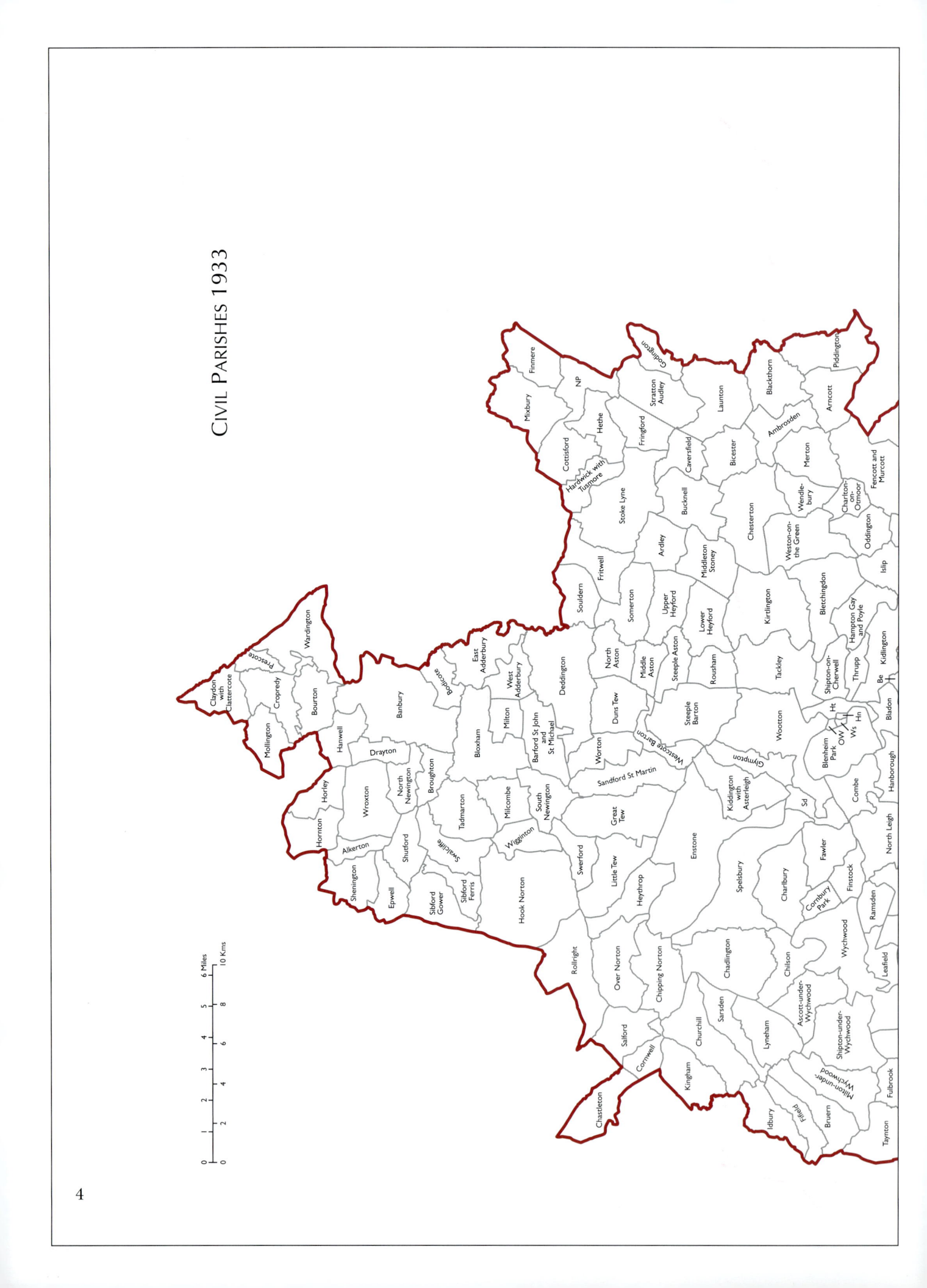

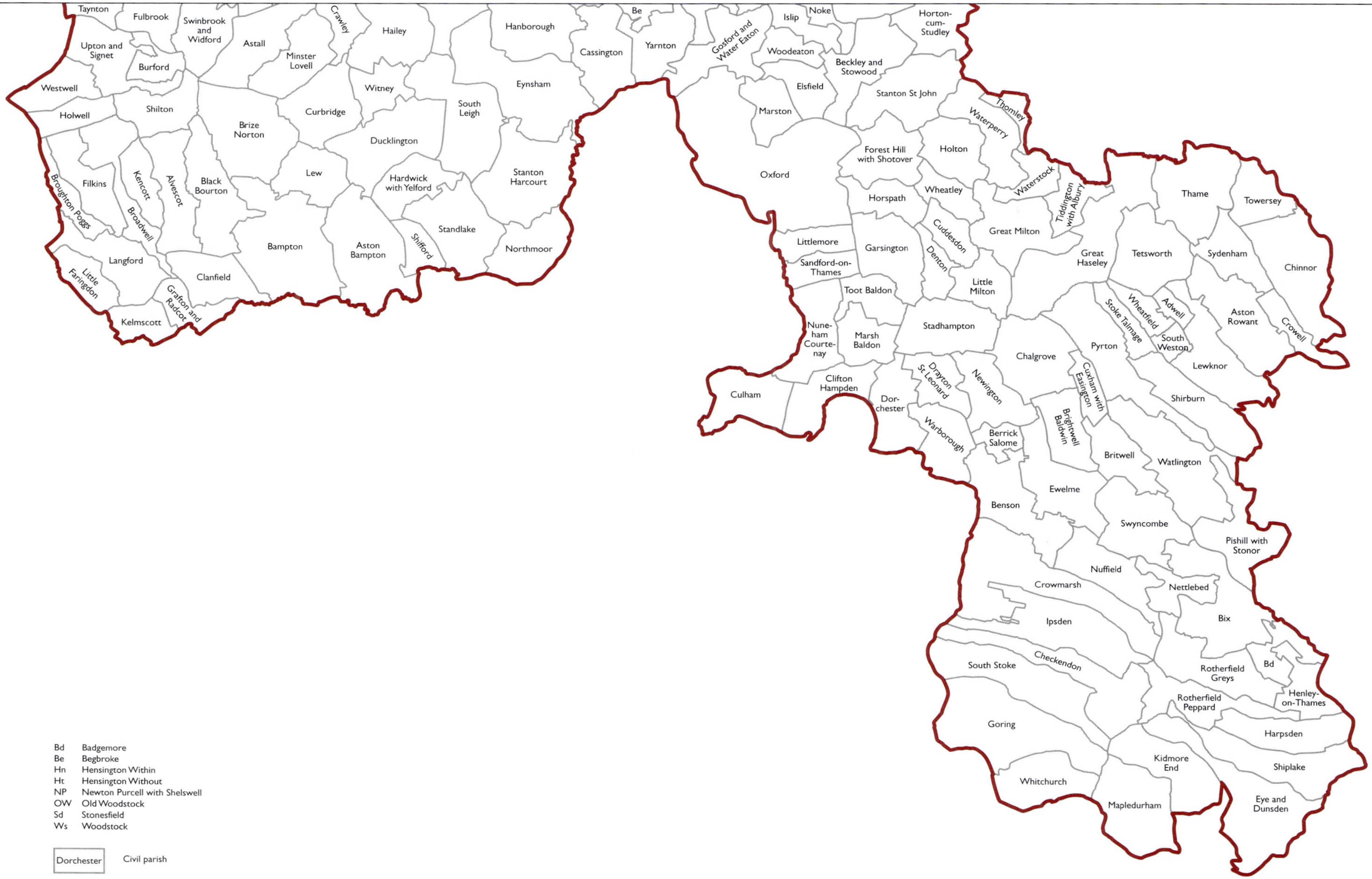

Bd	Badgemore
Be	Begbroke
Hn	Hensington Within
Ht	Hensington Without
NP	Newton Purcell with Shelswell
OW	Old Woodstock
Sd	Stonesfield
Ws	Woodstock

Dorchester — Civil parish

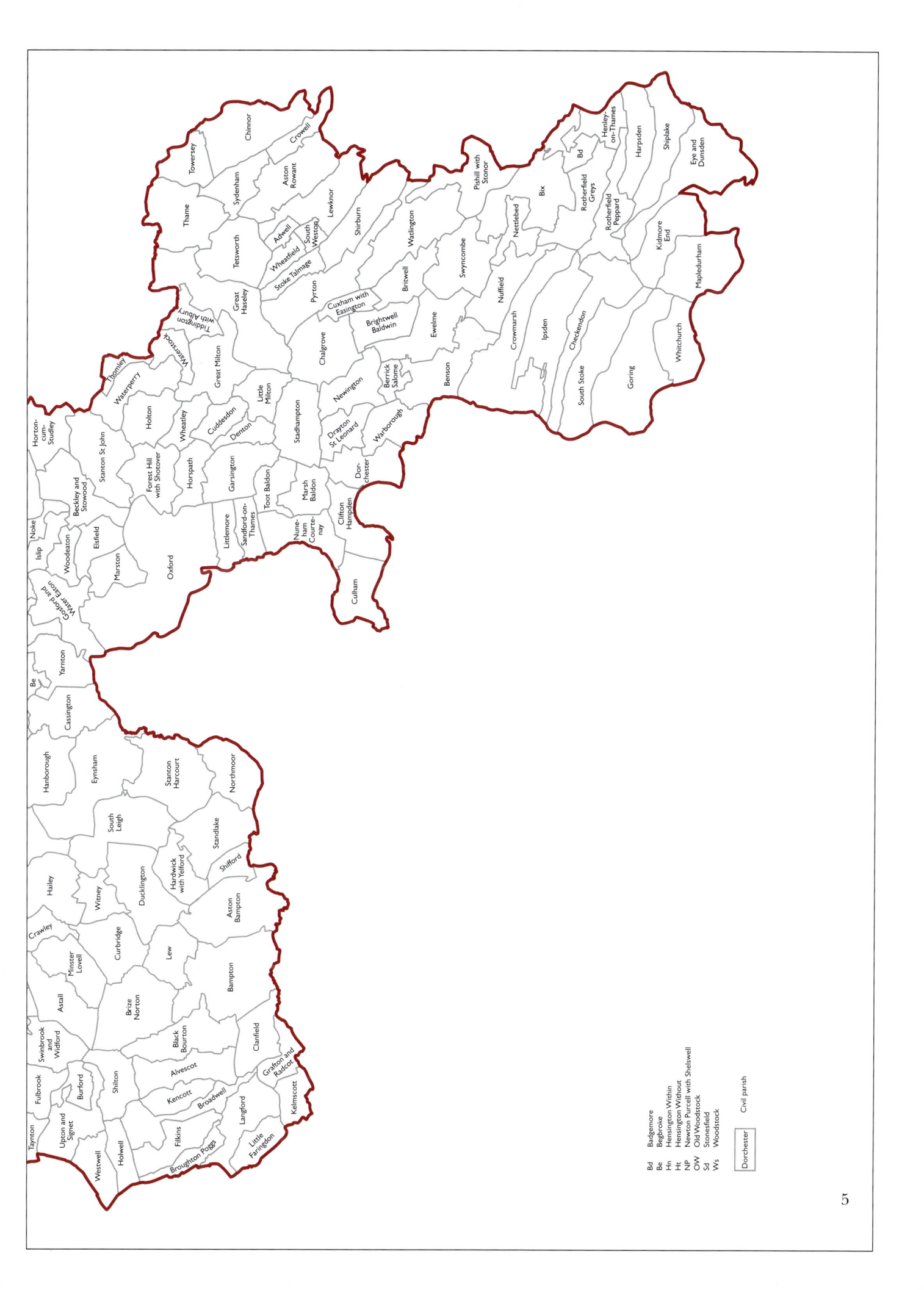

1 · Topography

Giles Darkes

The historic county of Oxfordshire occupies an area of approximately 193,990 ha (749 square miles) in mid-southern England. The county's maximum extent is about 80 km (50 miles) from Hornton in the north-west to Caversham in the south-east, whilst at its narrowest point it is only some 11 km (seven miles) between Oxford and the border with Buckinghamshire near Waterperry.

Lacking any natural physical boundaries other than the River Thames, it shares geomorphological and landscape characteristics with the counties which adjoin it. In some senses it is a transition county, showing aspects of landscape that are found more typically in adjacent areas: the limestone hills of the Cotswolds are predominantly in Gloucestershire and the chalk of the Chiltern Hills in Buckinghamshire, whilst the midland landscape begins properly in adjacent Warwickshire. As elsewhere, the topography of the county has historically influenced the position of lines of communication, as well as settlement patterns.

The natural topography of the county is orientated south-west to north-east, and divides into three predominant regions: the hillier landscape of the north Oxfordshire uplands, the broad central plain on which Oxford is sited, and the Chiltern Hills. The natural regions reflect closely the underlying geology (see entry 2). With no mountainous regions, and shaped by periglacial activity in the ice ages, the more hilly parts of the county are typically undulating rather than dramatic. The highest point is Shirburn Hill near Watlington at 255 m (837 feet) and the lowest about 32 m (106 feet) near Henley-on-Thames.

The north-west of the county is an area of upland which extends approximately from Burford to Mollington, north of Banbury. The area has two broad blocks of higher land, separated by the River Evenlode. In both blocks, the land reduces in height towards the south-east and is the tailing slope of a scarp-and-dip system whose scarp slopes lie out of the county. The landscape of the northern block reflects underlying Lias rock, dissected by tributaries of the Cherwell, while further south plateaus occasionally broken by valleys reflect the predominance of Oolitic limestones, typical of the Cotswold Hills. The Oolitic region is broken by the distinctive, broad valleys of the rivers Evenlode and Windrush. High points are on the county boundary at Shenlow Hill, Shenington, north-west of Banbury, at some 227 m (743 feet) and in Salford parish, west of Chipping Norton, where the land rises to 247 m (811 feet).

The central plain of the county lies to the south and east of the Oxfordshire uplands and, founded on Oxford and Gault clays, is much lower and less undulating than the regions which enclose it. The land is typically below 120 m (400 feet), declining gently towards the Thames valley, much of which is lower than 60 m (200 feet). The landscape is relatively flat and contains most of the county's floodlands. The only noteworthy exception to the flatness of the area is the Oxford Heights, a small escarpment, again lying south-west to north-east, which surrounds the city of Oxford and extends into both Berkshire at Cumnor Hill and Buckinghamshire near Brill, incorporating Shotover Hill and the higher area on which Beckley is sited.

The third region of the county is the Chiltern Hills. Oxfordshire contains part of the steep scarp slope of this chalk range, and the change in topography is very apparent when viewed from the central plain. Continuing south-east, the scarp slope reaches a height of 255 m and then changes to the dip slope which declines in height towards the Thames valley between Caversham and Henley-on-Thames. The chalk landscape has many dry valleys and a covering of beech wood, in contrast to the mostly cleared landscapes of the rest of the county.

Oxford receives an average of 643 mm (25.3 inches) of rainfall per year, and the higher ground of the county typically receives about 20% more. The county's rivers mostly drain to the south, as part of the Thames catchment area. North and west of Bicester a rise in the land to the east of Somerton forms a watershed, and streams from that area join the Great Ouse (itself forming the county boundary at Mixbury) at Buckingham and thence drain to the Wash. A few rivers in the north-west drain to the River Avon.

The Thames forms about a third of the county's boundary and is a winding river through much of its course. Its valley widens where it crosses clays, and narrows (as at Goring) where it negotiates gaps in limestone and chalk. It falls from about 73 m (240 feet) at Kelmscott to 32 m (106 feet) at Henley, and around Oxford divides into numerous branches, such is the flatness of the land. The Cherwell drains the centre of the county and is joined by a number of named tributaries from the uplands (including the rivers Sorbrook and Swere) as well as the River Ray to the north-east of Oxford. The rivers Evenlode and Windrush originate to the west of the county and flow in a series of incised meanders through the Cotswold Hills to join the Thames. Also worthy of note are the River Glyme and the River Thame, which drains much of the southern part of the central plain, joining the Thames at Dorchester.

The county's upland areas are characterised by numerous dry valleys and relatively few surface streams. In contrast parts of the central plain flood regularly and extensively. The rivers Thames, Thame, Cherwell, and to some extent Windrush and Evenlode, flood each winter and react rapidly throughout the year to heavy rains in their catchment areas. Hence much of the plain is also floodland (for example, Port Meadow in Oxford). There are no permanent natural lakes of any size, but the slight fall of the River Ray produces the county's only substantial wetland area, where it flows through Otmoor. Glacial meltwater deposited large quantities of waste rock (boulder clay, silts, pebbles, sands and gravels) in terraces across the county, both at high level and in river valleys. Much gravel has been commercially extracted, leaving artificial lakes. Oxfordshire's gravels are a key area for archaeological evidence (see entries 3, 4, 5, 6 and 7).

TOPOGRAPHY

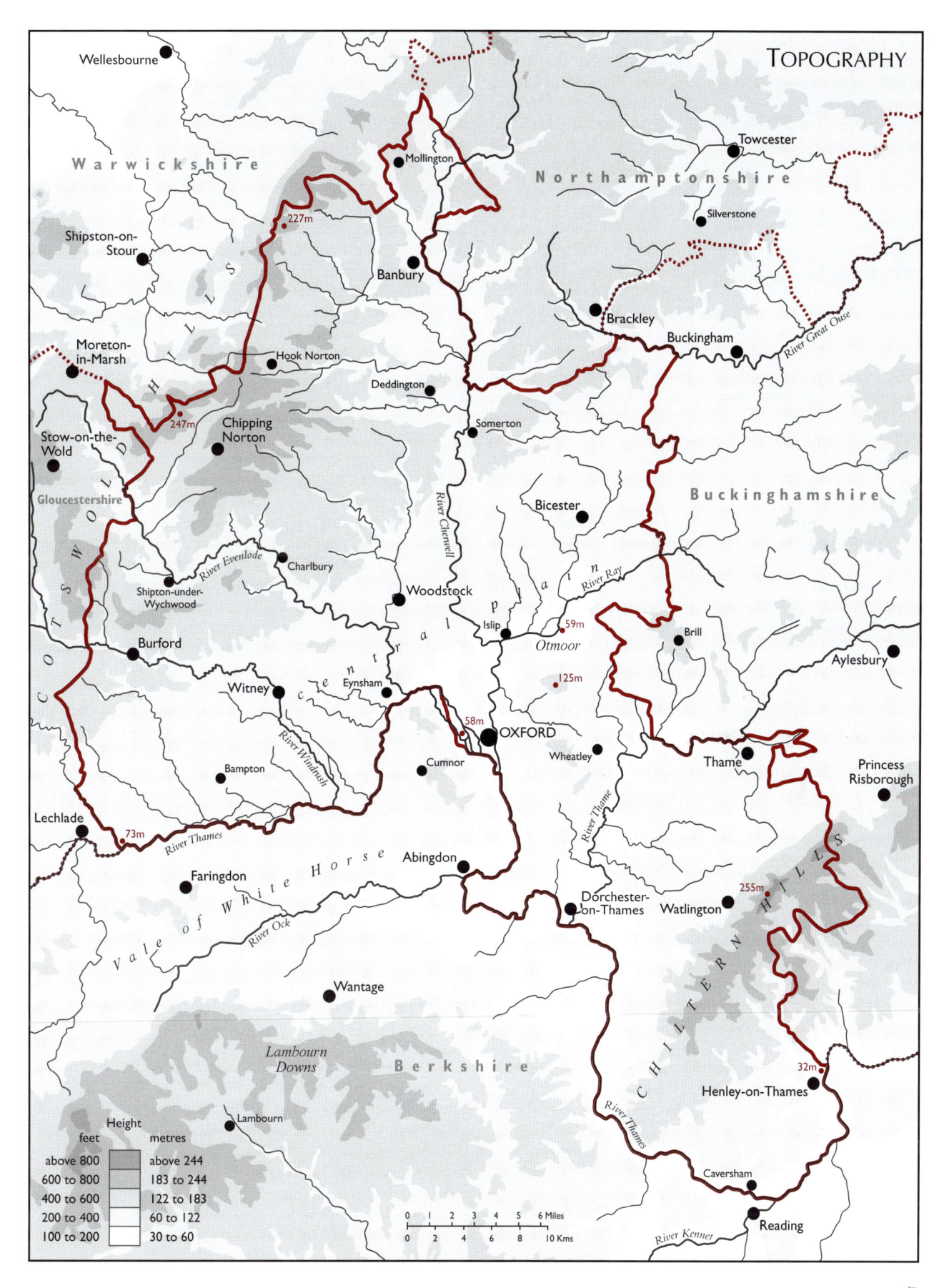

Wellesbourne

Warwickshire

Mollington

Towcester

Northamptonshire

Shipston-on-Stour

227m

Silverstone

Banbury

Brackley

Moreton-in-Marsh

Hook Norton

Buckingham

River Great Ouse

247m

Deddington

Stow-on-the-Wold

Chipping Norton

Gloucestershire

Somerton

Buckinghamshire

River Evenlode

Charlbury

Bicester

Shipton-under-Wychwood

Woodstock

River Cherwell

River Ray

Burford

Islip

59m

Brill

Aylesbury

Otmoor

Witney

c   e   n   t   r   a   l   p   l   a   i   n

125m

Eynsham

58m

Bampton

River Windrush

Cumnor

OXFORD

Wheatley

Thame

Princess Risborough

Lechlade

73m

River Thames

Abingdon

River Thame

Faringdon

Dorchester-on-Thames

255m

River Ock

Watlington

Vale of White Horse

C H I L T E R N   H I L L S

Wantage

32m

Lambourn Downs

Berkshire

Henley-on-Thames

Lambourn

River Thames

Caversham

River Kennet

Reading

Height	
feet	metres
above 800	above 244
600 to 800	183 to 244
400 to 600	122 to 183
200 to 400	60 to 122
100 to 200	30 to 60

0 1 2 3 4 5 6 Miles
0 2 4 6 8 10 Kms

2 · Geology

Philip Powell

The rocks of Oxfordshire include limestones, clays and sandstones that originated as beds of sediment in the seas of the Jurassic and Cretaceous Periods. They form a landscape of clay vales alternating with limestone ridges and uplands, each with its own special character. The rock layers are tilted gently to the south-east, so that the strata at the surface are progressively younger from north-west to south-east.

The oldest strata consist of the Lower Jurassic Lower Lias clay. These outcrop over a small area, mainly around Deddington and Banbury and in the upper valleys of the Evenlode and Cherwell, where they form heavy pasture land. The clay was formerly used for brick-making. The overlying Middle Lias, which forms the hilly country around Banbury, consists of thin sands and an iron-rich limestone known as the Marlstone. Builders refer to the Marlstone as Hornton Stone, and its warm, orange-brown colour gives a distinctive charm to the buildings of this district. Another name – Banbury Ironstone – refers to its former exploitation as iron ore. Above the Marlstone the thin clays of the Upper Lias form narrow outcrops that once supported brick pits.

The Middle Jurassic Inferior Oolite deposits mainly consist of brown sands and thin, rubbly limestones, but also include the limestone quarried in Cornbury Park that was used to build the mansion and much of Blenheim Palace. The overlying Great Oolite Group includes varied limestones, and forms a belt of upland characterised by arable fields and villages built of pale, local stone. At Taynton and Burford high-quality limestone occurs, and this can be seen in buildings across the county and beyond. Elsewhere, other beds provide roofing tiles, notably at Stonesfield.

The Upper Jurassic Oxford Clay forms the valley of the upper Thames and underlies Otmoor and Oxford itself. Its heavy, low-lying soils mainly support pastures. In the 19th century it provided brick clay for the expanding city of Oxford. The sands and limestones of the overlying Corallian Formation form the high ground from Cowley to Beckley. The Corallian limestone at Wheatley and Headington was quarried as freestone for centuries. It has been used in Oxford churches and colleges as well as for prestigious buildings such as Wallingford and Windsor castles.

The younger Kimmeridge Clay forms the bulk of the hilly areas of Forest Hill, Wheatley and the Baldons. Pits at Shotover, Wheatley and Culham once supported brickmaking. The upper part of the formation becomes sandy, indicating the onset of shallowing as sea levels fell near the end of the Jurassic. This is overlain by the Portland beds, consisting mainly of ochreous sands and rubbly limestones. However, around the Miltons and Haseleys the upper part is a pale limestone once much quarried for local buildings. The Purbeck beds, at the top of the Jurassic, occur on Shotover as a thin patch of limestones and clays deposited in coastal lagoons. They herald the retreat of the sea from this region and its emergence as dry land at the end of the Jurassic Period.

The earliest Cretaceous rocks are the river-laid Whitchurch Sands which cap Shotover and the Wheatley–Garsington ridge. On Shotover they include white pipe clay and high quality ochre. Near Wheatley the upper beds are purple sandstone, once dug as iron ore. The overlying Lower Greensand rocks are marine deposits and were laid down around 20 million years later. In their main outcrop, between Nuneham Courtenay and Culham, the sands are brown rather than green. Around Culham the rock is a coarse white grit, which provided stone for querns from Iron Age to mediaeval times.

The younger Gault Clay was deposited during the next major rise in sea level. This grey, silty clay has been used to make bricks which can be seen in many fine houses along the outcrop from Dorchester to Thame. It merges upwards into the Upper Greensand, a fine-grained, pale grey sandstone speckled with green grains of glauconite, a mineral rich in iron and potassium. This rock, known as Malmstone, forms a conspicuous ridge from Roke north-eastwards along the foot of the Chilterns.

The Upper Greensand grades upwards into the Chalk, the familiar soft, white, porous rock that forms the Chiltern scarp and underlies south-eastern Oxfordshire. The formation represents a time when all northern Europe was covered by sea in which calcareous ooze accumulated for more than 40 million years. The Lower Chalk is grey and contains a proportion of clay that makes it suitable for cement manufacture, as at Chinnor. The Middle Chalk is white chalk without flints. It forms the main part of the face of the escarpment. At certain levels it gives rise to springs such as those that feed the watercress beds at Ewelme. The Upper Chalk caps the scarp and forms the dip slope down to the Thames. It contains abundant flints which have been, and still are, an important building material in the area.

About 65 million years ago the sea retreated to leave dry land and erosion began to shape the modern landscape. Shortly afterwards, thin sands and clays of the Reading Beds were deposited in rivers and swamps on top of the Chalk. The patches that remain have long provided material for bricks and tiles, notably at Nettlebed. Sarsens, the hardened remnants of sand deposits, may also date from this time.

The Pleistocene Epoch, which began about two million years ago, was characterised by both glacial and interglacial conditions. Although Oxfordshire was never covered by ice, permafrost extended to considerable depths during glacial periods and erosion was severe. As a result, valley floors were covered with a jumble of ice-shattered fragments and clay, called Head or, in chalk areas, Coombe Rock. Clay-with-flints, a sandy clay mixed with broken flints and sarsen, may have originated during these times as a residue of dissolved Chalk and earlier deposits. The falling sea level in the Pleistocene also allowed rivers to deepen valleys, and resulted in the series of gravel deposits that extend from Wychwood Forest and the top of the Chilterns down to present-day flood plains.

Geology

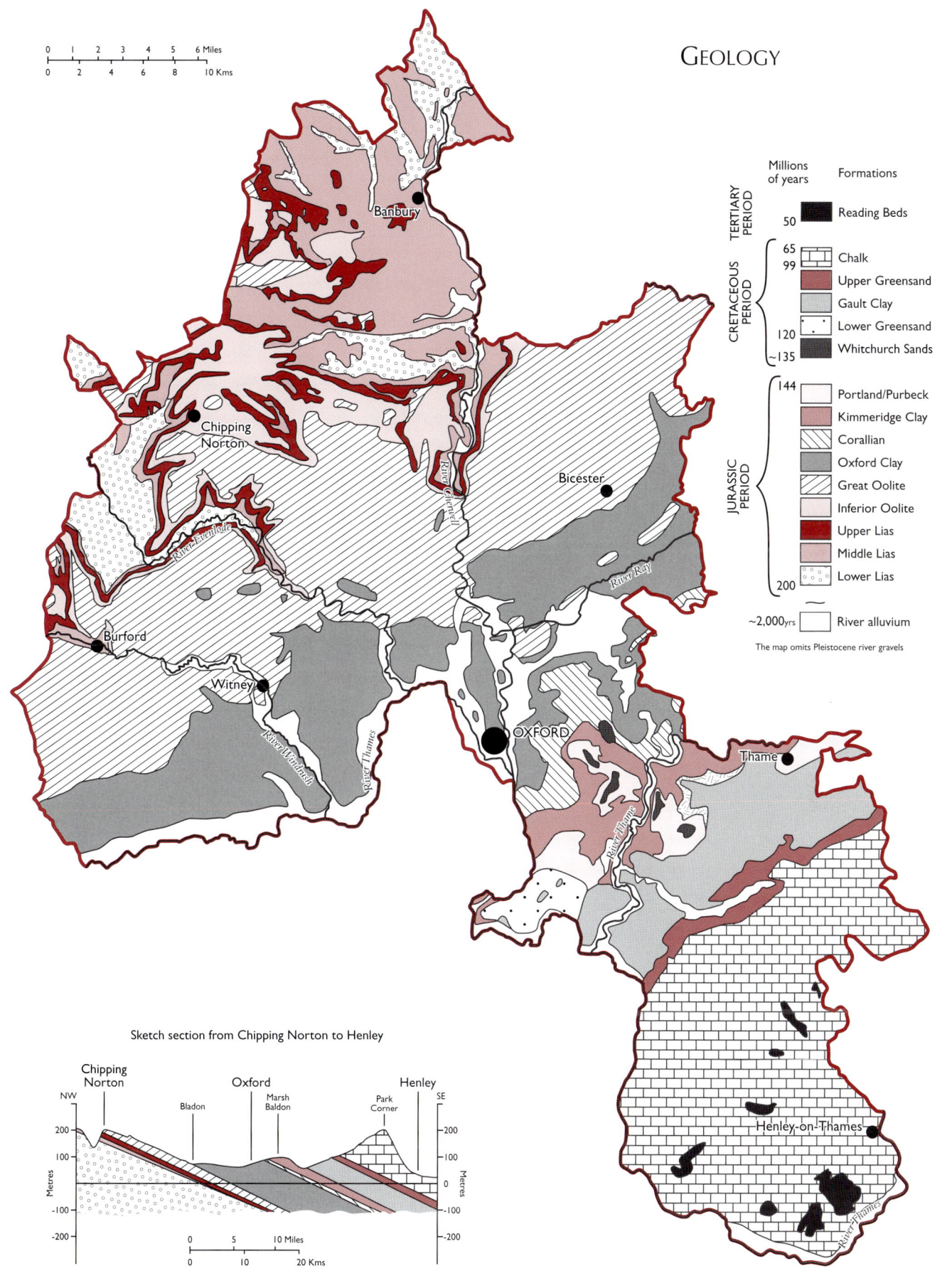

Millions of years		Formations
TERTIARY PERIOD		
50		Reading Beds
CRETACEOUS PERIOD		
65		Chalk
99		Upper Greensand
		Gault Clay
120		Lower Greensand
~135		Whitchurch Sands
JURASSIC PERIOD		
144		Portland/Purbeck
		Kimmeridge Clay
		Corallian
		Oxford Clay
		Great Oolite
		Inferior Oolite
		Upper Lias
		Middle Lias
200		Lower Lias
~2,000 yrs		River alluvium

The map omits Pleistocene river gravels

Sketch section from Chipping Norton to Henley

3 · Prehistoric Oxfordshire — Gary Lock

Palaeolithic The Palaeolithic is immense when compared with other archaeological and historical periods. Oxfordshire, like the rest of Britain, was at that time connected to the continent and saw extreme climatic and environmental change, from interglacials warm enough to support hippopotamus to sub-arctic tundra with roaming woolly mammoth. Although these processes were destructive of landscape and left very little archaeological evidence, the main physical features of the Cotswold limestone hills in the north-west of the county, the chalk downlands of the Chilterns in the south, and the clay vales of the Thames and its tributaries were broadly the same. Lithic sources for the manufacture of stone tools, mainly flint but also quartzite, and animals for food, were probably most important to the small groups of hunter-gatherers who colonised and recolonised central England as the ice sheets advanced and retreated. In the early period these were pre-sapiens hominids and by the middle period Neanderthals, eventually to be replaced by modern humans.

The chronology of the Palaeolithic is complicated by its relationship to the Pleistocene geological epochs, warm and cold phases, and Marine Isotope Stages. The cultural stages, or archaeological sub-periods, are based on stone tool typologies and can be simplified as the early Lower/Middle Palaeolithic ($c.700,000$ to $c.475,000$ BP,* simple cores, choppers and flakes, developing handaxes); the Anglian glaciation, when Britain was probably unoccupied ($c.475,000$ to $c.425,000$ BP); the later Lower/Middle Palaeolithic ($c.425,000$ to $125,000$ BP, later handaxes); the Middle Palaeolithic (or British Mousterian, restricted to $c.60,000$ to $c.40,000$ BP due to limited evidence, fine prepared core flaking and bout coupé handaxes, diagnostic of Neanderthal tool-making); and the Upper Palaeolithic ($c.40,000$ to $10,000$ BP, with sporadic episodes of occupation, various blade-tool industries and tool specialisation such as projectile points and burins).

Within Oxfordshire evidence for these periods is largely restricted to stone tools found in river gravels, often due to quarrying and therefore redeposited material. The Lower/Middle artefacts of the Upper Thames Valley and Cotswolds are mainly quartzite, crude handaxes, cores and flakes, whereas in the area around Oxford and further south more flint is available and was used to produce some finely made artefacts. A series of gravel pits have exposed various palaeo-channels of the early Thames, as at Stanton Harcourt and Wolvercote, some of them producing many hundreds of artefacts over the last hundred years or so. There are very few finds of individual artefacts from the Upper Palaeolithic in Oxfordshire, with a single excavated site at Gatehampton Farm, Goring, being a possible kill/butchery site producing typical 'long blades'.

Mesolithic Nationally the Mesolithic period is divided into early and late (7th to early 4th millennium BC locally), based on lithic typologies and particularly on the characteristic microliths of the later period, although much of the material from Oxfordshire makes this chronological distinction difficult. Limited environmental evidence, for example from Mingies Ditch, shows the increase in tree cover and species as the climate warmed through the period. The riverine distribution of sites suggests that people were moving by boat, exploiting the varied food resources of the rivers and valleys as well as the uplands, a diversity which required an equally diverse toolkit. Much of the Mesolithic evidence remains finds from river gravels together with surface finds. There are a small number of excavated sites in the uplands. At Windmill Hill, Nettlebed, and beneath the Neolithic long barrow at Ascott-under-Wychwood, palimpsest assemblages of tools, including microliths, suggest long periods of repeated visits and a range of subsistence activities, including tool manufacture, working bone, antler or wood, and skin processing. There is no evidence for structures and no human remains from the Palaeolithic or Mesolithic periods in Oxfordshire.

Neolithic and Early Bronze Age The transition to the Neolithic is poorly understood nationally and in Oxfordshire the often ambiguous character of the lithic assemblages reinforces this picture. The archaeological evidence for the established Neolithic comprises a much richer range of artefacts, including various forms of pottery, earthen and megalithic field monuments and sites identified from aerial photography. The Early Bronze Age (EBA), largely Beaker burials, is usually incorporated into any discussion of the Neolithic period, as many late monuments continue in use. Pottery is the main tool for dating, although radiocarbon dates from excavated material provide a more secure framework. For example, the earliest Neolithic dates in Oxfordshire are from midden deposits beneath the chambered tomb at Ascott-under-Wychwood ($c.3,900$ cal BC), and Beaker burials, such as those at Yarnton and Gravelly Guy, are in the range of $c.2,400$ to $1,900$ cal BC.*

The rivers probably remained important routeways through heavily wooded valleys and lowlands, now mixed deciduous woodland, although clearings were important for many of the ceremonial and communal monuments. There is some evidence for hunting. Domesticated cattle, pigs and sheep/goats are evidenced from the earliest Neolithic, along with the cultivation of wheat and barley, and even fragments of charred bread from Yarnton, although no fields are known in Oxfordshire. Excavations due to gravel extraction are of continuing importance, not least at Yarnton, revealing the only Neolithic houses in Oxfordshire. The largest, if a house rather than a communal building, is rectangular and at least 21 by 11 m. Other evidence is ephemeral, surface scatters and excavated pits, sometimes in clusters, suggesting a population of small groups which were mobile rather than permanently settled, perhaps staying in a single place for months at a time.

Despite this, Neolithic people did build considerable communal monuments, perhaps where mobile communities came together at certain times of the year. The longevity and attraction of places for building and reinforcing group identity is well illustrated by the remarkable complex of monuments at Dorchester which, even though most were destroyed by quarrying in the 1940s to 1980s, still

---

* For a note on dating see Notes and Further Reading

PALAEOLITHIC SITES

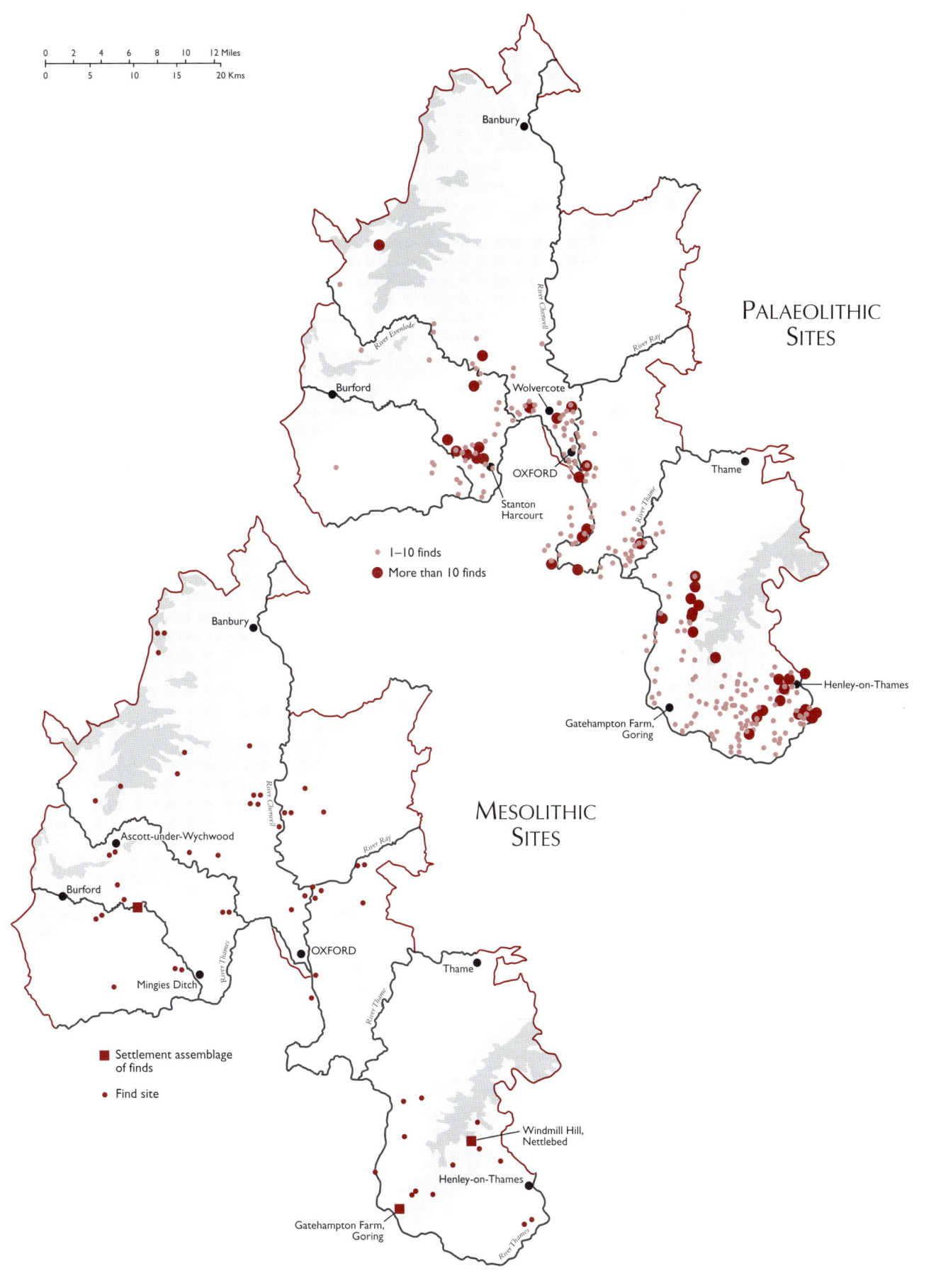

· 1–10 finds
● More than 10 finds

MESOLITHIC SITES

■ Settlement assemblage of finds
· Find site

3 · Prehistoric Oxfordshire (continued)

remain of national importance. This started with two small mortuary enclosures with burials linked around 3,400–3,200 cal BC by a cursus stretching over 1.8 km. This linear ditched enclosure may have been a ceremonial way connecting with and commemorating the dead. Over following centuries a series of ditched enclosures with burials were established around the cursus, culminating in c.2,500 cal BC with the building of the Big Rings henge monument over 200 m in diameter and providing a monumental meeting place. Through the EBA, perhaps c.2,200 to 1,600 cal BC, many round barrows were constructed around the henge, suggesting a continuing linking between the recently dead, the still living and past ancestors.

The main types of ceremonial earthworks are causewayed enclosures and cursuses in the early period and then henges, all most prevalent in valleys, and primarily the Thames valley, whereas the other main monument type, long barrows, is more known on the Cotswold uplands. There is a cluster of causewayed enclosures in the Upper Thames Valley and possibles at Burford and Banbury, close to the rivers Windrush and Cherwell respectively. Other than the Dorchester Big Rings, there are certain henges at the Devil's Quoits, Stanton Harcourt, and Westwell, near Burford, and other smaller possibilities have been identified from aerial photographs.

The earliest burial monuments may be the megalithic portal dolmens. The Whispering Knights at the Rollright Stones are the best example. All other possibilities are on the Cotswold uplands. Of the Cotswold long barrows Ascott-under-Wychwood has been the most thoroughly studied and is early Neolithic. Typical of these structures, it contained the partial remains of many individuals, possibly nearly 50, suggesting exposure and decomposition elsewhere. Recent statistical analysis of radiocarbon dates suggests a time span for the burials of perhaps only a few generations. The other well-known megalithic structures are stone circles, probably also some form of ceremonial communal place. One was built within the henge monument at the Devil's Quoits. The only other in Oxfordshire is the Rollright Stones. If stone was not readily available, then timber circles were built; recently discovered and excavated examples are at Dorchester and Gravelly Guy.

Once into the EBA the main funerary monuments are round barrows, many of which are known in Oxfordshire, either extant, mainly in upland areas, or as ploughed-out ring ditches, often in valleys and lowland areas and discovered by aerial photography, such as those in the University Parks, Oxford. These occur as single monuments, in small groups or often as barrow cemeteries. Grave goods are more common within EBA burials, good examples being from Dorchester and Stanton Harcourt. They include the distinctive Beaker pottery, the first metal objects and a range of artefacts, sometimes demonstrating long-distance contacts, although connections are also evident in the Neolithic through exotic artefacts such as polished stone axes. Beaker burials also occur in graves not covered by a barrow, so-called flat graves, as at Eynsham, Yarnton and Oxford.

Later Bronze Age The Middle and Late Bronze Age – starting c.1,500 and 1,000 cal BC respectively and sometimes together called the Later Bronze Age (LBA) – sees a shift of focus from funerary and ceremonial monuments to the organisation of agricultural and domestic landscapes with permanent settlements and associated field systems. This intensification of land use probably reflects increasing population, and aspects of the archaeological evidence continue into and through the following Iron Age period (starting c.8th century; see entry 4). The chronology of the LBA is based on bronze artefact and pottery typologies. Many hoards and individual artefacts are found within rivers, especially in the later part of the period, and probably represent votive deposits. Radiocarbon dating continues to be of importance. Because of the visibility of ploughed-out ditches on aerial photographs, the evidence for LBA settlement is heavily biased towards the Thames corridor, where many decades of photography and mapping have produced detailed later prehistoric landscapes, although differentiating between LBA and Iron Age features can be difficult. Commercial excavation in advance of quarrying continues to produce information about Bronze Age settlement and economy. Evidence for this period is sparse for the upland areas of the Cotswolds and Chilterns and patterns of settlement are poorly understood there.

Systematic field layouts are known from other parts of central England from the Middle Bronze Age, although in the Thames valley they may have developed at various times through the Bronze Age. Early ones have been suggested around Dorchester, possibly continuing to focus on earlier monuments. Elsewhere, environmental evidence suggests increasing stock raising and pasture, as at Berinsfield and Stanton Harcourt. Environmental evidence from Mingies Ditch and Gravelly Guy shows LBA woodland clearance on the gravel terraces and the establishment of open grassland. As with earlier periods, excavations at Yarnton, and nearby Cassington, are important, with groups of roundhouses on the floodplain perhaps representing extended family groups, some of which may be contemporary with trackways, with possible wheel ruts, water holes and also early evidence for the use of spelt wheat. At Cassington West there are 12 LBA roundhouses, together with groups of rectangular, four-post buildings, another type of structure that continued through the Iron Age. These large-scale excavations also show the relationship between LBA and Iron Age sites, with the latter shifting from the floodplain to a gravel terrace just a few hundred metres away.

Overall, the LBA saw agricultural intensification and increasingly well-organised and established settlements, focused on the Thames as an important routeway. A settlement near Wallingford has been interpreted as a possible entrepot for goods arriving by boat and there is evidence to suggest that the middle Thames to the south was an area with higher status settlements linked into wider bronze trading networks. In Oxfordshire the development of field systems and permanent settlements, both open and enclosed by a bank and ditch and with roundhouses, happened at different times through the LBA in different areas. It established the landscape and the social and economic foundations for the following Iron Age.

NEOLITHIC SITES

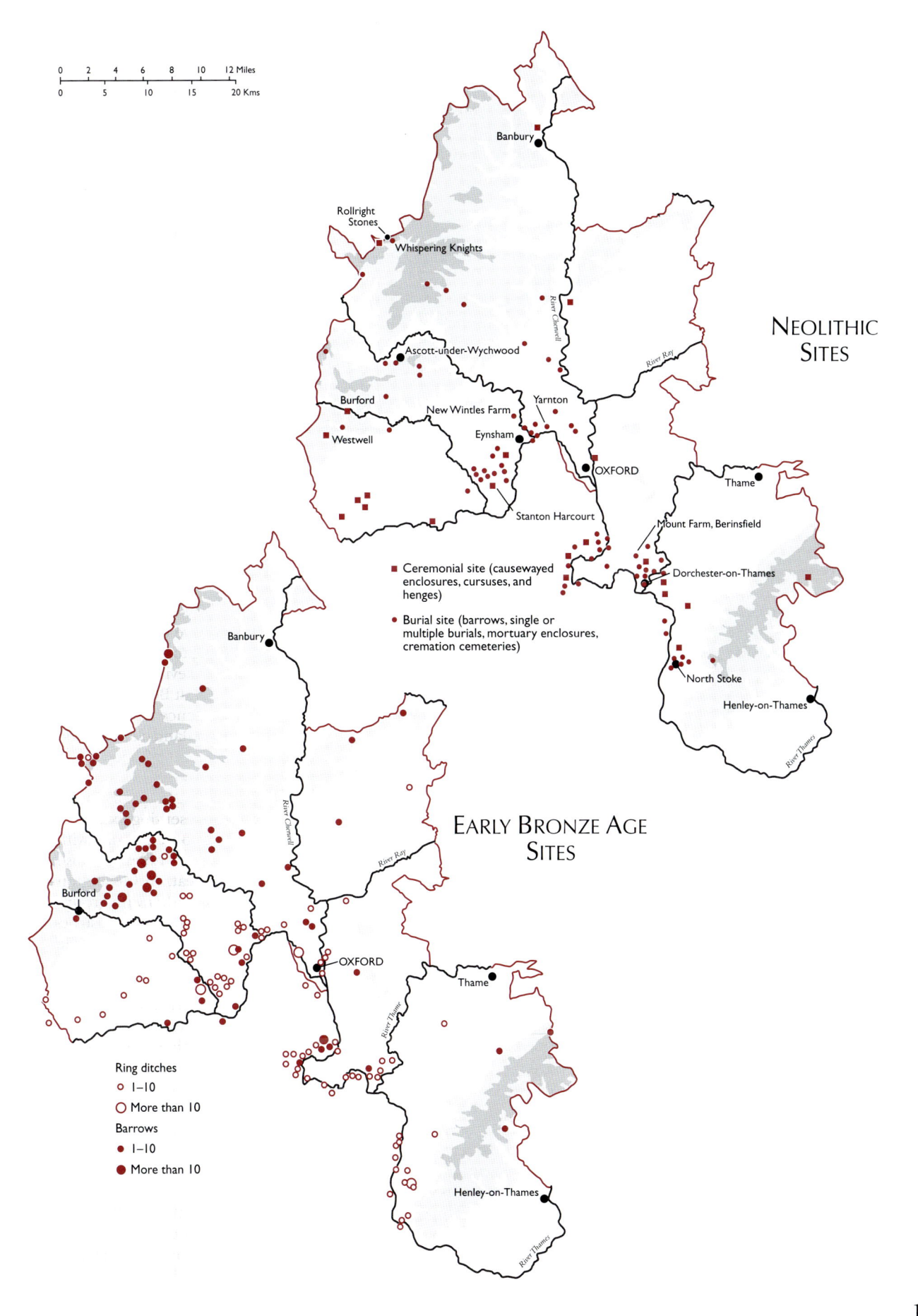

- ■ Ceremonial site (causewayed enclosures, cursuses, and henges)
- ● Burial site (barrows, single or multiple burials, mortuary enclosures, cremation cemeteries)

EARLY BRONZE AGE SITES

Ring ditches
- ○ 1–10
- ◯ More than 10

Barrows
- ● 1–10
- ⬤ More than 10

4 · Iron Age Oxfordshire

Alex Lang

Oxfordshire has been important in the development of British Iron Age studies, thanks to significant sites within its pre-1974 boundaries. Most archaeological work has taken place across the lowland gravels of the Thames valley. Here, a wealth of sites, excavated since the mid-Victorian period, have revealed important evidence about people, settlements, agriculture, resources, and the local landscape and environment.

This evidence shows that the Iron Age (c.800 BC–AD 43) saw significant and remarkable changes within the region. Settlements became larger (and more visible in the archaeological record) compared to those of the preceding Bronze Age. From the Early Iron Age (c.800 BC–400/300 BC) roundhouses emerge as the standard form of domestic structure. These were generally 8 to 15 m in diameter, usually made with wooden posts and walled using, probably, a wattle-and-daub technique and with roofs thatched using local resources such as meadow reeds or wheat straw. Other common features include pits, normally for storage of crops over winter but which often contained deposits that may have had religious or ritual significance, and four-post structures generally thought to be above-ground storage for harvested crops. All these continued in use throughout the Middle Iron Age (c.400/300 BC–c.50 BC).

Whilst domestic and storage structures were pretty similar across the region, settlement sites differed considerably. Some sites were surrounded by a boundary ditch, which archaeologists describe as enclosed. Good examples of this site-type are Mingies Ditch (Hardwick-with-Yelford) and Watkins Farm (Northmoor). These low-lying sites were in use for approximately 100 to 150 years and exploited the local environment to good effect. It appears that Mingies Ditch, extremely close to the Windrush, was a specialist husbandry site (possibly horses) able fully to exploit the lush pastoral meadows of the floodplain.

Other forms of sites were unenclosed, which often allowed them to expand or shift slightly over long periods of occupation. The two most intensively studied sites of this kind are at Stanton Harcourt and Yarnton. In both, large areas of landscape have been excavated, revealing dense levels of occupation. At Gravelly Guy (Stanton Harcourt), hundreds of pits were excavated, suggesting that the site was occupied for nearly 700 years. Yarnton is also particularly significant, as a Middle Iron Age cemetery was excavated there, one of only a few known in England for the period. Both sites (as well as many others) were well placed to exploit both the fertile gravels (excellent for arable cultivation) and the floodplain (pasture for animals). Sheep and cattle are the dominant species of the archaeological record, though pigs and horses were also husbanded. Typical crops included: wheat (spelt, emmer and free-threshing) and barley but other crops such as flax and beans and, where possible, reeds and floodplain grasses were also cultivated.

Beyond the Thames gravels the evidence is less clear-cut, with fewer large-scale excavations. Instead, small-scale excavations throughout the 20th century have provided snapshots of settlements and society. To the north, a number of Early Iron Age hillforts have been identified. Excavated examples include Chastleton, Lyneham and Bladon; others are known at Idbury, Ilbury (near Deddington), Heyford and Tadmarton and a further site lies on high ground overlooking the Thames valley in Eynsham Hall Park. Only one hillfort, Madmarston (Swalcliffe), shows evidence of settlement although this appears to relate to the Middle Iron Age phase of the site. The Middle Iron Age also marks an apparent expansion or increased visibility of settlements, especially in north Oxfordshire. Settlements at Steeple Aston, Banbury, Bicester, Bloxham, Kirtlington and a site near the Rollright Stones are similar to those of the Thames valley and show evidence of a mixed farming economy. Numerous cropmark sites from this region provide further evidence of settlement. The identification of over 40 'banjo' enclosures (named for their similarity in shape to the instrument) are the best indication of this, with numerous examples excavated elsewhere in southern Britain pointing to a Middle or Late Iron Age date, something backed up by minor excavations at Tomlin's Gate (Kiddington-with-Asterleigh).

Whilst there is strong continuity through the Early and Middle Iron Age, the changes marking the start of the Late Iron Age (c.50 BC–AD 43) are drastic and significant. Post-built roundhouses and pits are no longer in use, pottery styles change and coinage (with the first written words) starts to appear in the archaeological record. A general deterioration in climate increased exploitation along the Thames tributaries and the main river, which also meant that flooding towards the end of the Iron Age became more regular, forcing abandonment of many sites located on the lower terraces or floodplain. Rectangular boundaries start to appear at many settlement sites and a small number of much larger nucleated settlements develop at Cassington, Abingdon, further up the Windrush at Salmonsbury (Bourton-on-the-Water) and at Dyke Hills, near Dorchester-on-Thames. Whilst these generally show evidence of earlier settlement, it is in the Late Iron Age that large ditches and ramparts were constructed around them. These 'enclosed oppida' sites should not necessarily be considered towns but they certainly indicate greater complexity in settlement form. The appearance of coinage also helps to show us developing tribes and tribal regions. The Thames valley appears to have been a melting pot of different tribes overlapping and possibly trading. To the north-west lies the heartland of the Dobunni, the Catuvellauni to the north-east and the Atrebates to the south. The main boundaries seem to be marked by the Thames as a north–south divide and the Cherwell as a major boundary between the Dobunni and Catuvellauni. These are accentuated by the appearance of the nucleated settlements as well as by large dyke systems such as Aves Ditch and the south and north Oxfordshire Grim's Ditches, the latter a massive dyke system of unknown significance that covers some 8,800 ha of land just east of the Evenlode River.

Iron Age Settlement

- Farmstead site
- ⊙ Enclosed or earthwork site (hillfort or valleyfort)
- Late Iron Age linear boundary

Banbury
⊙ Madmarston
• Bloxham
⊙ Tadmarton
⊙ Rollright Stones
⊙ Ilbury
⊙ Chastleton
Steeple Aston
⊙ Heyford
Aves Ditch
• Bicester
Grim's Ditch
⊙ Idbury
⊙ Lyneham
River Evenlode
Tomlin's Gate
River Cherwell
River Ray
Grim's Ditch
River Windrush
⊙ Bladon
Yarnton
⊙ Eynsham Hall Park
⊙ Cassington
Mingies Ditch
Stanton Harcourt
Watkins Farm
Gravelly Guy
River Thame
Abingdon
⊙ Dyke Hills
South Oxfordshire Grim's Ditch
River Thames

DOBUNNI
CATUVELLAUNI
ATREBATES

0 1 2 3 4 5 6 Miles
0 2 4 6 8 10 Kms

15

5 · Roman Oxfordshire

Paul Booth

The pre-1974 county of Oxfordshire covers an area which in the Roman period formed parts of the territories of three of the major tribes or *civitates* of Britain, the Catuvellauni, centred on Verulamium to the east, the Dobunni centred on Cirencester to the west and the Atrebates with their centre at Silchester to the south. The extent to which these units, perhaps not formally constituted before the later 1st century AD, related to pre-Roman polities is uncertain. Legacies of the Iron Age were the linear earthworks of Aves Ditch and the south Oxfordshire Grim's Ditch, major local centres ('enclosed oppida') on the Thames, and further north the discontinuous earthworks of the north Oxfordshire Grim's Ditch, defining a much larger area, the significance of which remains unclear (see entry 4).

The impact of the Roman invasion of AD 43 was immediate and substantial. Alchester was established as a major military base, possibly a fortress of the legio II Augusta, as early as AD 44, at a strategically important junction of the south–north route from Chichester and Silchester up to the midlands with an east–west one linking the region with the new provincial centre of Colchester. These routes became formalised as the main Roman roads through the county and in due course nucleated settlements grew up along them. Alchester and Dorchester-on-Thames, the latter also the site of a fort, but one perhaps not established until after the rebellion of Boudica in AD 60/61, developed as walled towns. Alchester became the largest settlement in the county, covering an area of *c.*40–45 ha. West of Alchester there was a series of settlements on the main east–west road to Cirencester, Akeman Street, at Sansom's Platt, Wilcote and Asthall. Further settlements grew up on other elements of the road system, for example in the north of the county at Swalcliffe Lea on the road from Towcester to Stratford, while there may have been a minor settlement at the crossing point of a north–south road over the Thames at Oxford, and one further south-west at Wantage. There were other nucleated settlements in locations not obviously served by the major road network, such as Chipping Norton and Gill Mill, Ducklington.

These sites varied considerably in size and character. Stone buildings were common, for example at Alchester, Sansom's Platt and Asthall, and at Alchester included temples, a bath building and houses as well as the town walls. Elsewhere, for example at Gill Mill, which has been extensively excavated, only two such buildings, of simple rectangular plan, are known, although again the existence of a temple is likely on the basis of other evidence; such buildings were probably important features of all the major settlements. The presence of one at Dorchester is suggested by an inscription, erected by an officer who may have been based at a *mansio*, or official posting station. The provision of such services, and temples and markets, these two often associated, were amongst the major functions of the nucleated settlements.

The great majority of the population was based in the rural communities already in existence at the time of the Roman conquest – there is almost no evidence for disruption of settlement in the mid 1st century AD except in the vicinity of Alchester. With the passage of time distinct variations in settlement pattern began to emerge. Much of the Thames valley was occupied by farmsteads of simple character, sometimes in small clusters, while further north, on the Cotswold dip slope, there were more villas, some, like North Leigh and Stonesfield, very substantial establishments indeed. There was a notable concentration of villas within the area of the north Oxfordshire Grim's Ditch, several of which seem to have been established unusually early, in the later 1st century; elsewhere villas did not normally appear before the middle of the 2nd century, and sometimes rather later. The division between areas of settlement dominated by villas and those dominated by 'native type' sites was not a simple one, however, and in areas such as the Thames valley below Abingdon sites of both types were to be found. The extent of lower-status rural settlement in the northern part of the county is largely unknown because of the limited amount of work that has been carried out there.

A notable feature of the Thames valley is a phase of widespread disruption of the settlement pattern in the early 2nd century. Many sites were abandoned or relocated at this time, but their successors thereafter often continued in use through the later Roman period. The reason for this development is unknown, but it does not seem to have affected the villa sites in the north of the county.

Most settlements were involved in mixed agriculture, for which the best evidence comes from the Thames valley sites. Processes of intensification of production in the course of the Roman period included the introduction of 'corn driers' and animal- or water-powered mills, and the exploitation of hay meadows as a means of over-wintering increased numbers of animals. There is little evidence for large-scale industry, with the important exception of pottery production; a major industry centred on modern-day east Oxford was one of the largest in late Roman Britain, its specialist products being very widely distributed.

Settlements of all kinds were occupied up to the end of the Roman period, but it is not clear what happened after the conventional dating media of coins and pottery ceased to be renewed. Dorchester was an important focus of very late Roman activity, with large associated cemeteries and evidence for the presence of military personnel and perhaps sub-Roman mercenaries. Environmental evidence suggests continuing use of the countryside in the 5th century. This must indicate the survival of a significant Romano-British population in the first instance, but whether they were supplanted by immigrants or became acculturated in the course of the 5th century, adopting Anglo-Saxon architecture, artefacts and (up to a point) burial practices, remains highly contentious (see entry 6).

ROMAN SETTLEMENT

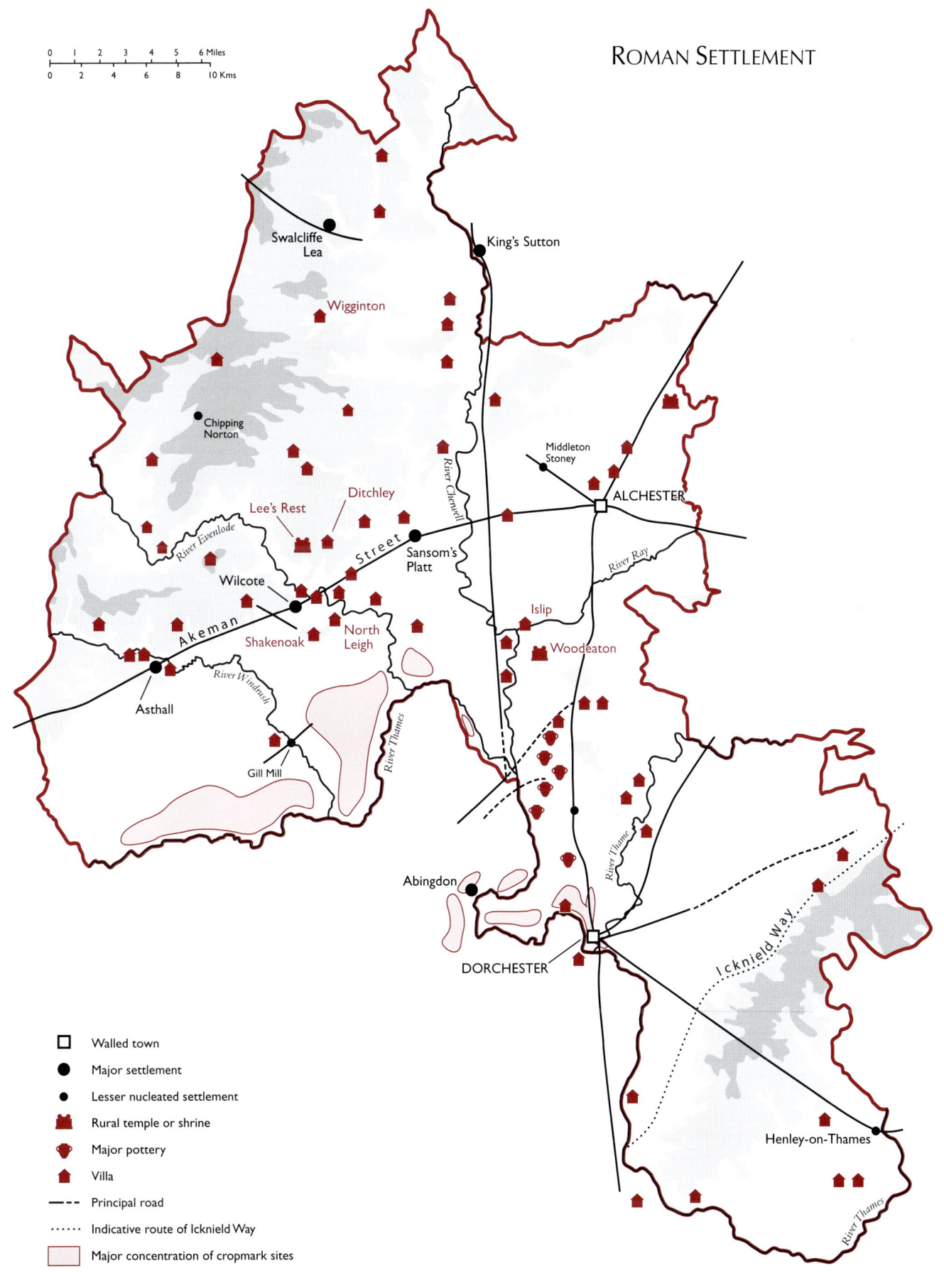

Legend:
- ☐ Walled town
- ● Major settlement
- • Lesser nucleated settlement
- Rural temple or shrine
- Major pottery
- Villa
- — — Principal road
- ······ Indicative route of Icknield Way
- Major concentration of cropmark sites

Labelled places:
Swalcliffe Lea, King's Sutton, Wigginton, Chipping Norton, Middleton Stoney, Alchester, Lee's Rest, Ditchley, Sansom's Platt, Wilcote, Islip, Akeman Street, Shakenoak, North Leigh, Woodeaton, Asthall, Gill Mill, Abingdon, Dorchester, Icknield Way, Henley-on-Thames

Rivers: River Evenlode, River Cherwell, River Windrush, River Thames, River Ray, River Thame

17

6 · Early Anglo-Saxon Settlement

Anne Dodd

The period from *c.* AD 450 to 650 saw a profound cultural shift across much of England. Although this process remains obscure in detail and even controversial, at a general level the spread of a new and distinctively Germanic culture is associated with the arrival of settlers originating from the north-west European coastal plains. These people are known to us as the Anglo-Saxons. They brought with them a very different way of life and a new language that is the basis of the English spoken today.

Many early Anglo-Saxon sites have been identified in the Thames valley, where they are readily visible as cropmarks on the gravel terraces. Many have come to light as a result of quarrying. Although the Thames was later a political boundary, at this time it is more likely to have linked people than divided them, and it seems to have been a corridor for early Anglo-Saxon movement, settlement and expansion. Cemeteries and settlements with distinctively Saxon cultural affinities have been found on both sides of the Thames, and particularly along the upper Thames valley between Standlake and Wallingford. Some of the earliest evidence comes from Dorchester, where signs of an Anglo-Saxon presence appear alongside the latest signs of the Roman town, providing key clues to the relationship between the late Roman population and the Anglo-Saxons (see entry 5).

Settlement in the early Anglo-Saxon period was much less intensive than in the preceding 4th century. There seems to have been a dramatic decline in population and considerable retrenchment in cultivation. Within this context, the confluences of the Thames and its tributaries in the Oxfordshire upper Thames valley seem to have become focal points, with cemeteries containing several hundred burials and widespread cropmark evidence for settlements. The main high-status focus probably developed just across the Thames from Dorchester during the 6th and 7th centuries. Here cropmark evidence for complexes of very large halls at Drayton/Sutton Courtenay and Long Wittenham can be associated with the West Saxon kings who emerge in the written record at this time. Bede tells us that the people of the region were known as the Gewisse, and how Dorchester became the seat of the first west Saxon bishopric in 635.

We know less about early Anglo-Saxon settlement in other parts of Oxfordshire, where there tend to be fewer opportunities for excavation. Finds and burials of the 5th and 6th centuries are known in smaller numbers, however, and their distribution suggests possible links with the valleys of the Windrush and Cherwell, earlier monuments, and the network of Roman roads and villas. The more reliably attested finds have come from near Burford, Minster Lovell, the Roman villa at Shakenoak near Wilcote, Lyneham Camp, Rollright, Souldern and Lower Heyford. Elsewhere, burials from Headington and Wheatley may reflect settlement on the Oxford Heights, and Chinnor early settlement at the foot of the Chilterns.

At face value, the distribution of 7th-century sites could seem a sign of expansion. However, numbers of datable burials suggest that, if anything, population declined in the 7th century from a peak in the early to mid 6th century. The increase in the number of known sites may be a result of changing settlement patterns rather than population growth. The large cemeteries of the 5th and 6th centuries were generally abandoned during the 7th century, and the burial sites of the 7th century tend to be smaller and more dispersed, perhaps more closely linked to individual settlements. An increasing propensity to reuse prehistoric barrows may also indicate smaller groups seeking to identify themselves with specific landholdings. A rich barrow burial found in the 19th century at Cuddesdon is datable to the late 6th or early 7th century and was possibly the grave of a member of the ruling family of the Gewisse.

Towards the middle of the 7th century the balance of power in the Oxfordshire region shifted, as the Saxon rulers of the Gewisse were forced south by the expansion of the kingdom of Mercia. At Asthall Barrow, overlooking the Windrush valley, a cremation burial was found with grave goods including drinking vessels and a gaming set, and the cremated bones of a horse and a sheep. This has marked affinities with Anglian and Scandinavian burial rites, and is thought likely to represent the burial of an early Mercian leader moving into the area. Around this time we see considerable expansion in the numbers of recognised sites in west and north-west Oxfordshire, with 7th-century finds from Great Tew, Chadlington, the former Roman villas at Shakenoak and North Leigh, Ducklington, Cokethorpe and possibly Brize Norton.

Settlements are harder to date than burials, but sites of the early to mid-Saxon period away from the major confluences have been identified at Black Bourton, at Wootton near Woodstock, at Kirtlington and near Littlemore, and scatters of early to mid-Saxon pottery found at places such as Cropredy, Banbury, Great Milton and North Stoke suggest that many more settlements remain to be identified. The recent find of a Kentish garnet-inlaid disc brooch at Bletchingdon hints that there may yet be much to discover about the Cherwell Valley and the hinterland of the Roman small town and later minster site at Bicester.

Although the West Saxons regained control of the land south of the Thames by the mid 9th century, the area that was to become Oxfordshire, north of the Thames, became thoroughly and lastingly integrated into Mercia. The development of key Oxfordshire places such as Oxford itself, the minster sites at Bampton, Eynsham and Bicester, and perhaps also the royal vills at Thame and Benson, is essentially datable to the period between the late 7th and early 9th centuries when the Mercians were consolidating their control. Early Anglo-Saxon archaeology is a key source of evidence for this lasting reorientation of the area that was to become Oxfordshire; from a corridor of Saxon expansion along the Thames Valley to a midland province of the kings of Mercia, and a key access route to the expanding port of *Lundenwic* (London).

ANGLO-SAXON SETTLEMENT

Chadlington	Site new in the 7th century
Souldern c.5–c.6	Site where a specific date range is indicated by finds of grave goods
Littlemore	Site with evidence of occupation over extended periods, or site where occupation cannot be dated more closely than early to mid Saxon
Carterton	Uncertain site

19

7 · Yarnton: Late Saxon Rural Settlement

Anne Dodd

Numerous settlement sites of the 5th to 7th centuries have been excavated in Oxfordshire, but we currently know much less about the later Anglo-Saxon period, when rural settlement patterns changed and the landscape began to assume the more familiar form recognisable in the later medieval period.

The extensive excavations of the Yarnton–Cassington project have revealed the first really good archaeological evidence for these processes of change in the county, and this can be set in the context of the increasing information available from documentary sources for the later Anglo-Saxon period.

During the 5th to 7th centuries Anglo-Saxon settlement at Yarnton, as was the case across wide areas of the Thames gravel terraces, was of low intensity, scattered, dispersed and unenclosed. However, in the 8th century a much more organised farmstead was established, focused on a large post-built hall set within a system of trackways, paddocks and enclosures. The farmstead was provided with a granary and a fowlhouse, and other structures probably represent subsidiary domestic buildings, barns and animal pens. During the 8th century the estate at Yarnton may have belonged to the nearby minster at Eynsham and there is evidence from plant remains for an intensification of farming to create more surplus. Hay was being grown for the first time since the Roman period, and heavier clay soils were being brought back into cultivation.

Evidence for similar 8th-century settlements was recovered nearby at Cresswell Field and Worton, where farmsteads comprising timber halls surrounded by paddocks and ancillary buildings were also recorded. This suggests that there was a significant reordering of the rural landscape in the area around this time. It is possible that this is linked to increasingly heavy demand for the production of surplus to support places such as the new minster communities. Renders payable to the king of Wessex, for example, included bread, honey, ale, cattle, geese, hens, cheese, butter, salmon, eels and fodder, and similar demands would have been made of the farmsteads of the Eynsham minster's estate.

During the 9th century the farmstead at Yarnton was reorganised. The focus shifted and a new hall, associated subsidiary buildings and wells were constructed within a system of enclosures to the east. The old 8th-century hall was rebuilt and enclosed within its own substantial boundary ditch. A small cemetery containing six or seven graves of 8th- to 9th-century date was located towards the western edge of the farmstead, and other human burials were found within the enclosure ditches surrounding the buildings. During the 9th century many minster estates were taken back into royal control and granted out to new, often secular, owners and this probably also happened to Yarnton. Does the changing layout of the 9th century represent the arrival of a new, secular owner? From analogy elsewhere, it is even possible that the name of a late Saxon owner is preserved in the name of Yarnton itself, in Old English 'Earda's tun'.

Subsequently, the focus of settlement at Yarnton shifted towards the site of the medieval church, manor and village. The area of the 8th- to 9th-century farmstead seems to have reverted to cultivation, and a series of small, regular enclosures were laid out to the north and south of a trackway along the terrace edge. The only building was a smithy located in the corner of one of the enclosures. Could the little enclosures have been the smallholdings of peasants on a reorganised estate of the 10th or 11th century, whose focus now lay much further to the north? In the early 11th century Yarnton was an estate of ten hides belonging to a man called Godwine, who exchanged it with his cousin Ealdorman Æthelmær to form part of the endowment of the newly refounded Benedictine abbey at Eynsham. Æthelmær, and by implication Godwine, belonged to a high-ranking aristocratic family which owned extensive estates locally, especially south of the Thames in Berkshire. The archaeological evidence suggests that it was around this time that the estate was reorganised, and this raises the possibility that the reorganisation of the field systems and peasant housing of the estate may have been an initiative of these big landowners, or even of the abbey itself.

The main hall under excavation at Yarnton, looking north. Copyright Oxford Archaeology.

Anglo-Saxon Yarnton

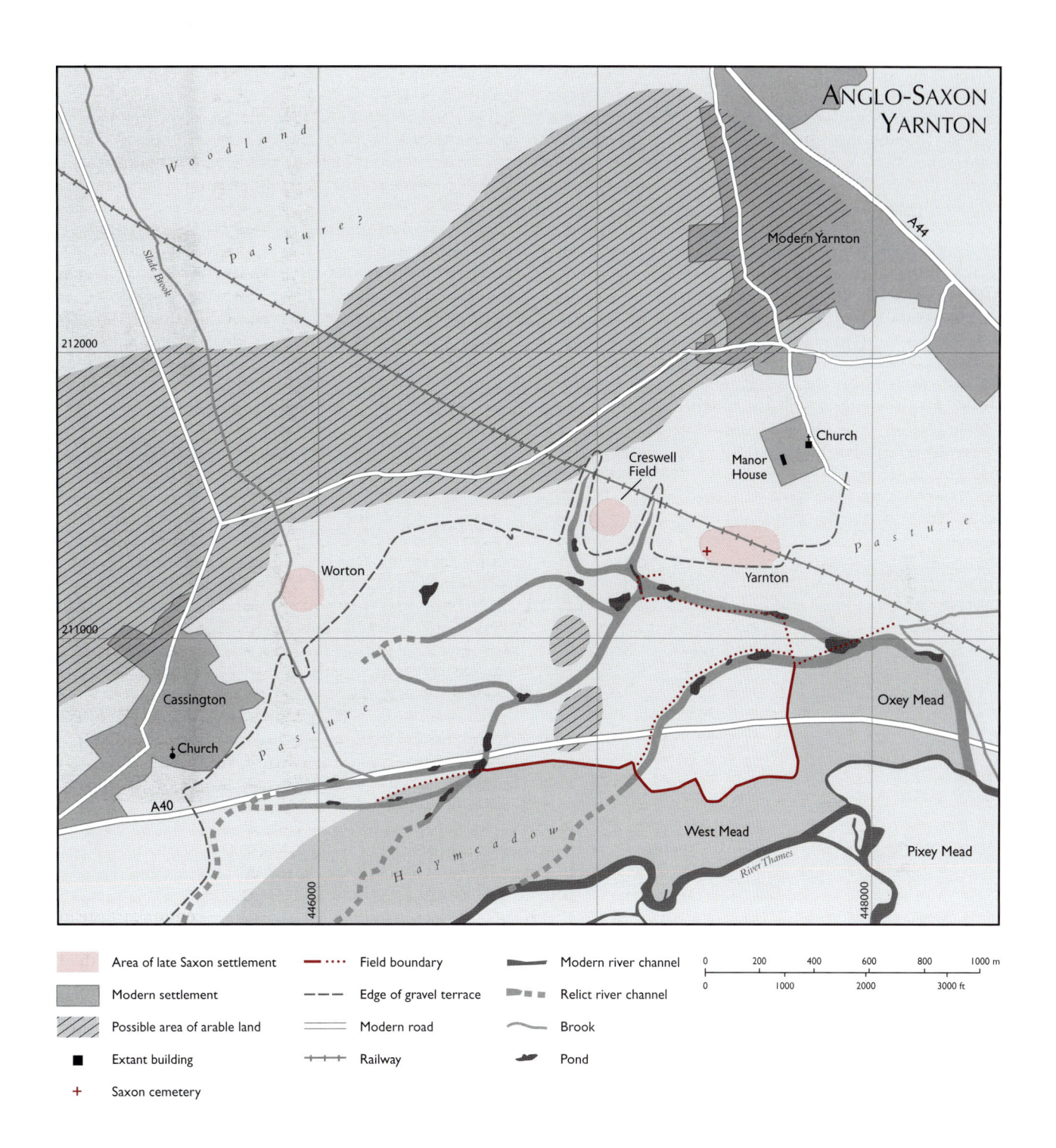

Legend:
- Area of late Saxon settlement
- Modern settlement
- Possible area of arable land
- Extant building
- Saxon cemetery
- Field boundary
- Edge of gravel terrace
- Modern road
- Railway
- Modern river channel
- Relict river channel
- Brook
- Pond

0   200   400   600   800   1000 m
0   1000   2000   3000 ft

Labels on map: Woodland Pasture?, Slade Brook, Modern Yarnton, A44, Creswell Field, Manor House, Church, Worton, Yarnton, Pasture, Cassington, Church, A40, Pasture, Haymeadow, Oxey Mead, West Mead, River Thames, Pixey Mead

21

8 · Place-Name Patterns

Ann Cole

Oxfordshire's place-names reflect both the physical features and human activities in the county. A few Celtic names survive as river names (e.g. Thames, Thame, Glyme, Windrush), and occasionally in settlement names including Taynton and Bladon embodying earlier names of the Hazelford Brook and Evenlode. French names are scarce: only Bruern ('heath') in the Cotswolds and Beaumont, Grandpont, Carfax and Rewley in Oxford. Most names derive from Old English (OE) terms which fall into two major groups – topographical and habitative.

The county's regions have their own distinctive assemblages of place-names describing the physical features and water supply. In the Chilterns, a dry chalk upland capped with clay-with-flints, the valleys were the most desirable settlement sites with names in *denu* ('long valley') such as Assendon, Checkendon, Dunsden, Harpsden and Ipsden on the dip slope, and *cumb* ('bowl-shaped valley') such as Swyncombe, Huntercombe and Watcombe (now Howe) on the scarp slope (see top map opposite). The scarcity of perennial streams means that only one *burna* ('clear stream') name, Shirburn, occurs. The water supply came from ponds (OE *mere*) found mainly on the interfluves, with names such as Homer, Kidmore and Uxmore. A series of *welle* ('spring') names characterise the scarp-foot spring-line settlements at Mongewell, Brightwell, Britwell, Cadwell, Adwell, and Crowell, while Ewelme (OE *æwielm*) means 'copious spring' (see middle map opposite).

The Gault and Kimmeridge Clay vale is well watered so *mere* names are replaced by *brōc* ('muddy stream'), as in Brookhampton, and *ford* names appear: Latchford, Rofford. *Hamm* occurs in Sydenham and Stadhampton (see below).

The Corallian ridge, north-east of Oxford, offered desirable settlement sites on a series of well-drained, whaleback-shaped hills (OE *dūn*): e.g. Baldon, Cuddesdon, Garsington, and Tiddington. West of Oxford, on slight rises on the upper Thames floodplain, the term *ēg* ('dry ground in a marsh') is found in Binsey, Medley, Osney, Chimney and Witney. The poorly drained soils on the Oxford Clay and in the Otmoor basin are noted in Otmoor and Murcott (OE *mōr* 'moor, wet ground'), Fencott (OE *fenn* 'linear marsh') and Marston and Menmarsh (OE *mersc* 'marsh'), but *dūn* names appear on the low Cornbrash ridge at Oddington and Ambrosden.

In the Cotswolds few valley terms occur – *cumb* (Combe, Milcombe) and *denu* (Dean, Ramsden, Sarsden) but bands of clay in the limestone throw out numerous springs, and *welle* names occur in Broadwell, Cornwell, Epwell, Holwell, Showell and Ledwell. The series continues east of the Cherwell with Fritwell, Fulwell and Shelswell. The smaller streams, often floored with clay, have settlements with *brōc* names, Broughton, Broughton Poggs, Begbroke, Fulbrook and Swinbrook, beside them (OE *brōc* 'muddy stream').

Place-names recording human activity and resources are well represented. Various rock types were recognised: there are two Sandfords, two Chalfords (*cealc* 'chalk, limestone'), Claydon and Clare ('clay') and *ceosol* ('wide scatter of small stones') in Chiselhampton. *Stān* is used of stones large enough to be potentially useful, as at Standlake, Stonor, Stowood, Stowford and Stanton St John, Wroxton and Lidstone. Standhill was a stone quarry, while Chalgrove was a chalk pit. Elsewhere, *stān* describes prehistoric structures: at Enstone for a burial chamber, at Taston for a standing stone, at Stanton Harcourt for a stone circle. Other prehistoric features are noted in Ditchley, the Dike Hills and Grim's Ditch (2) by use of *dīc* for prominent bank and ditch earthworks. The term for a tumulus (*hlāw, hlǣw*) appears in Cutslow and Lew. *Burh* is used of defended sites, some Iron Age forts (e.g. Idbury, Ilbury, Cornbury) and some Anglo-Saxon towns and manor houses. Roman settlements are noted in the names of Dorchester and Alchester, although it is not clear what *ceaster* refers to in Bicester. Chesterton means *tūn* by the Roman settlement (Alchester). The Roman roads are signified by the *strǣt* ('paved road') names: Stratton Audley and Stratford Bridge.

The most common habitative terms are *tūn* and *cot* (see bottom map opposite). *Tūn* ('enclosure, settlement') is absent from the Chilterns, but occurs widely elsewhere. Occasionally *tūn* is combined directly with a personal name: Wiggington, Willaston, or with a type of person, e.g. 'king' in Kingston, 'ceorl' in Charlton, but more often with the addition of a connective particle '-ing'

Some other Place-Name Elements found in Oxfordshire

Element	Meaning	Examples
Beorg	rounded hill	Warborough, Hanborough
Clif	steep slope, river cliff	Cleeve, Cleveley, Clifton (2), Swalcliffe
Healh	nook, hollow, corner	Holton, Asthall, Wainhill
Hyll	hill	Bucknell, Churchill, Pishill
Lacu	backwater, side channel	Bablock, Standlake, Shiplake
Hēah	high	Chiselhampton, Hempton, Henley, Heythrop
Holh	hollow	Holcombe, Homer
Lang	long	Langford (2), Langley (2), Launton
Middel	middle	Milcombe, Milton (3), Middleton Stoney
Fūl	foul, dirty	Fulbrook, Fulwell
Hālig	holy	Holwell, Holywell
Hwīt	white	Wheatfield, Whitchurch
Āc	oak	Oakley (2), Noke, Roke
Byxe	box-tree	Bix, Bixmoor Wood
Pirige	pear tree	Purwell, Pyrton, Waterperry, Woodperry
Wīthig	willow	Widford, Witheridge Hill, Withycombe
Hēg	hay	Hailey, Hayden, Heyford
Corn (cran)	crane	Cornbury, Cornwell
Crawe	crow	Crawley, Crowmarsh, Crowell
Fīna	woodpecker	Finmere, Finstock
Gōs	goose	Goose Eye, Gosford
Cīeping	market	Chipping Norton
Cirice	church	Church Enstone, Whitchurch, Churchill (?)

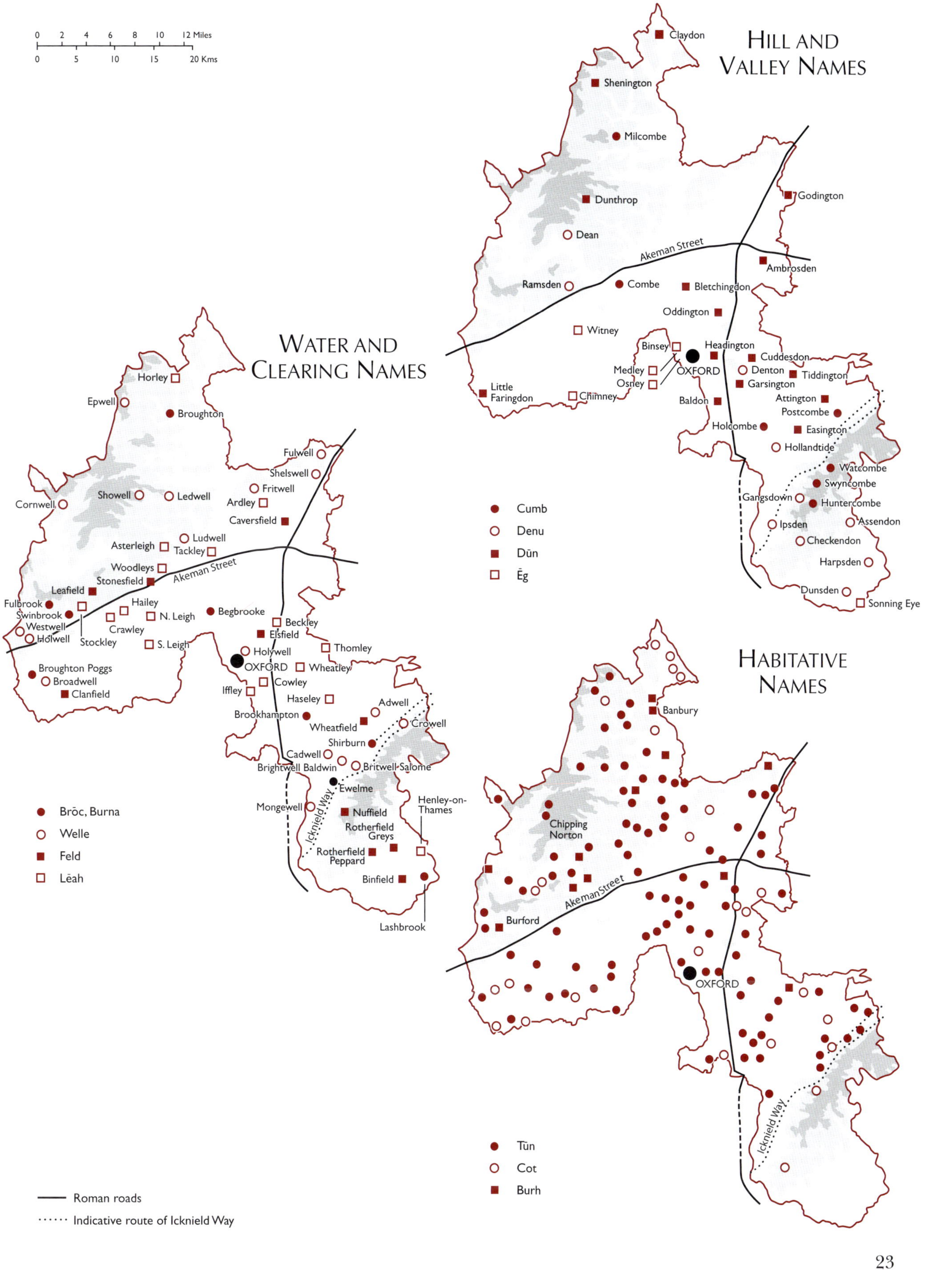
0 2 4 6 8 10 12 Miles
0 5 10 15 20 Kms
Hill and Valley Names
Claydon
Shenington
Milcombe
Godington
Dunthrop
Dean
Akeman Street
Ambrosden
Ramsden
Combe
Bletchingdon
Oddington
Witney
Binsey
Headington
Medley
OXFORD
Cuddesdon
Denton
Tiddington
Osney
Garsington
Little Faringdon
Chimney
Baldon
Attington
Postcombe
Holcombe
Easington
Hollandtide
Watcombe
Swyncombe
Gangsdown
Huntercombe
Ipsden
Assendon
Checkendon
Harpsden
Dunsden
Sonning Eye
Cumb
Denu
Dūn
Ēg
Water and Clearing Names
Horley
Epwell
Broughton
Fulwell
Shelswell
Fritwell
Showell
Ledwell
Cornwell
Ardley
Caversfield
Ludwell
Asterleigh
Tackley
Woodleys
Stonesfield
Akeman Street
Leafield
Fulbrook
Hailey
Swinbrook
N. Leigh
Begbrooke
Westwell
Crawley
Beckley
Holwell
Stockley
Elsfield
S. Leigh
Holywell
Thomley
Broughton Poggs
OXFORD
Wheatley
Broadwell
Cowley
Clanfield
Iffley
Haseley
Adwell
Brookhampton
Wheatfield
Crowell
Shirburn
Cadwell
Brightwell Baldwin
Britwell Salome
Ewelme
Henley-on-Thames
Mongewell
Icknield Way
Nuffield
Rotherfield Greys
Rotherfield Peppard
Binfield
Lashbrook
Brōc, Burna
Welle
Feld
Lēah
Habitative Names
Banbury
Chipping Norton
Akeman Street
Burford
OXFORD
Icknield Way
Tūn
Cot
Burh
Roman roads
Indicative route of Icknield Way

8 · Place-Name Patterns (continued)

to mean '*tūn*' associated with 'x' or 'y', e.g. Chadlington, Deddington, Emmington, Kiddington, Kidlington, Kirtlington, Piddington, Watlington, Yarnton. Many refer to position with respect to somewhere else: the Middletons, Astons, Westons, Nortons and Suttons. About a quarter are combined with topographical elements, some of them 'functional *tūns*' (certain *tūn* names indicate a settlement with functions or advantages beyond the normal agricultural ones).

Cot ('hamlet, humble dwelling') is well represented north of the Chilterns. A third are combined with personal names, e.g. Alvescot, Arncott, Balscott, Bodicote, Kelmscott, Kencott, Wolvercot; positional terms occur in a fifth of the names, while the rest mostly refer to the environment or vegetation: Caulcot ('cold'), Clattercote ('heap of stones'), Fewcot ('few'), Woodcote ('in a wood').

Throp, 'an outlying hamlet', represented by Thrupp, Astrop, Burdrop, Dunthrop, Heythrop, Southrop and Neithrop, is found mostly north of Oxford. *Hām*, 'homestead, farm', occurs in Bloxham, Mapledurham, Rousham, Newnham Murren and Nuneham Courtenay. Without OE spellings it is difficult to distinguish from *hamm*, 'river meadow, land in a river bend', e.g. Culham, Cuxham, Eynsham, Milham, Norham, Stadhampton Sydenham.

Farm crops and animals are noted in Wheatley (wheat), Rycote (rye), Pishill (peas), Cassington (watercress), Oxford, Uxmore (oxen), Horspath, Studley, Stadhampton (horses), Swinbrook, Swyncombe (pigs) and Shiplake, Shifford, Shipton (2) (sheep), Garsington (grassy), Barton, Berrick (barley farm, outlying grange).

Wudu is a general term for woodland as in Wychwood and Stowood. Otherwise it is mostly used as a distinguishing first element: Woodeaton, Woodperry and Woodstock in contrast to Water Eaton, Waterperry and Waterstock, the 'water' implying susceptibility to flooding.

Clusters of *lēah* names suggest the extent of Wychwood (Hailey, North and South Leigh), Stowood and Shotover (Beckley, Wheatley and Haseley) forests. *Lēah* probably refers to wood-pasture, but some names imply patches of woodland open enough to produce wheat (Wheatley) or hay (Hailey).

Grǣfe ('grove') is thought to mean coppiced woodland – careful management of a scarce resource. In parish and Domesday Book names, it occurs in predominantly arable areas, e.g. Warpsgrove. Grafton may have the function of collecting and despatching faggots to the Droitwich salt works.

Lēah is less frequent in the Oxfordshire than in the Buckinghamshire and Hertfordshire Chilterns, but it is replaced by *feld*, originally meaning 'rough, open pasture'. Nuffield ('tough'), Binfield ('bent grass'), Rotherfield ('cattle') and Turville (Bucks) ('dry'), implying poor quality pasture, occur on the 'plateaux' of the southern Chilterns.

Feld also occurs in Leafield (Le Feld), Stonesfield (Stunt's), Elsfield (Elesa's), Campsfield (Latin *campus*, 'field'), Clanfield (clean) and Wheatfield (white).

The road and river systems used during the early medieval period are indicated by the names for roads (*strǣt, weg, pæth*), crossing places, landing places (*hȳth*) and from some functional *tūn* names: among them (and occasional functional *cots*) are two Draytons and a Draycot situated where 'dragging' is necessary, because, on routes with steep inclines, very muddy conditions or frequent flooding, travellers may need local assistance. Merton and Tadmarton (*mere-tūn* 'settlement with a pond') indicate availability of water. Rivers needed to be kept navigable – free of weeds, fallen trees and gravel banks; the Eatons (*ēa-tūn* 'river settlement') were probably responsible for this. Water Eaton and Woodeaton kept the Cherwell navigable up to Islip, where it was crossed by the main road to Worcester. A series of Eatons on the Berkshire bank of the upper Thames kept that river navigable up to Cricklade. Landing places were signalled by the *hȳth* names: Bolney, Hythe Bridge in Oxford, Highcroft in Eynsham, and, later, Bablock Hythe. The hill term *ōra* ('flat-topped ridge with a convex shoulder' used as a visual 'signpost') is found by route-ways and in Oxfordshire picks out the Icknield Way with Bixmoor, Lewknor and Chinnor. An old track from Oxford via Shotover and Wheatley Bridge is marked by Golder, Clare, *Radenore* (now Pyrton) and Stonor en route to Henley and Bolney. Ford ('ford, causeway') is widespread, except in the streamless Chilterns. A few like Oxford, Shillingford and Stowford were on important route-ways but most represent either crossings of small rivers draining the Cotswolds, e.g. Burford, Widford (Windrush), Barford (Swere), Shutford (Sor Brook), or crossings of smaller streams by tracks linking neighbouring settlements, e.g. Rofford, Yelford. The most important routes thought from the place-name evidence to have been in use are shown on the map opposite.*

---

* In the key to this map 'Gough' refers to the Gough map of *c*.1360, held in the Bodleian Library, Oxford. See N. Millea, *The Gough Map: the earliest road map of Great Britain?* (Bodleian Library, 2007); and http: 143.117.30.60/website/goughmap/viewer.htm. 'Ogilby' refers to John Ogilby's linear maps of roads and their adjoining area, published in 1675. See *Ogilby's Road Maps of England and Wales from Ogilby's 'Britannia', 1675* (Osprey Publishing, Reading, 1971) for a modern facsimile. Roads and route-ways are also discussed in entries 10, 21, 31 and 43.

Route-Way Names

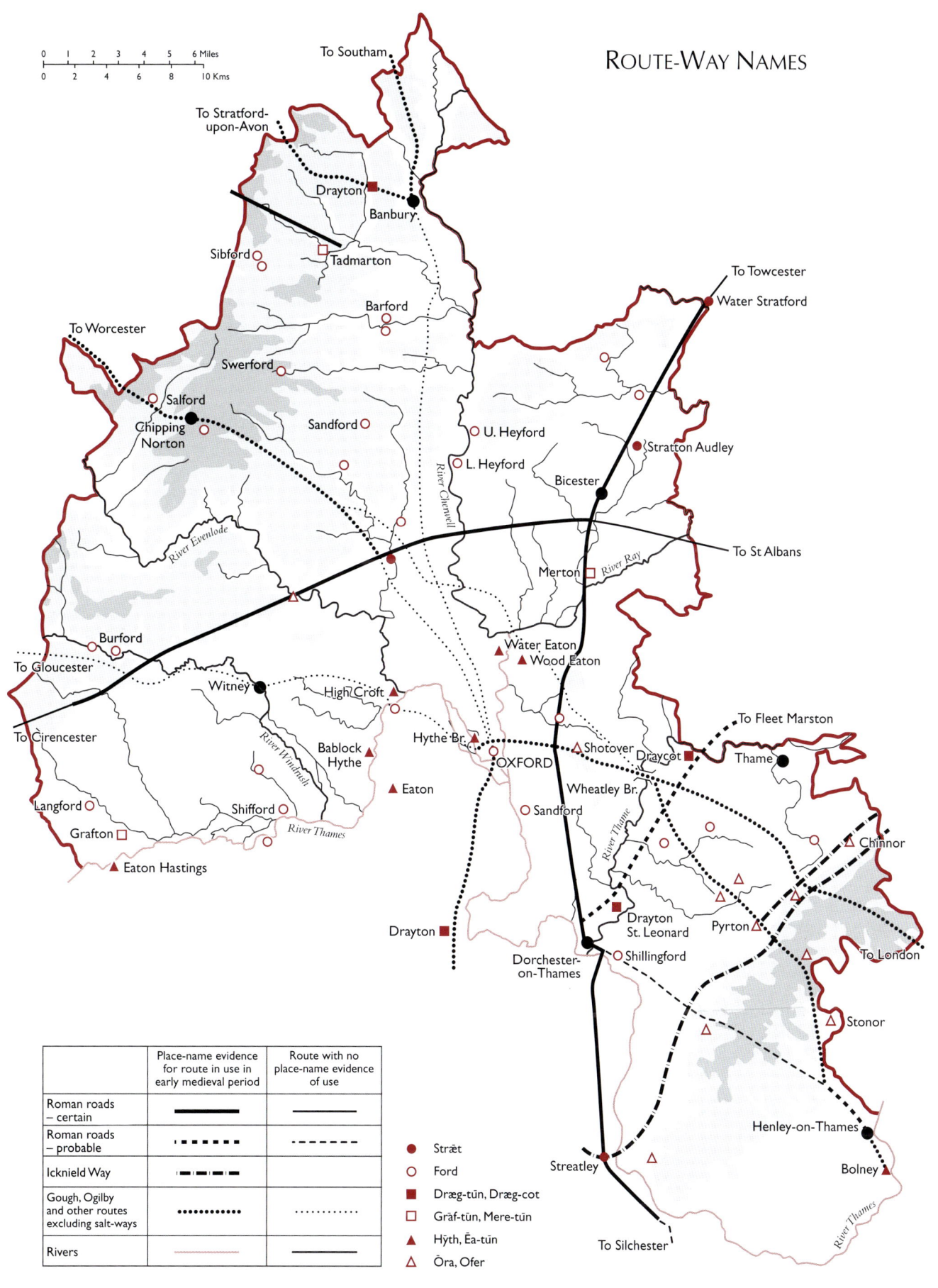

9 · The Anglo-Saxon Minsters

John Blair

It was between *c.*660 and 740 – nearly a century after the initial conversions – that English Christianity was established on its local basis, with the foundation of complex monastic sites (*monasteria* in Latin, *mynstru* or 'minsters' in English). These were elaborate and innovative in their buildings and material culture, often rich, and housed large communities, including nuns, monks, priests, and lower-class 'working brethren'. Their impact on the society and economy of England was transformative, and they seem gradually to have assumed the role of centres for pastoral care to the laity at large.

Across England, most minsters apparently started during this intense burst of activity, but are better recorded in some regions than in others. To the west of Oxfordshire, the unrivalled Worcester cathedral archive gives glimpses of many minsters in their earliest stages. For Oxfordshire, by contrast, charter survival is poor: to identify the minsters we must rely on scattered clues in much later sources, slowly but steadily augmented by archaeological data.

The most important minsters were concentrated heavily along the Thames. Dorchester, seat of the first West Saxon bishopric from the 630s, has pride of place, though in its later history it seems curiously obscure and impoverished, perhaps the victim of competition from more successful monastic and urban centres – Abingdon and Wallingford – across the river. More consistently prominent was Eynsham, the centre of a huge territory between the Thames, Cherwell and Windrush mentioned from the 820s; excavation has found traces of the 8th-century monastic buildings. Probably the other major minster of the upper Thames was St Frideswide's community at Oxford, first recorded in 1002 but the scene of vivid legends, set around the year 700, and preserved in later hagiography. The recent excavation there of a female burial, dated by radiocarbon determination to the late 7th century, illustrates dramatically the capacity of archaeology to give substance to shadowy traditions.

Archaeology is slowly bringing the earlier stages of other minsters to light, most substantially at Bampton (see entry 11), and at Bicester, where we are starting to see an agglomeration of late Anglo-Saxon settlement around St Eadburh's church. Charlbury, in Wychwood, housed the relics of St Diuma, a 7th-century missionary mentioned by Bede, which suggests that it was an important early centre. At nearby Minster Lovell, the recent discovery of burials outside the churchyard starts to substantiate the implications of the place-name, and of the richly jewelled head of a pointer – related to the Alfred Jewel – found there. At Shipton-under-Wychwood, too, dispersed groups of burials indicate a churchyard that was once much larger, and presumably served a larger population. In south-east Oxfordshire, important churches at Thame and Pyrton emerge from stray references in charters. Most obscure – perhaps because of vagaries of documentation – are the important mother churches of the upper Cherwell valley, Bloxham, Banbury, Adderbury and Cropredy: none of these is mentioned before the Conquest, though a site at Cropredy is the scene of St Freomund's hagiographical legend.

When they emerge into the light of record, most minster-places seem mere shadows of what they must once have been. Like minsters throughout England, they will have suffered progressively since the early 9th century from impoverishment, loss of independence, reduction of their communities, and above all from annexation as royal residences. The map of royal and hundredal centres in Domesday Oxfordshire (see entry 12) is to a large extent a map of minsters on to which those secular institutions had battened during the previous two centuries or so. At a reduced level, the communities could nonetheless retain some prosperity. Like Abingdon two generations earlier, Eynsham was refounded and re-endowed in 1005 as a strict Benedictine abbey on the currently fashionable model; for a few brief years it became one of the cultural centres of England under the abbacy of Ælfric, the great homilist and promoter of English as a written language. Other minsters probably retained, through the 10th and 11th centuries, their simplified communities of priests, which would sometimes (at Dorchester, Oxford and Bicester) be refounded in the 1100s as monasteries of regular Augustinian canons; Bampton retained its three portionary vicars, an extraordinary archaism, into the reign of Victoria.

It is likely, though the evidence is fragmentary and oblique, that minsters had for centuries provided pastoral care to big 'proto-parishes' around them. By 1100 these were breaking down into the small local parishes, centred on parish churches, that have existed ever since (see entry 17). By piecing together scattered references to continuing payments and other obligations owed by 'daughter' to 'mother' churches, we can begin to reconstruct this process. By the time of our first detailed local records, many of the Oxfordshire minsters' parishes had shrunk to little or nothing more than the rumps which they would control thereafter, but others, especially in the west of the county, can be discerned more completely. Bampton again stands out for its enormous parish, losing little of its probable original extent until the later middle ages.

Occasionally, as at Hook Norton or Great Tew, we can recognise substantial local churches that were, before the Conquest, starting to constitute a layer of parochial provision below the minsters. In general, however, it is not until well into the 12th century that the familiar framework of Oxfordshire local parishes can be seen coming into shape.

Reduced though they were as religious and cultural centres, the minster-places often retained distinctive characteristics, seen above all in their tendency to attract proto-urban growth around them (see entry 10). St Frideswide's was encapsulated within the new burghal town of Oxford around 890; others evolved into secular centres more slowly, but steadily. Coexisting with, but more topographically complex than, the planted market towns of the 12th and 13th centuries, the minsters assumed a new and continuing life among the urban centres of late- and post-medieval Oxfordshire.

Anglo-Saxon Minsters and Mother Churches

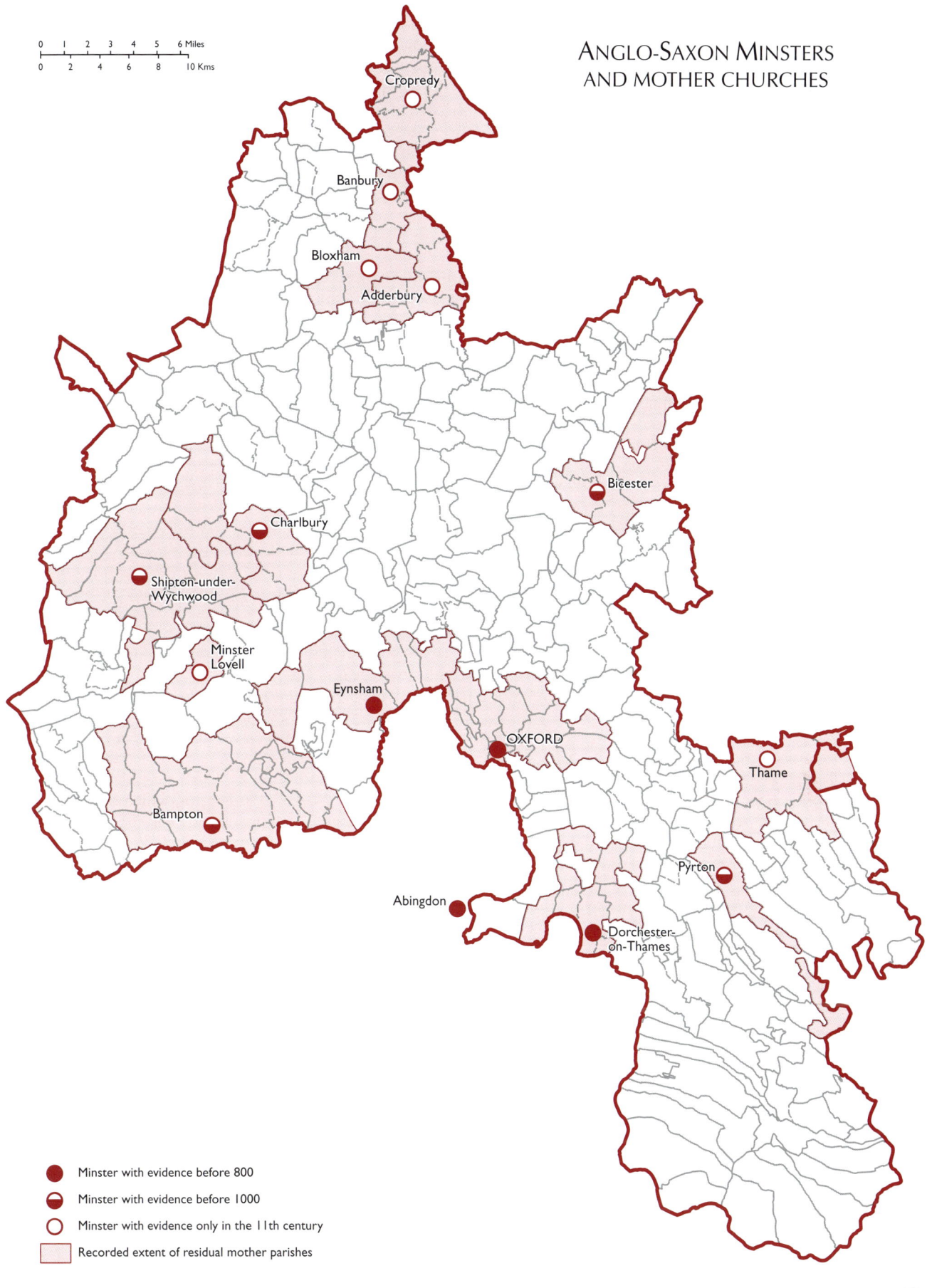

- Cropredy
- Banbury
- Bloxham
- Adderbury
- Bicester
- Charlbury
- Shipton-under-Wychwood
- Minster Lovell
- Eynsham
- OXFORD
- Thame
- Bampton
- Abingdon
- Pyrton
- Dorchester-on-Thames

Legend:
- ● Minster with evidence before 800
- ◐ Minster with evidence before 1000
- ○ Minster with evidence only in the 11th century
- Recorded extent of residual mother parishes

0 1 2 3 4 5 6 Miles
0 2 4 6 8 10 Kms

27

10 · Communications and Urban Origins before 1066 — John Blair

Accounts of early communication systems have traditionally emphasised ridgeways. More recent work has become sceptical about the long-term continuity of such routes, and has instead stressed the enduring importance for movement of people and goods, from late prehistory through to the central middle ages, of the major river systems draining to the south and east coasts. Roads were always there, of course, but they were less stable than waterways and will have varied in importance with fluctuations in the flow of trade and transport. In Oxfordshire, as elsewhere, we should see transport as an interplay between natural waterways – essentially fixed, but subject to obstruction by silt and weirs while also capable of being improved and extended – and roads, which often converged on crossing-points to create important nodes of human activity.

In Oxfordshire the main waterway was the Thames, with its tributaries the Windrush, the Evenlode, the Cherwell and the Thame. Hard to navigate above Henley by the late middle ages, the Thames seems in earlier centuries to have been usable, at least for downriver transport, from a much higher point. In several periods – notably the late Iron Age and the 5th to 11th centuries – the upper Thames region can be perceived as a 'gateway' zone, where luxuries from the Thames estuary, south-east Britain and a wider European world met bulk goods, from the west midlands and beyond, moving in the other direction. Recent work argues that, probably in the 10th to 12th centuries, the upper Thames was improved artificially, and augmented by tributary and bypass canals that have been recognised at Radcot, Bampton, Oxford and Wallingford: evidence of a more dynamic early medieval attitude to transport than is generally assumed.

Another important axis from the upper Thames, increasingly clearly indicated by metal finds and coins, was north-eastwards to the Wash. Some of this traffic was probably overland, but it is interesting to note later traces of a water route along the Ray and Cherwell to the Thames that could have been approached by portages from the Great Ouse river system near Buckingham.

Turning to roads, the Roman Akeman Street survived in fragments, but its continuing long-distance role is very unclear. The Icknield Way, crossing the Thames near Goring and following the Chiltern scarp foot to the east, can still (despite recent scepticism) be seen as an important through route, along which presumably travelled the merchant who left a coin hoard at Aston Rowant soon after 700. Roads to London from the west midlands and the south-west, running parallel with the upper Thames, were certainly important: the miracles of St Wulfstan show that he habitually took such a route from Worcester via the Chilterns. Nonetheless, it was especially the routes to Thames crossings and freighting-points that articulated the road system of the region. Most prominent were the pair of roads, one from the west midlands and the other from the north, converging on the 'oxen-ford' itself, using crossings over the broad Thames floodplain that may well go back to prehistory: recent excavation shows that Robert d'Oilly's great Oxford causeway of Grandpont (c.1080) replaced earlier structures, including a probable mid-Saxon timber bridge. Upriver, a similar convergence of roads from Gloucestershire and Shipton-under-Wychwood on one side and Enstone and Charlbury on the other may have passed through Bampton to a now lost crossing at Rushey Weir. Salt-ways from Droitwich met the Thames at various points from Lechlade downwards, taking bulk supplies for transport towards London, but also feeding local salt markets such as those recorded later at Faringdon and Piddington.

Grandpont is the prime example of what was apparently an 11th- to 12th-century fashion for bridging the river with causeways. This will have had a big impact on transport, both by causing the water to pound up and thus encouraging silting, and by concentrating road traffic at these easy crossing-points to the neglect of older fords and bridges. The bridge causeway at Radcot, serving what was evidently a new and deliberately constructed road, seems to have stimulated the eventual growth of Burford and Faringdon, which it linked, to the detriment of Bampton, now left isolated from through traffic.

As this illustrates, the transport pattern, and especially the road/river intersections, had an impact on the genesis of proto-urban settlements. Oxford was sited, like so many of the boroughs founded in the west midlands during c.880–930, at a river confluence which was also a major road junction: with its grid-plan and professionally constructed ramparts, it is locally in a class of its own, apart from Wallingford, downriver on the Berkshire bank. What Oxford shares with lesser centres, however, is urban growth around the nucleus of an old minster. The complex plans of several small towns reflect secular settlement on the fringes of a minster precinct. This phenomenon has been studied most intensively at Bampton (see entry 11) but is also now demonstrable at Bicester, where recent excavations have found peripheral groups of Anglo-Saxon buildings. A similar sequence may well be found in other small towns, such as Charlbury, Bloxham and Thame, when they are eventually explored archaeologically. Outside Oxford and Wallingford, urbanisation in the region was largely a post-Conquest phenomenon, but its earliest stages, in the form of these small but stable late Anglo-Saxon nuclei, are gradually coming to light.

Communications: Early Medieval

11 · Bampton: a Minster-Town

John Blair

Other essays in this atlas discuss the changing fortunes of the early minsters and the emergence of proto-urban places against a background of minster sites and developing communications (see entries 15 and 21). This essay looks at a single, well-investigated place that illustrates both those processes.

Bampton minster, in west Oxfordshire on the upper Thames, is first mentioned in a charter of 1069, which confirms land 'which King Eadwig gave to the holy man at Bampton and the community'. This shows that a religious community was in existence during Eadwig's reign in Mercia (955–7), housing the relics of a 'holy man' whom later sources name as St Beornwald. Throughout the middle ages Bampton church retained, to a remarkable extent, its huge parish and its rich living. In 1220 the clerical establishment there, apparently an informal college of canons, was reconstituted as a 'portionary vicarage' of three vicars, which survived – a bizarre anachronism – until the 1840s.

Since the 1980s, a research project has tried to flesh out this historical narrative, and to extend it backwards in time, through a combination of topographical analysis and small, strategically planned excavations. This has revealed a long and complex story, extending from an apparent site of Anglo-Saxon pagan cult to the present market town.

Underlying prehistoric and Roman monuments have helped to shape the religious topography of Bampton. Below and to the west of the main church were two Bronze Age barrows, of which the smaller may have suggested the location for the church itself, and the larger seems to have been adopted as an enclosure for the Deanery house and its chapel – or more probably their ritual predecessors – on the west side of the churchyard. Further east, outside the town, a late Iron-Age and Romano-British settlement became the site of a small Anglo-Saxon cemetery with simple 7th-century grave goods, and a chapel of St Andrew known in the later middle ages as 'the Beam'. This remarkably interesting name, meaning 'beam', 'post' or 'pillar' in Old English, is evidently the source of the name of Bampton itself (bēam-tūn, 'tūn by the bēam'). Given the cemetery and the later chapel, this was surely a ritual feature: it is an extremely rare instance where the sequence from Anglo-Saxon pagan shrine to later Christian site can be convincingly proposed.

At Bampton itself, excavations in the churchyard have proved that burial was taking place no later than c.850 – the firmest piece of evidence for a pre-Viking religious site here. The main topographical feature was a large oval enclosure, containing the church in its south-west corner but excluding the Deanery complex. Excavation has shown that this was bounded by a substantial ditch, four metres wide, apparently back-filled around 1100. This presumably monastic enclosure was the basis of the later town plan and helps to explain its otherwise puzzling complexity. On its south, where what was probably an early approach road from the Thames would have entered the enclosure, a wedge-shaped space, on the edge of which a late Anglo-Saxon sunken hut has been excavated, can probably be recognised as an early market-place (and indeed was used as a horse-market into modern times). A market at Bampton – the only one mentioned in Oxfordshire – appears in Domesday Book in 1086.

By then, Bampton was chiefly notable as a royal centre. The royal house probably stood west of the town across the Shill Brook, on the site of the later castle, and looks topographically peripheral to the monastic core: this is almost certainly one of those cases where a residence and administrative centre was attached to a formerly autonomous minster by one of the late Anglo-Saxon kings. Most of the large estate was in royal hands by the Conquest: Domesday Book, combined with earlier charters, reveals a remarkably orderly pattern in which different zones within the territory were allocated as private estates to be used for royal patronage, as holdings for the king's ministers and servants, as land for the earl, as land for the minster clergy, and as royal demesne.

The big triangular market-place south-east of the church complex is of classic post-Conquest form, and presumably represents an initiative by some lord – whether the clergy, the king, or his aristocratic successors at the castle – to realise economic potential. By 1300, then, Bampton had assumed a multi-layered aspect, with the castle and market-place peripheral to the ghosts of the former minster enclosure and early market. But the potential was to remain largely unfulfilled. It was probably changes in communication patterns, above all the building of the Radcot causeway which funnelled traffic between Burford and Faringdon, rather than through Bampton and its former Thames crossing at Rushey, that caused this formerly central place to be bypassed and left behind: by the 17th century it was so cut-off as to encourage the nickname 'Bampton-in-the-Bush'. For us, therefore, it is a particularly good place for studying those early stages of urbanism that later growth has often obliterated.

But Bampton remained distinctive and special. The grand 12th- to 15th-century church still looks more monastic than parochial in scale. Grouped around it, the rectory or 'Deanery' house to the west and the three vicarages on the other three sides have the air of a cathedral close in miniature; the clergy (mostly from Devonshire, since the minster belonged to Exeter cathedral from the 1050s) and their dependents must have constituted a distinctive community at the heart of the town. Through the later middle ages, Bampton remained a place where royal and other officials with business in London or at the court kept country residences – a situation oddly perpetuated today by the many senior solicitors and accountants working from home. Bampton is also a famous centre for continuing folkloric practices, notably morris-dancing in May and the mummers' play on Christmas eve. Not all these phenomena may be closely connected, but they add up to make a place that is different because of its long and complex history, and where the layers of religious, royal, commercial and social activity can be perceived with unusual clarity.

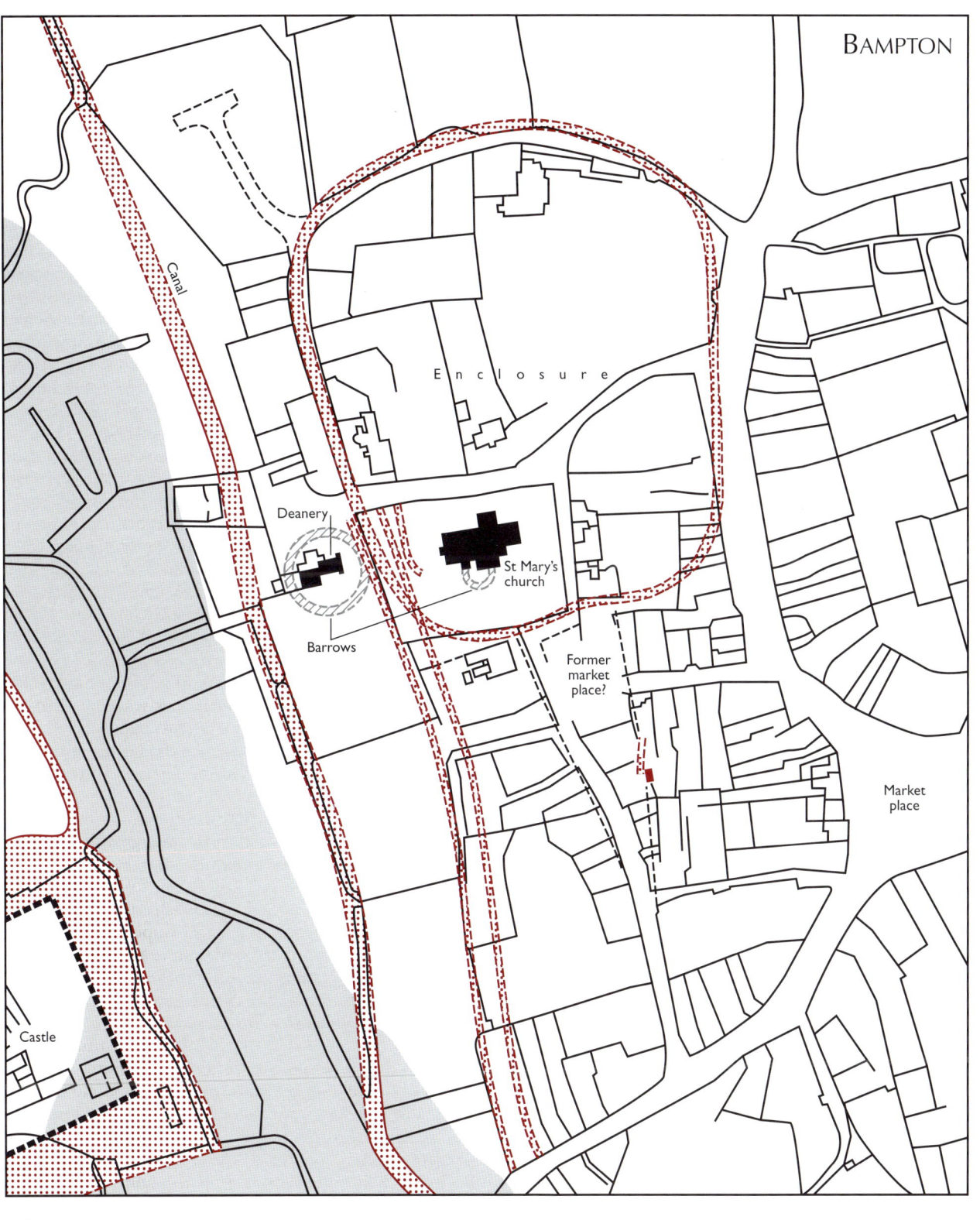

BAMPTON

Bronze Age barrows
Medieval ditches
Alluvium
Late Anglo-Saxon building

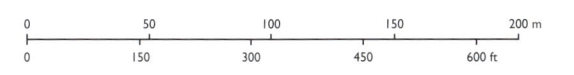

0   50   100   150   200 m
0   150   300   450   600 ft

31

12 · Domesday Landholdings and Settlement

Mark Page

The Domesday Survey of 1086 was commissioned by William the Conqueror to find out what land each person held, its value, and its assets (including arable, meadow, pasture, wood, mills and tenants). The aim was to take stock of the kingdom's resources following the Norman Conquest. Some 91 landholders (or tenants-in-chief) were listed in Oxfordshire, headed by King William. The royal manors were scattered across the county, and though few in number were mostly large and valuable, including Bampton and Benson, each worth over £80. Most also had the jurisdictional rights of hundreds (local administrative units) annexed to them. Oxfordshire's Domesday hundreds were imperfectly recorded, and their boundaries mapped here are reconstructed from later evidence. The high value of royal manors meant that overall the king possessed around a fifth of the county's revenues, though he owned less than a tenth of its productive arable land.

The Church's landholdings were extensive, comprising two-fifths of the county's revenues and more than a third of its plough-teams (see entry 13). The Church's manors were divided among six bishops of English sees, three Norman bishops, four English and two French abbeys, St Frideswide's minster in Oxford, and four other priests. The largest estates belonged to Odo Bishop of Bayeux until his fall in 1082. Like many large landholders, Odo kept a few manors in hand (called the demesne), including Deddington (worth the substantial sum of £60), but granted the rest to his retainers, usually in return for military or other services, a process known as subinfeudation. One of Odo's chief supporters was Wadard, who appears armed and mounted on the Bayeux Tapestry, and held several Oxfordshire manors of the bishop, including Cogges (worth the middling sum of £10).

Most of the county's manors were held by lay tenants-in-chief. The most extensive estates belonged to trusted followers of the king, including Robert d'Oilly, Roger d'Ivry, and Miles Crispin, each of whom held over 20 manors and together possessed almost a quarter of the county's revenues and around a fifth of its plough-teams. However, most of the county's lay estates were relatively small, often consisting of only one or two manors, although some of the county's landholders also held extensive estates elsewhere. The Conqueror's half-brother, Robert Count of Mortain, for example, held a single manor in Oxfordshire at Horley, but was one of England's largest post-Conquest landholders. Together these smaller estates accounted for around a sixth of the county's revenues and more than a third of its plough-teams.

A substantial part of the county's revenues was received not by the tenants-in-chief themselves but by those to whom they had subinfeudated their manors (known as mesne tenants). Domesday Book often gives no more information about these individuals than their Christian name, such as the Anglo-Saxon called Alfred, who held Cuxham (worth £6) and Harpsden (£5) of Miles Crispin, and only occasionally can a connection be established between them and later holders of the manor. Like Alfred, a number of other mesne tenants possessed English names and were probably survivors of the Conquest, but they were relatively few and mostly poor. By 1086 the wealth of Oxfordshire was largely in Norman hands.

Domesday Book is a list of manors; it does not record individual parishes, villages, or other settlements. Some 251 places in Oxfordshire were named, but many others in existence by 1086 were excluded. Some large manors comprised several separate places, subsumed under a single heading in the survey. In the upper Thames valley, Broadwell incorporated the neighbouring settlements of Filkins, Holwell and Kelmscott; though not recorded until the 12th or 13th century, their Anglo-Saxon names suggest that they were inhabited before the Norman Conquest. In a number of cases settlements belonged to manors some distance away. These detached properties often contained resources unavailable locally. The Bishop of Lincoln's manor of Banbury, for example, lacked woodland, but included Charlbury in Wychwood Forest, until the bishop granted it to Eynsham Abbey.

The absence of a place-name in Domesday Book does not, therefore, indicate a lack of habitation. The Chilterns settlement of Stonor was recorded in an Anglo-Saxon charter but is absent from Domesday Book, subsumed in the extensive manor of Pyrton. Conversely, some villages or parishes were divided among several manors. The parish of Bix near Henley-on-Thames was split between three manors, later called Bix Brand, Bix Gibwyn and Bromsden (recorded in Domesday Book as part of Benson), the internal boundaries of which can only be reconstructed imperfectly. Bix lay in an area of dispersed settlement, but nucleated villages, too, might be divided between owners. Two medieval manor houses lay next to the church in the small village of Shipton-on-Cherwell near Woodstock, belonging to the Domesday manors of Hugh de Grantmesnil and Ilbert de Lacy.

Domesday Book's description of manors does not reveal whether settlement was nucleated or dispersed. No indication is given, for example, that Miles Crispin's manors of Upper Heyford (nucleated) and Rotherfield Peppard (dispersed) contained very different settlement types. Nor, as a snapshot of a single year, does the survey illuminate the dynamics of settlement change. Nevertheless, some manors mentioned in 1086 evidently had sizable settlements which later contracted or were deserted, including Alwoldsbury in Alvescot and Bolney in Harpsden.

Domesday Book is probably accurate in describing the manors of 11th-century Oxfordshire as overwhelmingly rural. The only place with identifiably urban characteristics was Oxford, while the only market mentioned was at Bampton. Later medieval towns, including Banbury, Burford, Thame and Witney, appear as wholly rural settlements, and Henley-on-Thames is not even named. While the level of market activity was almost certainly greater than the survey suggests, most Oxfordshire towns developed in the 12th century and later. Although it undoubtedly has shortcomings, Domesday Book offers an unparalleled guide to Oxfordshire's early medieval settlement geography.

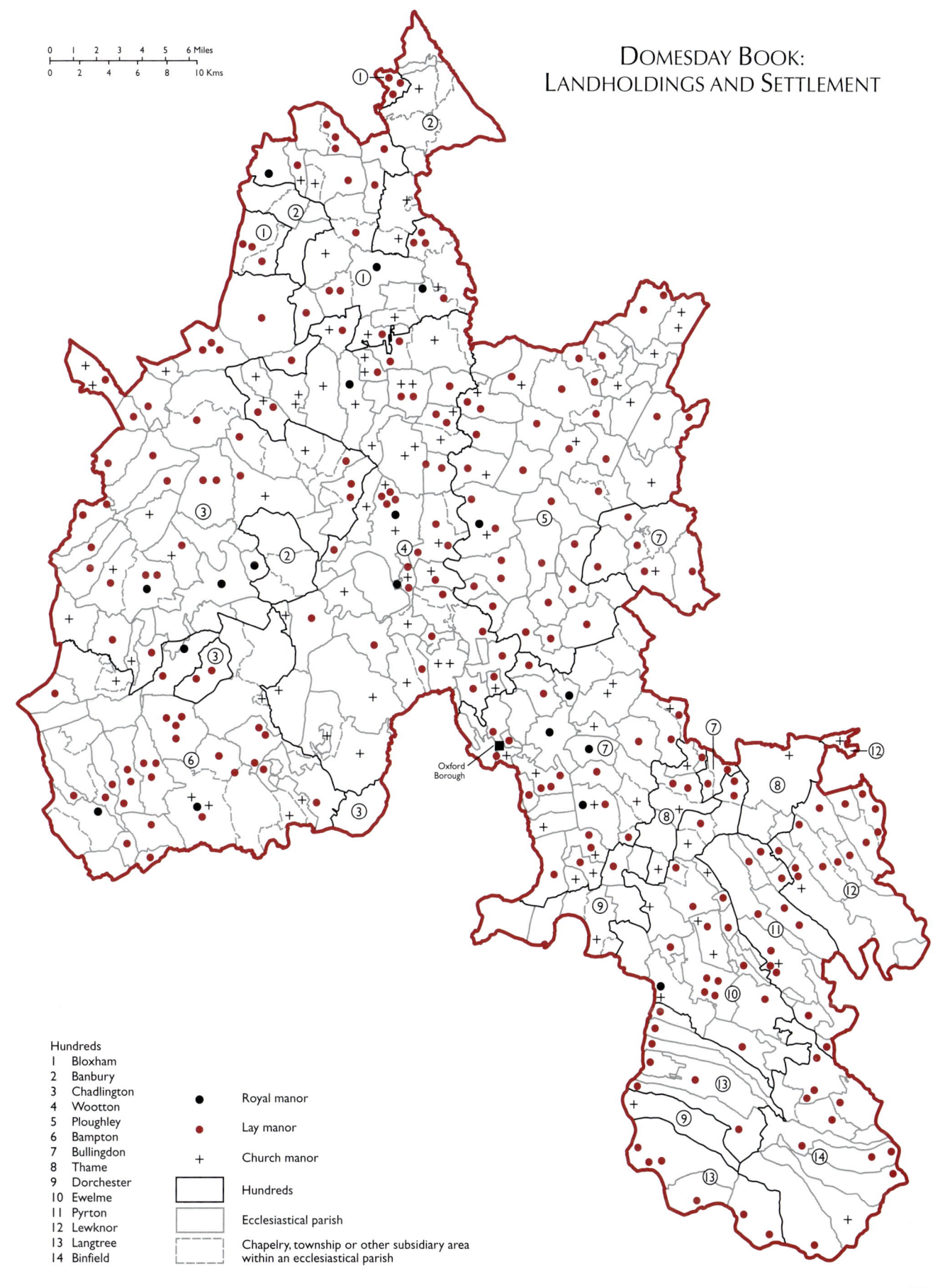

Domesday Book: Landholdings and Settlement

Hundreds
1. Bloxham
2. Banbury
3. Chadlington
4. Wootton
5. Ploughley
6. Bampton
7. Bullingdon
8. Thame
9. Dorchester
10. Ewelme
11. Pyrton
12. Lewknor
13. Langtree
14. Binfield

- ● Royal manor
- ● Lay manor
- + Church manor
- ☐ Hundreds
- ☐ Ecclesiastical parish
- ┊ Chapelry, township or other subsidiary area within an ecclesiastical parish

Oxford Borough

33

13 · Domesday Landscape and Land Use — Mark Page

By 1086 the Oxfordshire countryside was already extensively worked and carefully managed. The Normans took possession of a long-settled and thoroughly exploited land. Domesday Book provides valuable (though highly abbreviated) information about the county's farmland, describing its arable in terms of plough-lands and plough-teams, with more straightforward measurements of meadow and pasture. Woodland and waste are also mentioned, as are the many mills and fisheries located on rivers and streams, while more occasional references are made to other resources, including gardens (in Holywell, Oxford) and a pottery (at Bladon).

Most 11th-century Oxfordshire communities practised mixed farming, primarily intended for their own subsistence rather than for the market. The demands of self-sufficiency help to explain the many manorial and parish boundaries which encompassed lands of different quality (such as the strip-shaped parishes in the Chilterns) and which in turn were reflected in the Domesday descriptions of mixed resources and land use. Nevertheless, the county's varied geology and topography affected the ways in which particular manors were exploited, resulting in an uneven distribution across Oxfordshire of the available arable, meadow, pasture and woodland.

Arable, expressed as the number of plough-teams in 1086, was most heavily concentrated in the north and west, including Adderbury, Banbury and Cropredy on the marlstone uplands, and extending in an arc across the limestone uplands to the west of the river Cherwell north of Woodstock over to Shipton-under-Wychwood and Taynton on the border with Gloucestershire. Another area of dense arable cultivation lay south-east of Oxford in the plain between the rivers Thame and Thames at the base of the Chiltern escarpment. By contrast, arable farming was less intense in Wychwood Forest, the upper Thames valley, the area around Otmoor, and in the Chilterns. The precise meaning of Domesday's description of arable is contested. A plough-land is usually taken to represent around 100 acres, the land one plough could cultivate in a year, while a plough-team referred to an actual implement of wood and iron, most likely pulled by eight oxen. In Oxfordshire it has been suggested that the number of plough-lands indicated the plough-teams in operation in 1066, not always the same as the number of teams in use 20 years later. On manors with fewer plough-teams in 1086, there was probably understocking and room for expansion; where there were more plough-teams than plough-lands, the extension of arable farming may already have occurred.

Understocking was particularly marked in the Chilterns and north Oxfordshire east of the Cherwell, where the heavy stonebrash soil was difficult to work. Among the manors affected was Hethe near Bicester, an Anglo-Saxon word meaning heath or uncultivated ground; in 1086 it had eight plough-lands but only three teams. Manors with surplus plough-teams were prominent on the fertile loams at the foot of the Chilterns: Cuxham was typical in having four plough-lands and five teams. Arable farming had also been extended around Wychwood, indicating woodland clearance; North Leigh, for example, had ten plough-lands and 14 teams. Whilst Domesday Book reveals the distribution of arable, it tells us little about land organisation, whether in large open fields farmed in common by the community, or in small individual closes.

The draught animals (mostly oxen in 1086) on which arable farming depended were largely grass fed. Meadow was highly prized because it yielded a hay crop which could be mown and stored over winter; however, it was labour-intensive, and this may have limited its exploitation. Widely available along the county's many rivers and streams, the amount of meadow belonging to individual manors nevertheless varied from a few acres (or none at all) to several hundred, and to some extent was probably determined by the need to feed plough-oxen. Thus, relatively little meadow was recorded in the Chilterns (where plough-teams were also few in number), though most manors had access to Thames-side meadows, which were more fully exploited in later centuries. In Domesday Book pasture probably meant grazing land which could not be mown. Its concentration on the north-western edge of the Oxfordshire Cotswolds and in the clay vales, and its absence from the Chilterns, suggests that the county's pasture was inconsistently recorded. Perhaps only enclosed pasture, which could be measured in terms of acres or perches, was included. Large tracts of unenclosed grazing land was probably available in Oxfordshire's woodland, the distribution of which was roughly in inverse proportion to the area under pasture. Domesday woodland was most heavily concentrated in the forested areas of Wychwood, Shotover and Stowood, and on the clay-with-flints soils of the Chilterns.

Oxfordshire's landscape and land use were constantly changing to meet the needs of its population, as a comparison of Domesday Book with later records shows. Some changes were made by landholders, for example investment in mills and fisheries; others were undertaken collectively or individually by manorial tenants. Domesday lists some 6,784 tenants in rural Oxfordshire. Of these, over 54% were villeins, usually considered to have occupied relatively large holdings (15 to 30 acres), and probably largely self-sufficient. Tenants known as bordars made up a further 29% of the observed population. These were probably low-status estate workers occupying smallholdings of perhaps five acres or less, and often succeeded in the later middle ages by cottars. Despite considerable local variation, villeins and bordars were a slightly larger proportion of the population in eastern rather than western Oxfordshire, where slaves were more prominent. Slavery was in steep decline by 1086, but nevertheless around 1,022 slaves were recorded in Oxfordshire, 15% of the population. Finally, a small number of other groups were mentioned, including freemen, fishermen, and knights. The total population of the county cannot be recovered, but taking into account up to 1,070 urban properties in Oxford, and using a common multiplier of five to allow for whole families, the survey produces an estimate of around 40,000 people.

DOMESDAY BOOK:
LANDSCAPE AND LAND USE

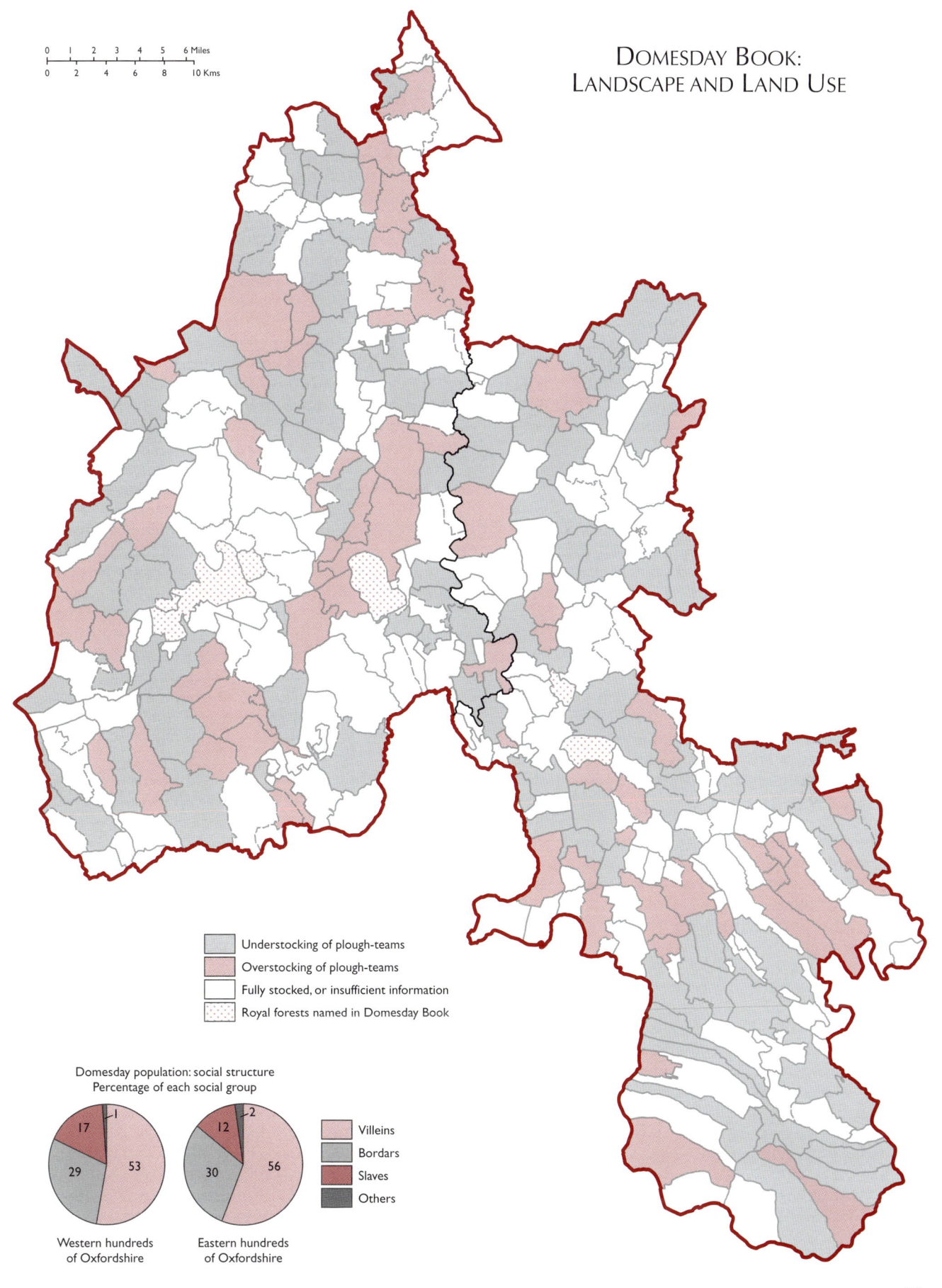

- Understocking of plough-teams
- Overstocking of plough-teams
- Fully stocked, or insufficient information
- Royal forests named in Domesday Book

Domesday population: social structure
Percentage of each social group

Western hundreds of Oxfordshire: Villeins 53, Bordars 29, Slaves 17, Others 1

Eastern hundreds of Oxfordshire: Villeins 56, Bordars 30, Slaves 12, Others 2

14 · Castles and Moated Sites

James Bond

Castles can be defined as the fortified private residences of a medieval lord, as distinct from communal defences, such as town walls, and forts, housing army detachments. The map depicts a range of medieval sites whose principal shared feature is the presence of some ostensibly defensive component. They date from the late 11th to the early 16th century. Classification is difficult because the structures themselves were subject to change.

Although the dwellings of some Anglo-Saxon thegns had some form of defensive perimeter, true castles are generally agreed to have been introduced into England by the Normans. The first constructions were of earth and timber. The simplest form was the ringwork, where domestic buildings lay within a more or less oval enclosure protected by a bank, palisade and external ditch. The more distinctive motte and bailey included the additional feature of a high earthen mound with a timber palisade and timber tower. Within a few years of the Conquest the more important castles were being reinforced with stone curtain walls and keeps.

Locally the first priority for the Norman invaders was to subdue the Saxon *burh* of Oxford, the largest and potentially most hostile centre of population. Control over a strategic crossing of the Thames was a secondary objective. Both were achieved in 1071 by Robert d'Oilly's construction of a large motte and bailey over a previously settled area on the western side of the *burh*. During the 12th century the bailey was strengthened by a stone wall with interval towers, and a polygonal stone keep was built on top of the motte; in 1216 a semicircular barbican was added to the south-east. By the mid-13th century, however, Oxford's strategic importance had diminished, and the castle began to fall into decay.

Smaller earthen castles associated with local lordships appeared in some numbers during the late 11th and 12th centuries. The most remarkable group is at Ascott-under-Wychwood, where three small castles lie within a few hundred yards of each other. Two are of motte-and-bailey form, while the central one had a stone tower from the outset, with clay mounded up around its base. A stone tower was also used instead of a motte at Middleton Stoney. Aerial photography has revealed an oval enclosure, probably Roger d'Ivry's original stronghold, antedating the visible earthworks of Beaumont Castle at Mixbury. A moated ringwork at Cogges may reasonably be equated with the fortified manor of the Arsic family. At Chipping Norton much more substantial earthworks survive of the FitzAlans' castle, a large ringwork with footings of stone internal buildings and two subsidiary outer enclosures. The earliest phase of Deddington Castle, built before 1100, consisted of an embanked enclosure some eight and a half acres in extent. Here a polygonal stone-walled inner bailey was inserted in the early 12th century, and timber domestic buildings were replaced in stone after about 1160.

Oxfordshire was a cockpit of conflict during the Anarchy of 1139–53. Oxford Castle was held for Matilda, and in 1141 was besieged by Stephen's army, which threw up siege works outside the northern wall. A succession of siege works was also made at Crowmarsh during actions against Wallingford Castle, on the Berkshire bank of the Thames, in 1139, 1145–6 and 1152. Two adulterine 'castles' built in 1141 by Matilda, at Woodstock and Bampton, probably represent makeshift strengthenings of existing buildings; the latter was simply a temporary fortification of the church tower. Investigations at Radcot in 2008 revealed a large keep built in the late 11th century, defended by Matilda in 1142, and then demolished in the later 12th century. Many castles garrisoned during the Anarchy were subsequently slighted: the tower of Ascot d'Oilly was dismantled around 1180 and that at Middleton Stoney in the early 13th century.

Despite a reduction in the number of castles after the Anarchy, the most important remaining sites continued to be elaborated. New techniques of fortification, involving concentric defences with curtain walls, round towers and moats, employed most conspicuously in the conquest of north Wales by Edward I, were introduced to Oxfordshire in a major reconstruction of Banbury Castle somewhere around 1300. Subsequently the Crown began to exert more control over the fortification of private manor houses by granting crenellation licences, and between 1315 and 1406 licences were acquired for five sites in Oxfordshire. The Edwardian style of quadrangular enclosure with corner towers, with or without a moat, was also employed at Ham Court, Greys Court and Shirburn. Increasingly, however, the outward display of military strength was more for show than for any serious defensive purpose. By the time that Hanwell Castle was begun, in about 1500, requirements of domestic comfort took precedence over defence, and the corner towers, gatehouse and battlemented parapets were entirely for show, robbed of any defensive value by large outward-facing windows.

Moats represent a form of quasi-fortification particularly characteristic of the 13th and early 14th centuries. Their distribution is concentrated in the flat clay vales, where construction of water-holding ditches or ponds is relatively easy. About 70% of moated houses in Oxfordshire are located within existing or deserted nucleated settlements, and it is likely that most of these are manorial sites. A few isolated moats in the southern Chilterns and around the Wychwood Forest margins may represent farmsteads of sub-manorial rank associated with assarting and colonisation of waste. The majority of moats are simple quadrilateral enclosures between three-quarters of an acre and two acres in extent, surrounding the main dwelling. Some have more than one island, the subsidiary enclosures normally accommodating farm buildings or gardens. Many moats, especially in the clay vales, are linked with fishpond complexes. Concentric moats, such as the triple ditches which surround the Beckley Park lodge, are rare in Oxfordshire and limited to sites of particular prestige. The practice of making moats round dwellings went out of fashion in the later middle ages, but the digging of moats as garden features continued well into the 17th century, and the latter practice may account for rather more sites than was appreciated in earlier accounts.

Castles and Moated Sites

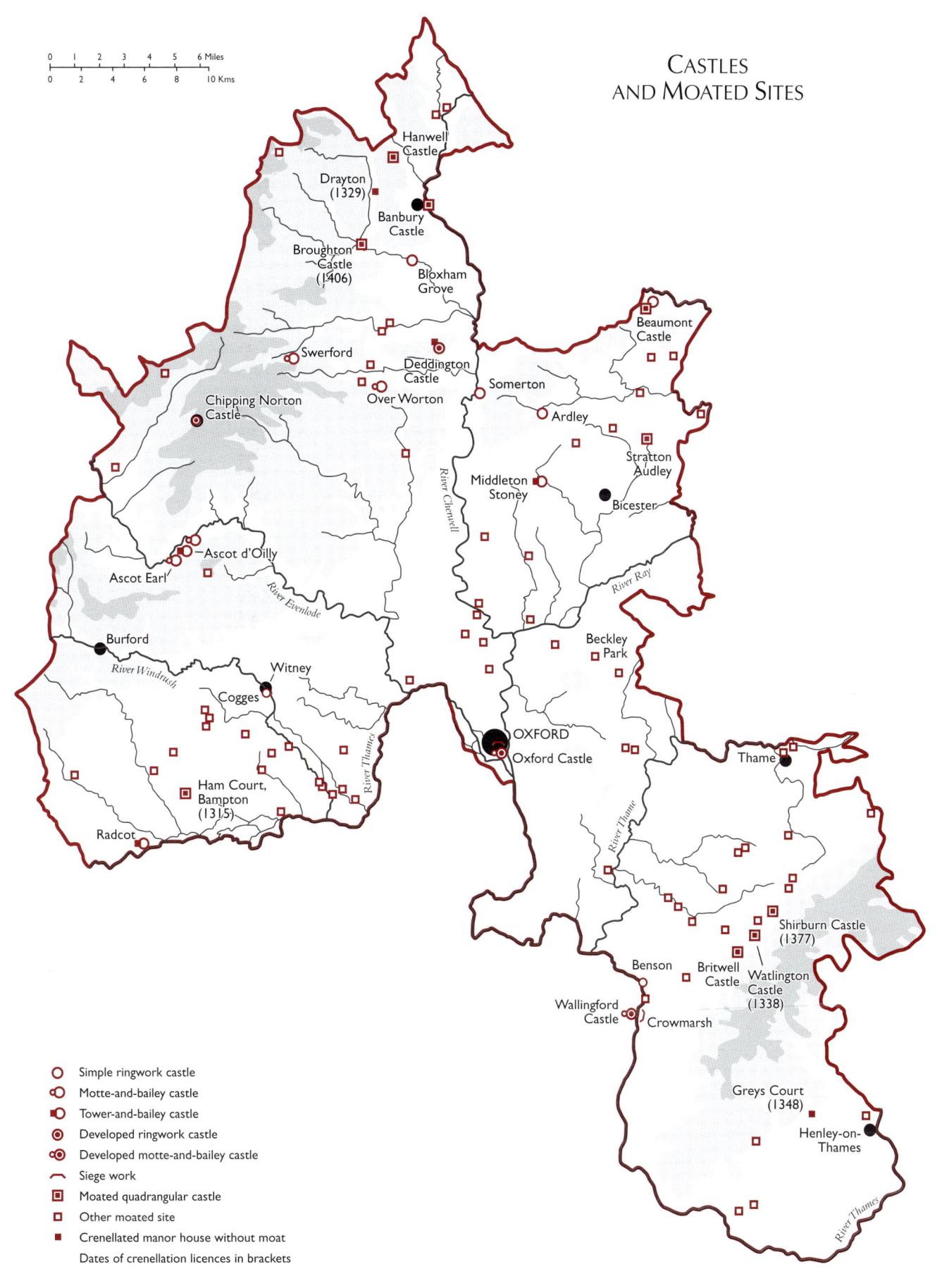

Scale: 0–6 Miles / 0–10 Kms

Labelled sites:
- Hanwell Castle
- Drayton (1329)
- Banbury Castle
- Broughton Castle (1406)
- Bloxham Grove
- Beaumont Castle
- Swerford
- Deddington Castle
- Over Worton
- Somerton
- Ardley
- Chipping Norton Castle
- Stratton Audley
- Middleton Stoney
- Bicester
- Ascot d'Oilly
- Ascot Earl
- Beckley Park
- Burford
- Witney
- Cogges
- OXFORD / Oxford Castle
- Thame
- Ham Court, Bampton (1315)
- Radcot
- Shirburn Castle (1377)
- Benson
- Britwell Castle
- Watlington Castle (1338)
- Wallingford Castle
- Crowmarsh
- Greys Court (1348)
- Henley-on-Thames

Rivers: River Cherwell, River Ray, River Evenlode, River Windrush, River Thames, River Thame

Legend:
- ○ Simple ringwork castle
- ⊙◯ Motte-and-bailey castle
- ◐ Tower-and-bailey castle
- ⊙ Developed ringwork castle
- ⊙⊙ Developed motte-and-bailey castle
- — Siege work
- ▣ Moated quadrangular castle
- □ Other moated site
- ■ Crenellated manor house without moat
- Dates of crenellation licences in brackets

37

15 · Medieval Towns, Markets and Fairs — Robert Peberdy

In the mid 11th century there was probably a network of trading centres, with regular markets and fairs, which included some places with minster churches. Although some centres had developed quasi-urban features such as resident craftsmen and even a market-place (as at Bampton), they remained essentially agricultural settlements. Trading probably took place mainly in churchyards or on greens. Only Oxford was clearly urban, with a large concentrated population, distinctive layout, and extensive non-agricultural economy (see entry 29). But urban development, including a market-place, has also been suggested at Dorchester, a cathedral centre until 1072.

From c.1100 small towns were developed, sometimes alongside existing settlements, each providing a weekly market and annual fair (trading on consecutive days). Trading was also started on some rural manors. The outcome was a new network of trading centres, in which towns were pre-eminent. It subsumed some pre-existing markets which had been transferred to new towns. Urban societies were established throughout Oxfordshire, and the rural economy and peasant life became to some extent dependent on towns. The foundation of towns and much trading on manors were lords' initiatives, though royal charters were increasingly obtained to give legal status to markets and fairs. By the mid 1200s, possibly 17 small towns existed, of which 13 proved successful, though foundation dates are mostly unknown. Small towns were visibly different from other settlements, e.g. most had a prominent market-place. Although Normans contributed to urban development (e.g. Robert fitz Hamon at Burford by 1107), the foundation of Oxfordshire's small towns was part of a Europe-wide movement.

At least five towns were founded near lords' households: Banbury, Chipping Norton and Deddington, associated with castles; and Witney and Woodstock, associated with other residences. Lords encouraged traders and craftsmen who could provide goods and services. But they created towns primarily to stimulate economic activity and increase their own incomes – from rents, tolls and courts. Founding a town required conversion of demesne land from agricultural to urban use. Risk was minimised by upgrading important settlements or selecting places with concentrations of traffic. Six towns were founded at settlements with important churches (Bampton, Banbury, Bicester, Charlbury, Eynsham, Thame), an 'urbanising' of centres already having quasi-urban activities. Most towns were located on main route-ways. There were unsuccessful towns: Middleton Stoney is documented in the 13th century; Standlake, a cloth-making and market centre in the 13th to 15th centuries, has a town-like layout; Islip, on a major route-way, received market grants (1245, 1364) and has a possibly urban topography; and Chinnor contained burgages (townsmen's tenements) in 1338.

By 1260 urbanisation was relatively dense, presumably reflecting a prosperous rural economy. The 14 successful towns (including Oxford) represented an average of one town per 54 square miles (140 sq. km). In this Oxfordshire was similar to the highly urbanised west Midlands rather than the less urbanised east Midlands. Each town was on average 8.8 miles (14.1 km) from neighbouring towns, and 6.3 miles (10.1 km) from its nearest neighbour, slightly less than the desirable minimum separation between markets (6.66 miles) recommended in the 13th-century legal treatise 'Bracton'. Most Oxfordshire small towns were founded by barons, bishops or monasteries and remained under lordly control. Only Woodstock and Henley were royal foundations. Lords normally granted liberties to householders, such as the right to sell tenements. Townsmen were occasionally allowed to form a merchant gild with jurisdiction over trading. But most towns were governed through manorial courts, either a portmoot or manor court. The strongest corporate liberties developed in the royal towns. Oxford became self-governing during the 12th century. In Henley, a royal town until 1244, a gild acquired extensive authority by the late 13th century. In Woodstock, a gild existed by the early 14th century and was replaced by a chartered corporation in 1453. Townsmen sometimes formed religious and social gilds as parallel centres of authority. Towns were often designated as boroughs, denoting legal status, but this usually recognised personal rather than corporate liberties.

Inhabitants of small towns engaged in craftwork (leather, wood, metal, cloth), victualling (e.g. as bakers, butchers) and distribution (e.g. as chapmen, mercers). There were typically at most about 30 occupations. The scope for specialisation was limited; it occurred only at advantageous locations. Burford exported high-quality Cotswold wool. Witney and Banbury, with access to capital, water, wool and fuller's earth, became cloth-making centres (like Oxford). Between the 1290s and 1340s Henley was a foremost centre for grain-buying by London cornmongers. The extent of rural trading is unclear. Markets and fairs may have gone unrecorded because they lacked royal authorisation. (An unchartered market at Crowmarsh Gifford is known in the 12th and 13th centuries only because it allegedly damaged Wallingford's market.) Many rural places for which markets and fairs were authorised in the 13th and 14th centuries were near towns. Most chartered rural markets evidently failed to become established, though Hook Norton market, granted in the 15th century, apparently flourished. Most fairs were held during May to September.

Around 1300 Oxfordshire's leading small towns probably had 1,000 to 1,200 inhabitants each. They were: Banbury, Bicester, Chipping Norton, Henley, Thame, and Witney. Towns were affected by demographic and economic change. Populations were halved by the Black Death (1348–9), but many towns recovered as the purchasing power of peasants increased. In the mid 15th century towns suffered further depression caused by shortage of coin. Populations declined, but widespread conversion of arable land to pasture enabled some townsmen to prosper from wool and other trades (see entry 16). Town economies began to change in the 16th century as rural and urban populations increased, wool-exporting declined, inland trading expanded and London became more influential.

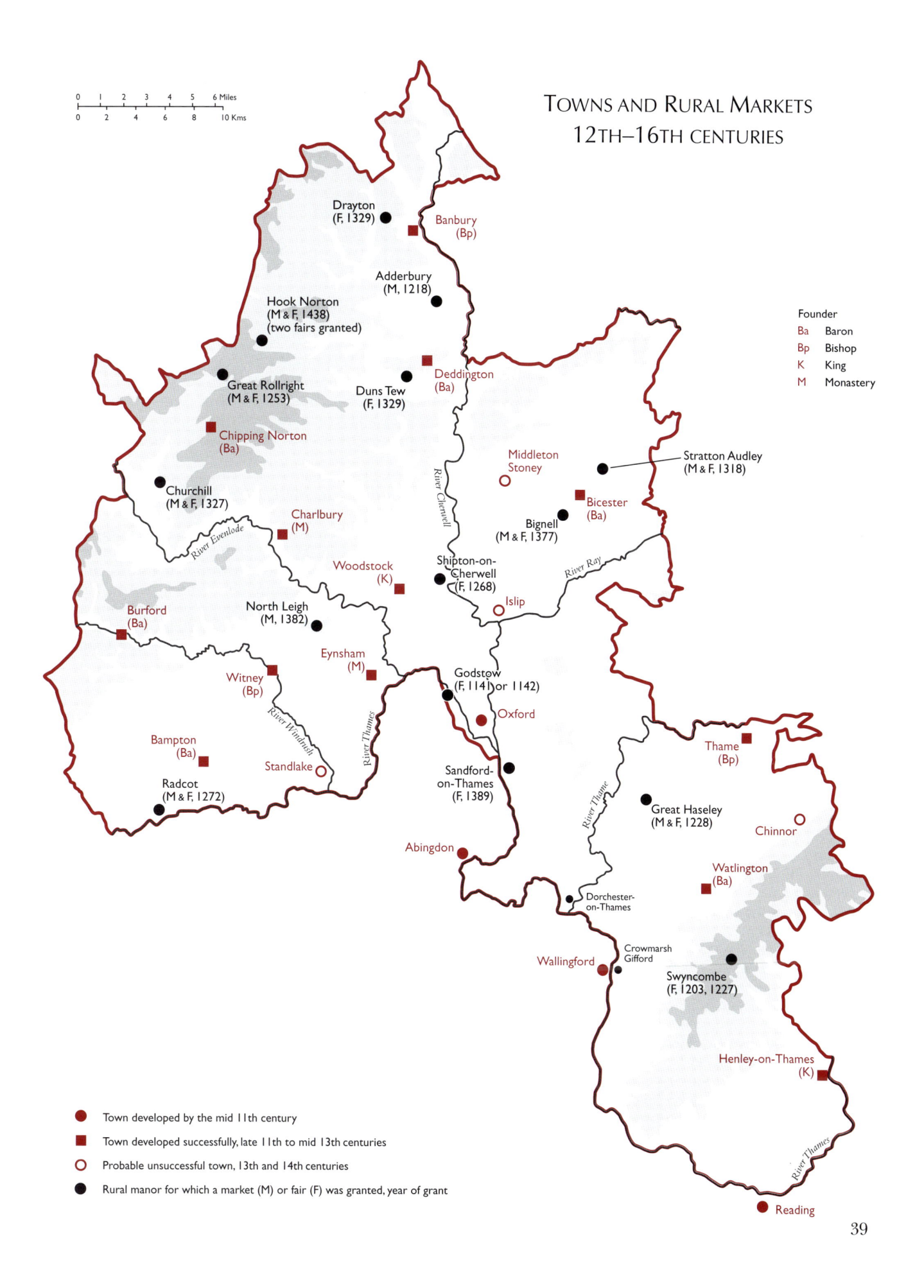

Towns and Rural Markets 12th–16th Centuries

Founder
- Ba Baron
- Bp Bishop
- K   King
- M   Monastery

- ● Town developed by the mid 11th century
- ■ Town developed successfully, late 11th to mid 13th centuries
- ○ Probable unsuccessful town, 13th and 14th centuries
- ● Rural manor for which a market (M) or fair (F) was granted, year of grant

Drayton (F, 1329)
Banbury (Bp)
Adderbury (M, 1218)
Hook Norton (M & F, 1438) (two fairs granted)
Great Rollright (M & F, 1253)
Duns Tew (F, 1329)
Deddington (Ba)
Chipping Norton (Ba)
Middleton Stoney
Stratton Audley (M & F, 1318)
Churchill (M & F, 1327)
Bicester (Ba)
Bignell (M & F, 1377)
Charlbury (M)
Woodstock (K)
Shipton-on-Cherwell (F, 1268)
Islip
Burford (Ba)
North Leigh (M, 1382)
Eynsham (M)
Godstow (F, 1141 or 1142)
Witney (Bp)
Oxford
Thame (Bp)
Bampton (Ba)
Standlake
Sandford-on-Thames (F, 1389)
Radcot (M & F, 1272)
Great Haseley (M & F, 1228)
Chinnor
Abingdon
Watlington (Ba)
Dorchester-on-Thames
Wallingford
Crowmarsh Gifford
Swyncombe (F, 1203, 1227)
Henley-on-Thames (K)
Reading

39

16 · Medieval Wool and Cloth Trades — Robert Peberdy

In Oxfordshire, a county with little permanent pasture, sheep-keeping and wool production have been shaped by agricultural priorities rather than natural conditions. In the 11th century wool was a by-product of a rural economy focused primarily on cereal production. Corn was grown in large fields (usually two or three per village), whilst in the Chilterns smaller fields were characteristic. Sheep were used to maintain soil fertility, manuring fallow fields and stubble. Wool production was ubiquitous, but flock sizes and wool output were limited by the extent of commons for grazing. Much wool was used in local, domestic cloth making, as part of peasant self-sufficiency. Women spun wool into yarn with weighted spindles, and laboriously wove it on upright looms.

In the 11th and 12th centuries, cloth was industrialised and commercialised. Concentrations of artisans' workshops developed, mainly in towns. The more efficient horizontal loom and elaborate 'finishing' resulted in cloth of higher quality. Finishing included fulling (pounding cloth with water and soap and scouring with fuller's earth), tentering (stretching and drying), napping (shearing loose fibres) and sometimes dyeing. Most cloth makers were men. Cloth industries diverted wool from domestic use into markets and supply networks. Peasants increasingly bought cloth from the market, though peasant women continued to spin wool. Industrial cloth making became established in Oxfordshire. A centre existed at Oxford by 1130, when a weavers' gild was recorded. Products included russets (grey cloths) and burrels (coarse cloths). The gild's royal licence conferred a monopoly within 5 leagues (7½ miles). By the 13th century there were also sizable industries at Witney, Standlake and Banbury. Underlying factors included availability and quality of water and provision of capital. Other small towns probably contained a few cloth makers meeting local demand.

Between the late 1100s and early 1400s the fortunes of Oxfordshire's cloth industries varied. Efficiency grew with the introduction of water-powered mechanical fulling. Purpose-built fulling mills or modified corn mills were funded by lords. The earliest known was at Minster Lovell by 1197; more were installed in the 13th century. However, by the later 1200s the industries were in difficulty. Oxford weavers claimed that merchants were undercutting them by using cheaper rural weavers (e.g. in Cowley, Beckley, Islip). But though there were some village weavers, a cloth-making district did not develop. Oxford's industry revived: in 1381 the town contained 149 cloth makers, including 62 weavers. Banbury's industry was also strong, and cloth making continued, probably at reduced levels, in west Oxfordshire. Oxford's industry declined in the early 15th century.

Wool trading was significant by *c.*1100 at Oxford and Burford and expanded during the 12th and 13th centuries, when wool was England's major export, principally to the Flanders cloth industry. Wool was produced on peasant holdings and lords' demesnes. The best was Cotswold wool from west Oxfordshire, which was rated as the second or third finest English wool. Other Oxfordshire wool was of slightly lower quality. Wool exporting – initial purchase, inland transport and shipping – involved foreign and English merchants, and local 'woolmen' (or 'broggers'). In the later 1200s much Oxfordshire wool was bought by English merchants based elsewhere, mainly in London but also in Andover (Hants) and Ludlow (Salop). A few exporters lived in Oxfordshire: at Thame, Oxford, Burford and Chipping Norton. At Banbury woolmen gathered Midland wool; and in the early 14th century Witney and Deddington were important trading centres. Oxfordshire wool was normally shipped from London or Southampton. Exporting was probably sustained during the 14th century.

Oxfordshire agriculture remained corn-oriented while population continued to increase. It was the religious houses which notably saw wool production as a relatively easy way to increase income. They sometimes consolidated open-field holdings and converted them to pasture in the 12th and 13th centuries. In Oxfordshire five houses emphasised wool production: Eynsham, Osney, Bicester, Thame and Bruern. Houses also acted as middlemen for local peasants.

From the early 1400s changed demographic and economic conditions altered agricultural strategy. Smaller populations meant reduced demand for cereals and resulted in surplus arable land. Throughout Oxfordshire many landholdings were consolidated and used as sheep pastures, despite lower wool prices. Sheep flocks and wool production expanded, benefiting local woolmen. Some built substantial businesses, selling to Italian merchants at Southampton, exporting via London, or possibly supplying cloth-making districts in southern England. Between the mid 15th and mid 16th centuries there were wealthy wool merchants in most Oxfordshire small towns. For example, from Henley John Elmes (*fl.* 1417–60) traded wool in Southampton and imported alum and wine. He was wealthy enough to buy a manor and leave a chantry.

From the mid 1400s Witney's cloth making revived. Wool merchants such as Thomas Fermor (d.1485) possibly provided investment and marketed cloths, and the Bishop of Winchester contributed a new fulling mill (1458–9). From the 1470s national exports expanded, doubling in 80 years. Witney, Standlake and probably Banbury benefited but, mysteriously, not Oxford. Cloth making grew elsewhere, notably at Henley (five weavers recorded 1494–1511) and Burford. The main late-medieval product was 'broadcloth', woven on two-man looms.

Wool and cloth were among the principal commodities produced in medieval Oxfordshire and traded there and more widely. Their main impact was to raise incomes across a wide range of society. The wool and cloth trades continued beyond the 1550s. Wool declined in importance as overseas exporting lessened and population growth put greater emphasis on grain and dairying. However, cloth making prospered at Banbury and Witney, with the new Witney blankets achieving international repute.

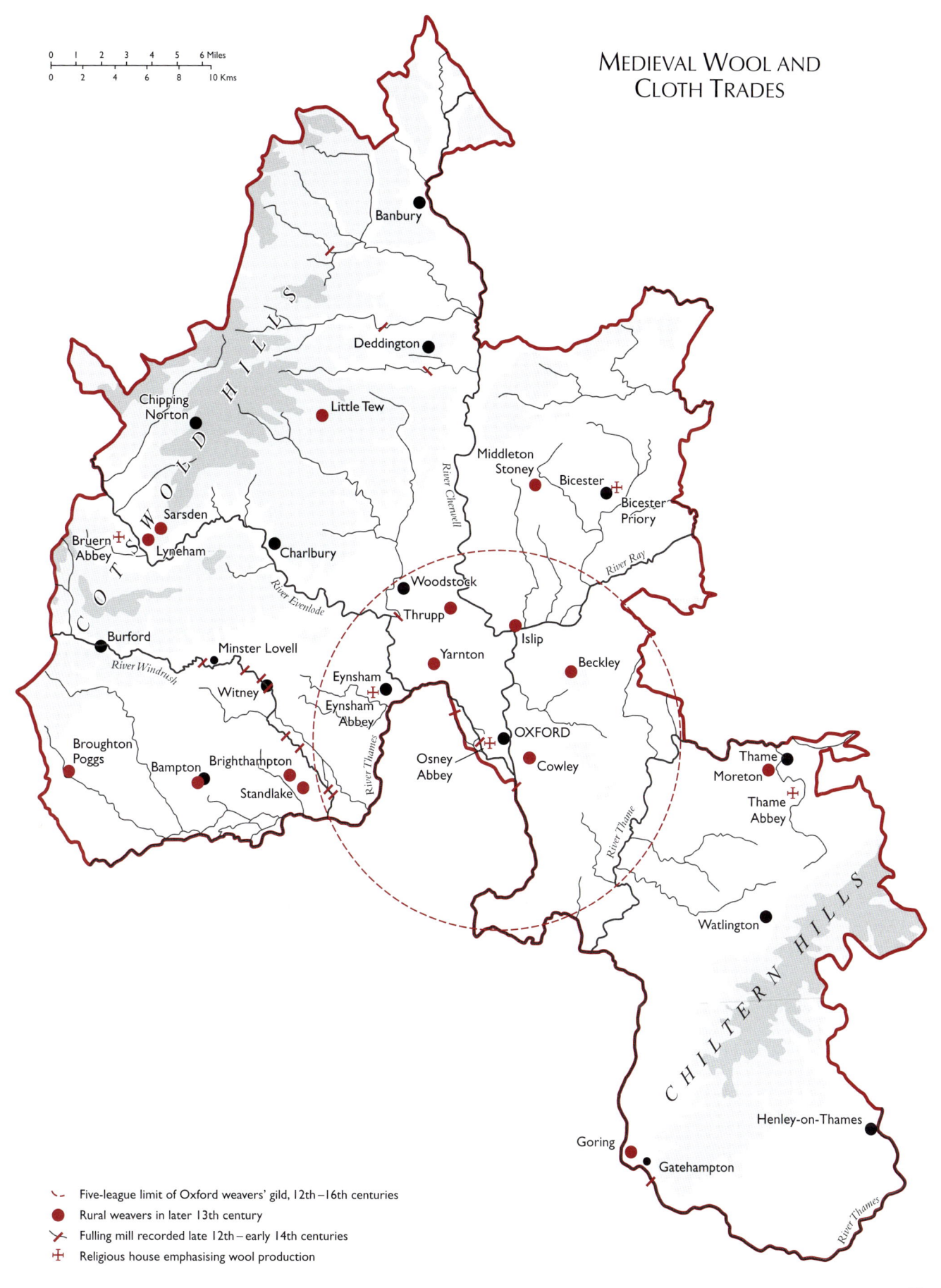

MEDIEVAL WOOL AND CLOTH TRADES

- ⌇ Five-league limit of Oxford weavers' gild, 12th–16th centuries
- ● Rural weavers in later 13th century
- ✕ Fulling mill recorded late 12th – early 14th centuries
- ☩ Religious house emphasising wool production

41

17 · The Development of Parishes
Elizabeth Gemmill

Between the 10th and 12th centuries, the ecclesiastical landscape of England changed dramatically. The network of large minster parishes came to be overlaid by a finer mesh, made up of many more local churches, in smaller parishes, usually served by a single priest. The large parishes of many minsters were eroded and divided, although some retained vestiges of their former status. The broad outlines of these developments are well established, although the timing and local details are less well known, and the parish structure that was in existence by the end of the 12th century was to be the pattern for the remainder of the medieval period and well beyond.

The change resulted from developments in the late Anglo-Saxon society and economy. As the population increased, and as nucleated village communities developed, there came a need for locally situated churches in which villagers could worship, receive the sacraments, and be buried. Large units of landownership were breaking up, and there developed a wider class of local lords, holding smaller estates. For them, ownership of a church was an adjunct of lordship. Thus the development of the village or manorial church responded to the needs of the local community and the desire of its lord. Often the parish coincided with the extent of the lord's estates. In his charter to Osney Abbey of c.1130–5, Robert d'Oilly gave 'these churches of my estates', which included Kidlington, Weston-on-the-Green, Hook Norton and Chastleton.[1]

We rarely know who exactly was responsible for building individual churches, but it is clear that manorial lords claimed ownership of them, including the right to dispose of tithes, to appoint clerks on their own authority to serve in the churches, and to grant them out. But the impact of papal reforms in the 12th century was to restrict the rights of patrons in churches, leaving only the right (called the right of advowson) of presenting clerks to the bishop for admission. Since it was no longer possible for laymen to receive income from churches, some granted their rights to monasteries and cathedral chapters. Even so, advowsons were highly valued by patrons who retained them, as they could still use 'their' churches as a way of providing for their protégés. Meanwhile the bishop ensured that the needs of the local community were also met. Thus when Ingram was admitted to North Leigh on the presentation of Robert, Count of Dreux, in 1225, he had to provide a suitable chaplain since he himself did not know 'our' language.[2]

The proliferation of new local churches inevitably reduced the importance of the minsters, since they were built within the minster parishes and diverted their revenues, most obviously their entitlement to tithes and burial fees. Some minsters lost their rights; others, more powerful, retained theirs. An example of a compromise was when, in the early 12th century, the Bishop of Lincoln consecrated Cassington chapel, built by Geoffrey de Clinton within the former minster parish of Eynsham. The Abbot of Eynsham gave up his church's right to the tithes of Cassington and Worton but retained the burial dues from Cassington and half the offerings of the two feasts of St Peter.[3] The church of Bampton retained, throughout the later medieval period, the right to bury the dead of a number of churches in the surrounding area. Some former minsters, such as Thame and its dependent chapels, became prebendal churches; others, like Dorchester, were re-established as religious houses and retained rights over the churches with which they had long been associated. The rights of the new, local churches were in turn safeguarded, and indeed the bishop had authority to license the building of any new chapel which might infringe on the rights of the parish church.

The richest source for the development of parish churches is the architecture of the churches themselves, and the archaeology associated with their sites. Many were built in the 10th and 11th centuries, but the greatest period of new building was between the mid 11th and 12th centuries, and by the mid 12th century most were complete. Unfortunately Domesday Book, a vital source of information for the existence of churches in some counties, is most disappointing for Oxfordshire; but monastic cartularies (Abingdon, Eynsham, Osney and St Frideswide) and the early charters of the cathedral church of Lincoln contain many post-Conquest grants and confirmations of grants of Oxfordshire churches.

From the early 13th century the evidence becomes much more comprehensive. Bishops' registers survive from 1209, and contain institutions to parish churches and chapels and ordinations of vicarages. Later, there are papal assessments of the value of churches, most importantly the Taxatio of Pope Nicholas IV made in 1291–2. This is the main source for the information in the map opposite. The parish boundaries shown on the map are, however, those of the 19th century, which were not identical with what we know of parish boundaries in the medieval period.

Although not every church known to have existed in the late 13th century was mentioned in the Taxatio, and certainly not every chapel, it nonetheless reveals clearly how parochialisation had advanced. It listed, deanery by deanery, the value of churches and chapels in England and Wales, and included details of pensions, of portions, and, in some cases, of patrons. The sheer number of churches with a value of £10 or less suggests in itself that many churches were founded to serve small, local communities. The map shows that there was a fair distribution of churches and chapels over the county as a whole, although with a greater concentration of churches in the centre and east and, of course, in Oxford. The distribution of churches in the south of the county reflects the topography. At the same time, some of the wealthier churches, with their complexes of daughter churches and chapels, were the survivors of the former minster system which the newer churches and their parishes overlaid.

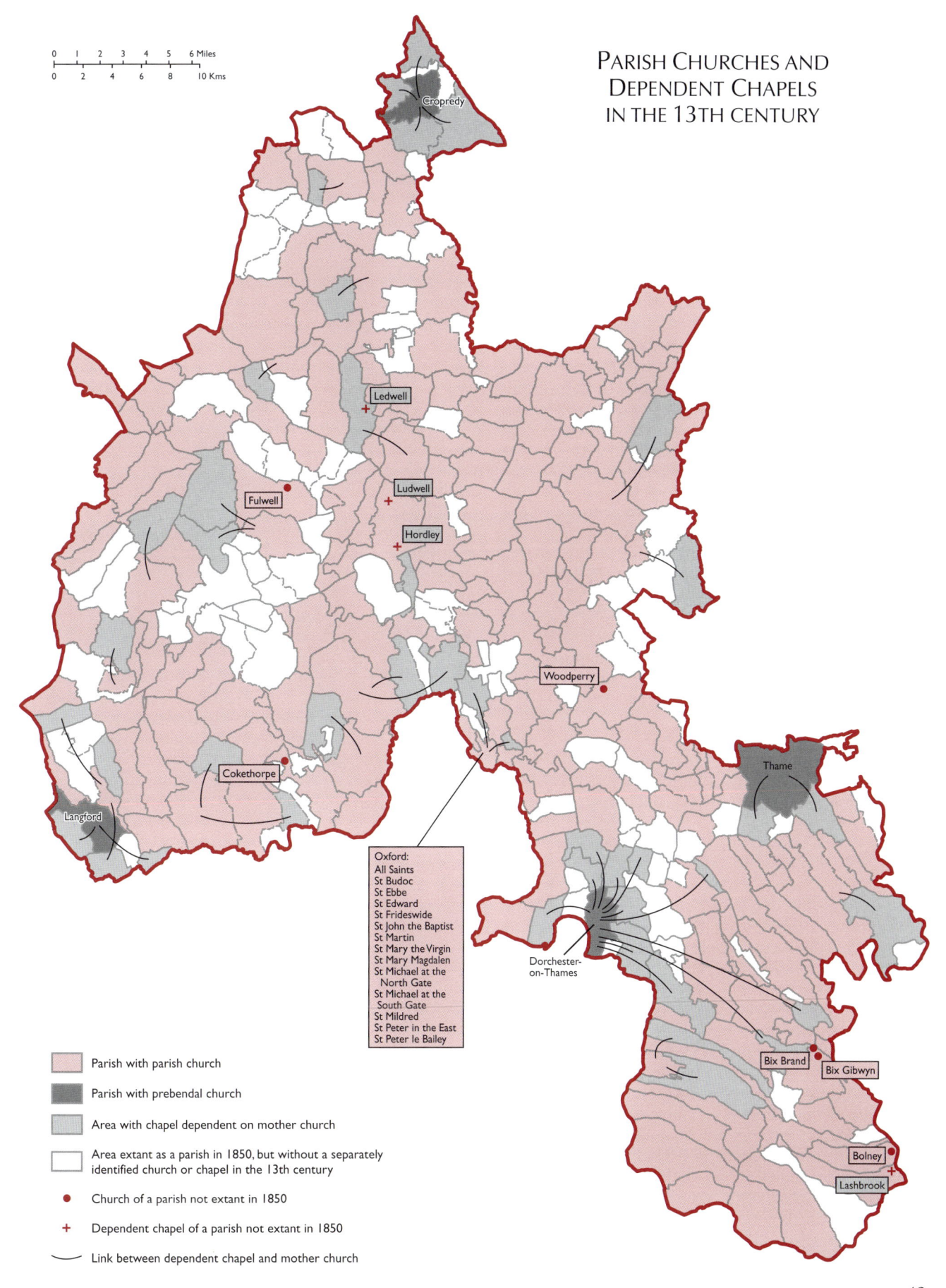

Parish Churches and Dependent Chapels in the 13th Century

18 · Vicarages and Appropriated Church Livings — Simon Townley

At their foundation most churches were endowed with glebe, tithes and offerings (the 'rectory') to support a resident priest. But from the 11th and 12th centuries many such endowments were transferred to religious houses or other institutions for pious motives, usually by laymen whose ancestors had built the churches on their estates. From the 1150s reforming bishops strove to control the process and, where they allowed it, to ensure an adequate income for a resident vicar, who received an agreed stipend or a share of the church's revenues.

Some Oxfordshire appropriations, to cathedral chapters or former minsters, pre-dated the Conquest. The pace accelerated in the 12th century, with the large-scale endowment of established Benedictine houses such as Eynsham, and of newly founded or reordered ones such as Osney Abbey, Dorchester Abbey and St Frideswide's Priory (by then all houses of Augustinian canons). From the 13th century episcopal control reduced new appropriations, but the 14th and 15th centuries still saw over 20, with Stanton Harcourt appropriated to Reading Abbey as late as 1506. By the Dissolution, around 53% of Oxfordshire livings had been appropriated along with a substantial number of dependent chapelries, a proportion higher than in many counties. Total diversion of church revenues was even greater, since many religious houses had pensions or a share of demesne tithes in unappropriated rectories. Eynsham abbey's £5 pension from Souldern, for instance, amounted to half the church's income. Overall, Dorchester Abbey's income from church revenues far exceeded that from its land.

In Oxfordshire the largest number of appropriations (over 50) were to Augustinians, in particular the Oxfordshire houses of Osney (15), Dorchester (12) and St Frideswide's (7). Dorchester's were concentrated near the abbey, and included a core of churches which had formed cathedral prebends before the see was transferred to Lincoln in 1072. Osney's were more scattered, reflecting extensive foundation grants by Robert d'Oilly, the abbey's acquisition of churches belonging to St George's in the Castle, and subsequent piecemeal gifts.

The second largest appropriators were Benedictines (28 appropriations, some lost in the Middle Ages), headed by Eynsham Abbey with nine. By contrast, Cistercians (5), Hospitallers (3), and secular colleges (2) acquired far fewer. Most monastic appropriators were Oxfordshire houses, though others (excluding three French foundations) were spread across a dozen counties. Another nine livings, including the large multi-township parishes of Cropredy, Shipton-under-Wychwood, Langford, Bampton, and Great Milton, were appropriated to the secular cathedral chapters of Lincoln, Salisbury or Exeter, mostly to provide prebends. Oxford colleges acquired a dozen rectories before the 1530s (see entry 25).

During the Middle Ages several appropriated rectories changed hands. Four were confiscated from French houses during the Hundred Years War and used to endow Eton College, while two passed to Oxford or Cambridge colleges after Cold Norton and Bromhall Priories were dissolved through poverty. Several other Oxford college rectories were acquired from earlier owners, including Abingdon and Eynsham abbeys, the bishops of Lincoln and Winchester, and St John's Hospital, Oxford.

Perpetual vicarages were ordained in most such churches, but from the outset vicars' incomes varied considerably. In 1254 Sandford-on-Thames vicarage was worth under £3 (below the 5-mark legal minimum), and by the 15th century Chastleton and Fulwell churches were so impoverished that they could no longer support a vicar. In 1535 nearly half recorded vicarages were worth only £5 to £10. Conversely, Burford, Cropredy and Charlbury were worth over £25 – considerably more than many rectories – while at Bampton, served (uniquely in Oxfordshire) by three portionary vicars, the total endowment was £30. Vicars' responsibilities and costs also varied, with many responsible for multiple settlements and outlying chapelries. Some vicarage ordinations provided for assistants (e.g. Langford and Broadwell), though not all these arrangements persisted. Most vicarages included altarage, small tithes, and sometimes glebe, while many of Hugh of Wells's ordinations mentioned a house. Some such stipulations were ignored (e.g. Combe).

Bishops had to balance parish needs with those of religious houses, and consequently not all appropriated churches had a vicar. Most of Dorchester Abbey's and several of Osney's were served by stipendiary chaplains and occasionally by the canons, prompting widespread neglect and occasional interventions by the bishop (e.g. at Forest Hill and Pishill). Such arrangements persisted beyond the Reformation, with many such churches continuing as impoverished curacies until the 19th century. Even where vicarages were ordained they did not always survive. Those at Kidlington, Combe and Wroxton were themselves appropriated or revoked on the bishop's authority, and the churches served by stipendiary chaplains, while in the 1530s Osney Abbey leased Black Bourton's vicar's share to a layman. Occasionally bishops reinstated the rectory, as at Chastleton in 1459.

Vicarages were also ordained in parishes where the rector was a licensed absentee or pluralist (or, as at Alkerton in 1250–1, barely literate). Most such arrangements were temporary (and not mapped here), though at St Peter in the East, Oxford, a short-term vicarage continued after Merton College appropriated the living, while the wealthy living of Witney had both a rector and a perpetual vicar from the 13th century to 1633.

By the Dissolution the pattern of appropriation and vicarages was largely complete, although Northmoor rectory was appropriated to St John's College, Oxford, as late as 1555. Otherwise the most obvious change was the wholesale transfer of appropriated rectories to new owners. Most passed to laymen, and a substantial number to Oxford colleges (particularly Christ Church, Exeter, St John's and Trinity), while a few were given to the new bishopric of Oxford. Earlier college appropriations and many of the cathedral prebends continued, as did most vicarages, though the Oxford churches of St Giles and St Peter in the East were temporarily downgraded to curacies.

VICARAGES AND APPROPRIATED CHURCH LIVINGS

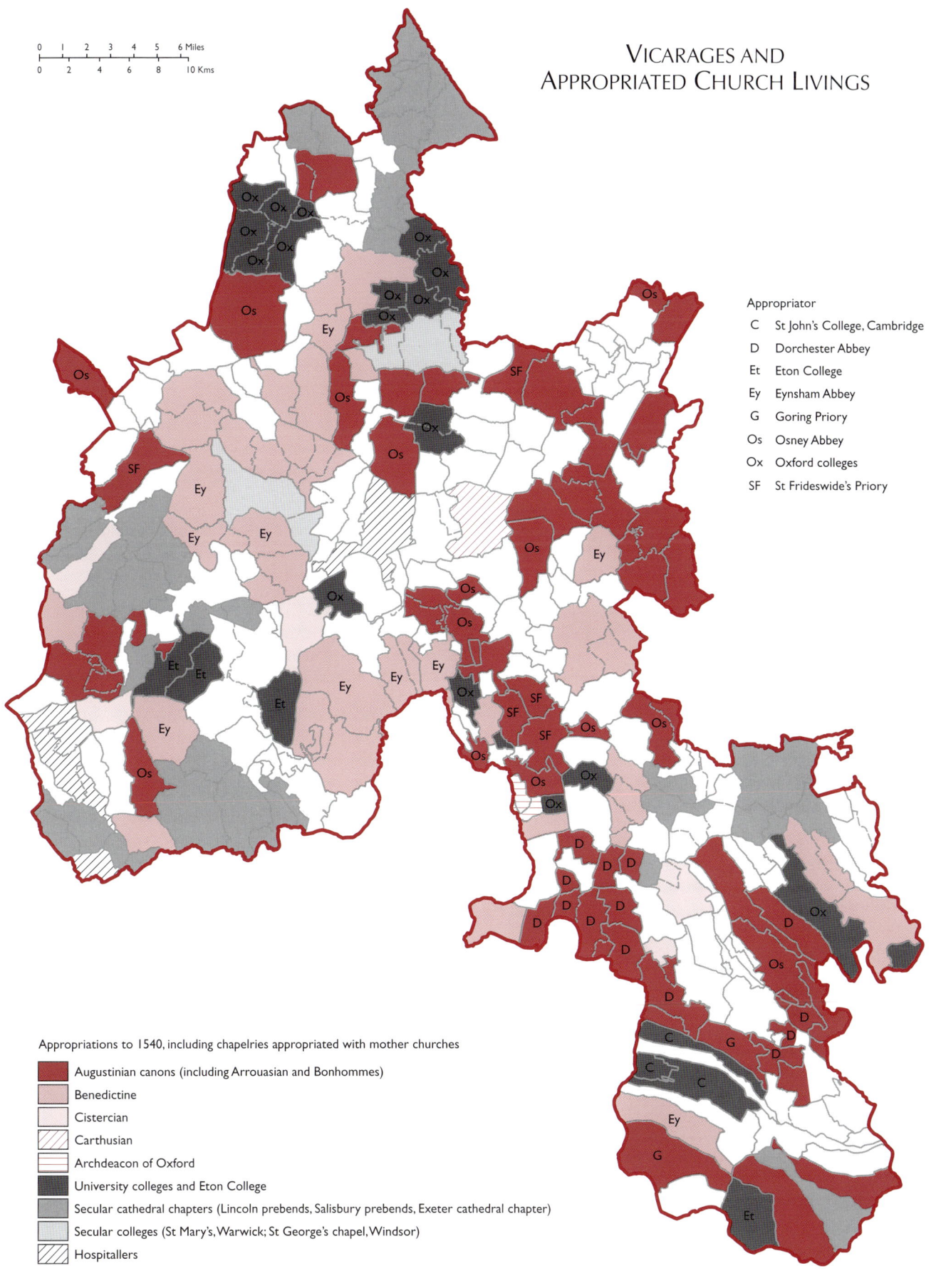

Appropriator
- C St John's College, Cambridge
- D Dorchester Abbey
- Et Eton College
- Ey Eynsham Abbey
- G Goring Priory
- Os Osney Abbey
- Ox Oxford colleges
- SF St Frideswide's Priory

Appropriations to 1540, including chapelries appropriated with mother churches

- Augustinian canons (including Arrouasian and Bonhommes)
- Benedictine
- Cistercian
- Carthusian
- Archdeacon of Oxford
- University colleges and Eton College
- Secular cathedral chapters (Lincoln prebends, Salisbury prebends, Exeter cathedral chapter)
- Secular colleges (St Mary's, Warwick; St George's chapel, Windsor)
- Hospitallers

19 · Religious Houses

James Bond

Bede and the Anglo-Saxon Chronicle record an episcopal see founded at Dorchester by the missionary Bishop Birinus in 635 for King Cynegils of Wessex. This did not long survive Birinus's death. A new see established there by Archbishop Theodore in 672 to serve South Mercia was also short-lived. Even its re-establishment in the 880s may have started as a temporary measure during Danish occupation of the ancient diocesan centres of Leicester and Lindsey. In the event, however, the bishops remained at Dorchester until 1072, supervising an increasingly unwieldy diocese spreading from the Thames to the Humber. Its first Norman bishop, Remigius, transferred his see to Lincoln. Thereafter Oxfordshire remained without a cathedral until the 1540s.

The minsters forming the earliest generations of religious communities are discussed elsewhere (see entry 9). In the mid 10th century Wessex and Mercia were affected by a great monastic reform spearheaded by Archbishop Dunstan. New monasteries were founded and old minsters revived under Benedictine rule. Monks leading a stricter, more contemplative way of life replaced the secular clerics in the minsters. The ancient Berkshire minster at Abingdon was at the forefront of this change, being refounded in 954. Eynsham, reformed as a Benedictine house at the relatively late date of 1005, was the only Oxfordshire minster to follow this course. Its monks were dispersed after the Norman Conquest, but the abbey was re-endowed by Bishop Remigius, who then removed the monks to Stow in Lincolnshire in 1091. The community returned to Eynsham in 1094 and remained until the suppression in 1539, becoming Oxfordshire's second richest abbey. Several Benedictine abbeys outside Oxfordshire, including Abingdon, Winchcombe and Battle, also held valuable demesne estates in the county.

The number of religious houses increased considerably through the 12th and 13th centuries. The most important of the new Benedictine foundations was the nunnery of Godstow, settled in a meadow north of Oxford with royal support in 1133; its income in 1535 ranked third of all religious houses in Oxfordshire. Smaller Benedictine nunneries followed, at Littlemore (c.1140) and Studley (c.1175). Two alien priories were founded by Norman lords as dependencies of Benedictine abbeys in their homeland: a cell of Fécamp at Cogges (1103) and a cell of Ivry at Minster Lovell (c.1183). Both were suppressed in 1414–15, their property subsequently granted by Henry VI to Eton College. A few Benedictine monks briefly settled on the site of a hermitage at Pheleley near Charlbury, but this establishment was abandoned 40 years later, its endowments absorbed by Eynsham Abbey.

New religious orders arrived during the 12th century. The most significant group in Oxfordshire were regular canons following the Rule of St Augustine of Hippo. Three of Oxfordshire's ancient minsters were reformed or re-established under Augustinian rule: St Frideswide's in Oxford in 1122, Dorchester in about 1140 and Bicester before 1185. The Dorchester canons were, in their early years, attached to the stricter Arrouaisian congregation, who were influenced by contemporary Cistercian reforms.

Three more Augustinian priories, Osney (1129), Cold Norton (1148–58) and Wroxton (1217), together with the Augustinian nunnery of Goring, were entirely new foundations. Osney, founded by Robert d'Oilly in 1129, was soon promoted to abbatial status, and became the richest religious house in Oxfordshire, and one of the most important houses of regular canons in England.

Three colonies of Cistercian monks were settled in Oxfordshire, none of more than local importance. Two display the characteristic Cistercian preference for remote, isolated locations. The monks who settled in 1137–8 at Otley near Otmoor found this too waterlogged, and a couple of years later Bishop Alexander of Lincoln offered them an alternative site within the old episcopal park at Thame. Bruern Abbey was settled on a heath on the north-west side of Wychwood, removing an existing village in the process. The third site, Rewley, initially planned in 1280 as a monastic college, was uncharacteristically located on the western fringes of Oxford. Thame and Bruern both established several granges or estate farms within the county. Other granges belonged to Cistercian abbeys outside Oxfordshire, such as Beaulieu Abbey's farm at Shilton.

Of the reformed orders of regular canons only the Gilbertines settled in Oxfordshire, their priory at Clattercote developing out of a leper hospital in about 1150. The two military orders both had bases in the county. The Knights Templars established their first preceptory at Temple Cowley in 1136, followed by another at Merton, but in 1240 were offered a more substantial endowment of land at Sandford-on-Thames. This became their principal local administrative base. *Camerae*, available for temporary occupation on business, were maintained at Sibford and Warpsgrove. On the suppression of the Templars in 1308, some of their property passed to the Hospitallers of St John, who had established their own commandery near Clanfield before 1279.

Miscellaneous religious foundations included a college of secular canons attached to St George's church in Oxford Castle in 1074, and absorbed by Osney Abbey in 1149. Hospitals and almshouses, mapped here, are discussed in entry 24. The mendicant friars, the last major group of religious orders, appeared during the 13th century and settled only in Oxford. The Dominicans arrived in 1221, the Franciscans in 1224, the Carmelites in 1256, the Austin friars in 1267 and the Trinitarians (conventionally regarded as friars, though not mendicants) before 1286; each group initially occupied makeshift premises until they were able to acquire sufficient land on which to erect churches and domestic ranges. The Friars of the Sack and Crutched Friars also had brief tenures in Oxford before their suppression. Monastic colleges were founded to serve monks or canons studying at the University of Oxford. Three were for Benedictines: Gloucester College, developed in 1283–91, Durham College in 1286–91 and Canterbury College in 1363–70. The Cistercians founded St Bernard's College in 1437. Their sites and buildings were all absorbed within later college foundations. Only the Augustinian college of St Mary, founded in 1435, was not re-occupied by a post-Dissolution college.

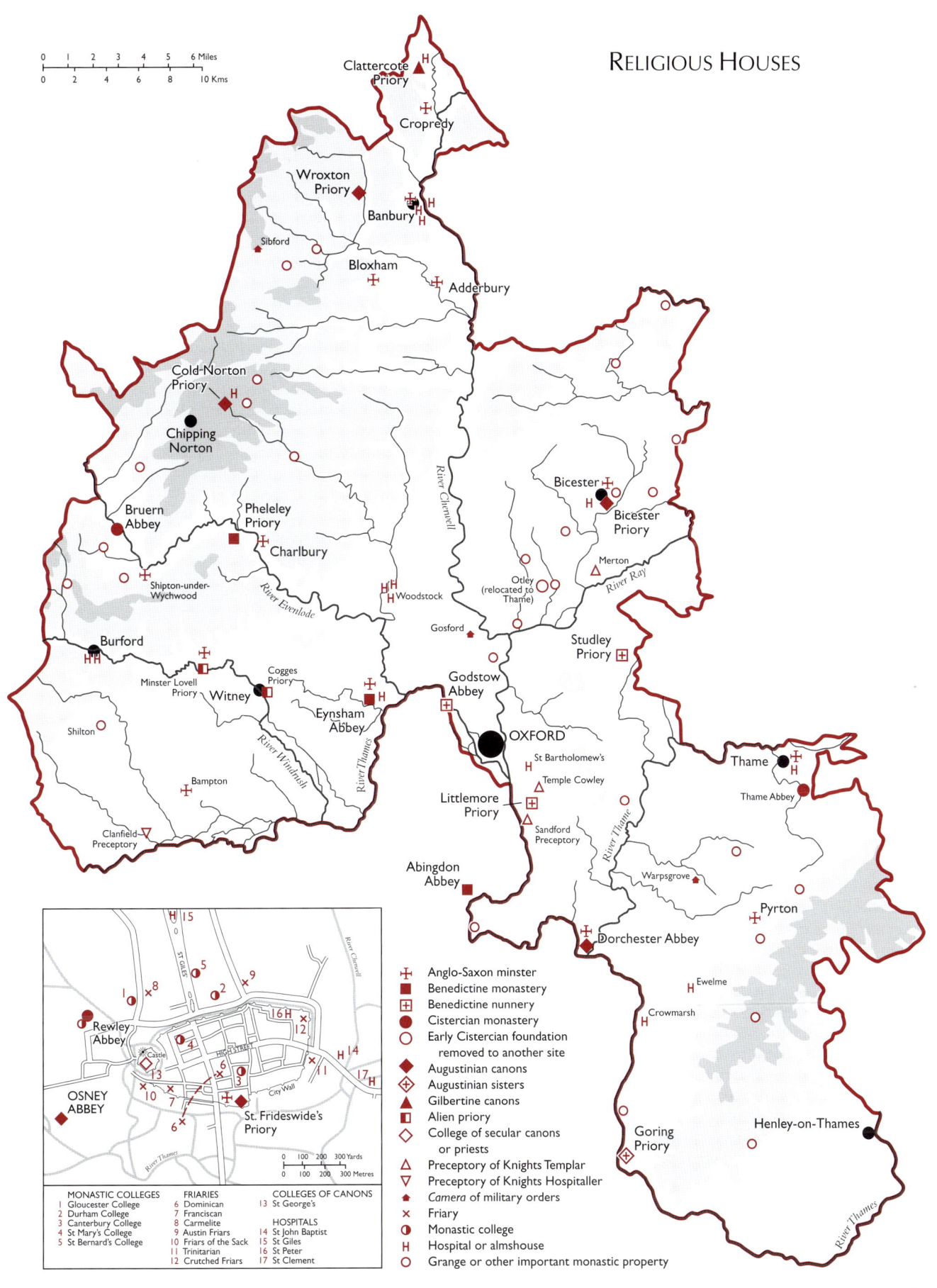

RELIGIOUS HOUSES

Legend

- ✠ Anglo-Saxon minster
- ■ Benedictine monastery
- ⊞ Benedictine nunnery
- ● Cistercian monastery
- ○ Early Cistercian foundation removed to another site
- ◆ Augustinian canons
- ✧ Augustinian sisters
- ▲ Gilbertine canons
- ▢ Alien priory
- ◇ College of secular canons or priests
- △ Preceptory of Knights Templar
- ▽ Preceptory of Knights Hospitaller
- ★ *Camera* of military orders
- × Friary
- ◐ Monastic college
- H Hospital or almshouse
- ○ Grange or other important monastic property

Oxford inset

MONASTIC COLLEGES
1. Gloucester College
2. Durham College
3. Canterbury College
4. St Mary's College
5. St Bernard's College

FRIARIES
6. Dominican
7. Franciscan
8. Carmelite
9. Austin Friars
10. Friars of the Sack
11. Trinitarian
12. Crutched Friars

COLLEGES OF CANONS
13. St George's

HOSPITALS
14. St John Baptist
15. St Giles
16. St Peter
17. St Clement

20 · Medieval Forests and Parks
Stephen Mileson

Hunting was a major pastime of medieval kings and aristocrats and their love of the chase resulted in the establishment of a range of hunting reserves. Some were designed primarily to protect deer and their habitat, including large wooded or moorland forests, which were the preserve of the crown and nobility, and smaller enclosed parks, which were enjoyed more widely, including by the richer gentry. Many lords also obtained charters of 'free warren' from the king, giving them control over hunting smaller game animals on their manors. The creation of exclusive hunting grounds was a lengthy process, beginning before 1066 and continuing throughout the Middle Ages. It was often controversial because intimately connected with the expression of power and lordship. Oxfordshire was well provided with hunting reserves, including the most prestigious and important: forests and parks.

Three royal forests were spread across the wooded central part of the county: Wychwood in the west, Shotover in the middle, and a small part of the Buckinghamshire forest of Bernwood in the east. Each was overseen by local officials, and was also part of a national administrative and judicial system. The extent of forest jurisdiction changed a good deal during the Middle Ages. In 1086 the king's Oxfordshire forests were said to be nine leagues long and nine leagues wide, but their bounds were hugely increased by Henry II (1154–89). He enlarged Wychwood forest so much that it included around a third of the county, incorporating many lordly as well as royal estates. This expansion of forests was highly unpopular, since the enforcement of forest law not only affected lords' own hunting, but also imposed restrictions and financial charges on the exploitation of land in forest areas, including settlements and farmland as well as woods and wastes. Not surprisingly, landowners were quick to secure reductions in forest bounds at times of royal weakness. Henry II's enlargements were reversed in the early 13th century, and further reductions in 1294–1327 limited the Oxfordshire forests largely to the king's demesne manors. In 1284 the Bishop of Winchester even managed to establish a private forest or 'chase' in his manor of Witney, on the edge of Wychwood.

The forests were hunting reserves and manifestations of royal authority, but also an important source of income and materials. Forest jurisdiction brought in money, from fines against those who poached deer or felled trees, and from charges on grazing and other activities managed by forest courts. Further revenue was generated from ordinary farming activities on the large royal estates within the forest. By the 14th century the regularisation of taxation and the reduction of forest bounds had made forest jurisdiction an unimportant source of revenue, and the forest bureaucracy entered a long decline as a result. Nevertheless, the forest remained a vital source of timber, firewood and venison. These products were used by the royal household, and also granted to subjects as a reward or favour, as were certain positions in the forest hierarchy.

For ordinary people the effects of living in a forest were mixed. Obligations to attend forest courts, exactions by foresters, and damage caused to crops by deer were partly balanced by the mixture of resources available for arable and pastoral husbandry. Locals were able to clear (or 'assart') certain areas of woodland to create additional farmland under the oversight of the crown, which benefited from the resulting fines. The forest also provided grazing and wood for nearby settlements, partly through 'common' rights secured by small customary payments. It was likewise a home for industry, including wood production in coppices and pottery making. The deer themselves were a tempting target for peasant poachers. Forests were imperfectly policed and much unauthorized hunting, grazing and felling must have gone undetected.

The growth of population and spread of farming in the 12th and 13th centuries made it increasingly difficult to preserve deer and provide space for hunting in forests and open woods and wastes, and parks were created to help solve this problem. These fenced or walled enclosures were stocked principally with fallow deer, a species introduced from overseas which survived better in restricted spaces than the native red or roe deer. Kings themselves were among the first to create parks, notably at Woodstock, but park-making was also taken up by nobles, religious houses and knights, eager to secure their own hunting grounds. Kings sometimes helped to stock lords' parks by providing gifts of deer, and lords might seek royal permission to create these reserves, especially on manors in or close to forests. Over 30 parks were created in medieval Oxfordshire. They varied greatly in size, from a few score to many hundred acres. The great majority were in wooded areas, especially around Wychwood and in the Chilterns. Most were enclosed before the Black Death, but some were created later, partly making up for the loss of earlier parks which had been disparked.

Parks, like forests, provided a very visible reminder of their owners' aristocratic leisure priorities and control of resources and they seem to have been regarded as important markers of high status. Some parks surrounded or lay next to lords' residences and may have been intended as an impressive setting, but others were well away from any associated manor house. Most parks were used for subsidiary activities to help offset the cost of deer-keeping, including the pasturing of livestock or horses and production of timber and fuel. They also provided secure locations for rabbit warrens (or coneygarths) and fish ponds. Park-making restricted access to substantial areas of wood-pasture and could lead to the repossession of tenants' arable land, disruption to roads, and displacement of settlement. Not surprisingly, parks sometimes became embroiled in disputes between lords and peasants over access to resources, as well as being targets for aristocratic rivals or gangs of poachers, but their appeal to the landowning classes ensured that they remained important features of the Oxfordshire landscape into the 16th century and beyond.

MEDIEVAL FORESTS AND PARKS

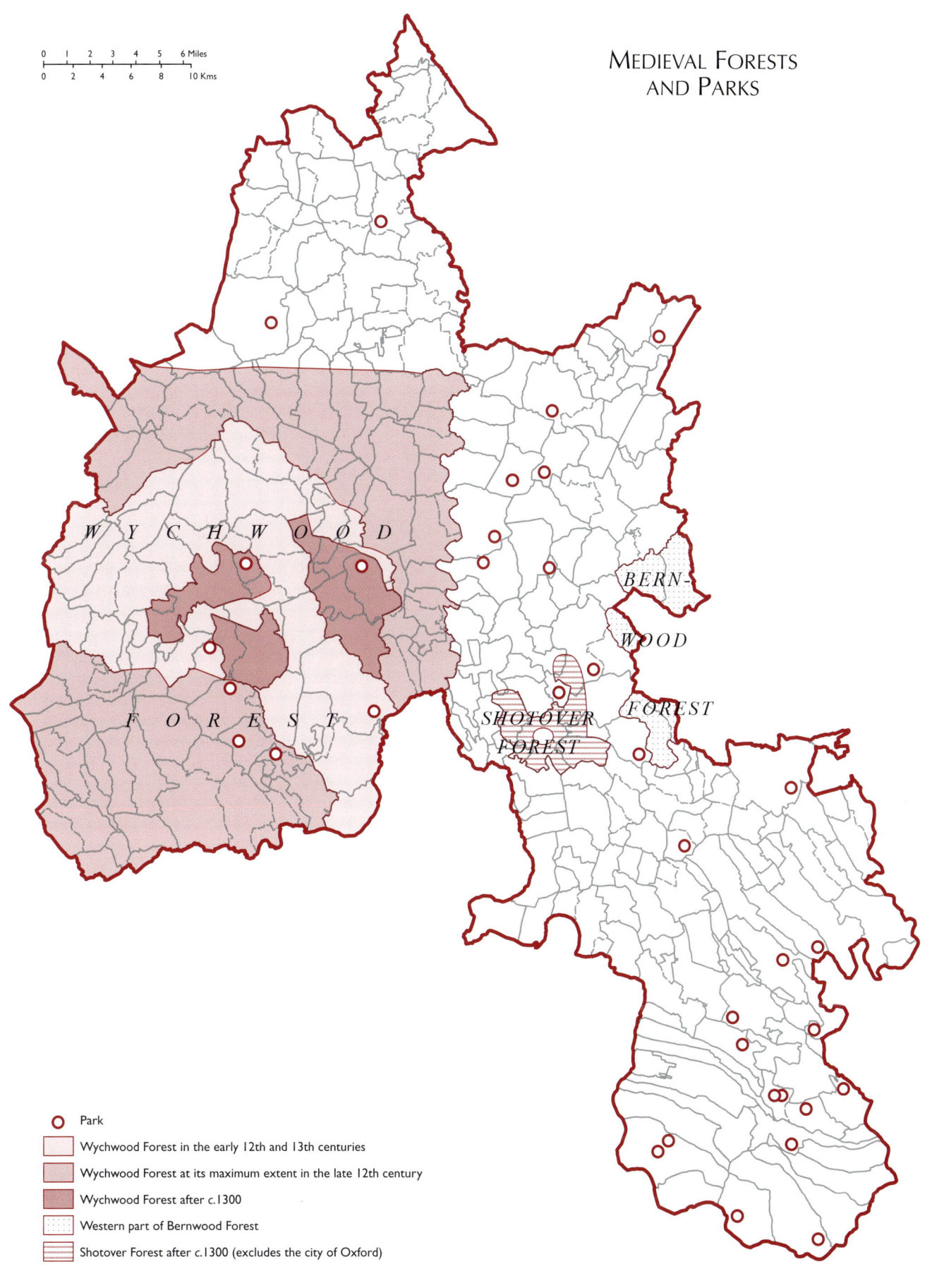

WYCHWOOD FOREST

BERNWOOD FOREST

SHOTOVER FOREST

○ Park
  Wychwood Forest in the early 12th and 13th centuries
  Wychwood Forest at its maximum extent in the late 12th century
  Wychwood Forest after c.1300
  Western part of Bernwood Forest
  Shotover Forest after c.1300 (excludes the city of Oxford)

49

21 · Late Medieval Communications — Robert Peberdy

Post-Conquest Oxfordshire inherited numerous inter-regional route-ways. They included prehistoric ridgeways, Roman roads and Anglo-Saxon salt-ways. Many intersected or converged, particularly near the two main river-crossings, at Banbury and Oxford. Long-distance, through traffic benefited the county, and Oxfordshire people could communicate readily with important regions and towns. The convergence of routes on Oxford encouraged development of a university from the late 12th century.

Between the 11th and 16th centuries the pattern changed little, reflecting landscape and settlement stability and the route-ways' adequacy for the volumes and types of traffic. The only significant alteration, mainly in the 12th and 13th centuries, was the modification of routes with bridge building and diversion of roads through market places at new or expanded small towns (e.g. Burford, Thame). Both developments facilitated economic expansion. The relative importance of particular routes was probably altered by various factors: changing trade patterns, increasing use of carts (from the late 12th century), early common carrying services (mentioned from the 1390s) and changing relationships with river navigation. But continuance of foot traffic – walking, horse-riding, droving, packhorses – meant that routes suitable for these purposes but difficult for carts remained in use, such as the Icknield Way and Knightsbridge Lane.

The most important route-way was probably north–south from the west midlands via the Banbury–Oxford ridgeway to Winchester and Southampton. In the late 11th and 12th centuries Winchester had quasi-capital status, while Southampton was a major port and embarkation point for Continental royal territories. The route's importance was indicated by Robert d'Oilly's construction at Oxford in the later 11th century of a massive stone bridge (Grandpont) and causeway across the Thames floodplain. In the late 14th and 15th centuries the route was important for wool-exporting via Southampton.

Two other important route-ways, from Worcester and Gloucester, the principal crossing-points of the River Severn, reached Oxfordshire from the west midlands (and Wales). The route from Worcester (via Chipping Norton) bypassed Oxford, crossing the Cherwell near Bletchingdon and the Ray at Islip. It continued via Wheatley, where the Thame was bridged by the late 12th century, and on to London. The route from Gloucester (through Burford, Witney and Eynsham) reached Oxford via Wytham Hill. (Travellers could alternatively approach Oxford via Long Hanborough and the road from Woodstock.) Both routes connected premier wool-growing areas with London. Travellers to Oxfordshire from the south-west could take various routes to Newbury (the Bristol–London route, routes from Exeter and Salisbury) and then go north. Travellers from Bristol could alternatively travel via Chippenham and Faringdon.

Two other major routes crossed eastern Oxfordshire. One diverged from the Oxford–Banbury ridgeway north of Oxford (Jordan Hill), crossed the Cherwell at Gosford (bridged by c.1250) and headed to Northampton, from where routes led to the north-east (e.g. York) and east (e.g. Cambridge). The other led from Oxford to London. Its initial course was difficult. After crossing the Cherwell at Pettypont (now Magdalen Bridge), travellers had to climb up Cheney Lane to Shotover Plain before joining the Worcester–London road at Wheatley. Another route went from Pettypont south to Dorchester and Henley.

Banbury, situated by the River Cherwell (bridged by 1294), was the meeting point for eight routes. The Coventry–Southampton route passed through the town, and other routes joined the Cotswolds and west midlands with the east midlands and places beyond.

Oxfordshire's main navigable river, the Thames, continued to provide an inter-regional route between the south-west midlands and south-east England, usable from both adjacent areas and distant places with routes to trans-shipment points. Where land and river transport were alternatives (e.g. between Oxford and Henley from the 12th to the 15th century), such matters as commodity value in relation to carriage costs (journey times, tolls), availability of boats, and risk had to be assessed. The extent of long-distance navigation altered in response to changing physical and economic conditions, which in turn affected the relative importance of trans-shipment points.

Before 1066 the Thames was possibly used from Cricklade downriver, while salt from Droitwich was probably carried downstream from Lechlade. From the 11th to the 13th century conditions changed with the spread of riverside mills, mill-dams and flashlocks. By 1086 there were 17 mills between London and Oxford, mostly in Oxfordshire; by c.1300 there were 25. Fish-weirs also hindered navigation. The building of mill-dams improved navigability below Oxford by raising water levels, but the need for boats to pass through flashlocks increased travel times and costs. This appears to have deterred navigation between the upper Thames and the river below Oxford from the 13th century.

Between Oxford and London, economic forces stimulated a considerable navigation, and from the 12th century Henley-on-Thames was an important trans-shipment point. In the late 13th and 14th centuries it was the main centre for shipment of grain from south Oxfordshire to London. Navigation upstream from London was used to supply heavy and bulky goods (e.g. wine, salted fish, metal) to towns and rural wharfs. Several boat types were used, with the 'shout' (a long, flat-bottomed boat with pointed ends) prominent below Oxford from the 13th century.

Possibly from the mid 15th century, economic depression caused long-distance navigation to cease between Oxford and Reading or Henley, thereby enhancing Henley's trans-shipment role (e.g. for conveyance to Oxford). Demand for imports revived at places above Reading from the mid 16th century. By the 1560s the Thames was reused upriver to Culham (near Abingdon). Beyond Culham navigability proved difficult for the new, larger 'western barges' (recorded from 1548), and goods for Oxford were trans-shipped at Burcot. The Burcot–Oxford section was improved from 1624 (e.g. with installation of poundlocks on the Swift Ditch near Abingdon and at Sandford and Iffley), and the Thames was reopened to Oxford and beyond for large vessels in 1635.

COMMUNICATIONS: LATE MEDIEVAL

51

22 · Wealth and Population in 1334 and 1524   Simon Townley

The only source to give an overview of wealth (and to a lesser extent population) between the 13th and 16th centuries is the lay subsidies levied by the Crown. These were taxes assessed at the level of the vill, which can generally be identified with the parish or its constituent townships. Until 1332 and again in the 16th century the subsidies listed all those who fell above the tax threshold, with their individual assessments and the total received from the community. In 1334, however, a quota system was adopted based on the 1332 subsidy, by which each vill became collectively responsible for raising a particular amount. This entry maps the data recorded in the subsidies of 1334 and 1524, both of which are available in print.

The medieval subsidies were assessed on movables, usually surplus goods or produce available for sale. By 1334, however, exemptions were commonplace, notably of wool, coin and plate. Probably this means that some places (e.g. towns with large numbers of wool merchants or vills with significant sheep flocks) were under-assessed. Clerical income (e.g. glebe and tithes) was also exempt. The 16th-century subsidies were more comprehensive, but conflated taxes (charged at different rates) on goods, land and wages. In all subsidies, taxpayers generally appeared only once, under the place where they lived or had substantial assets; consequently a vill's assessment will sometimes include wealth from other places, or, conversely, exclude a major property holder. Taxable wealth might also be concentrated in a few hands, or spread among large numbers of people.

If these caveats are borne in mind, the subsidies provide an invaluable comparison of taxable wealth. By this measure medieval Oxfordshire ranked among the wealthiest counties in England: between sixth or seventh per square mile in the late 13th and early 14th century, first (after London) in 1334, and 16th in 1524, its slippage reflecting growth in other areas rather than contraction in Oxfordshire itself. Factors underpinning its prosperity included: a wide variety of soils and agricultural resources, which could variously support intensive arable farming, intensive sheep-rearing, or mixed sheep–corn husbandry; a well-developed marketing network of prosperous small towns, including Banbury, Burford, Witney and Henley; and good access to London, both by road and by river. Oxford itself was the eighth wealthiest English town in 1334, and the 30th in 1524–5. Even so some other counties enjoyed comparable natural advantages, prompting Campbell (2006) to judge Oxfordshire's exceptional wealth 'something of an enigma'.

Mapping by regions within the county (see maps on this page and on p. 54) can produce differing results depending on the units chosen (see Martin and Steel (1959) and Sheail and Hoyle (1998)). Nonetheless the 1334 data largely confirm the picture presented by Hoskins and others, with particular pockets of wealth showing up in the clay vales and limestone hills between Oxford and Watlington, on the clay and river gravels around Bampton and Witney in the south-west, and on the light and fertile redland soils in the north around Banbury. The Chilterns, with their dispersed settlement set amidst woodland, wood pasture, and small arable fields on chalk-with-flints, were collectively the poorest area, despite the presence of Henley with its market and river-borne grain trade with London.

Mapping at parish level shows much greater variety. In particular the prominence of the south-west upper Thames area was due largely to the taxable wealth of Witney and Bampton (with its market and extensive parish), while average wealth south-east of Oxford was pushed up by exceptional payments from Cowley,

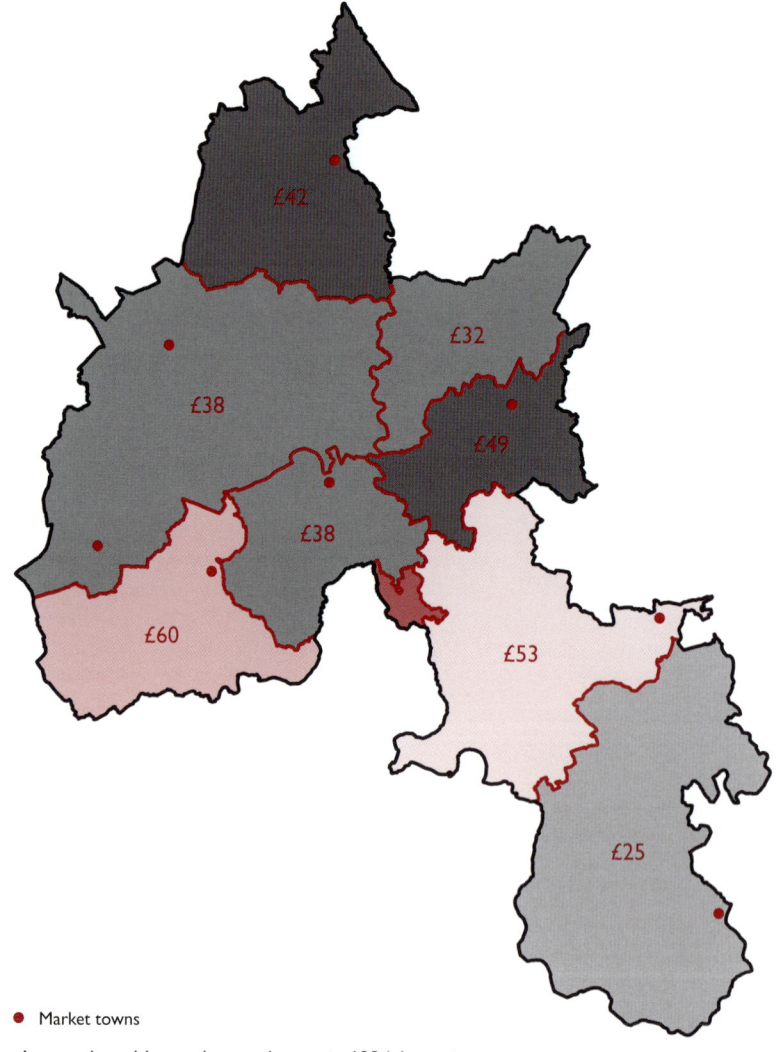

● Market towns

Assessed wealth per thousand acres in 1334, by region

WEALTH IN 1334

Assessed wealth per thousand acres, 1334, in pounds

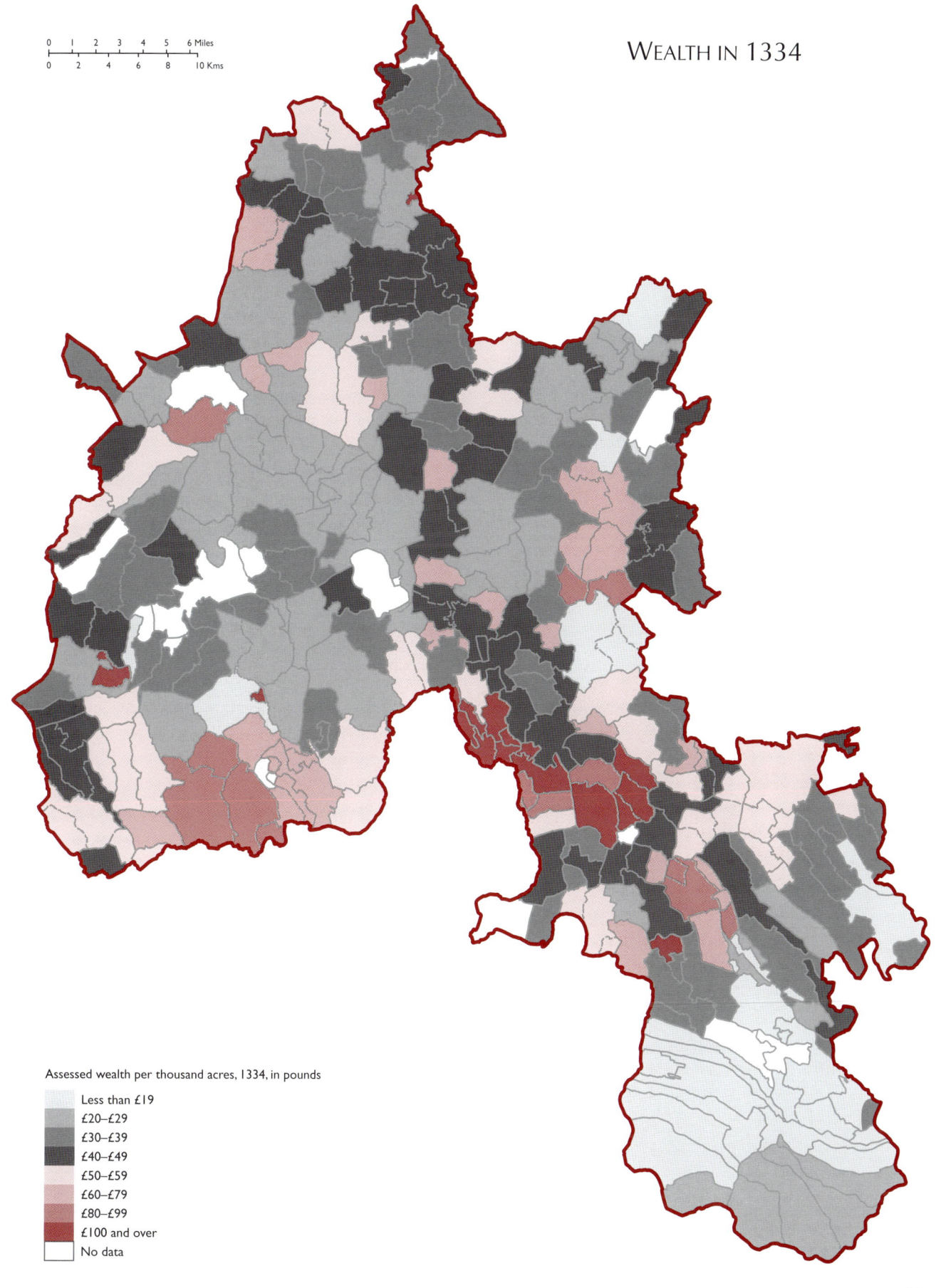

- Less than £19
- £20–£29
- £30–£39
- £40–£49
- £50–£59
- £60–£79
- £80–£99
- £100 and over
- No data

22 · Wealth and Population in 1334 and 1524 (continued)

Garsington and Cuddesdon. Burford (with its emerging role in the international wool trade) also stands out, though further north around Wychwood and up to Chipping Norton assessments were relatively low. The northern redlands, too, showed considerable variation, while even in the poorer north-east there were some pockets of high assessment. What lay behind the parish or township variations cannot be determined from the 1334 returns, which exclude information on the number or wealth of individual taxpayers, and have to be supplemented from earlier assessments or from other sources. Standlake's relatively high assessment of £161, for instance, probably reflects the presence of four demesne farms, a market and small-scale cloth manufacture.

The 1524 subsidy gives a less clear-cut geographical picture, which is perhaps to be expected given that its raw tax yields represent an amalgam of different types of wealth. Nonetheless they show the presence or otherwise of taxable wealth in particular vills, whether this was in the form of a wealthy individual (e.g. a resident lord or the farmer of an enclosed demesne) or of an emerging group of prosperous yeomen working newly consolidated farms. The tiny enclosed hamlet of Yelford in west Oxfordshire, for instance, yielded well over 100s. per 1,000 acres on the basis of a single payment from the resident lord (who paid on goods worth £40), while nearby Minster Lovell appears even more wealthy on account of a prosperous demesne farmer who may have leased the manor house. The increase in the taxable wealth of some Chilterns parishes similarly reflects the emergence of prosperous yeoman farmers, for example at Harpsden, where three or four prominent yeomen paid the bulk of the total yield. Conversely, the apparent poverty of Curbridge (near Witney) may reflect the fact that it included the Bishop of Winchester's demesne, which was taxed elsewhere. Similar explanations probably underlie many of the variations, and argue against an overly deterministic view of prosperity based solely on geography and soil types. The returns for towns require similar caution. Witney paid the highest amount after Oxford, but of that, four-fifths was paid by the wool stapler and sheep farmer Richard Wenman, whose exceptional wealth extended way beyond the town. Some other towns (e.g. Henley) were taxed with the surrounding rural area, for which allowance must be made.

Numbers of taxpayers are not easily translated into population, since an unknown number of people (possibly 15 to 20 times the number of taxpayers) never paid tax. Nonetheless, early 14th-century subsidies suggest that Oxfordshire was one of the most populous and densely settled counties as well as one of the wealthiest. Poll tax figures for 1377 are not strictly comparable because of intervening population collapse and settlement desertion following the Black Death; however, they show some correspondence, confirming that the lowest population densities were in the Chilterns, and some of the highest in the north, the south-west, and the area between the Chilterns and Oxford. Thereafter no comprehensive sources for population exist before the protestation returns and Compton Census of the 17th century. The latter (arranged by deanery) recorded the highest numbers (probably of adult inhabitants, and categorised as either conformists, papists or Nonconformists) in Witney deanery, with relatively high numbers in central and north Oxfordshire, and a total of 3,768 in Henley deanery, which confirms that the Chilterns population (though still relatively low) was rising. In 1801 the densest settled areas remained the north and south-west, along with Oxford itself and the vale and limestone uplands to its south-east.

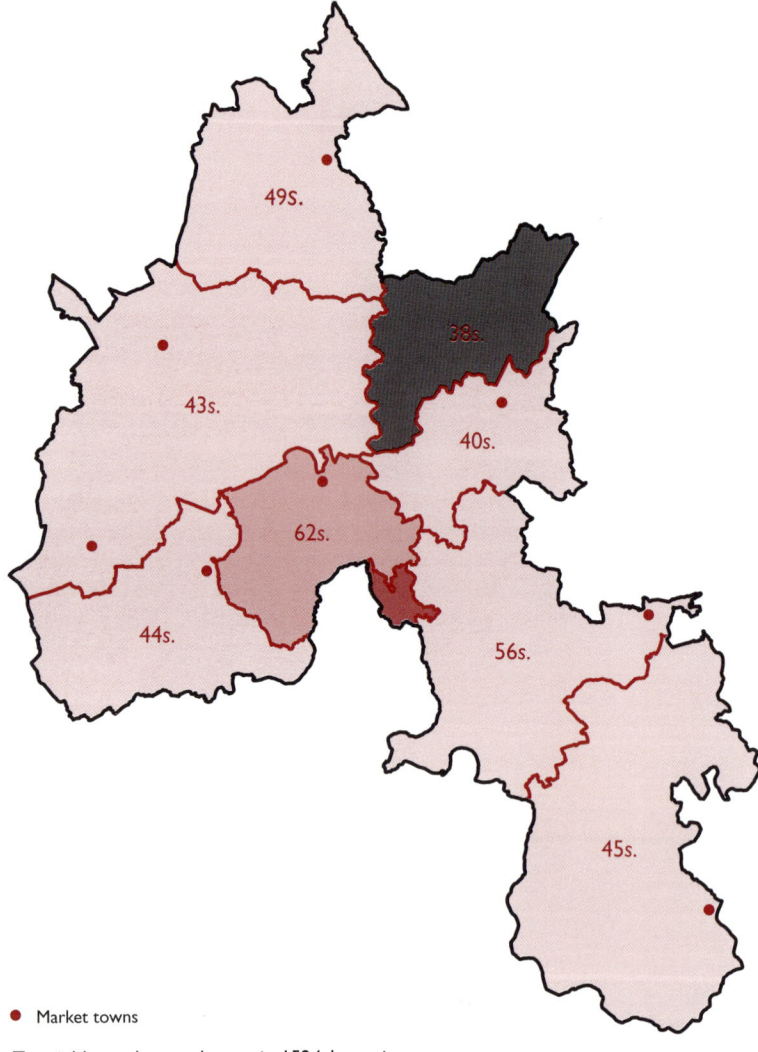

● Market towns

Tax yield per thousand acres in 1524, by region

WEALTH IN 1524

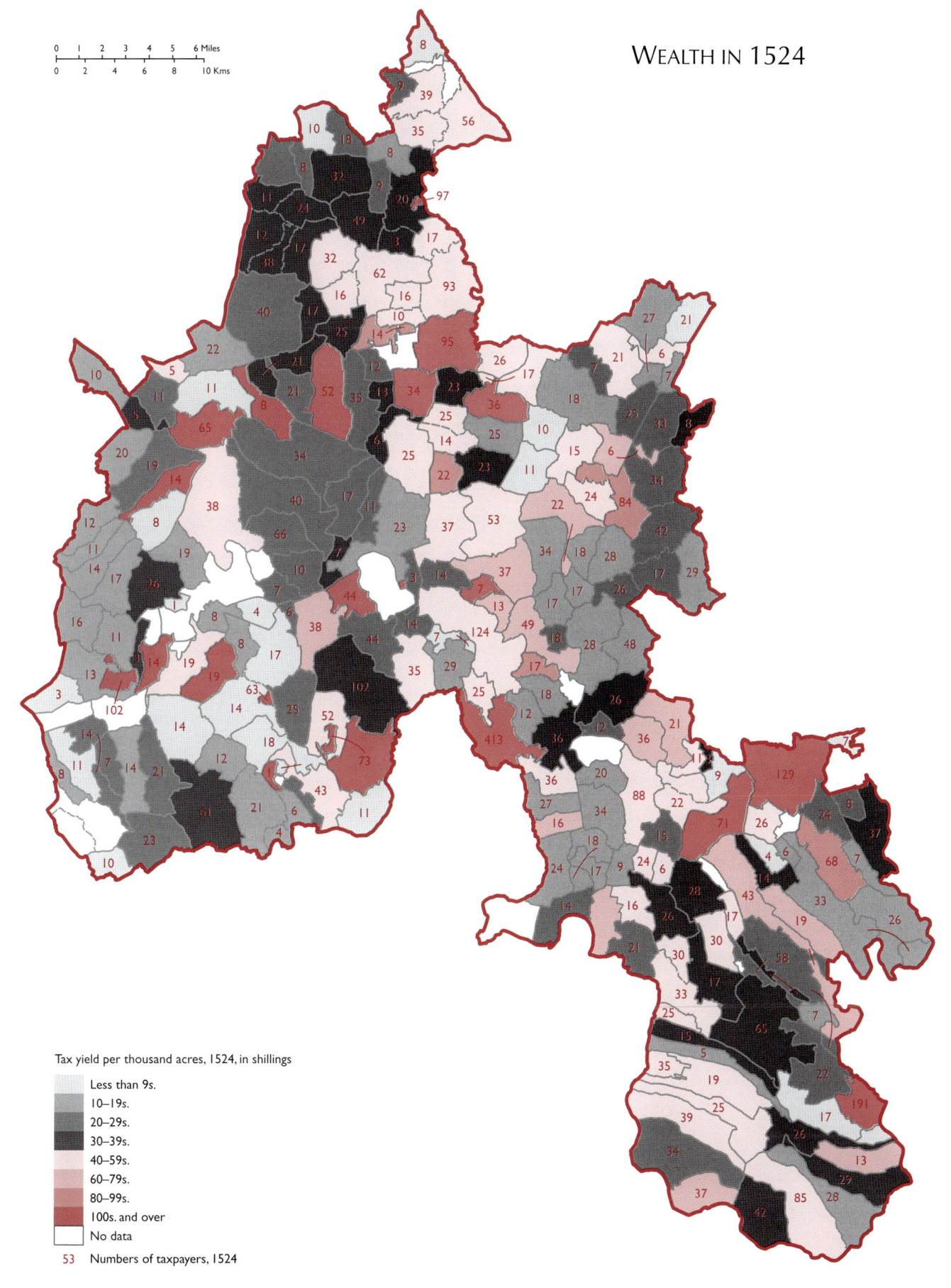

Tax yield per thousand acres, 1524, in shillings
- Less than 9s.
- 10–19s.
- 20–29s.
- 30–39s.
- 40–59s.
- 60–79s.
- 80–99s.
- 100s. and over
- No data

53 Numbers of taxpayers, 1524

23 · Deserted and Shrunken Settlements — Stephen Mileson

The later Middle Ages saw the reduction of settlement across much of Britain and Europe in the face of population decline and economic difficulties. In England many towns and rural settlements shrank, and over 2,000 villages disappeared entirely. This reversal came after a long phase of uneven growth from the 9th to the late 13th century, when rising population and economic expansion were accompanied by a major increase in the number and size of occupied sites and a fundamental and enduring change in the character of settlement. An efflorescence of urban life was matched by the development of denser and more fixed rural settlements, which in many areas replaced a less stable pattern of scattered farmsteads. For all its problems, the later Middle Ages was a period of dynamic reorientation rather than collapse. An examination of late medieval settlement decay provides valuable insights into the earlier expansion and into the scope of medieval social and economic achievement as a whole.

Oxfordshire, like much of the midlands, was strongly affected by late medieval settlement contraction. A quarter of the county's medieval village sites are now deserted, and though Oxfordshire comprises only 1.5% of the area of England it accounts for 5% of its abandoned villages. A few of these disappeared earlier in the Middle Ages and others were not finally deserted until the 17th or 18th century, but the decay and disappearance of the majority occurred between 1300 and 1530. Most surviving settlements became less fully occupied and many towns as well as villages decreased in size. Evidence for deserted or severely shrunken settlements comes from various sources: tax lists, manorial records, early maps and the landscape itself. Some former villages are still visible as hollow ways and earthworks in pasture fields, e.g. Shifford, near Bampton; others are indicated by an isolated church or a dense scatter of medieval pottery found in a ploughed field. Many abandoned villages were survived or succeeded by more limited settlement – often single manor houses or a few isolated farms.

The underlying cause of late medieval desertions and shrinkages was a prolonged reduction in population, which lasted well into the 16th century. The decline of human numbers began because of famine and farming problems in the early 14th century, and it was greatly accelerated by the Black Death of 1348–9 and subsequent outbreaks of plague which continued into the 15th century. Birth rates failed to make up for deaths and by 1500 the population was around half what it had been in 1300. A handful of places in the county seem to have been totally depopulated by the first onset of plague, including the already struggling village of Tusmore, but normally decline was a more gradual process, frequently culminating during the economic slump of the mid to later 15th century.

Reduced population was general, but the survival or loss of individual settlements was determined by human agency. The actions of landlords could be crucial, for instance where they evicted the last few inhabitants from dwindling villages to create large grazing grounds, as seems to have occurred at Little Rollright in the Cotswolds and Chippinghurst by the river Thame. But most lords tried for a long time to retain rent-paying tenants and more often it was decisions made by several generations of ordinary locals that provided the main impetus towards desertion. Since land and jobs were more readily available in the late middle ages, existing inhabitants simply left unpromising settings to look for better opportunities, and newcomers were not tempted in. For this reason smaller and poorer places were worst affected, especially satellite hamlets which lay in the shadow of larger and better endowed settlements, like Thomley in the east of the county, close to Waterperry and Worminghall.

Villages and hamlets were abandoned throughout the large part of Oxfordshire dominated by nucleated settlement, but the areas worst hit were the early settled and densely populated clay vales and the Cotswold dip slope. Communities here were heavily reliant on cereal cultivation and had a limited number of by-employments. They suffered badly from the fall in grain prices which occurred after the mid 1370s. Thereafter, attempts to respond to the new conditions by adopting less labour-intensive animal husbandry frequently led to local tensions and conflicts which encouraged emigration. In particular, the consolidation of holdings and enclosure of pastures by lords, demesne farmers or ambitious tenants tended to disrupt the highly developed open-field farming systems of these areas, harming the interests of those below the village elite. Mobility among lesser folk was also encouraged by the prevalence of unfree tenure and its associated dues, which many hoped to leave behind by taking up land on more favourable terms in a different village.

In areas of dispersed settlement like the wooded Chilterns dip slope there were no nucleated sites to be deserted, but there were numerous straggling road- and green-side hamlets and many of them declined as individual houses and farmsteads were abandoned. It is hard to assess the precise scale of decay in such areas since the medieval settlement pattern is difficult to reconstruct, but recent research shows that some localities were badly affected. So much is evident from the amalgamation of parishes and abandonment of churches at places like Bix and Harpsden in the 15th century. Scattered settlement and relatively loose community bonds in such regions remained fundamentally unaltered, but the location of homes and underlying social and economic structures were probably undergoing as much change as elsewhere.

Late medieval settlement desertion was the result of demographic decline and material hardship, but it did not simply reflect vulnerability to outside forces. In all its variety it was also an active response to changing circumstances, reflecting positive choices made by a widening group of people at a time of better overall balance between population and resources. Most settlements survived, and even where there was decay this at least presented ambitious individuals with opportunities to consolidate land and engage in new activities.

Deserted and Shrunken Settlements

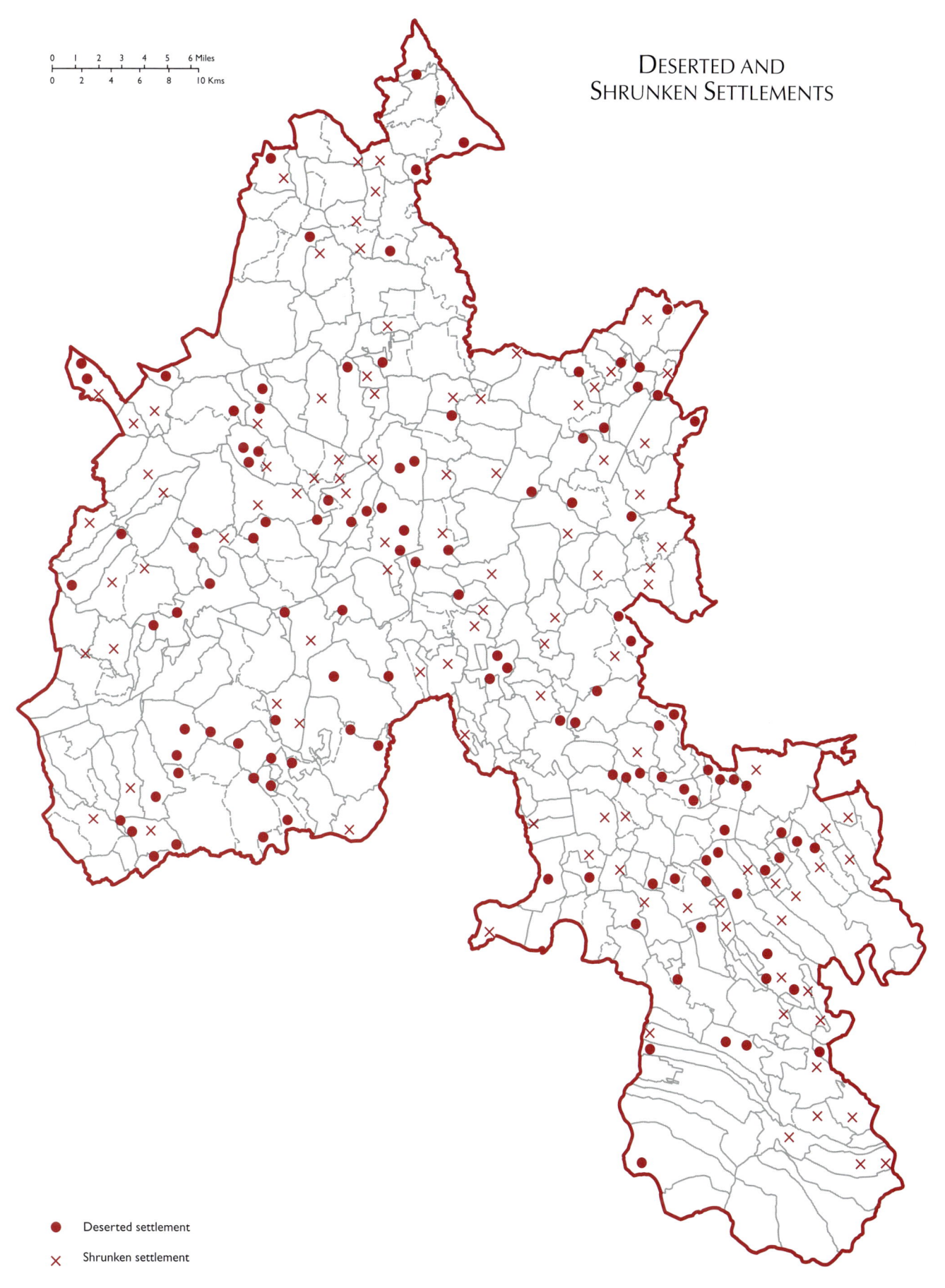

- Deserted settlement
- × Shrunken settlement

24 · Medieval Chantries and Hospitals

Diana Wood

Chantries and hospitals, although different institutions, were both part of the 'economy of salvation'. The founders and benefactors of each had performed a charitable act, and hoped it would earn them credit in heaven, lessening their time and pain in purgatory. The masses and prayers offered by chantry priests were specifically to intercede for souls there. Both chantries and hospitals were dissolved when the doctrine of purgatory was condemned. Henry VIII's Act of 1547 vested chantries and hospitals in the king's hands, although Edward VI's Act dissolving the chantries omitted hospitals.

A chantry, from the Latin *cantare*, was a foundation which provided daily masses and prayers for the souls of the founders, of others named, and often of all Christians. It might be established in perpetuity or for a limited time. Usually specific rents or a parcel of land would be assigned to provide income for its upkeep and pay a priest. A perpetual chantry could be anything from a college or chapel to a side altar set against a pillar in the parish church to an endowment to pay a priest to celebrate masses at an existing altar. Those who could not afford such foundations could join a religious gild or fraternity, a principal aim of which was to ensure members a fitting funeral and then to offer masses and prayers for their souls. A gild might found or administer a chantry: at Banbury the Gild of Blessed Mary took over a chantry originally founded by townsmen, while at Deddington the Gild of Holy Trinity was associated with a chantry at the altar of Holy Trinity and St Mary, originally founded to benefit the souls of Henry VI and others. Oxford itself had numerous chantries, some of them particularly grand. Often colleges were founded as chantries: All Souls was founded in 1438 by Archbishop Chichele for the salvation of Henry V, the Duke of Clarence and the Englishmen who fell in the Hundred Years War against France.

Although the doctrine of purgatory was not authorized until 1274 at the Second Council of Lyons, prayers of intercession and masses for the dead had long been known in England. Religious houses would have been expected to intercede for the souls of their founders and benefactors. The emphasis here, however, is on perpetual chantries in parish churches and colleges.

Chantries are difficult to enumerate because many have left little or no trace. It is likely that every parish church would have had several. Documentary evidence occurs in the chantry certificates; in returns made to commissioners on their dissolution; in bishops' registers, where the institution of a chantry priest might be recorded (although many were privately employed and unlicensed); in licences to alienate land to the Church in mortmain (necessary after 1279, and found in the patent rolls); and in wills and cartularies. Often physical evidence is all that remains. Traces of a piscina on a south wall might well indicate the site of a chantry chapel. In Oxfordshire there are about 50 churches which exhibit features of possible chantries. There is evidence of about 70 named chantries, with an additional 66 in the city churches, two-thirds of which were founded in the 14th century. Ten colleges were established partly as chantries, including Rewley Abbey, originally intended as a college or chantry for the soul of Edmund Earl of Cornwall, and there were a few chantries within colleges, such as that of Sir Thomas Ingledew, a Yorkshire cleric, in Magdalen (*c*.1448).[1] The first university scholarship was provided in conjunction with a chantry. In 1243 the Prior of Bicester used a bequest from Alan Bassett to pay two chaplains to celebrate mass daily for Bassett and his wife and also to study in the schools at Oxford.[2]

Occasionally a chantry and a hospital might coincide. They

CHANTRIES OF MEDIEVAL OXFORD

Churches	Number of chantries		Number of chantries
1 St Mary Magdalen	3	10 St Frideswide	10
2 St Michael at the Northgate	3	11 St Thomas	1
3 St Mildred	1	12 St Mary the Virgin	10
4 St Peter le Bailey	7	13 St Peter in the East	4
5 St Martin	5	14 St George in the Castle	1
6 All Saints	8	15 St Giles	1
7 St Ebbe	3	16 St John the Baptist	2
8 St Aldate	4	17 St Cross	1
9 St Michael at the Southgate	1	18 Trinitarian Friars' chapel	1

Chantries within colleges

	Number of chantries
19 Balliol College	1
20 Magdalen College	2
21 Oriel College	1
22 University College	2

● Colleges founded partly as chantries

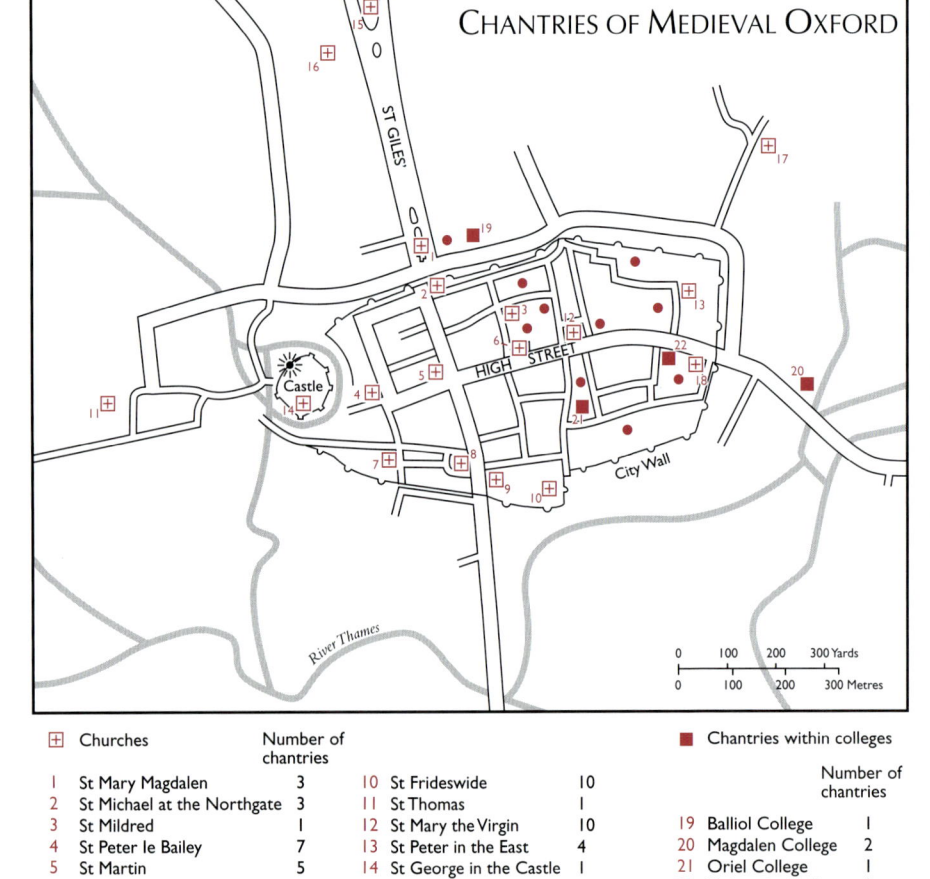

Perpetual Chantries

0 1 2 3 4 5 6 Miles
0 2 4 6 8 10 Kms

CROPREDY

WROXTON PRIORY
• John de Broughton, 1340

BANBURY
• John Forest et al, 1413, Gild of Blessed Mary

SWALCLIFFE LEA
• Ralph of Wilby, 1227

NORTH NEWINGTON

BROUGHTON

SWALCLIFFE
• Richard Whitewell, Rector, 1359, Lady chapel

DEDDINGTON
• Gild of Holy Trinity, 1445

SOUTH NEWINGTON

GREAT TEW

SOMERTON

CHASTLETON

COLD NORTON PRIORY

CHIPPING NORTON 5
• Richard Wale, St Mary, pre-1290
• Trinity Gild, c.1450, St Catherine's altar, Gild chapel
• Margaret Gervys, St John the Baptist, 1481
• Margaret Prynner, St James the Apostle (Chantry of John Rogers, alias Prynner), 1481

ENSTONE

ROUSHAM

BICESTER 2
• conventual church of St Mary: Walter of Fotheringay 1323, 1327

WOOTTON

TACKLEY

WOODSTOCK 3
• St Mary/St Mary Magdalen, 1453
• Thomas Croft, pre-1488, St Margaret
• Manor house chapel chantry, pre 1520s

HAMPTON POYLE

BURFORD
• John Pinnock, c.1486, Trinity chapel
• Richard Bishop, c.1508, Trinity chapel
• Merchant Gild, c.1200, Lady chapel

NORTH LEIGH
• Wilcote, c.1440

ASTHALL 3

COGGES 4

ISLIP
• Abbot of Westminster, 1258, Edward the Confessor

THAME
• Richard & Sybil Quatremain, St Christopher, 1447

THAME
• Anon, 15th/early 16th c. St John's aisle

MINSTER LOVELL 1
• John Lovel, 1273, St Cecilia

EYNSHAM ABBEY

DUCKLINGTON

SOUTH LEIGH

STANTON HARCOURT

OXFORD See separate map

HOLTON

WATERSTOCK

BAMPTON 2
• c.1402, chapel, Queen St
• Churchyard chapel of the Virgin, 1235

HORSPATH

RYCOTE
• Richard Quatremain, 1449

GARSINGTON
• Edward Audley, Bp Salisbury, 1520s

SOUTH WESTON

STANDLAKE 2
• Simon of Evesham, 1354
• 'Standlake chantry', pre-1535

CHALGROVE

WITNEY
• Richard of Standlake, pre-1348
• William Edington, Bp Winchester, 1346-66, chapel of the Virgin
• Thomas Richards of Fermor, 1485, S. transept aisle
• Thomas Richards of Fermor, 2nd chantry, unknown site
• Anon, pre-1270s, Virgin Mary

BENSON

EWELME
• Wm & Alice de la Pole, St John the Baptist, 1437

STONOR
• Sir John Stonor, 1349

HENLEY-ON-THAMES 4
• Merchant gild, pre-1317
• John Havelle & Thomas Clobber, 1382, St Catherine
• John Elmes, 1460
• John of Harwell, 1338

HARPSDEN

MAPLEDURHAM
• Robert & Amice Bardolf, 1381

● Church with a chantry
●² Church with more than one chantry
• John Lovel Chantry founder
○ Probable chantry, but lacking documentary evidence

59

24 · Medieval Chantries and Hospitals (continued)

God's House at Ewelme, exterior of the church from the south showing the Chapel of St John the Baptist

did so in the foundation at Ewelme by William de la Pole, Earl of Suffolk, and his wife Alice, née Chaucer, which comprised an almshouse (God's House), the fine chantry chapel of St John the Baptist in St Mary's Church and the grammar school. The term hospital came from the Latin *hospes,* meaning hospitality, and by transference a guest or traveller. Some hospitals were founded as hostels for travellers, such as St John the Baptist, Oxford, founded between 1180 and 1190 by Henry II, and St John the Baptist, Banbury, founded before 1225. Hospitals of whatever type were essentially religious houses, with an emphasis as much on healing the soul as the body, if not more so. There would have been no doctors. The hospital community who cared for the inmates would have lived a quasi-monastic life, and later strict religious obligations were imposed on the inhabitants of almshouses.

Founded from the late 12th century by the Church or royalty, hospitals, and especially almshouses, were later established by the nobility and townsfolk. They were usually outside the town walls, and the leper hospitals were often near bridges to facilitate begging. Wealthy or important foundations, like St John the Baptist, Oxford, or Ewelme, have left copious evidence, such as cartularies and foundation deeds, but the evidence for almshouses can often be limited to a stray reference, such as that for St Clement's, Oxford, known only from a grant of alms in 1345.[3]

Gradually hospitals evolved into three main types: leper hospitals, founded mainly before 1250, when the disease was widespread; hospitals for the non-leprous poor and sick; and almshouses, mainly late medieval.[4] Oxfordshire had well-documented examples of each of these – respectively, St Bartholomew's, Cowley, St John the Baptist, Oxford, and Ewelme. But the categories were by no means watertight, and often houses changed their function. Leper hospitals changed when leprosy became less prevalent in the late medieval period: St Bartholomew's, Cowley, granted to Oriel College in 1328, became a rest home for members of the College; St Leonard's, Clattercote, north of Banbury, became a priory of Gilbertine canons. Other communities were also transformed in the late medieval period either because they were in decline or because they were dissolved: St John the Baptist, Oxford, became Magdalen College, and St John the Baptist, Banbury, became a grammar school. Ewelme was one of the few to survive unchanged at the Reformation.

Bartlemas Hospital and Chapel (from J. H. Parker, *A Guide to the Architectural Antiquities in the Neighbourhood of Oxford,* 1846)

Medieval Hospitals

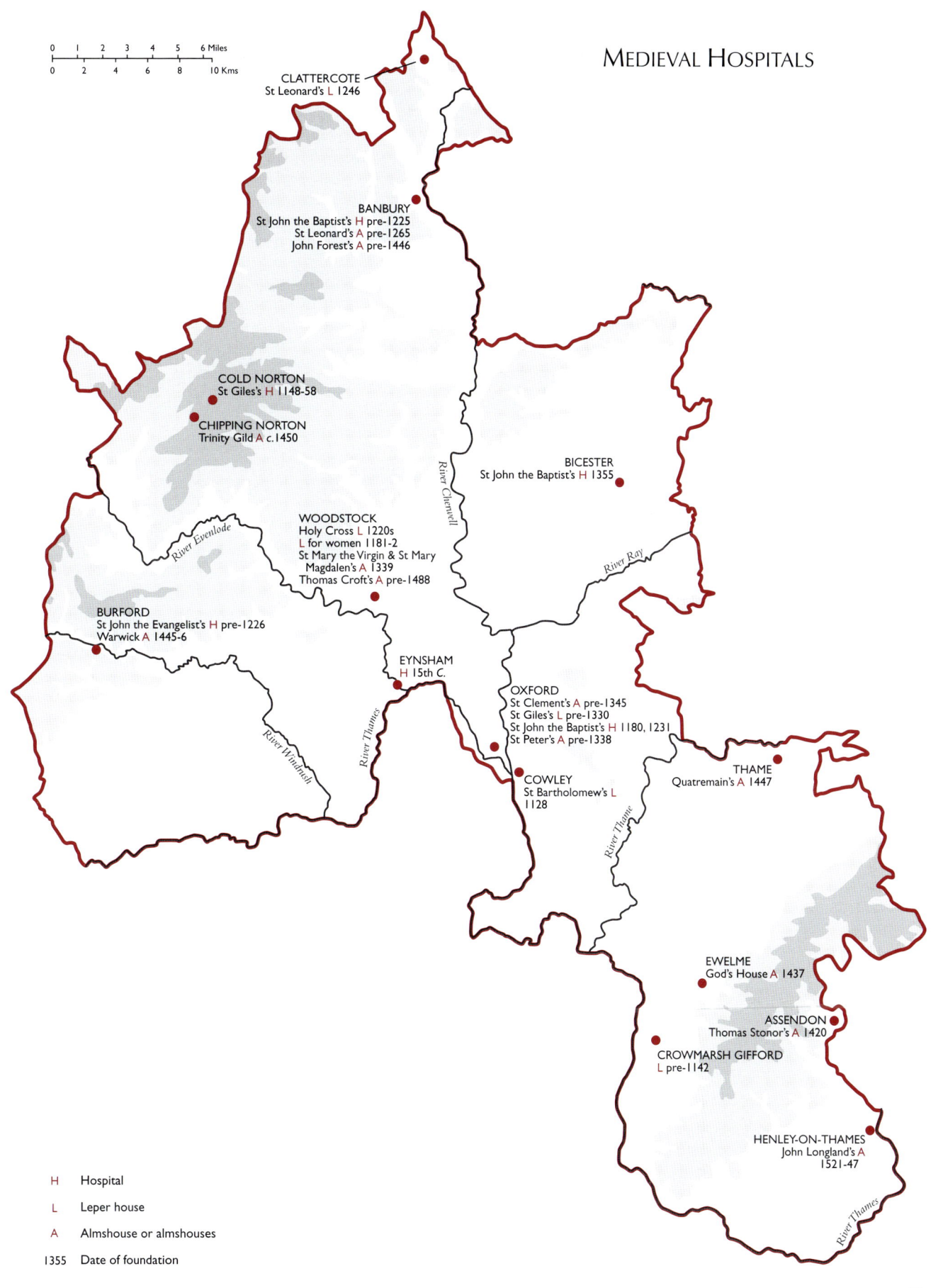

CLATTERCOTE
St Leonard's L 1246

BANBURY
St John the Baptist's H pre-1225
St Leonard's A pre-1265
John Forest's A pre-1446

COLD NORTON
St Giles's H 1148-58

CHIPPING NORTON
Trinity Gild A c.1450

BICESTER
St John the Baptist's H 1355

WOODSTOCK
Holy Cross L 1220s
L for women 1181-2
St Mary the Virgin & St Mary Magdalen's A 1339
Thomas Croft's A pre-1488

BURFORD
St John the Evangelist's H pre-1226
Warwick A 1445-6

EYNSHAM
H 15th C.

OXFORD
St Clement's A pre-1345
St Giles's L pre-1330
St John the Baptist's H 1180, 1231
St Peter's A pre-1338

COWLEY
St Bartholomew's L 1128

THAME
Quatremain's A 1447

EWELME
God's House A 1437

ASSENDON
Thomas Stonor's A 1420

CROWMARSH GIFFORD
L pre-1142

HENLEY-ON-THAMES
John Longland's A 1521-47

H Hospital
L Leper house
A Almshouse or almshouses
1355 Date of foundation

61

25 · University and College Properties before 1500 — Ralph Evans

A university emerged at Oxford in the latter part of the 12th century. Its establishment can be assigned to no particular year, but by 1209 it was functioning as an effective corporation. Like the university created very slightly later at Cambridge it was much favoured by the English crown and soon acquired a remarkable range of rights and privileges. From an early date it had a strong corporate identity, a carefully regulated constitution, a relatively autonomous position within the English church, a significant place in the English state, and a European reputation for its scholarship, but it held hardly any real property.

The business of the medieval university, including teaching, was largely conducted in premises it did not own. Not until the 1320s did it construct its own building for the meetings of its governing body; in the 15th century it added the ostentatiously magnificent theology school, with a new university library on the upper floor. From the 1250s the university held a few tenements in Oxford that generated a small rental income. Acquired at various dates by gift, bequest or purchase, they were often academic halls. The greater part of the university's modest annual revenue derived not from rents but from fees or fines of one kind or another.

Most of medieval Oxford's students lived in academic halls, rented from private landlords by masters licensed by the university. The halls were tightly structured communities with strong identities, and some endured for long periods, but they were intrinsically ephemeral, their existence renewable annually. Crucially they were unendowed. Colleges by contrast, which exercised an influence disproportionate to the small number of their fellows, were permanent legal corporations endowed with real property. Typically a college received the bulk of its property at its foundation, and added to it by benefaction or purchase.

By 1500 there were ten non-monastic colleges in Oxford: Merton (founded 1264–74), University (1280), Balliol (c.1283), Exeter (1314), Oriel (1324–6), Queen's (1341), New (1379), Lincoln (1427), All Souls (1438) and Magdalen (1458). They varied greatly in size and in the value and distribution of their estates. Most were founded by bishops who were senior servants of the crown, and two more by lesser clerks with royal support. These were men well placed to acquire property on favourable terms, whose contacts and position might be as significant as their financial resources. Walter of Merton held one of England's poorest sees, but his professional knowledge of Jewish business enabled him to buy up manors mortgaged to Jews by impoverished gentry, including Cuxham in Oxfordshire. William Waynflete, bishop of England's wealthiest see, established Magdalen College on the site of the hospital of St John the Baptist. Many of the hospital's lands passed to Magdalen, making its Oxfordshire estate more extensive than any other college's, and over three further decades Waynflete and his agents carefully acquired additional properties. Even powerful founders were constrained by what was on the market, but it seems significant that a disproportionate number of college properties were in Oxfordshire or adjacent counties, where they could more easily be supervised.

Like the university itself all the medieval colleges held some tenements in the town of Oxford. In the countryside a college might hold a full manor or more or less extensive lands of another lord. A manor might, like Cuxham, coincide quite closely with a village and parish or, like Golder, have appurtenances in several parishes (in such cases only the manor itself is named on the map). Colleges' holdings could be of very different sizes. Magdalen held several yardlands at the deserted settlement of Ilbury in the parish of Deddington, while at Waterperry Oriel held just two acres of meadow. There might be a mill on a college's estate, as Merton's at Cuxham, New College's at Kingham, or Lincoln's at Iffley. Very occasionally colleges relinquished properties after a short period; these are not included on the map.

Another form of property often held by a college was an appropriated church: the college as rector would receive the major tithes of the parish while a vicar might take the lesser, much less valuable, tithes (see entry 18). The revenue of an appropriated church, even after the deduction of necessary expenses, could easily be as great as that of a manor, and might well be simpler to extract. The rectory of Adderbury was one of New College's most valuable properties; in addition to tithe the rectory's glebe land at Adderbury was treated as a manor with a court for its tenants. Adderbury was let to wealthy laymen, but a rectory was sometimes leased by the vicar, as on occasion was that of All Souls at Lewknor. A college might hold the advowson of a church, the right to present a new incumbent, but such occasional patronage was not a source of income.

Colleges were perpetual ecclesiastical corporations, in some ways comparable to medium or small religious houses, and they probably managed their estates in much the same way. Until the mid 14th century Merton College exploited its manors directly, and the warden and fellows were closely involved in the minutiae of farm management. But even when estates were leased out the heads and bursars or treasurers of colleges were active in the management of estates and might be obliged by statute to visit them each year, and colleges retained control of their manorial courts. Although Merton was not a large or powerful lord it was able to engineer significant social and economic change on its estates. At Cuxham it continued the policy of previous lords in buying up free holdings and consolidating the demesne; in the 1290s it created new villein tenements, increasing the supply of unfree labour available for the production of wheat for the London market. The contribution of the colleges and their lessees to the building stock of the county includes the fine surviving barn built for New College at Swalcliffe, very possibly by the mason–architect who began the imposing theology school of the university itself.

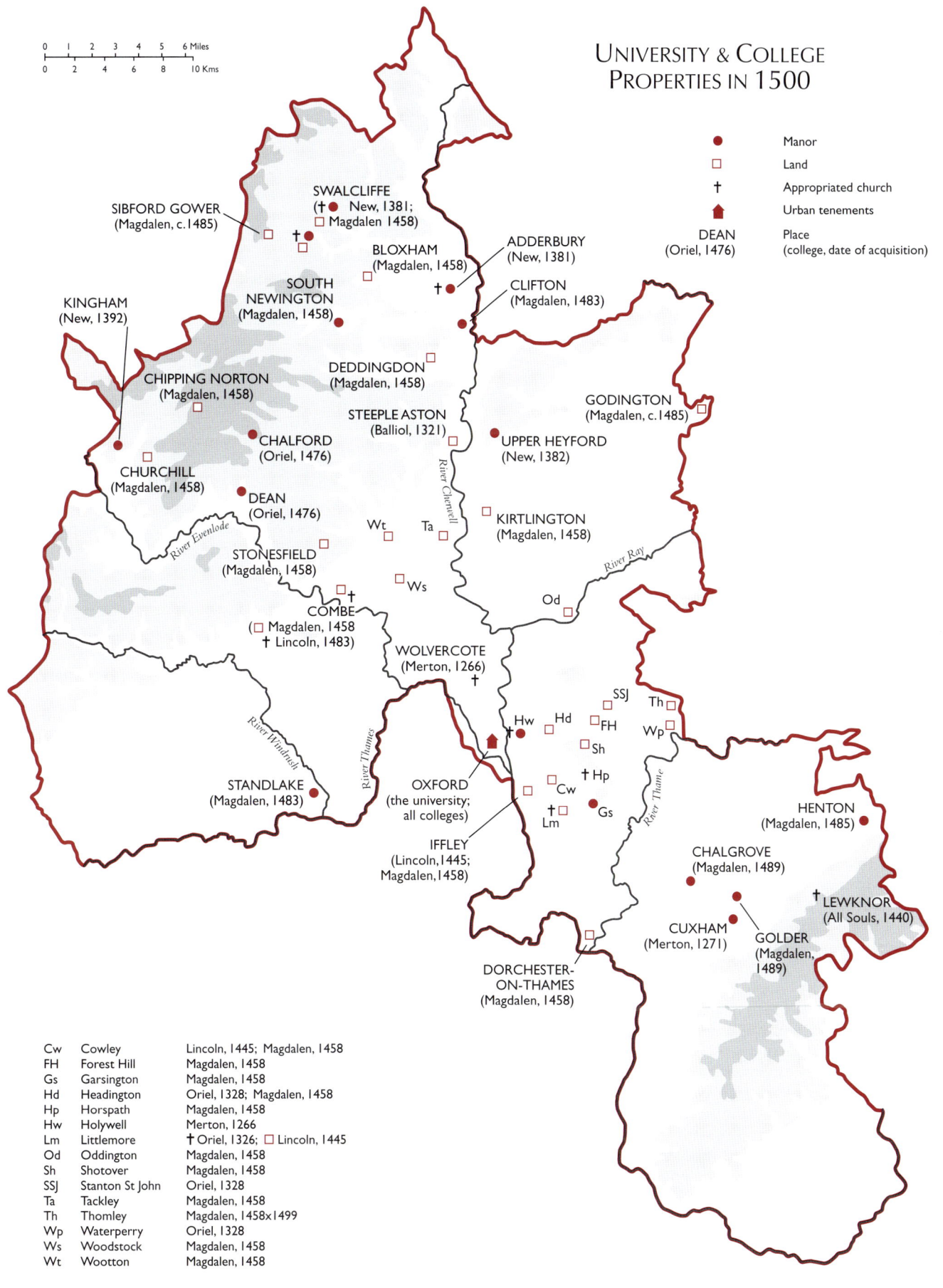

University & College Properties in 1500

Legend:
- ● Manor
- □ Land
- † Appropriated church
- 🏠 Urban tenements
- DEAN (Oriel, 1476) Place (college, date of acquisition)

Places:
- SIBFORD GOWER (Magdalen, c.1485)
- SWALCLIFFE († New, 1381; □ Magdalen 1458)
- BLOXHAM (Magdalen, 1458)
- ADDERBURY (New, 1381)
- CLIFTON (Magdalen, 1483)
- KINGHAM (New, 1392)
- SOUTH NEWINGTON (Magdalen, 1458)
- DEDDINGDON (Magdalen, 1458)
- GODINGTON (Magdalen, c.1485)
- CHIPPING NORTON (Magdalen, 1458)
- STEEPLE ASTON (Balliol, 1321)
- UPPER HEYFORD (New, 1382)
- CHALFORD (Oriel, 1476)
- CHURCHILL (Magdalen, 1458)
- DEAN (Oriel, 1476)
- KIRTLINGTON (Magdalen, 1458)
- STONESFIELD (Magdalen, 1458)
- COMBE (□ Magdalen, 1458; † Lincoln, 1483)
- WOLVERCOTE (Merton, 1266)
- STANDLAKE (Magdalen, 1483)
- OXFORD (the university; all colleges)
- IFFLEY (Lincoln, 1445; Magdalen, 1458)
- HENTON (Magdalen, 1485)
- CHALGROVE (Magdalen, 1489)
- LEWKNOR (All Souls, 1440)
- CUXHAM (Merton, 1271)
- GOLDER (Magdalen, 1489)
- DORCHESTER-ON-THAMES (Magdalen, 1458)

Abbreviations:

Cw	Cowley	Lincoln, 1445; Magdalen, 1458
FH	Forest Hill	Magdalen, 1458
Gs	Garsington	Magdalen, 1458
Hd	Headington	Oriel, 1328; Magdalen, 1458
Hp	Horspath	Magdalen, 1458
Hw	Holywell	Merton, 1266
Lm	Littlemore	† Oriel, 1326; □ Lincoln, 1445
Od	Oddington	Magdalen, 1458
Sh	Shotover	Magdalen, 1458
SSJ	Stanton St John	Oriel, 1328
Ta	Tackley	Magdalen, 1458
Th	Thomley	Magdalen, 1458×1499
Wp	Waterperry	Oriel, 1328
Ws	Woodstock	Magdalen, 1458
Wt	Wootton	Magdalen, 1458

26 · Pottery and Potters

Maureen Mellor

Pottery is the signature of the Viking and later medieval period in most of Europe. For the early Anglo-Saxon period it is central to our understanding of death, burial and funerary customs. By comparing and contrasting assemblages for the later period, pottery gives an insight into a changing society, through the patterns of pottery use in great households and in everyday peasant life.

In the 10th to 12th centuries, jars comprised the bulk of vessels. They were vermin-proof, made excellent storage and were used in conjunction with woven baskets and leather, wooden and metal containers. They were also used in cooking. A new form was introduced – the spouted pitcher. By the mid 13th century the majority of ceramic assemblages in towns were colourful glazed pitchers. Metal vessels were now preferred for cooking. However, ceramic vessels were still needed as multifunctional storage vessels until the end of the medieval period.

The processes of pottery making were complex and required access to clay, water and fuel, supplies abundant in Oxfordshire. Making and firing pots was often a seasonal and hazardous occupation. Dense smoke and sparks were a risk in densely populated settlements.

Along the Thames corridor, a variety of clays tempered with sand and particularly chaff- or grass-tempered were in use during the 5th to 7th centuries. These fashioned plain and decorated cremation pots and vessels for use in the home and in the farmed landscape.

The Christianisation of most of England in the 7th century saw the demise of pottery funerary vessels. Minimal change in the use of everyday pottery is evident and until recently archaeological evidence suggested little movement of pottery within mid-Saxon Oxfordshire. The recognition of Ipswich wares (720–850), the most common type in use in London's *wic*, indicates contact, either via the Thames or with visitors who navigated waterways from the Wash. Its presence locally may merely represent the personal equipment of an individual or may possibly be evidence of trade in goods that commanded a higher economic value (quernstones, hone stones).

The Danish settlement at the end of the 9th century and the unification under Cnut are reflected in the ceramic record. By the 10th to 11th centuries the regional character of pottery production and consumption is apparent and reflects political boundaries. Late Saxon shelly ware, produced close to Oxford, included hand-built vessels. Later jars were also made on the wheel, which enabled potters to produce more as the population rose in the *burhs* and rural settlements. Scientific analysis corroborates the visual identification of this tradition and its largely riverine distribution from Eynsham to London.

A change in pottery supply is evident across Oxfordshire by the end of the 10th century. St Neot's-type ware, apparently brought great distances from within the Danelaw, is found in the *burhs* (Oxford, Wallingford), isolated castles (Deddington) and rural settlements (Fawler, Grimsbury). The non-local potters made wheel-thrown jars of smaller capacity than many of the locally made jars. This must have caused problems in ordinary households in an age where measuring and weighing were the exception. A wider repertoire of forms, deep-sided bowls, lamps and storage jars is also evident. The presence of glazed, Stamford-type spouted pitchers, inspired from the Continent, and more importantly of crucibles for fine metalworking suggests transportation over an even greater distance from within the Danelaw. The Anglo-Scandinavian culture appears to have encouraged greater commercial enterprise than the Anglo-Saxon cultures of Wessex and Mercia. St Neot's-type ware may have travelled with the Viking armies and then supplied the newly won territories, only to contract and retreat from Oxfordshire around Cnut's death (1035).

Continental imports, though rare in late 10th- and early 11th-century Oxfordshire, were made in France, the Rhineland and the Low Countries and may reflect commerce with Southampton (Wessex) and London (Mercia), both ports where international exchange is documented, rather than direct trade with the Continent. Regional imports, mainly pitchers and decorated storage jars, often travelled further, as illustrated by glazed, spouted pitchers and the stamp-decorated Michelmersh-type vessels from Winchester and its Wessex hinterland.

The hand-built calcareous gravel wares produced to the north-west of Oxfordshire, a region tied to a seasonal agrarian cycle typical of a feudal society, encouraged a conservative pottery tradition with part-time potters. A continuation of this local ware is mentioned in Domesday Book (1086), where potters at Bladon returned a hefty 8% of the total value of the manor.

Changes to Oxfordshire's political structure are evident post-1066, when new traditions emerge to the north-east of Oxford, and at Ashampstead, where kilns were identified recently. The bulk of the vessels were jars, variably sized, and a new style of pitcher – the glazed, spouted tripod pitcher, designed to rest on a flat surface. The potters at Ashampstead sometimes employed white slip to decorate pitchers, which travelled as far as Newbury and Abingdon on the Berkshire side of the Thames.

By the later 12th century a handmade coarseware industry centred on the Savernake Forest supplied domestic wares to Oxford and Abingdon. Abingdon's market was frequented by inhabitants of south Oxfordshire (e.g. Chalgrove), while other markets supplied the same wares to Witney and to the castle at Middleton Stoney. Work in advance of the Newbury bypass located two pottery kilns. Around Nettlebed, ceramic industries are documented in the 14th and 15th centuries and Henley, a transhipment port on the Thames, boasted kilns dated to the 13th century. In the north-west of the county a coarseware industry, possibly influenced by Minety (Wilts), operated from within the Wychwood Forest. Other regional wares include pottery from Minety. Banbury and its hinterland were supplied by products from Potterspury and Brackley.

The outstanding ceramic industry of the region was centred on Brill, just over the Buckinghamshire border, and its surrounding parishes. The skilled potters supplied local consumers and the markets of Oxfordshire with highly decorated tablewares, including lamps, and storage vessels of varying sizes. The medieval ceramic tradition continued there until disafforestation in 1632.

POTTERY AND POTTERS

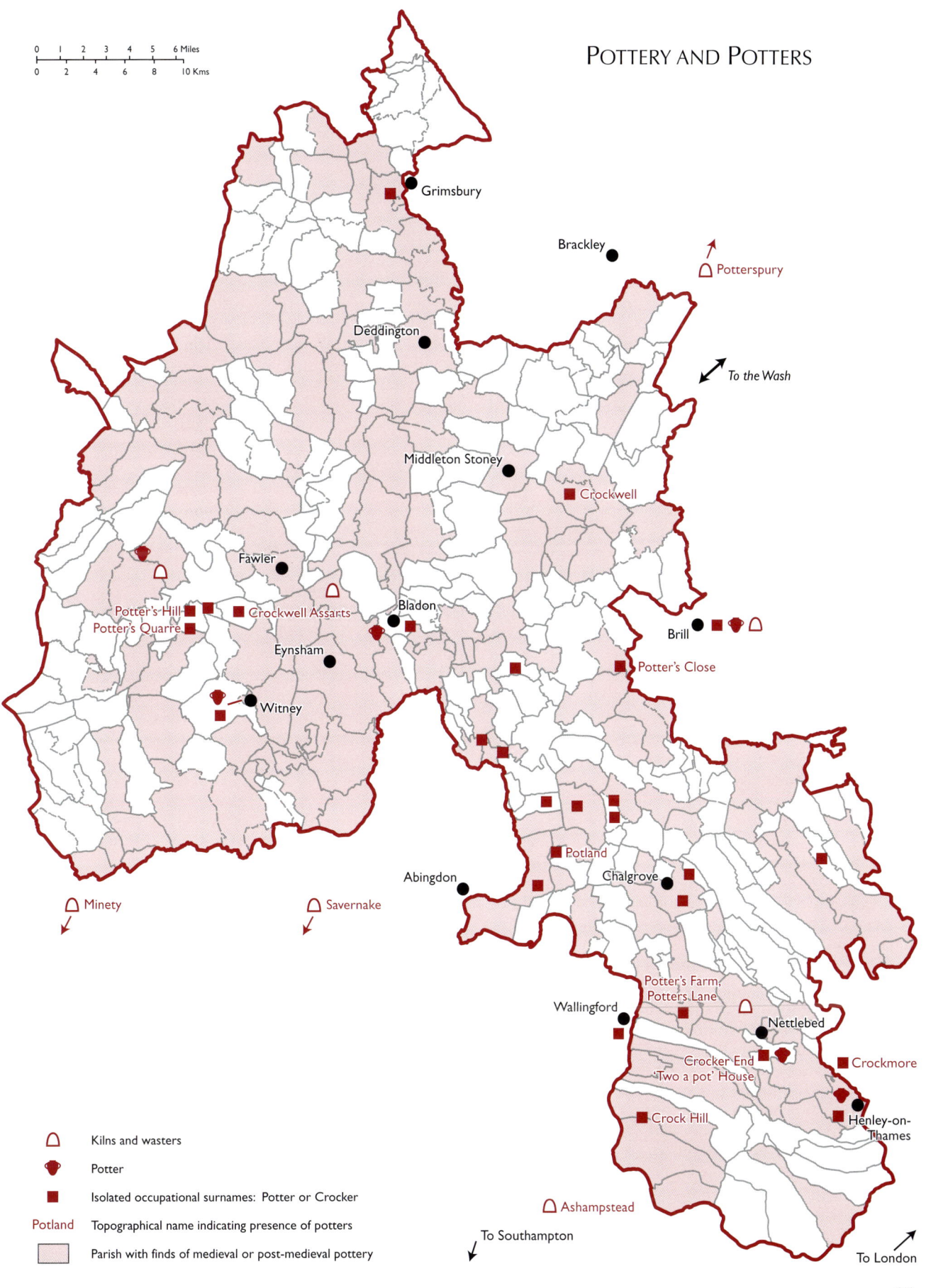

27 · Medieval Vernacular Buildings — David Clark

There has been no systematic survey of Oxfordshire's vernacular buildings – by which we mean those structures which use local building materials and were built for 'ordinary' people in a local style reflecting their period. In the Middle Ages the standard house was based on a hall which was entered through opposing doors at one end (the low or service end) and was heated by means of a central hearth, the smoke from which rose to the rafters and percolated through the thatch or, in stone or tile roof houses, some form of louvre or chimney. Beyond the hearth, the 'high' end often had a dais lit by a large window and was differentiated from the rest of the hall by finer carpentry or decoration. The layout can be seen at its clearest in many Oxford college dining halls (New College and Christ Church, for example). In the simplest rural examples, the hall was a communal, family space used for cooking and sleeping as well as eating and sitting. Beyond the high end a door might lead to a further room (solar) or even a two-storey wing containing a parlour and/or private sleeping chambers. At the low end beyond the cross-passage would typically be a pantry (for dry goods) and a buttery (for liquids), while higher-status houses might have a third doorway leading to a kitchen, often detached from the house because of the potential fire hazard. The finest example of a detached kitchen is at Stanton Harcourt Manor, but there are vernacular survivals in Dorchester and Newnham Murren. Mill Farm Cottage, Mapledurham (1334), is a surviving example of what was originally a simple three-bay hall house. Yelford Manor had a hall with jettied cross-wings at either end, built in one phase of c.1500, while at the apparently similar Chalgrove Manor (hall of 1488) one of the wings is earlier than the hall, suggesting the process of 'alternate rebuilding' of the various parts as greater wealth demanded higher status spaces.

Surviving hall houses are found in all parts of the county; for example in the ironstone area at Swalcliffe (Manor) and Deddington (Leadenporch House), in the Oolitic Limestone zone in Burford (Bull Cottage), and in the examples above from the Thames Valley and Chiltern foothills, where timber was the building material of choice. While vernacular buildings are characterised by their use of local materials, only a handful of stone houses can confidently be dated to the medieval period, and most of these are in urban locations. What survives today may not be representative of the medieval built environment: it seems likely that most rural medieval houses were timber, with a thatched roof. In Burford, where stone quarrying was an important local trade, there also seems to have been a tradition of timber building (109, 111–3 High Street) and of stone ground floors with timber above, for example at the Tolsey (1525) and Calendars (1473). Recent research using dendrochronology has enabled more of medieval Oxfordshire's buildings to be dated (see upper map).

Timber buildings fall broadly into two traditions, box-frame and cruck. A cruck is a curved timber through which the weight of the roof is taken to the ground, either directly or via part of a solid wall. Their overall distribution is broadly north and west of a line between the Solent and the Wash, including Oxfordshire, where cruck frames are found throughout. Most are medieval.

Crucks are classified according to the way they are joined at the apex. Many of these distributions are national, but one of these, the so-called Type W, is found mainly in north Hampshire, Berkshire, Buckinghamshire and Oxfordshire (see lower map).

Box frames, on the other hand, are found all over the country, but their carpentry often shows regional or local characteristics, many of which changed over time. One early form was the aisled hall, similar in form to some barns, where the principal posts supporting the roof structure are internal to the building, allowing the roof to come down on each side over narrow aisles. The Queen's Head at Crowmarsh Gifford (1341) is a good example. By the 15th century, box frames with square panels of wattle-and-daub infill would have been ubiquitous. Higher-status versions had more vertical timbers, and less infill. This 'close-studding' can be found over a wide area in the south of the county, from Burford in the west (Calendars) to the Witney area (Church Farm, South Leigh, Yelford Manor and Standlake Manor) and eastwards to Chalgrove Manor, Grey's Court and Henley.

Oxfordshire roof structures seem to follow a pattern typical of the south of England. In the 13th century, rafters were pegged at the apex in pairs with no form of lateral strengthening (St Giles church, Oxford, chancel roof 1288) but by the 14th century this had been superseded by the crownpost roof. Here, the collars of the paired rafter roof were linked by a single axial timber (crown plate or collar purlin) supported by crownposts at intervals pegged into tie-beams, braced to the collars and crown plate. A dated example of 1381 survives within 26–28 Cornmarket, Oxford. By the 15th century the side purlin roof was established, usually with the purlin clasped between the principal rafter and the collar, which in turn was supported by queen-posts tenoned into the tie-beam. The guesthouse at Dorchester Abbey has an example of 1444–5.

Brick has an early history in Oxfordshire. The kilns at Nettlebed were an important source of brick and tile (the words were interchangeable in the Middle Ages) for Wallingford Castle and the early part of the encyclopaedia of brickwork at Stonor. In the 1450s the de la Poles used brick to great advantage in their school and almshouses at Ewelme.

Oxfordshire is rich in examples of medieval farm buildings. Of singular importance is the set of barns built by New College in the early 15th century (Adderbury, Swalcliffe, Upper Heyford and Oxford) Other survivals are in Minster Lovell (which also boasts a fine 15th-century dovecote), and the cruck barns at Church Farm, Enstone (1382), and Rectory Farm Barn, Northmoor (now a house).

VERNACULAR BUILDINGS

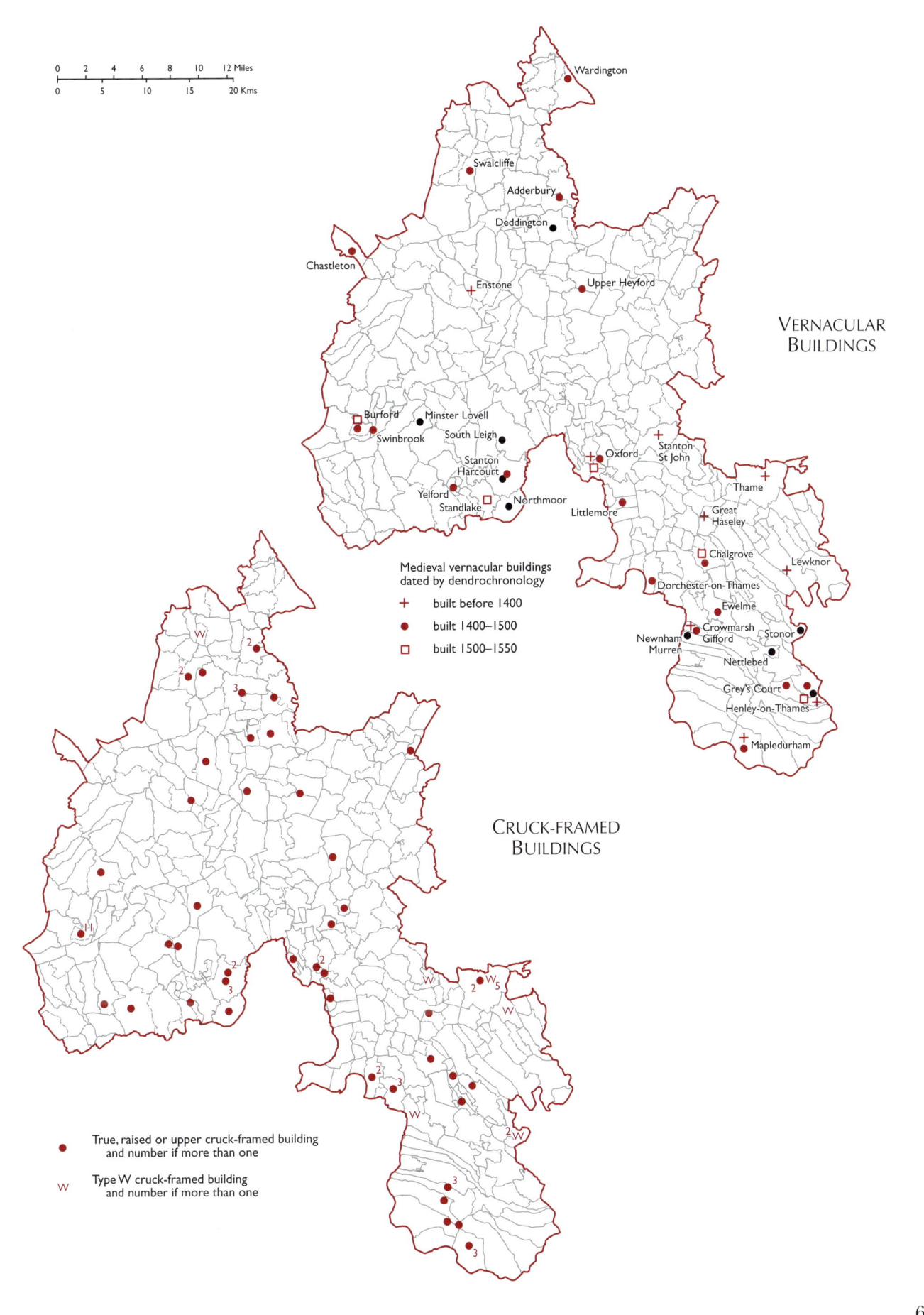

Medieval vernacular buildings dated by dendrochronology
- + built before 1400
- ● built 1400–1500
- ☐ built 1500–1550

Locations labelled: Wardington, Swalcliffe, Adderbury, Deddington, Chastleton, Enstone, Upper Heyford, Burford, Minster Lovell, Swinbrook, South Leigh, Stanton Harcourt, Yelford, Standlake, Northmoor, Oxford, Stanton St John, Littlemore, Thame, Great Haseley, Chalgrove, Lewknor, Dorchester-on-Thames, Ewelme, Crowmarsh Gifford, Stonor, Newnham Murren, Nettlebed, Grey's Court, Henley-on-Thames, Mapledurham

CRUCK-FRAMED BUILDINGS

- ● True, raised or upper cruck-framed building and number if more than one
- W Type W cruck-framed building and number if more than one

67

28 · Medieval Watermills

James Bond

The use of water-power for grinding corn was a Roman introduction, though no Romano-British mill sites have yet been recognised in Oxfordshire. Watermills were costly to construct and maintain and, when they reappeared in the early middle ages, they were initially restricted to royal and monastic estates where sufficiently large and reliable supplies of grain could be ensured. Abingdon Abbey claimed to have been deprived of a mill at Cuddesdon during the Danish wars; if true, this would represent the earliest Oxfordshire record. The same abbey held land at Tadmarton, where a mill featured as a charter boundary landmark in 956. A mill-weir at Ducklington, mentioned on the charter bounds of Witney in 1044, had appeared since the earlier bounds of 969.

Before the Conquest, many mills were probably simple structures worked by a horizontally mounted wheel which rotated a vertical spindle affixed directly to the upper stone. A wooden paddle, probably from a late Saxon horizontal waterwheel, has been recovered from the Trill Mill Stream in Oxford. The more familiar vertically mounted waterwheel, which employed gearing to generate more power, was also in use long before the Conquest. By the 13th century vertical-wheeled mills had superseded the horizontal type, the change probably reflecting the expansion of feudal monopolies, each lord compelling his tenants to bring their grain to the manorial mill to be ground and imposing a toll upon them for doing so.

Over 200 mills are recorded in the Oxfordshire Domesday survey, mentioned in connection with 116 out of the 251 vills. Twenty of those places had three or more mills: five are noted at Cropredy, Adderbury, Dorchester and Chalgrove, six at Shipton-under-Wychwood. In some cases such multiple records almost certainly represent separate buildings: at Cropredy, for example, two mills recorded in 1086 on the Bishop of Lincoln's demesne appear to equate with the later Upper and Lower Mills in Cropredy itself, while three mills on lands held by tenants can probably be identified with the later Wardington, Prescott and Slat Mills. Elsewhere multiple mill entries may refer to one wheel driving two or more sets of stones, or two or more wheels, under the same roof. Where Domesday Book ascribes more than one mill to a vill, the number appears on the map, and links suggest whether single or separate sites are implied.

The annual cash value of Oxfordshire mills in 1086 ranged from 20d up to 30s, with mills in half a dozen places also rendering between 100 and 450 eels. Domesday Book does not distinguish between different types of mills, but some of the least-profitable examples may still have had horizontal wheels. Most mills probably now employed vertical undershot wheels, rotated by the kinetic energy of water flowing beneath. Undershot wheels can be turned by streams with only a slight fall, and minimal earthworks are required to form the mill-race.

Mills which yielded no taxable profit may have been excluded from Domesday, so the record in 1086 may be incomplete. However, the quantity of mills noted in later manorial accounts and extents suggests that the actual number of mills did increase significantly between the late 11th and 13th century. Their proliferation resulted in many conflicts caused by flooding or interrupted water flow to other mills downstream. The biggest concentration of medieval mills was around Oxford, but only a few of these survived into later centuries. By the end of the 12th century the overshot wheel, turned by potential energy or weight of water, had been introduced; the stream was led in a trough or launder over the top of the wheel and directed into buckets on the wheel, which thus rotated in the opposite direction to an undershot wheel. Overshot wheels require only about 25% of the water needed to turn an undershot wheel effectively, but they do need an adequate fall, and are more suited to faster-flowing streams with a steeper gradient. The record of new mills after 1086 reveals an upstream extension of milling capacity towards the watershed on some streams, perhaps reflecting the increasing use of overshot wheels.

Some medieval mills had a relatively short life. In 1293 a new mill is recorded inside Woodstock Park, but in 1334 Edward III ordered its removal and re-erection on a new site outside the park. However, overshot wheels in particular required millponds, dams, weirs, leats and sluices, and the effort of construction meant that, once a suitable site had been selected, it would often remain in use at least into the 18th or 19th century. Mill buildings, by contrast, were vulnerable to strains through movement and vibration of machinery, timber rotting in damp conditions, and sparks from millstones in dusty atmospheres causing fire risk. As a result, the buildings were often reconstructed, and the structure of most extant watermills dates predominantly from the 18th and 19th centuries.

Most conspicuous in the overall distribution of medieval mills is their absence from the Chilterns, where there were few suitable streams. Mills were most common on the faster-flowing tributaries from the Cotswolds and north Oxfordshire uplands. Of the eight mills built on the sluggish waters of the Ray catchment only two remained in use in 1750. On the Thames, mills find their greatest concentration between Dorchester and Henley, but this gives a somewhat false picture, since there were more mills on the Berkshire bank further upstream.

The vast majority of medieval watermills were employed solely in grinding corn. However, the invention of the cam-shaft and trip-hammer paved the way for several other industrial applications, such as fulling cloth. The earliest record of a fulling mill in Oxfordshire occurs in 1197, when William Lovell gave a corn mill and fulling mill at Minster Lovell, both probably under the same roof, to Thame Abbey. Over 20 fulling mills are documented in Oxfordshire before 1540, though in some cases this function may have been short-lived. The greatest concentration was always on the Windrush, though several appeared on the Thames, on the Cherwell and its tributaries and on the Glyme.

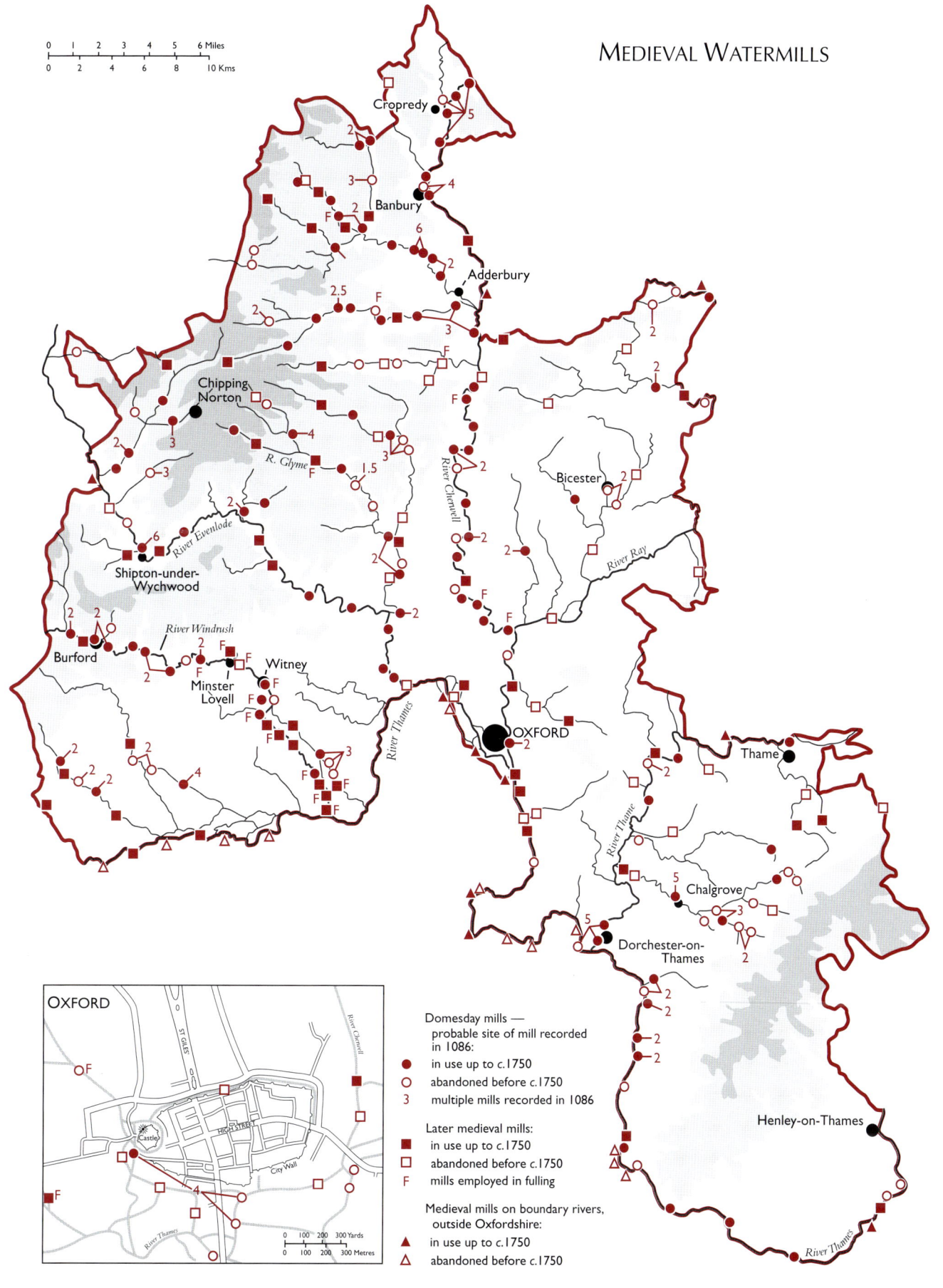

Medieval Watermills

Domesday mills —
probable site of mill recorded in 1086:
- ● in use up to c.1750
- ○ abandoned before c.1750
- 3 multiple mills recorded in 1086

Later medieval mills:
- ■ in use up to c.1750
- □ abandoned before c.1750
- F mills employed in fulling

Medieval mills on boundary rivers, outside Oxfordshire:
- ▲ in use up to c.1750
- △ abandoned before c.1750

Oxford (inset)

69

29 · Oxford before 1800 — Alan Crossley

Saxon and Medieval Oxford The town was first mentioned in 911, when Edward the Elder took control of London and Oxford, presumably in preparation for the movement against the southern Danes which marked his reign. By then, Oxford belonged to a system of fortified *burhs* organized by Alfred or Edward the Elder to defend Wessex, but its earlier history remains uncertain. The river Thames had long been a frontier between Wessex and Mercia, and the unidentified ford from which Oxford took its name was presumably of military significance as well as carrying an important north–south trading route. The site on which the town developed was part of a royal estate centred on Headington, but mid-Saxon finds in the vicinity have been largely confined to the approaches to a river-crossing south of the later *burh*; there is also some archaeological support for a supposition (from literary evidence) that the nearby St Frideswide's monastery (on the site of Christ Church) had originated as a Mercian royal foundation of *c*.700. In general, however, the paucity of early finds suggests that Oxford may have become a major settlement only after the deliberate creation of a fortified *burh*, probably on vacant land, close to whatever small riverside settlement there was. An early 10th-century document suggests that Oxford's Saxon rampart was much shorter than the medieval town wall, and the later street plan hints at an original fortress which was roughly square, centred on the highest point (Carfax), whence straight streets, aligned on the four cardinal points, ran to gates near the centre of each peripheral wall. The north gate was probably on its later site, but the east gate on High Street perhaps stood just west of Catte Street, and outside it, curving down to a crossing of the river Cherwell, a road later preserved as the famous 'bend' in High Street; the west gate perhaps stood just west of the junction of Queen Street and New Inn Hall Street, with outside it a road curving west (through the later castle site), crossing the river into St Thomas's High Street; even the original south gate may have stood further north, near St Aldate's church, before St Frideswide's priory was brought within the town walls. This symmetrical layout, surely achievable only through deliberate planning, is notably similar to other Saxon planned towns such as Wareham (Dorset): moreover, the length of the suggested rampart would be in accord with the documentary evidence. Archaeological confirmation is lacking and, if indeed Oxford was a planned fortress, its likely date and founder remain uncertain.

The late-Saxon town prospered, benefiting from its position on major trade routes at the heart of the kingdom. It had an important mint and its townsmen enjoyed privileged trading rights in London and a status comparable to the men of London and Winchester. There was a royal residence, frequently the venue for great councils. By the early 11th century the town had expanded eastwards towards the Cherwell crossing and westwards (over the site of the later castle); the walled town acquired its familiar lozenge shape when both those areas were fortified, perhaps after sack by the Danes in 1009. In 1066, with over 1,000 recorded houses and perhaps 11 churches, Oxford ranked in size behind only London, York, Norwich, Lincoln and Winchester. There was considerable post-Conquest devastation, attributable only partly to the destruction of houses for Robert d'Oilly's castle, built across the western entrance to the town; d'Oilly also built (or improved) Grandpont, the great causeway on the south.

In the early Middle Ages Oxford remained politically important, the Court and great councils coming to the royal palace (the 'king's houses') outside North Gate. The town's corporate identity was confirmed in the 1190s, when it acquired a common seal and a royal charter. Its flourishing economy was based chiefly on wool and cloth, but it gained, too, from a position at the centre of a great corn-growing area and on important routes between the midlands and Southampton, and from Wales through Gloucester to London. In 1227 Oxford paid the same tallage as York, more than all other provincial towns. Prosperity was reflected in intensive building, subdivision of properties and suburban expansion. During the 13th century the town walls were rebuilt in stone. By 1279 some 1,400 properties were crowded into the town and suburbs and there were 18 parish churches as well as the houses of most major religious orders. The university, which began in the 12th century as a small and loose association of scholars, had developed as a major element in the town's economy and also, after prolonged and violent clashes with townsmen, a formidable political power, united under its chancellor.

In the 13th century Oxford began to suffer from the (national) movement of cloth production from town to country. Later other factors – the cessation of royal visits, competing markets within its region, the decline of Thames navigation, new routes by-passing Oxford towards an increasingly dominant capital, the transfer into ecclesiastical hands of a disproportionate share of town property – all contributed to the town's late-medieval decline. Having ranked eighth among provincial towns in taxable wealth in 1334, Oxford fell to at least 29th place by the early 16th century, and, except for the university, became a county and market town of only local significance, with a population of *c*.3,000 (excluding scholars). Its economic base changed from manufacture and commerce to service trades heavily dependent on the university. The suburbs contracted and intramural properties fell vacant, a process accelerated by the Black Death, which killed perhaps a third of the population. Houses once occupied by merchants and craftsmen were acquired as academic halls, of which there were some 70 in the early 15th century, declining to fewer than ten as colleges expanded. Grand university and college buildings came to dominate the eastern part of the town where decay had been most widespread: New College was built over some 50 vacant plots and Merton College took into its garden most of the south-east corner of the town.

Oxford 1500–1800 In 1524 Oxford was small and not prosperous. Its economy was heavily dependent on the university, which directly employed a fifth of tax-paying inhabitants. Its medieval primary industries – fulling,

Oxford in 1279

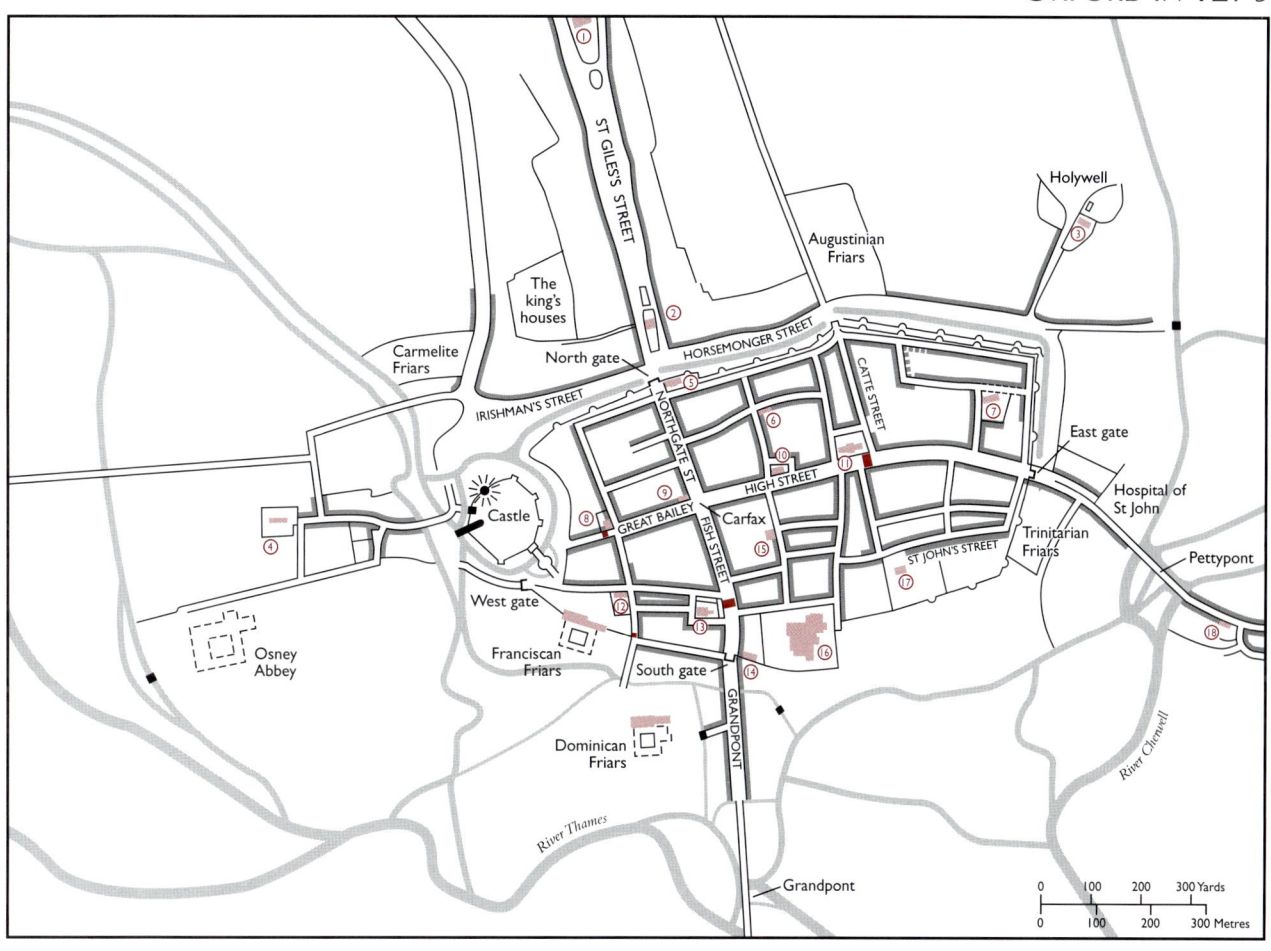

	Church		Churches	7	St Peter in the East	14	St Michael at the South gate
	Built-up street frontage	1	St Giles	8	St Peter in the Bailey	15	St Edward
		2	St Mary Magdalen	9	St Martin	16	St Frideswide's Priory
	City Wall	3	St Cross	10	All Saints	17	St John
		4	St Thomas	11	St Mary the Virgin	18	St Clement
	Possible sites of original west, south and east gates	5	St Michael at the North gate	12	St Ebbe		
	Mill	6	St Mildred	13	St Aldate		

71

29 · Oxford before 1800 (continued)

weaving, tanning – had largely disappeared, and leading townsmen were mostly small tradesmen and craftsmen in the victualling, distributive, clothing and building trades, supplying a local market. Road and river communications were poor, so even semi-industrial enterprises such as brewing served only a restricted hinterland. Late-medieval depopulation had resulted in falling rents and a reduced housing stock: there were vacant plots in the central streets and large open spaces once occupied by houses and academic halls. The Reformation brought the dissolution of monasteries and friaries which had dominated the medieval town, and a temporary sharp decline in university numbers to a low point in the mid 16th century.

Oxford was deemed a city from 1542, when it became the seat of a bishop. Then, chiefly between the 1580s and the Civil War, it grew in population and prosperity until, by the 1660s, it ranked eighth among English provincial urban centres. Its growth owed much to the revival of university education, which had a similar impact on Cambridge. There were not many more than 1,000 scholars and servants in Oxford in the 1550s, but numbers probably doubled by the end of the century and approached 3,500 by the 1630s. The total population, not much more than 3,000 in the 1520s, grew to *c.*5,000 in the 1580s, then probably doubled by the 1630s. After the disruptions of the Civil War and Interregnum it reached a similar level of over 10,000 in the 1660s. Oxford thus outstripped national demographic trends: England's population roughly doubled (from 2.5 to 5 million) between the 1520s and the 1630s, but Oxford's population tripled.

Its economy was stimulated by demand from an increasingly prosperous rural hinterland and by the general revival of internal trade. Road communications improved and Thames navigation was opened up to Oxford in the 1620s, but the city still relied chiefly on supplying a local market, particularly the university. Growth was characterised by an expansion of existing crafts and trades, and small household enterprises remained the norm. Immigration was crucial, since there was little natural population increase. The number of apprentices flooding into the city rose from fewer than 30 a year in the 1560s to about 85 a year by the 1630s. Tailoring, gloving and shoemaking accounted for nearly half the intake in the early 17th century. Numbers in the distributive trades, which involved more capital, were fewer but grew steadily from the 1590s. The food and drink trades expanded somewhat later, but by the 1630s, in terms of apprentice numbers, ranked third after the leather and clothing workers. By then a tenth of all masters and apprentices were engaged in the building trades. The wealthiest occupations, reflected in membership of the city's ruling elite, were the distributive and food and drink trades, notably mercers, drapers, brewers and innkeepers.

The maps of Ralph Agas (1578) and David Loggan (1675) show that Oxford's population growth resulted in much greater housing density but very little expansion of the built area. In 1578 the city retained its medieval town walls, its castle and its great south and east bridges. The

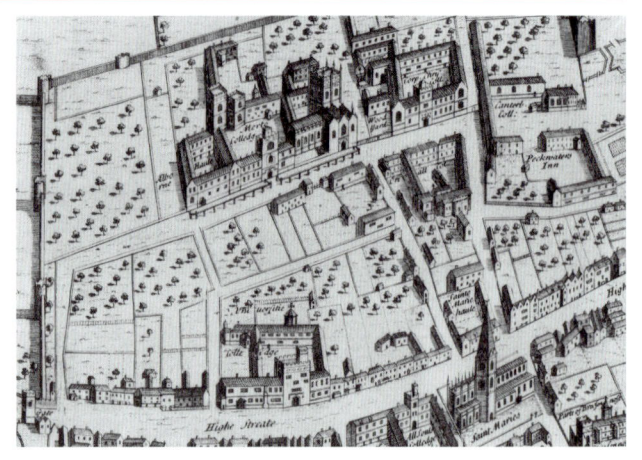

Detail from Ralph Agas's map of Oxford looking south, showing the area between Merton College at the top and University College and High Street at the bottom. In 1578, open space around the colleges was still evident.

intramural streets were notably spacious, and outside were the thinly populated suburbs (mostly single streets) of St Giles, Holywell, St Clement's, Grandpont and St Thomas, and the ruins or rebuilt remnants of Osney and Rewley abbeys and the houses of the Black, Grey, White and Augustinian Friars. Grand quadrangular college buildings were beginning to dominate the eastern part of the city, the most spectacular being the unfinished Christ Church on the site of St Frideswide's priory. Three monastic colleges in the northern suburbs had been replaced by Trinity and St John's Colleges and Gloucester Hall.

Loggan in 1675 depicted a much more crowded city, the result of a century of infilling along the main streets, subdividing plots, narrowing and heightening street frontages, building back along plots behind them, and redeveloping deserted medieval side streets. Similar transformation had taken place in the suburbs. The chief extensions of the medieval built area were on the waste around the northern city wall and ditch, with the creation

By 1675 David Loggan's map of the same area records dense building between High Street and Merton Street.

OXFORD IN 1578

	University and college buildings and academic halls
	Churches
	Other buildings as shown by Ralph Agas
	City Wall

Based on the map of Oxford by Ralph Agas, 1578

1. Gloucester Hall
2. Site of Whitefriars
3. West gate
4. Site of Grey Friars
5. New Inn Hall
6. Little gate
7. Site of Black Friars
8. North gate
9. St John's College
10. Broadgates Hall
11. Balliol College
12. Trinity College
13. Christ Church almshouses
14. South gate
15. Jesus College
16. Christ Church
17. Lincoln College
18. Exeter College
19. Part of Christ Church (formerly Peckwater Inn)
20. Divinity School and University Schools
21. Brasenose College
22. Part of Christ Church (formerly Canterbury College)
23. Smith gate and bastion chapel
24. Site of Augustinian Friars
25. Corpus Christi College
26. Oriel College
27. St Mary's Hall
28. All Souls College
29. Merton College
30. New College
31. University College
32. St Alban Hall
33. The Queen's College
34. St Edmund Hall
35. East gate
36. Site of Trinity Hall
37. Magdalen Hall
38. Magdalen College
39. Magdalen Bridge

29 · Oxford before 1800 (continued)

of entirely new streets of houses (the later Broad, George, Ship and St Michael's streets, and most of Holywell); there had been some building around the castle ditch and on the edge of the later Gloucester Green. The city walls had been broached in many places and the castle largely slighted, but much remained of the zigzag earthworks thrown up around the outskirts in the Civil War, when Oxford was the Royalist headquarters. University buildings now covered much of the central area and dominated the skyline. The Bodleian Library, Sheldonian Theatre, Botanic Gardens, Wadham and Pembroke Colleges, large new quadrangles at a dozen other colleges, and Tom Tower in Christ Church were all 17th-century creations.

In the 18th century the university declined and the city's growth came to an end. Even so, rising standards of consumption in a reduced undergraduate population ensured that Oxford's shopkeepers and craftsmen, untouched by the industrial revolution, remained reasonably prosperous, and the economy was boosted by the city's development as a coaching, tourist, county and social centre. Total population fell to perhaps 9,000 to 10,000 in mid-century, and was still below 12,000 in 1801. Taylor's map of 1751 shows no significant expansion of the city since Loggan, but many important buildings had been added, notably the Old Ashmolean, the Clarendon Building, and the Radcliffe Camera, major new college buildings at Queen's, Worcester, Christ Church, All Souls, Corpus Christi, Magdalen and University, and also a new town hall, the Holywell Music Room, and that notable feature of Oxford's skyline, All Saints church.

The Davis map of 1794 shows the extensive topographical changes of the later 18th century. Paving Commissioners appointed in 1771 had removed the narrow gateway tower (Friar Bacon's Study) from south bridge, the east and north gates (the latter including Bocardo prison), the butcher's shambles in the middle of Queen Street, Carfax conduit and various encroaching houses in Turl Street, in St Aldate's and near St Mary Magdalen church. The city's street-markets had been moved to the large surviving indoor market in 1774. New Road, laid out through the castle precinct, provided much better access to Oxford from the west by linking Botley Causeway directly to Queen Street, while on the east, Magdalen Bridge had been rebuilt and a new road opened up towards Henley (Iffley Road). The canal had reached Oxford in 1790, ending at New Road wharf. Important public institutions had been established on the northern fringes – the Radcliffe Infirmary (1759), the Radcliffe Observatory (1772), the United Parishes workhouse near the later Wellington Square (1772) and the city gaol on Gloucester Green (1789).

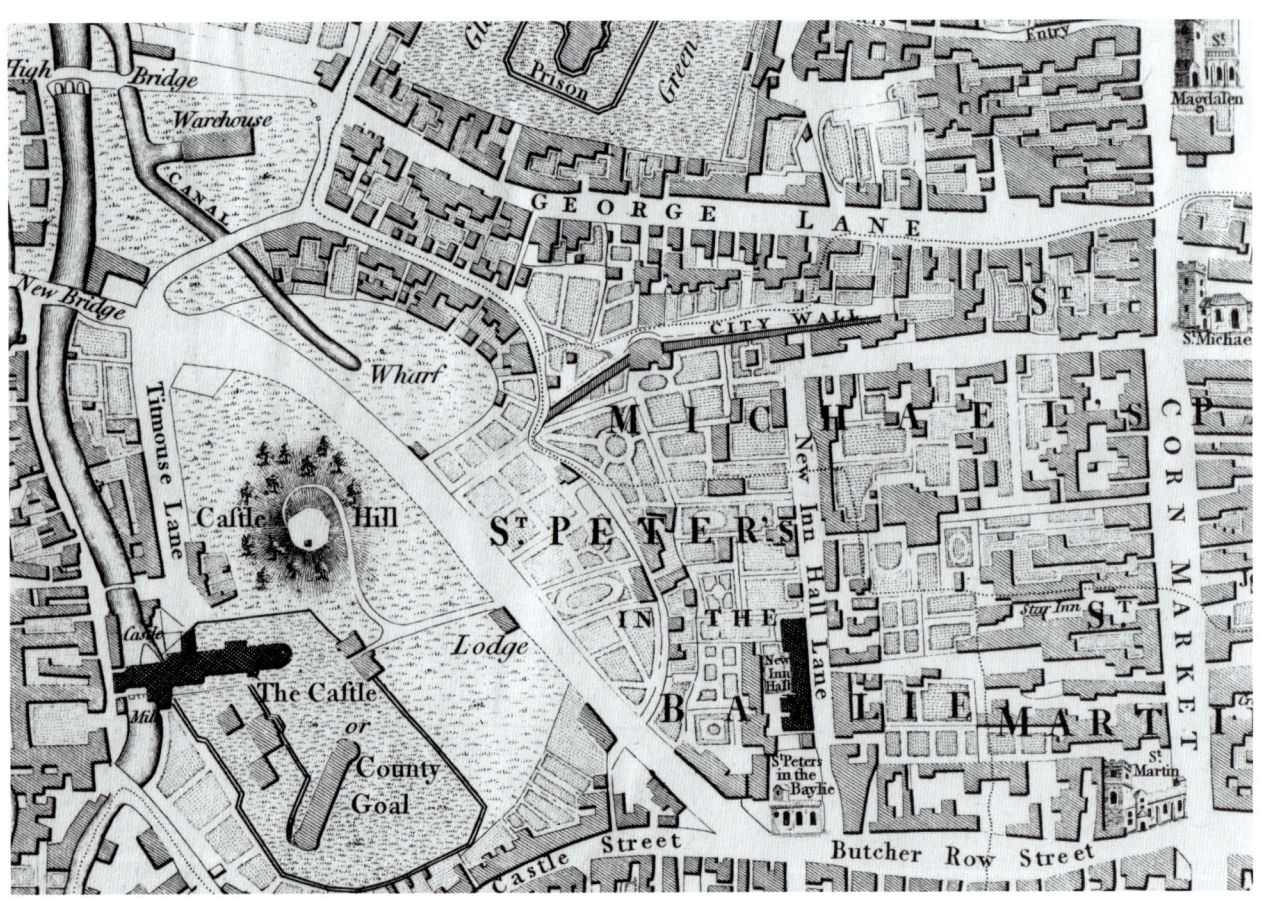

Detail from Richard Davis's map, showing major late 18th-century changes. New Road through the castle precinct formed the new western approach to the city. The canal, opened in 1790, ended close to the city centre.

OXFORD IN 1794

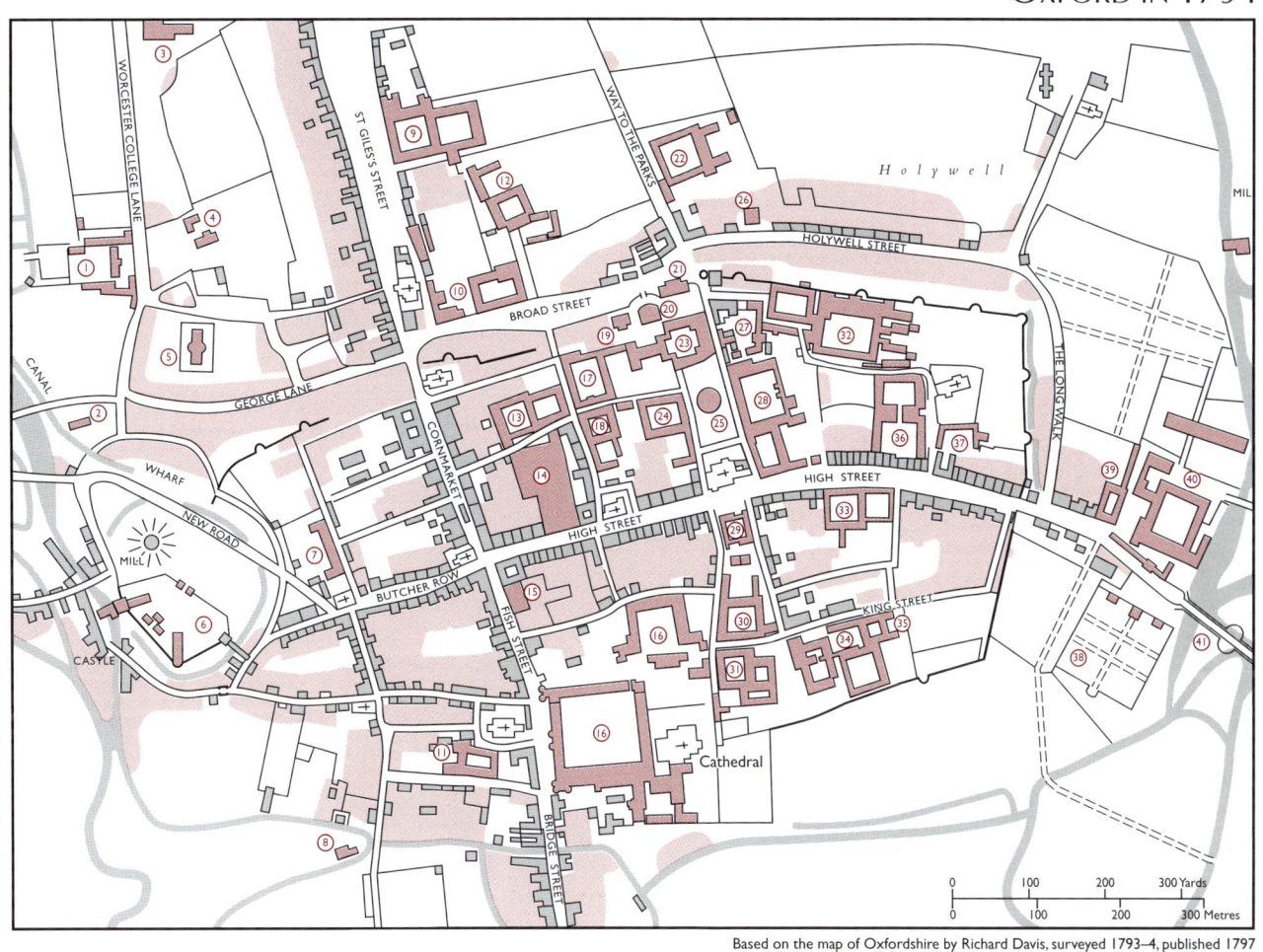

Based on the map of Oxfordshire by Richard Davis, surveyed 1793–4, published 1797

Legend:
- University and college buildings, academic halls and principal public buildings
- Churches
- Buildings shown on Agas's map of 1578
- Areas built up between 1578 and 1794
- City Wall
- New roads

1. Worcester College
2. Canal warehouse
3. New workhouse
4. Old workhouse
5. City Gaol
6. County Gaol
7. New Inn Hall
8. Tan yard
9. St John's College
10. Balliol College
11. Pembroke College
12. Trinity College
13. Jesus College
14. New (covered) market
15. Town Hall
16. Christ Church
17. Exeter College
18. Lincoln College
19. Museum (Old Ashmolean)
20. Theatre (Sheldonian)
21. Printing House (Clarendon Building)
22. Wadham College
23. The Schools (Bodleian Library)
24. Brasenose College
25. Radcliffe Library (Radcliffe Camera)
26. Holywell Music Room
27. Hertford College
28. All Souls College
29. St Mary's Hall
30. Oriel College
31. Corpus Christi College
32. New College
33. University College
34. Merton College
35. St Alban Hall
36. The Queen's College
37. St Edmund Hall
38. Physic Garden
39. Magdalen Hall
40. Magdalen College
41. Magdalen Bridge

30 · Agriculture and Farming Regions 1500–1700   Mark Page

Farming in Oxfordshire in the 16th and 17th centuries was influenced by three main factors: first, the consumption needs of the local population; secondly, the opportunities for marketing agricultural produce; and thirdly, the suitability of topography and soils to particular types of farming practice. Different farmers responded to these influences in different ways, according to whether they were mainly concerned with their own subsistence needs or were producing for the market. Farming practices, moreover, changed over time, as fluctuations in population levels affected the demand for produce, and as developments in agricultural technology and commercial infrastructure transformed the opportunities for trade.

Taken as a whole, the county's early modern farmers grew four major cereal crops: wheat, rye, barley and oats, together with the pulse crops of peas and beans; they also kept cattle, sheep, pigs and poultry. Although almost all farms had to combine crops and livestock, if only because animals were needed for draught and as a source of manure, the precise mix of arable and pastoral husbandry was capable of almost infinite variation. Notwithstanding the often complex and subtle diversity of practice adopted by individual farmers, however, four main farming regions can be distinguished in Oxfordshire in this period.

The fertile red loam soils of the marlstone upland district around Banbury were well suited to both arable and livestock farming. This flexibility of land use probably encouraged the proliferation of small farms in the area, whose occupiers engaged in little specialisation because they tended to be self-sufficient. Across the largely open arable fields, which were mostly enclosed after 1750, villagers were permitted to graze a specified number of cattle and sheep after harvest and during fallow. Additional fodder for livestock was also provided in the 17th century by creating leys (temporary areas of pasture) in the open fields.

From 1630 an increase in the acreage devoted to wheat probably reflected changing demand from local consumers. A lack of water transport meant that grain from the marlstone uplands was rarely marketed over long distances. Farmers instead drove their livestock on the hoof, especially beef cattle and sheep, to Oxford or other market towns in the region, and carried high-value goods such as wool and Banbury cheeses, which were greatly prized in London. New division of the open fields and the planting of fodder crops allowed an increase in cattle rearing and dairying (probably at the expense of sheep farming) during the 17th century, though compared to other parts of the county there was relatively little agricultural change.

To the south, the limestone uplands of the Oxfordshire Cotswolds witnessed similar developments but on a larger and more intensive scale. The region had long been dominated by traditional sheep-and-corn husbandry, and during the 17th century the sheep population undoubtedly increased. However, heavier stocking of cattle, horses and pigs also occurred, made possible by the introduction of improved legumes and grasses, including clover, lucerne, and especially sainfoin, which were more productive and nutritious than indigenous grasses.

The thin stonebrash soils of the district were particularly suited to barley production, which was used to make beer and bread and could also be fed to animals. But in places where the stonebrash was mixed with heavier clays, wheat could also be grown, and was increasingly substituted for barley in the 17th century. The rising class of yeomen who dominated the region, and who began to enclose land earlier than on the marlstone uplands or in the clay vale, probably sold some of their agricultural produce in local market towns such as Chipping Norton, Witney and Woodstock, though an increasing amount was destined for the voracious London market (see entry 47).

The fertile clay vale of central Oxfordshire, between the Cotswolds and the Chilterns, also supplied the capital, notably with large quantities of wheat and malt, which were shipped down the Thames on barges. Although the rich, heavy soils of the region were best suited to arable farming, the small, open-field farmers who predominated in the vale also raised beef cattle and sheep, and kept a few pigs and horses. Common grazing rights were usually stinted in order to avoid overstocking, though allowances were generous enough for many farmers to build up valuable herds and flocks. As well as cereals, other crops grown included hops, flax and hemp for the brewing and clothing industries.

Mixed farming remained the principal feature of agricultural enterprise in the region during the 16th and 17th centuries, though there were significant changes. Enclosure (albeit on a limited scale) increased the acreage under grass, which in turn allowed the size of flocks and herds to grow. Wheat, beans and peas were substituted for barley, oats and rye, and convertible husbandry systems (in which land alternated between arable and grass) seem to have been widely adopted. However, gains in arable productivity were perhaps less pronounced in the vale than on the uplands to the north.

Finally, in the Chilterns, most farmers practised sheep-and-corn husbandry, though with the distinctive added element of timber-growing. Woodland flourished on the clay-with-flints soils of the steep slopes and uneven plateaus of the area's numerous narrow valleys, with arable and grazing land concentrated on (but not restricted to) the more fertile gravels and sands overlying the chalk subsoil. Most land was already enclosed by the 16th century, when the region's farmers entered upon a long period of prosperity, based on the export of grain and firewood to London via the river port of Henley-on-Thames.

The principal grain was barley, much of which was malted for brewing, while during the 17th century wheat was increasingly substituted for oats and rye. Sheep were mostly kept for their wool and manure, but flock sizes fell following a decline in the Berkshire cloth industry, while heavier applications of lime and chalk, which reduced the soil's acidity, lessened the demand for dung. Many farmers kept a few cattle and pigs for their own subsistence needs but there was little commercial dairying or breeding. John Leland's comment, made in the 1530s, that there was 'plenty of wood and corn about Henley', applied equally in 1700.

FARMING REGIONS 1500–1700

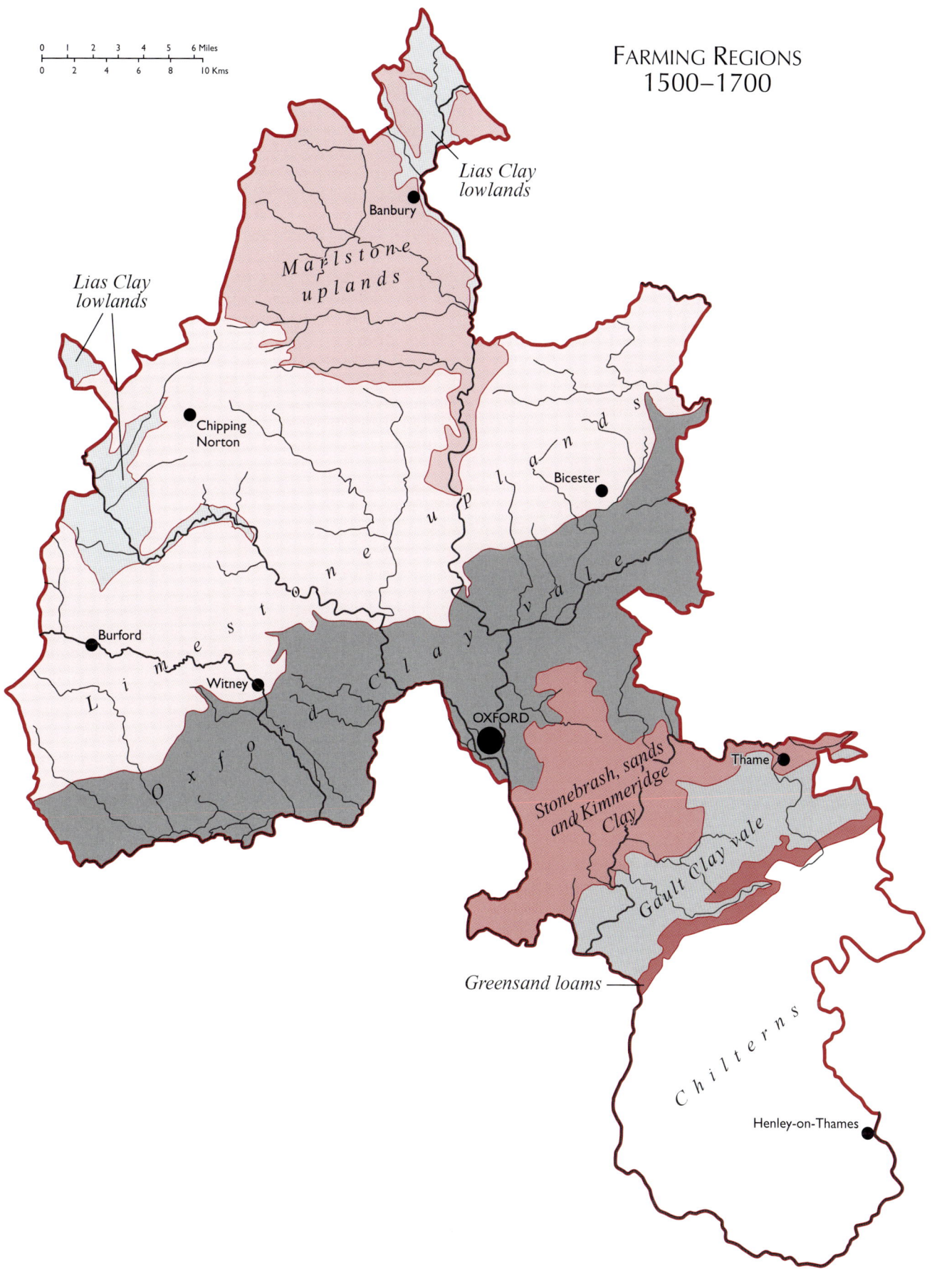

Lias Clay lowlands

Banbury

Marlstone uplands

Lias Clay lowlands

Chipping Norton

Bicester

Limestone uplands

Clay vale

Burford

Witney

Oxford Clayland

OXFORD

Thame

Stonebrash, sands and Kimmeridge Clay

Gault Clay vale

Greensand loams

Chilterns

Henley-on-Thames

77

31 · Early Modern Market Towns

Adrienne Rosen

Early modern Oxfordshire inherited a well-established network of market towns. Competition had eliminated most medieval village markets, and all the 15 market centres trading in 1500 were still recognisably urban 250 years later, with the exceptions of Eynsham and Hook Norton, where markets petered out, and Charlbury, whose market was intermittent until it was restarted in 1678. Of the county's estimated 67,000 inhabitants in 1676 almost 40% lived in towns and nearly two-thirds of those in towns other than Oxford. Oxfordshire in the 17th century was more urbanised than any of the midland counties, with a stable urban system that changed little thereafter.

The county's second town was Banbury, the dominant centre in north Oxfordshire. At the confluence of major drove routes from Wales and north-west England towards London, Banbury had a large weekly cattle and sheep market and seven annual fairs selling horses and cattle. In east Oxfordshire, the market and fairs at Thame also specialised in cattle and attracted graziers and butchers from London. Markets in the smaller towns were generally less specialised, offering a range of local produce and livestock as well as manufactured goods.

The expansion of inland trade from the mid 16th century encouraged the building and elaboration of market houses throughout Oxfordshire. Witney's Butter Cross, built soon after 1606, apparently incorporated the steps of the medieval market cross. More common was a two-storey structure with a meeting room above shops or an open market space, as at Deddington. Local lords might provide a building, such as Thomas Stonor's gift of a new market house with grammar school above at Watlington in 1664-5, but townsmen themselves often contributed. Goods were also offered for sale in shops throughout the week. Probate inventories show a proliferation of shops (see entry 37) in Oxfordshire towns from the later 16th century, apparently flexible spaces for workshops and storage as well as retail trade.

Agriculture remained integral to the market town economy. At Bicester 16% of townsmen with known occupations were mainly engaged in farming, and at Witney 10%. In addition many townsmen combined urban occupations with agriculture. In smaller towns leading tradesmen were commonly also major agricultural landholders, whereas civic leaders at Banbury invested in urban property.

Urban industry was generally small-scale, aimed at local markets. Burford moved from wool-trading to cloth-making in the early 16th century but its industry soon declined. Tanning and leather-working were prominent at Banbury, Chipping Norton and Burford, with numerous shoemakers at Banbury before 1640, and gloving was well established at Charlbury by 1700. Banbury also manufactured cloth and had five woollen drapers in 1600.

Two local industries did develop on a larger scale. Witney had emerged as a centre of cloth manufacture before 1500, aided by the water-power of the Windrush, and in the 16th century the town and its hinterland produced undyed broadcloths for export. National difficulties in the cloth industry in the 1620s prompted a shift to blankets, a specialised form of broadcloth. About 60 clothiers in the 17th century provided work for craftsmen in the town and for cottage spinners throughout west Oxfordshire, and Witney blankets were sent to London for national and international distribution.

The second newly important industry was malting, a lucrative activity in many Oxfordshire towns in the 17th century: a fire at Banbury in 1628 destroyed 20 kilns, and in the early 18th century Burford and Witney maltsters were shipping malt down the Thames to London. But the most specialised malting centre was Henley, where the industry expanded rapidly from the late 16th century. Henley was already a major inland port, where grain, wood and malt were collected and trans-shipped for London, and by 1700 a fifth of its male population worked on the river.

Although the social and cultural facilities of Oxford surpassed anything offered by a small town, all urban centres provided services for local customers. Medical practitioners became more widely available from the later 17th century. Schools were founded in almost all Oxfordshire towns between 1550 and 1670, in many cases re-establishing pre-Reformation foundations. Alehouses and inns were central to urban life. Larger inns provided rooms for local government business and commercial transactions, as well as lodging for travellers. Inns were essential to towns on major roads and to markets attracting long-distance buyers and sellers, and a survey of beds and stabling in 1686 found Henley, Thame and Banbury especially well provided for. Woodstock was unusual as a small town specialising in upper-class custom: the royal palace in Woodstock Park, succeeded after 1705 by Blenheim Palace, brought royal visits and gentry customers to the town's shops and well-furnished inns. The gentry also patronised race-meetings close to Woodstock, Burford, Chipping Norton, Bicester, Banbury and Oxford in the late 17th and early 18th centuries.

Gentry custom might be welcome, but most towns preferred independence in their administration. Forms of urban governance varied from manorial courts leet and parish vestries at Deddington and Bampton to fully fledged corporations in Oxford and, on a smaller scale, in Woodstock. Witney was a seignorial borough of the Bishop of Winchester but had its own borough court in the 16th century. Banbury's lord, the Bishop of Lincoln, sold the borough in 1547. The Reformation swept away the town gild, which had provided a form of corporate life, and the town was incorporated in 1554. Henley's merchant gild, responsible for the bridge, survived, but in 1568 the town nonetheless acquired a charter. Chipping Norton lost its town gild and sought incorporation when a new lord threatened the borough's accustomed independence in 1607, but Burford townsmen were less fortunate in 1621 when their customary administration of the court and market was challenged and overthrown. At Bicester leading townsmen bought the manor as feoffees after 1597 and acclaimed the town's unincorporated status: '. . . for such as be in debt and danger need not shun it, neither are there any polling officers . . . to enrich themselves and impoverish others, which maketh a market town to flourish so much the more'.

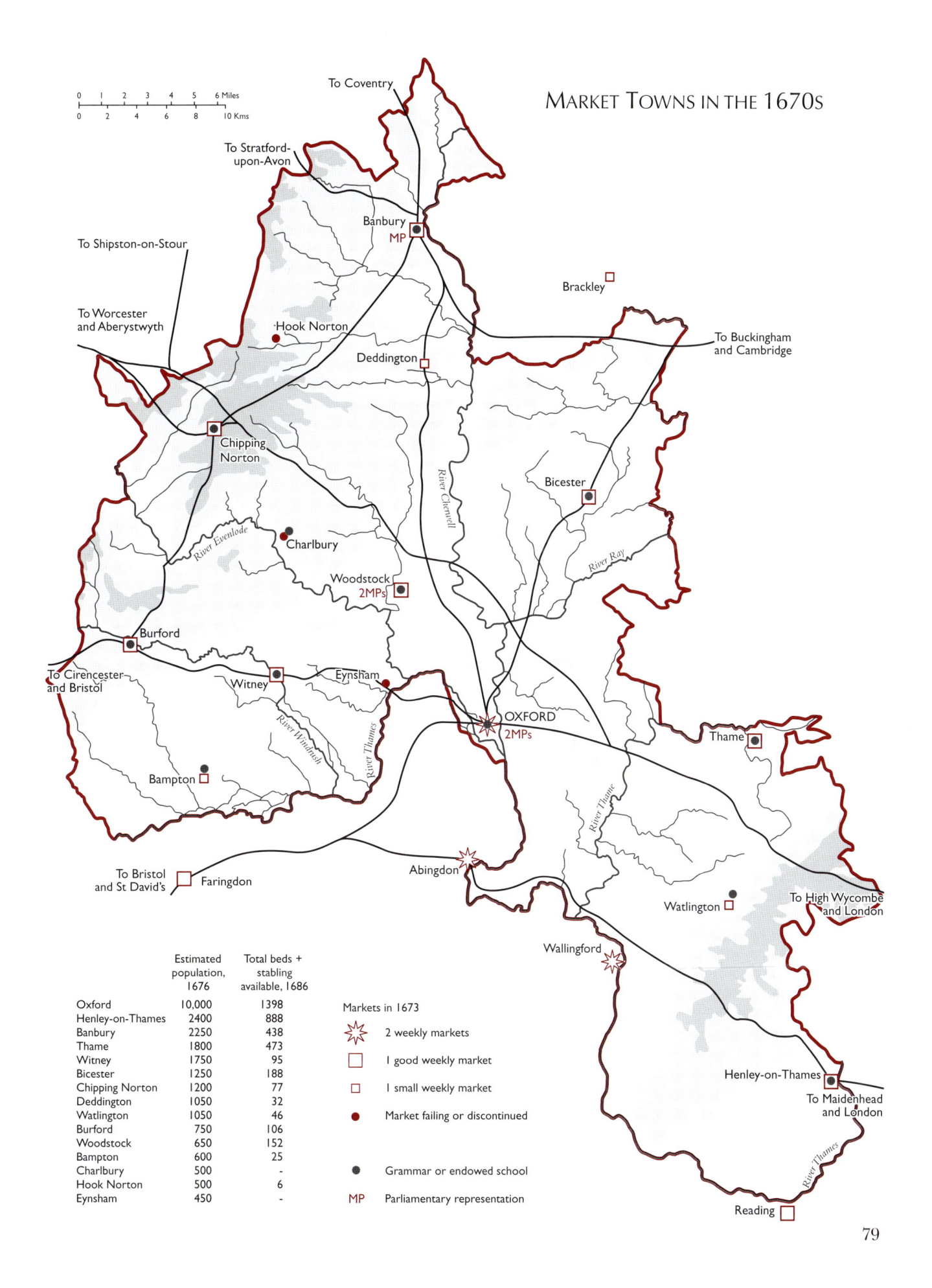

Market Towns in the 1670s

	Estimated population, 1676	Total beds + stabling available, 1686
Oxford	10,000	1398
Henley-on-Thames	2400	888
Banbury	2250	438
Thame	1800	473
Witney	1750	95
Bicester	1250	188
Chipping Norton	1200	77
Deddington	1050	32
Watlington	1050	46
Burford	750	106
Woodstock	650	152
Bampton	600	25
Charlbury	500	–
Hook Norton	500	6
Eynsham	450	–

Markets in 1673:
- 2 weekly markets
- 1 good weekly market
- 1 small weekly market
- Market failing or discontinued
- Grammar or endowed school
- MP: Parliamentary representation

79

32 · The Dissolution of the Monasteries — Adrienne Rosen

Three of Oxfordshire's religious houses closed in the early 16th century before the general dissolution: Cold Norton Priory was suppressed on the death of its last canon in 1507, and in 1524 St Frideswide's Priory in Oxford, and Littlemore, a notoriously scandalous nunnery, were dissolved to endow Wolsey's new Cardinal College. More than 20 institutions remained, more than half in Oxford with the wealthy Augustinian abbey at Osney and houses at Rewley and Godstow nearby, four houses of friars and five monastic colleges for monks studying in the university. Bishop Longland of Lincoln (1521–47) carried out several visitations which found half-hearted observance of the monastic rule and monks mixing freely with local laity, notably at Dorchester and Thame, but the reports suggest apathy rather than a crisis in monastic life.

In autumn 1536 most of the smaller Oxfordshire houses – Bicester, Bruern, Dorchester, Goring, Rewley and Wroxton – were visited by commissioners and suppressed, despite the Abbot of Rewley's offer to Cromwell of £100 if his house were saved or converted into a college. Clattercote Priory, said to be 'old, foul and filthy', was dissolved in August 1538, as were the four Oxford friaries, and Eynsham Abbey followed in December. A commissioner also visited Godstow but the abbess appealed and temporarily saved her house. Finally in November 1539 the axe fell on Thame, Studley, Osney and, last of all, Godstow.

If there was resistance or regret in Oxfordshire it went unrecorded, and it is probably impossible to gauge the psychological impact of the dissolution. Monastic churches were quickly demolished and their materials and fittings sold and reused; part of the shrine of St Edburg from Bicester Priory survives in Stanton Harcourt church. The grand church of Osney Abbey was spared and in 1542 designated cathedral of the new diocese of Oxford, but a change of plan in 1546 transferred the see to Christ Church; Osney's church was dismantled and its materials, including the great bell Tom, carried across Oxford to the new cathedral. Christ Church was the former church of St Frideswide's Priory, where Wolsey's fall in 1529 had halted demolition of the church and priory buildings. His unfinished college was eventually refounded as King Henry VIII's College, succeeded in 1546 by Christ Church and united with the new cathedral and dean and chapter under the first Bishop of Oxford, Robert King (1542–57), formerly Abbot of Bruern, Thame and Osney. The only other monastic church to survive the dissolution was Dorchester Abbey. Bishop Longland's kinsman Richard Beauforest, described by Leland as a 'great riche man' of Dorchester, paid £140 for the chancel of the church, previously used by the canons and separated by screens from the nave where the lay community worshipped, and gave it to the parishioners as a spacious but expensive parish church.

Monastic precincts and buildings were put to a variety of new uses. Sites with watermills were often proposed as premises for cloth manufacture: the Black and Grey friars' sites in Oxford were suggested for a scheme to employ the poor, and a Witney clothier tried to secure a lease of Eynsham Abbey. Osney Abbey's site was rented in 1547 to William Stumpe of Malmesbury for cloth-making and a new fulling mill was built there although any charitable purpose was soon forgotten. Within Oxford, four of the five monastic colleges became the sites of new university colleges and halls, and the Carmelite friars' refectory was used as a parish poorhouse. Elsewhere, monasteries made desirable residences. The Stanleys occupied part of Eynsham Abbey and at Thame Park the Wenmans preserved the abbot's lodgings which had been sumptuously rebuilt in the early 1500s. Substantial new houses were built in the 16th and 17th centuries on monastic sites, incorporating parts of the original buildings, by the Pope family at Wroxton Abbey, the Crokes at Studley Priory and the Copes at Bruern Abbey.

The monasteries owned many forms of property – land, manors, farms, advowsons, tithes, urban housing – all of which passed to the Crown at the dissolution. Much changed hands again in the active property market of the 1540s and 1550s as monarchs granted and sold properties and new owners resold and exchanged their holdings. Further research is needed on changing patterns of landholding. The maps show one aspect, the ownership in 1535 and 1600 of Oxfordshire advowsons, 50% of which had belonged to religious houses. These rights to present clergy to the livings of local parishes were of particular interest to Oxford colleges, which doubled their share by purchase and gift to almost 25% of the county's livings by 1600. The Crown generally exchanged advowsons for manors and by 1600 was left with only 20 livings (10%). The greatest beneficiaries were laymen, whose share doubled to 50%. The list of purchasers was dominated by a small group of ambitious local men who were already well-connected at Court. Sir John Williams, Master of the King's Jewels, amassed a large estate centred on Thame where he established a grammar school and almshouse. Sir Thomas Pope, treasurer of the Court of Augmentations, bought extensively and used some of his acquisitions to found Trinity College in 1555. Monastic property created a few new gentry such as the Powells of Sandford on Thames, but more significant was its elevation of certain families – Popes, Wenmans, Norreys, Chamberlains and others – into the first rank of Oxfordshire's social and political elite. It is interesting to note that many of these families had Catholic sympathies.

Other effects of the dissolution gradually became apparent. Places with a religious house would have felt the loss of local employment and charitable giving, especially at a time of rising food prices. The transfer of rectories from religious houses to laymen contributed to reluctance to pay tithes; tithe payments on former monastic demesne land were also disputed, as at Eynsham in the 1590s. The dissolution touched local life in ways that were certainly not foreseen by its initiators and triggered major shifts in ownership, power and influence in Oxfordshire.

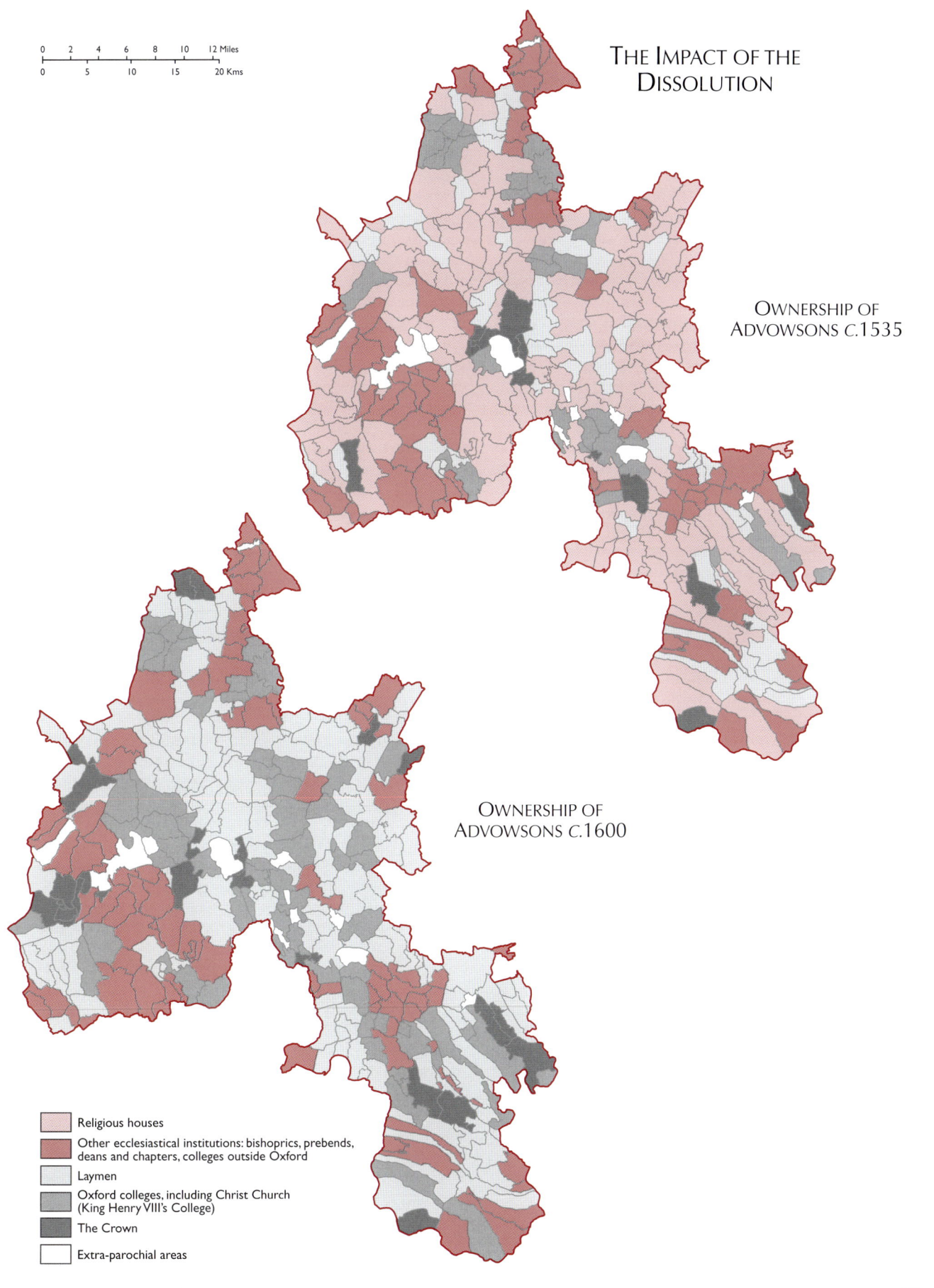

THE IMPACT OF THE DISSOLUTION

OWNERSHIP OF ADVOWSONS C.1535

OWNERSHIP OF ADVOWSONS C.1600

- Religious houses
- Other ecclesiastical institutions: bishoprics, prebends, deans and chapters, colleges outside Oxford
- Laymen
- Oxford colleges, including Christ Church (King Henry VIII's College)
- The Crown
- Extra-parochial areas

33 · Tudor Rebellions

Adrienne Rosen

Tudor governments feared nothing more than rebellion and disorder, and Oxfordshire twice caused alarm during the 16th century.

In July 1549 a crowd of several hundred attacked Sir John Williams's deer-parks at Thame and Rycote, killed all his deer, and feasted on his wine and sheep. From there they proceeded to Oxford and threatened Magdalen College. The vice-chancellor ordered colleges to take precautions and many posted guards, although Corpus Christi also supplied food and drink to the rebels. The mob then headed to Woodstock, perhaps with the intention of attacking the royal park. Here news reached them that government troops were in pursuit; some of the rebels dispersed, but a group continued to set up a camp at Chipping Norton. Evidence for the rebels' motives is sparse but their rising coincided with rebellions in Devon and Cornwall against the new Book of Common Prayer, introduced in June, and it seems likely that in Oxfordshire too religious grievances were uppermost. Sir John Williams and Leonard Chamberlain (steward of the royal park at Woodstock) were prominent government officeholders and purchasers of local church lands. Williams had acted as a commissioner for the dissolution of the chantries in 1547. Earlier in 1549 he and Chamberlain had visited Oxfordshire parishes to draw up inventories of church goods, arousing fears that these too would shortly be confiscated by the Crown. The rebels focused their attacks on property associated with those most actively involved in the implementation of religious change.

The government of Protector Somerset, preoccupied with rebellions in the West Country and East Anglia, had not expected trouble in Oxfordshire and sent Lord Grey of Wilton, an experienced soldier, to control the situation. He went first to Rycote and then followed the rebels' route north-west at the head of 1,500 horsemen and foot-soldiers with local gentry. A pardon may have been offered during negotiations, but it was refused. The outcome was swift and brutal. Edward VI's journal recorded that 'more than half of them ran their ways, and other[s] that tarried were some slain, some taken and some hanged'; Somerset reported that 200 rebels had been captured. The location of the battle is unknown but a contemporary poem refers to deaths on 'the open highway'.

Fourteen men – four priests and ten laymen, all commoners – were selected by Grey for execution, to be carried out in parishes and market towns for maximum public effect, although all but three were later pardoned. James Webbe, Vicar of Barford St Michael, was tried for high treason and hanged, drawn and quartered at Aylesbury, while Henry Joyes, Vicar of Chipping Norton, was hanged from his own church and Thomas Bowldry of Great Haseley was executed in Oxford. The government blamed a small number of 'troublemakers' rather than the commonalty as a whole. Order was restored and Oxfordshire offered no further opposition to the Reformation.

Almost 50 years later, the Oxfordshire rising of 1596 proved abortive and failed to threaten public order, yet Elizabeth I's government responded vigorously. In that year England faced a third harvest failure. Grain prices at Oxfordshire markets rose steeply and the landless poor, obliged to buy food, suffered great hardship. Rumours of food riots, sedition and conspiracy spread rapidly and a nervous government feared popular disorder or even rebellion. The crisis was exacerbated in midland counties by recent enclosure. In north Oxfordshire and the Vale of Oxford enclosure of arable land for sheep-pasture had been taking place since the late 15th century. Very few villages were completely deserted but piecemeal small enclosures were widespread as landlords took land from common fields to create parks and closes, evicted tenants and curtailed rights of common. The process continued in the 1580s and 90s and popular opinion blamed enclosure for the plight of the poor. A number of gentlemen aroused particular resentment – Francis Power of Bletchingdon, William Frere of Water Eaton, Sir William Spencer of Yarnton, Vincent Barry of Hampton Gay and Sir Henry Lee of Ditchley, all from families recently risen to gentry status and often recent purchasers of church lands. Most unpopular of all was Henry, Lord Norreys, one of Sir John Williams's two sons-in-law and heir to his house and estates at Rycote.

Food prices preoccupied the poor in 1596. The first concerted action was a petition in September to Lord Norreys, Oxfordshire's lord lieutenant, for relief; gentlemen were understood to have obligations of hospitality and care for their tenants, as well as a duty to the state to maintain order. When no help resulted, attention turned to more desperate action. Bartholomew Steer, a carpenter at Hampton Gay, and James Bradshaw, a miller, formulated a plan to attack unpopular landlords, destroy their enclosures, seize their grain and weapons, and march to London as a 'rising of the people'. As they travelled between Oxfordshire mills, to markets at Bicester, Witney and Oxford, at village feasts and the homes of kin and neighbours, Steer and Bradshaw tried to persuade others to join them, promising a merrier world where food would be abundant and work no longer a necessity. Many supporters were young single men, their prospects blighted by poverty. Steer's brother, a weaver, expected support from the unemployed of Witney's cloth industry. Many promised to join once others had taken the lead.

On the appointed November evening Bartholomew Steer met three fellow conspirators at Enslow Hill. They waited in vain for others to arrive, and then dispersed. Enslow Hill stood close to the 'great road' from London to the midlands where it crossed the Cherwell; Steer was aware of a tradition of an earlier popular rising there, perhaps the rout of 1549. Word of the intended rising soon reached the authorities and five conspirators were arrested, sent to London and interrogated by the attorney general, Sir Edward Coke, using torture. Steer and Bradshaw probably died in prison, and two others were tried for high treason and executed at Enslow Hill. Despite its failure this Oxfordshire rising prompted the government into action, and in 1597 legislation against enclosure was revived. Agrarian Oxfordshire offered no support a decade later to the anti-enclosure Midland Rising of 1607.

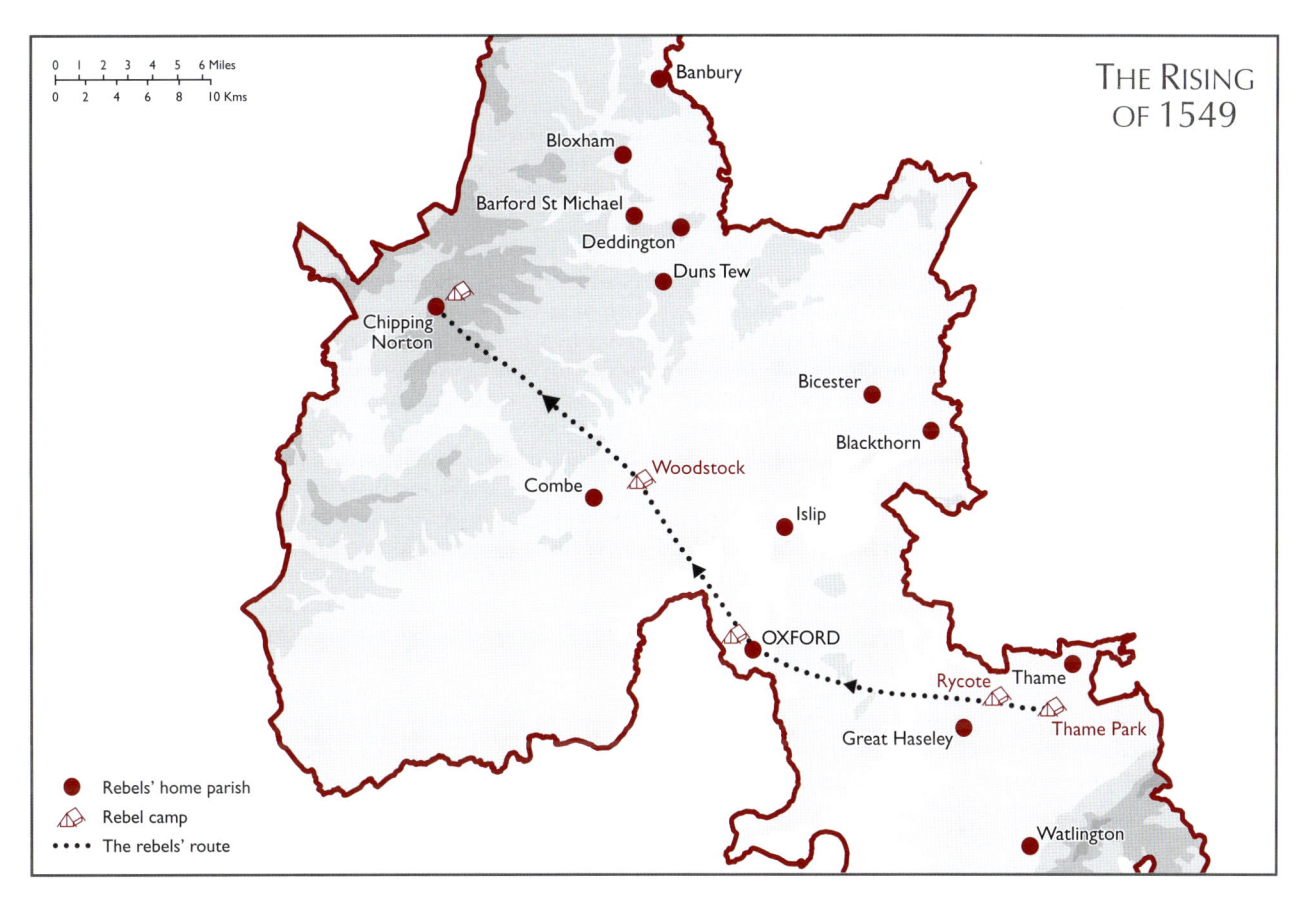

THE RISING OF 1549

- ● Rebels' home parish
- ⛺ Rebel camp
- ⋯ The rebels' route

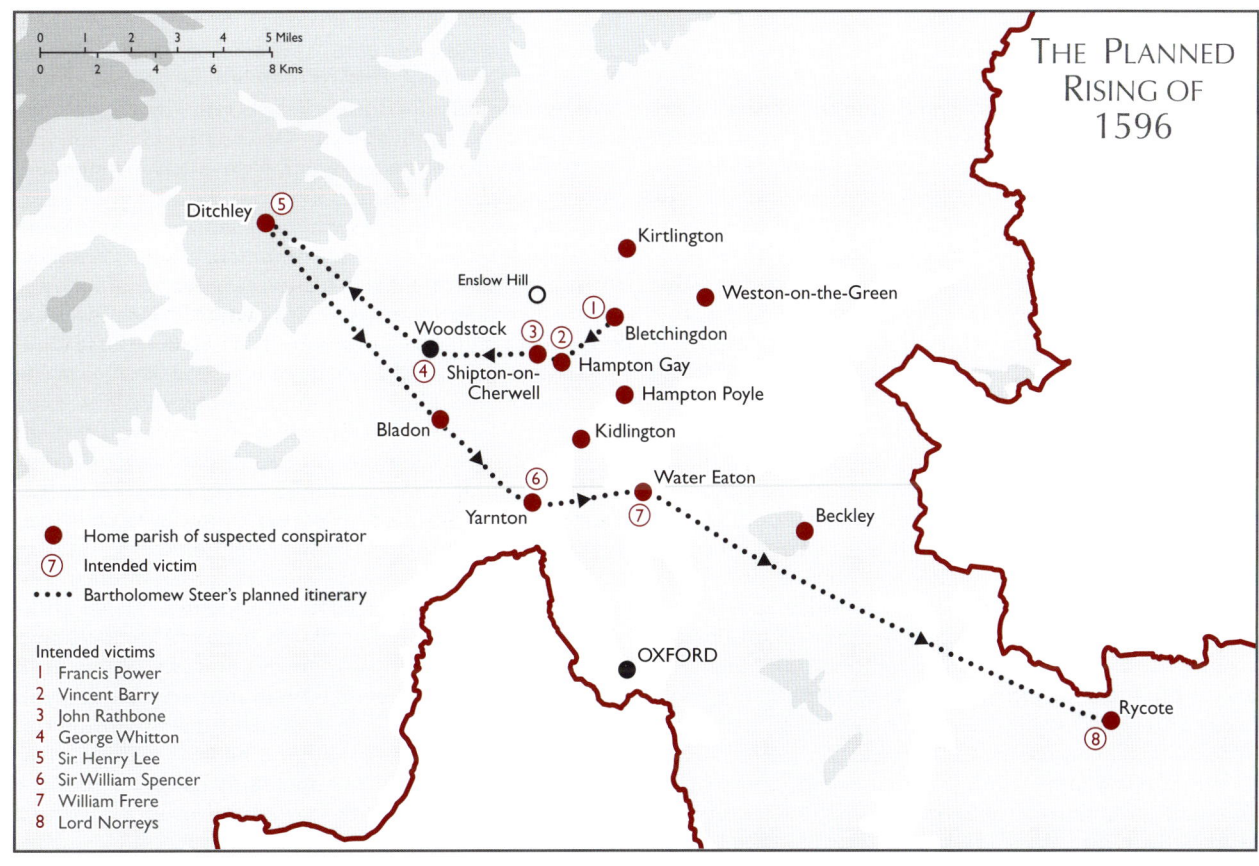

Locations: Banbury, Bloxham, Barford St Michael, Deddington, Duns Tew, Chipping Norton, Bicester, Blackthorn, Combe, Woodstock, Islip, OXFORD, Rycote, Thame, Great Haseley, Thame Park, Watlington

THE PLANNED RISING OF 1596

- ● Home parish of suspected conspirator
- ⑦ Intended victim
- ⋯ Bartholomew Steer's planned itinerary

Intended victims
1. Francis Power
2. Vincent Barry
3. John Rathbone
4. George Whitton
5. Sir Henry Lee
6. Sir William Spencer
7. William Frere
8. Lord Norreys

Locations: Ditchley, Enslow Hill, Kirtlington, Weston-on-the-Green, Woodstock, Bletchingdon, Shipton-on-Cherwell, Hampton Gay, Hampton Poyle, Bladon, Kidlington, Yarnton, Water Eaton, Beckley, OXFORD, Rycote

83

34 · Roman Catholic Recusants 1558–1800 — Mary Hodges

Recusants refused (Latin *recusare,* to refuse) to conform to the Church of England as established in 1559. Oxfordshire already had some history of opposition to religious change (see entry 33), whilst the university was always a centre of religious controversy. Some colleges resisted the new Established Church. Trinity and St John's were loyal to the old religion. Almost 30 of the priests ordained at Douai (the seminary in the Netherlands founded in 1568 by William Allen of Oriel College for the training of English priests) were Oxford graduates, most famously Edmund Campion, Jesuit and martyr. In 1581 the Privy Council noted the numbers leaving the university to become Catholic priests overseas, and from that year undergraduates had to subscribe to the 39 Articles of the Church of England. However those in halls, such as Gloucester and St Mary's, did not have to subscribe and some Catholics continued to study and teach in Oxford.

During Elizabeth's reign up to a third of Oxfordshire gentry were identified as loyal to Catholicism, and recusancy was often linked to places dominated by a Catholic landowner. As many as 171 Oxfordshire parishes have some history of recusancy. For Catholics the presence of a priest was vital, at least periodically, enabling people to hear mass, receive communion and make confession. The government concentrated on the pursuit and imprisonment or execution of priests, although after 1581 lay people also risked imprisonment and occasionally death. This increasing severity drove many to appear monthly in the parish church whilst attending mass at home or in other recusant houses. Known as 'Church papists', the menfolk attended services whilst the women did not, paying fines or occasionally facing imprisonment. Priests were sheltered in a network of 'safe houses', some with hiding places designed and built by Nicholas Owen, an Oxford carpenter, martyred in 1606. Priests seldom stayed for more than a day or two and servants and local villagers, often also recorded as recusants, had to be relied on. Safe houses included Stonor, Holton, Tusmore, Holywell in Oxford and Haseley Court.

In Oxford priests served townspeople as well as the university. Five inns, the Mitre, the Star, the Blue Boar, the Dolphin and the Catherine Wheel, were known centres to hear mass, as were the homes of recusant families like the Nappers of Holywell Manor and Temple Cowley. In 1561 the mayor reported that there were not three houses in the town without papists. A 1577 return listed 49 recusants and one priest in the city and 23 recusants and two priests in the university. There were recusant printers and booksellers. Oxford graduates, trained overseas as priests, worked under cover with the recusant community. In July 1589, George Nichols, graduate of Brasenose College and Douai, with his companion Thomas Belson, from a prominent recusant family, were executed as traitors at the public gallows in Broad Street. With them were Richard Yaxley, priest and Humphrey Pritchard, a serving man at the Catherine Wheel Inn. The inn's landlady was imprisoned for life. In 1610 George Napper, of the Oxford recusant family and ordained at Douai, was captured in Oxford and executed.

In Oxfordshire at least 40 landholding families vital to recusancy can be listed, among them Babington, Belson, Blount, Brome, Catesby, Chamberlayne, Dormer, Fettiplace, Fortescue, Lenthall, Napper, Plowden, Rainolds, Stanley, Stonor and Wenman. A network of kinship and marriage linked many of them. Round them gathered tenants and servants, particularly stewards, also recusants. In 1630 villagers in Holton and Wheatley conspired to bury the Catholic Elizabeth Houseman (née Brome) in Holton church, defying the Bishop's excommunication. In 1635 the Vicar of Pyrton recorded the baptism of Stonor children by their Catholic chaplain. The Cursons of Waterperry sheltered Jesuit priests and their house, like that of the Daveys at Dorchester (unusually a more humble, yeoman family), was a Catholic centre for their area. Between 1603 and 1659, 11 priests were recorded in the counties of Oxfordshire, Berks and Bucks. Jesuit priests acted as itinerant missionaries and established centres in Oxfordshire at Britwell, Kiddington, Mapledurham and Waterperry.

The 17th century saw frequent religious conflict, in which Oxfordshire often figured prominently. During the Civil War, when Charles made Oxford his capital, mass was celebrated in some colleges and elsewhere in the city. Suspicions of Catholicism remained and periodically flared up. There were anti-Catholic riots in Oxford following the Popish Plot of 1678 and again under James II. His determination to give Catholics some freedom to worship and occupy public office provoked the university to oppose this dangerous attack on the Church of England. Catholics were identified in the university. At University College the master opened a chapel where mass was said, and at Magdalen College the king's attempts to impose a president and fellows were resisted. For the county, the Compton Census of 1676 gives a useful picture of the numbers of Catholics during this period, with the greatest presence in the south and east (see map).

Although recusants were not persecuted by imprisonment or death in the early 18th century they continued to feel the pressure of fines, taxation, limited rights and popular antipathy. The 1767 Return of Papists proved almost the last attempt to deprive recusants of land and income. Gradually some toleration, although still controversial, began. The Catholic Relief Act of 1778 meant that Catholics could buy and inherit land; prosecution and imprisonment of Catholic priests was abolished. After 1791 Catholic places of worship could be registered, though towers or bells were forbidden and the building had to be set back from the road. Catholics could enter the professions (although the universities of Oxford and Cambridge remained closed to all but members of the Church of England until 1871). By 1793 it seemed safe to move the Jesuit mission at Waterperry into Oxford, based in St Clements on land given by the Boulters of Haseley. About 60 Catholics lived in Oxford at this time. In 1796 French Catholic priests, refugees of revolution, were housed and welcomed in Thame. The University Press reprinted a Bible in French for the priests and six of them went on to serve Oxfordshire missions including Tusmore, Brailes, Mapeldurham and Oxford. The scene was moving towards Catholic emancipation, finally enacted in 1829.

Roman Catholic Recusants 1558–1800

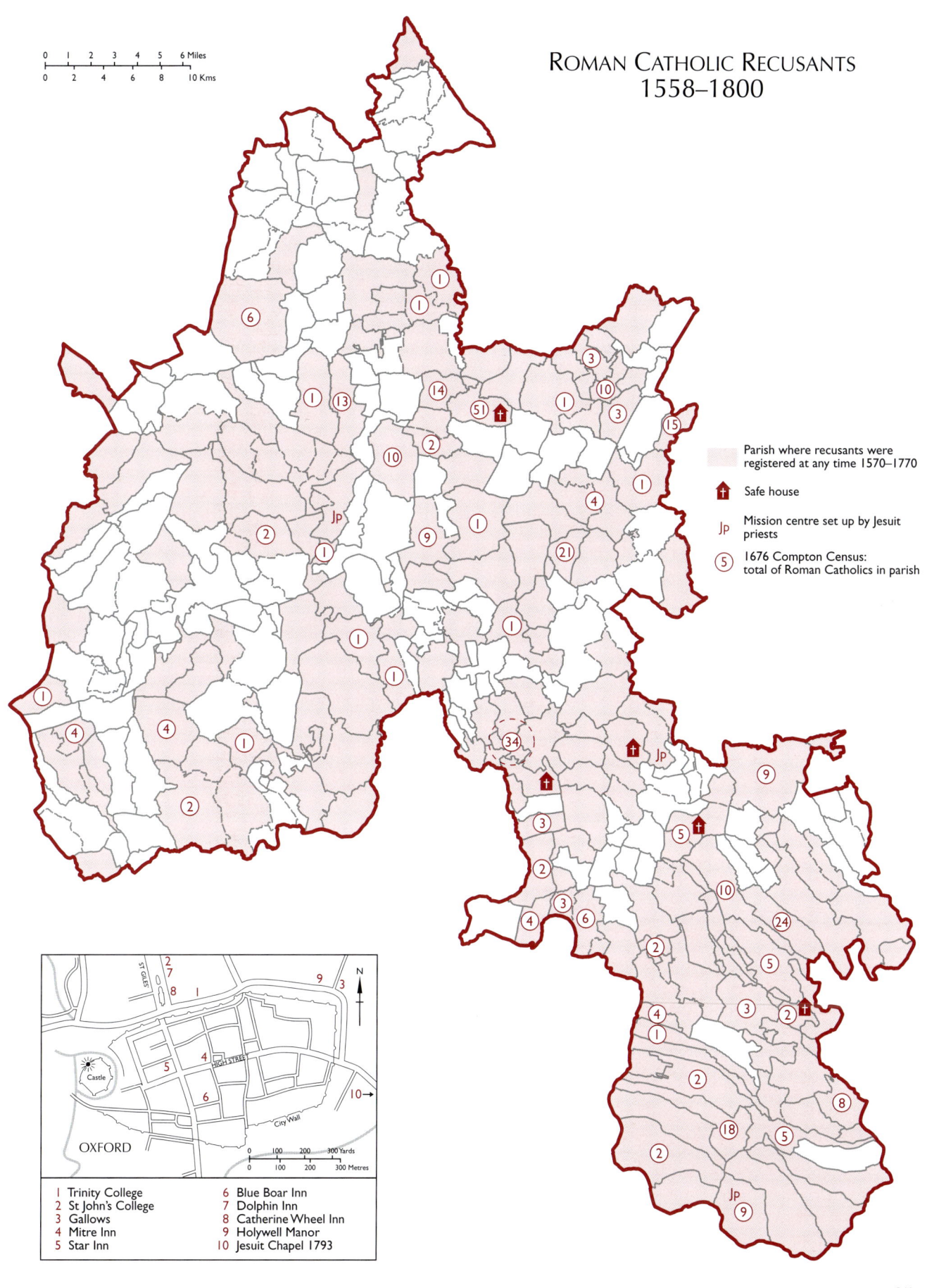

Legend:
- Parish where recusants were registered at any time 1570–1770
- ✝ Safe house
- Jp Mission centre set up by Jesuit priests
- ⑤ 1676 Compton Census: total of Roman Catholics in parish

Oxford inset:
1. Trinity College
2. St John's College
3. Gallows
4. Mitre Inn
5. Star Inn
6. Blue Boar Inn
7. Dolphin Inn
8. Catherine Wheel Inn
9. Holywell Manor
10. Jesuit Chapel 1793

35 · Early Protestant Nonconformity — Mary Clapinson

The confusion in church and state during and after the Civil War encouraged a ferment of debate on religious beliefs and forms of church government, and a variety of sects quickly took root. The Baptists developed a system of 'associations' and the Quakers a network of 'meetings'. Despite Charles II's promise of religious toleration in his Declaration of Breda in 1660, the Cavalier Parliament passed a series of acts between 1662 and 1665 which enforced conformity to the re-established Church of England, and penalised Nonconformists, now legally designated as such for the first time. About a thousand clergy, unable to accept the 1662 Act of Uniformity with its insistence on episcopal ordination and use of the Book of Common Prayer, were ejected from their livings. Around them dissenting congregations, chiefly of Presbyterians and Independents (or Congregationalists) were established.

In 1669 the replies of the Anglican bishops to Archbishop Sheldon's enquiries about the strength and distribution of dissent provide the first overview of Protestant Nonconformity. In Oxfordshire, they reveal three distinct areas of activity. Most notable of these was a band across the north of the county with conventicles meeting in adjacent parishes: Presbyterians in Deddington and Adderbury, Baptists in Hook Norton, Swalcliffe, Bloxham and Adderbury, and Quakers in Bloxham, Sibford Gower, Tadmarton and Adderbury. The conventicles in the south-east formed another group. All, except the three meetings in Warborough (of Quakers, Sabbatarians and Baptists), were in parishes adjoining the Buckinghamshire border: Presbyterians and Anabaptists were reported as meeting at Thame, Watlington and Kingston Blount in Aston Rowant parish, with Quakers and Sabbatarians apparently joining them in Kingston, and Sabbatarians in Watlington; in Henley, Presbyterians and Quakers held separate meetings, and a Baptist conventicle was reported in Lewknor. In the west, conventicles were more scattered: Quaker meetings flourished in Brize Norton, Shipton-under-Wychwood, North Leigh and Charlbury; Independents met in Chipping Norton, and Baptists in Wilcote; there was a large congregation of Presbyterians and Independents at Cogges, and a smaller one of Presbyterians and Baptists at Chadlington. In the north-east only one conventicle was reported – at Bicester, where 100 or 200 'separatists of all sorts' met regularly in a baker's barn furnished with pulpit, seats and galleries.

The 1669 return demonstrates the role of ejected clergy as preachers to conventicles. The largest congregations of Nonconformists (those at Henley, Thame, Adderbury, Cogges and Bicester) were all served by ejected ministers, many granted licences to preach following Charles II's Declaration of Indulgence in 1672. The licensing of meeting houses at the same time confirms the 1669 pattern of dissent (Presbyterians being licensed to meet in Adderbury, Bicester, Deddington, Thame and Watlington; Independents in Chipping Norton, Henley, Thame and Watlington; Baptists at Finstock in Charlbury parish), with the addition of Presbyterians, Baptists and Independents in Oxford, Presbyterians in Banbury, and Independents in Dorchester. The Quakers did not apply for licences, maintaining, as did some Baptists and Independents, that the king had no more right to grant religious toleration than to take it away. In 1668 a Quaker Quarterly Meeting was established in Oxford, with constituent Monthly Meetings at Banbury, Warborough and Witney taking responsibility for Preparatory Meetings in the north, south and west of the county. This pattern of Quaker activity survived, despite forcible breaking up of meetings, long terms of imprisonment, heavy fines and punitive distraint of goods under the penal laws, until they were revoked by the Toleration Act in 1689.

In 1676, Sheldon again sought information about the strength of dissent, instructing the bishops to ascertain from incumbents the number of inhabitants, papists and Nonconformists in each parish. The resulting 'Compton Census' shows that the general pattern of dissent in Oxfordshire remained the same, with large numbers of Nonconformists reported in parishes like Hook Norton, Bloxham, Chipping Norton, Thame and Henley. It suggests that although the dissenters met in these places, they were widely scattered, with Nonconformists being reported in 120 of the 231 parishes that made returns.

At his diocesan visitations, John Fell, Bishop of Oxford from 1676 to 1686, sought to identify dissent and try to reduce it. In 1682 he asked clergy not just to provide numbers and names of Nonconformists in their parishes, but also to visit them at home, discuss their reasons for dissent, and seek to persuade them to return to the fold. Thirty-five incumbents' replies survive. They reveal that in north Oxfordshire, the conventicles at Adderbury, Bloxham, Deddington and Banbury continued to alarm local clergy, as did the conventicles in the west at Bampton, Leafield, Chipping Norton, Burford, Witney, Charlbury and Hook Norton, and in the south at Aston Rowant, Lewknor, Warborough and Henley. The Anglican clergy believed that until these conventicles were suppressed, dissent would flourish. Many were convinced that most dissenters were too set in their ways to be argued back into the established church.

Fell, with the help of the Archdeacon of Oxford, continued to gather information about dissent, and followed up with prosecutions of leading Nonconformists; but neither persuasion nor coercion had the desired effect, as is revealed in the 1715 survey of dissenting congregations undertaken by a committee of London ministers (Presbyterian, Congregational and Baptist). The survey (preserved in the Evans manuscript in Dr Williams's Library) shows that large dissenting congregations continued in Banbury (with 600 hearers), Bicester (between 300 and 400 hearers), Witney and Henley (between 400 and 500 each), and Bloxham (500), with smaller ones, of between 100 and 200 hearers, in Oxford, Chipping Norton, Thame, Combe, Horley and Burford. When in 1738 Thomas Secker, Bishop of Oxford, asked Oxfordshire clergy about dissenters in their parishes, their replies confirm that many conventicles reported in 1669 had survived, most notably those in Henley, Oxford, Bicester, Banbury, Witney and Hook Norton.

PROTESTANT NONCONFORMITY

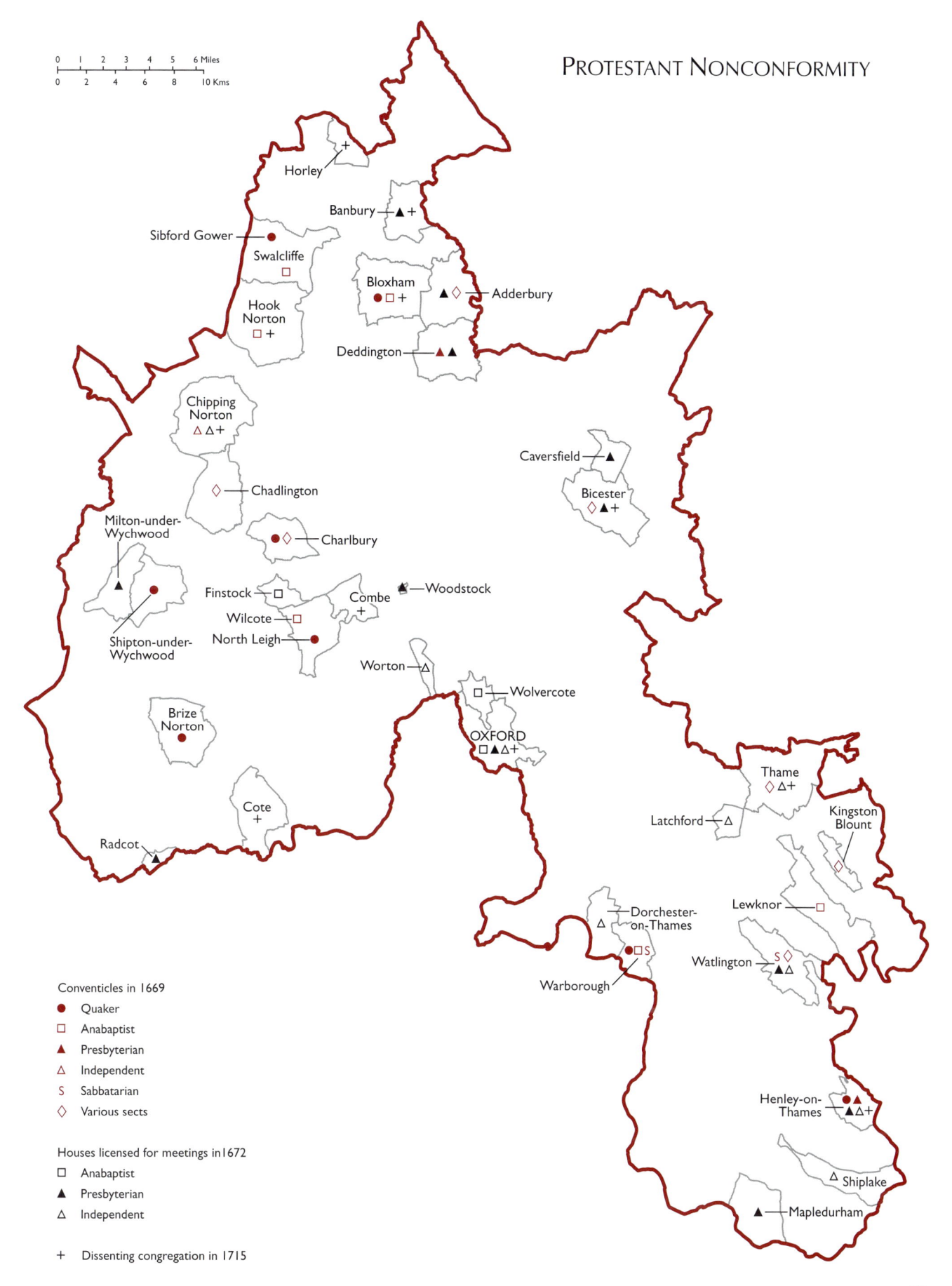

Conventicles in 1669
- ● Quaker
- □ Anabaptist
- ▲ Presbyterian
- △ Independent
- S Sabbatarian
- ◇ Various sects

Houses licensed for meetings in 1672
- □ Anabaptist
- ▲ Presbyterian
- △ Independent

\+ Dissenting congregation in 1715

87

36 · Elites and Office-Holders: mid 17th Century — Vivienne Larminie

Commentators at the time and since have characterised the mid 17th century as a 'world turned upside down', in which traditional forms of authority were replaced and new men emerged, imposing unprecedented policies. There is truth in this, but the picture is far from simple. There were already social and political tensions in the 1630s. These were readily apparent in Oxfordshire.

Early modern local government was based on the county and parish units, but the 'county community' was not hermetically sealed. Ties of kinship, landholding, patronage, politics and religion complicated the loyalties of the ruling elite upon whom Charles I most relied to impose crown policies in Oxfordshire during his personal rule (1629–40). The sole peer with an ancient title, William Fiennes, 8th Baron and 1st Viscount Saye and Sele, seated at Broughton Castle, was a commanding figure in north Oxfordshire and neighbouring Northamptonshire, but Saye and 'Banburyshire' were bywords for puritanism and political and fiscal recalcitrance; king and viscount distrusted each other profoundly. Among a clutch of recently created peers, whose aristocratic authority had yet to establish deep roots, were highly able men also critical of the government, notably Lucius Cary, 2nd Viscount Falkland, Thomas Wenman, 2nd Viscount Wenman, and Henry Danvers, 1st Earl of Danby. It was a weakness of Charles's rule that his lord lieutenant was Thomas Howard, 1st Earl of Berkshire, whose lands were chiefly outside the county and whose family was tinged with Catholicism. From 1637 to 1641, amid widespread fear of creeping popery, he mustered troops to fight an unpopular war against the king's rebellious Scottish protestant subjects.

Meanwhile, successive Oxfordshire sheriffs dragged their feet over the collection of extra-parliamentary taxes like Ship Money, among them John D'Oyly, from a family with rare claims to gentility dating from 1066. Lacking credible alternatives, Charles had no option but to name such men as subsidy commissioners in 1640. Perennial tensions between the city and University of Oxford were heightened as the vice-chancellor, William Laud, promoted the university's superior power. That, as Archbishop of Canterbury, he also championed controversial ceremonialism and greater clerical autonomy exacerbated confrontations.

Parliamentary elections in March and October 1640 offered opportunities for the political elite to relay county grievances. Ship Money defaulters James Fiennes and Thomas, Viscount Wenman were returned in both elections to the two shire seats. Banbury (one seat) predictably elected another Fiennes, James's brother Nathaniel. Woodstock, under the influence of its steward, disaffected courtier Philip Herbert, 4th Earl of Pembroke (based in Wiltshire), was represented by its puritan recorder William Lenthall and by park ranger Sir William Fleetwood (spring) and a Herbert (autumn). In Oxford, gratitude to the city's steward, the Earl of Berkshire, for assistance in disputes with the university twice led to the election of his son Charles Howard, Viscount Andover, but after he was called to the Lords in November, recorder John Whistler and alderman John Smith made a less compliant pairing. The university, as ever, chose outsiders to champion scholarly priorities. Secretary of State Sir Francis Windebanke, Laud's candidate, and Sir John Danvers were replaced in the Long Parliament by diplomat Sir Thomas Roe and the internationally respected lawyer John Selden. Windebanke had fallen foul of suspicions of encouraging the machinations of foreign Catholics.

The outbreak of war in 1642 fragmented the political elite. The Howards joined the king enthusiastically, Falkland reluctantly. Along with representatives of leading gentry families like Sir Thomas Pope and Sir Robert Dormer they were among commissioners of array for the county appointed by Charles at York on 4 July. Inclusion is not an infallible guide to allegiance: Sir Francis Norreys was not the only gentleman named who failed to do duty. Meanwhile, Wenman and the Fienneses adhered to Parliament. They may be found, with Speaker of the House of Commons William Lenthall, John D'Oyly and the lawyer Bulstrode Whitelocke, among assessment commissioners named by Parliament in 1644. Two sets of county administrators were established, one Royalist and operating from the king's headquarters in Oxford, the other Parliamentarian and operating where it could with assistance from London. Little evidence survives of their activities.

The surrender of Oxford in June 1646 ushered in a series of changes in personnel. The Parliamentarian county committee revealed that month included names long prominent in local administration like D'Oyly and Cobb but also a relative newcomer, Thomas Appletree. A mixture of old and new men persisted. Oxford MPs Whistler and Smith, who after suffering much at the hands of Royalists were compromised by association with the city and the rival Parliament held there in 1644, were disabled from sitting and replaced by D'Oyly and mercer John Nixon, three times mayor and a powerful force on the corporation in the ensuing decade. Unsurprisingly, since they had much to gain and relatively little to lose, it was men like Appletree who spearheaded the activities of the sequestration commission which assessed and confiscated the estates of Royalist and papist 'delinquents'. His chief partner in this was William Draper, a Kentishman who had married an Oxfordshire gentlewoman in the 1630s; he stayed to become governor of Oxford castle during the 1651 invasion scare and a county representative in the Nominated ('Barebones') Parliament of 1653. Such men seemed to demonstrate the triumph of upstarts, but elsewhere the make-up of administration was complex.

The commission of the peace remained fluid. Periodic purges of JPs in the later 1640s and 1650s – removing, replacing and reinstating men according to their standing with central government – echoed earlier remodellings. A listing of 1650, in the wake of the king's execution, included both nationally and locally significant office-holders, like Appletree, Draper, D'Oyly and Nixon. But there were others of longer standing and of less proven political loyalty like the aristocratic maverick Sir John Danvers and Robert Jenkinson, whose father had been sheriff for Charles I in 1645. Not all actually served – some

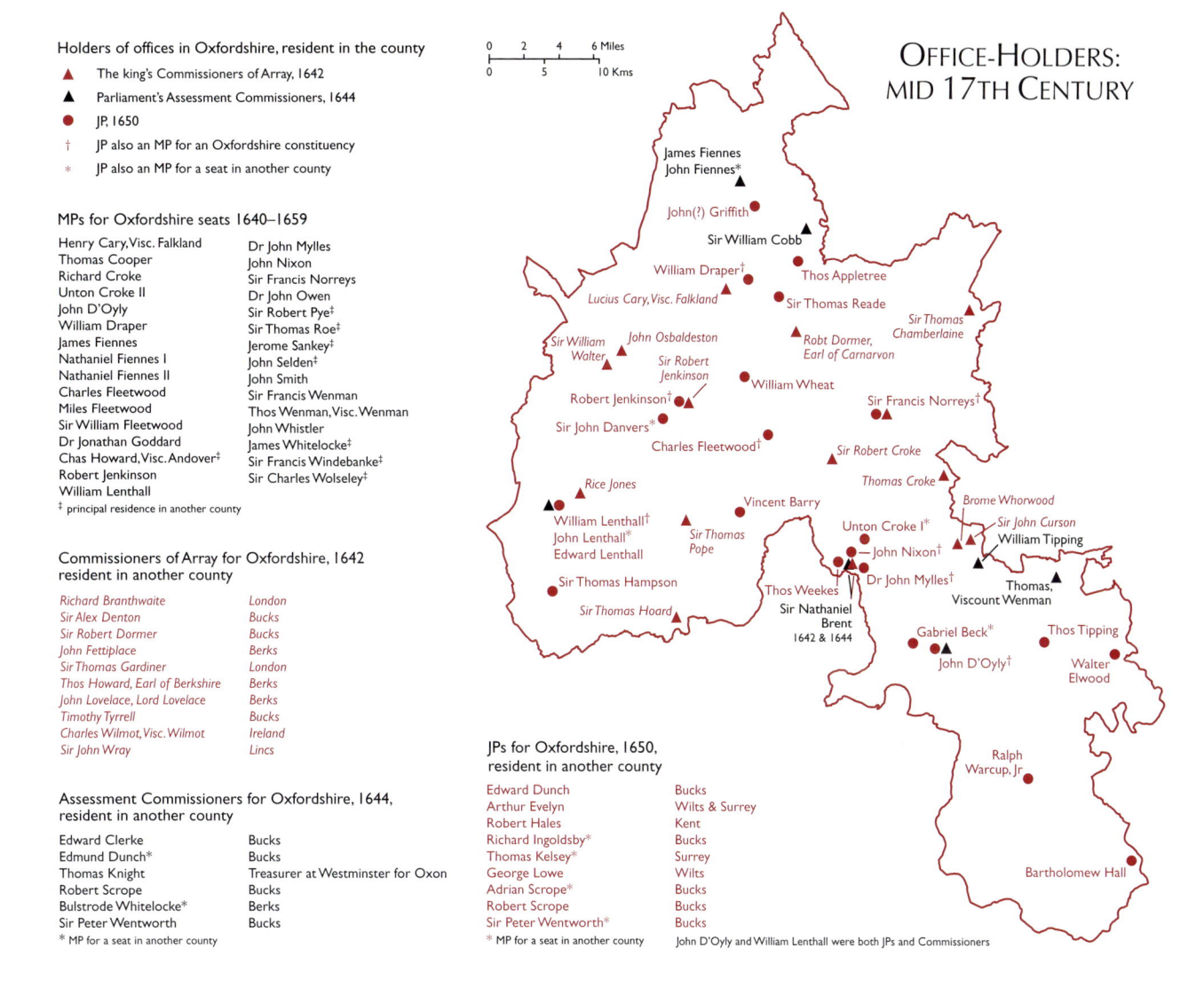

OFFICE-HOLDERS: MID 17TH CENTURY

Holders of offices in Oxfordshire, resident in the county
- ▲ The king's Commissioners of Array, 1642
- ▲ Parliament's Assessment Commissioners, 1644
- ● JP, 1650
- † JP also an MP for an Oxfordshire constituency
- * JP also an MP for a seat in another county

MPs for Oxfordshire seats 1640–1659

Henry Cary, Visc. Falkland	Dr John Mylles
Thomas Cooper	John Nixon
Richard Croke	Sir Francis Norreys
Unton Croke II	Dr John Owen
John D'Oyly	Sir Robert Pye‡
William Draper	Sir Thomas Roe‡
James Fiennes	Jerome Sankey‡
Nathaniel Fiennes I	John Selden‡
Nathaniel Fiennes II	John Smith
Charles Fleetwood	Sir Francis Wenman
Miles Fleetwood	Thos Wenman, Visc. Wenman
Sir William Fleetwood	John Whistler
Dr Jonathan Goddard	James Whitelocke‡
Chas Howard, Visc. Andover‡	Sir Francis Windebanke‡
Robert Jenkinson	Sir Charles Wolseley‡
William Lenthall	

‡ principal residence in another county

Commissioners of Array for Oxfordshire, 1642, resident in another county

Richard Branthwaite	London
Sir Alex Denton	Bucks
Sir Robert Dormer	Bucks
John Fettiplace	Berks
Sir Thomas Gardiner	London
Thos Howard, Earl of Berkshire	Berks
John Lovelace, Lord Lovelace	Berks
Timothy Tyrrell	Bucks
Charles Wilmot, Visc. Wilmot	Ireland
Sir John Wray	Lincs

Assessment Commissioners for Oxfordshire, 1644, resident in another county

Edward Clerke	Bucks
Edmund Dunch*	Bucks
Thomas Knight	Treasurer at Westminster for Oxon
Robert Scrope	Bucks
Bulstrode Whitelocke*	Berks
Sir Peter Wentworth	Bucks

* MP for a seat in another county

JPs for Oxfordshire, 1650, resident in another county

Edward Dunch	Bucks
Arthur Evelyn	Wilts & Surrey
Robert Hales	Kent
Richard Ingoldsby*	Bucks
Thomas Kelsey*	Surrey
George Lowe	Wilts
Adrian Scrope*	Bucks
Robert Scrope	Bucks
Sir Peter Wentworth*	Bucks

* MP for a seat in another county

John D'Oyly and William Lenthall were both JPs and Commissioners

---

fell foul of the oath of engagement to the Commonwealth imposed on all officeholders during 1650–1 – but significantly men like Jenkinson and Sir Francis Norreys appeared content to fulfill traditional roles in a novel context. Both were MPs for the county in the 1650s, the latter while his much-loved son was consorting with Royalists in France. It is testament to altered circumstances that for much of this time there was no peer visibly active in Oxfordshire politics – even Saye and Sele had retired to the Isle of Lundy. The identity of those who were dominant demonstrates the subtlety of change. The most powerful was probably Charles Fleetwood, brother of royal servant Sir William and son-in-law of Oliver Cromwell. MP, JP and absentee major-general for the county during the short-lived experiment in military rule, he had taken over William's offices in London and Woodstock without any apparent family disharmony. More visible locally were the Crokes of Marston: Unton the elder, from an important lawyer dynasty with branches in and beyond Oxfordshire, and throughout these decades a local commissioner and sub-steward of the university; elder son Richard, who became recorder and MP for Oxford; and Unton the younger, army officer and (irregularly) simultaneously sheriff and MP.

The death of Oliver Cromwell heralded the reappearance of some old names. Among local men who sat with the Croke brothers in the 1659 Parliament were not only another Fleetwood and another Fiennes but also the youthful Sir Henry Lee of Ditchley (representing a Wiltshire seat) and Henry Cary, 4th Viscount Falkland. Lee and Cary had spent their adolescence abroad among Royalist exiles and used their voice in Parliament to subvert the regime. Later that year Falkland headed an abortive rising in the county, seeking the return of the monarchy.

Following the Restoration in 1660 there was further flux: some reaped the reward of their interregnum allegiance and some did not. While Royalists like the Lees were more than recompensed for their sufferings, Falkland was sidelined in Irish office. The Fleetwoods were finally eclipsed and Appletree lost office, but the Fienneses still dominated Banburyshire and men like Richard Croke reinvented themselves to retain their places.

37 · Early Modern Shops and Shopkeepers — Kate Tiller

Shops were an established part of life in Oxfordshire in the 16th, 17th and 18th centuries. Their location and the variety of goods available to local people offer an important insight into standards of living and patterns of consumption in a period when historians have suggested that a consumer revolution was underway. This process saw what were formerly accounted luxuries becoming the decencies of life, and previous decencies increasingly perceived as necessities. Effective demand arose where a range of goods was available at a cost affordable to a growing number of buyers. Belongings were being acquired by purchase as well as inheritance. Considerations of fashion and social emulation were at work. Havinden has estimated that between 1580 and 1640 the prosperity of husbandmen, the small farmers of Oxfordshire, increased by some two-thirds. These were the circumstances behind the material culture of the homes of the Great Rebuilding. Taking place during the same period, this saw the vernacular houses of Oxfordshire substantially rebuilt or newly erected with greatly enhanced levels of comfort and privacy (see entry 38). Many hundreds of detailed contemporary listings of the goods and chattels to be found in these houses, and related farms and businesses, are available through probate inventories. These list and value movable goods for the purposes of probate, which was regulated through the courts of the Church of England until 1858. The form of inventories was codified in 1529, and from then until around 1730 they provide particularly detailed descriptions of the property of most kinds of Oxfordshire people (married women and some of the poorest excepted). This entry uses the probate inventories of Oxfordshire shopkeepers to explore their distribution, the goods they offered and changes in the pattern of the county's shops during the early modern period.

Mercers were the most numerous type of shopkeeper recorded between 1516 and 1800.[1] There were 31 in Oxford, 12 in Banbury, and others in 28 different places (see top map). The greatest numbers were in the north and west. Mercers were the least specialised of all shopkeepers. They sold fabrics, sometimes in rich variety, but also a wide range of other goods. William Brock, mercer, who died in 1685, was the village shopkeeper at Dorchester. He stocked relatively few fabrics but many haberdashery items, ready-made hose (an item needing frequent replacement), candles, rice, oatmeal, sugar, salt, spices and spirits. His customers would also have found blue pots, speckled cups, beer glasses, earthenware, writing paper, small books (cheap paperbacks of ballads, stories and godly texts), as well as beehives, balls and nets. Other mercers kept simple medicines. The Johnsons of Woodstock were a rare example of a dynasty of mercers. Most were more transitory, and their number declined over the period. Between 1516 and 1640, 55 mercers in 21 places left inventories; 1641–1732, 38 in 14 places; and 1732–1800, 20 in 9 places.

Goods were not only available from the keepers of permanent shops. Another way was to buy from chapmen, hawkers and pedlars. Sometimes called the mercers of the poor, they provided a peripatetic shop, travelling on foot or horseback with a hamper of goods, and sometimes setting up a regular stall on local market days. The inventories of 25 Oxfordshire chapmen (see top map) show how they fitted into the hierarchy of trading and supply below the mercers. As G. H. Dannatt wrote of Ellis Edwards, chapman of Bicester who died in 1714, he played 'his many parts of wood-merchant, rag and bone man, scrap metal dealer, supplier of dainty trimmings for the use of ladies, and general merchant, all concealed under the word "chapman"'.[2]

Other terms often interchangeable with mercer were draper, grocer and chandler or tallow chandler. Alongside the 113 mercers' inventories are 86 for chandlers, 44 for tallow chandlers, 62 for grocers and 40 for shopkeepers. Drapers and haberdashers were relatively few in number (47 and 12 respectively) and confined to the towns. Between 1641 and 1732 the chandlers (see middle map) were the most numerous amongst these designations, 91 of 104 traders. Like the mercers, they were concentrated in north and west Oxfordshire, but more in the villages than towns. By contrast, 'grocers' are rare before 1733, but became the largest group amongst mercers, chandlers, shopkeepers and grocers thereafter. It is also between 1733 and 1800 that the term 'shopkeeper' is widely adopted, and that of 'chandler' dwindles. Also after 1733 many more retailers appear in south Oxfordshire (see lower map). This is associated with the increase in shopkeepers and grocers, and in the proportion of retailers outside Oxford generally. The shift from concentrations of shopkeepers in the north and west to the south of the county seems to reflect general changes in the relative prosperity of parts of Oxfordshire at this period. Proximity to London markets and increasing contacts and business generated by the main routes to and from the capital particularly benefited south Oxfordshire.

When ranked in terms of the total number of probate inventories for mercers, chandlers, tallow chandlers, shopkeepers and grocers, the towns and villages demonstrate a clear hierarchy. Oxford dominated with 91, outstripping Banbury (29) and Witney (22). A smaller group of towns – Bicester, Burford, Chipping Norton, Deddington, Thame and Woodstock – followed (13 to 16 references). Then came Henley and Watlington (10). Dorchester and Bampton had seven references each and Eynsham and Islip five.

Oxfordshire retailers certainly offered a wide range of goods in the early modern period, and not just in the larger towns. Of the items identified by historians as characteristic of the revolution in consumption – stockings, caps, cheap earthenware, nails, tobacco pipes, lace, ribbon, processed food and drink – most were on offer relatively early on. Although still short of the mass provision and specialism that were to follow – for example in 1847 Dorchester had 17 shopkeepers, including butchers, bakers, grocers, tailors, a dressmaker, a straw-hat maker and a linen draper – decencies as well as necessities were commonly to be had from Oxfordshire's shops in the 16th, 17th and 18th centuries.

Chandlers and Tallow Chandlers 1516–1800

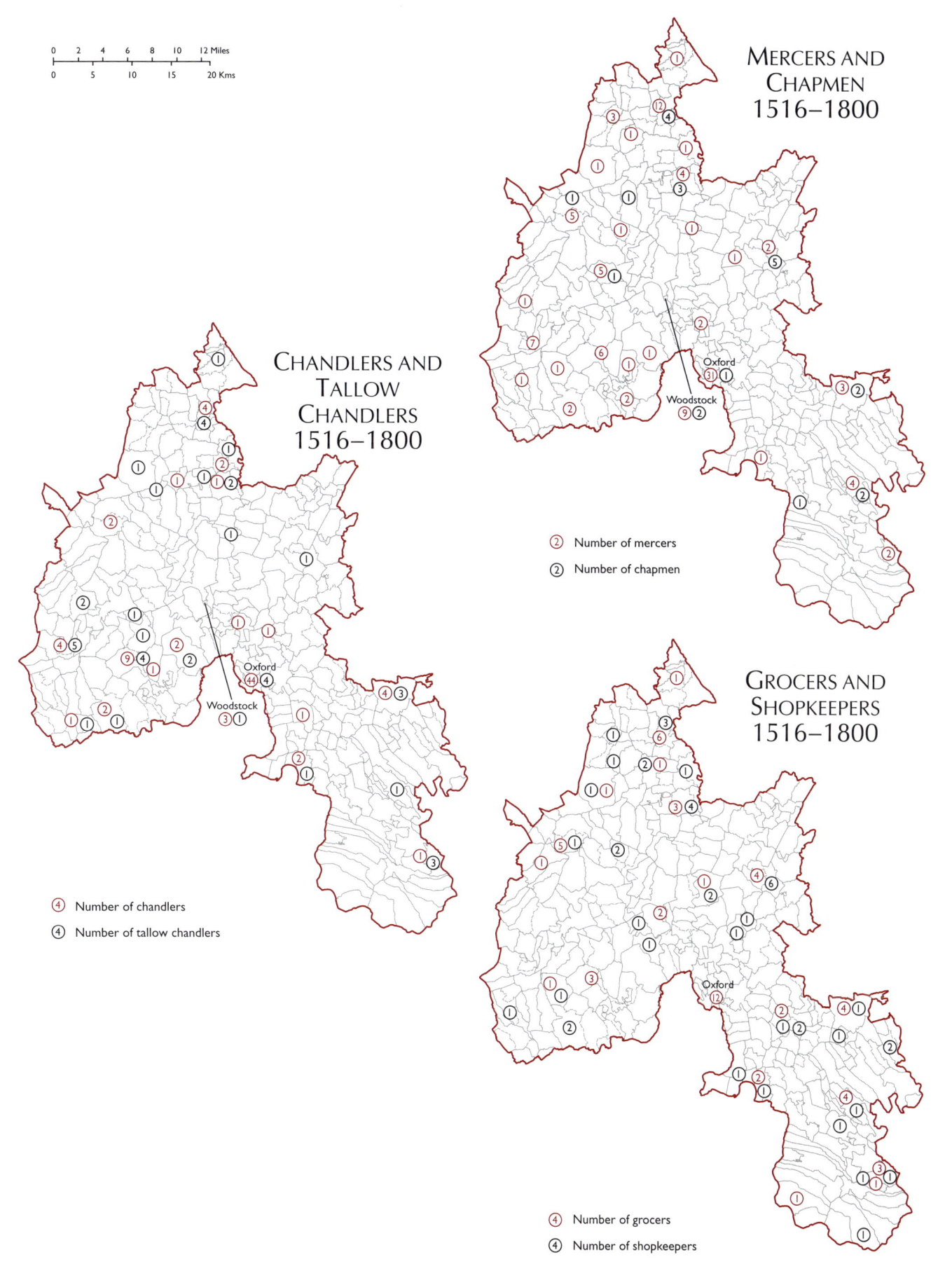

- ④ Number of chandlers
- ④ Number of tallow chandlers

Mercers and Chapmen 1516–1800

- ② Number of mercers
- ② Number of chapmen

Grocers and Shopkeepers 1516–1800

- ④ Number of grocers
- ④ Number of shopkeepers

38 · The Great Rebuilding

Malcolm Airs

W. G. Hoskins was living at Steeple Barton in north Oxfordshire when his seminal essay, 'The Rebuilding of Rural England, 1570–1640', was first published in 1953. Its opening sentence proclaimed that 'Between the accession of Elizabeth I and the outbreak of the Civil War, there occurred in England a revolution in the housing of a considerable part of the population.'

Hoskins focused on rural evidence but indicated that this revolution was equally applicable in towns. He suggested that the years of greatest activity were between 1575 and 1625. The revolution took the form of a rebuilding or substantial modernisation of existing buildings and a remarkable increase in household furnishings and equipment. In the early 1950s the scholarly examination of smaller rural buildings was only just beginning and Hoskins's essay helped set the research agenda over the next 25 years until, in 1977, R. Machin published a revisionist essay, attacking both the methodology and broad conclusions of Hoskins. The subsequent debate has established that the regional timing of improvements was far more diverse than the original proposal but also a general consensus that there was a major transformation of housing for much of the country during the early modern period.

The Oxfordshire evidence reflects this national complexity. The standard medieval house plan was abandoned in the upland limestone areas of north Oxfordshire a generation or so later than in the south and east where a timber-framed tradition persisted. The net result was broadly similar. The hall, open from ground to roof and heated by an open hearth, ceased to be the dominant element in the design of the vernacular house. Enclosed fireplaces became the norm and this revolutionary advance in heating and comfort permitted a more flexible use of space within the house. The hall remained in name the most important room but, now that there was no need for smoke from the hearth to escape through the rafters, it could be reduced in height to a single storey with another room above. For the first time the upper storey could be fully utilised for domestic purposes throughout its full length and the practice of going upstairs to bed gradually became universal. This was made possible by a new emphasis on the staircase, which was often contrived next to the chimneystack for structural support, although in some parts of the county, such as the stone belt of the north and around Dorchester in the south, staircases were housed in attached turrets, which allowed a more spacious ascent and an architectural flourish.

Enclosed fireplaces enabled cooking to be brought within the body of the house and the separate detached kitchens which still survive in some parts of the county were abandoned to new uses as ancillary outbuildings. The new kitchens within the house replaced medieval storage rooms next to the entrance as part of a rearrangement of traditional service functions. In larger houses, the chamber or parlour on the ground floor beyond the other end of the hall was provided with a fireplace and by the 1640s many upper-storey bedrooms were also heated. Chimneystacks rising above the ridge of the roof were a highly visible symbol of growing domestic comfort and proliferated to such an extent that in 1662 hearths became a basis of taxation for central government.

Of equal prominence was the systematic replacement of wooden shutters by glazed casement windows, which admitted more light whilst protecting the occupants from weather. The creation of well-lit, smoke-free rooms stimulated interior decoration largely in the form of painted wall surfaces but also of decorated chimneypieces, shaped balusters on staircases, plaster ceilings and decorative glazing. For those who could afford it there was wooden wall panelling to further reduce draughts and to impress visitors with the taste and wealth of the householder. Wall-painting was ubiquitous but ephemeral and generally only a few fragments survive. These range from simple repetitive patterns in the roof space at Church Farm, South Leigh, to the grand figurative scheme with black-letter inscriptions that once covered the walls and ceiling in the first floor chamber of 34 Upper High Street, Thame. These bright new interiors, furnished with a growing inventory of personal possessions as described in contemporary probate records, represented a startling departure from medieval standards.

Surviving buildings suggest the transformation began in the timber-framed areas of southern Oxfordshire c.1550 and was well under way by the early 17th century, when it finally reached the limestone uplands. By the outbreak of the Civil War most of Oxfordshire's surviving medieval housing stock had been radically remodelled, although even such substantial buildings as Leadenporch House and Castle End, both in Deddington, were not fully modernised until the mid 17th century. Many medieval houses were able to survive the process. Typically, a chimneystack was inserted in the open hall, which was then divided horizontally into two floors. A new staircase to the upper floor was provided, either within the existing house or as an addition. The window openings were glazed, ceilings were plastered and further fireplaces were introduced to serve the more specialised functions carried out in individual rooms. It was far cheaper than building a new house from scratch and probably only took a few months to achieve. Just across the Thames in Berkshire, Robert Loder carried out just such a modernisation of his farmhouse in Harwell for an outlay of only £6 10s.

New house types were also devised, to meet the demands of a rising population or to replace medieval houses incapable of modernisation. In lowland Oxfordshire, around 1600, new domestic arrangements were characteristically provided by house plans with a brick chimneystack placed directly opposite the entrance and rising centrally through the roof. The houses were two-storeyed from the outset, although in more humble examples the upper storey was partly within the roof space lit by dormer windows. The central chimneystack could heat rooms to either side on both floors and created a draught-free entrance lobby, with space for a staircase on the other side of the stack. Most early examples of these lobby-entry plans had rooms of equal dimensions either side of the stack, giving the house an architectural symmetry. More accommodation could be provided by additional units at one or both ends although these required additional chimneystacks if the rooms were to be heated. Originally devised within the timber-framed tradition, the lobby-entry plan was equally suitable for walling materials such as brick, flint and stone that became fashionable in the area in the 17th and 18th centuries. Indeed, the lobby entry was so ubiquitous that it continued into the second half of the 20th century.

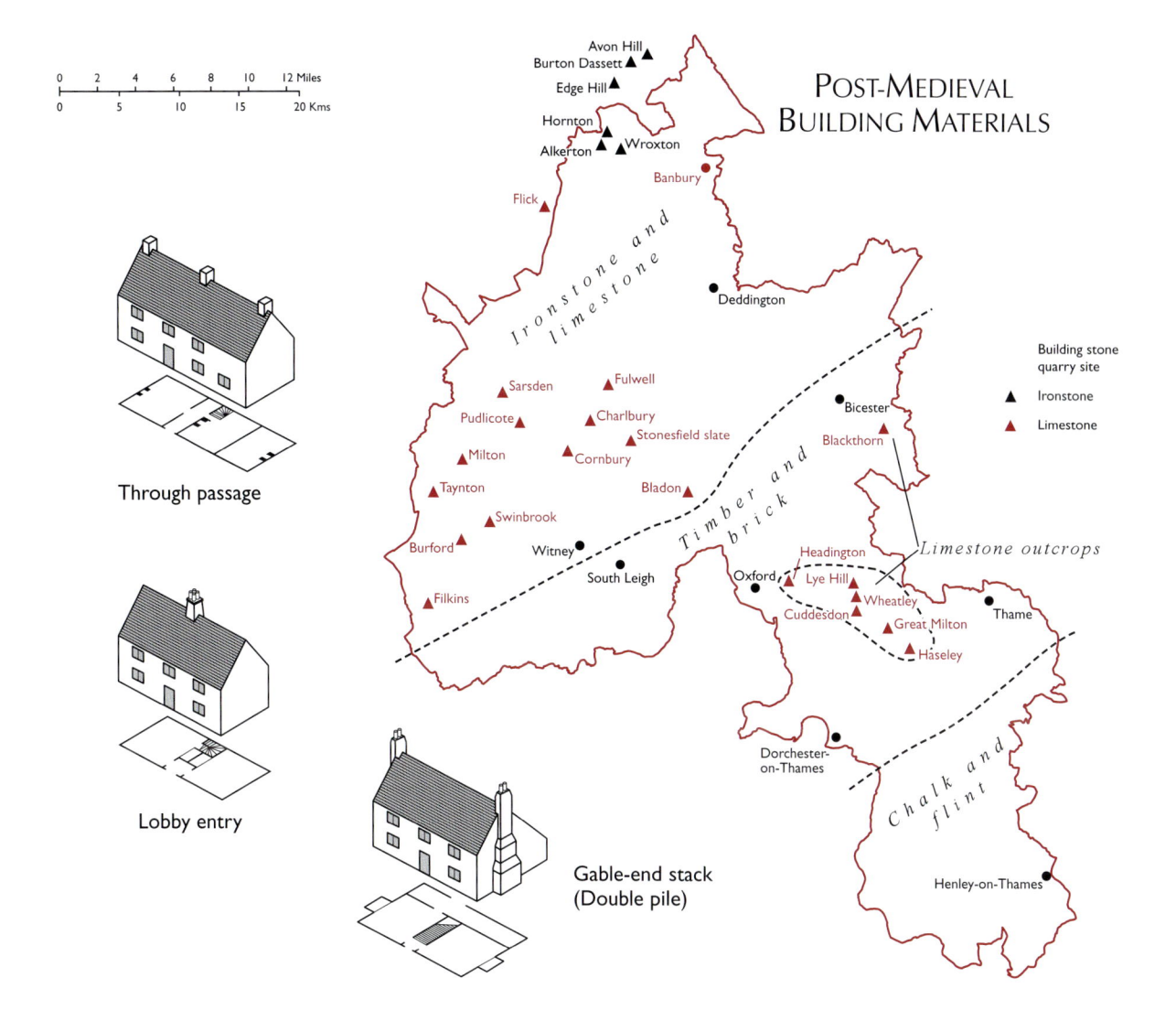

In upland Oxfordshire the peak of building activity came c.1650–75. Here the medieval tripartite plan with the entrance into a through passage was retained in new, storeyed houses that began to be built in stone around c.1615. The kitchen, heated by a gable-end stack, was placed to one side of the passage with a ground floor hall and its associated chimneystack on the other side. There was usually a parlour beyond the hall, heated by another gable-end chimneystack. The staircase rose from within the hall. This arrangement separated the services from the domestic areas of the house and provided direct access to the yard at the rear, but needed the construction of three separate chimneystacks and resulted in an asymmetrical entrance front.

By c.1680, the two distinct regional traditions were joined by a third new house type, found throughout the county when solid wall construction became common for all but the very poor. This adopted earlier elements to provide a symmetrical façade with a central entrance and the chimneystacks in the gable-end walls. The services were placed in a lean-to outshot at the rear, which introduced a double-pile plan at ground floor level. Unencumbered by a chimneystack, the central doorway gave on to a more spacious entrance hall and staircase. By the 18th century this new plan had superseded the through-passage plan and rivalled the lobby-entry plan as the preferred regional choice.

It is now clear that what Hoskins identified as a revolution was more correctly the beginning of a process of domestic transformation that continued long after 1640. It was forged in a radical rethinking of the function of the house, involving rebuildings and then the development of distinctive new house plans. Examples of the Great Rebuilding are to be seen throughout Oxfordshire.

39 · Civil War 1642–1649

Kate Tiller

Oxfordshire was deeply embroiled in the Civil War of 1642 to 1649. Its people, towns and villages were caught up in the conflict, willingly or not. In the build-up to war, during Charles I's personal rule from 1629, the county showed many of the accumulating tensions at work (see also entry 36). Religious differences were clear, with some areas known for their puritanism, like Banbury and the north, and others for their high churchmanship. William Laud, Charles I's anti-Calvinist Archbishop of Canterbury, was President of St John's College (1611–21) and influential as Chancellor of the University from 1629. He promoted changes at parish level to worship and leisure pastimes which inflamed puritan opinion. The king's exploitation and sometimes sale of Crown lands affected royal manors and forests in the county. Oxfordshire men were involved in growing conflicts over authority and taxation, at national, parliamentary and local level; the county was notoriously reluctant to pay Ship Money. Key meetings of the king's opponents were held at Broughton Castle, home of Lord Saye and Sele. Most famously, William Lenthall of Burford, Speaker of the House of Commons, resisted the king when Charles attempted to arrest five MPs in the House in 1641, declaring that he would act only 'as the House is pleased to direct me, whose servant I am.'

When open warfare began the first great battle took place, in October 1642, just over Oxfordshire's northern border at Edgehill, as Parliamentarian forces sought to stop Charles reaching London. This reflected the county's strategic position, on main routes from London to the midlands and to the west. Oxfordshire lay between Royalist strongholds to the north and west, and Parliamentarian areas to the south and east. This 'front line' position was reinforced when, after Edgehill, Charles made Oxford his capital. Although there were no major battles on Oxfordshire soil, clashes at Chalgrove Field in June 1643 (leading to the wounding and death at Thame of leading Parliamentarian John Hampden) and Cropredy Bridge in June 1644 were violent and shocking.

By 1643 there were garrisons and houses of known sympathies around the county. Banbury Castle, Burford and Woodstock Manor were held for the king, as were the nearby key towns of Abingdon and Wallingford. Reading and Thame changed hands several times. Bletchingdon, Gaunt House, Mapledurham, Radcot, Rousham, Shirburn Castle and (just into Bucks) Brill and Boarstall were also Royalist strong points. The principal Parliamentary garrisons were Compton Wynyates, Brackley, High Wycombe and Henley. At Henley, Phyllis Court was fortified and its garrison commanded by the lawyer and parliamentarian, Sir Bulstrode Whitelocke, whose diary provides an important description of the period. The town was raided by Royalists, and threatened by their garrison at Greenlands House, between Henley and Mill End. Greenlands finally surrendered in summer 1644, after Parliamentarian bombardment from across the river. Banbury Castle, a Royalist garrison in a Puritan town, was subjected to a 13-week siege in 1644.

Perhaps the greatest impact on Oxfordshire people was having to endure four years of militarisation, with the disruption and uncertainty caused by persistent skirmishing, pillaging and raiding, requisitioning and billeting, and heavy taxation from both sides. Vehicles, livestock, crops and timber were taken, including some 2,000 horses in 1643. Farming was disrupted. As study of the registers of some Oxfordshire and Berkshire parishes has revealed, troops brought disease and there were outbreaks of typhus or camp fever, some of epidemic proportions, in Thame and Henley and in some rural parishes in 1643–4.

Oxford was occupied by the royal court and government for four years. The king kept court at Christ Church, his queen at Merton, New College cloisters was a magazine, and the Bodleian Library a warehouse for stores. College plate was melted down, and a mint established. The medieval city walls were repaired and fortifications were created to the north of the city between the Thames and Cherwell, in the present area of the University Parks, and linked to the natural barriers provided on other sides of the city by rivers and meadows. Navigation was barred by booms on the river. Oxford became a crowded place, hit in 1643 by fire and epidemic disease. The support of the town for the king was uncertain. During 1645 troops led by Cromwell and Fairfax were active round Oxford, and Bletchingdon House and Gaunt House were seized for Parliament. In April 1646 Charles left Oxford for the last time and it came under siege. A surrender was negotiated, in the house of Unton Croke at Marston, and took effect in June. Woodstock Manor, Banbury Castle, Shirburn and Boarstall also fell to Parliament during the summer. In July 1646 Wallingford became the final Royalist garrison in the area to surrender.

The legacy of the war long outlasted local hostilities. The ferment of ideas continued, showing the war as a struggle not just amongst elites, but by men and women throughout society involved in debate and asserting independent choices. Levellers, radical democrats within the Cromwellian army, appeared in 1649 in Banbury, Oxford and Burford. Cromwell and Fairfax came to restore discipline and some 350 Levellers were imprisoned in Burford church, three of whom were shot in the churchyard as an example to the rest. New religious congregations, many with members who had fought on the side of Parliament, emerged as the precursors of Oxfordshire's earliest Nonconformist churches (see entry 35). Tithes and church courts were abolished. Major landmarks – Wallingford and Banbury castles, part of Oxford Castle and Woodstock Manor – were dismantled by Parliament. Many parish churches had suffered damage through fighting or iconoclasm. Some places in Oxfordshire celebrated Charles II's restoration in 1660, and former institutions returned, including tithes and church courts, under the energetic leadership of John Fell, a former Royalist soldier now Bishop of Oxford. Yet issues of monarchical power and religious conscience continued to be worked out up to the Glorious Revolution of 1688, and beyond, with memories of civil war still strong in Oxfordshire, a county which had experienced it so directly.

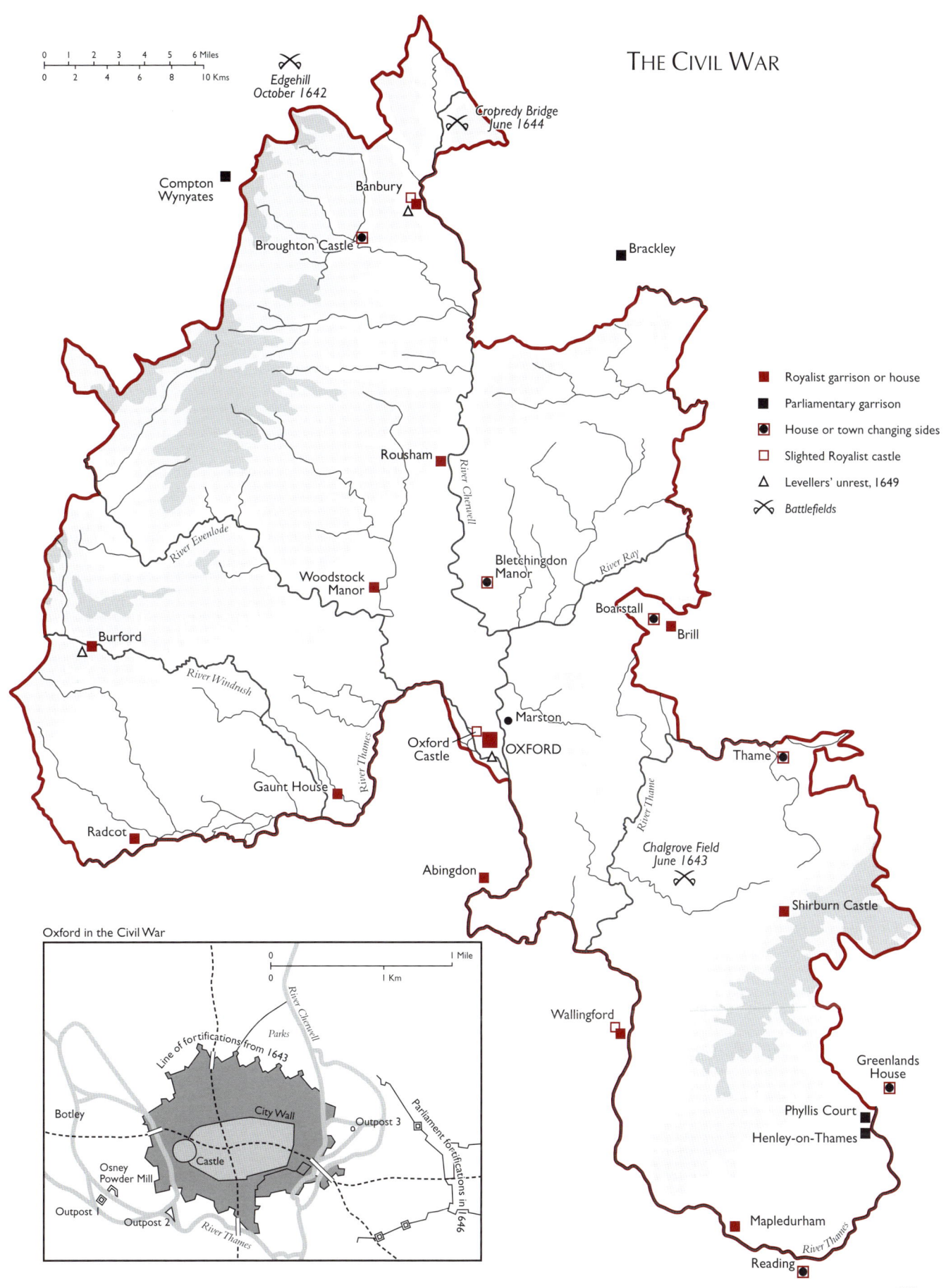

THE CIVIL WAR

Legend:
- ■ Royalist garrison or house
- ■ Parliamentary garrison
- ⊙ House or town changing sides
- ☐ Slighted Royalist castle
- △ Levellers' unrest, 1649
- ⚔ Battlefields

Locations and features:
- Edgehill October 1642
- Cropredy Bridge June 1644
- Compton Wynyates
- Banbury
- Broughton Castle
- Brackley
- Rousham
- River Cherwell
- Woodstock Manor
- Bletchingdon Manor
- River Ray
- Boarstall
- Brill
- River Evenlode
- Burford
- River Windrush
- Marston
- Oxford Castle
- OXFORD
- Thame
- Gaunt House
- River Thames
- River Thame
- Radcot
- Abingdon
- Chalgrove Field June 1643
- Shirburn Castle
- Wallingford
- Greenlands House
- Phyllis Court
- Henley-on-Thames
- Mapledurham
- Reading

Oxford in the Civil War

- Line of fortifications from 1643
- River Cherwell
- Parks
- Botley
- City Wall
- Castle
- Outpost 3
- Parliament fortifications in 1646
- Osney Powder Mill
- Outpost 1
- Outpost 2
- River Thames

95

40 · Country Houses 1500–1670 — Geoffrey Tyack

The religious and political upheavals of the 16th century brought about a major change in land ownership, in Oxfordshire as in all English counties (see entry 32). Formerly monastic land was sold on by the Crown to new owners, and the monarchy's continuing need for cash led to the piecemeal alienation of the once-considerable royal forests in the county (see entry 20). Price inflation in the second half of the 16th century benefited landowners, both 'new men' and those from longer-established local families which managed to hold on to their estates. These developments all contributed to an increase in country-house building, especially in the years of the so-called Great Rebuilding (see entry 38) between the accession of Queen Elizabeth and the outbreak of the Civil War in 1642.

In 1665 the largest house in Oxfordshire, judging by numbers of hearths, was Cornbury, a former hunting lodge in Wychwood Forest.* There were other very large houses, of 30 hearths or more, at Rycote, Swyncombe, Great Tew, Rotherfield Greys, Burford, Ditchley, Wroxton, Shirburn, Bletchingdon and Caversham. Most of these stood on or near the sites of medieval houses, and some – notably Greys Court and Shirburn Castle – incorporated, and still to some extent do incorporate, medieval fabric. This is also true of Stonor House and Broughton Castle, both of which can boast continuous descent through the same family from the Middle Ages to the present; and Minster Lovell Hall and Stanton Harcourt Manor, two largely 15th-century houses of long-established Oxfordshire families which were abandoned in the early 18th century but never totally demolished. Burford Priory and Wroxton Abbey were, on the other hand, built by 'new' men – Sir Lawrence Tanfield and Sir William Pope – on the sites of monasteries whose buildings have entirely disappeared, and the same was true of Studley Priory, built by the descendants of John Croke, the new purchaser. But at Thame Park the early 16th-century lodgings of the last abbot were incorporated into the new house built by Lord Williams, an energetic despoiler of monastic houses, and parts of the Gilbertine priory at Clattercote were also incorporated into a house which only survives in fragmentary form.

In the early 16th century most of the largest houses were built, like the colleges of Oxford University, around courtyards. The so-called castle at Hanwell, built *c*.1500 by William Cope, cofferer to Henry VII, originally had a courtyard plan, and at Rycote, built probably by Henry VIII's treasurer Sir Richard Heron in the 1520s, there were two courtyards, with corner turrets of a type seen in many early Tudor houses. Both houses were built of brick – a material already used at Stonor House in the 15th century – and brick was also used at Beckley Park, a hunting lodge rather than a full-scale country house built by Lord Williams of Thame *c*.1540. It continued to be employed in the southern part of the county in the late 16th and early 17th centuries, as at Hardwick House and Mapledurham, but elsewhere locally quarried stone was the favoured building material for the rest of the 16th century and long after.

Most of Oxfordshire's Elizabethan and Jacobean country houses were planned more compactly than their early Tudor predecessors, with a main block of two or even three storeys, usually one room deep and containing the hall, flanked by wings. This could give an H or a half-H plan, seen originally at Burford Priory (partially demolished), at the ruined manor house at Hampton Gay, and, rather later, at Rousham, built *c*.1635. Windows grew larger after the mid 16th century and were usually disposed symmetrically across the main facade, as in the north front of Broughton Castle, completely remodelled *c*.1554, and at the long-demolished house of the Cobb family at Adderbury. External enrichment usually came from rows of gables and tall chimneystacks, both notable features at Broughton, and carved porches. Internally the most impressive fixed features were wooden staircases, carved wooden hall screens (also a feature of Oxford colleges), chimneypieces, and ornamental plaster ceilings. All these features can be found at Chastleton, the best-preserved Oxfordshire house of the period, built by a lawyer, Walter Jones, 1607–12; it also retains some of its original furniture and its garden layout of walled 'outdoor rooms'.

Classical architecture made only very slow inroads into Oxfordshire in the 16th and early 17th centuries. For almost all country-house owners the architectural language of the Renaissance was something only to be employed decoratively, in chimneypieces (e.g. at Broughton Castle, Hardwick, Chastleton, etc.) and around porches, as at Burford Priory and Studley Priory. A more thoroughgoing approach only appears in 1631–3 at Cornbury, when a new wing was added for one of Charles I's courtiers, Henry Danvers, Earl of Danby – the patron of the Botanic Garden in Oxford – by Nicholas Stone, Inigo Jones's master mason at the Banqueting House in Whitehall. Stone's restrained, dignified approach to classicism was shared by Hugh May, Charles II's Paymaster (and later Comptroller) of Works, who was employed by the Earl of Clarendon, the most powerful man in Restoration England after the King himself, to continue the rebuilding of Cornbury with a new east range, stable block and chapel of 1663–8. Its completion marked an epoch in Oxfordshire's country-house architecture, and echoes of May's design can be traced in the county throughout the 18th century and beyond.

---

* The royal manor house in Woodstock Park was not assessed.

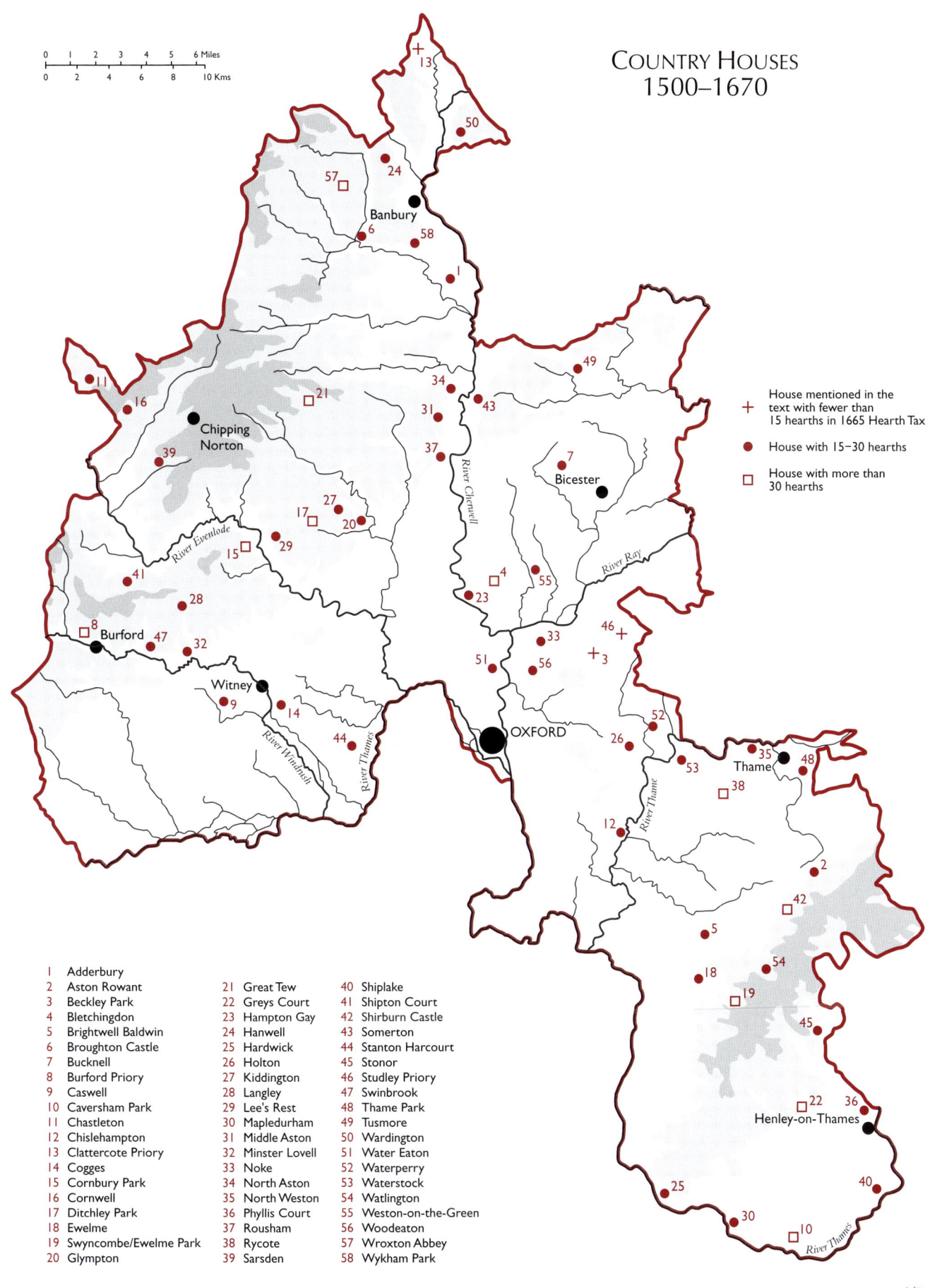

COUNTRY HOUSES 1500–1670

Legend:
- ✚ House mentioned in the text with fewer than 15 hearths in 1665 Hearth Tax
- ● House with 15–30 hearths
- ☐ House with more than 30 hearths

1. Adderbury
2. Aston Rowant
3. Beckley Park
4. Bletchingdon
5. Brightwell Baldwin
6. Broughton Castle
7. Bucknell
8. Burford Priory
9. Caswell
10. Caversham Park
11. Chastleton
12. Chislehampton
13. Clattercote Priory
14. Cogges
15. Cornbury Park
16. Cornwell
17. Ditchley Park
18. Ewelme
19. Swyncombe/Ewelme Park
20. Glympton
21. Great Tew
22. Greys Court
23. Hampton Gay
24. Hanwell
25. Hardwick
26. Holton
27. Kiddington
28. Langley
29. Lee's Rest
30. Mapledurham
31. Middle Aston
32. Minster Lovell
33. Noke
34. North Aston
35. North Weston
36. Phyllis Court
37. Rousham
38. Rycote
39. Sarsden
40. Shiplake
41. Shipton Court
42. Shirburn Castle
43. Somerton
44. Stanton Harcourt
45. Stonor
46. Studley Priory
47. Swinbrook
48. Thame Park
49. Tusmore
50. Wardington
51. Water Eaton
52. Waterperry
53. Waterstock
54. Watlington
55. Weston-on-the-Green
56. Woodeaton
57. Wroxton Abbey
58. Wykham Park

97

41 · Country Houses 1670–1815

Geoffrey Tyack

Apart from Cornbury, there was relatively little documented country-house building in the 40 years after the Restoration. A new Bishop's Palace was built at Cuddesdon to replace its timber-framed predecessor, damaged in the Civil War. Sarsden House was rebuilt after a fire of 1689 by William Walter, and in about 1685–8 a new(?) house was built by the Baskerville family at Crowsley, set within a new deer park. Like Cornbury, these houses had regular classical facades and hipped roofs, and so too did smaller houses like Newington House, probably built in the 1660s and heightened by an extra storey in 1777.

The building of Blenheim Palace inaugurated a new phase of country-house architecture in Oxfordshire. Sir John Vanbrugh described his gargantuan, publicly funded pile, begun in the royal park at Woodstock in 1705, as both 'a Royall and a National Monument' and a 'private habitation' for the first Duke of Marlborough and his family, and it has always surpassed all other Oxfordshire houses in size and magnificence, and in the grandeur of its collections. It was followed by a group of noblemen's houses, each set in an extensive, formally planned private landscape and each employing to a greater or lesser extent the architectural and decorative language of the Baroque: Heythrop, by Thomas Archer for the first Duke of Shrewsbury (1707–10); Caversham Park for the first Earl of Cadogan (c.1718–23); and Ditchley Park, by James Gibbs and Francis Smith of Warwick for the second Earl of Lichfield (1720–42). Echoes of the Baroque can also be seen in a group of gentlemen's houses built in the years following the end of the French wars in 1713: Shotover Park, for James Tyrrell (c.1713–20), which still retains its formal garden layout; Bruern Abbey, for the Cope family, on the site of a long-vanished Cistercian monastery (c.1720); Britwell House, a miniature Ditchley for Sir Edward Simeon (1727–8), with a main block fronting an open courtyard flanked by lower service blocks; and the rather similar Woodperry House, possibly by the Oxford master-mason William Townesend, for John Morse, a London banker (1728–31). Townesend also worked for the second Duke of Argyle at Adderbury House in 1723–4 (later extended by Roger Morris). This is a plain, even austere, house, and some other early 18th-century Oxfordshire houses were even plainer, such as Haseley Court (1710: extended 1754), Waterperry (c.1713), etc.

The largest mid-18th-century country houses were Kirtlington Park (William Smith of Warwick and John Sanderson for Sir James Dashwood, 1742–8); Thame Park, where the sixth Lord Wenman employed William Smith to add a large new wing c.1745; Middleton Park, where the Earl of Jersey built a new house on the site of one burnt down in 1753 (remodelled 1806–7); and Ambrosden, begun on the site of an earlier house by Sir Edward Turner c.1739, completed with the help of the Warwickshire gentleman-architect Sanderson Miller and demolished after Turner's death in 1766. All were externally plain, but Kirtlington and Thame Park had richly decorated interiors in the neo-Palladian style developed by William Kent, who worked at Ditchley in 1724–5 and at Rousham, remodelled internally for General James Dormer in 1738–41. Kent was also involved in designing garden buildings at Shotover in 1724–5 and was responsible for the present layout of the garden at Rousham, one of the most beautiful of all early English landscape gardens.

Several 18th-century country house owners chose, like General Dormer at Rousham, not to replace their existing houses but to remodel or extend them, often in conjunction with a landscaping scheme. So the first Earl of Macclesfield, a successful lawyer, remodelled and modernised Shirburn Castle soon after purchasing the estate in 1716, retaining what survived of the 14th-century corner towers and rebuilding the rest. More commonly, as at Stonor in the 1750s, the exterior was given a plain classical face-lift, though the hall was redecorated in the Gothic style. Gothic was only rarely used externally, first by Kent in the wings added to Rousham and then, much later in the 1790s, at Braziers Park, Ipsden, by Daniel Harris, keeper of Oxford gaol, for J. G. Manley, and subsequently at Bradwell Grove by William Atkinson for William Hervey, c.1804. Meanwhile, several genuinely medieval houses, such as Minster Lovell Hall, were allowed to fall into ruin, or to disappear almost completely, like the old house of the Quartremain family at North Weston.

Most new Oxfordshire houses of the later 18th century had classical facades and compact villa-like plans, and were isolated in parkland laid out in the manner of 'Capability' Brown, one of whose grandest schemes survives at Blenheim. The first of these houses was Nuneham Courtenay, built in 1756–61 on a new site overlooking the Thames south of Oxford by the art-loving first Lord Harcourt, who chose the site in preference to his existing houses at Stanton Harcourt and Cokethorpe (c.1720) because of its 'superior landscaping possibilities'; his architect, Stiff Leadbetter, was also responsible for the Radcliffe Infirmary in Oxford. Later villa-like houses include Watlington Park, built c.1760 for John Tilson on land purchased from the Stonors; Chislehampton, for a London merchant, Charles Peers (1767–8); Tusmore, by Robert Mylne for William Fermor, representative of a long-established local family (1766–70: demolished); Bletchingdon Park (James Lewis for Arthur Annesley, 1782); and Waterstock House (S. P. Cockerell for Sir Henry Ashurst, 1787–90: demolished).

COUNTRY HOUSES 1670–1815

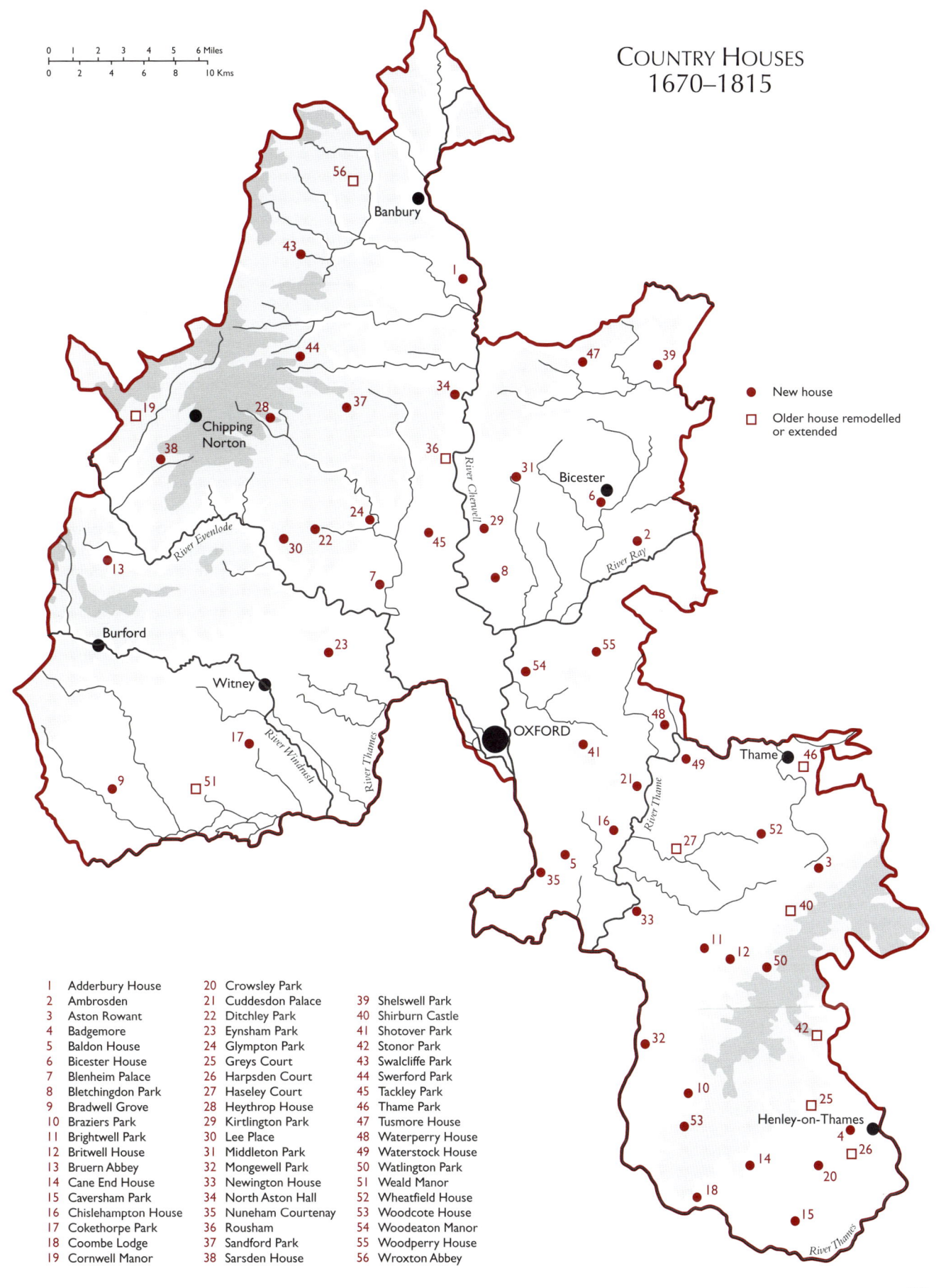

- New house
- Older house remodelled or extended

#	Name	#	Name	#	Name
1	Adderbury House	20	Crowsley Park	39	Shelswell Park
2	Ambrosden	21	Cuddesdon Palace	40	Shirburn Castle
3	Aston Rowant	22	Ditchley Park	41	Shotover Park
4	Badgemore	23	Eynsham Park	42	Stonor Park
5	Baldon House	24	Glympton Park	43	Swalcliffe Park
6	Bicester House	25	Greys Court	44	Swerford Park
7	Blenheim Palace	26	Harpsden Court	45	Tackley Park
8	Bletchingdon Park	27	Haseley Court	46	Thame Park
9	Bradwell Grove	28	Heythrop House	47	Tusmore House
10	Braziers Park	29	Kirtlington Park	48	Waterperry House
11	Brightwell Park	30	Lee Place	49	Waterstock House
12	Britwell House	31	Middleton Park	50	Watlington Park
13	Bruern Abbey	32	Mongewell Park	51	Weald Manor
14	Cane End House	33	Newington House	52	Wheatfield House
15	Caversham Park	34	North Aston Hall	53	Woodcote House
16	Chislehampton House	35	Nuneham Courtenay	54	Woodeaton Manor
17	Cokethorpe Park	36	Rousham	55	Woodperry House
18	Coombe Lodge	37	Sandford Park	56	Wroxton Abbey
19	Cornwell Manor	38	Sarsden House		

42 · Schools in the 18th Century

Geoffrey Stevenson

Schooling in 18th-century Oxfordshire involved a varied and uneven mix of old, sometimes decayed, historic endowments and new, voluntary, charitable and religious initiatives. There is no comprehensive source for these provisions, but a general picture is offered by responses to the Bishop of Oxford's visitation questions of 1738 and by a diocesan survey compiled for the Archbishop of Canterbury in 1808. Every school reported in 1738 and 1808, alongside others known from a variety of sources to have functioned at some point in the century, is mapped here. The picture is of necessity incomplete, the only central records available being those of the Society for the Promotion of Christian Knowledge (SPCK), established in 1699. Most likely omissions are some dame and petty schools, as well as some small schools for gentry sons kept largely by clergymen, though these may have advertised in the county newspaper, *Jackson's Oxford Journal*, established in 1753. The lack of educational provision in many places is indicated by the fact that of 179 parishes recorded in the 1738 returns, only 53 mentioned a school. Little had improved by the 1759 visitation, when schools figured in only 41 of 163 parish returns. By 1808 progress had been made, but over a quarter of Oxfordshire parishes still did not return any school.

The 18th century began with the promotion of charity schools, to be maintained by subscription, to function beside those funded by the more traditional endowment. The map distinguishes endowed schools, charity schools, and those schools financed, in whole or in part, by parental fees, amongst which are many small examples stated to be run by women, often called 'dame' schools. A third type of school, added from the 1780s, was the Sunday school, in effect a one-day charity school. Other provision included workhouse, industrial or evening schools. The dominant provider was the Church of England, with a small number of Protestant Nonconformist or Roman Catholic institutions. Parishes reporting no school provision before 1808, along with some extra-parochial areas (mainly emparked or forest land), are distinguished from those with poor reporting by the clergy. One explanation for the seemingly high number of these is the proportion of college livings. McClatchey suggests that 'Oxfordshire villages suffered from their proximity to the university', with high levels of non-residence a 'toll exerted from the country parishes by the University . . . in return for affording them one day out of seven the advantage of its scholarship'.[1]

Endowed schools were prominent well before this time, but continued to attract legacies from those disposed to improve schooling, support apprenticeship of boys or alleviate the problems of old age, a set of aims which were not always distinct, as in the case of the joint school and hospital foundation at Ewelme. Some, particularly in the market towns, offered a grammar or classical curriculum, whilst others specifically forbade this and concentrated on limited, elementary skills useful to the rural poor. At Islip, the teaching of French, Latin, Greek or Hebrew was forbidden. By 1800 some grammar schools had lapsed into elementary village schools, such as Steeple Aston, with its change of master from a cleric to an ex-army drummer once responsible for regimental education in the 55th Border Regiment. Literacy at that time could be acquired, not merely in schools, but through apprenticeships, trade and even military service.

Charity schools depended not on endowment but on recurrent subscriptions 'moved by prevailing enthusiasm' through sermons and other means. The SPCK now sought to give impetus nationwide, though this flagged after one generation. Its primary aim, to enhance morality with attention to the catechism, was a duty which many incumbents took upon themselves informally. The SPCK 1712 list of 21 Oxfordshire schools shows a concentration on the larger centres, yet several listed prove also to have endowments.[2] Moreover, the combined use of subscriptions as well as parental fees was common in many other initiatives, the distinction being not well understood. The Vicar of Witney in 1759 clarified his visitation response by adding 'by a voluntary charity school I understand one that is supported by present voluntary subscriptions or charity'.

The development of Sunday schools after 1780, producing institutions with much larger attendances than most day schools, was a re-emergence of the fervour of the Charity School movement in the guise of one-day-a-week schooling. Sunday schools began to produce new teaching methods in the towns, and in the view of some recent historians (like Laqueur, who uses Bicester as an example) to generate a distinctive culture in the lives of many working-class people.

Beyond endowed, charity and Sunday schools, a plethora of small schools is recorded, often quite temporary, and run by older women called 'dames'. These provided much of the patchwork of teaching of reading, writing, catechising or needlework. They might be seen as compensating for gaps in other provision, as for example Mrs Oglander's school in extra-parochial Stow Wood, which was presented by the vicar of neighbouring Elsfield as the excuse for the lack of a school in his parish.

By 1800, two questions were emerging: how was the Anglican church to respond to the numbers of schools owned, or run by, Nonconformist congregations – Quakers, Baptists, Presbyterians and newer Wesleyan Methodists – and also by Roman Catholics? The former were strongest in the north of the county and in the Chilterns, whilst the latter only appeared close to wealthy Catholic families at Tusmore, Stonor and Mapledurham.

The second question related to the role of the state in the education of the poor. This saw its first airing in the failed bill of 1807 proposed by Samuel Whitbread, which would have entitled the children of poor parents to two years' free schooling: interestingly, it was lamented as a 'missed opportunity' by the curate at Westwell responding to the bishop in 1808. These questions dominated developments in schooling in the 19th century as population grew and became proportionately more youthful, and debates on voluntary and denominational versus state educational provision intensified (see entry 55).

Schools in the 18th Century

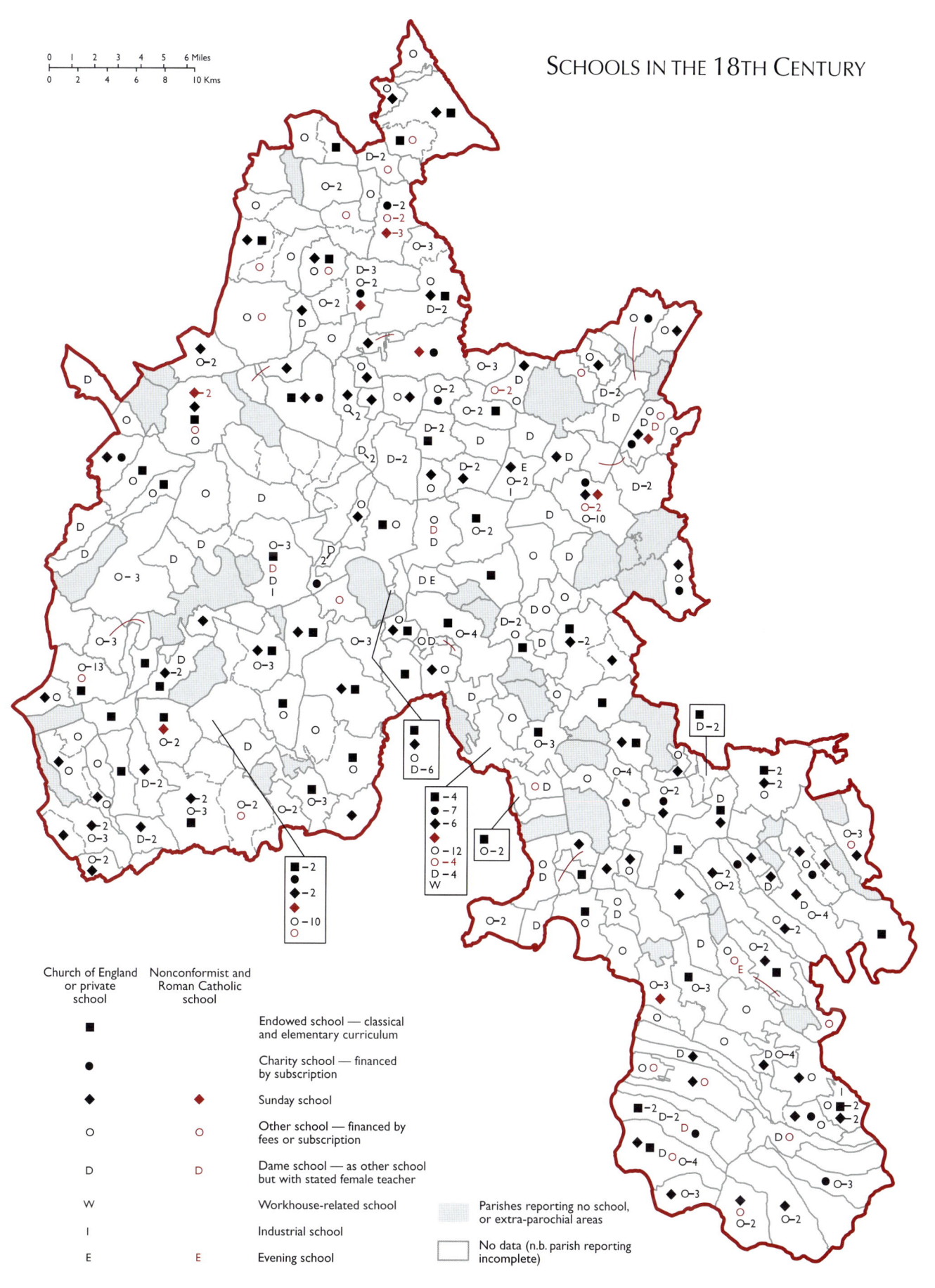

Church of England or private school / Nonconformist and Roman Catholic school

- ■ Endowed school — classical and elementary curriculum
- ● Charity school — financed by subscription
- ◆ ◆ Sunday school
- O O Other school — financed by fees or subscription
- D D Dame school — as other school but with stated female teacher
- W Workhouse-related school
- I Industrial school
- E E Evening school

Parishes reporting no school, or extra-parochial areas

No data (n.b. parish reporting incomplete)

43 · Roads in the 18th and 19th Centuries

Barrie Trinder

Many long-distance road services already passed through Oxfordshire in 1700. Gerhold has shown that by the 1680s almost every county had both packhorse and wagon services to London. There were regular passenger coaches between London and Oxford in the late 17th century and in summer 1679 Banbury could be reached within a day by 'flying coach' from London. The 1703 *Oxford Almanack* shows many long-distance services from the capital, ranging in frequency with distance – twice weekly to Banbury, fortnightly to Birmingham, Northampton and Bristol, monthly to Shrewsbury, every five weeks to Exeter, quarterly to North Wales and three times a year to Westmorland. Some carriers can be identified. John Jordan of the Hollybush, Banbury, worked a weekly wagon to London in 1681. In 1689 he left 'horses, wagons and other things as belongs to a carrier' worth £40 (out of a total movable estate of £245). His son John died the following year, when the chattels relating to the trade were defined as 'Twelve horses, one wagon, the harnesse and implmts belonging to them'. The presence of grain and cheese worth £10 in his granary may give some indication of the goods that he carried. Similar ponderous vehicles continued to make their way slowly to the capital until the dawn of the railway age, their journeys doubtless shortened by the gradual improvement of roads. In 1861 Thomas Eustace was still the London carrier from Chinnor and ten years later Henry Palmer, then in his 80s, continued to work a wagon from Benson to the capital.

The turnpike system, which transferred responsibility for main roads from the authorities in the parishes through which they passed to trusts made up of local notables, transformed the pattern of transport in England during the 18th century. The first turnpike act relating to Oxfordshire covered the main road from London, from the county boundary near Stokenchurch through Oxford to Woodstock, and was passed in 1719, doubtless in conjunction with an act covering the route in Buckinghamshire from Beaconsfield to Stokenchurch (5 Geo I c.1. 2). Three more acts relating to Oxfordshire roads were passed in the 1730s, six in the 1750s, five in the 1760s and five in the 1770s, with a further seven between 1780 and 1802. Arthur Young in 1813 commended Oxfordshire's turnpike trustees, observing that all the towns in the county were linked by good roads.

The improvement is reflected in the pattern of road services. Packhorses ceased to make their way to the capital during the 1750s, while stage coaches, posting (or private hire) coaches and, from the 1780s, mail coaches proliferated. Turnpike roads also made possible the development of networks of country carriers. Oxford became one of the principal towns of thoroughfare in southern England, the hub of services from the length of the Welsh border as well as of cross-country services to and from the south coast and the eastern counties. No other town in the county experienced the same density of traffic, although Henley was busy with traffic between Oxford and London, and Banbury was a modest hub for coaches. A few villages, of which Benson was the prime example in Oxfordshire, made a large parts of their living from serving road travellers.

Some isolated roadside inns were so renowned that they functioned in effect as villages of thoroughfare. The Chapel House near Chipping Norton was outstanding in England, commended by Dr Samuel Johnson in 1776 and accounted 'quite a principality' by John Byng, later 5th Viscount Torrington, in 1785. The brothers La Rochefoucauld, also visiting in 1785, found 'a considerable inn standing on its own in the countryside'. Less than ten years old, its 'parlours and bedrooms are of a luxury and comfort that can't be compared with anything in France. The stable-block is immense . . . they have fifty-two horses . . . arriving and departing every minute of the day.' A Scottish farmer in 1802 concluded that it was 'as civil a house as any in Britain'.

Oxfordshire Turnpikes and Turnpike Acts

Date	Route	Act
1719	Stokenchurch–Oxford–Woodstock (Enslow Bridge)	5 Geo I c.2
1730	Woodstock (Enslow Bridge)–Rollright	3 Geo II c.21
1731	Chapel-on-the-Hill–Bourton-on-the-Hill	4 Geo II c.23
1736	Henley-on-Thames–Oxford	9 Geo II c.14
1751	Crickley Hill–Oxford (Oxon & Glos)	24 Geo II c.28
1753	Burford–Preston (Oxon & Glos)	26 Geo II c.34
1753	Banbury–Edge Hill	26 Geo II c.42
1755	Southam–Banbury	28 Geo II c.46
1756	Chilton Pond (Oxford)–near Faringdon	29 Geo II c.81
1757	Towcester–Weston-on-the-Green	30 Geo II c.48
1764	Shillingford–Reading	4 Geo II c.42
1765	Banbury–Lutterworth	5 Geo III c.105
1767	Oxford–near Fyfield	7 Geo III c.66
1768	Reading–Hatfield (Herts, Bucks, Berks, Oxon)	8 Geo III c.50
1769	Stony Stratford–Woodstock	9 Geo II c.88
1770	Aylesbury–Little Molton (Bucks, Oxon)	10 Geo III c.58
1770	Burford–Banbury	10 Geo III c.101
1771	Witney–Clanfield	11 Geo III c.73
1771	Great Faringdon–Burford	11 Geo III c.84
1777	Asthall–Buckland (Oxon, Berks)	17 Geo III c.104
1781	Weston-on-the-Green–Kidlington	21 Geo III c.87
1791	Bicester–Aynho	31 Geo III c.103
1791	Great Marlow–Stokenchurch	31 Geo III c.135
1792	Burford–Lechlade	32 Geo III c.153
1793	Clay Hill–Bicester	33 Geo III c.180
1800	Witney–Tew	39/40 Geo III c.16
1802	Banbury–Barcheston (Oxon, Warwks)	42 Geo III c.38

Sources: W. Albert, *The Turnpike Road System in England 1663–1840* (Cambridge University Press, 1972); E. Pawson, *Transport and Economy: the Turnpike Roads of Eighteenth Century Britain* (London: Academic Press, 1977).

ROADS

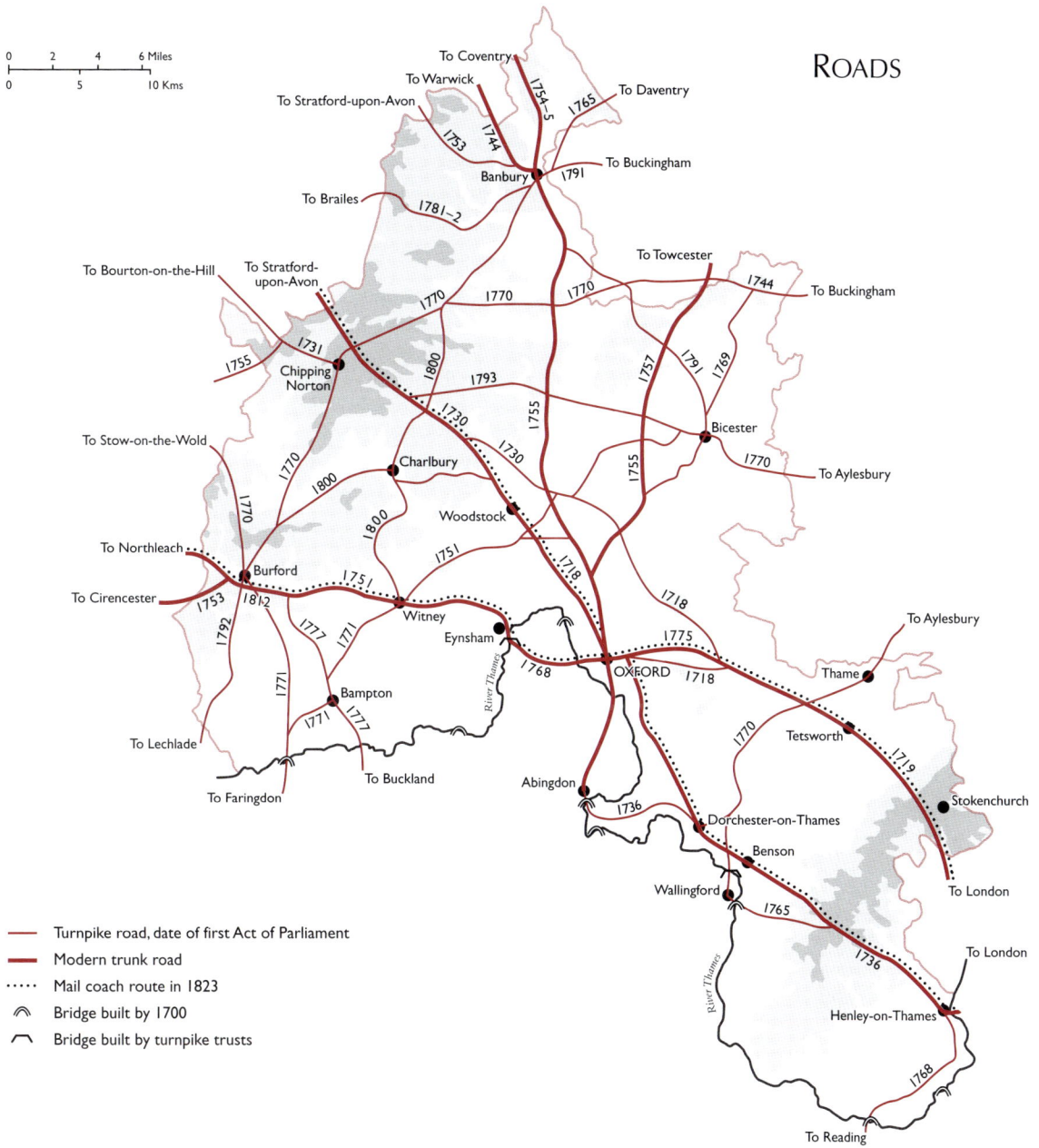

Legend:
- Turnpike road, date of first Act of Parliament
- Modern trunk road
- Mail coach route in 1823
- Bridge built by 1700
- Bridge built by turnpike trusts

Stagecoach routes through Oxfordshire, 1830

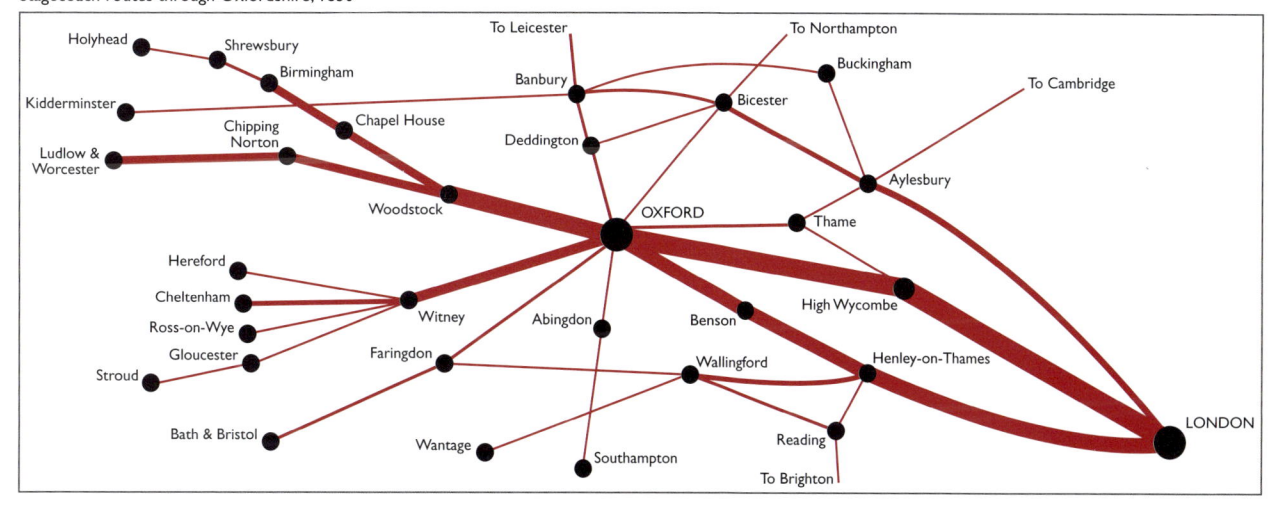

103

44 · Rivers and Canals

Barrie Trinder

Inland navigation in Oxfordshire centred on three distinct waterways which, for about a century after 1790, served as a network that profoundly influenced the county's economic development. On the lower Thames, navigation between Oxford and London was established by Acts of 1606 and 1624, the latter authorising a commission for the river between Oxford and Burcot. By repute the first barge reached Oxford from London on 31 August 1635. A community of bargeowners working to and from London grew up around Folly Bridge, bringing upstream shop goods, coal from north-east England and imported softwoods. Subsequent legislation created the Thames Commissioners in 1751, and enabled the building of a succession of pound locks and towpaths, allowing horses to be used for haulage. But a journey from Oxford to London could still take six days in the 1790s.

Navigation on the upper section of the Thames has been analysed by Mary Prior in her study of Fisher Row, the community from which small boats carried goods to and from the area upstream to Lechlade or even Cricklade, as well as fishing on waters near Oxford. The community was well established in the 16th century, prospering from the carriage of agricultural produce, and stone from Taynton loaded at Radcot Bridge. By 1800 both sections of the Thames were probably losing traffic to road transport.

The third element in the system was the Oxford Canal. North Oxfordshire had long suffered from fuel shortages. There was relatively little woodland and 18th-century enclosures reduced supplies of furze from open heaths. Sanderson Miller, a Banbury draper, operated flat-bottomed boats on the Cherwell between Oxford and Banbury, probably until *c*.1714. Agitation for a canal linking the Cherwell with the Warwickshire coalfield began in Banbury in 1768. The Oxford Canal was opened from its junction with the Coventry Canal at Longford to Banbury in 1778 but not extended southwards until the late 1780s. Coal was available at Enslow in 1788. In 1789 the opening of the Duke's Cut linked the canal with the upper Thames, a wharf in north Oxford opened, and on New Year's Day 1790 the first boats reached Hythe Bridge wharf. In 1796 a link to the Thames was opened through the Isis Lock. The completion of the Coventry Canal to Fradley Junction on the Trent & Mersey Canal, with its junction at Fazeley linking to the Birmingham Canal Navigation, made the Oxford Canal part of a developing national network of inland waterways. Six weeks before its terminal basin was opened a second link to the network was completed when the Thames & Severn Canal was opened to the Thames upstream from Lechlade (see inset map).

Oxfordshire's waterways reached a peak of national significance between 1790 and 1805. The Oxford Canal and the Thames provided the principal route for goods between London and the midlands. Little coal went to the capital by this route, but it was sold at wharfs along the Thames and Kennet. The Thames & Severn Canal enabled barges from the Thames to reach the Severn at Framilode, and sailings from Hambros Wharf in London offered through transits to Worcester, Bridgnorth and Shrewsbury. It also provided access to the upper Thames valley for coal from South Wales, the Forest of Dean and the Black Country. A new route from the Midlands to London was provided by the Warwick & Birmingham, Warwick & Napton and Grand Junction canals, completed by the opening of Blisworth Tunnel in 1805. Vessels following this route used the section of the Oxford Canal between Napton and Braunston, generating tolls that made the company exceedingly prosperous. However, the new route reduced the number of vessels passing Claydon summit. Two other canals connected with the Oxfordshire network, although neither entered the historic county. The Wilts & Berks Canal opened in 1810 from Abingdon and provided a link with the Thames & Severn Canal near Cricklade. The canals were disused by 1906 and formally abandoned in 1914, although parts are being restored.

Of more consequence in Oxfordshire was the establishment of local wharfs along the Thames and on the Oxford Canal, locations for coal merchants, kilns for bricks, lime and malt, and public houses, often kept by coal merchants or boat owners. For example, the Grantham family's wharf at Heyford was Bicester's link to the waterways system, and for a time the inmates of its workhouse collected coal there. On the upper Thames there was competition between coal suppliers from the Thames & Severn Canal and those who carried it from Leicestershire and Warwickshire along the Oxford Canal and the Duke's Cut, hoping to supply Burford, Witney and Faringdon.

Several distinct canal communities grew up in Oxfordshire, in Banbury in the vicinity of the wharfs and boat-building yard in Mill Lane, and in Oxford in Fisher Row, where the old-established Beesley family became prominent canal boat men. One of the most influential was at Eynsham. In 1800 the Oxford Canal Company leased an ancient wharf at the confluence of the Chil and Limb brooks, where they had employed a wharfinger since 1792, and built a flash lock, the Clay Weir, to improve access for narrow boats entering the Thames from the Duke's Cut. The wharf became the base of the Parker family, who dealt in coal, corn, salt and bricks, and worked barges down the Thames to London in the 1830s, and of several canal boating families, amongst them the Hathaways and the Humphrises.

After 1850 the majority of boats using the southern part of the Oxford Canal were worked by Oxfordshire families. There were few commercial vessels on the lower Thames, which was increasingly a place of pleasure, depicted by Henry Taunt, Francis Frith, Kenneth Graham and Jerome K. Jerome, its principal vessels not commercial barges but cruising steamers, particularly Salter's, established when John Salter, boatbuilder, moved from Fulham to Folly Bridge in 1858. Narrow boats continued the canal trade in the 20th century, with a boost in carrying during the Second World War, but the subsequent decline was accelerated by the severe winter of 1947. Through the 1950s commercial narrow boats gave way to pleasure craft, and by 2000 the county's waterways were busier and providing more employment than at any time in history, except perhaps for the 15 years after 1790.

Navigable Rivers and Canals

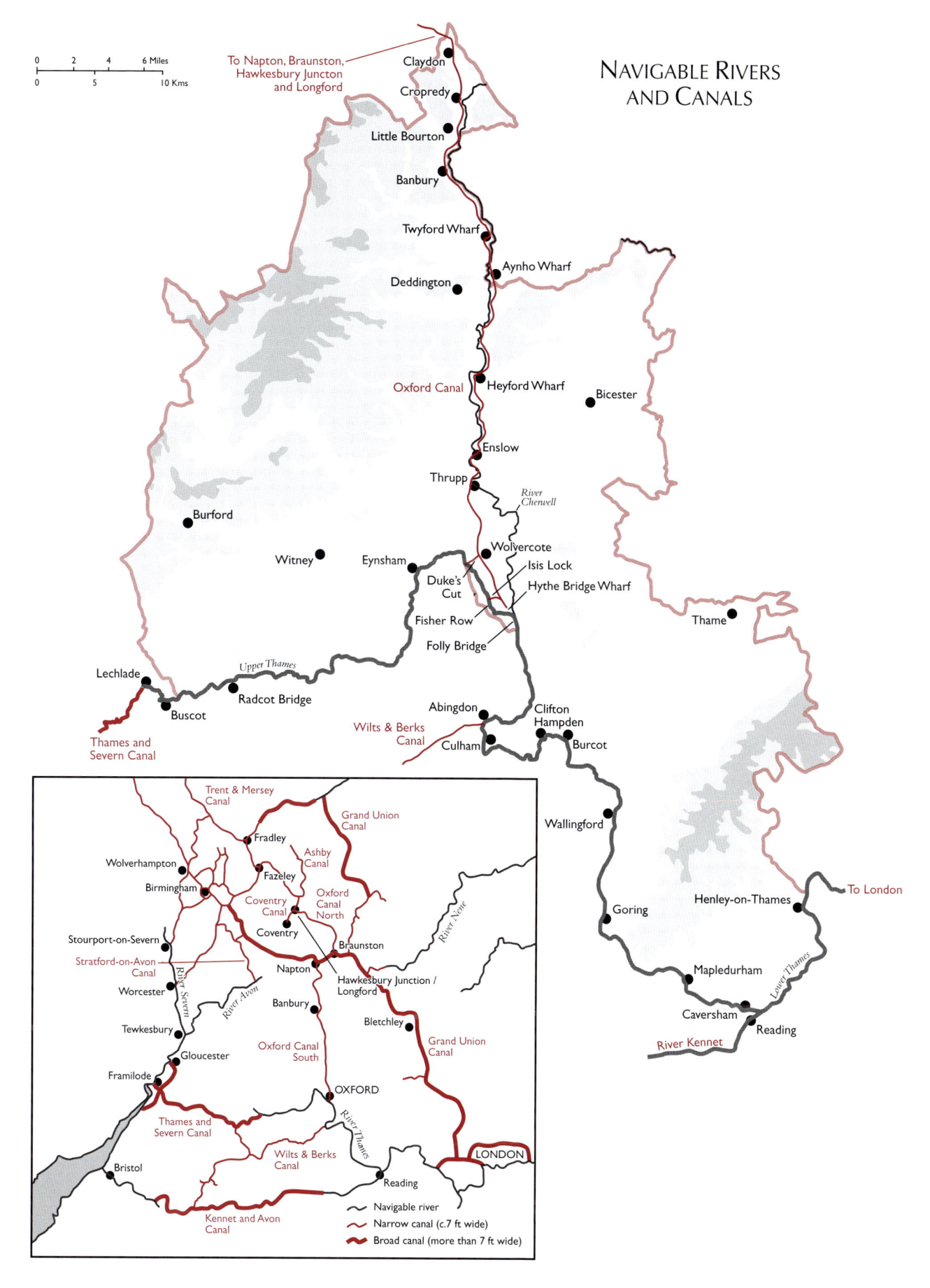

Main map labels:

- To Napton, Braunston, Hawkesbury Junction and Longford
- Claydon
- Cropredy
- Little Bourton
- Banbury
- Twyford Wharf
- Aynho Wharf
- Deddington
- Oxford Canal
- Heyford Wharf
- Bicester
- Enslow
- Thrupp
- *River Cherwell*
- Burford
- Witney
- Eynsham
- Wolvercote
- Isis Lock
- Duke's Cut
- Hythe Bridge Wharf
- Fisher Row
- Folly Bridge
- Thame
- Lechlade
- *Upper Thames*
- Radcot Bridge
- Buscot
- Abingdon
- Clifton Hampden
- Burcot
- Culham
- Thames and Severn Canal
- Wilts & Berks Canal
- Wallingford
- Goring
- Henley-on-Thames
- To London
- Mapledurham
- Caversham
- Reading
- *Lower Thames*
- River Kennet

Inset map labels:

- Trent & Mersey Canal
- Fradley
- Grand Union Canal
- Wolverhampton
- Fazeley
- Ashby Canal
- Birmingham
- Coventry Canal
- Oxford Canal North
- Stourport-on-Severn
- Coventry
- *River Nene*
- Stratford-on-Avon Canal
- Braunston
- Worcester
- Napton
- Hawkesbury Junction / Longford
- *River Severn*
- *River Avon*
- Tewkesbury
- Banbury
- Bletchley
- Grand Union Canal
- Gloucester
- Oxford Canal South
- Framilode
- OXFORD
- *River Thames*
- LONDON
- Thames and Severn Canal
- Wilts & Berks Canal
- Bristol
- Reading
- Kennet and Avon Canal

Legend:
- Navigable river
- Narrow canal (c.7 ft wide)
- Broad canal (more than 7 ft wide)

Scale: 0 2 4 6 Miles / 0 5 10 Kms

105

45 · Towns 1700–1900: Nodality, Growth and Decay   James Bond

Many different criteria can be used to identify towns in the 18th and 19th centuries. They are normally larger than villages. Urban functions invariably included the holding of regular markets, usually also fairs. Some towns were formally constituted as boroughs, with special privileges such as rights of self-government. Some formed the centres of administrative units such as counties or poor law unions. While all market towns retained links with an agricultural hinterland, they also offered employments in trade and industry. Urban status can usually be recognised by its reflection in the fabric of the settlement. During the middle ages towns had acquired distinctive plan elements such as market-places and burgage plots, while subsequently they acquired specialised buildings such as town halls, shops, distinctive types of urban housing and concentrations of industrial premises.

Despite having many features in common, however, towns have never been of uniform importance. Even in the middle ages distinctions had been made between towns with 'full markets' and those with 'local markets'. By the early 19th century a more complex hierarchy can be recognised, based upon population size and social and economic functions. Oxford itself remained dominant as the regional capital. Banbury was an important secondary regional centre, comparable in rank with Abingdon, Newbury or Aylesbury in neighbouring counties. A third tier was represented by a group of five large market towns, Chipping Norton, Witney, Bicester, Thame and Henley, generally spaced at intervals of nine to 13 miles. Beneath these was a group of smaller centres, Deddington, Charlbury, Burford, Bampton, Woodstock, Eynsham and Watlington, which reduced the distance between market towns to between five and nine miles.

Amongst the various urban functions the right to hold regular markets was probably the most consistently important over the longest period. The map employs Thiessen polygons to outline theoretical market hinterlands.* Each fourth-tier centre had 15 to 20 rural villages within its hinterland, but it did not hold a monopoly on the provision of services for those villages, and some requirements could only be met by travelling further to a higher-tier centre. Some markets were prescriptive, held by ancient custom, others were acquired or legitimised by royal charter, particularly during the 12th and 13th centuries (see entry 15). However, markets had not always been an exclusive prerogative of towns: during the middle ages market rights had also been acquired for at least 15 communities in Oxfordshire which would now be regarded as no more than villages or hamlets. What disqualifies those places from consideration as towns is that none succeeded in retaining trading functions over the longer term: in every case their markets had failed, or been suppressed, before the 18th century.

Leaving aside the failed village markets, the basic distribution of towns established during the middle ages remained unchanged throughout the 18th century. This reflected the limited means of transport available; most people attending markets went on foot, livestock were driven along the roads and other goods were carried by cart or packhorse. However, significant advances in transport began in the 18th century, first with the turnpiking of the main cross-country roads between market towns, then with the improvement of navigation on the Thames and the construction of the Oxford Canal. The most decisive influence on the fate of Oxfordshire's market towns came in the mid 19th century, with the expansion of the railway network (see entries 43, 44 and 46). Accessibility had always been a vital factor in the economic success of a town, but the abstract portrayal of routes on the map emphasises how some towns were more advantageously placed in relation to the developing transport system than others. Every town was accessible by turnpike road, but Oxford and Banbury were focal points upon which about ten major roads converged, whereas towns like Deddington and Woodstock were served by only one major through road. The economy of Burford suffered a significant blow when the old coach road from Oxford to Cheltenham, which had passed through the town, was replaced by a new turnpike road keeping to the high ground to the south. Before 1800 Oxford, Henley and, to a limited extent, Eynsham, were the only Oxfordshire towns with direct access to water transport, but completion of the Oxford Canal in 1790 linked Banbury and Oxford with the industrial Midlands. The railway reached Oxford in 1844, and within 20 years railways had been extended to most other Oxfordshire towns, reaching Banbury (1850), Bicester (1850–1), Charlbury (1853), Chipping Norton (1855), Henley (1857), Eynsham (1861), Witney (1861) and Thame (1862). Watlington became the terminus of a branch line only in 1872 and Woodstock in 1890. Bampton and Deddington were left two miles from the nearest railway and Burford four miles.

Census figures (arranged by parish or township and requiring manipulation to match them to urban areas) reflect a widening gulf between the four tiers of towns. Oxford's pre-eminence increased, as its population grew from just under 12,000 to over 49,000 between 1801 and 1901. Banbury, with about 3,800 people in 1801, grew rapidly and, despite faltering slightly in the 1880s, its population had just exceeded 10,000 by 1901. The population range of the third-tier towns increased, with some fluctuations, from between 1,800 and 2,900 in 1801 to between 2,900 and 3,800 in 1901. However the fourth-tier towns, with populations ranging from 980 to 1,600 in 1801, experienced only modest growth before entering a protracted decline. Each of those seven failing towns was fundamentally disadvantaged by its limited transport connections; in particular, three were without direct rail links and three more on cul-de-sac branch lines. Deddington, Burford and Bampton had all lost their markets by the end of the 19th century, and markets in the other smaller towns were in terminal decline. Unable to attract other urban functions, in effect they slipped out of the urban league table, and the hinterlands of the third-tier towns expanded at their expense.

* For a note on Thiessen polygons see Notes and Further Reading.

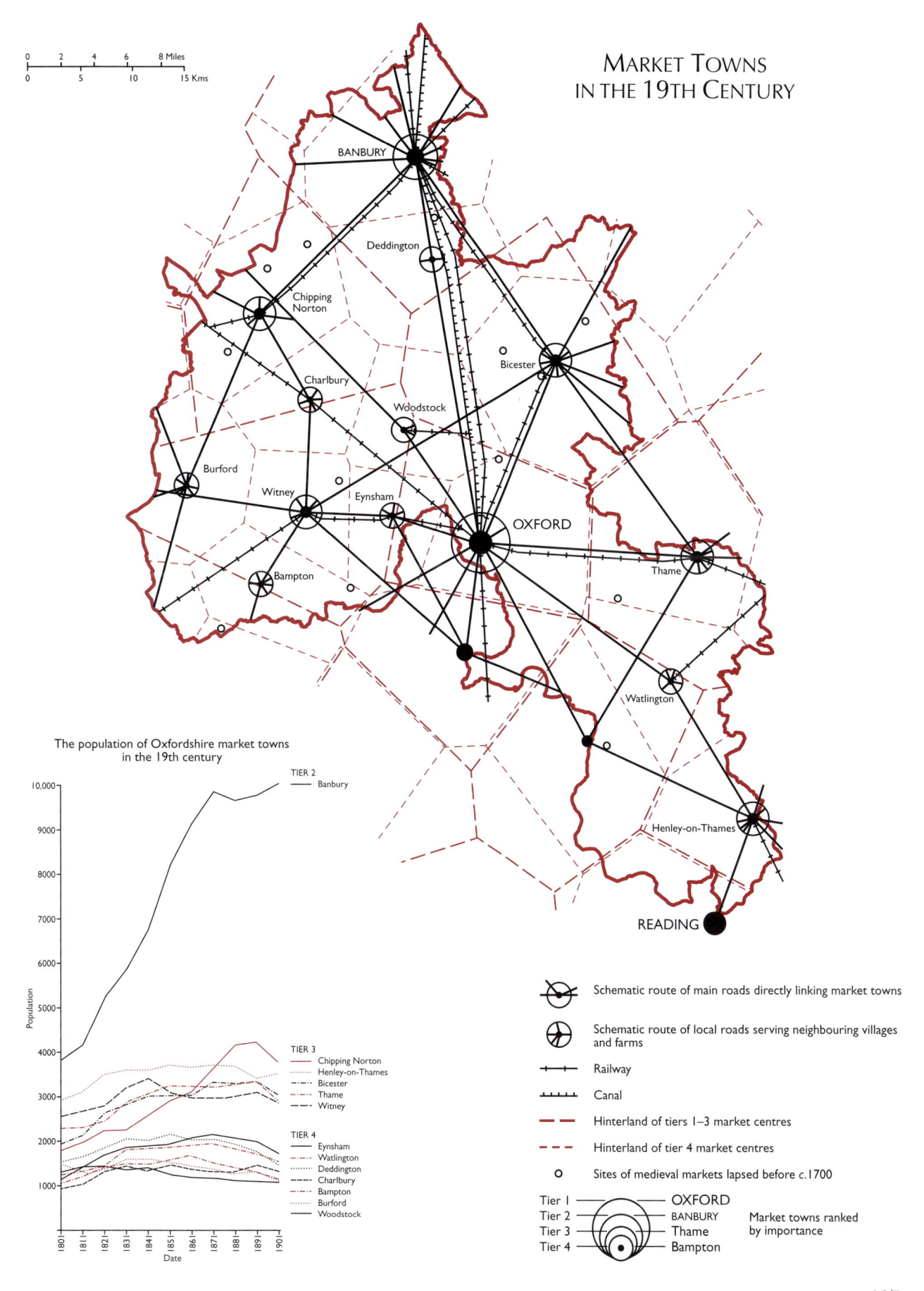

Market Towns in the 19th Century

The population of Oxfordshire market towns in the 19th century

TIER 2
— Banbury

TIER 3
— Chipping Norton
⋯ Henley-on-Thames
–·– Bicester
–··– Thame
– – Witney

TIER 4
— Eynsham
— Watlington
⋯ Deddington
– – Charlbury
–·– Bampton
⋯ Burford
— Woodstock

Legend

- Schematic route of main roads directly linking market towns
- Schematic route of local roads serving neighbouring villages and farms
- Railway
- Canal
- Hinterland of tiers 1–3 market centres
- Hinterland of tier 4 market centres
- ○ Sites of medieval markets lapsed before c.1700

Tier 1 — OXFORD
Tier 2 — BANBURY
Tier 3 — Thame
Tier 4 — Bampton

Market towns ranked by importance

46 · Railways

Barrie Trinder

In the early 1840s a national railway system was evolving and it was clear that, with two incompatible systems in use, the south midlands would be a major battlefield in the war of the gauges. George and Robert Stephenson had employed the standard (or narrow) gauge of 4 ft 8½ in for the London & Birmingham Railway (L&B), opened in 1838, whilst Isambard Kingdom Brunel's broad-gauge Great Western Railway (GWR) opened from Paddington to Maidenhead in 1838 and through to Bristol in 1841. The GWR main line runs for about 3½ miles through Oxfordshire, west of its bridge over the Thames at Lower Basildon. The magnetic power of the main-line railways quickly attracted the custom of Oxfordshire towns (see entry 45). Steventon on the GWR became the railhead for Oxford, Faringdon Road (Challow) for Witney, and Weedon, Wolverton and Tring on the L&B for Banbury. The GWR opened its branch from Didcot to Oxford on 12 June 1844.

The battle continued with a lengthy parliamentary enquiry into proposed lines north of Oxford, the Oxford, Worcester & Wolverhampton (OWW) and Oxford & Rugby (O&RR) railways. Construction of the broad-gauge O&RR began in Port Meadow in August 1845 but proceeded slowly. It opened as far as Banbury in 1850, when passenger trains at Oxford began to use a station on the present site, abandoning that at Grandpont to the use of freight trains. A northward extension was opened in 1852, but it ran through Leamington to Birmingham, and its route to Rugby was abandoned near Knightcote. The OWW was intended as a broad-gauge route but Brunel, who had underestimated the costs of construction, resigned as engineer in 1852, and the railway was completed in 1853–4 with rails of mixed gauge and with most of the pointwork impossible for broad-gauge trains to use. Meanwhile the ambitions of narrow-gauge companies were embodied in the Buckinghamshire Railway from Bletchley on the L&B main line to Banbury and Oxford, the lines bifurcating at Verney Junction, east of Buckingham. The Banbury line was opened, with much local support, in 1850 and the company planned to extend its route north-west. The Oxford branch was opened into Rewley Road station in time to take excursionists to the Great Exhibition in 1851. Of more consequence in the battle of the gauges was the completion in 1854 of a 1½ mile loop from Oxford Road Junction, south of Kidlington to Yarnton on the OWW, which, with the building of a south curve at Bletchley, enabled narrow-gauge trains from the West Midlands to travel through to London Euston.

The battle subsequently slid into stalemate. The GWR extended broad gauge from Birmingham to Wolverhampton in 1854, giving it a through route to Merseyside. In 1860 the OWW joined two other companies to form the West Midland Railway, which from 1863 amalgamated with the GWR, ending the use of the Yarnton Loop by trains to Euston. Thereafter broad gauge through Oxfordshire was altered to mixed gauge as increasing amounts of traffic reached Wolverhampton and Wolvercote Junction, requiring transhipment for onward carriage to London and southern England. As early as 1858 excursionists from Banbury went all the way to Portsmouth in narrow-gauge carriages. The line from Reading to London Paddington was converted to mixed gauge. The first narrow-gauge train entered the London terminus on 14 August 1861. A second route from Oxford to London, the London, Buckinghamshire & West Midland Junction Railway, eventually took shape as the broad-gauge route opened from Maidenhead to High Wycombe in 1854, to Thame in 1862 and to Kennington Junction, south of Oxford, in 1864. Within six years it was converted to narrow gauge. This phase of railway development in Oxfordshire also saw branch lines extended to some small towns, from the GWR main line to Henley-on-Thames in 1857 and Abingdon in 1856 (not passing through historic Oxfordshire), and from the OWW to Chipping Norton in 1855 and Witney in 1861.

The following decades of railway development in Oxfordshire saw proposals to build a line across the north of the county that could take ironstone to south Wales. Two new lines resulted. The Northampton & Banbury Railway opened in 1872 from Blisworth through Towcester to the Buckinghamshire Railway, on whose metals its trains travelled into Banbury. In 1910 the railway became part of the Stratford-upon-Avon & Midland Junction Railway. The Banbury & Cheltenham Direct Railway was authorised in 1874, and its western section from Kingham opened in 1881. In 1887 the railway was completed by linking the existing Chipping Norton branch from Kingham with the GWR main line at King's Sutton. A loop at Kingham, enabling the Ports-to-Ports Express route from Newcastle and Hull to Cardiff and Barry, was completed in 1906. Otherwise this period saw only extensions to small market towns, from Witney to Fairford in 1871, from Princes Risborough to Watlington in 1872 and from Kidlington to Woodstock in 1890.

Oxfordshire's remaining public railways were part of the final fling of railway building before the First World War. In 1899 the Manchester, Sheffield & Lincoln Railway renamed itself the Great Central Railway and opened its 'London Extension' from Annesley, near Nottingham, to Quainton Road, north of Aylesbury, beyond which it used the Metropolitan Railway's tracks into London but built its own terminus at Marylebone. Its station at Finmere, lay in Oxfordshire. The company also built 8¾ miles of line from Woodford, Northamptonshire, to the GWR at Banbury, creating for over 60 years from 1900 an important link between the north and south of England, particularly for freight. The GWR's route to the north, neglected with the demise of the broad gauge, was revived in the 1890s, when the first British vestibuled corridor train was used on the route, and through coaches to the Welsh coast were introduced. In 1910 the GWR opened its 'Bicester cut-off', which entered Oxfordshire near Blackthorn and passed through Bicester to join the old GWR main line at Aynho. It reduced the distance from Paddington to Banbury from 86 to 67 miles. Oxfordshire's railway system was at its maximum extent at the time of the 1923 legislation to group companies.

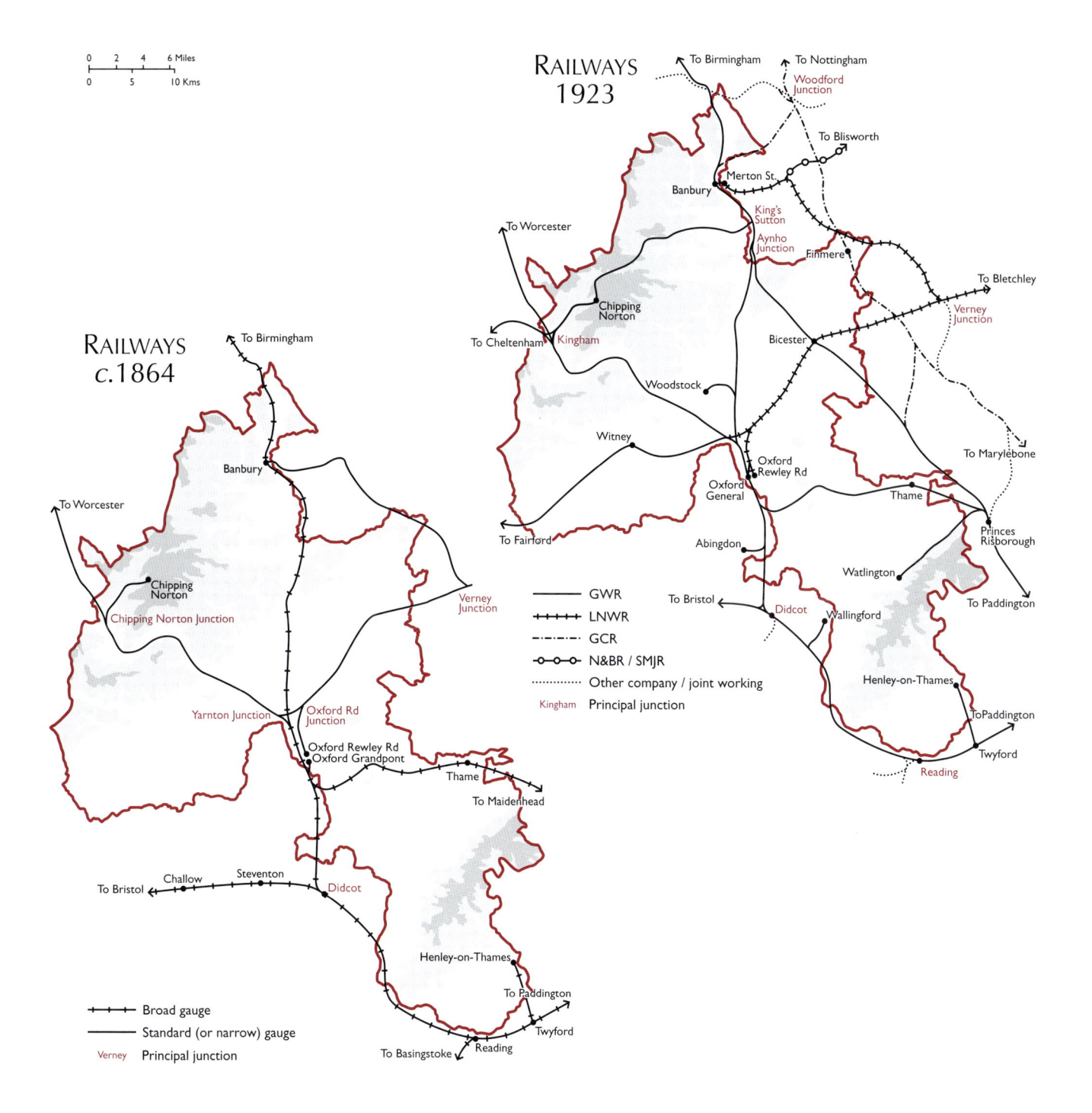

Branch lines in Oxfordshire were rigorously pruned from the early 1950s and the main line of the Great Central Railway with its branch to Banbury was abandoned after the Beeching Report. The county's rail network now consists of the former GWR main line to the north through Oxford and Banbury, a very busy route with commuter traffic to London; an intensive service of cross-country trains between the north and the Midlands and the south coast; and heavy freight traffic, notably trains carrying containers to and from Southampton. The OWW line remains as the 'Cotswold Line' and carries some express trains to and from London from Hereford, Malvern and Worcester. The 'Bicester cut-off' came near to closure in the late 1960s but has been revived by Chiltern Railways. Sections have been restored to double track and several trains an hour link Banbury and Bicester with London and Birmingham. The Henley-on-Thames branch remains open and passenger trains have been restored to the Oxford branch of the Buckinghamshire Railway between Oxford and Bicester.

47 · Agriculture 1750–1970   Kate Tiller

Agriculture in 1750 stood, according to many influential accounts, on the threshold of a revolutionary modernisation. This involved new crops, improved rotations and livestock, mechanisation, and enclosure of ancient openfield systems to create privately owned farms and larger units of ownership, directly controlled for commercial production for burgeoning outside markets. The result was transformed farming practice and landscape, rising outputs and rents, and dislocated social relationships. How far was Oxfordshire part of such a revolution?

Historians have increasingly argued that the agricultural changes so vital nationally to industrial, urban and demographic growth were already underway in the 16th and 17th centuries. During that time predominantly arable areas, organised in common field systems, achieved major internal modernisation, allowing crop specialisation and innovation, improved grasses and leguminous crops, drainage and water meadows, more and better animal fodder, convertible husbandry, changed rotations and improved layouts, engrossment and consolidation of holdings and pre-parliamentary enclosure. Oxfordshire was part of this picture. South Oxfordshire responded to London markets in the 17th century. In north Oxfordshire, Hook Norton provides just one example of flexibility and change. Before 1700 its medieval two-field system was reoriented from east and west to north and south fields, each further divided into quarters, allowing rotations of increasing complexity and variety. In the north of the parish Lodge Farm, a smart new yeoman farmstead, built in 1646, was probably associated with enclosure for sheep farming. Further enclosure for grazing at Cowberry was agreed in 1672 between a local grazier and mercer, a Chipping Norton mercer and a cooper from Battersea, London. North Oxfordshire and the mid-county clay vales feature in Robert Allen's 1992 account of 'a biological revolution in grain growing' brought about by 1700 through the enterprise of yeoman, family farmers in the south midlands.

Contemporary observers of Oxfordshire farming after 1750 struggled to generalise. The government-funded Board of Agriculture (1793–1822) strove to promote modern improvements and reported twice on Oxfordshire (1793 and 1807). William Marshall referred in 1807 to a county 'unnatural, in regards to its lands . . . inconvenient with respect to its outline. . . . Its awkward limbs extend themselves into three natural departments.' Certainly much of Oxfordshire lacked natural boundaries and was not a distinct farming terrain. Running from south-west to north-east, the ironstone uplands and the Cotswold Oolite are features shared with neighbouring counties. Likewise, the clays of central Oxfordshire adjoin the vales of White Horse and Aylesbury. The Oxfordshire Chilterns are part of a much longer divide, the boundary between contrasting, national landscape zones (inset map opposite). Most of Oxfordshire lay in the midland, fielden area, dominated by arable cultivation, large fields, nucleated villages, intensively regulated land use, and early and strongly developed manorial and parish structures. By contrast, the Chilterns marked the start of an 'ancient' landscape, more wooded, with limited arable cleared as small, irregularly shaped fields, and with areas of common and dispersed settlement. These topographical, agricultural and social distinctions within the county remained important throughout the period of modernisation, despite commercialisation and increasing means of overcoming natural constraints, by drainage, new crops or fertilisers.

Arthur Young, secretary to the Board of Agriculture, surveyed Oxfordshire in 1807. He identified four districts, the Redlands in the north, the Cotswolds, a district of 'miscellaneous loams' (he placed surprisingly little emphasis on clays), and the Chilterns. (A more detailed soil classification of Oxfordshire, from the 1930s is mapped opposite.) This was a county of mixed farming, dominated by arable. Young particularly praised the Redlands with their variants on the four-course rotations originated in Norfolk, and typically featuring wheat, barley, oats and turnips with clover and beans. Parliamentary enclosure was well advanced. Oxfordshire was not a grassland county, and common meadow tended to be neglected. Only two major wastes, Otmoor and Wychwood, remained unimproved. Young wrote in a time of high produce prices, with a growing home market of non-producers protected from outside competition by prolonged wartime conditions. After 1815, post-war slump and fluctuating trade conditions slowed the pace of change, investment declined, and distress increased, albeit with some recovery after *c.*1835.

The third quarter of the 19th century, the era of Victorian High Farming, saw an improvement in fortunes, when enthusiasm for the application of science, engineering and modern production methods to farming coincided with relative lack of competition, high demand and capital investment. New, efficiently laid out farm buildings, water supply, drainage, chemical fertilisers, stock improvement, and transport (particularly railway development) all figured. Model Farm at Shirburn, with its decidedly industrial appearance, was built in 1856–7, indicative of this phase. Oxfordshire saw a final spike of parliamentary enclosure. Most dramatic was the final taming of Oxfordshire's only remaining unimproved waste, Wychwood. The disafforestation of the ancient royal forest took place in 1856–8, when 2,843 acres were cleared creating seven new arable farms, with modern farmsteads for stock and determined tenants like J. S. Calvertt, answering (in the words of a contemporary) 'the first supreme command to man, "Replenish the earth and subdue it".' The Crown estate was showing the way. This period proved the high water mark of landed estates. The governmental Return of Owners of Land, 1873, revealed that Oxfordshire was the English county fourth least dominated by great estates (over 10,000 acres). Only Blenheim fell into this category. It was gentry estates (1,000–10,000 acres) which characterised the county. In these terms, Oxfordshire was the third most gentrified of all English counties.[1]

The prosperous confidence of High Farming did not survive the mid 1870s, which saw the beginning of a deep

Soil Classification

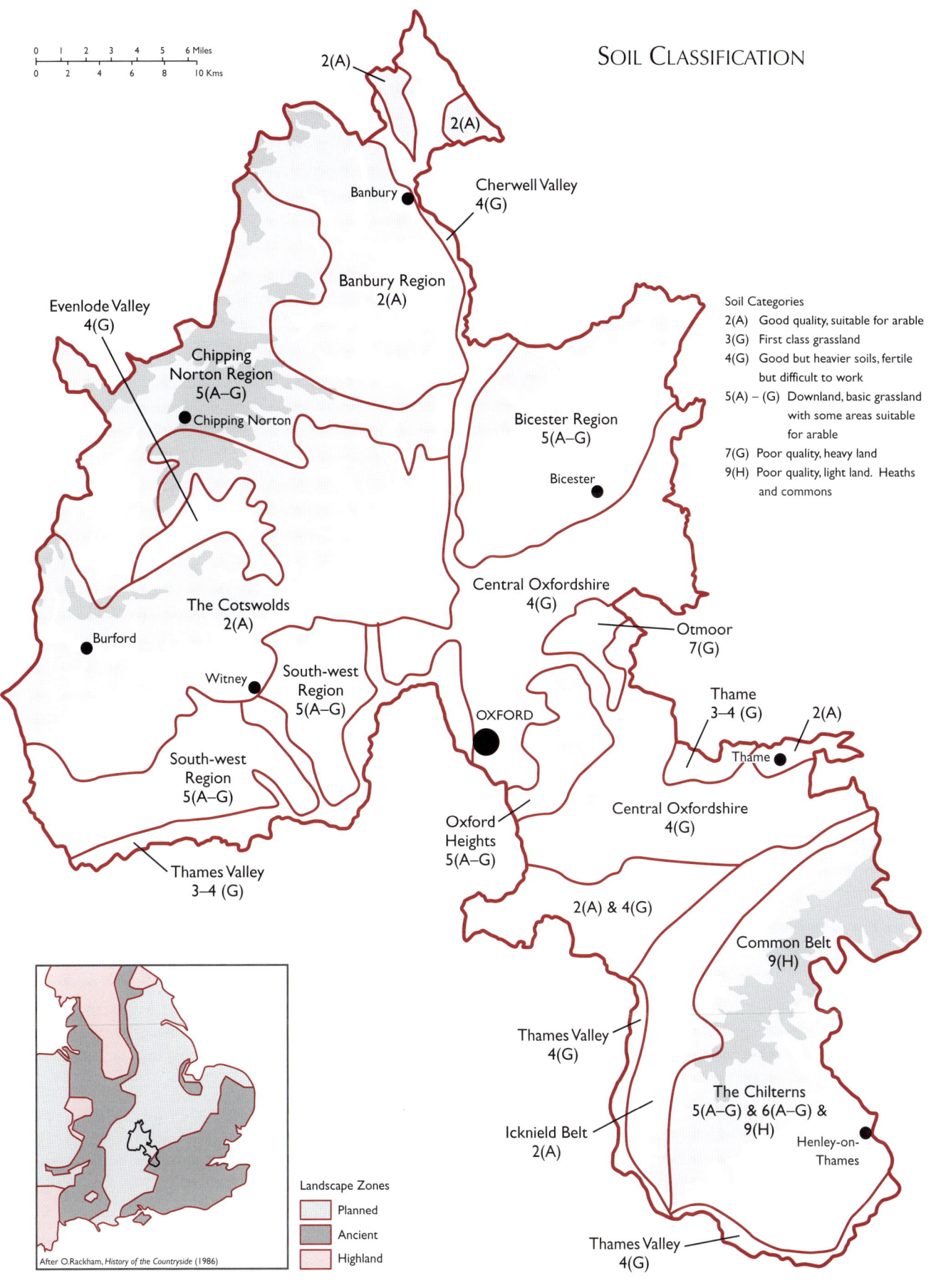

Soil Categories
- 2(A) Good quality, suitable for arable
- 3(G) First class grassland
- 4(G) Good but heavier soils, fertile but difficult to work
- 5(A) – (G) Downland, basic grassland with some areas suitable for arable
- 7(G) Poor quality, heavy land
- 9(H) Poor quality, light land. Heaths and commons

Regions labelled on map:
- Cherwell Valley 4(G)
- Banbury Region 2(A)
- Evenlode Valley 4(G)
- Chipping Norton Region 5(A–G)
- Bicester Region 5(A–G)
- The Cotswolds 2(A)
- Central Oxfordshire 4(G)
- Otmoor 7(G)
- South-west Region 5(A–G)
- Thame 3–4(G), 2(A)
- South-west Region 5(A–G)
- Central Oxfordshire 4(G)
- Thames Valley 3–4(G)
- Oxford Heights 5(A–G)
- 2(A) & 4(G)
- Common Belt 9(H)
- Thames Valley 4(G)
- Icknield Belt 2(A)
- The Chilterns 5(A–G) & 6(A–G) & 9(H)
- Thames Valley 4(G)

Landscape Zones
- Planned
- Ancient
- Highland

After O. Rackham, *History of the Countryside* (1986)

111

47 · Agriculture 1750–1970 *(continued)*

and prolonged agricultural depression which was to last until 1939 (alleviated only by war-related upturns). It began with the collapse of prices for home-produced grain. In the 1870s free trade came home to roost, as agriculture in other countries began to export large volumes of grain, and later meat, and affordable, quick and reliable means of transport and subsequently refrigeration enabled supply of the British market. Oxfordshire, with its emphasis on arable farming and lack of other large-scale employments, was particularly vulnerable. In 1871 in Oxfordshire 23,220 males were employed in agriculture. By 1911 there were 15,128. Wages were low and the farming workforce was ageing. Rider Haggard was told in 1901 by the schoolmaster at Great Rollright that 'three-quarters of the young men and all the young women left the village at nineteen or twenty years of age, only the dullest staying at home.' Landlords reluctantly reduced rents, even on the recently created Wychwoods farms. Capital investment and maintenance slowed or ceased. Tenants were difficult to get or keep. There was a major shift to pasture, a fall in sheep numbers and an increase in cattle. Oxfordshire, against all historical trends, was 'greening'. This was partly enforced. Grass needed less labour and often received less management. However, the change also reflected new opportunities. The railways opened up markets for milk in London, Oxford, Reading and the Midlands. Dairying became increasingly important to Oxfordshire agriculture. Rider Haggard heard in the Cherwell valley that 'the railroad [was] nicknamed the Milky Way', and that as 'the old yeoman class had gone under' so outsiders to Oxfordshire were taking on farms.

The First World War brought unprecedented government intervention to ensure national food supplies. Price and wage control, increase in arable (Oxfordshire arable increased by over 15,000 acres in 1914–19), technical improvements, mechanisation and good husbandry (e.g. hedging and ditching neglected during the depression) were all enforced. Wartime arrangements of county and district agriculture committees, wage boards and minimum cereal prices were maintained until 1924. Tough times followed. The post-war years saw sales of land estimated at 168,000 acres between 1918 and 1939. Numbers of owner-occupiers increased, but agricultural labouring jobs continued to decline. One Oxfordshire farmer, George Henderson, took on 85 acres at Enstone in 1924 and claimed (in his best selling *The Farming Ladder* (1944)) that success could be achieved with family labour, hard work, limited capital, and diversification into specialist markets (poultry, eggs, pullets, milk, pigs). However, surveys of Oxfordshire agriculture in the 1930s make more depressing reading. Farming was run down and struggling. The county had reached the turning point when farming no longer determined its fortunes. Increasing numbers of people had rural homes but worked elsewhere. Parts of Oxfordshire were becoming 'rurban' and losing cultivated land for urban and industrial development, especially round Oxford. Beyond that, Oxfordshire was now a grassland county; in 1939, of its cultivated land, 34% was arable, 63% permanent pasture and 3% rough grazing.

This is the picture found by the Land Utilisation Survey in the late 1930s (see map opposite). Dairying was the largest source of income for Oxfordshire farmers. Crop yields were below national averages, cultivation lacked variety, there were labour shortages and 'a fair proportion of bad farmers'. This verdict was borne out by the wartime National Farm Survey of all farms over five acres (insets opposite). Quality of management was graded A, B or C. Category C farmers could be ordered to change crops or even be compulsorily replaced by a tenant. Oxfordshire's farms fell below national averages and there were marked differences within the county. Bullingdon district, including the Icknield belt and Thame area, had the highest incidence of A-rated farms; Witney district, with the SW dairying area, had high A and low C ratings; Ploughley, including the Bicester region, with Oxfordshire's largest farms amalgamated because of depression, had the fewest top-rated farms and by far the most C-category reports.

Once more war galvanised agriculture, organised through the County War Executive Committee and six District Committees with extensive powers of direction. A return to arable was again vital. Amidst this emergency action, planning was already underway for post-war agriculture, and Oxfordshire played a vital part in this, particularly through the work of C. S. Orwin. His 1944 survey *Country Planning*, and the subsequent film *24 Square Miles*, used the area between Banbury and Chipping Norton to analyse the problems of pre-war agriculture and the relatively deprived lives of country dwellers, going on to propose a future where improved agriculture, new small-scale industry and planned housing, educational, health and welfare facilities would be brought to the countryside. Mains gas, electricity and water, metalled roads, bus services and active citizenship would be enjoyed by all. Such thinking underpinned the post-war settlement, the 1947 Agriculture Act and farming's development as a state-led industry.

The period up to Britain's entry to the European Economic Community in 1973 saw overall agricultural prosperity in a context of continuing government involvement. Although direct government purchase of produce ended after 1953, annual price reviews, subsidies, funding for buildings, drainage and fertilisers, and research and scientific advice continued. This, and an emphasis on increased productivity, were reflected in Oxfordshire in larger farms and mechanisation. Less labour was needed and 'efficiencies' like hedgerow removal changed the working landscape, outside planning-protected areas. In 1951 in Oxfordshire, 6,116 males were in regular agricultural employment; by 1971 there were 2,608. In 1951, of cultivated land in the county 59% was arable, 39% permanent grass, and 2% rough grazing. By 1971 the proportions were 68% arable, 31% grass, and 1% rough grazing. Oxfordshire was again an arable county, but farming and its role in the county were very different.

LAND-USE REGIONS

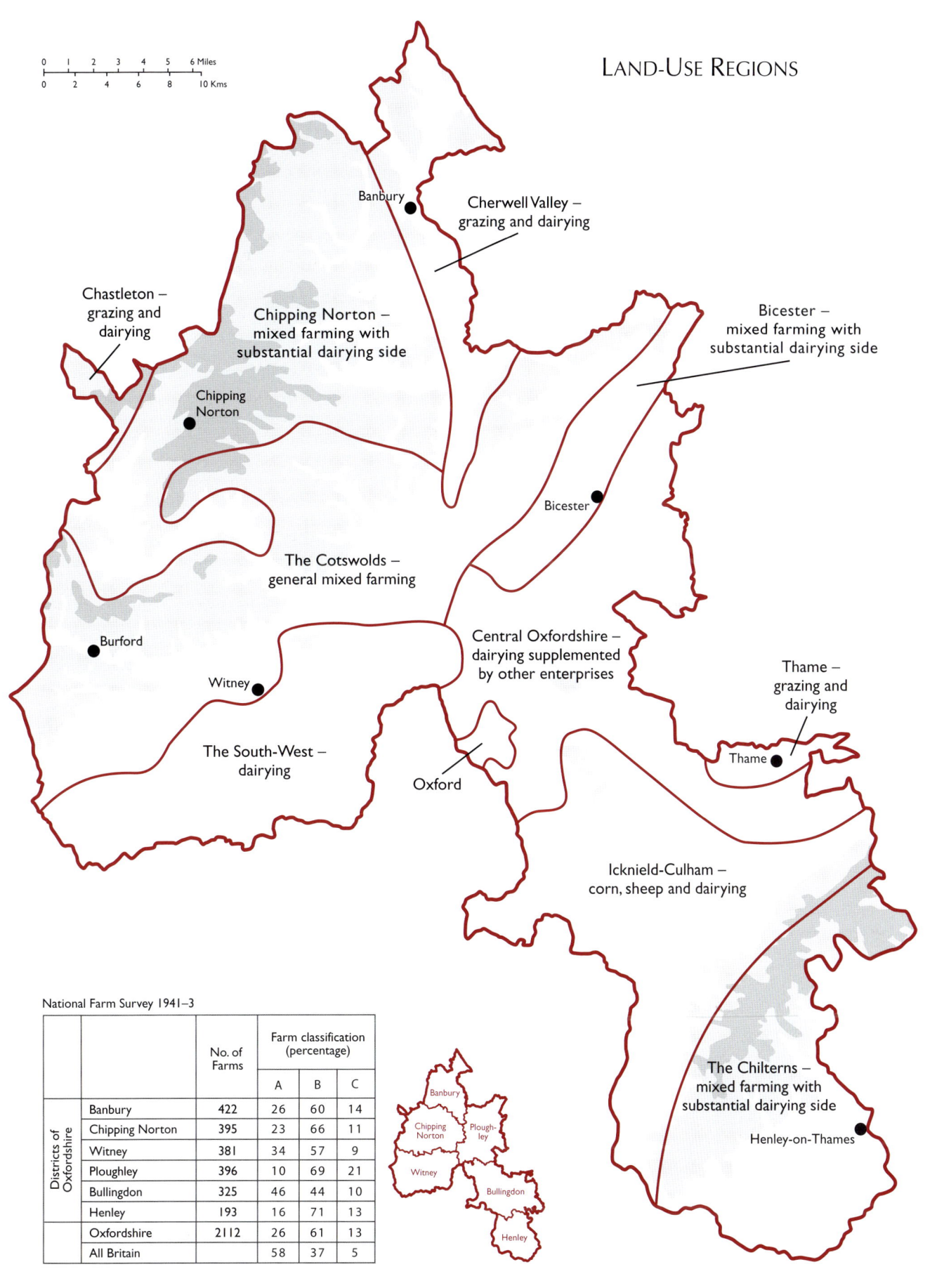

Cherwell Valley – grazing and dairying

Chastleton – grazing and dairying

Chipping Norton – mixed farming with substantial dairying side

Bicester – mixed farming with substantial dairying side

The Cotswolds – general mixed farming

Central Oxfordshire – dairying supplemented by other enterprises

Thame – grazing and dairying

The South-West – dairying

Icknield-Culham – corn, sheep and dairying

The Chilterns – mixed farming with substantial dairying side

National Farm Survey 1941–3

		No. of Farms	Farm classification (percentage)		
			A	B	C
Districts of Oxfordshire	Banbury	422	26	60	14
	Chipping Norton	395	23	66	11
	Witney	381	34	57	9
	Ploughley	396	10	69	21
	Bullingdon	325	46	44	10
	Henley	193	16	71	13
	Oxfordshire	2112	26	61	13
	All Britain		58	37	5

48 · Parliamentary Enclosure 1758–1882
Keith Parry

Enclosure changed agricultural practice; many small strips held in shared open fields were consolidated into larger, fenced areas held by individuals in severalty. The rights of commoners to use open fields and manorial wastes for pasture and other purposes were removed. Parliamentary enclosure started as a Bill supported by more than two-thirds of the local land ownership by value, often measured by area or land tax. If successful, the Bill became an Act. Appointed independent commissioners elaborated the Act at local level into an Award, allotted new land to owners, laid out new roads, allocated responsibility for fencing the new fields and produced surveyed maps. Old enclosures, land exchanges and commutation of tithes could be included. The General Enclosure Act of 1836 reduced direct involvement of Parliament.

Oxfordshire is one of the counties most heavily affected by parliamentary enclosure. Approximately half the county was enclosed, though a third of Oxfordshire parishes had no parliamentary enclosure (see map, bottom right). For Oxfordshire 190 Acts were passed between 1758 and 1882, leading to 184 Awards. Of these, 137 were made under a Private Act, and 53 under the General Enclosure Acts. Over 50 of the awards included more than one parish and 20 parishes were the main subject in more than one Award. The most complex Enclosure Acts in Oxfordshire were for the waste of Otmoor and the disafforestation of Wychwood.

Little is known about the initial discussions at parish level before preparing a Bill, though some of the larger landowners, e.g. the Duke of Marlborough and the Earl of Macclesfield, bought out smaller freeholds and/or common rights to waste before initiating a Bill. In most Oxfordshire enclosures conversion of the Bill to an Award took two to four years. Delays between the Bill and the Act could occur in Parliament as a result of administrative mistakes or strong local opposition, e.g. Otmoor. In a small number of parishes, the delays were considerable, up to 60 years.

The bar chart (below) shows the number of Awards made every five years for Oxfordshire from 1750 to 1874 and the table (below right) analyses the numbers of Awards and the area affected by time periods.

The geographical distribution of enclosures by phase is mapped opposite. Phase One, 1758–1784, was concentrated in the rich Redlands in the north and the limestone Cotswold landscape to the west. Phase Two, 1785–1835 shows a shift in focus from the north and west to the central lowlands and the valleys of the rivers Ray and Thame. In Phase Three, 1836–1882, areas in the south-east on the chalk uplands of the Chilterns were affected, using mainly the General Enclosure Acts. Many small residual areas around Wychwood were also enclosed.

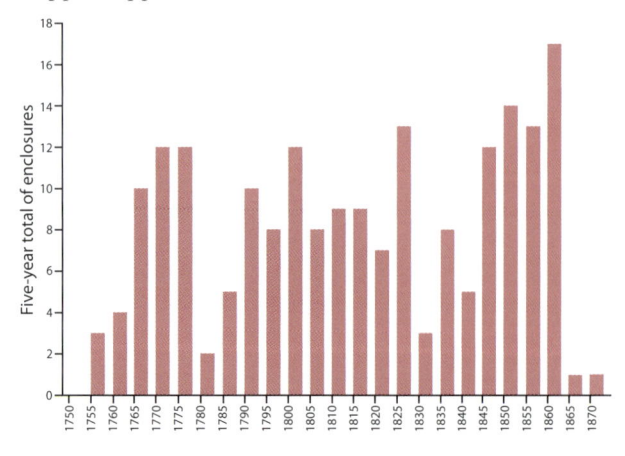

There is no single factor which determined the date of an Award; every parish was different. However, some broad explanations of the Oxfordshire chronology have been proposed. One of the earliest studies argues that the north and west of the county had recently moved from a two- to a four-field system to improve agricultural returns and landowners were more likely to use enclosure for a further gain than in the south and east, which had adhered more firmly to existing three-field systems. Others suggest that parliamentary enclosure started in the midland counties, particularly Northamptonshire, and diffused outwards, reaching north and west Oxfordshire earliest. More recent studies see the main cause as economic. Commercialisation of agriculture emphasised improving the returns from land to feed the growing population, particularly of London. Enclosure enabled owners to raise rents significantly, up to double, and to improve productivity to obtain returns that were more than enough to offset the investment required to enclose. Owners with the richest soils in the north had more scope to increase land productivity and rents, usually by increasing pasture, and were therefore in the vanguard to enclose. Later, as corn prices reached high levels during the Napoleonic Wars, more marginal lands in the Oxford vales were enclosed for arable farming. The areas of poorest soils and where woodland management was a key part of the local economy as in the Chilterns were the last to change.

There has been much debate about the social consequences of enclosure – particularly with respect to poverty leading to emigration and impoverishment. Studies of Oxfordshire show little evidence for increasing depopulation in country parishes after enclosure. In some areas there were increasing Poor Law payments, maybe more as a result of the general economic situation than enclosure specifically.

An undoubted consequence of enclosure was landscape change. Landowners consolidated scattered holdings and built farmhouses in the centre of these new areas. Open fields were replaced by large, mainly rectilinear fields bounded by hedges and ditches. New footpaths and straight roads with wide verges were constructed.

Phase	Date of Award	Number of Awards	Number of Awards p.a.	Acres enclosed*
1	1758–1784	51	1.9	76,884 (16%)
2	1785–1835	78	1.5	111,329 (23%)
3	1836–1882	61	1.3	53,633 (11%)
Total		190		241,846 (50%)

* For phase 1 the area is understated, as some early Awards did not cite area size.

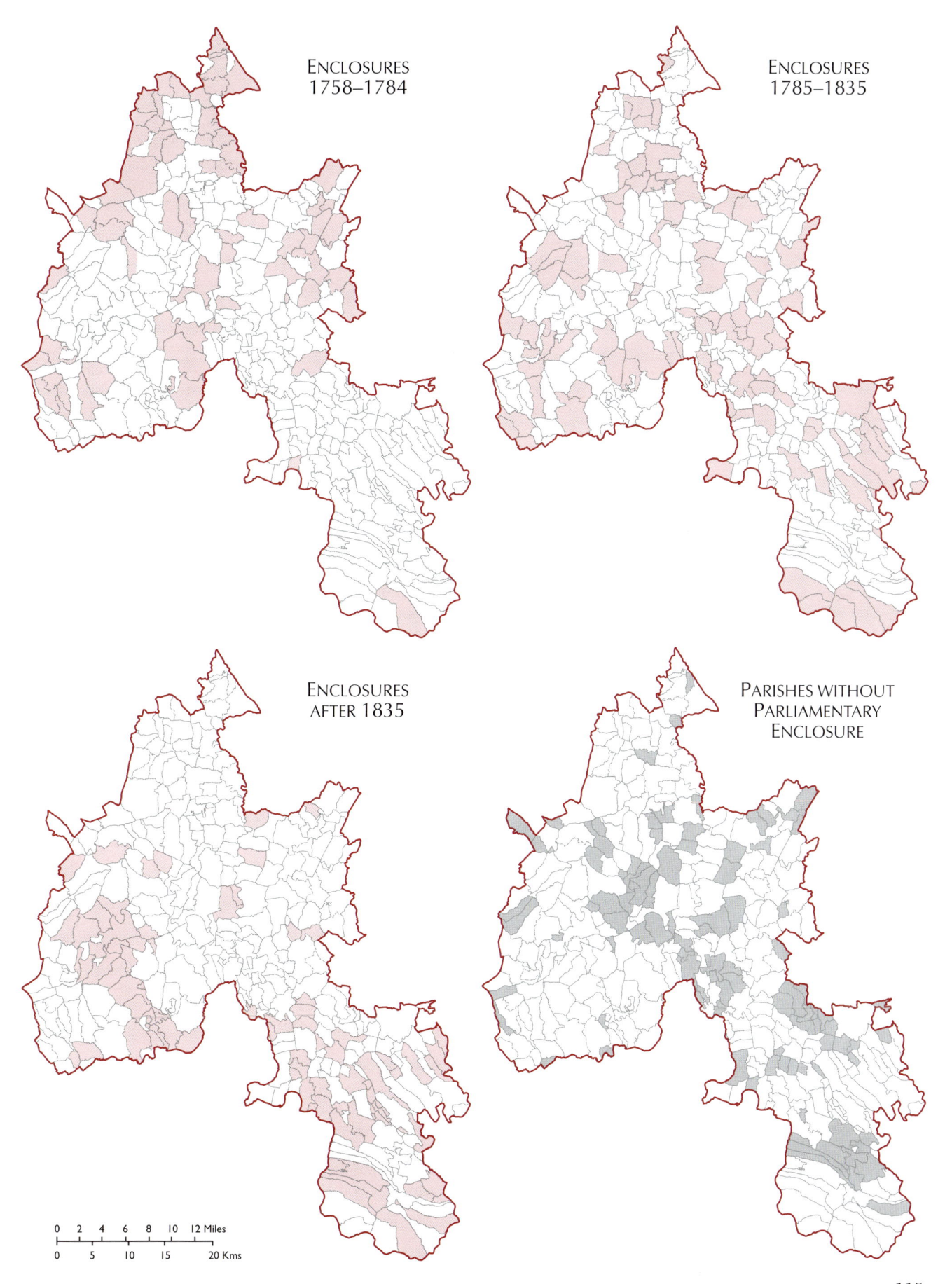

ENCLOSURES
1758–1784

ENCLOSURES
1785–1835

ENCLOSURES
AFTER 1835

PARISHES WITHOUT
PARLIAMENTARY
ENCLOSURE

0 2 4 6 8 10 12 Miles
0 5 10 15 20 Kms

115

49 · Labouring Lives

Kate Tiller

From the mid 18th century the population of Oxfordshire began to rise. Parish registers and (from 1801) national censuses reveal a rapid natural increase, with baptisms outstripping burials. Despite some out-migration the numbers of people in rural as well as urban parishes increased, especially up to the 1830s. The consequences were far-reaching, mirrored in rising local expenditure on poor relief, the responsibility until 1834 of each parish or township, through its ratepayers, elected vestry, and overseers of the poor. Where there had generally been some equilibrium between wages, prices and population numbers, with poverty experienced chiefly at vulnerable times of the life cycle, by widows, orphans, the old and chronically ill, or in occasional emergencies of dearth, epidemic, flood or fire, now significant proportions of the adult, able-bodied were falling into need. Oxfordshire communities struggled under the pressure of more people, changes in agriculture, and limited alternative or additional jobs.

The experience of Bampton between 1780 and 1834 vividly illustrates this phase of Oxfordshire life. It was a large village, and growing (population 1,003 in 1801, and 1,605 by 1831). In the 1790s and 1800s poor rates and expenditure boomed. As David Eastwood has put it, Bampton found itself at 'the sharp end of social policy' and responded by creating 'a republic in the village'. A select vestry structure was adopted, focusing power with the principal ratepayers. Sophisticated schemes were developed locally, for wage subsidies, work creation, rating revaluation, sliding scales of relief related to bread prices, family size and employment record, and (as in 28 other Oxfordshire parishes by 1815) a parish workhouse was set up. The running of this was contracted out, the beginnings of salaried officials. Other Oxfordshire parishes had schemes for apprenticeships, assisted emigration and allotments. The tensions between controlling local taxation and expenditure, responding morally to genuine need, and guarding against glaring inequality at a time when unrest was feared, are widely apparent in the county.

Structural unemployment was an underlying reality of these times. Evidence collected by an 1831 Parliamentary commission on the poor laws spells out the situation at Kidlington. There were 150 men and boys in agricultural labour; 80 could be found work by local farmers; 30 were put to public works on roads and in gravel pits; 40 (27%) were on parish relief. Things were worse in winter. This was a classic case of labour surplus. The map shows the position in Oxfordshire by 1851. Based on research by John R. Walton, it plots the difference for each township or parish between the number of male agricultural labourers resident and the number of men and boys employed on local farms, as returned in the decennial census. Although not all farmers returned numbers, and women and children doing farming work are missing, the results are revealing.

Labour surplus was more widespread in Oxfordshire, but a smaller number of places show labour deficits, with fewer agricultural labourers resident than were employed on local farms. Places with labour surplus and deficit are intermingled, and this is likely to relate to a pattern of village types observed in the 19th century, and analysed by modern historians, that is, open and closed villages. As another Parliamentary investigator observed, on a visit to Oxfordshire in 1868–9, 'Deddington with its hamlets is an open parish into which labourers have been driven from surrounding close parishes.' Closed parishes, often estate dominated, were identifiable by relatively small populations, concentrated landownership, controlled development, large farms, low poor rates, limited but high-standard tied housing, few crafts, trades, shops or pubs, and strong Anglicanism. By contrast, open parishes had larger populations, rapid growth to 1851, diverse ownership, more and smaller farms, high poor rates, more small industries and crafts, plentiful but poorer-quality rented housing, more shops and pubs, more religious Nonconformity and less social deference. These village types did not develop in isolation, but related to each other, as the map suggests. A large labour surplus can be seen at Deddington, with a number of deficit parishes just to the south. Hook Norton, a classic open village, shows a labour surplus. Closed or estate villages with a labour deficit would need villages or towns in surplus and near enough for labourers to walk to work on their farms; the adjoining surplus and deficit symbols for Kingston Blount and Aston Rowant suggest such a symbiotic relationship. Some of the largest labour surpluses adjoin the Blenheim estate. (Unfortunately numbers of those employed were not returned for the Blenheim estate villages where complementary labour deficits would be anticipated.)

The fortunes of Oxfordshire agricultural labouring families remained uncertain. In 1907 the average weekly wage was the lowest in England and Wales, at 14s 11d. When the social investigator B. Seebohm Rowntree turned from his famous studies of urban poverty to consider the lives of rural families, he estimated that for a family of two adults and three children to survive the weekly minimum income needed was 20s 6d. The diet involved would sustain the breadwinner for physical work but be 'more austere than that provided in any workhouse in England or Wales', with no butcher's meat, a little bacon, scarcely any tea, and no butter or eggs. Food took up 67% of the 20s 6d, the rest providing fuel, rent, clothing (5d a week for each child), insurance and sundries. Tobacco, beer, newspapers, amusements and holidays were amongst the many things that did not figure. Compulsory schooling and a decline in married women's work meant the possibilities for additional household earnings were more limited than historically. Garden and allotment produce and charitable and neighbourly gifts could help. However, Rowntree and Kendall's study, *How the Labourer Lives Now* (1913), includes numbers of detailed household budgets from Oxfordshire which show that many families in the county lived in a state of chronic poverty at the start of the 20th century.

LABOUR SURPLUS AND
LABOUR DEFICIT IN 1851

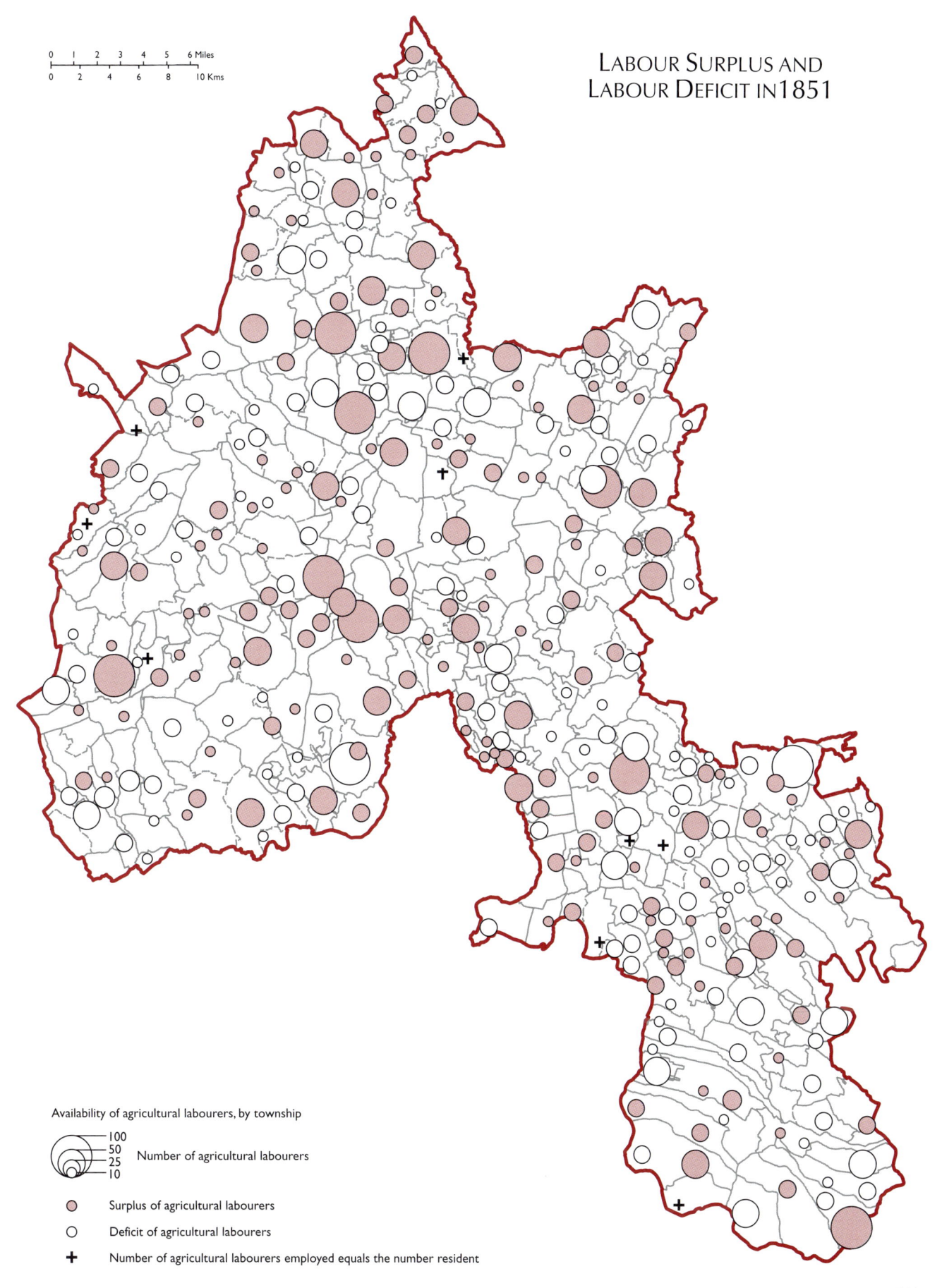

Availability of agricultural labourers, by township

- 100
- 50
- 25
- 10

Number of agricultural labourers

● Surplus of agricultural labourers

○ Deficit of agricultural labourers

✛ Number of agricultural labourers employed equals the number resident

117

50 · Industrial Oxfordshire: the mid 19th Century — Barrie Trinder

Oxfordshire was not regarded in the 19th century as one of the 'manufacturing counties'. It lacked coal mines and blast furnaces and had only a few multi-storey textile mills. Industry was nevertheless a significant factor in the county's economy. It can be examined at three levels, long-established industries, manufactures related to 19th-century industrialisation (both covered here) and proto-industries (see entry 51).

Long-established industries included tanneries and maltings in market towns, while in towns and countryside centuries-old watermills provided power for grinding grain, with some adapted for textile manufacturing and paper-making. Rural quarries yielded various sorts of stone. Tanning continued in the 1850s and 60s in most towns. Typical in 1861 were Thomas Hunter in Henley, employing ten, and Stephen Johnson in Thame with three workers. Some leather-processing concerns developed specialisms. The Hulberts employed over 20 people making parchment in Caversham in 1861, and 16 in 1871. There were maltings in every town, although by the late 19th century an increasing proportion were incorporated in breweries. Rope and sack makers also traded in almost every town.

Most Oxfordshire paper-mills originated in the second half of the 17th century and were still working in the mid 19th, although only two or three remained in 1900. Hazelford Mill, Broughton, was converted from fulling to making paper in the late 18th century but closed in the 1850s. The nearby mill at North Newington was producing paper by the 1680s and employed 20 people in 1861, but was subsequently adapted to make superphosphates. Deddington Mill was adapted for paper production in 1684, employed only two or three people in the 1850s and by 1870 had been readapted as a corn mill. Eynsham Mill was also established in the 1680s and by the 1720s was producing high-quality paper for Bibles. Under the management of Thomas Routledge, a pioneer in the use of esparto grass for paper production, it employed 63 people in 1861. The nearby mill at Wolvercote made white paper for books as early as the 1680s. It was steam operated from 1811, soon after the opening of the Oxford Canal. Although out of use for a spell in the 1850s, following a bankruptcy, by 1881 it employed nearly a hundred people. Sandford Mill was adapted to make paper in 1826, was purchased by Oxford University Press in 1880 and remained in operation until 1980. There were also mills at Hampton Gay, Rotherfield Peppard and Shiplake.

The historic Taynton quarries, from which stone was extracted for Blenheim Palace and for Oxford colleges, were not being intensively worked in the 1850s. There was rather more activity at Wheatley and Headington. Quarries occupied about 20 men at Hornton, and there were further workings just over the county boundary in Radway. In 1871 two merchants were dealing in the 'slates' mined by less than a dozen men in Stonesfield. Two new kinds of quarrying were to have a profound influence in the county in the 20th century. Limestone was extracted for cement production around Bletchingdon, as it was at Chinnor after 1900. Ironstone quarries at Fawler employed ten men in 1861, and at Adderbury in 1881 there were seven 'ironstone miners', as well as a clerk recording their production, but the scale of the industry was small and in 1891 there were only 19 ironstone miners in the whole county, compared with over 1,000 in Northamptonshire.

Other Oxfordshire industries in the 19th century reflected the revolution in mining and manufacturing further north. Commercial breweries were established, chiefly in towns, using steam engines for pumping, copper sheeting in mash tuns and vats, and specific grades of coal for malting (see entry 52). Foundries making agricultural implements brought in pig iron and wrought iron, and shaped castings and forgings on machine tools made in Manchester and London. They flourished in almost every town. Works active in the 1850s and 60s included: Samuelson's, Lampitts and Barrows & Stewart in Banbury; Grafton & Ward and W. Hood in Oxford; J. Tomlinson in Watlington; Charles Haslam in Henley; George Roberts in Bicester; J. Dean in Woodstock; and Thomas Troy in Caversham. Coach makers cut and beat metal from elsewhere and incorporated into their products springs, couplings and locks made in the Black Country. They flourished in every town in the county.

Metal workers, other than blacksmiths catering for local needs, also appeared in Oxfordshire. The largest concern was the works of the brothers Benjamin, Joseph and Samuel Mason. Established in Deddington in 1820, it made wrought-iron axles, and continued until the early 1890s. The Masons employed 40 people in 1861. A colony of nail makers flourished in Great Bourton, numbering 14 in 1861, several of them natives of Bromsgrove, although the principal entrepreneur, employing six people, was a local man, John Hales. There were also rural foundries. John Dimmock employed four men making castings at Pyrton, while John Stevens had a foundry worked principally by his sons, at Britwell Salome.

Coal delivered by water made it possible to make bricks in every part of Oxfordshire. The workings of brick makers occupied the fringes of most towns, as at Headington in Oxford, and on the Broughton and Middleton Roads in Banbury. Joseph Castle on the Cowley Road in Oxford employed 153 men in building, farming and brick making in 1861. In the countryside in that year nine people made drainpipes, tiles and bricks for Richard Breakspear in Long Hanborough, and brick making on Beggar's Bush Hill at Benson was on a sufficient scale to employ not just brick burners but also a bookkeeper. William Pollinger of Bishopland Farm, Dunsden, combined brick making with farming, employing 29 people. A widow, Catherine Aldridge, and her son Andrew made red-ware pots at Fortnam's Yard, Barford St Michael, as did George Hooper of Stoke Row Farm, Ipsden, who employed eight men making red ware and six brick makers. James Thompson of Nettlebed employed 75 in his farm, sawmill and pottery, where a decade later Benjamin Thompson employed 48 people in the manufacture of stoneware, pipes and bricks.

INDUSTRIAL OXFORDSHIRE IN THE 1850s AND 1860s

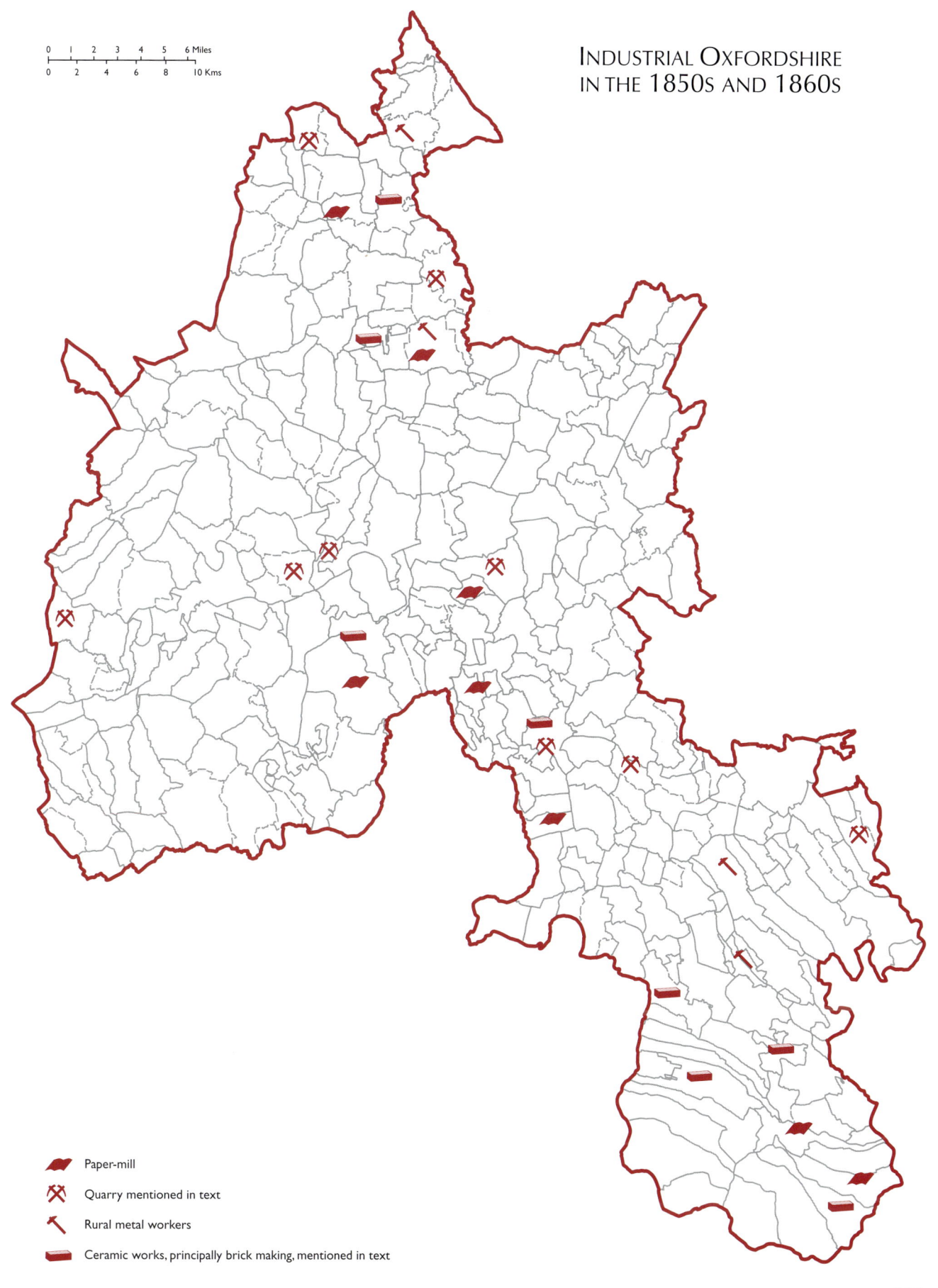

- Paper-mill
- Quarry mentioned in text
- Rural metal workers
- Ceramic works, principally brick making, mentioned in text

51 · Proto-Industries of 19th-Century Oxfordshire — Barrie Trinder

Proto-industries constituted the most significant level of industry in 19th-century Oxfordshire. The county was notable for the extent of such manufactures, in which materials were distributed by factors based in towns to craftspeople in the countryside, who returned to them completed or semi-finished products for marketing. The making of woollen textiles, slop clothing, gloves, lace and chairs employed several thousand people in the mid 19th century, many of them women.

Woollen fabric making remained proto-industrial in the early 19th century, but the concerns that prospered adopted the factory system. Textile manufacturers in the Banbury area specialised in the production of plush by the 1790s. In the 1830s plush-making remained a rural and domestic industry, with 35 weavers at Shutford, 34 at Bloxham, 34 at Adderbury and 105 in Banbury itself. A factory system developed gradually. The trade suffered recession in the 1840s, and by 1851 was more concentrated in Banbury, where there were 123 weavers and 16 ancillary workers. Baughans employed a steam engine for spinning but there were no power looms in the town. Subsequently the trade contracted. By 1871 there were only 52 weavers in Banbury, employed at the factories of William Cubitt and James Hill. Smaller factories grew up in villages where there had been concentrations of handloom weavers. William Wrench employed 23 at Shutford in 1861 and 28 in 1871, while James Gascoigne employed nine weavers at Bloxham in 1861 and seven in 1873. A few weavers worked in their homes at Adderbury, the Barfords, Milton, the Sibfords and Wroxton.

There were four textile manufacturers in Chipping Norton in the 1790s, all of them taking in cloth from domestic weavers. By 1851 the descendants of one of them, Thomas Bliss, had built a mill for making woollen cloth, managed by a Yorkshireman. It was replaced in 1872 by one of Oxfordshire's most spectacular industrial buildings. By 1891 William Bliss was employing 581 people, most working in the factory and living in Chipping Norton. They included many migrants from other textile regions, tweed warpers from Galashiels, cloth dressers from Stroud, scourers (i.e. those who washed wool to remove grease) from Trowbridge and cloth finishers from Dedham, Essex.

Witney blanket manufacture also moved from proto-industrial to factory-based organisation by the 1850s. In the 1790s much of the yarn used in weaving blankets was spun over a wide area, extending from south of the Thames and into Gloucestershire. The trade flourished with the introduction of mechanised spinning and carding, spring looms and, from the 1850s, power looms. Production was concentrated in Witney itself, where manufacturers continued to build new mills into the 20th century. In the 1860s the industry employed over 600 people, scarcely any living beyond the boundaries of the extended parish of Witney. Worsham Mill in Astall parish, used for woollen-cloth manufacture in the 1860s, was taken over by a Witney blanket manufacturer in the 1890s and remained in use until the mid 20th century.

John Hyde's company, established in Abingdon in the 1840s, pioneered large-scale manufacture of clothing. In 1851 Hyde was supposedly employing 1400 people making garments. Outworkers were spread over surrounding parishes, principally in Berkshire, but in the 1860s there were more than 30 slop (i.e. cheap, ready-made) tailoresses in Clifton Hampden, 27 in Culham, 20 in Dorchester, a considerable number in Eynsham, and some in Warborough and Benson. Isolated shirt makers as far away as Thame and Fritwell, as well as some of the many dressmakers at Drayton St Leonard and women 'engaged in needlework' in Chiselhampton and the Baldons, may also have worked for Hyde's. (Tracing the extent of slop tailoring is made difficult by the inconsistency of terms used by census enumerators. Vest makers, trouser makers or slop tailoresses are easily identifiable.)

Woodstock was celebrated for leather glove making before 1700. The trade employed over 40 men in 1768, and numbers expanded during the Napoleonic Wars. By 1839 about 150 men and around 1,000 women were employed, almost all in their own homes. In the 1860s glove making extended from the Thames at Eynsham, with 33 glovers in 1861, through Handborough (190), North Leigh (53), Combe (81) and Bladon (31), to the centre of the trade at Woodstock. There were 133 glove-makers in Woodstock itself in 1871, and 88 in Old Woodstock. There were six glove manufacturers, five of whom employed respectively nine, 20, 30, 32 and 42 workers. (The 1861 census returns for Woodstock are lost.) Related specialisms included glove cutters, sewing machinists and tyers for sewing-machines, indicating the extent to which the industry had been organised. Glove making was also extensive in the parishes to the north and east, with 110 glovers in Steeple Barton and Westcott Barton in 1861, 115 in Stonesfield and 88 in Wootton in 1871. Glove making was almost as important in Witney and its townships. In 1861 there were 82 glovers in Cogges, 63 in Hailey, 28 in Witney itself and 16 in Minster Lovell, with a few in Crawley, Curbridge and Ducklington. William Prichett of Newland, Witney, employed over than 500 people. In 1861 there were 128 people involved in gloving in Charlbury, including 'grounders', men who prepared leather for glove makers. Many more glovers lived in nearby villages: 140 in Finstock and Fawler, 116 in Leafield, 25 in Shipton-under-Wychwood and 17 in Ascott-under-Wychwood, 11 in Chadlington and 11 in Chilson and Shorthampton. Chipping Norton was a smaller hub of the trade; one firm in 1861 employed 15 people and glovers were fairly sparsely scattered in parishes near the Gloucestershire border.

Chair making in the Chilterns centred on High Wycombe, but extended into Oxfordshire. Chairs were assembled in urban workshops from components shaped by 'bodgers' working in the woodlands. The median factory labour force was around 30. However, John Phipps of the Bull, Nettlebed, employed 57 people in 1861, including a sawyer, three chair makers, a chair framer and a 'stainer and grainer of chairs', who all lodged with him. None of the other 'factories' in

Proto-Industrial Manufacturing

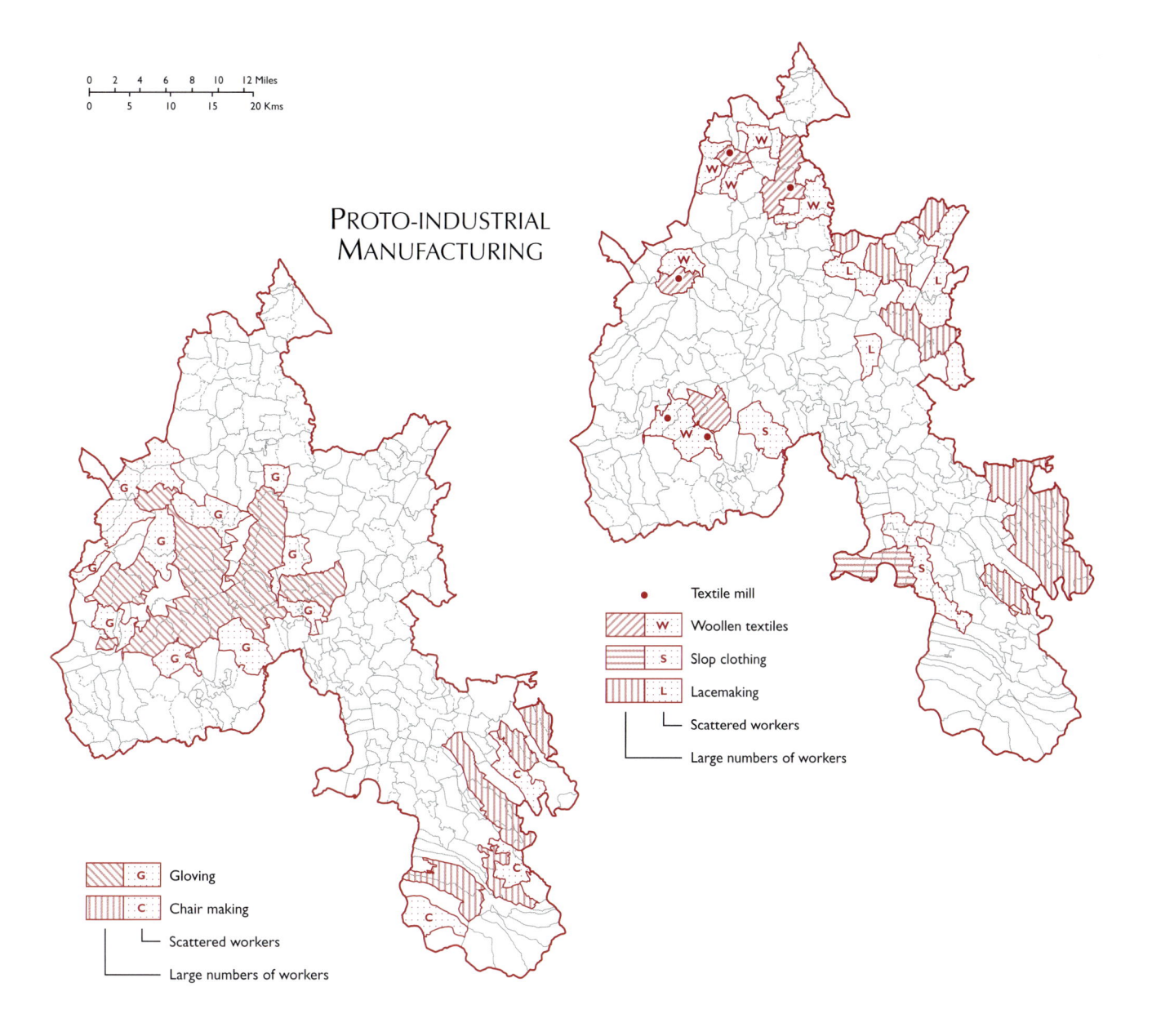

Watlington or Nettlebed appears to have employed more than seven people, but many chair turners made components, 57 in Chinnor, more than a dozen each in Pyrton, Lewknor, Rotherfield Greys and Aston Rowant, and appreciable numbers in Goring, Ipsden, Watlington and Caversham. Many more 'hewers of wood' and 'woodmen' were probably concerned with the furniture trade, creating jobs for 300–400 men.

In the 19th century pillow lace was manufactured across a large area of Buckinghamshire, Bedfordshire and Northamptonshire, and on the eastern fringes of Oxfordshire. Factors distributed work to, and collected finished products from, women working mostly at home. Oxfordshire lacemaking was concentrated around Thame and Bicester, separated by the salient of Buckinghamshire around Brill Hill, also the home of many lacemakers. The principal lacemaking parishes in the south in 1861 were Chinnor (249 lacemakers), Aston Rowant (185), Sydenham and Emmington (100), Thame (58), Towersey (57) and Lewknor (45). The industry did not extend significantly south of Watlington. Further north, Bicester had 77 lacemakers in 1861. The density in other parishes varied considerably, with 53 in Souldern in the Cherwell valley, but only four at Fritwell, and six each at Somerton and Ardley. By contrast there were 52 in Stoke Lyne, 35 in Mixbury, 32 in Ambrosden and Blackthorn, 17 at Weston-on-the-Green and 15 in Piddington, with a few in Launton, Stratton Audley, Finmere, Caversfield and Shelswell, and a few isolated individuals in parishes further west, but none at Fringford, Tusmore, Hardwick, Cottisford, Wendlebury and Chesterton.

52 · Brewing and Malting

John Rhodes

From the middle ages, the growing of barley for malting, in Oxfordshire as elsewhere along the Thames and around London, generated an important local industry and downriver trade. In medieval villages a surplus of barley allowed some to brew and sell ale to their neighbours, and by the 15th century a new class of regular brewers had emerged. Brewing for sale, in towns as well as villages, was matched by medieval brewing in the greater households, monasteries and Oxford colleges. The Queen's College had a brewer in 1340–1, and continued brewing until the Second World War, probably the longest record of brewing on a single site anywhere.

The addition of hops, imparting flavour and preservative qualities, turned ale into beer and allowed the common brewers in London to expand sales throughout the 16th century. Increased production created fresh demands for malt, which Oxfordshire was well placed to supply. Early malting centres were the riverside towns of Oxford, Abingdon, Wallingford and above all Henley. Many maltsters also set up as brewers. From 1700 Oxfordshire's breweries grew in number and size and the brewery became the most conspicuous industrial building in all the towns and many villages. The most important factor was the general increase in population, while a decline in domestic and alehouse brewing meant better sales for the common brewer.

In Oxford the 18th century saw the emergence of the great brewing families – the Halls, Treachers, Morrells and Tawneys – but there were also numerous small concerns and publican brewers. These breweries were concentrated in the town centre, in St Aldate's and Brewer Street, Queen Street and Cornmarket, with others in St Giles and St Thomas, where many maltsters were also located. Elsewhere in the county the pattern was repeated, with a succession of short-lived concerns, but also the establishment of soundly based common breweries – Wells of Wallingford (1720), Brakspear's of Henley (1779), Hayward's of Watlington (late 18th century), and Hitchman's of Chipping Norton (1796). Their success was due to good business sense, capital for new equipment, and in some cases the acquisition of tied houses. In south Oxfordshire from the 1780s competition was intense, with Brakspear's, Hayward's, Wells of Wallingford and Simonds of Reading all seeking control of tied houses. Other breweries appeared in the first half of the 19th century to meet a growth in demand. Thomas Hunt's brewery in Banbury was established in the 1830s, and Clinch's at Witney and John Harris's at Hook Norton in the 1840s.

The later 18th and early 19th century saw new industrial techniques, particularly steam power, become available in brewing. A good local example of the industrial Victorian brewery was Hunt Edmunds of Banbury. Thomas and John Hunt of the Unicorn Inn bought a small malthouse in 1835, turned to brewing and gradually expanded, forming a partnership with William Edmunds. An 1858 valuation shows their investment – large cast-iron vessels, a refrigerator, a malt-dressing machine and a Patent Mashing Machine. Development was completed in 1866 with a great new malthouse. Some brewers, like Hunt Edmunds and Brakspear's of Henley, modernised piecemeal. Others replaced old premises with a new type of building – the tower brewery. Phillips in Oxford, Morland's in Abingdon, and the Hook Norton Brewery built such towers, creating prominent landmarks extensively used in their advertising.

The mid 19th century was the high point for both brewing and malting. Improved river navigation in the 1770s allowed expansion in the London malt trade, and the opening of the Oxford Canal in 1790 connected the county to the brewing centres of Birmingham and Burton, and to sources of coal for steam power and malting. The malthouse became a common industrial building in Witney, Burford, Banbury and Bicester, as it already was in the riverside towns. By 1860 every town had at least one brewery, and some had many more: 14 in Oxford, ten in Banbury, seven in Bicester, five in Abingdon, four in Deddington, three in Witney, and two each in Eynsham, Watlington and Henley, with single ones elsewhere, making an overall total of 70. By 1910 these had dwindled to 18. This reflects a national trend – of 50,000 breweries in the UK in 1840 barely 3,000 were left by 1900. Beer production had not declined, but brewing was concentrated within fewer and larger concerns.

Industrial development needed capital, and the late 19th century saw some family breweries becoming limited companies and expanding at the expense of weaker competitors, with a spate of take-overs from the 1880s. This was a sign of vigour in local brewing, and most of the resulting firms survived until the 1920s, when they started to be hit by very different take-overs. Some were local arrangements but others involved brewers from outside the region. The Wallingford Brewery fell to Ushers of Trowbridge in the 1920s, and Hall's of Oxford to Allsop in 1926. A fresh wave followed in the 1960s, with Garne's of Burford acquired by Wadworth's; Clinch's Brewery, Witney, by Courage; and Hunt Edmunds by Mitchells & Butlers.

Twenty years later only four brewers remained in Oxfordshire and along the Thames: Brakspear's at Henley, Morland's at Abingdon, Morrell's in Oxford and the Hook Norton Brewery. Today only the last of these remains. Morrell's closed on its ancient site in 1998, Morland's was bought and closed in 2000 and Brakspear's ceased brewing in 2002. At the same time there has been a revival of the small or publican brewer, with half a dozen micro-breweries in Oxfordshire in 2010. At Witney, in the former malthouse revived in 1983, the Wychwood Brewery took over production of some of Brakspear's beers in 2002, using the old fermenting vessels from Henley. The most dramatic loss was the great maltings at Wallingford, the last local representative of the historic industry, which closed in 1999 and was demolished in 2000.

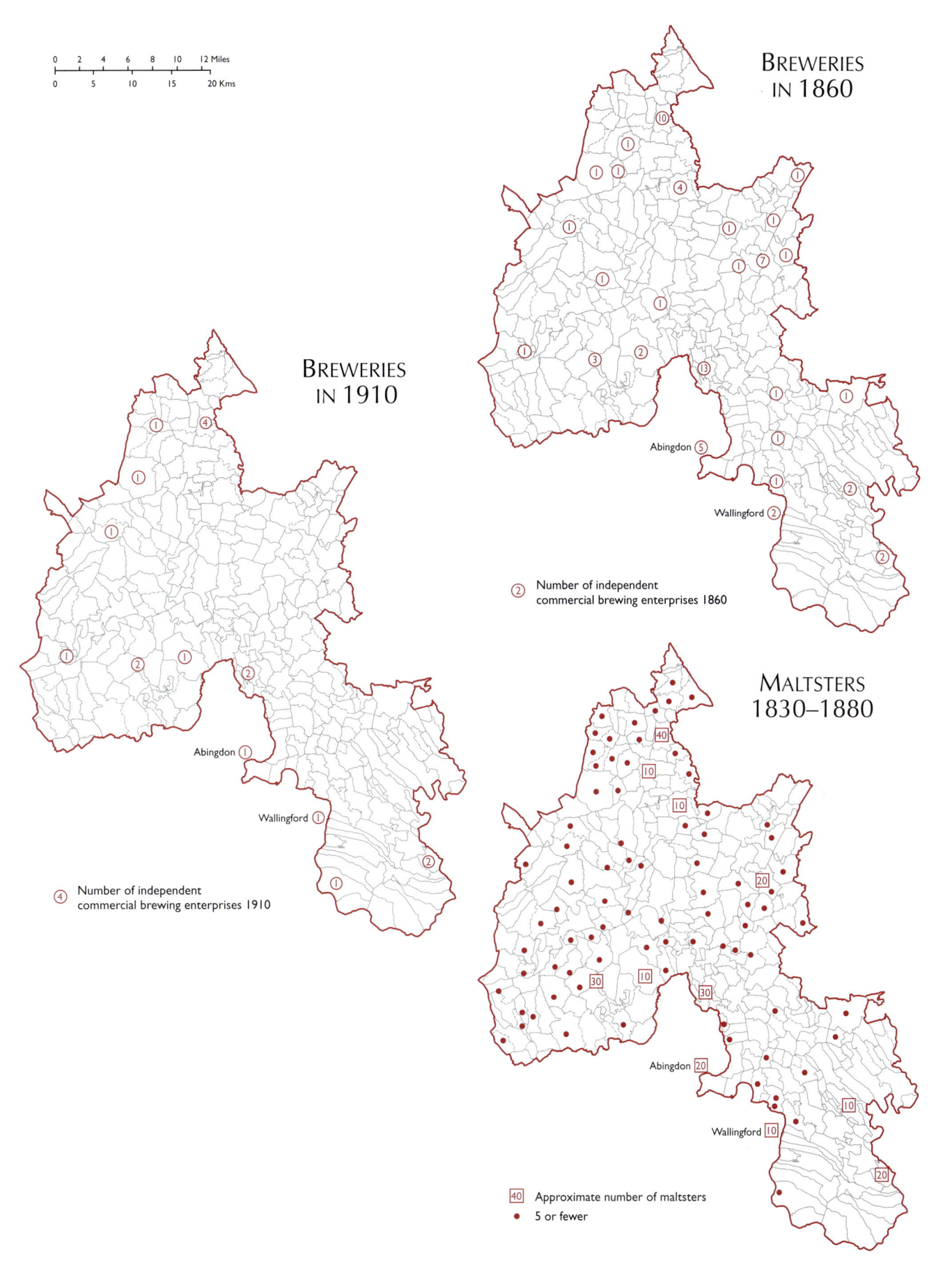

Breweries in 1860

Breweries in 1910

② Number of independent commercial brewing enterprises 1860

④ Number of independent commercial brewing enterprises 1910

Maltsters 1830–1880

[40] Approximate number of maltsters
• 5 or fewer

53 · Country Houses 1815–1939   Geoffrey Tyack

Nineteenth-century Oxfordshire was, with one exception, a county of moderately sized rather than huge landed estates; in 1873, at the time of the 'New Domesday' survey of land-ownership in Britain, only 15% of land in the county formed part of estates of over 10,000 acres, compared with a quarter nationally, but the percentage of land in estates of between 1000 and 10,000 acres was higher than the national average. The exception was Blenheim, with 21,944 acres; the next largest estate belonging to an Oxfordshire resident was that of Tew Park, with 7,945 acres. Tew Park belonged to Matthew Boulton, whose family bought the estate out of the profits of industry in Birmingham. But most of the larger Oxfordshire landowners came from families established in the county since at least the 18th century and sometimes much longer: the Dashwoods of Kirtlington, the Harcourts of Nuneham Courtenay, the Stonors of Stonor, the Dormers of Rousham, etc. With a handful of exceptions, newcomers who moved into Oxfordshire, such as the Crawshays, who used the profits of their South Wales ironworks to buy Caversham Park, bought smaller estates.

The rather conservative pattern of land-ownership helps explain the dearth of really large new country houses in the county between the end of the Napoleonic Wars and the onset of agricultural depression it the 1870s and 1880s. The largest completely new house was probably Caversham Park, rebuilt after a fire in 1850 by the City of London architect Horace Jones. It is classical in style, as are Caversfield House, built in 1842–5 for the warden of Merton College by C. R. Cockerell, architect of the Ashmolean Museum, Kiddington Hall (c.1850), by Sir Charles Barry, and Headington Hill Hall (1856–8), by John Thomas for the brewer James Morrell. But the surprisingly modest Tew Park is loosely Jacobean in style, and the same style was also employed at Swyncombe House (1830s, demolished), Howbery Park at Crowmarsh Gifford, Joyce Grove, Nettlebed, and Freeland House (1885, etc). Bignell House, Chesterton (1866), and Shelswell Park (1875), both in the Bicester hunting country – then enjoying its peak of popularity – and both demolished, were in the ponderous version of Gothic favoured by the Witney-born William Wilkinson and seen all over North Oxford. But the most impressive Gothic Revival country house in the county was the extravagantly turreted, French-looking Wyfold Court, Rotherfield Peppard, by Charles Barry's pupil George Somers Clarke for a cotton manufacturer, Edward Hermon (c.1872–8).

Rather than building anew, most landowners in Victorian Oxfordshire chose to remodel or extend their houses. Swerford Park was given a classical face-lift by Sir John Soane's draughtsman Joseph Gandy in 1824–9, and substantial alterations were carried out at Sarsden House in the 1820s by George Stanley Repton, son of the famous landscape gardener who had made improvements to the grounds in the 1790s. Some relatively modest 18th-century classical houses – e.g. Shotover, Watlington Park, Tusmore – were enlarged by new wings, mostly later removed. Heythrop House was rebuilt internally by Alfred Waterhouse for the railway contractor Thomas Brassey in 1871. There were also alterations to the county's large stock of medieval and 16th- and 17th-century houses. At Mapledurham the Elizabethan facade was tidied up and the Georgian sash windows removed c.1828–31, and Weston Manor acquired its neo-Tudor facade at about the same time. Wroxton Abbey, left unfinished in 1631 and altered in the 18th century, was completed in a rich neo-Jacobean style in 1858, and Barton Abbey (so-called), a relatively modest Elizabethan house, was successively enlarged in a similar style by members of the Hall family, inheritors of another Oxford brewing fortune.

The cult of 'Old English' architecture and decoration burgeoned in the last third of the 19th century. William Morris was in the vanguard of fashionable taste when he took over an old farmhouse, Kelmscott Manor, as a second home in 1871, and in the succeeding decades several old Oxfordshire houses were lovingly restored, many of them by architects who shared Morris's values and outlook: Fritwell Manor by Thomas Garner, who lived there himself (1893), Water Eaton Manor, by Garner's partner G. F. Bodley (1890s), Yarnton Manor by Garner (1897), Checkendon Court by Guy Dawber (1920), and Asthall Manor, remodelled by the Birmingham architect C. E. Bateman for Lord Redesdale, father of the Mitford sisters, c.1920 (he later built a new house at Swinbrook, near the site of the long-demolished seat of the Fettiplace family).

As agricultural profits fell in the wake of depression, the traditional idea of a country house as the centre of a flourishing landed estate gave way to that of 'a place in the country': a rural retreat for occasional residence and weekend entertaining, as famously practised from 1915 to 1928 by Philip Morrell and his wife, Lady Ottoline, at the 17th-century Garsington Manor. Here the setting was beautified by new formal gardens, and there are other memorable gardens of this period at Friar Park, Henley (1896), and, of the interwar period, at Ditchley Park and Cornwell Manor. New houses include Ernest George's Shiplake Court, built overlooking the Thames – and conveniently close to a railway station – for a London stockbroker in 1889; Ewelme Down (Walter Cave, c.1910); Flint House, Goring Heath (Ernest Newton, 1913); and Nuffield Place (Oswald Milne, 1914, latterly home of Lord Nuffield, founder of Morris Motors). All are in an Arts and Crafts-inspired 'Old English' or neo-Georgian style and all, significantly, are in the south of the county. Other new houses replaced older ones, such as the neo-Georgian Mongewell Park (R. S. Wornum, 1890–1), in an 18th-century landscaped park by the Thames; the neo-Jacobean Eynsham Park (Ernest George, 1900–4), on an estate formed in the 1770s out of the former Eynsham Heath; and Sir Edwin Lutyens's neo-Georgian Middleton Park (1938), perhaps the last big house built before the Second World War put an end – temporarily as it turned out – to the country-house building tradition in Oxfordshire.

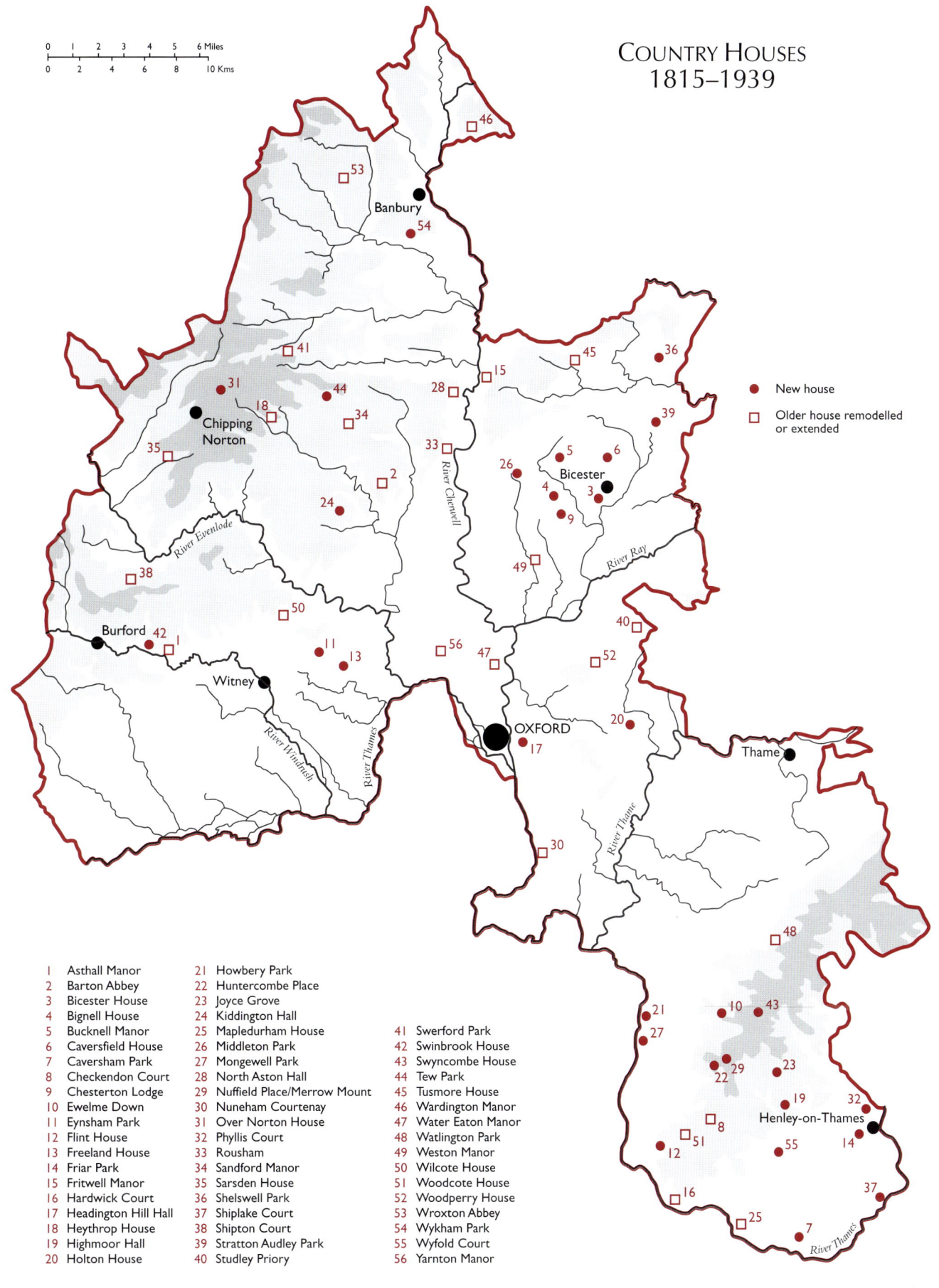

COUNTRY HOUSES 1815–1939

- ● New house
- ☐ Older house remodelled or extended

1 Asthall Manor	21 Howbery Park	
2 Barton Abbey	22 Huntercombe Place	
3 Bicester House	23 Joyce Grove	
4 Bignell House	24 Kiddington Hall	
5 Bucknell Manor	25 Mapledurham House	41 Swerford Park
6 Caversfield House	26 Middleton Park	42 Swinbrook House
7 Caversham Park	27 Mongewell Park	43 Swyncombe House
8 Checkendon Court	28 North Aston Hall	44 Tew Park
9 Chesterton Lodge	29 Nuffield Place/Merrow Mount	45 Tusmore House
10 Ewelme Down	30 Nuneham Courtenay	46 Wardington Manor
11 Eynsham Park	31 Over Norton House	47 Water Eaton Manor
12 Flint House	32 Phyllis Court	48 Watlington Park
13 Freeland House	33 Rousham	49 Weston Manor
14 Friar Park	34 Sandford Manor	50 Wilcote House
15 Fritwell Manor	35 Sarsden House	51 Woodcote House
16 Hardwick Court	36 Shelswell Park	52 Woodperry House
17 Headington Hill Hall	37 Shiplake Court	53 Wroxton Abbey
18 Heythrop House	38 Shipton Court	54 Wykham Park
19 Highmoor Hall	39 Stratton Audley Park	55 Wyfold Court
20 Holton House	40 Studley Priory	56 Yarnton Manor

54 · Parliamentary Representation

Philip Salmon

Oxfordshire has played host to some of the most striking anomalies in the English electoral system, according it a special place in the representative history of the United Kingdom. Most conspicuous of these was the existence of the university constituency at Oxford, for which both Peel and Gladstone served as MPs before becoming prime minister. Distinct from the city, and with a franchise based on the possession of a doctorate or MA rather than a property qualification, Oxford University elected two MPs from the early 1600s until 1948, and for a brief spell (1644–5) even accommodated Parliament itself. One of two such university constituencies before 1801, and even at the peak of university representation one of only nine such places, its elections rarely involved actual polling, but were usually settled in advance through pre-electoral campaigning. These uncontested elections without rival candidates – once the norm in most types of constituency but increasingly less common after 1832 – all but ceased in 1918, when the university, in an experiment, moved to the single transferable vote, yet another electoral 'first', alongside postal ballots (1864) and expatriate voting (1918).

The university did not provide Oxfordshire's only electoral novelty. Before 1832 Banbury was one of just five English boroughs (out of 203) that elected a single MP (one of whom was another prime minister, Lord North), and among a handful of places where a 'modern' first-past-the-post election might occur. Unfortunately, the influence of the earls of Guilford and their successors left few opportunities for a poll prior to the enfranchisement of the £10 householders by the 1832 Reform Act. Thereafter, lacking the usual 19th-century safety-valve of a second seat, Banbury became the scene of intense party conflict and electoral violence, the dynamics of which have been neatly captured by Barrie Trinder. In 1885 it was incorporated into North Oxfordshire by the Redistribution of Seats Act.

The role of multiple seats in providing opportunities for electoral compromise and enabling hard-pressed voters to satisfy both their landlord and conscience, at a time when all polling was performed in public, was well illustrated in Woodstock, another Oxfordshire pocket borough. The removal of Woodstock's second seat by the 1832 Reform Act left its squabbling family patrons, the Duke of Marlborough and his estranged son, the Marquess of Blandford, with little option but to fight it out at the polls, as they did at both the 1837 and 1838 elections, leaving a trail of evicted tenants and harassed voters in their wake. Marlborough's death in 1840 ended their feud for the solitary seat, which thereafter provided a safe berth for nominees of the Blenheim interest, most notably Lord Randolph Churchill, father of the 20th-century prime minister, before its absorption into Mid Oxfordshire in 1885.

It was the allocation of a third MP to the county constituency, however, that really singled out Oxfordshire. Just one of seven counties to elect three MPs from 1832, its additional seat considerably lessened the prospects for competition between candidates, of the kind that had resulted in intense polling in all three previous general elections and infamously in 1754. (This election, one of the most notorious of the 18th century for bribery and chicanery, inspired Hogarth's 'An Election Entertainment'.) The third seat also made polling itself far more complex on the rare occasions when a contest took take place. In 1837, for instance, four contenders stood for three seats, and since each elector could vote for any one, two or three of them, casting what were known as 'plumpers' or 'split' votes, they each had 14 different ways of voting. (Amazingly, the surviving pollbook shows that only one elector in a turnout of 4,120 messed things up, by choosing all four.) Just two general elections were contested like this, however, before the county was separated into the single-member divisions of Mid, North and South Oxfordshire in 1885.

Many of the names of the MPs for Oxfordshire's constituencies – Harcourt, Norreys, Stonor etc. – will be immediately familiar to anyone acquainted with its historic houses and street signs. It would be wrong to assume, however, that Oxfordshire elections were simply muster-rolls of tenants on landed estates and that voters exercised no autonomy in their political choices, as David Eastwood has clearly demonstrated. Indeed, the more votes electors possessed – and in this county they possessed more than most – the more easily they could balance a range of obligations, to landlord, community, profession, and, of course, to all those without the vote, a group that before 1918 included all women. A lack of contests was no indicator of political inactivity. Canvassing and pre-electoral skirmishes could be intense, settling outcomes before a poll, whilst the registration system introduced in 1832 provided local parties with a yearly opportunity to enlist their supporters and object to their opponents on the electoral rolls. These local 'battles of the registers' made many results inevitable.

In the city of Oxford, the region's only other constituency prior to 1885, more traditional means were deployed to win over electors, especially its notoriously venal freemen, who, despite the restrictions imposed on this ancient franchise by the 1832 Reform Act, still accounted for one-fifth of the electorate in 1868. After a succession of investigations into bribery, which exposed payments of £1 for a 'plumper', 10 shillings for a 'split' vote and the 'treating' of electors with pies and beer, the city was deprived of first one and then both of its parliamentary seats in 1881. Following its reinstatement as a single-member borough four years later the Conservatives, who had hitherto always struggled, more or less dominated until 1966, notwithstanding the addition of the industrial behemoth of Cowley in 1948.

Oxfordshire has long since ceased to display so many electoral curiosities and unique features, setting it apart from the rest of England, but in 2010 David Cameron, MP for Witney, became yet another prime minister to sit for one of its constituencies.

Parliamentary Representation Before 1832

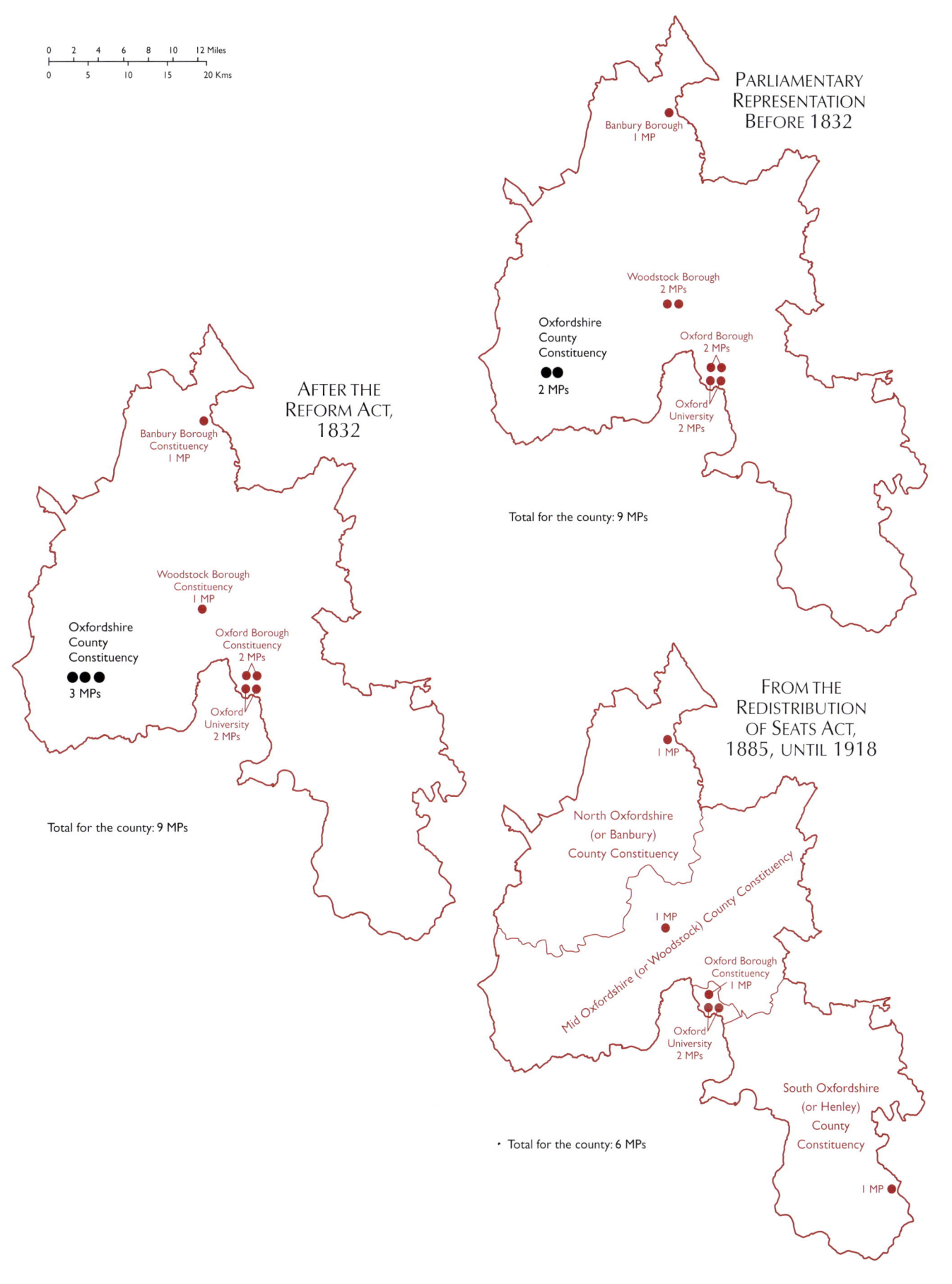

Banbury Borough
1 MP

Woodstock Borough
2 MPs

Oxfordshire County Constituency
2 MPs

Oxford Borough
2 MPs

Oxford University
2 MPs

Total for the county: 9 MPs

After the Reform Act, 1832

Banbury Borough Constituency
1 MP

Woodstock Borough Constituency
1 MP

Oxfordshire County Constituency
3 MPs

Oxford Borough Constituency
2 MPs

Oxford University
2 MPs

Total for the county: 9 MPs

From the Redistribution of Seats Act, 1885, until 1918

1 MP

North Oxfordshire (or Banbury) County Constituency

1 MP

Mid Oxfordshire (or Woodstock) County Constituency

Oxford Borough Constituency
1 MP

Oxford University
2 MPs

South Oxfordshire (or Henley) County Constituency

1 MP

Total for the county: 6 MPs

0 2 4 6 8 10 12 Miles
0 5 10 15 20 Kms

127

55 · Education in the 19th century: Elementary Schools   Kate Tiller

During the 19th century the educational experience of Oxfordshire children was transformed. From an uneven mix of old, endowed schools with some newer charity, day and Sunday schools and private enterprise schools in certain localities, there was by 1902 a universal provision of state-funded elementary schools for children aged 5 to 13. These great changes were achieved in a series of stages.

In 1833 the first state funding of local elementary education was finally introduced. This was not direct governmental provision. Instead, initially modest sums were provided in support of existing, voluntary schools, and of pupil teaching and teacher training. These were principally organised through two national organisations, born out of the widespread movement of the preceding 50 years to provide some limited mass education. These efforts involved fierce rivalries between religious denominations. The British & Foreign School Society, founded in 1808, was supported primarily by Dissenters. The National Society (for Promoting the Education of the Poor in the Principles of the Established Church) was its Anglican counterpart, established in 1811. By 1833 the number of Oxfordshire schools had already increased greatly and only 15 parishes were without any school.[1]

By 1858, 403 public weekday schools (counting girls, boys and infants departments separately) were operating in the county. Of these, 370 were Church of England, 28 British or Nonconformist and five Roman Catholic. Anglican dominance was equally overwhelming in Sunday schools: 445 Church of England and 88 Nonconformist.[2] Anglican schools were educating 82% of weekday pupils and 72% of Sunday scholars. This reflected National Society and local funds for school building, followed up by continued local fundraising and collection of scholars' pence, typically 1d or 2d per week. Church schooling was further underpinned by the Oxford Diocesan Education Board, established in 1839, and its associated school inspection. In 1853 a new diocesan teacher-training college opened at Culham. Contact with education was typically brief, as the experience in 1867 of an agricultural labouring family, the Herveys of Epwell, shows.[3] John, the father, was unemployed in the winter. He had a wife and six children, aged between 15 and 3. The four eldest were at work, three boys in agriculture starting aged 9 and their sister in domestic service. Only one child, an 8-year-old boy, was at school, with siblings aged 5 and 3 still at home. Economic realities and doubting attitudes to book learning limited commitment to school, although generational differences were beginning to emerge. John could not read or write, but his two elder sons could.

Increasing government funding brought scrutiny and gradual imposition of controls. The visits of Her Majesty's Inspectors (from 1839) loom large in accounts of school life. The Newcastle Commission (1858–61) resulted in the Revised Code of 1862. This imposed a centralised curriculum, centred on the three Rs, scripture study, and needlework for the girls, compliance with which was a condition of funding. Payment was by results, measured in attendance and tests in the core subjects, a utilitarian model which applied into the 1890s. This pattern of schooling was subsumed into the first universal elementary education provided for 5- to 10-year-olds under Forster's Act of 1870. This used existing schools but, if local places were insufficient, decreed the establishment of School Boards, locally elected, undenominational and partly funded by local rates. The map shows elementary schools receiving government funds in 1875–6. Some places had schools but continued to resist state support and are not listed. School Boards established following the 1870 Education Act are also shown, with the year of their first election.

Reactions in Oxfordshire to Forster's Act were strong. Loss of child labour was felt by employers and parents, whilst Anglicans resented state intervention in a sphere they regarded as properly theirs. One response was renewed voluntary effort, with a spurt of new and extended schools built to avoid imposition of School Boards. There was a battle to enforce attendance and a basic standard of education before pupils could receive a school leaving certificate and begin work. School attendance officers were employed, and rules tightened by further Acts of 1876 and 1880. Nevertheless closure of schools at peak harvest times and major village events remained part of the Oxfordshire calendar. Epidemic disease was another cause of closures, at a time when medical facilities remained rudimentary. This was the education portrayed in north Oxfordshire in the 1880s by Flora Thompson.[4] These village children were 'only the second generation to be forcibly fed with the fruit of the tree of knowledge'. This some 45 of them received in a single room, taught by one female teacher, assisted by lowly-paid monitors, themselves recent pupils. The curriculum followed the Revised Code, reinforced by rote learning and daily visits from the rector. Thompson pictures a limited and limiting education of often reluctant pupils guided towards unquestioning absorption of values of belief, respect and gratitude ahead of lives of restricted options. Only gradually did this regime widen, nationally and locally. During the 1890s fee-paying was effectively abolished, as was rigid payment by results. The minimum leaving age was raised to 11 and then 12. Gardening, object lessons, history, geography and physical exercise were to be found in Oxfordshire schools. By the 1890s illiteracy (measured by ability to sign the marriage register) was 5% for men and 2.7% for women. In 1860 it had been 30.5% and 28.3% respectively.[5]

The Education Act of 1902 represented state co-ordination of existing provision. School Boards (there were only 25 in Oxfordshire) were abolished and county and borough councils made local education authorities (LEAs). All schools were now rate-aided, and all were 'council schools', although religious affiliations remained within a framework of freedom of conscience for parents and pupils. LEAs could establish secondary schools, but opportunities for most Oxfordshire children to progress remained negligible. In 1924 there were only six LEA secondary schools (Banbury, Bicester, Burford, Henley, Thame and Witney) and less than 5% of Oxfordshire children from only 40 of the county's 212 primary schools were selected 'as capable of profiting from secondary education'.[6]

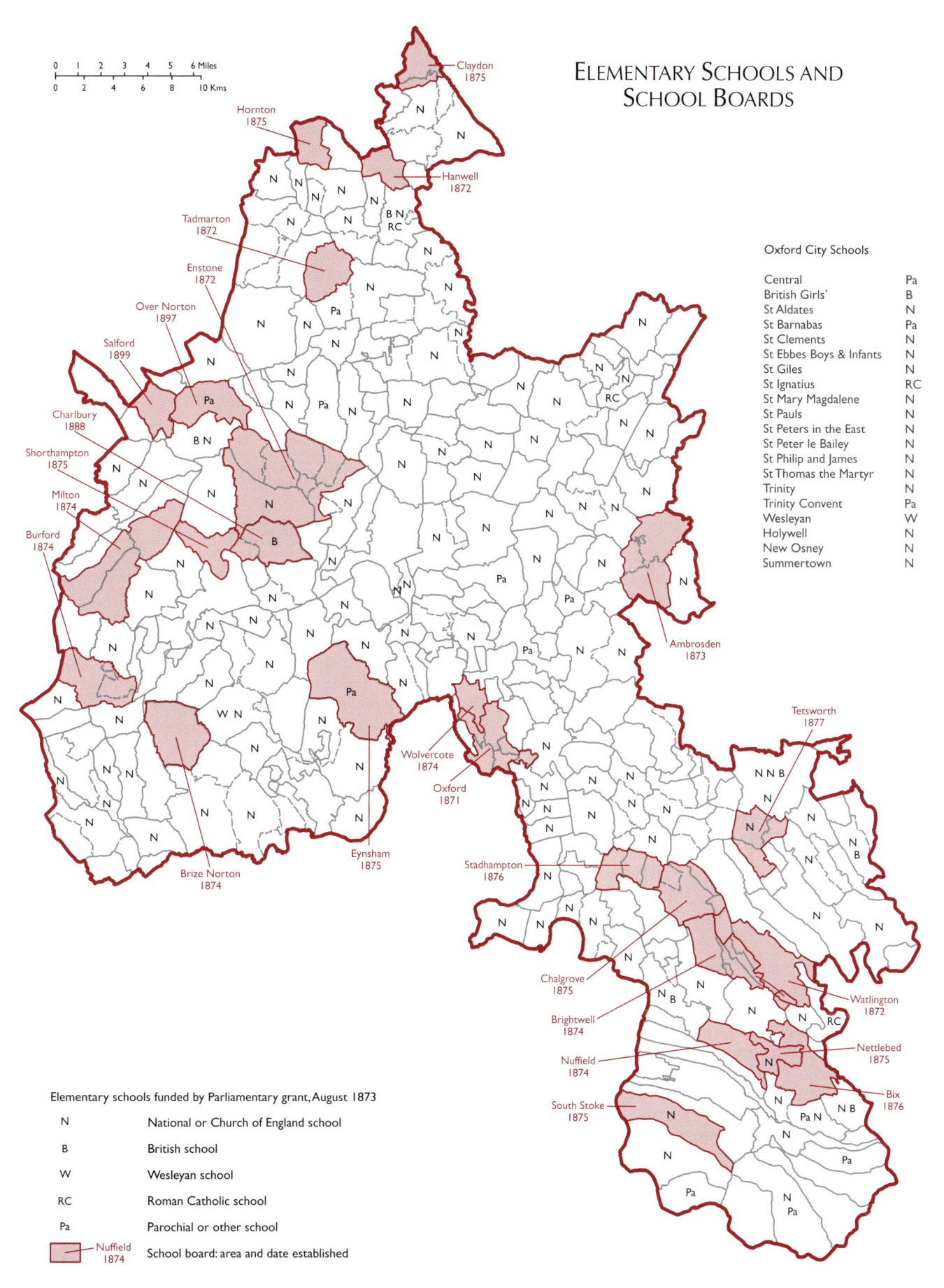

ELEMENTARY SCHOOLS AND SCHOOL BOARDS

Oxford City Schools

Central	Pa
British Girls'	B
St Aldates	N
St Barnabas	Pa
St Clements	N
St Ebbes Boys & Infants	N
St Giles	N
St Ignatius	RC
St Mary Magdalene	N
St Pauls	N
St Peters in the East	N
St Peter le Bailey	N
St Philip and James	N
St Thomas the Martyr	N
Trinity	N
Trinity Convent	Pa
Wesleyan	W
Holywell	N
New Osney	N
Summertown	N

Elementary schools funded by Parliamentary grant, August 1873

- N — National or Church of England school
- B — British school
- W — Wesleyan school
- RC — Roman Catholic school
- Pa — Parochial or other school
- Nuffield 1874 — School board: area and date established

129

56 · Education in the 19th Century: the Private Sector — Kate Tiller

A parallel world of Oxfordshire schools, privately run and catering for predominantly middle-class customers, was to be found alongside the county's developing public elementary provision (described in entry 55). Parts of an earlier 'private sector' were dwindling, dame schools being gradually superseded by public provision, and endowed and charity schools (if they survived) changing in character. Some, like the grammar schools at Ewelme and Dorchester, respectively 15th- and 17th-century endowments, were subsumed into the new public system as local National schools. Others, like Lord Williams Grammar at Thame and Abingdon School, just across the Thames in Berkshire, developed independently, constructed new buildings and took significant numbers of boarders and not just local pupils.

However, most of the private schools, meeting the demands of fee-paying parents from Oxfordshire and beyond, appear to be new enterprises, sometimes transitory in nature, set up in both towns and villages, and often run in private homes with numbers of pupils ranging from two to over 40. They left little or no mark in contemporary institutional, denominational or national educational records, but something of their presence may be pieced together – for example by using newspaper advertisements, census enumerators' books, rate and tithe records, parish registers and family papers.[1] Private schools were dependent on being known and are therefore well covered in commercial directories. It is on these listings that the accompanying maps are based, showing the location and number of private schools in 1852, 1883 and 1915, and distinguishing those specifically stated to offer boarding places.[2]

In 1852 a total of 104 private schools was found, 41 in Oxford, the remaining 63 in 29 places outside the city. In 1883 the total listed was 75, with 23 in Oxford and 52 elsewhere, in 23 different places. By 1919 the figures were 34, of which 15 were in Oxford and the other 19 in 12 different places. At all dates the high proportion of women involved in running private schools is apparent; of named proprietors in 1852, 60 were female, in 1883 the proportion was even higher, at 51 out of 75 schools, and in 1915, 23 out of 34. Most were widowed or unmarried, pursuing an independent livelihood in one of the few respectable jobs open to them.

The nature of private schooling is further revealed from individual cases. For example, the Garlick School in the village of Ewelme in south Oxfordshire appears to have run for some 35 years. It accommodated over 40 pupils in a large house, the Mount, and in an adjoining cottage. The proprietors were a local family, headed by James Garlick (1783–1843), who seems to have turned to schoolmastering late in life. After his death the business was taken forward by his widow, Elizabeth, and survived until she died in 1875. The Garlicks' main and established trades were as publicans of the Greyhound Inn in Ewelme and as butchers. Their pupils were aged 7 to 14 and half to three-quarters came from outside Oxfordshire, mostly from London. They were taught by three people, members of the family and usually one other. For a brief period girls were admitted, but this was chiefly a boys' school. Those children for whom information can be discovered were from families in trade, coming to Ewelme between early years at home or dame school and before possible further education at grammar or minor public schools (one boy went on to St John's College at Hurstpierpoint in Sussex). There was no aspiration to university entry, but to involvement in government service or family business. The curriculum included grammar, arithmetic, geometry and French, and (judging by a surviving exercise book) strong moral and disciplinary messages. An exercise in copperplate read, 'There is frequently a worm at the root of our most flourishing condition.' Pupils attended the village church, but they also gardened and played cricket on the Cow Common.

Some Oxfordshire communities consistently supported clusters of private schools, for example, Bampton in west Oxfordshire. Here there were four private schools in 1852. In neighbouring households in the High Street were Elizabeth Steede's Ladies School, with nine pupils taught by her sister, and Thomas Forestier's establishment, with 17 boys taught by himself. He offered the desirable combination of classical and commercial education. Seven of his pupils were Oxfordshire-born, including two Earlys from Witney and a Druce from Eynsham, well-known families in blanket manufacture and farming respectively. At West Weald, Bampton, was a further school with 19 young gentlemen. It later became 'St Mary's College', a typical touch of public school emulation. Bampton's fourth private school was much more modest, supporting a farmer's widow and her two unmarried daughters, who taught just three local girls aged 6 to 11. This was school-keeping as a survival strategy.

By 1915 the numbers of private schools seems to have fallen markedly. Amongst those continuing were local examples of that late-19th century growth area, middle-class boarding and public schools, as at Sibford, where the Quaker boarding school had been established in 1842, and at Bloxham and Radley, just into Berkshire, both Anglican public schools, opened in 1860 and 1847 respectively. Bloxham catered 'chiefly to boys who go direct from school into the business of life'. Elsewhere more private schools were designating themselves as 'preparatory'. A high proportion continued to cater for girls. Gradually alternative opportunities, changing parental attitudes, and outside regulation and standardisation had begun to overtake this relatively unknown but significant sector of 19th-century educational and local life, found in many Oxfordshire towns and villages.

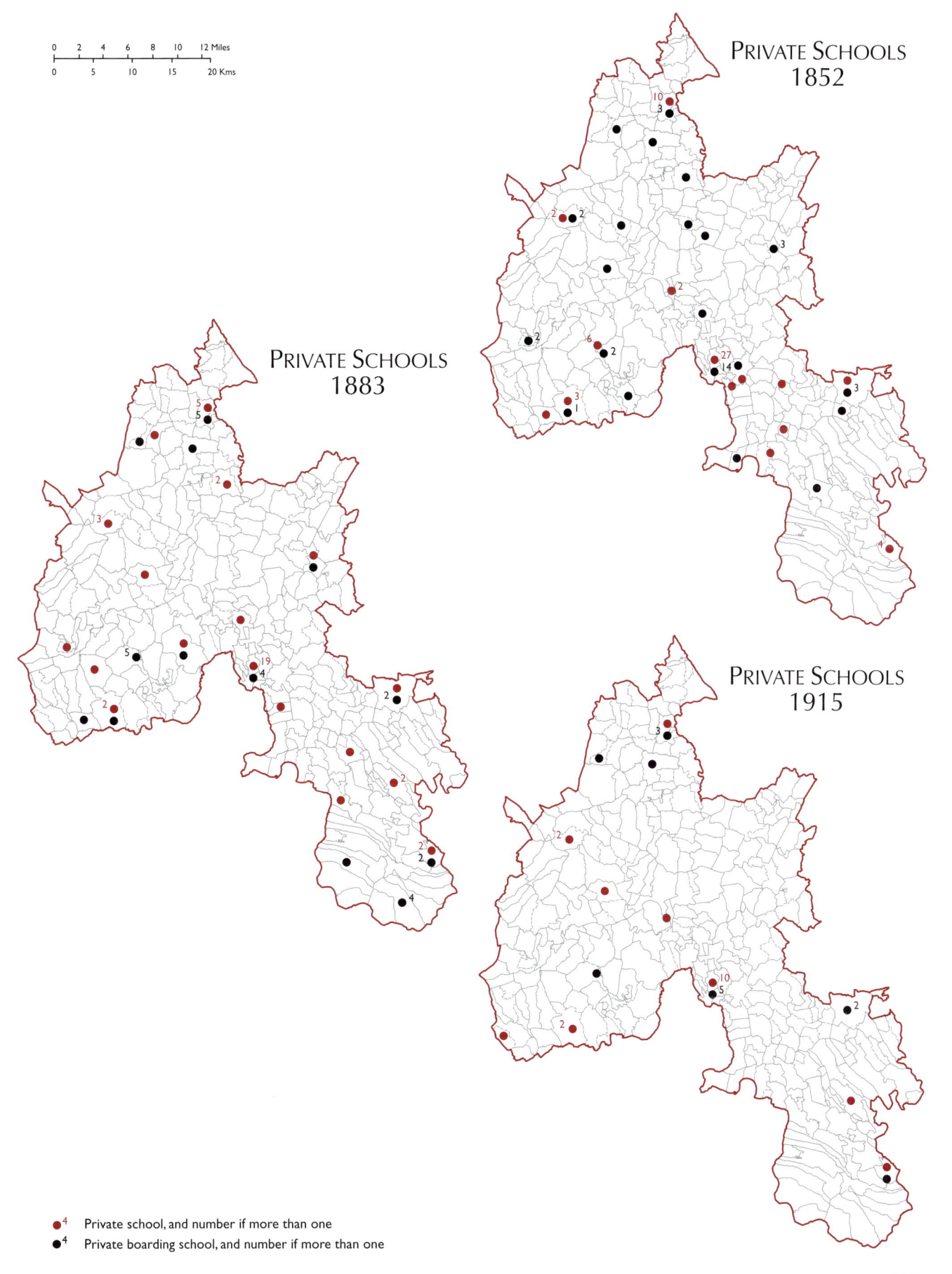

PRIVATE SCHOOLS
1852

PRIVATE SCHOOLS
1883

PRIVATE SCHOOLS
1915

● 4 Private school, and number if more than one
● 4 Private boarding school, and number if more than one

57 · The Church of England in 1835   Mark Smith

The constitutional revolution of 1828–32, which saw full political rights being extended to Roman Catholics and Protestant Nonconformists and an extension and redistribution of Parliamentary representation, brought with it pressures for the reform of many other parts of the establishment. Prominent among the targets for reform was the Established Church and one of the first fruits of this initiative was the Ecclesiastical Revenues Commission established in 1832 to investigate the distribution of patronage and wealth within the Church. Its report, presented to Parliament in 1835, represented the first systematic survey of the Establishment as a whole since the Reformation and provides a snapshot of the state of the Church on the eve of the great reorganisation of the Victorian era. The three maps presented here chart four elements of the Commission's report: patronage; the value of benefices to their incumbents; and the Commission's estimate of parish populations in 1835, combined with the information it received on the church accommodation available in each parish.

Patronage The distribution of ecclesiastical patronage within the county reflects a continuation of trends already visible in 1600. Much of the large share accruing to the Crown in the immediate aftermath of monastic dissolution had disappeared by then but by 1835 it had shrunk even further with only five livings in the county and a further three in Oxford. The Bishop of Oxford remained relatively poorly provided with patronage within his own diocese with only eight benefices, mostly in the north and west. Much patronage, especially in south-west Oxfordshire, remained securely in the hands of ecclesiastical and collegiate patrons elsewhere in the country, especially the Dean and Chapter of Windsor, which presented to three benefices, and Eton College, which presented to six. However, much the most numerous were those benefices in the hands of private patrons and of the university and its colleges. In a county characterised by small and medium-sized gentry estates, the private patronage was correspondingly dispersed. The owner of the county's one really large estate – the Duke of Marlborough – had five benefices in his gift, along with a share in the patronage of two others, but most other private patrons had one or at most two presentations to make. So though in aggregate they were much more important, it was the crown and the bishop that remained the most significant individual patrons in the county. Moreover, while many of the benefices in private hands produced respectable incomes for their incumbents, few were real plums: of the nine Oxfordshire benefices with an average gross income of over £700 only one, Kingham, had a private patron. A particular feature of ecclesiastical patronage in Oxfordshire was the role of the university and its colleges, which, while not quite as influential as the religious houses prior to the dissolution, were nevertheless the most important collective patrons in the county. They included the largest patron of all, Christ Church, whose dual role as college and cathedral chapter carried with it 15 advowsons and a number of other significant holdings, for example New College with seven benefices and Merton and St John's with six each. Five of the nine most wealthy benefices were in college hands and the total size of collegiate holdings seemed likely to increase, given the utility of Oxfordshire benefices to their Fellows.

Income The Ecclesiastical Revenues Commission collected a range of data on the value of benefices to their incumbents, the most important of which was the gross income, before any mortgage payments or curates' salaries, averaged over three years ending in 1831 (see middle map). Parishes are grouped into four categories – those worth less than £150 a year (a figure which represented a minimum respectable income for a clergyman in the early 19th century) and three categories of higher income which might be taken as representing respectability (£150–£249), comfort (£250–£349) and wealth (£350 and above). The map reveals a complex picture with no clear pattern. Oxfordshire had a considerable number of benefices yielding an income below the £150 mark and no fewer than 19 benefices with a gross average income of less than £70. These were not concentrated in the poorer farming areas such as the Chilterns (which in fact contained a number of the most wealthy benefices in the county) but could be found with considerable frequency in the prosperous vales region of central Oxfordshire. This phenomenon reflects one of the central economic problems affecting the church – the impropriation of tithes (see entry 18). This creamed off major income to a third party (often the patron) before it reached the incumbent, often leaving even prosperous parishes with low benefice incomes.

Accommodation The final map brings together two pieces of information from the 1835 survey: an estimate of parish population and a statement of church accommodation available in the parish. In a handful of cases the incumbents merely stated that accommodation was 'sufficient' for the parish but the majority returned actual numbers. This allows an estimate to be made of the percentage of the parish that might be accommodated in the church at any one time. This is an incomplete measure of the health of the church, since a building that accommodated only half the parishioners might still be regarded as adequate if it held two services every Sunday, while a church that accommodated 80% might be thought inadequate if it held only one. Nonetheless, taken at an intermediate point in the rise of rural population in the county, this is a useful indicator of where the church was already under significant pressure (accommodating less than 50%) and where it might soon expect to be so (accommodating 50% to 75%). It is significant that pressure was already being felt not just in urban parishes like those in Oxford but also in large rural parishes, especially in north and west Oxfordshire. In this context the major reconstruction of the church that was to be such a feature of the Victorian period may not have come a moment too soon.

GROSS INCOME PER ANNUM

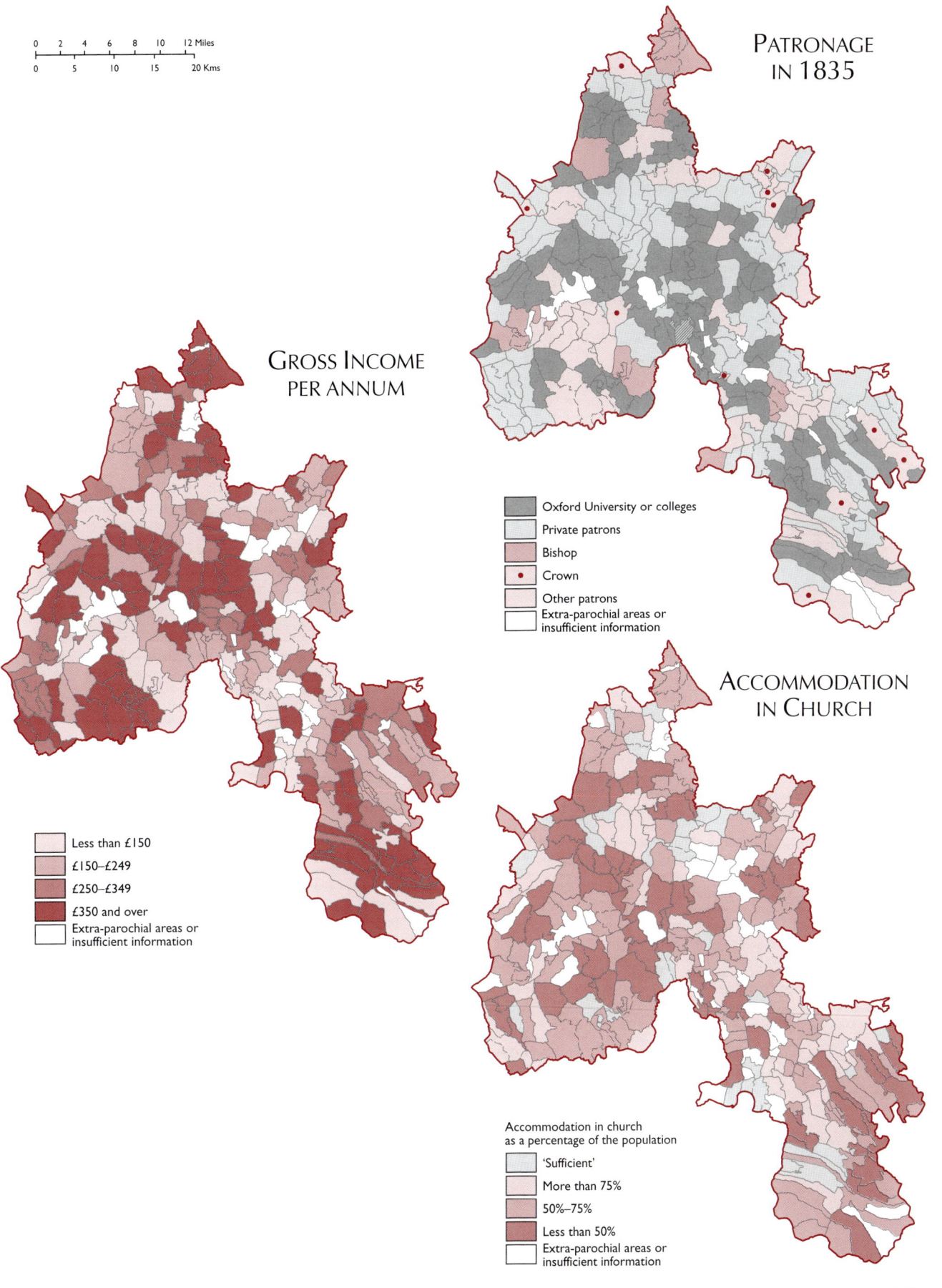

Less than £150
£150–£249
£250–£349
£350 and over
Extra-parochial areas or insufficient information

PATRONAGE IN 1835

Oxford University or colleges
Private patrons
Bishop
Crown
Other patrons
Extra-parochial areas or insufficient information

ACCOMMODATION IN CHURCH

Accommodation in church as a percentage of the population

'Sufficient'
More than 75%
50%–75%
Less than 50%
Extra-parochial areas or insufficient information

58 · Church and Chapel in 1851

Kate Tiller

On Sunday 30 March 1851, the first and only national census of accommodation and attendance at places of worship was conducted. Special forms were distributed to the clergy or officials of churches, chapels, meeting houses or cottage meetings of all denominations in towns, villages and outlying hamlets. The returns, with their figures of sittings, free or otherwise, and of attendances at services on the morning, afternoon or evening of census Sunday reveal the religious geography of Oxfordshire. The rich details in individual returns have been published in full elsewhere. Here it is the overall patterns of religious provision, observance and denominational allegiance, and some of the marked variations of experience within the county, which are summarised

Accommodation for worship in Oxfordshire was dominated by the Church of England, with 67% of the 109,301 sittings available. Oxfordshire was the third most Anglican of 41 English counties in this respect. Dissenters had 33% of sittings, but their presence varied considerably between Registration Districts (RDs coincided with Poor Law Unions, see p. 145). Dissenting provision was strongest in Banbury RD at over 44%; it ranged from 33% to 35% in Thame, Witney and Henley RDs; the lowest rates of Nonconformist sittings (18%) were in Headington RD, followed by the Woodstock, Chipping Norton, Oxford and Bicester areas. Overall there were sittings for some 65% of Oxfordshire's population, should they choose to worship.

It is less easy to determine exactly how many Oxfordshire people did choose to worship on 30 March 1851. No individual names are recorded, only total attendances at each service. Since most churches and chapels held at least two services (the Church of England typically in the morning and afternoon, the Dissenters in the afternoon and evening), the number of people attending more than once is uncertain. From census officials in the 1850s to recent historians, much debated attempts have been made to adjust the results of the religious census to allow for double counting. Here a simpler and widely used method is adopted: all the morning, afternoon and evening attendances are aggregated and expressed as a percentage of the population of the area concerned, giving an index of attendance or IA. The percentage of total attendances gained by denominations may also be calculated (the percentage share or PS). On this basis and accepting some inevitable double counting of 'repeat' attenders, 64% of Oxfordshire's population worshipped on Census Sunday, and 63% of those attendances were Anglican. Oxfordshire's level of observance (IA) was above the national average of 58%, and higher than Warwks or Glos, but slightly lower than Berks and distinctly lower than Wilts and Bucks.

Of 235 Oxfordshire settlements with at least one place of worship, 103 were solely Anglican, and 132 'mixed' (with some form of Dissent). By 1851 the Church of England was reforming and energising its ministry and organisation. This included new church building, as recorded in the census (see top map), particularly in west Oxfordshire. The diocese of Oxford was a leading example of Anglican activism under the high-profile leadership of Bishop Samuel Wilberforce, who in 1851 also headed national opposition to the taking of the religious census. This episcopal lead is reflected in the exceptionally high rates of non-compliance by incumbents; some 70 Anglican returns (27%) had to be completed by someone other than the incumbent, or were filled in by them partially or expressing protest. The 'religiosity' of Anglican only and mixed places varied significantly: in the former, the IA averaged 48%; in the latter, it rose, with 62% of the population attending a place of worship and an Anglican IA of 33%.

Protestant Dissenting denominations of 17th-century origin (Old Dissent) were locally rather than generally strong (centre map). Overall they accounted for 42% of Nonconformist attendances. Baptists and Independents or Congregationalists were most numerous. Their geographical distributions suggest continuities from 17th-century strengths (see entry 35), with Baptists concentrated particularly in the north and west, and Independents or Congregationalists in the south and near the eastern border with Bucks. The dates of chapel buildings, recorded in the religious census, show that like all denominations Old Dissent had felt the effects of evangelical revival, with a notable upsurge of building and rebuilding in the preceding 25 years. For example, Bicester Independent chapel was built in 1729, the effects of its 19th-century revival reflected in Independent chapels built between 1841 and 1850 in the nearby villages of Blackthorn, Ambrosden and Launton. Quakerism was confined to 12 traditional meetings, with attendances of 10 to 20.

New Dissent, Methodism, with 55% of Nonconformist attendances, was the most widespread form of Dissent in Oxfordshire in 1851 (bottom map). Of 240 chapels or meeting houses returned, 73 were Wesleyan Methodist and 42 Primitive Methodist (compared with 43 Independent or Congregational and 40 Baptist). Wesleyans had built prodigiously in the 1830s and 1840s, reaching parts of the county, notably the centre and north-east, previously resistant to Dissent. They were widespread in towns and countryside. It was in the towns that the lowest IAs, but the greatest choice of organised religion, were to be found. Primitive Methodism was still relatively new to Oxfordshire, the denomination most likely to meet in cottages or barns rather than purpose-built chapels. The 'Ranters', as they were often called by Anglican clergy, were predominantly working-class and rural. They were found in the areas historically most hospitable to Dissent and, unlike the Wesleyans, did not break through to other parts of the county.

Roman Catholicism in Oxfordshire was localised and far flung. There were eight churches, typically linked to the presence of leading Catholic families, e.g. at Chipping Norton, Heythrop and Radford, where the common factor was the patronage of the Talbots, earls of Shrewsbury. Oxfordshire in 1851 had no centres of urban, working-class and Irish Catholics. There was one synagogue, in Oxford, with ten attending on Saturday 29 March.

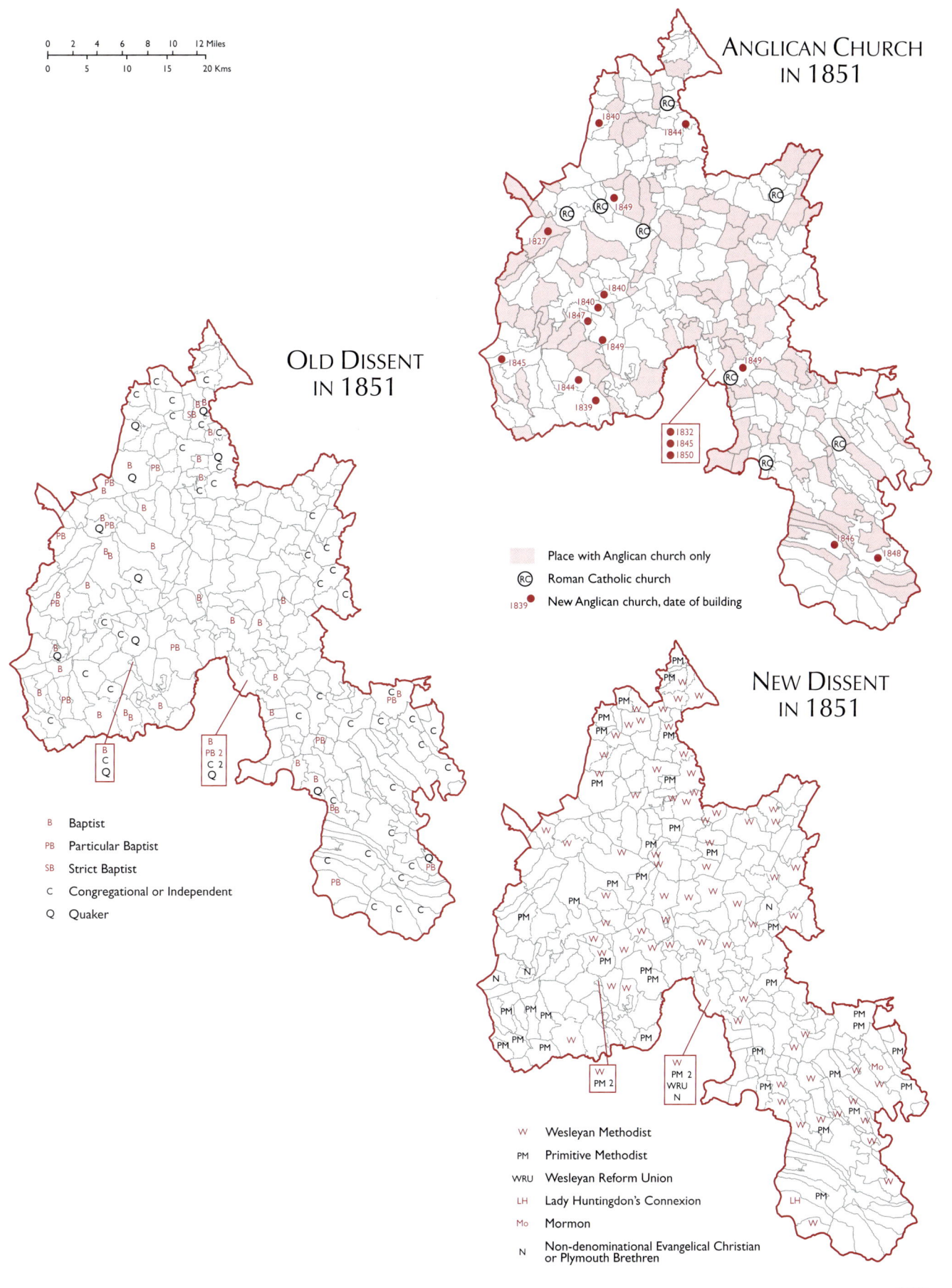

Anglican Church in 1851

Old Dissent in 1851

- **B** Baptist
- **PB** Particular Baptist
- **SB** Strict Baptist
- **C** Congregational or Independent
- **Q** Quaker

Place with Anglican church only

RC Roman Catholic church

1839 ● New Anglican church, date of building

New Dissent in 1851

- **W** Wesleyan Methodist
- **PM** Primitive Methodist
- **WRU** Wesleyan Reform Union
- **LH** Lady Huntingdon's Connexion
- **Mo** Mormon
- **N** Non-denominational Evangelical Christian or Plymouth Brethren

135

59 · Population Change 1801–1851   James Nash

Like England as a whole, the population of Oxfordshire rose faster in the first 50 years of the 19th century than at any time before or since. Nationally the peak came in the decade 1811–21, when the population of England and Wales rose by 18%, spurred principally by a higher birth rate. The same decade saw Oxfordshire's greatest rate of growth, of 16.2%. Over the 50 years the county's population grew by 52.2%, from 111,977 in 1801 to 170,434 in 1851. The question of parish population sizes and rates of increase or decline is complicated by boundary changes and by local factors such as the closure of workhouses or the temporary presence of workmen constructing railways. For the purposes of this entry the numbers for each parish have been accepted at face value.

Even at this rate of expansion Oxfordshire lagged behind most of the country. Over the same period the population of England and Wales grew by 101.6%. Among the southern rural counties of England, only Wiltshire grew significantly more slowly, by just 38%. The main reason for this variation in growth was internal migration, as families and individuals moved from one county to another, and in particular from the countryside to towns and cities.

Compared to most other counties, Oxfordshire had few towns. In 1801 only Oxford had more than 5,000 inhabitants, and by 1851 only Banbury and Witney had reached this size. The other Oxfordshire settlements which could claim to be called towns – Chipping Norton, Henley, Bicester, Thame, Charlbury, Eynsham, Watlington, Deddington, Burford, Bampton and Woodstock – were very small: none had more than 3,000 inhabitants in 1801 or 4,000 in 1851, though each performed some urban functions (see entry 45). Only Oxford, Banbury, Witney and Chipping Norton had any manufacturing capacity. Rural-to-urban migration, therefore, tended to be out of the county towards large centres of population, though there continued to be strong intra-county migrant flows from one village to another. Although emigration from Oxfordshire took place, it was less than in most other rural counties.

Population growth in Oxfordshire, 1801–51: urban and rural growth compared

	1801	1851	% growth
England & Wales (000)	8,893	17,928	101.6
Oxfordshire	111,977	170,434	52.2
Oxford (inc. suburbs)	13,421	30,410	126.6
Banbury (inc. suburb)	3,810	8,206	115.4
Urban Oxfordshire (Oxford + Banbury)	17,231	38,616	124.1
Rural Oxfordshire (inc. small towns)	94,746	131,818	39.1

Within Oxfordshire, the highest growth was, not surprisingly, in the larger towns. The population of the city of Oxford rose by 114%; growth was concentrated not in the city centre, where there was little room for new households, but in the inner suburbs of St Ebbe's to the south (up from 853 in 1801 to 4,656 in 1851), St Giles to the north (from 1,241 to 4,882) and St Thomas to the west (from 1,020 to 4,205), as land sales or the break-up of estates or market gardens freed land for development. By 1851 these three parishes housed 53% of the city's population, compared to 26% in 1801. Just outside the city three more suburban parishes saw exceptional growth: St Clement's (from 413 to 2,139), Headington (from 669 to 1,653) and Iffley (from 331 to 969), while the development of a fourth, Cowley, was held back by late enclosure.

Most other Oxfordshire towns were too small, and offered too few opportunities for employment, for suburbs to develop. Neithrop township, the western suburb of Banbury, was an exception: it quadrupled in size from 1,055 to 4,180, while Banbury itself grew by only 46%. In the south of the county, the parish of Rotherfield Greys (up from 677 to 1,518) benefited from an overspill of population from Henley. These were the only suburbs in the county in 1801–51.

Apart from Oxford and Banbury, there were some variations in the rates of growth from parish to parish, though there does not seem to be any general pattern pointing to common causes, rather than local factors. The mean rate of growth among the rural parishes was 39% over the period. A scattering of such parishes, among them Cogges, Hanborough, Bladon, Steeple Barton, Stoke Lyne and Cottesford, showed an increase of 80% or more. At least ten parishes, also scattered through the county, experienced actual decline, including four parishes fringing Otmoor, where a particularly controversial and strongly resisted enclosure took place in the 1830s. Some pattern is detectable by grouping parishes into their hundreds. The large hundred of Wootton (20,062 persons in 1851), running from Eynsham and Wolvercote in the south to Deddington in the north, grew by 56%; apart from the parishes named above, Steeple Aston, Eynsham, Kidlington, Sandford and Stonesfield showed strong growth. On the other hand, the western hundred of Bampton (including Burford, Witney and surrounding villages) increased by only 29%, the lowest rate of growth amongst the 14 hundreds of rural Oxfordshire. Alvescot, Black Bourton, Burford and Kencot all grew by less than 10% in the 50 years. Conversion of land use from arable to pasture may have been a factor in this area. But the other hundreds show little variation in the rates of population increase, nearly all growing by 35 to 45%. 'Push' and 'pull' factors affecting the decision to leave, including in particular the availability of work, evidently applied at similar rates to them all.

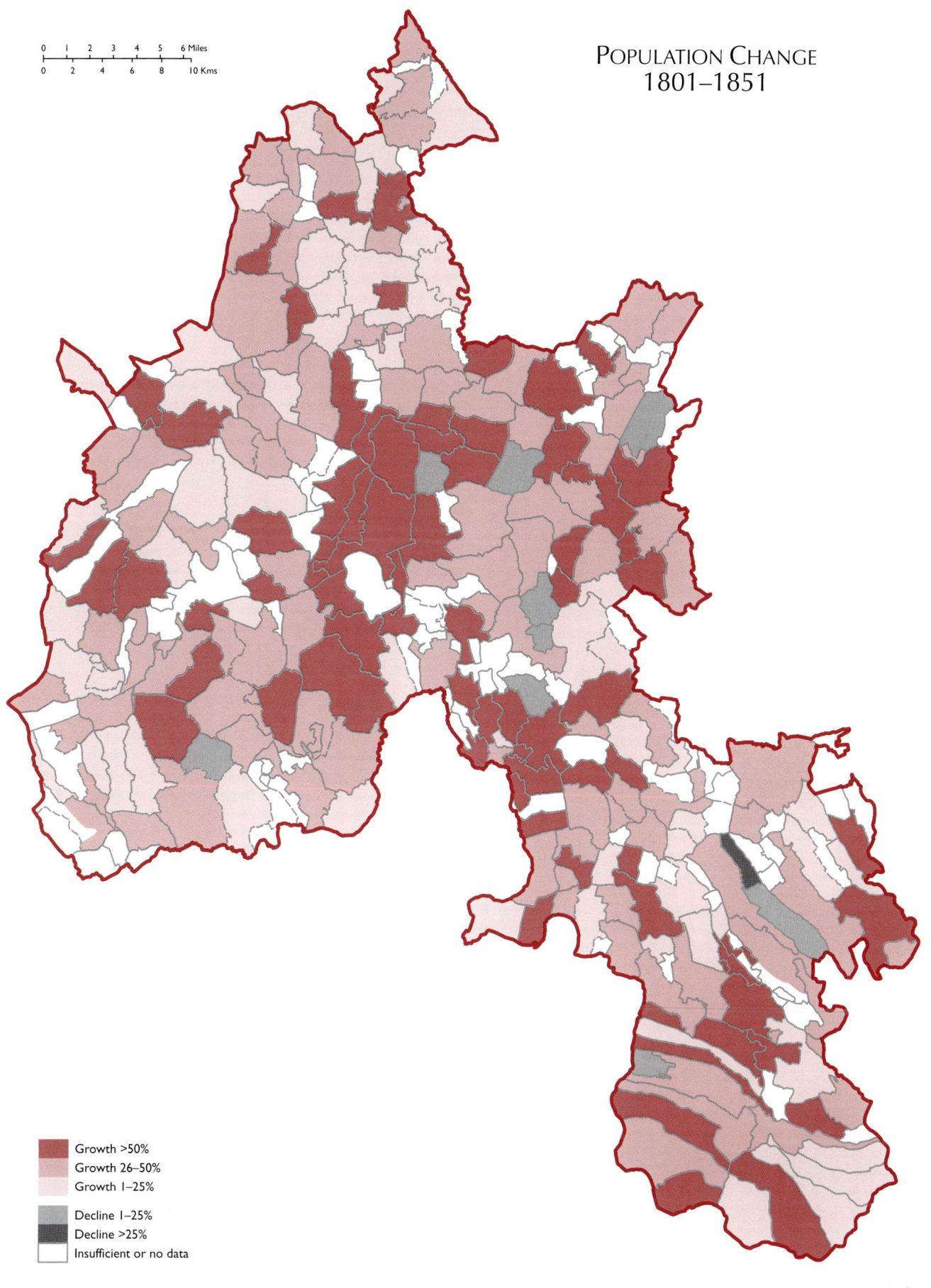

Population Change 1801–1851

Growth >50%
Growth 26–50%
Growth 1–25%
Decline 1–25%
Decline >25%
Insufficient or no data

60 · Population Change 1851–1901

James Nash

Population change in the second half of the 19th century presents a distinct contrast to the first. While the population of England and Wales continued to grow strongly between 1851 and 1901, rising by 81% from 18 to 32½ million, Oxfordshire's population stagnated.*

Oxfordshire was not alone in losing population: other southern rural counties without important towns or cities also declined. Dorset and Wiltshire, like Oxfordshire, grew by less than 10%. The populations of Somerset and Cornwall actually dropped. It is noticeable that large-scale out-migration from Oxfordshire started well before the agricultural depression of the last quarter of the century took hold. However, out-migration was particularly severe in the 1890s, when agricultural conditions were especially bad.

What growth there was, was concentrated entirely on Oxford and the suburbanised parishes immediately surrounding it, the extreme southernmost part of the county nearest Reading, and the two market towns of Chipping Norton and Banbury in the north (see also entries 45 and 64). Oxford itself continued to change. St Ebbe's was fully developed, and its population peaked in 1881. The inner suburbs of St Thomas and St Giles both doubled in size, the latter after St John's College began a cautious programme of development in the 1850s.[1] The most rapid growth was in the outlying parishes, which were transformed into suburbs. The population of St Clement's rose by 250%, from 2,100 to 5,200; Headington's from 1,700 to 3,700; Iffley's from 1,000 to 2,400; and, most remarkably, Cowley's from 800 to 9,300, after the very late enclosure of its fields in 1854. By 1891, over 50% of the city's population lived in the suburbs. Overall, Oxford's population rose from 30,000 in 1851 to 53,000 in 1901, an increase of nearly 80% and close to the national average.

Apart from Oxford, the largest four towns in the county were Banbury, Henley, Witney and Chipping Norton, with populations of between 10,000 and 4,000, respectively, in 1901. All these towns had some importance outside the county. Banbury, Witney and Chipping Norton had local industries with a national market – agricultural machinery in Banbury, blankets in Witney and tweed in Chipping Norton. Banbury also had an important place in the communications network between the south and the Midlands and was a market and trading centre out of proportion to its size.[2] The fourth town in this category, Henley, developed not because of industry but as a market town-cum-middle-class resort, due in part to the growing appeal of the Royal Regatta, established in 1839.

Town growth was uneven. Banbury and Chipping Norton grew fairly rapidly between 1851 and 1871, Banbury by 20% from 8,200 to 9,900; Chipping Norton by 21% from 3,400 to 4,100; but then both towns stagnated. Witney declined slightly but steadily, from 5,400 in 1851 to 5,100 in 1901. By contrast Henley grew rapidly, especially after 1881, when its development spilled over into the adjacent rural parish of Rotherfield Greys. Its population expanded from 5,250 in 1851 to 6,850 by 1901, making it the fastest growing town in the county after Oxford, overtaking Witney in size.

The next largest settlements, with just over 3,000 residents in 1851, were the market towns of Bicester and Thame. They also lost population by 1901, by 1% and 11% respectively, the decline mostly happening in the 1890s. These towns all depended mainly on their agricultural hinterland and did not have any substantial local industry. Despite considerable out-migration they held their place in the local economy, with local newspapers, markets and services, and as administrative centres.

The seven smallest towns – Deddington, Eynsham, Watlington, Burford, Bampton, Charlbury and Woodstock, with between 1,250 and 2,200 inhabitants each in 1851 – all lost population, as local transport links improved and as the larger towns gathered up administrative functions at the expense of the smaller. All in all, these towns declined even more than the villages. Eynsham and Watlington made small gains between 1851 and 1871, while the other towns made small losses; after 1871 all these towns declined. Burford, Bampton and Deddington suffered in particular. The populations of the seven towns declined by 20% overall between 1851 and 1901, evidence of their loss of position in the local community.

The rural population of Oxfordshire, i.e. all the population outside the towns mentioned above, declined between 1851 and 1901. Until 1871 it was just stable, at about 100,000; from 1871 to 1901 it went down to 86,500, a decline of 13%. Again, this reduction was particularly marked in the 1890s. As we have seen, suburbanised parishes round Oxford grew rapidly, but the effect of Oxford as an employment or foodstuff market for surrounding villages seems to have been very limited, and other parishes less than five miles from Oxford, e.g. Beckley, Noke, Islip and Cassington, lost more than 25% of their populations. The area in south Oxfordshire which shared in the greater prosperity of east Berkshire extended only a few miles to the north of the river Thames, to Rotherfield Greys and Ipsden; and none of Oxfordshire's small towns showed the vigour of those in Berkshire. Instead these pockets of modest growth were surrounded by three areas of sharp decline: the villages on the Chiltern edge from Ewelme to Chinnor, to the north of the county around Banbury, and in the west from Stanton Harcourt to Burford. Here villages declined by more than 25%; in the rest of the county very few showed any growth.

Oxfordshire towns and villages, 1851–1901

	1851	1901	Growth %
Oxford[a]	29,900	52,900	+77
Banbury	8,200	10,000	+22
5 'middling' towns[b]	20,400	22,000	+8
7 smallest towns	12,200	9,700	-20
Villages	99,700	86,500	-13

a. Including suburbs of St Clement, Headington, Iffley and Cowley
b. Chipping Norton, Witney, Henley (including Rotherfield Greys), Bicester and Thame

* For table, see Further Reading and Notes.

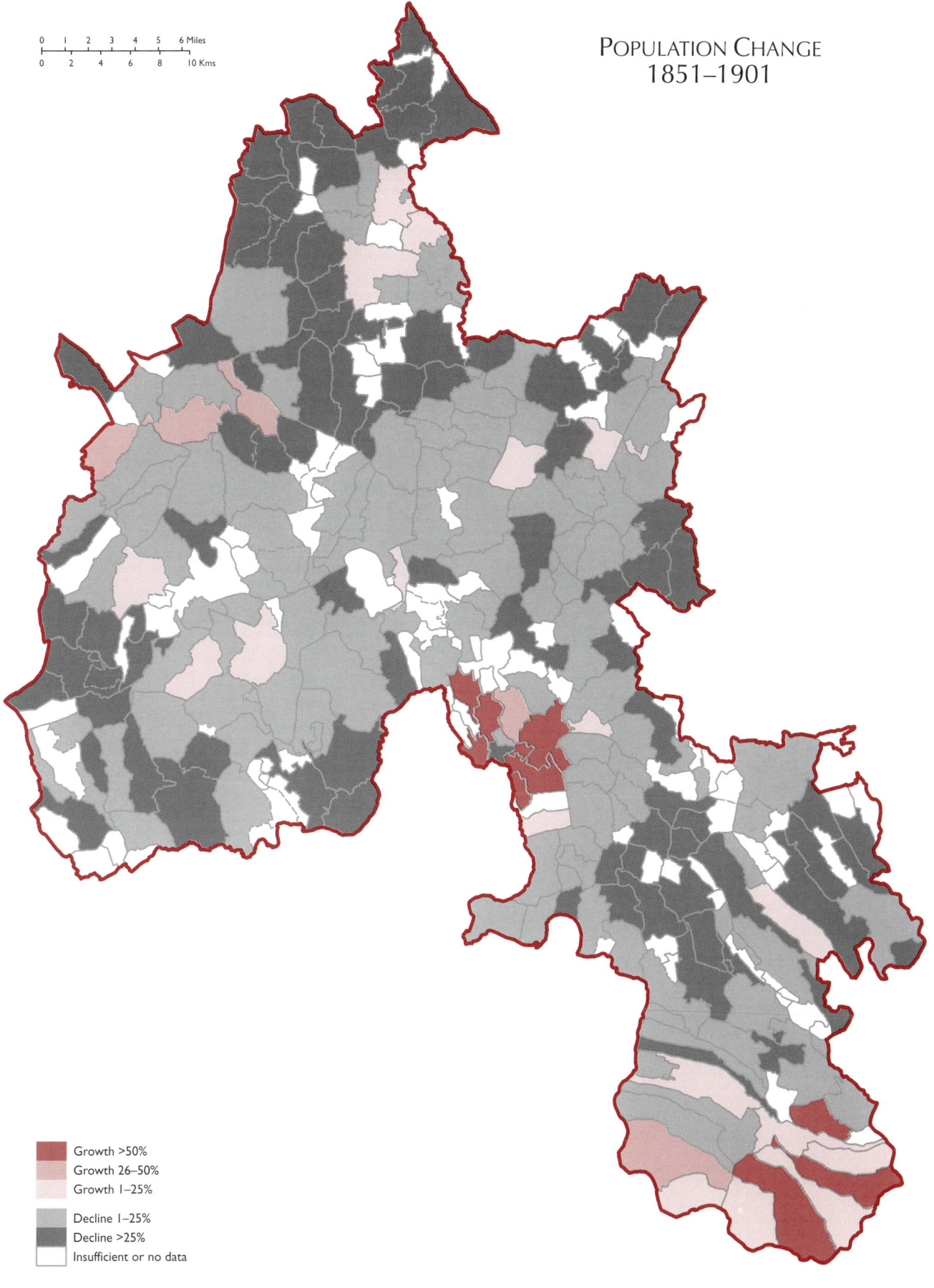

Population Change 1851–1901

Legend:
- Growth >50%
- Growth 26–50%
- Growth 1–25%
- Decline 1–25%
- Decline >25%
- Insufficient or no data

61 · Migration Patterns 1851–1901   James Nash

Between 1851 and 1911 rural England experienced a net loss of over four million people through migration, and the urban areas a net gain of over two and a half million. The peak of this activity was in the 30 years between 1841 and 1871, when the rural population of England and Wales dropped from 53% to 35%. By 1901 the rural exodus was nearly over.

Oxfordshire was one of the least urbanised counties and experienced strong migration out of the county, especially in the second half of the century. Whilst the population of England and Wales nearly doubled between 1851 and 1901, Oxfordshire's stagnated, and in the 1890s actually declined.

Any measure of migration flows within Great Britain (this entry does not attempt to count overseas migration) must be an underestimate, as many movements, especially where a family or individual moved more than once between census years, would have gone undetected. A convenient method of measuring these flows is to analyse other county populations by place of birth, thus counting the number of Oxfordshire-born residents in one census year, in this case 1881.

The largest population flow was to adjacent counties, in order of popularity, Berkshire, Warwickshire, Buckinghamshire, Gloucestershire, Northamptonshire, Worcestershire* and Wiltshire. Some 36,300 Oxfordshire-born people (or Oxonians) were living in these counties in 1881, 13.8 per thousand of the resident population. The most popular, Berkshire, had the longest mutual boundary with Oxfordshire. Of Oxonians in Berkshire, 2,700 were in Reading, just over the border from Oxfordshire; the rest were in small towns – Cookham, Windsor, Wokingham and Sandhurst – and villages. In 1881, 51 Berkshire residents per thousand were Oxfordshire-born. These were local, short-distance migrants, many seeking similar, rural-based work to that which they or their families had done in Oxfordshire.

Some 33,000 out-migrants moved to the London area. There were 19,200 Oxonians living in Middlesex in 1881 and 8,400 in Surrey (which included London south of the river, with suburbs such as Lambeth and Camberwell). They tended to cluster in west London, near the roads or railway stations of arrival. In Paddington, for example, at 12.5 per thousand, there was twice the density of Oxonians than in Islington (5.4 per thousand). Many were young unmarried women working as servants. Families were less likely to move to London than to neighbouring counties; London was more attractive to young, single people, though not exclusively so.

Other regions drew fewer Oxonians. No non-contiguous county outside the south-east had an Oxonian population of more than four per thousand. Northern industrial cities, despite higher wages, had little appeal, except where existing personal links eased the difficulties of migration and home-and-job-seeking. Some 5,600 Oxonians were living in the northern counties (5,300 in Lancashire and Yorkshire), but this was only 0.7% of the resident inhabitants. Apart from Warwickshire, the midlands drew few Oxonions, except for Staffordshire with 2,400.

Remote and rural regions had the least appeal. About 1,700 migrants had moved to the south-west, mainly to Somerset and Dorset. East Anglia attracted very few and Scotland almost none. No Oxonians at all were found in Cumberland or Northumberland. Overall, the ten most popular counties for Oxfordshire migrants, in relation to their size, were Berkshire, Buckinghamshire, Northamptonshire, Warwickshire, Gloucestershire, Middlesex, Surrey, Worcestershire, Wiltshire and Hertfordshire; the least attractive were Cumberland, Northumberland, Cornwall, Durham, Norfolk, Westmorland, Lincolnshire, Lancashire, Cheshire and Suffolk.

There were counter-currents of migration where families and individuals moved from other counties to Oxfordshire, or left only to return later. On the whole, migration currents into the county were strongest from counties which also received large numbers of Oxonians. About 26,400 Oxfordshire inhabitants (146 per thousand) were born in adjacent counties; there were 7,300 from the south-east, including 4,100 from Middlesex; and 1,400 from Hampshire. However, out-migrants from Oxfordshire to other counties exceeded in-migrants from those counties in most cases. In particular Surrey, Lancashire, Middlesex, Staffordshire and Yorkshire received more than four times as many Oxonians as sent migrants to Oxfordshire.

Out- and in-migration from British regions and counties to and from Oxfordshire, 1881

Region (Counties)	From Oxon	Oxon-born[1]	To Oxon	Ratio[2]
Adjacent counties (Berks, Bucks, Northants, Warwks, Glos, Worcs, Wilts)	36,293	13.8	26,412	1.4
London & South-East (Middx, Surrey, Herts, Kent, Essex)	32,947	5.4	7,270	4.5
South (Hants/IOW, Sussex, CI)	3,728	3.2	1,933	1.9
West Midlands (Staffs, Hereford, Salop, Cheshire)	3,502	1.7	1,178	3.0
East Midlands (Leics, Rutland, Derby, Notts, Lincs)	2,255	1.4	986	2.3
East (Beds, Hunts, Cambs, Suffolk, Norfolk)	1,387	1.2	1,417	1.0
South-West (Somerset, Dorset, Devon, Cornwall)	1,697	1.1	2,179	0.8
North (Yorks, Lancs, Westmorland, Durham, IOM, Cumb, Northumb)	5,589	0.7	1,396	4.0
Wales	1,044			
Scotland	46			

Regions and counties in each region are listed in order of attractiveness to Oxon out-migrants, relative to population size
1. Oxon-born per thousand population
2. Ratio of out-migrants per in-migrant

* At this period Worcestershire was adjacent to Oxfordshire.

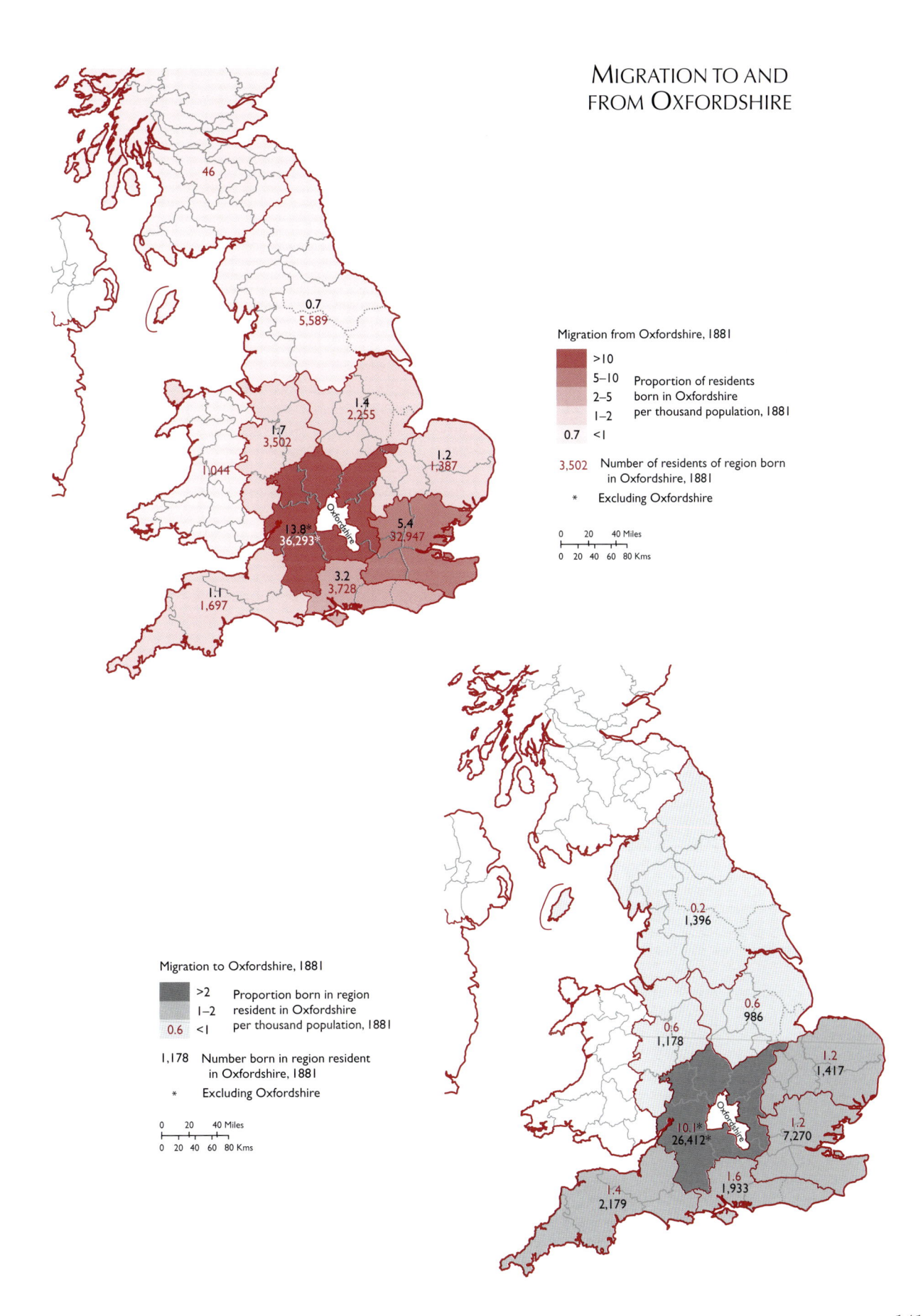

Migration to and from Oxfordshire

Migration from Oxfordshire, 1881

- >10
- 5–10   Proportion of residents
- 2–5   born in Oxfordshire
- 1–2   per thousand population, 1881
- 0.7   <1

3,502 Number of residents of region born in Oxfordshire, 1881

* Excluding Oxfordshire

Values on map:
- 46
- 0.7 / 5,589
- 1.7 / 3,502
- 1.4 / 2,255
- 1,044
- 1.2 / 1,387
- 13.8* / 36,293* (Oxfordshire)
- 5.4 / 32,947
- 3.2 / 3,728
- 1.1 / 1,697

Migration to Oxfordshire, 1881

- >2   Proportion born in region
- 1–2   resident in Oxfordshire
- 0.6   <1   per thousand population, 1881

1,178 Number born in region resident in Oxfordshire, 1881

* Excluding Oxfordshire

Values on map:
- 0.2 / 1,396
- 0.6 / 986
- 0.6 / 1,178
- 1.2 / 1,417
- 10.1* / 26,412* (Oxfordshire)
- 1.2 / 7,270
- 1.6 / 1,933
- 1.4 / 2,179

62 · Friendly Societies

Shaun Morley

The friendly society was the most popular form of organised association in rural 19th-century England. These were mutual aid societies to insure members against sickness and burial costs. But much more than that, friendly societies provided security in vulnerable times, fraternity, socialising and, through their rules, a self-regulating behavioural code. Membership was almost exclusively male. Independent village clubs were local in nature, many with rules that allowed membership only to those living in the village or immediate vicinity. Club meetings were normally held at a local inn or school room and on club nights the quarterly dues were paid. Most independent clubs varied in size between 40 and 100 benefit members. Some had substantial membership in relation to their village size. Somerton peaked at 310 members in 1877 against a total parish population of around 350, so must have drawn members from further afield, despite neighbouring villages being well served by clubs. Friendly societies were the most prominent of a range of local organisations, aimed at mutual aid and practical survival such as coal, clothing or pig clubs.

Many clubs also had honorary members, who subscribed each year as a show of support for the club, but drew no benefit. Independent societies came in two forms – permanent and dividing, with sharing of assets after one, five or seven years being the most common cycle of the latter. The dividing clubs were seen by contemporary commentators as an inferior form, encouraging short-term returns rather than sustained thrift, but they fulfilled a purpose as useful as their permanent counterparts.

The affiliated orders, centrally organised with branches, became popular in the industrial north in the early 19th century but struggled to take hold in Oxfordshire, even in the urban areas. Numerically – both in terms of number of clubs and membership – independent clubs exceeded the affiliated orders for most of the century. The 1874 Royal Commission reported that the Banbury Union district was 'swarming with local clubs of a good average character', many of which were registered but the number unregistered was also large.[1] Up to 40% of Oxfordshire societies remained unregistered and many of these remain largely hidden from the modern view.

Friendly societies first appeared in the 17th century and it is likely that some were present in the county by the early 18th century, especially in Oxford, which had a wide range of associational clubs. Standlake Benefit Society (formed 1761) and Charlbury Old Club (1762) are two of the earliest known, whilst Stonesfield (1765) was longest lived, surviving until 1911.

In 1802–3 a national survey revealed just 69 registered societies in Oxfordshire with 5,030 members.[2] This was one of the lowest levels of clubs and membership in England and Wales, with only 1% of the population being members. While the numbers had grown by 1857 to 167 clubs, only the smallest counties had fewer, with the sole exception of Hampshire, which had a similar distribution. However, where clubs existed frequently over 50% of adult males of the community were members. Only a small proportion of clubs accepted female members whose subscriptions and benefits were half. The Oxford Working Women's Benefit Society was formed in 1882 and Whitchurch Women's Friendly Society, an unregistered dividing society, lasted for 20 years in mid century, with benefit including 12 shillings for four weeks 'lying in' following child birth.[3]

The societies supported members with payments for sickness, burial and occasionally other benefits. Membership was governed by strict rules and those receiving sick pay could not visit a public house, work, engage in gaming or walk far from home without losing benefit. They were visited at home by club stewards as a sign of support, but also to ensure they were actually sick. Most independent clubs were wholly democratic with all officials elected, generally by simple majority voting. Rather than social control by the elite, the evidence points strongly to a preference for self-regulated standards. In almost all independent clubs, the membership decided on the direction of the club, whilst affiliated order branches were increasingly regulated by their central governing body.

The annual club day was one time in the year when the whole community engaged in a celebration, with marching bands, stalls, music, dancing and a club dinner at the clubhouse. Those sons or daughters who had migrated from the village returned to meet family and friends, often bringing with them money or gifts. It was a whole community event, exceeding the popularity of the religious festivals. Club day provided a further opportunity for the members to display their independence. The reinvention of the parish perambulation made a strong statement. Led by a brass band, the members would process to be seen, to publicise their importance and to entertain. The noise generated was a sign of their presence, as was the calling at the larger houses in expectation of a cash contribution or goods. In towns, several clubs would frequently hold their club day at the same time forming an impressive display. Establishment observers of club days, such as clergy or newspapers, frequently referred to significant drunkenness and violent behaviour but few actual examples are now apparent.[4]

The maps show those parishes where friendly societies existed in 1802–3 and makes comparison with societies registered in 1891 (independent societies) and 1886 (affiliated order branches).[5] A total of 130 societies and branches were registered at these later dates, fewer than in 1857, with affiliated order branches representing 26% of clubs. Evidence from newspapers and other contemporary accounts indicates unregistered clubs were still a significant feature. Throughout the century, Oxford and the northern and western part of the county exhibited the greater concentration and south Oxfordshire a relative dearth of registered societies. Affiliated order branches were grouped in the Banbury and Oxford areas and dominated by two orders, the Independent Order of Odd Fellows Manchester Unity and the Ancient Order of Foresters. By 1905 these branches exceeded independent clubs by 83 to 58. The main functions of the friendly societies were significantly superseded by the Liberal welfare reforms of 1911 and they dwindled in significance from their 19th-century heyday.

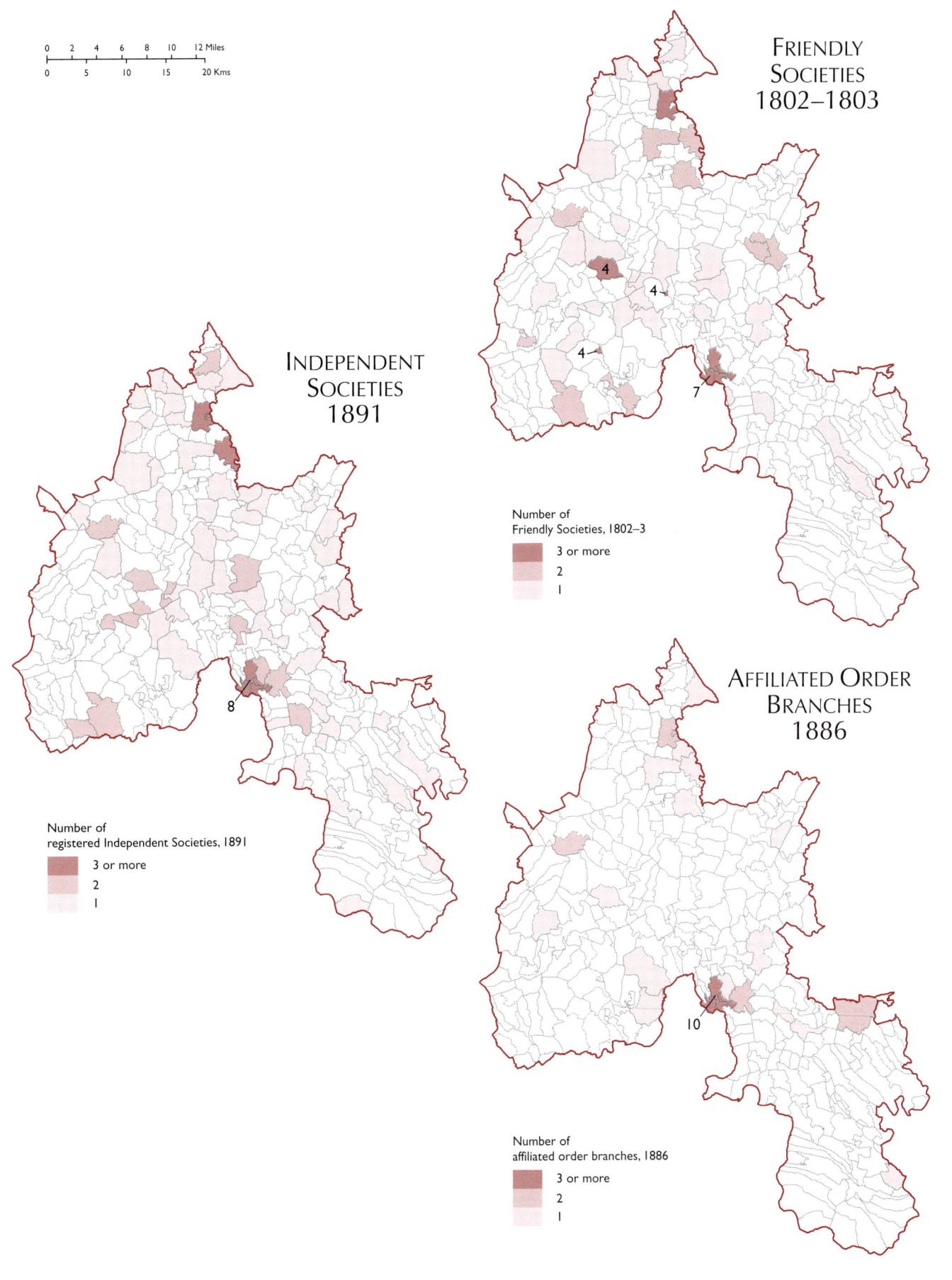

FRIENDLY SOCIETIES 1802–1803

Number of Friendly Societies, 1802–3
- 3 or more
- 2
- 1

INDEPENDENT SOCIETIES 1891

Number of registered Independent Societies, 1891
- 3 or more
- 2
- 1

AFFILIATED ORDER BRANCHES 1886

Number of affiliated order branches, 1886
- 3 or more
- 2
- 1

143

63 · Poor Relief 1834–1948
Chris Gilliam and Kate Tiller

The Poor Law Amendment Act of 1834 swept away a system of local government established in 1601, with responsibilities for the poor and needy exercised through individual parishes or townships. The new act was a watershed, moving from the persistent diversity of the old parish government to a standardised system, rooted in Utilitarian orthodoxy and directed centrally from London. The state superseded the locality using a solution defined by theories of political economy rather than by the personal relationships of a moral economy. A financial remedy was sought to the rising costs of the previous, variable provision, increasingly overwhelmed by the volume and nature of need. The New Poor Law was also intended as a social and psychological tool, a disincentive to pauperism.

Its terms were clear. It was not sufficient to be poor to qualify for public relief. Recipients must be destitute. Relief was to be given to the able-bodied only in a workhouse where conditions were 'less eligible' than any found in the applicant's outside life. This was designed as a deterrent, self-acting test. Parishes were grouped into new poor law unions (PLUs), locally administered by salaried staff, overseen by a Union Board of Guardians elected on a property-based franchise. The whole was regulated by the Poor Law Commission (PLC) in London and its itinerant inspectors.

In Oxfordshire the structures to deliver the New Poor Law were rapidly established. Eight PLUs were set up between March and September 1835, and seven new workhouses opened in 1836–7.* The aim was that Unions should be of equal size, centred on a market town and its hinterland of social and economic connections. This proved easier said than done, and the county's nine PLUs varied somewhat in population and area (see table).

The changed geography of poor relief demonstrated new thinking by overriding traditional patterns, in this case county boundaries. Five Oxfordshire PLUs included parishes in other counties. Thus Banbury Union reflected the town's extensive sphere of influence, stretching into Northants and Warwickshire. Similarly, seven PLUs centred in other counties included Oxfordshire parishes; Abingdon (including 12 Oxfordshire parishes), Brackley (2), Bradfield (3), Faringdon (5), Wallingford (12), and Wycombe (3). Until they were transferred to Buckinghamshire in 1844, Buckingham Union included two Oxfordshire settlements, Lillingstone Lovell and Boycott. The new system proved a focus for vigorous and political local debate; the *Banbury Guardian* newspaper began life in 1838, debating the New Poor Law.

The reformed arrangements cut costs and re-energised private charitable effort. The most potent symbols of change were the workhouses, typically located on the edge of towns, with accommodation for 200 to 450 inmates. The buildings generally followed standard designs of spare grandeur with impressive gatehouses and wings radiating from a central hub, enabling both oversight of the inmates and the segregation of young and old, male and female required by the workhouse system. Paupers came together for meals and religious worship. All aspects of expenditure and management, down to the daily menus, were subject to direction by the PLC (from 1847 to 1871 the Poor Law Board and from 1871 to 1919 the Local Government Board (LGB)).

In practice outdoor relief, provided in the poor's own homes, continued after 1834. Ten years later, in 1844, some 22% of local inhabitants were reported as being in receipt of some poor relief in a six-month period, the overwhelming majority of outdoor relief.[1] This was supposedly given only in restricted circumstances, like sickness, but it sometimes suited local farmers, prominent amongst ratepayers and Guardians, to agree to take on otherwise unemployed local labourers rather than send them to the workhouse. The task of administering the New Poor Law outside the workhouses fell to Relieving Officers (ROs). The diary of George Dew, RO for the Bletchingdon district of Bicester Union from 1870 to 1923, shows the tensions between theory and practice. Dew, of Lower Heyford, left school at 15, was RO aged 24, and visited paupers in their homes. In 1879 in the 18 parishes of his district there were 116 people receiving outdoor relief (14 able-bodied, 81 not, and 21 children). Sometimes the workhouse became inevitable, as when, in December 1870, Dew took an 81-year-old man on a bed by carrier's cart to the Bicester workhouse. In 1873 the Union moved from giving outdoor relief mainly in bread to cash payments. The LGB feared that the able-bodied might misuse cash, but the change went ahead.

Union workhouses in the later 19th century developed a range of facilities – medical services, dispensaries, special provision for deaf and blind, care for mothers and babies, vagrants' wards – and from the 1870s sent pauper children to local schools. This reflected the dominance of the old, sick and young amongst inmates. Outside the workhouse significant proportions of the labouring population experienced poverty at some stage in their lives (see entry 49). Awareness and understandings of poverty were changing. After years of debate, the 1906 Liberal government legislated on welfare reform, including old-age pensions (1908), and the National Insurance Act (1911). In 1913 workhouses were retitled poor law institutions, but it was not until the Local Government Act of 1929 that the system was radically changed. Boards of Guardians were replaced by Public Assistance Committees, dispensing means-tested benefits. Numerous workhouses (six in Oxfordshire) became hospitals or homes, albeit still tainted by the spectre of 'less eligibility'. For many people it was only the post-1945 creation of the Welfare State that really changed things. As one of its creators, Ernest Bevin, said of the 1948 National Assistance Act, 'At last we have buried the poor law.' Only three of the county's workhouses have escaped post-war demolition, Henley (Townlands Hospital), and Chipping Norton and Thame, now developed for private housing.

---

* Oxfordshire had nine Unions in all; that in Oxford continued a Union and Board of Guardians, or Incorporation, established in 1771, with a large workhouse in what is now Wellington Square, Oxford. This was replaced in 1864 by the Cowley Road workhouse. One PLU, Henley, initially used a pre-existing, parish workhouse, which was subsequently expanded and modernised. All the other Unions built afresh immediately after their establishment.

Poor Law Unions

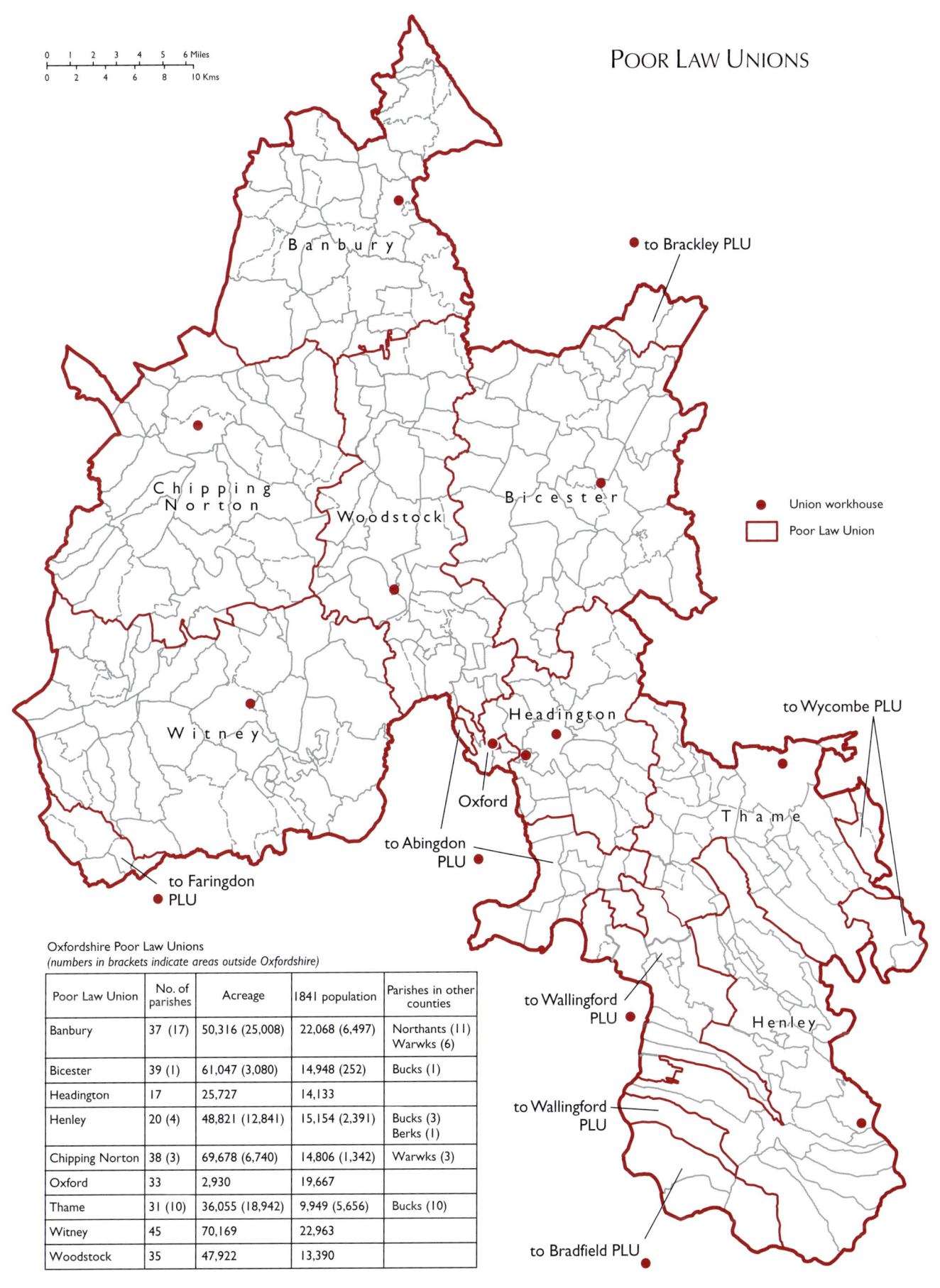

Oxfordshire Poor Law Unions
(numbers in brackets indicate areas outside Oxfordshire)

Poor Law Union	No. of parishes	Acreage	1841 population	Parishes in other counties
Banbury	37 (17)	50,316 (25,008)	22,068 (6,497)	Northants (11) Warwks (6)
Bicester	39 (1)	61,047 (3,080)	14,948 (252)	Bucks (1)
Headington	17	25,727	14,133	
Henley	20 (4)	48,821 (12,841)	15,154 (2,391)	Bucks (3) Berks (1)
Chipping Norton	38 (3)	69,678 (6,740)	14,806 (1,342)	Warwks (3)
Oxford	33	2,930	19,667	
Thame	31 (10)	36,055 (18,942)	9,949 (5,656)	Bucks (10)
Witney	45	70,169	22,963	
Woodstock	35	47,922	13,390	

64 · The Growth and Impact of Oxford after 1800   Malcolm Graham

The built-up area of Oxford scarcely extended beyond its medieval limits in 1801 and had a population of under 12,000. Today, the city covers 4,560 hectares and houses an estimated 151,000 people.

The population of Oxford rose by 314% during the 19th century – nationally, the increase was 267% – and this in a rural county with a declining population (see entry 60). The city contained 11% of the county's population in 1801 and 27% by 1901. Without major industrial development, Oxford continued to offer much employment as a provider of goods and services to the university, to the surrounding agricultural region and to an increasing residential population. Printing, especially the University Press, brewing and the building trade were locally important and college service employed 609 males in 1901; a wholesale clothing industry and retail trade employed growing numbers of females.

Migrants from Oxford's hinterland and people unhoused by clearances in the city centre generated a surge of house-building in the 1820s, particularly in St Ebbe's and Jericho and in St Clement's; the latter was incorporated into the municipal boundary in 1836. Enclosure of Cowley Field, south-east of Magdalen Bridge, in 1853 opened up a large area to freehold development and the growing Cowley St John district became part of the Oxford Local Board district in 1864. Development of North Oxford, controlled largely by St John's College, began in the 1850s and its leasehold villas accommodated not only prosperous town and gown households but also many newcomers of independent means who found the city attractive and easily accessible by rail. By 1889, when Oxford became a county borough, North Oxford had virtually merged with Summertown, a village planted on old enclosures in 1820, and the new boundary incorporated that area. South of Folly Bridge, New Hinksey originated in 1847 as a detached suburb, still in Berkshire, which was added to the Oxford Local Board district in 1875. The coming of the railways to St Thomas's parish in 1850–1 encouraged development in West Oxford and, as the city had 451 railway employees by 1901, this area became a virtual railway suburb.

Henry Taunt, the Oxford photographer, humorously depicted the outcome of 19th-century development as the Oxford Ass. Middle-class North Oxford rode a donkey with its head in Headington and its tail in West Oxford; East Oxford and Cowley were its front legs and South Oxford the back ones. The topography of the city to some extent dictated this pattern of development by limiting house-building on the flood plains of the Thames and Cherwell. Land ownership was equally important since Oxford colleges owned much of the land in and around Oxford and were reluctant to initiate development which might prove prejudicial to their long-term interests.

The shortage of development land in 19th-century Oxford encouraged building beyond the city boundary. Headington and Iffley continued to provide idyllic settings for country estates and Boars Hill began to attract wealthy residents from the 1880s. New villages were planted at Headington Hill in 1824 and at New Headington in 1851, while freehold building plots were made available at Cowley, New Marston and Kennington in 1866, 1871 and the 1900s respectively.

Oxford seemed destined to remain a university city at the beginning of the 20th century but William Morris, later Lord Nuffield, swiftly added an industrial dimension at Cowley. The motor industry attracted many new residents and encouraged house-building, especially in an arc to the east and south-east of the old city and north of Summertown in Wolvercote and Cutteslowe. The Cutteslowe Walls, built in 1934 to separate a private estate from a council estate, achieved national notoriety before their demolition in 1959. The population of the city rose by 73% between 1921 and 1951 – the national increase was 17% – and house-building spread beyond the extended 1929 boundaries to places like Botley, Kennington, Kidlington and Risinghurst which were readily accessible by bus, cycle and car.

Unrestrained development threatened the special character of Oxford and, in the post-war years, planners tried to limit the growth of the local motor industry and formally proposed a Green Belt around the city in 1959 (see entry 70). Cowley thrived in the 1950s and many new workers were housed at Blackbird Leys, a large estate south-east of Oxford, where building began in 1957. Slum clearance reduced the city centre population and employment in the motor industry began to fall in the 1970s. Rising car ownership and the flight to the suburbs also encouraged housing developments in communities within commuting distance of the city. From 1979, County Structure Plans directed development towards other centres and Oxford's population remained virtually static between 1961 and 1991.

A flourishing economy generated renewed growth in the 1990s and the city's population increased from 110,103 in 1991 to 134,248 in 2001. Key employment sectors included education, particularly at the city's two universities, health, public administration, retail, publishing and high-technology businesses, many of them spin-offs from university research. Extensive house-building took place at Greater Leys, beyond Blackbird Leys, and on former industrial land beside the Oxford Canal in North Oxford, but much development has continued beyond the city boundary. Oxford University and Oxford Brookes University now have over 40,000 students and their housing needs continue to fuel the demand for more houses for the working population. The 2009 South-East Plan required the building of 8,000 new houses in the city by 2026 and another 4,000 houses in a controversial incursion into the Green Belt beyond Greater Leys. Oxford's population is expected to reach 186,000 by 2031.

The number of jobs in Oxford is much larger than the resident working population and about 25,000 commuters come into the city every weekday. Many of these people live in communities which are effectively suburbs but remain outside the city. Meanwhile, a shortage of development sites within the city has spawned a ring of science parks around Oxford. Oxford has far outgrown its administrative boundaries and it now impacts upon much of central Oxfordshire.

The Growth of Oxford

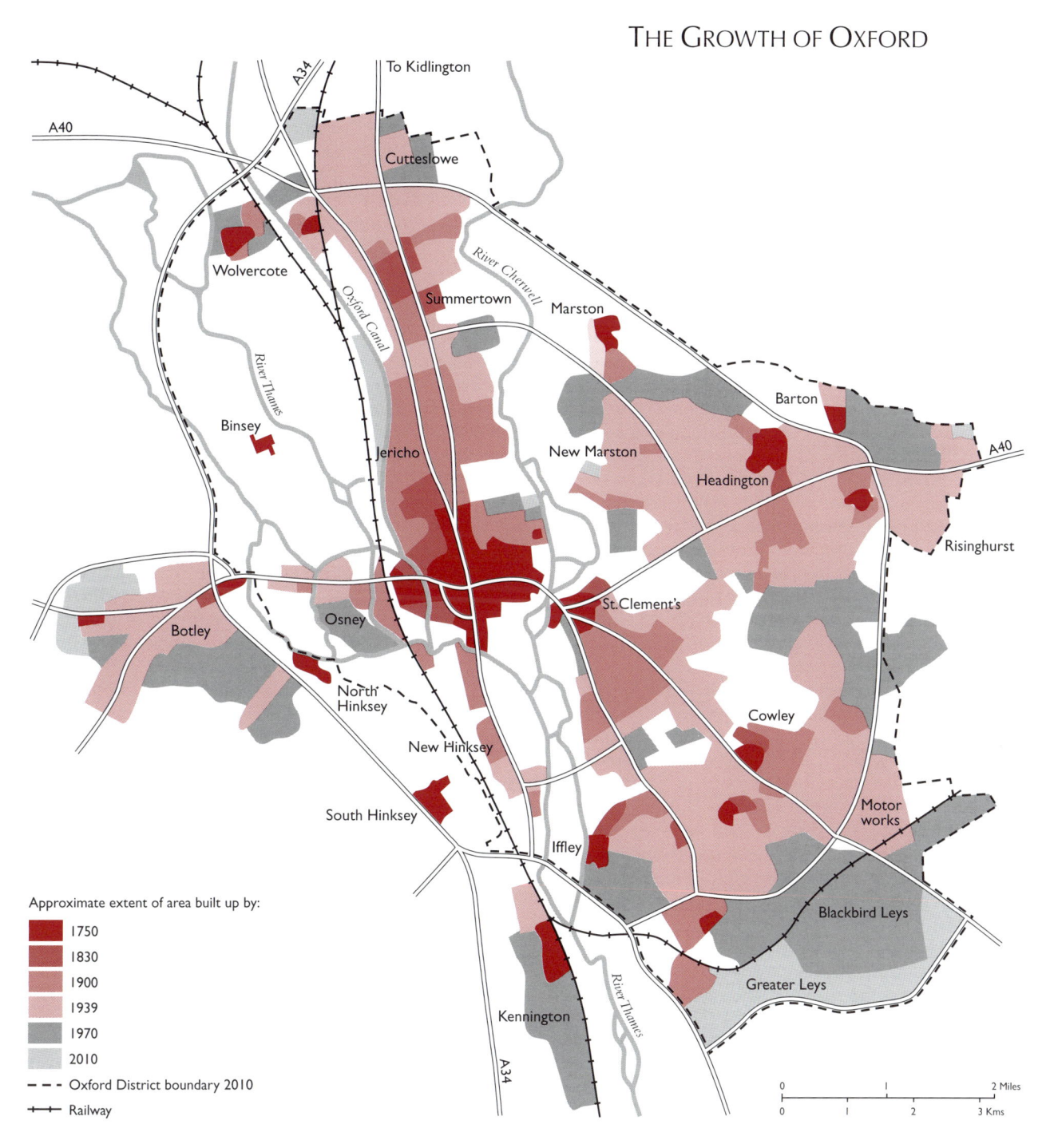

Approximate extent of area built up by:
- 1750
- 1830
- 1900
- 1939
- 1970
- 2010
- – – – Oxford District boundary 2010
- ┼┼┼ Railway

The population of Oxford (* estimated)

Year	Area (ha)	Area (acre)	Population	Year	Area (ha)	Area (acre)	Population	Year	Area (ha)	Area (acre)	Population
1801	1,186	2,931	11,921	1881			40,837	1961	3,555	8,784	106,291
1811			13,257	1891	1,908	4,715	45,742	1971			108,805
1821			16,446	1901			49,336	1981			107,770
1831			20,710	1911			53,048	1991	4,560	11,268	110,103
1841	1,421	3,511	24,258	1921			57,036	2001			134,248
1851			28,843	1931	3,405	8,414	80,539	2007			*151,000
1861			28,601	1941			*107,000	2011			*161,700
1871			34,482	1951			98,684	2031			*186,000

147

65 · The Motor Industry — Malcolm Graham

It seemed in 1899 that 'Oxfordshire was fated never to be an industrial county.' There were traditional industries such as the Witney blanket industry and Bliss's Tweed Mill at Chipping Norton. In Banbury, Samuelson's Britannia Works introduced large-scale manufacture of agricultural implements in the 1850s but a proposal to build a railway carriage factory in Oxford in 1865 had come to nothing.

The motor industry changed Oxfordshire within a generation. Two early initiatives were short-lived but the third one proved decisive. In Bampton, Oliver Collett, a jeweller, built a motorcycle in 1898 before constructing a light car, the Bampton Voiturette, in around 1902 but he soon abandoned work on motor vehicles. The Berwick Motor Company, in Banbury, enjoyed brief success building Berwick motorcycles in the late 1920s. William Richard Morris, later Lord Nuffield (1877–1963), was behind the third dramatically successful enterprise, making bicycles behind the family home in East Oxford by 1893 and motorcycles by 1898. He diversified into the sale, repair and hire of motor cars at premises in Longwall Street by 1903 and built a palatial garage on the site in 1910. He assembled his prototype Bullnose Morris there in 1912 and began production in April 1913 at the former Oxford Military College in Cowley. The site was ideal, close to Oxford but beyond the city boundary (until 1929) and with ample space for expansion. Morris's was largely diverted into munitions work during the First World War but, by increasing output and cutting prices, the firm became the country's largest producer of cars by 1925. Exports boomed and nearby Cowley station became Morris Cowley in 1928, when facilities opened for delivering new cars by rail to British ports. Morris Radiators opened in Summertown in 1919 and moved to new premises in Woodstock Road in 1925. Growing demand for MG (Morris Garages) sports cars led to the building of the world's first special-purpose sports-car factory at Edmund Road in 1927; production moved to Abingdon two years later. Morris also encouraged the establishment of the Pressed Steel Company next to the Cowley plant in 1926.

The number of people employed in the Oxford motor industry rose from around 100 in 1914 to over 11,000 by 1939. Many people, particularly from south-west England and south Wales, moved to Oxford between the wars to find work. Morris did not consider workers' housing to be his responsibility, and private building firms, notably Moss & Son, builders of Florence Park in 1934, erected a number of estates in Cowley and Headington which were largely rented by factory workers. Smaller developments in many communities around Oxford provided cheaper housing for other incomers, while local recruits, attracted by higher pay, often chose to commute to Cowley daily by bike, bus or train rather than pay high rents in the City. By 1936, around 40% of the workforce was living outside the City, mostly within ten miles of the plant. Significant numbers were also travelling longer distances, particularly from Banbury, Bicester and Witney and from outside the county.

Cowley was diverted into munitions work during the Second World War and became a crucial part of the export drive in postwar Britain. Despite planning constraints aimed at preserving Oxford's setting, the local motor industry continued to grow and employed 28,500 people in 1973. New council estates, particularly Blackbird Leys from 1957, helped to house some of these factory workers and their families. The county began to attract related firms in 1950, when Smith & Sons Ltd, a London firm which had been supplying Morris's with clocks and speedometers since the 1920s, opened a motor accessories division at the former Witney airfield. Smith's manufactured vehicle heaters and soon employed 1,500 staff with plans to double the workforce; the firm built a housing estate off Burford Road by 1961 to accommodate key workers. Automotive Products Co. Ltd established a services and spares factory at Banbury in 1962 which employed 1,700 people in the early 1970s. Neither firm survives today – AP closed down in 1985 and the hydraulics section at Smith's was the last part to close in 2001. The Oxford motor industry shrank because of global competition and currently employs around 4,000 people. The former Cowley assembly plant was cleared for Oxford Business Park in 1994 and the Military College buildings were converted into flats. BMW acquired the Pressed Steel factory from Rover in 1999 and, after completely modernising the plant, the company launched its new MINI there in 2001.

Since the 1970s, Oxfordshire has been at the heart of England's Motorsport Valley, benefiting from existing automotive expertise and relevant training at Rycotewood College, Thame and Oxford Polytechnic, now Oxford Brookes University. Reynard Motorsport began as Sabre Automotive Ltd in Bicester in 1973 and relocated to Brackley in 2000. Also in Brackley is the Brawn 2009 F1 world champion team (now Mercedes). Wirth Research, established in 2003, is based in Bicester, building racing cars. TWR, founded at Kidlington in 1976, operated from the Leafield Technical Centre between 1993 and 2002; the Super Agari F1 team was at Leafield between 2006 and 2008. Prodrive Ltd has operated from headquarters in Banbury since 1986 and Ascari Cars Ltd has developed and built racing cars at Banbury since 2000. Benetton F1 opened the Whiteways Technical Centre at Enstone in 1992, continuing as Renault since 2001. Williams, one of the most successful F1 teams, began at Didcot in 1977, moving to Grove in 1998. Jaguar Cars manufactured XJR-15 sports cars at Wykham Mill in Bloxham between 1990 and 1992, followed by Aston Martin building DB7 cars between 1994 and 2004. These companies have been among Oxfordshire's largest high-tech employers and employed 2,500 people in the county in 2001.

The motor industry brought new jobs and a new prosperity to Oxfordshire, encouraging many people to move into the county. Its visual impact in terms of factories and associated housing has been most obvious in and around Cowley but the industry and its products have had far-reaching implications for Oxfordshire and the wider world.

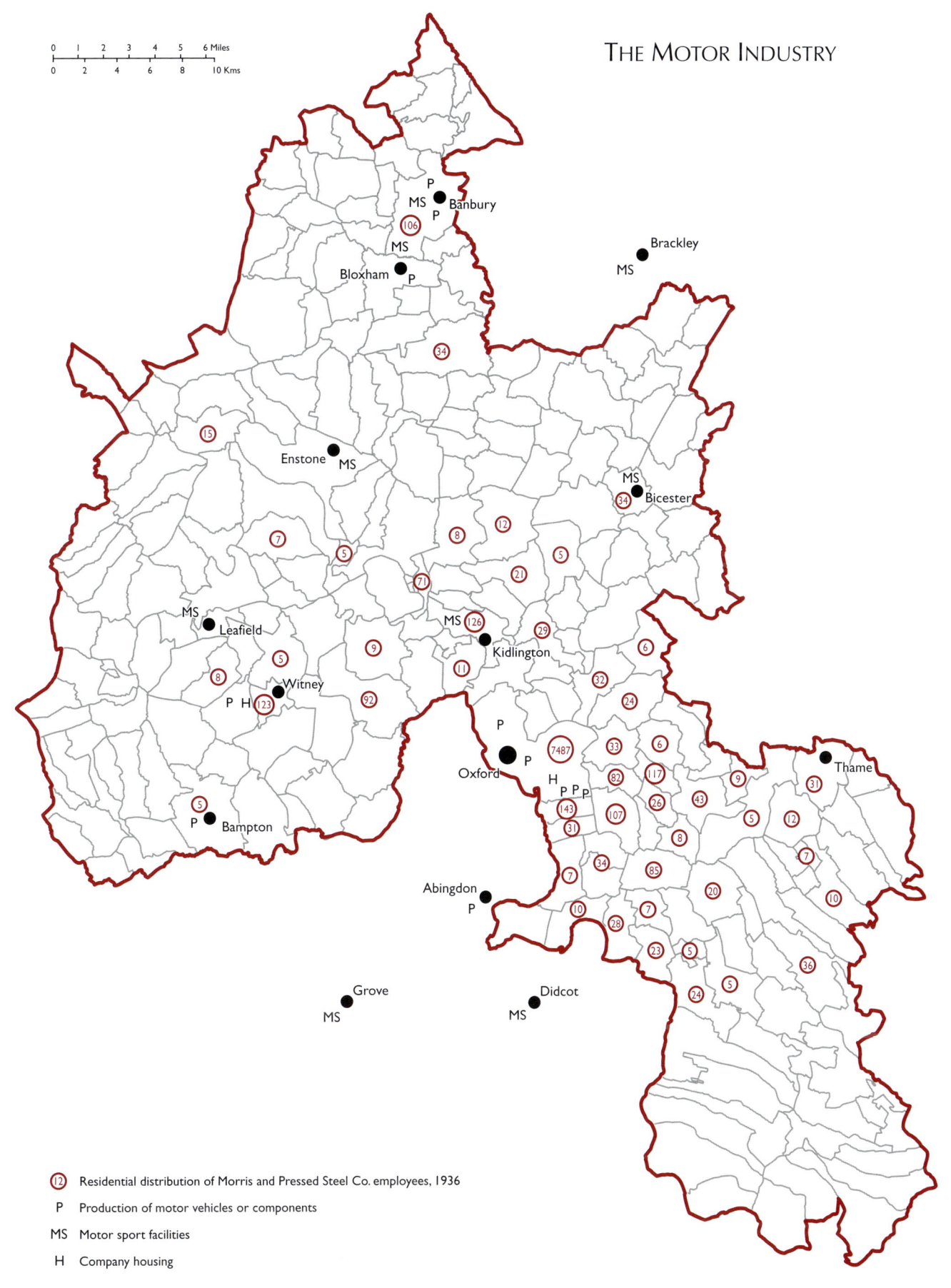

THE MOTOR INDUSTRY

⓵② Residential distribution of Morris and Pressed Steel Co. employees, 1936
P   Production of motor vehicles or components
MS Motor sport facilities
H   Company housing

149

66 · Local Government in the 19th and 20th Centuries   Chris Gilliam

Modern local government began with the poor law unions (PLUs) of 1834, new districts centred on towns with boards of guardians elected by ratepayers, and the Municipal Corporations Act of 1835, with ratepayers electing members of borough corporations (mostly established by ancient charter). During the 19th century additional, ad hoc local authorities were established, notably urban and rural sanitary authorities, created under the 1872 and 1875 Public Health Acts and based on rural and urban areas of PLUs.

The principle of ratepayer elections was extended to counties and districts under the 1888 and 1894 Local Government Acts. County Councils (CCs) succeeded quarter sessions, whilst rural and urban sanitary authorities became rural and urban district councils (RDCs and UDCs). The 1894 Act completed the evolution of ancient parishes into civil parishes and finally separated ecclesiastical and civil powers, many having already passed to other authorities. CCs had to ensure that boundaries of lower-tier authorities did not cross those of higher tiers but there was little change, except that new rural districts were created for Oxfordshire parishes of non-Oxfordshire PLUs (see entry 63). This resulted in an uneven spread of area and population of districts, with consequences for their financial resources and capacity to provide services. Although Oxford City was not originally amongst county boroughs created in 1888 (CBs, with populations over 50,000), its boundaries were extended and it received CB status in 1889–90, giving it independence from the county. The 1888 and 1894 legislation gave CCs slightly enhanced powers (e.g. over major roads) and improved funding from central government. Older authorities, boroughs, PLUs and school boards continued to operate as before.

By 1932 the remaining ad hoc authorities had been abolished and the powers of district and county councils significantly extended. The first major change, in 1902, saw transfer of responsibility for state-provided elementary education to county and county borough councils, henceforth local education authorities (LEAs).[1] The new LEAs were also given specific powers to provide post-elementary education. County and district councils gained increasing powers under public health, housing and planning legislation. Various laws created an embryo county health service, which included the county medical officer of health, inspector of midwives, school medical officers and district health visitors, the supervision of midwives and nursing homes, provision of hospitals and treatment for tuberculosis and other infectious diseases, and duties relating to blind persons and adopted children.[2] A series of housing and planning laws gave district councils powers to improve housing conditions. In 1919, district councils were required to ascertain housing needs and prepare housing schemes (if necessary for building 'council houses') with some financial help from the Exchequer. CCs were to monitor district schemes and could in some cases assume their powers.

Between 1928 and 1932 the boundaries and functions of local government were greatly changed. The Oxford Extension Act 1928 provided the first increase in the city's boundaries since 1890: from 4,719 acres and 57,052 people in 1921 to 8,416 and 80,539 in 1931.[3] The CC petitioned the House of Lords against this 'aggression'. Shortly afterwards, the 1929 Local Government Act greatly extended the powers of county and county borough councils in four key areas: responsibility for the poor law; as sole highway authorities (except for unclassified roads in urban districts); as planning authorities with equal powers to the districts; and in undertaking a general review of district and parish boundaries in their areas. The Oxfordshire Review Order 1932 redrew the map of Oxfordshire in the first (and only) major rationalisation of local government boundaries between 1895 and 1974. Seven rural districts[4] and one urban district[5] were abolished, with most of their areas included in two new rural districts.[6] The remaining rural districts,[7] urban districts[8] and three of the municipal borough (MBs)[9] were altered. Woodstock MB was unchanged (see lower map). The object was to provide for development needs,[10] to remove boundary anomalies,[11] and to ensure that rural districts were large enough to provide adequate services[12] and an equitable distribution of the rate burden. The only significant boundary change before 1974 was a further extension of Oxford CB in 1957 to include the new housing estate of Blackbird Leys.

The 50th anniversary of CCs in 1938 saw celebrations of the enormous progress in provision of services. Local government involvement in individual lives – the provision of basic needs and regulation – increased in wartime, through air-raid protection and civil defence, the Government Evacuation Scheme and provision of billets. Further functions, particularly at county level, resulted from the social welfare legislation of the post-1945 Labour government, including provision of universal secondary education, designation as local health authorities within the new National Health Service and as chief planning authorities under the 1947 Town and Country Planning Act, and transformation of the poor law and public assistance facilities into universal social services.

Local government was now costly and complex. There was growing dissatisfaction with existing organisation and boundaries, which were regarded as inefficient, expensive and amateurish. Discussions of local government reform began in 1941, and in 1945 the Local Government Boundary Commission was established. With little political support, it was abolished in 1949 and nothing significant was achieved until a Royal Commission was set up in 1966 under Lord Redcliffe-Maud. Its radical proposals for reorganisation were overtaken when a Conservative government, essentially committed to reform within the traditional structure, was elected in 1970. Its proposals were eventually implemented as the first major change since 1888 and 1894. The Local Government Act of 1972 led to the abolition in 1974 of the existing districts – RDCs/UDCs/MBs – and their replacement by three new ones.[13] Oxford lost its independent CB status but expanded its boundaries yet again to become a fourth district. A further significant expansion to the county saw the transfer of the Vale of White Horse area from Berkshire as the fifth district. This remains the situation in 2010.

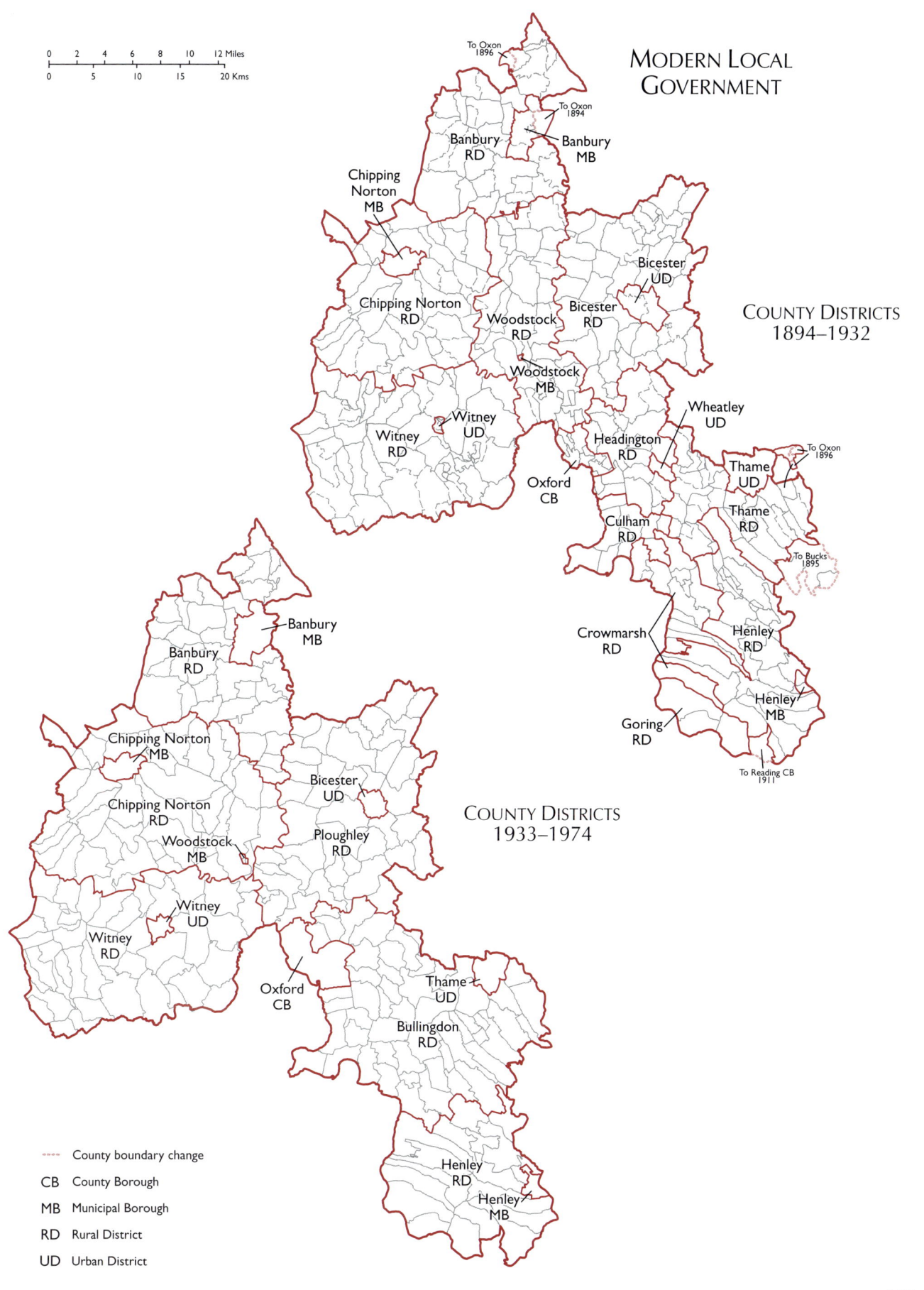

Modern Local Government

County Districts 1894–1932

County Districts 1933–1974

- - - - County boundary change
- CB County Borough
- MB Municipal Borough
- RD Rural District
- UD Urban District

151

67 · Housing and Urban Renewal: Oxford 1918–1985   Alan Crosby

Before 1914 undiluted laissez-faire attitudes predominated on Oxford City Council, in the field of housing as in other municipal activity. The council was notoriously unwilling to enforce sanitary improvements and impose building controls, and made almost no use of national legislation to deal with the worst unfit housing. The working-class districts which developed after 1830 in St Ebbe's, Jericho and St Thomas were generally recognised as grossly unsatisfactory in terms of overcrowding, sanitation, public health and building standards. As early as 1848 St Ebbe's was described as 'a swamp converted into a cesspool', but no remedial action was taken.

After 1918 the Council, with extreme reluctance, intervened, undertaking slum clearance and building council houses, but remained exceptionally hesitant. Its modest initial plan was to build 400 houses in ten years; only 215 actually materialised. Council house rents were among the highest in the country, because until 1925 the city, almost uniquely, refused to borrow from the Treasury to fund schemes, preferring to buy and develop sites using profits on the housing revenue account. Thus, the poorest and most needy citizens were not to be the beneficiaries.

Between 1923 and 1930 the city built a further 1,647 houses, but opportunities were increasingly constrained by external factors – rapid industrialisation and a huge influx of population generated intense competition for building land, and colleges were reluctant to sell sites on the urban fringe except for high-status private housing. The interwar council estates were therefore a miscellany of small schemes, in an arc from Headington to New Hinksey at a distance of two to three miles from Carfax. In total, Oxford had 3,085 council houses in 1939, 543 built by Bullingdon RDC in semi-rural areas annexed by Oxford in 1929.

The Victorian policy towards slum housing endured through the 1920s. Individual houses or small groups were tackled, but only 129 properties demolished between 1911 and 1929. However, the 1930 Housing Act required councils to prioritise slum clearance, and between then and 1939 Oxford demolished 872 houses, mostly in St Ebbe's and other inner city districts, or in older village cores like Wolvercote, Cowley and Headington. Much more ambitiously, the comprehensive redevelopment of St Ebbe's was approved in 1939, envisaging the clearance of a further 590 houses and the building of blocks of workers' flats in landscaped settings: 500 residents would be displaced to new peripheral housing estates.

After 1945 the shortage of sites for new housing became acute. The City Council, though now enthusiastic to intervene and build on a large scale, found itself severely limited. The main schemes were on the uncompleted ring road, at Northway/Barton, Summertown Farm and (partly in Bullingdon RD) Rose Hill, and in the early 1950s new estates were built on the disused airfield at Cowley; at Wood Farm, Slade and Town Furze on the eastern ring road; and at Minchery Farm in the south. These largely exhausted the stock of developable or affordable land.

A 1949 council report concluded that the only answer was to develop sites straddling the city boundary or lying beyond it: between Cowley and Headington; beyond Cowley towards Garsington; and around Littlemore. The city was now locked in a protracted struggle with the county and rural district councils, which saw such projects as prefiguring major extensions of the city boundary.

In 1953 both county and city accepted that new housing was needed for 16,000 people in Oxford, but the draft county development plan proposed that they should be accommodated by the major expansion of Kidlington, and in eight other communities between five and ten miles from the city. That would remove the risk of a 'Greater Oxford' emerging. The city council put forward a radically different approach, arguing for the housing of at least 10,000 people in a de facto new town at Blackbird Leys, greatly extending the urban envelope and encroaching into the semi-rural fringe. In 1954 the minister, faced with these diametrically opposite strategies, and forced to take account of the proposed green belt and its impact on future expansion, authorised the Blackbird Leys scheme.

The land was brought within the city boundary and the huge, and subsequently troubled, estate constructed between 1957 and 1970. Within the city lack of building land meant that only small, fragmented schemes were possible. Taking the interwar and post-war estates together, the map demonstrates the overwhelming concentration of council housing in the eastern and south-eastern outer city, and its virtual absence from the north, the west and the belt between Marston and Iffley. The impact of council building on the social and physical geography of the city is clear.

As Blackbird Leys grew, the clearance of St Ebbe's progressed, a sorry tale which became a matter of embarrassment and shame to the city council for over 25 years. The displacement of its population, and the likelihood of the process being repeated in Jericho, placed great pressure on the future housing programme. Furthermore, the failure to redevelop St Ebbe's produced a major shortfall in replacement housing. In the mid 1960s the City Council therefore began to promote a regional approach, envisaging a series of schemes whereby much of Oxford's council housing would be built in places as distant as Bicester and Abingdon. The only tangible outcomes were the small estate at Berinsfield (1968–70), a joint scheme at Kidlington between Oxford City and Cherwell District Council (1975–80), and the purchase by the City Council of the privately built Barton Court estate at Abingdon (1975). By then, the entire housing picture had changed irrevocably as a result of social and political reorientation.

Chastened by the bitter experience of St Ebbe's, the City Council decided in 1965 to scrap plans for comprehensive clearance in Jericho, adopting instead a pioneering policy of 'gradual renewal' which obviated the displacement of population and retained, at least in some form, community coherence. The Jericho experiment, though controversial at the time, marked the abandonment of comprehensive urban renewal in Oxford. Within a decade such policies had been espoused by central government. And by 1985, when the sensitive redevelopment of the dereliction in St Ebbe's was being planned, Oxford City Council was no longer an active housebuilder – Margaret Thatcher's policies had made that impossible.

COUNCIL HOUSING IN OXFORD
1918–1974

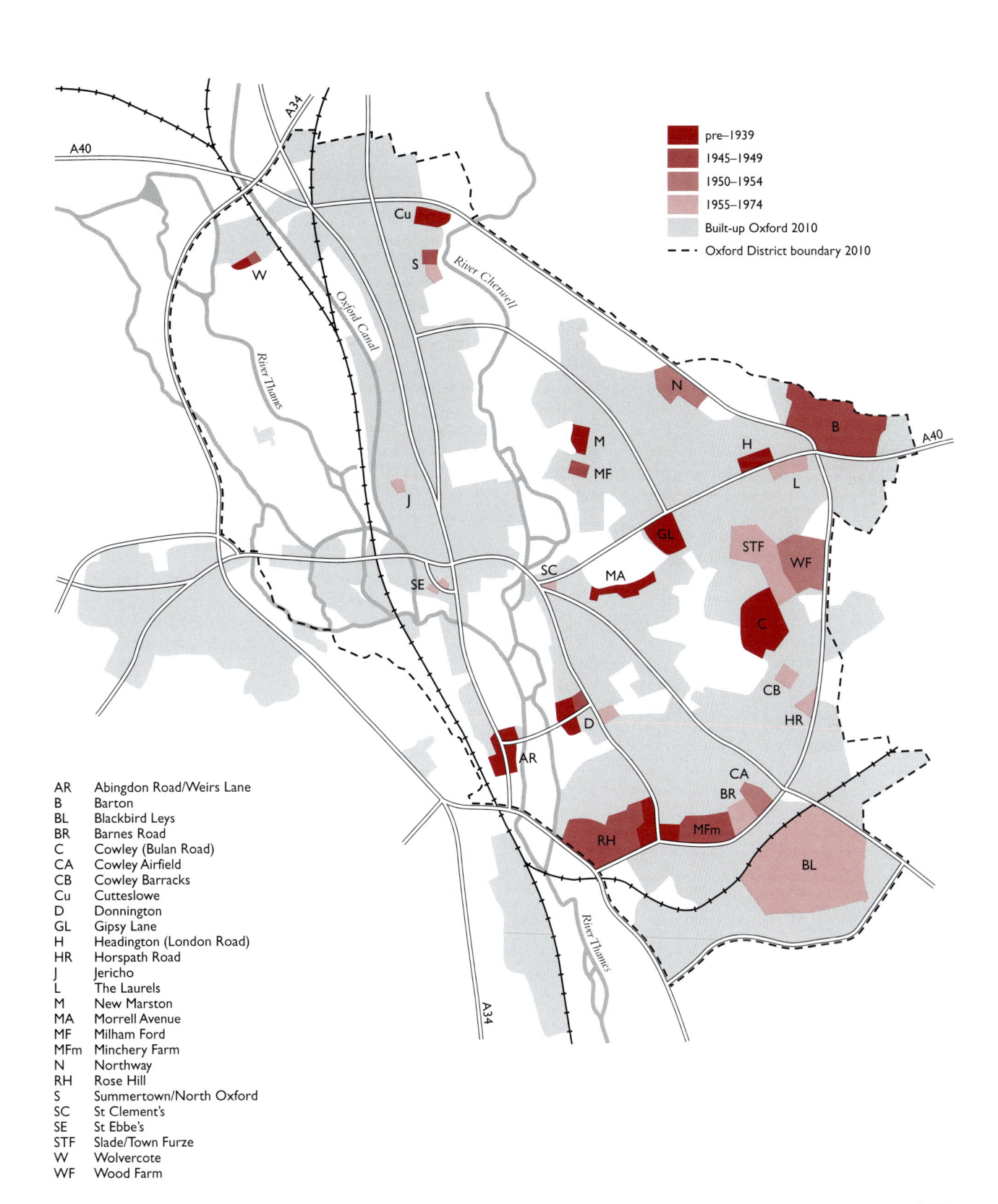

Legend:
- pre–1939
- 1945–1949
- 1950–1954
- 1955–1974
- Built-up Oxford 2010
- Oxford District boundary 2010

AR	Abingdon Road/Weirs Lane
B	Barton
BL	Blackbird Leys
BR	Barnes Road
C	Cowley (Bulan Road)
CA	Cowley Airfield
CB	Cowley Barracks
Cu	Cutteslowe
D	Donnington
GL	Gipsy Lane
H	Headington (London Road)
HR	Horspath Road
J	Jericho
L	The Laurels
M	New Marston
MA	Morrell Avenue
MF	Milham Ford
MFm	Minchery Farm
N	Northway
RH	Rose Hill
S	Summertown/North Oxford
SC	St Clement's
SE	St Ebbe's
STF	Slade/Town Furze
W	Wolvercote
WF	Wood Farm

153

68 · The Second World War — Malcolm Graham

Oxfordshire lay well behind the front line in the Second World War, providing a safe haven for military activity and supporting the war effort through its industries and farms.

The Royal Air Force had five airfields in Oxfordshire by 1939, at Benson, Bicester, Brize Norton, Upper Heyford and Weston-on-the-Green. In wartime, training became their priority and many satellite airfields were needed, partly to disperse aircraft at risk from air raids. By 1944, there were over 20 military airfields in Oxfordshire, including American bases at Chalgrove and Mount Farm and a Fleet Air Arm unit at Culham. Many pilots and paratroops were trained at local airfields and vital photographic reconnaissance missions were flown from Benson, Mount Farm and Chalgrove. RAF Broadwell, opened in 1943, was used for the D-Day landings and the Arnhem campaign. The RAF also had a depot at Woodcote and an ammunition park at Eynsham.

A hutted camp off The Slade was built by March 1940 to increase the capacity of Cowley Barracks, the Oxfordshire & Buckinghamshire Light Infantry depot, and large houses such as Eynsham Hall, Howbery Park in Crowmarsh and Wykham Park near Bloxham were requisitioned as army camps. In 1941, Arncott was chosen as the site for a massive Ordnance Depot built with the help of Italian prisoners of war from Windmill Camp near Blackthorn. The depot sent trainloads of supplies to the South Coast before D-Day, utilizing extensive Hinksey marshalling yards built at Oxford in 1942. Hutted army camps hidden by trees were established at Cornbury Park and Nettlebed.

GHQ Stop Lines were built in southern and eastern England to meet the threat of invasion in 1940. They used concrete pillboxes and anti-tank defences to reinforce the obstacles provided by waterways, and the River Thames through Oxfordshire formed part of Stop Line Red. The line crossed to the Berkshire bank at the Wittenhams and, to avoid the long loop around Oxford, it continued as an anti-tank ditch from Culham through Marcham to Northmoor. More pillboxes were built in the Cherwell valley between Kidlington and Banbury on Stop Line Yellow. The value of these defences was soon questioned but pillboxes continued to be built around airfields and major towns; four one-man pillboxes survive in the Windrush meadows at Witney. Loop-holed walls, at Charlbury and Bicester for example, were probably formed by local Home Guard units to strengthen temporary roadblocks.

The prospect of military and civilian casualties led to a rapid expansion of hospital services. The Radcliffe Infirmary in Oxford took over Rycote Park as a children's hospital and maternity hospitals for evacuees were established in Oxford and at Chippinghurst Manor in Garsington. The War Emergency Medical Service took over the Wingfield Morris Hospital at Headington and built a large new hospital, later the Churchill, nearby in 1940. The Churchill Hospital became an American military hospital between 1943 and 1945 and US forces operated other hospitals at Ramsden and Bradwell Grove. The Examination Schools in Oxford were converted into a military hospital and St Hugh's College became a head injuries hospital. Middleton Park became a military hospital and a hutted military hospital was built at Holton Park in 1942.

The first bombs landed in Oxfordshire in June 1940 and the county recorded 222 incidents and the dropping of 3,831 bombs by July 1944. No bombs fell on Oxford and there was no intensive bombing elsewhere. Air raids in Oxfordshire killed just 20 people and injured 60; the most serious incidents were an air raid on Stanton Harcourt and Brize Norton in August 1940 which killed seven people and an attack on Banbury in October 1940 which killed six. Military sites were most frequently bombed – there were 12 raids on Weston-on-the-Green – but most bombs, including four V1s in 1944, fell in open country and caused little damage. Heavy anti-aircraft battery sites were established around Banbury and Oxford and some concrete bases to which the guns were fastened have survived. Camouflage was used to disguise factories and airfields from enemy raiders and a dummy Northern Aluminium Company (NAC) factory was built at Bourton, three miles north of Banbury. Five decoy airfields were also established in the county, using dummy runway lighting to divert night raids.

Wartime farming and industry changed the Oxfordshire landscape. The Oxfordshire War Agricultural Executive Committee directed farmers to increase grain production and organised the clearance of unproductive land. A rail-served grain silo was built at Water Eaton in 1943 and food depots were established at South Leigh and Hanborough stations. The Oxford motor industry was diverted into war production, including the repair of military aircraft, for which Cowley airfield was built in 1940, and a cartridge case factory was added in 1941. The aircraft manufacturers De Havilland used Witney aerodrome to repair damaged planes and the NAC at Banbury opened a metal reprocessing plant at Adderbury. Oil pipelines from Avonmouth and Southampton docks were brought to a distribution centre at Islip in 1942.

Most evacuees to Oxfordshire found accommodation in private houses but nurseries for young unaccompanied children were established at Bruern Abbey and Sandford St Martin. Institutions, particularly schools and government departments, also moved to the county. Blenheim Palace provided a temporary home for Malvern College in 1939–40 while the Admiralty retreated to Malvern and it then took in MI5 for the rest of the war. The Government backed the creation of British or Municipal restaurants across the county to minimize the waste of food. Like wartime nurseries and services canteens, they took over existing buildings or occupied new prefabricated concrete structures. Investment in recreation facilities was minimal but a riverside lido at Benson, complete with Spitfire fountain, was built in 1943.

Many features of wartime life proved ephemeral but major infrastructural change left a lasting legacy. Some abandoned military camps became temporary homes for squatters, refugees and former prisoners of war. They later became a focus for new industrial and housing development. More profoundly perhaps, the war ushered in an era of intensive farming which thoroughly changed the Oxfordshire landscape within two generations.

The Second World War

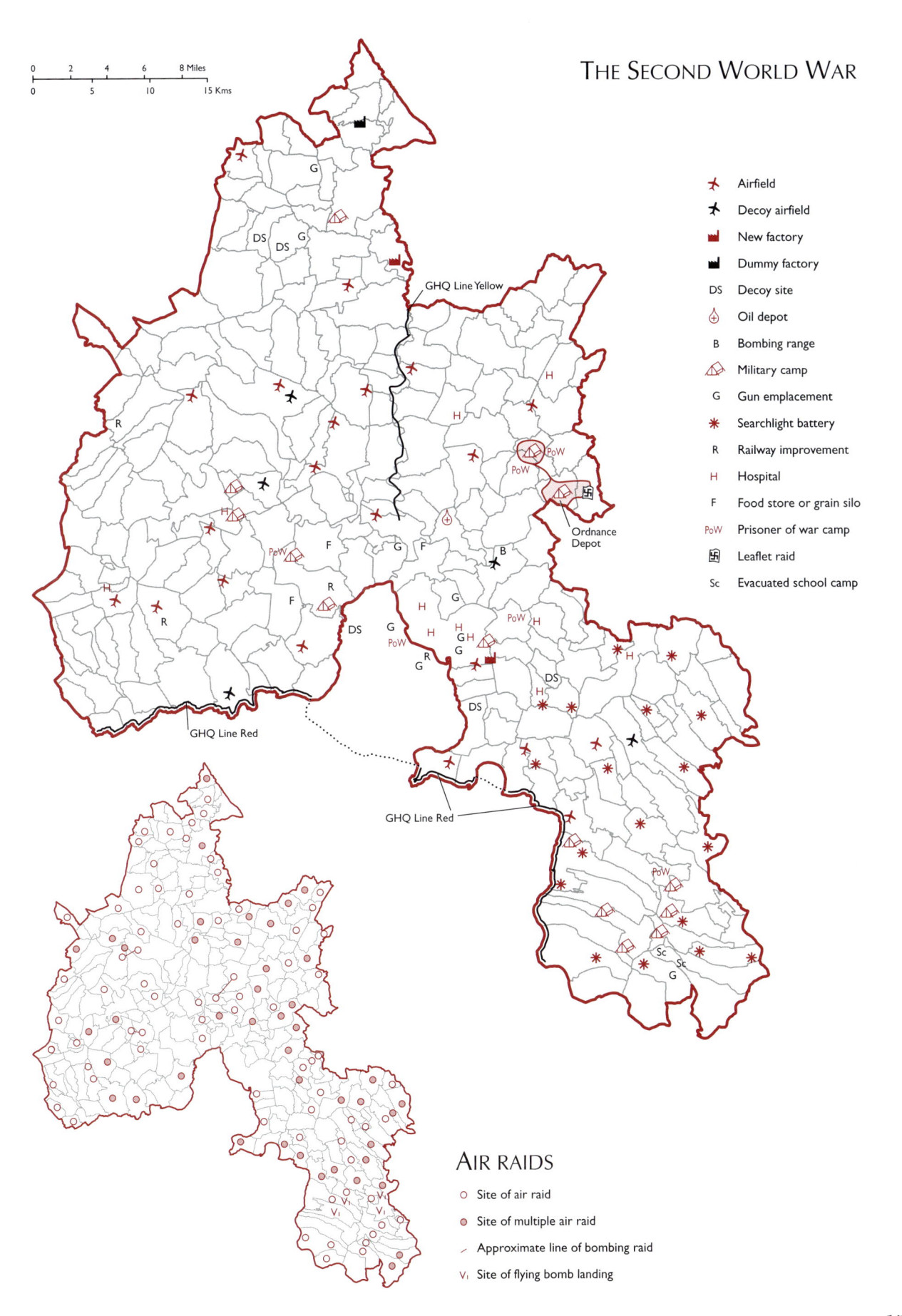

Legend:
- ✈ Airfield
- ✈ Decoy airfield
- 🏭 New factory
- 🏭 Dummy factory
- DS Decoy site
- Oil depot
- B Bombing range
- ⛺ Military camp
- G Gun emplacement
- ✴ Searchlight battery
- R Railway improvement
- H Hospital
- F Food store or grain silo
- PoW Prisoner of war camp
- 卍 Leaflet raid
- Sc Evacuated school camp

GHQ Line Yellow

GHQ Line Red

Ordnance Depot

Air Raids

- ○ Site of air raid
- ● Site of multiple air raid
- Approximate line of bombing raid
- V₁ Site of flying bomb landing

155

69 · The Cold War

Trevor Rowley

Although the military presence in Oxfordshire diminished after 1945, the county's strategic importance increased significantly, as during the Cold War its airbases formed part of NATO's frontline. In response to the perceived growing nuclear threat from the Soviet Union, in 1951 Strategic Air Command decided to base a force of American nuclear bomber aircraft in Britain. Two of the four sites chosen for conversion to United States Air Force (USAF) bases, Upper Heyford and Brize Norton, were in Oxfordshire. Both runways were extended from 1,830 to 2,540 metres and over the next 40 years, there was an intensive programme of fortification at Upper Heyford. This included the construction of 56 hardened aircraft shelters for strategic nuclear bombers, tactical reconnaissance and fighter aircraft. The swing-wing F111 fighter-bomber aircraft were on permanent standby here for three decades. A small American town was built for the 10,000 military personnel and their families based here. After the base closed in 1993, its redundant military structures were identified as a unique assemblage of Cold War facilities. After a protracted planning dispute, in 2010 it was decided that the site should have various uses, to include housing, industry and car storage. Only parts of the Cold War buildings, the Instant Response section, were to be protected and conserved.

Brize Norton was a USAF base from 1952 to 1965, after which it was developed as a military transport facility. By 2010 it was a 'super base' forming the largest RAF operation in the UK. It incorporates a passenger terminal, cargo-handling shed and extensive married-quarters (in Carterton). The 'Base-Hangar', opened in 1967, was then Europe's largest cantilever construction hangar. The base was used in the Falklands campaign, both Gulf Wars and in NATO operations in Bosnia and Kosovo. During the Cold War RAF Benson was used for reconnaissance and from 1962 formed part of RAF Transport Command Fleet. Now it is chiefly a helicopter base, forming part of Joint Helicopter Command as well as the home for police and ambulance helicopters.

RAF Barford St John was closed in 1946, but was re-opened during the Cold War as a USAF satellite communications station for the communications base at RAF Croughton, just across the Northamptonshire border. During the Korean War RAF Weston-on-the-Green was under the control of Bomber Command and the Air Positioning Plotting Unit, but after 1954 it was used almost exclusively for parachute training by the UK military. Weston became the Drop Zone for the RAF Parachute Training School based at Brize Norton and aircraft from RAF Lyneham (Wilts). Nearby RAF Bicester became a transit centre for the despatch of equipment to troops based in Germany after WW2 and from 1947 to 1961 housed the HQ of No 40 Group (Maintenance Command). RAF Bicester closed as an operational base in 1976, but between 1978 and 1994 was used by the USAF as a military hospital and medical storage facility. The Central Ordnance Depot at Bicester, the largest in Europe, was the only Regular Army facility in the old county to function throughout the Cold War, along with the Defence Clothing and Textile Agency at nearby Caversfield. After the Second World War RNAS Culham, operating as HMS *Hornbill*, was used by several naval units, including the Photographic Development Unit, before it was closed in 1953. Parts of the airfield have been home, since 1978, to the Joint European Torus, the world's largest fusion experimental facility. Other former military sites with subsequent research, industrial or commercial uses include Harwell (the Atomic Energy Research Establishment, Rutherford Appleton Laboratory and Diamond Light Source) and Milton Park.

In 1957 the United Kingdom Warning and Monitoring Organization (UKWMO) was established to warn of any impending nuclear air attack. The Royal Observer Corps (ROC) was to report any bomb strike and monitor the resulting level of radioactive fallout. Fallout warnings were to reach the public via a broadcasting system known as HANDEL, using the speaking clock as a means of communication. The code 'Tocsin Bang' would confirm that a nuclear bomb had fallen. ROC posts were mostly on higher open ground and typically consisted of a stairwell leading to a monitoring room with Atomic Weapons Detection Recognition and Estimation of Yield (AWDREY) instruments, some rudimentary furniture and a small room containing a chemical lavatory. The only visible above-ground features were ventilation shafts. Sixteen of the 1500 underground monitoring posts constructed nationally between 1958 and 1961 were in Oxfordshire. Seven of these closed in 1968 and the remainder in 1991.

Several stations were demolished completely; the Kidlington post lay under what is now Gosford Hill School's playing field and the Shipton-under-Wychwood post was replaced by a television relay mast, but those at Middleton Stoney and Boars Hill remain virtually intact. The Oxfordshire HQ of ROC Group 3, adjacent to the old Oxford and Bucks Light Infantry barrack block in Cowley, consisted of a semi-sunken bunker, with about a dozen rooms, including male and female dormitories, a generator, ventilation and filtration plants and scientific and monitoring rooms. The barracks were converted for use as the HQ of UKWMO in the 1980s. Both the ROC and UKWMO sites were closed in 1992. The above-ground features of the monitoring post were demolished for a car park, but the bunker and barracks are now part of Oxford Brookes University.

Oxfordshire was part of Emergency Government Region 6, which initially had its HQ at Warren Row, Maidenhead, and later Basingstoke, but there were also County and District Emergency Centres. The Oxfordshire Emergency Centre was below the grounds of Woodeaton House, with sufficient room to house a skeletal local authority administration. The bunker is intact with many of its original features and is now used as a meeting and conference facility. Oxford City (Oxford Town Hall basement), Cherwell District (Banbury Town Hall basement) and West Oxfordshire Districts had their own Emergency Centres. The latter was in a bunker underneath the council offices in Woodgreen, Witney, with a suite of rooms, including a decontamination shower. The entrance has a cover on rails, apparently copied from an East German Stasi design.

The Cold War

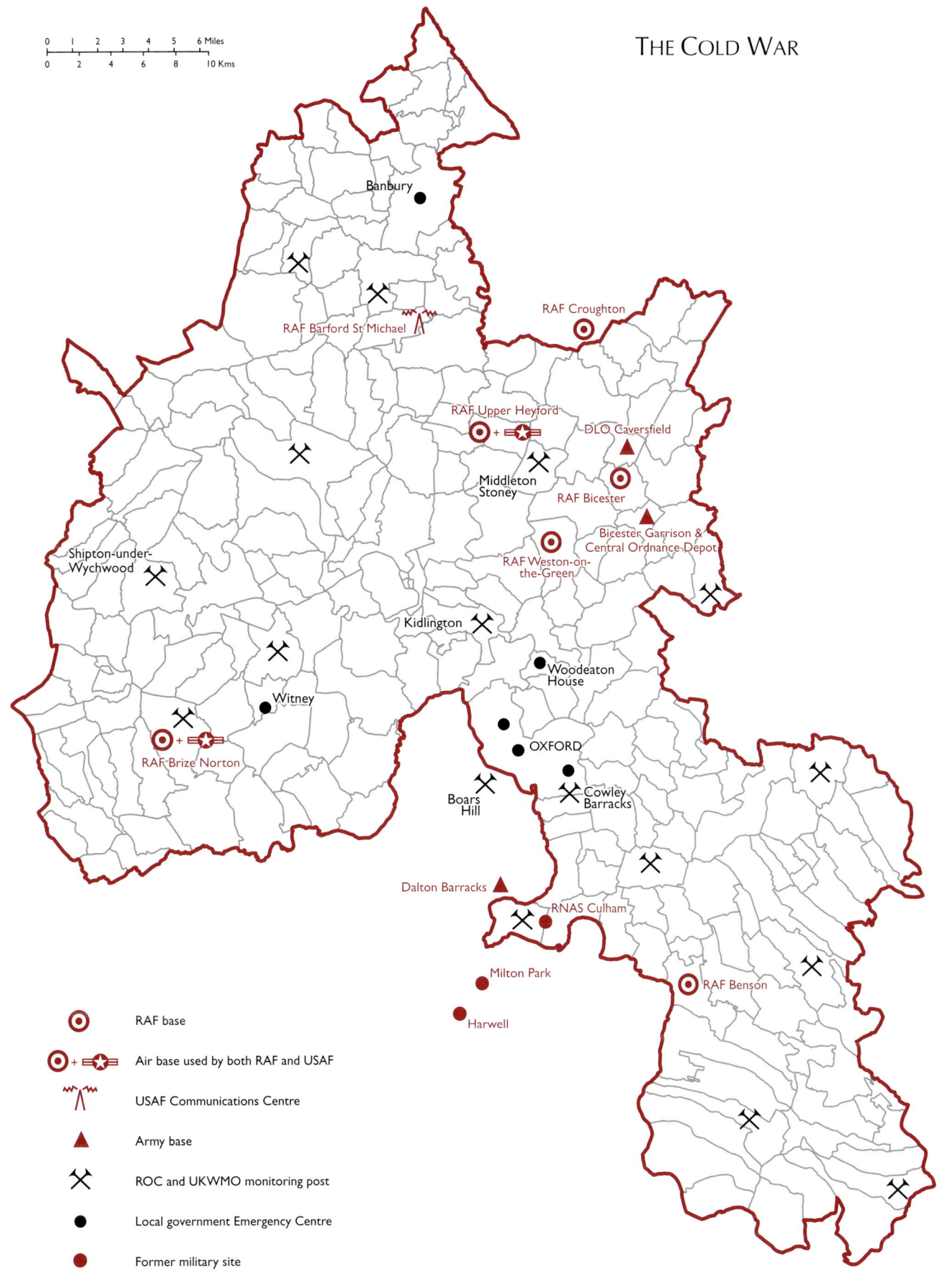

Legend:
- ◉ RAF base
- ◉ + ✪ Air base used by both RAF and USAF
- ⋀ USAF Communications Centre
- ▲ Army base
- ✕ ROC and UKWMO monitoring post
- ● Local government Emergency Centre
- ● Former military site

Labelled locations:
- Banbury
- RAF Barford St Michael
- RAF Croughton
- RAF Upper Heyford
- DLO Caversfield
- Middleton Stoney
- RAF Bicester
- Bicester Garrison & Central Ordnance Depot
- Shipton-under-Wychwood
- RAF Weston-on-the-Green
- Kidlington
- Woodeaton House
- Witney
- OXFORD
- RAF Brize Norton
- Boars Hill
- Cowley Barracks
- Dalton Barracks
- RNAS Culham
- Milton Park
- Harwell
- RAF Benson

157

70 · Town and Country Planning in the 20th Century — Liam Tiller

The control of urban expansion, and the protection of the landscape setting of Oxford and of the countryside in general were the dominant planning themes in Oxfordshire throughout the 20th century.

The 1909, 1919 and 1932 Housing and Town Planning Acts required borough and district councils to prepare planning schemes to guide and control development. A planning scheme, proposing land use zones, housing densities, height limits for new building and new roads was prepared for a Joint Regional Advisory Committee of the city and adjoining district councils and approved by the Ministry of Health in 1927. In 1926 two pressure groups were formed, the Oxford Preservation Trust (OPT) and the Council for the Preservation of Rural England (CPRE), the latter founded by Sir Patrick Abercrombie, to limit urban sprawl and ribbon development. In 1927 the CPRE prepared the county's first regional plan, focusing on preserving and enhancing the landscape of the Thames valley from Cricklade to Staines.

In 1931 a Regional Survey of the county was published. It was commissioned by the Oxfordshire Regional Planning Committee and prepared by Abercrombie and Adshead, both architects, and the Earl of Mayo, a civil engineer. The survey concentrated on preserving the rural character of Oxfordshire in the face of the pressures being generated by the Cowley motor industry and from London along the trunk roads. It proposed a reduction of designated housing land around Oxford, and schemes for an Oxford bypass and a series of satellite villages around the city. The 1930s also saw the first town-planning schemes for Banbury, Chipping Norton, Henley-on-Thames, Thame, Witney and Woodstock. In 1939 another planning scheme for Oxford was published. It was not submitted for approval because of concern about possible compensation claims but was used for 'interim development control'.

The 1947 Town and Country Planning Act established a new planning system. County councils and county borough councils became the planning authorities, and henceforth all development required planning permission. Private reports on Oxford had been prepared by OPT in 1942 and Thomas Sharp in 1947. The Oxford City Development Plans of 1955, 1967 and 1972 all had the prime aim of reconciling the roles of the city as county town, industrial centre and university city. The County Development Plan, approved in 1954, was supplemented by more detailed town maps for Witney, Kidlington, the Oxford Fringe area, the Reading Fringe area, Bicester, and Banbury. The County Council's concern was to control Oxford's growth, protect the countryside and, in rural areas, to concentrate new development in a number of 'specified' small towns and larger villages where public services and infrastructure could be provided.

In 1949 the National Parks and Access to the Countryside Act introduced Areas of Outstanding Natural Beauty (AONBs), in which development was to be very strictly controlled. Two AONBs were designated in Oxfordshire, the Chilterns in 1964 and the Cotswolds in 1966.

The 1952 Town Development Act (TDA) encouraged the movement of industry and population out of the major conurbations. Banbury Borough Council entered into TDA agreements with both Birmingham, under which the Birds Custard factory moved to the town, and with London. Banbury had already, before the Second World War, encouraged inward investment by facilitating the establishment of the Alcan aluminium factory.

In 1959, under pressure from OPT, proposals were submitted to the government for an Oxford Green Belt to check the city's growth, to prevent it merging with surrounding villages and to protect its special character. Approval of the Green Belt took the Minister of Housing and Local Government 15 years and even then only the outer boundaries were approved. The inner boundaries were given only interim status to allow for further consideration in the preparation of Local Plans. By this time the amount of undeveloped land in and on the edge of Oxford to meet its local housing and other needs was becoming very limited. The final definition of the inner boundaries dragged on into the 1980s with disagreements between the local authorities involved.

From 1974 a new system was introduced of a County Structure Plan, to which Local Plans had to 'conform generally'. The former was prepared by the County Council and the latter by the new district councils set up by local government reorganisation. The county, concerned by the rapid growth of the 1960s and 1970s and the potential of Oxford to attract development that would put unsustainable pressure on infrastructure and threaten the special character of Oxford, adopted a 'Country Towns Strategy'. This strategy sought to divert development pressures from Oxford to four towns, Banbury, Bicester, Witney and Didcot. Rural development was to be constrained and plans for new road building were culled as both unaffordable and likely to encourage unwanted growth. The M40 motorway extension to Birmingham, completed in 1991, was built on a route to the east of Otmoor away from Oxford, where, in the County Council's view, it was less likely to foster unwanted development pressures in the city. A proposal for a third Thames bridge in Reading was opposed because of the growth pressures it would help generate in south Oxfordshire. In Oxford plans for new roads were abandoned and a 'balanced transport strategy' adopted, limiting parking space in the city centre and introducing a pioneering park-and-ride system.

The City Council opposed the Structure Plan strategy. It wanted more housing and employment close to the city but an alternative proposal to develop a linear urban area from Kidlington through Oxford to Abingdon was rejected. Subsequent local plans for the Oxford Fringe, prepared in the 1980s, did however include the major new housing area at Greater Leys, south of the city, and finally fixed the boundaries of the Green Belt. In the 1990s the development of the 'country towns' continued rapidly. The agreed strategy for the early 21st century is to continue to constrain development near Oxford and provide for further growth in Bicester and Didcot.

Planning in the 20th Century

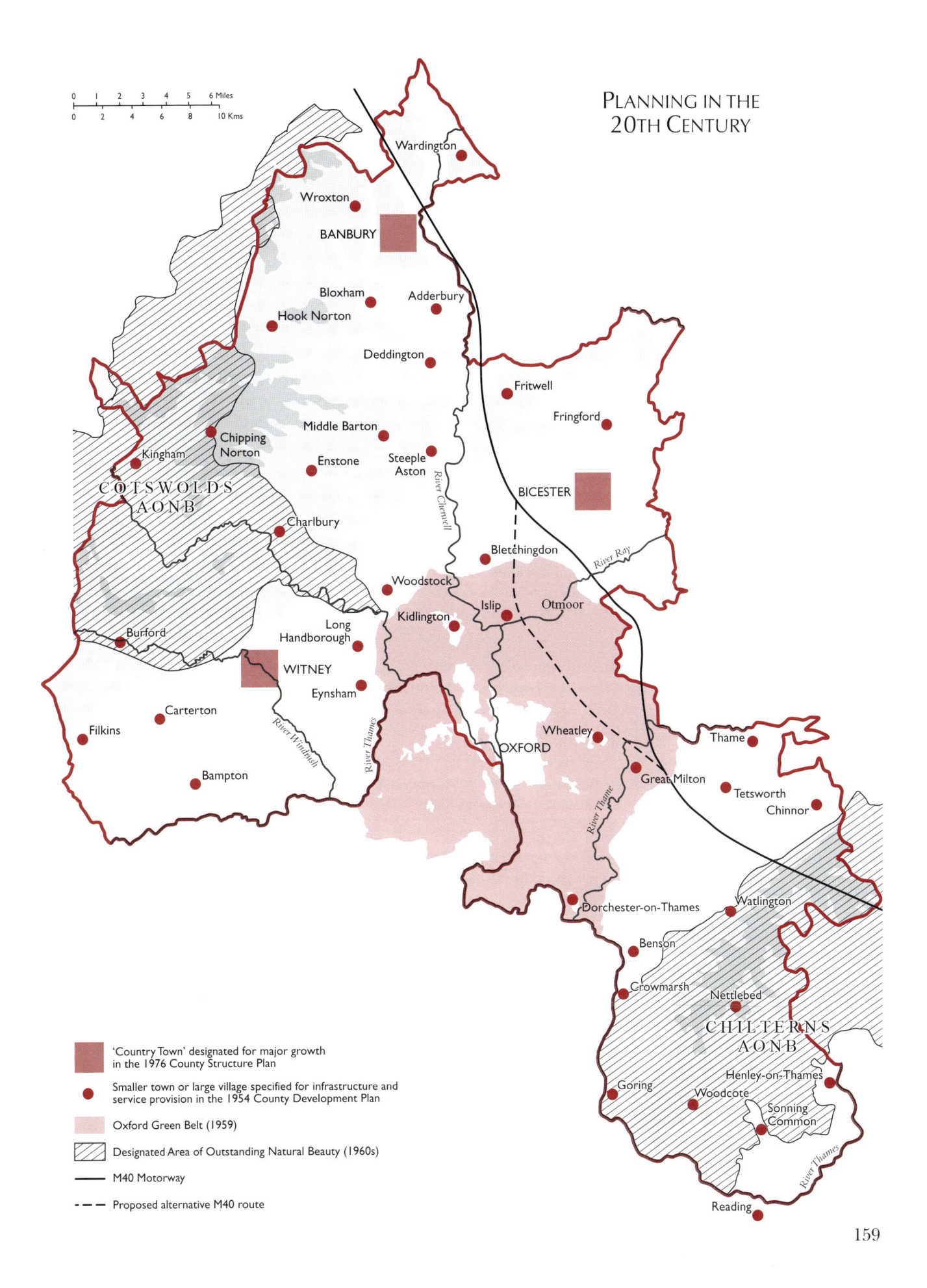

- ■ 'Country Town' designated for major growth in the 1976 County Structure Plan
- ● Smaller town or large village specified for infrastructure and service provision in the 1954 County Development Plan
- Oxford Green Belt (1959)
- Designated Area of Outstanding Natural Beauty (1960s)
- —— M40 Motorway
- --- Proposed alternative M40 route

71 · Education in the 20th Century

William Whyte

In most counties, one of the biggest changes in education wrought by the 20th century was the foundation of a university. That was certainly true of Oxfordshire's neighbours. Here, however, the university already existed – and that has made the development of the county's education somewhat unusual. Nonetheless, Oxfordshire was not immune to the changes that swept across the nation. For the three trends that reshaped Britain's education – greater systematisation, greater centralization and wider access – also reformed learning and teaching in the county.

By 1900, Oxfordshire, like the rest of the country, had achieved universal state elementary education (see entry 55). Secondary education, by contrast, was patchy and beyond the ambitions of most children. Further and higher education was almost unheard of. Although there was some teacher training, many of those running schools had little more than experience to offer. All this was to change. The key turning points were the 1902 and 1944 Education Acts.

The 1902 Act made county and borough councils responsible not only for schools but also for secondary and technical education. The Act was controversial, not least with Nonconformists, who objected to the fact that their rates would now pay for a number of schools run by the Church of England. Nonetheless, it marked a revolution: creating a national system of education. In Oxfordshire, it left the councils responsible for ten grammar schools as well as for all elementary provision.

The 1944 Act represented a still greater change. It envisaged a tripartite system of secondary education, across the country. Selected at 11, pupils would be sent to grammar schools (for an academic education), technical schools (for a scientific education), or secondary modern schools (for a vocational education). Oxfordshire County Council offered to experiment with a more comprehensive system of larger, mixed-ability schools, but the national plan won out. The result was a further growth in the system: with a dozen grammar schools joined by two dozen secondary moderns and three technical schools, in Banbury, Oxford and Witney.

From the mid 1960s, encouraged by changed government policy, the county and city councils turned these secondary schools into comprehensives. Oxfordshire adopted a two-tier system; Oxford went for primary, middle and high schools. The unification of the Local Education Authority in 1974 did nothing to change this, but at the turn of the millennium the city was brought into line with the rest of Oxfordshire. The 1980s and 1990s saw further pressure to systematize, with the introduction of a national curriculum in 1988 and school league tables from 1992.

The Education Acts also made local councils responsible for further education. After 1944, in particular, a whole network of colleges was created. Rycotewood College for Rural Crafts in Thame was founded in 1938 and taken over by the county council ten years later. The Witney Day Continuation School became the West Oxfordshire Technical College in 1950. The Technical Institute in Banbury became the North Oxfordshire Technical College in 1961. At about the same time, the county council turned the Henley Technical Institution into the South Oxfordshire Technical College. And in Oxford, the College of Further Education was created in 1963.

Reform also reshaped adult education. The 19th-century tradition of university extension classes and night schools had begun in Oxford and was enhanced by the foundation, in 1903, of the Workers' Education Association. By 1950 evening classes were meeting at no fewer than 33 places. Ten years later, the councils were supplementing this with adult education centres at Kidlington, Watlington, Sonning Common and Oxford.

Even the independent schools were transformed. Rising academic standards in the state sector meant they had to change. Small private schools simply did not have the resources to keep up: they dwindled from more than 40 to fewer than six in the first 50 years of the century. Larger and more academic schools, by contrast, thrived. By 2000, secondary schools like Magdalen College School and preparatory schools like the Dragon School had national – even international – reputations.

The growth of educational provision required more teachers. In the first half of the century, there was a mixed economy of training. Some teachers attended colleges like Culham (1852–1978), Felstead House (1873–1923) or Cherwell Hall (1902–20). Others took courses elsewhere. Most elementary teachers simply learnt on the job. After the 1944 Education Act, however, the need to raise standards led to a national programme of teacher training. The Lady Spencer-Churchill College of Education was founded in 1948 and moved to Wheatley in 1965. Westminster College came to Oxford in 1959. Increasingly, teaching came to be seen as a graduate profession and these two colleges were subsequently absorbed into what is now Oxford Brookes University. From 1897 Oxford University also granted Diplomas in Education to trainee elementary teachers, and by 1903 there were 320 students. The training of secondary teachers was added, and in 1919 the University Department for the Training of Teachers was created. Its successor, the Department of Educational Studies, still has close links with local schools.

This involvement in teacher training was just one way in which higher education changed. The University of Oxford grew enormously: from over 3,000 students in 1900 to more than 20,000 in 2000. Oxford School of Art, founded in 1865, became, first, the City Technical College and, in 1970, Oxford Polytechnic. In 1992 it was retitled Oxford Brookes University, and grew to nearly 20,000 students. The Royal Military College of Science moved to Shrivenham in 1946, was chartered in 1953 and is now linked to Cranfield University, becoming the UK Defence Academy in 2002. When county boundaries were redrawn in 1974, it became a third Oxfordshire university.

Thus the 20th century created a countywide network of schools and further education colleges, and hugely increased the provision of higher education. By the beginning of the 21st century, the system was changing again, but it was now truly a system, rather than a collection of discrete developments.

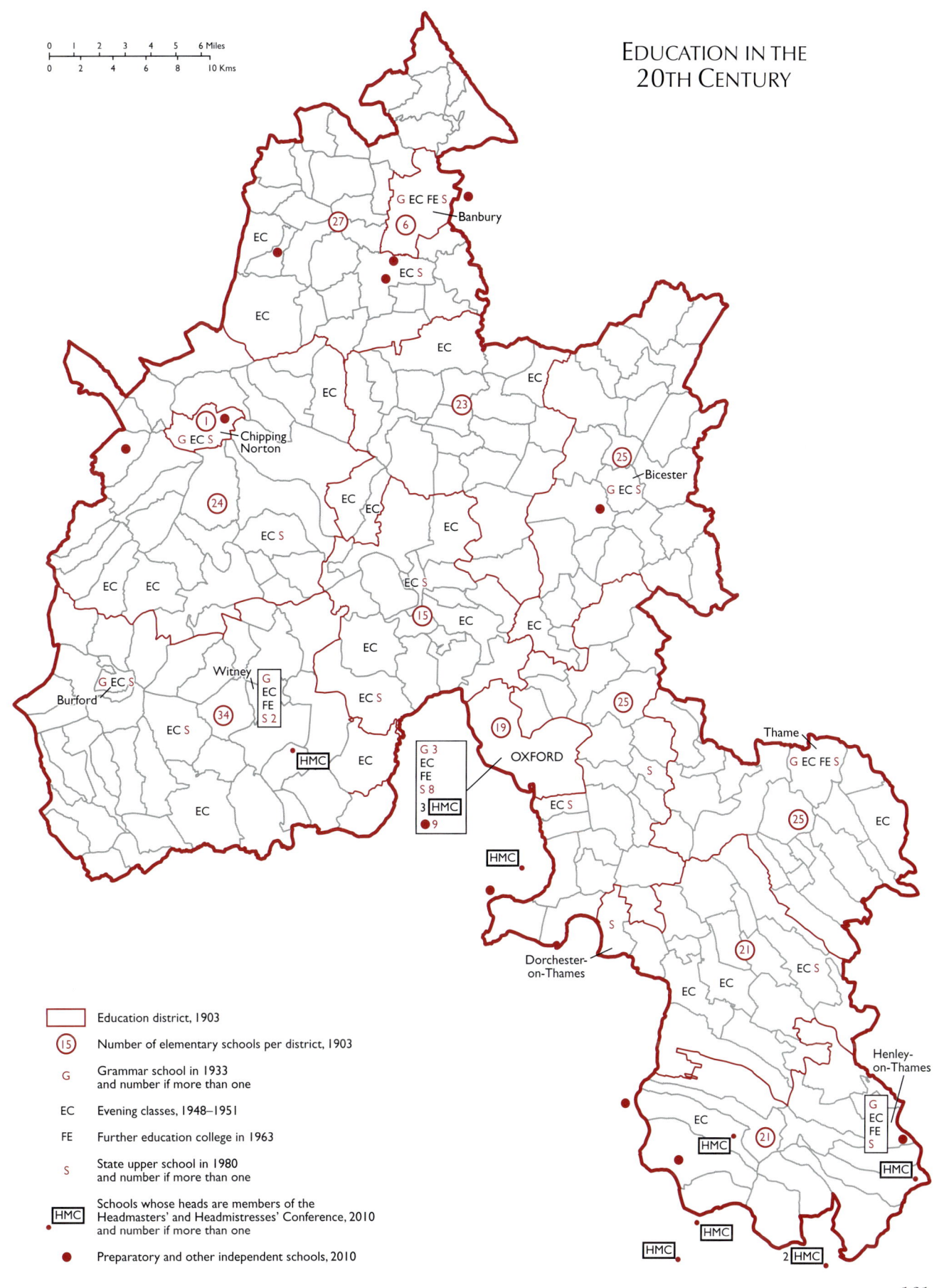

Education in the 20th Century

Legend:

- ☐ Education district, 1903
- ⑮ Number of elementary schools per district, 1903
- G Grammar school in 1933 and number if more than one
- EC Evening classes, 1948–1951
- FE Further education college in 1963
- S State upper school in 1980 and number if more than one
- [HMC] Schools whose heads are members of the Headmasters' and Headmistresses' Conference, 2010 and number if more than one
- • Preparatory and other independent schools, 2010

72 · Religion in the 20th Century

William Whyte

Until comparatively recently, the story of religion in 20th-century Oxfordshire would have seemed remarkably uncomplicated, presenting a narrative of decline and fall: of the diminishing importance of the Church of England and of religion as a whole. Current research has started to challenge this consensus. Not only have historians revealed that the place of religion in the 19th century was more complex than previously thought, but also that the 20th-century experience is equally complicated and far more interesting than an unproblematic description of decline.

It would be wrong to downplay the difficulties of institutional religion in this period. Church attendances fell; the place of religion in public life became more problematic; churches and chapels closed. Indeed, the most obvious manifestation of apparent decline was the number of ecclesiastical buildings declared redundant. Over the century, this happened to 17 Anglican churches and more than 100 Nonconformist chapels in Oxfordshire. The Methodists were worst hit. The county's religious landscape was redrawn. The area around Witney alone lost three churches, in addition to a Methodist chapel, a Quaker Meeting House, and a Christian Science reading room. It saw its Congregationalist chapel bulldozed to make way for a supermarket.

Yet it would be a mistake to see the closure of churches as nothing more than evidence of religious collapse. It is important not to ignore the ways in which the churches themselves were making strategic decisions rather than simply abandoning hope. When the Methodists and Congregationalists of Thame started worshipping together, for example, they had no further requirement for two chapels; so one was closed. Likewise, the village of Nuneham Courteney had never needed two churches, and, when Lord Harcourt sold the estate, the Anglican diocese swiftly shut one down. Methodist reunion in 1932 similarly made many chapels surplus to requirements. Population changes also made some churches unnecessary. As the county was suburbanised, some rural churches had shrinking populations to serve and were consequently closed.

If population changes rendered some churches redundant, they also created the need for other, new buildings. The growth of Oxford's and Reading's suburbs and the development of new estates like Carterton, Berinsfield and Bicester led to a considerable building programme. During the century, over 30 new churches were erected. More than a dozen were built in the City of Oxford alone. After the Second World War, Kidlington acquired four new places of worship: new Anglican and Roman Catholic churches; and new Methodist and Baptist chapels. Some new buildings were highly original – like the Holy Family Church in Blackbird Leys (1964–5), which possesses an extremely avant-garde hyperbolic paraboloid roof. Others were more architecturally run-of-the-mill, but they all stand as testament to a period of development as well as decline.

These new churches also illustrate the ways in which denominational adherence changed. Oxfordshire in 1900 was an overwhelmingly Protestant county, made up of Anglicans and Nonconformists, as it had been throughout the Victorian era. One of the big shifts in this period was the decline in Nonconformist church attendance. Another was the rising number of Roman Catholics. New Catholic churches were built in Henley, Bicester, Littlemore, Eynsham and elsewhere. Four were erected in Oxford. Together they mark a revolution in the county's religious history.

Still more strikingly, the 20th century witnessed the advent of non-Christian religions within the county. By 2000 there were five mosques – four in Oxford and one in Banbury; two Sikh Gurdwaras – one in Marston, one in Banbury; and a Synagogue in Oxford. There were also plans to build Buddhist and Hindu Temples. The growth of these non-Christian religions was sometimes difficult. Not only did they face opposition from some parts of the population, but they also could find it difficult to establish a long-lasting institutional presence. The Baha'i faith briefly ran a centre in the 1950s, but although there is still an assembly in Oxford, it does not possess a permanent meeting place. The Jewish Carmel College, with its remarkable modernist Synagogue, lasted nearly 50 years in Mongewell – but closed in 1997. And even the Muslims – by far the largest non-Christian group in the county – were forced to make a mosque redundant. The opening of the Central Mosque on the Cowley Road at the turn of the millennium led to the closure of the county's first ever Mosque: Bath Street, in Oxford, established in 1968. Nonetheless, even more than the growth of Roman Catholicism, the arrival of these faiths unquestionably changed the religious life of the county.

Is this, then, a story of decline? The picture is mixed, as the results of the 2001 Census indicate. These showed that in the old county of Oxfordshire, something like 73% of the population identified themselves as Christians. About 1% identified themselves as Muslims; less than that as Jews, Muslims, Sikhs or Hindus; and about a quarter either had no religion (17%) or would not give a religious affiliation (7%). There were some significant variations across the county. The City of Oxford was home to the fewest Christians (60%) and the largest number of atheists or agnostics (33%), as well as the most Muslims (4%) Jews (1%), and Hindus (1%). In West Oxfordshire, by contrast, 77% of the population declared themselves Christian, making it one of the most homogenous areas in the country.

Taken together, the evidence suggests that a simple narrative of decline just will not do. There are clear signs both that institutional religion struggled, and that new religions made headway in this period. But levels of some belief in religion – and, specifically, in Christianity – remained high. Church building programmes reveal something more dynamic than mere collapse. Other religious upsurges, as amongst evangelical, charismatic and pentecostal Christians, sometimes took place in house churches, not in separate, formal buildings. The history of religion in Oxfordshire in the 20th century is still to be written. But it seems likely that this is not the end of the story.

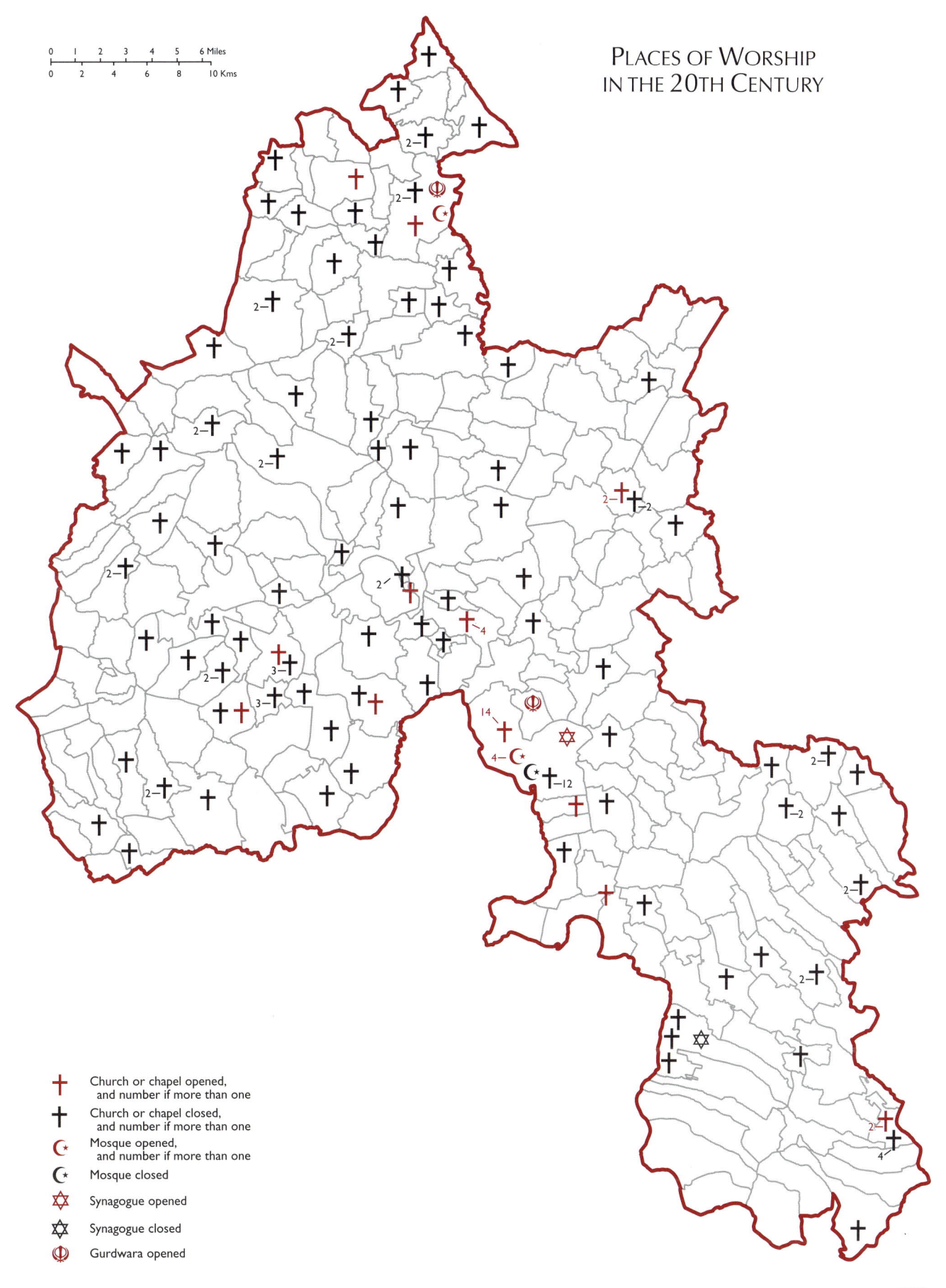

PLACES OF WORSHIP
IN THE 20TH CENTURY

† Church or chapel opened,
  and number if more than one
† Church or chapel closed,
  and number if more than one
☪ Mosque opened,
  and number if more than one
☪ Mosque closed
✡ Synagogue opened
✡ Synagogue closed
☬ Gurdwara opened

163

73 · Maternal and Infant Welfare in the 20th Century — Angela Davis

The first two decades of the 20th century saw a considerable expansion in the provision of maternal and infant welfare, both through voluntary enterprise and pubic legislation. The Second Boer War (1889–1902) focused attention on the ability of mothers to rear fit children. Forty per cent of recruits were found to be unfit for active service. These facts shocked the country and in 1902 the Interdepartmental Committee on Physical Deterioration was set up to consider how the situation might be improved. Oxfordshire's social elite responded to this call to action. One of Oxford's foremost voluntary societies, the Infant Welfare Association, began operation in 1905 to educate poor mothers in child-rearing.

Concern about the wastage of infant life further intensified in the years preceding World War I. In 1918, the Maternity and Child Welfare Act made it legal for local authorities to make any arrangements sanctioned by the Local Government Board for attending to the health of expectant mothers and children under five. The Act began a change in the relationship between voluntary and statutory agencies with services increasingly provided under the auspices of the county council. Voluntary infant welfare centres had been set up in Oxford during the first decade of the century. By the late 1930s 13 clinics existed in Oxford, and a further 30 around the county. They were now run by the council although still staffed by volunteers. The county centres suffered from a lack of suitable premises with many held in draughty rooms in village halls. Distance and expense prevented many women from attending. Rural infants did not escape all surveillance, however, with domiciliary health services taking the form of visits from the Health Visitors. Once-a-month antenatal clinics had started up in the mid 1920s, serviced by out-of-area General Practitioners (GPs). The clinics were poorly attended though, as they were often hard to reach, and were disbanded in the late 1930s, with GPs undertaking antenatal visiting themselves.

The interwar years saw a rapid extension in the number of salaried midwives employed by voluntary local nursing associations – principally the Oxfordshire Nursing Federation (ONF). By the late 1930s the ONF was responsible for 49 village nursing associations and had appointed 54 village nurses throughout rural Oxfordshire (excepting the rural district of Banbury, which was served by the Cottage Benefit Nursing Association). One domiciliary midwife, based in Henley, was directly employed by the council. GPs were the only doctors called in to help midwives in the Oxfordshire system. As part-time antenatal medical officers for the county, they could refer pregnant women to the maternity department at Oxford's Radcliffe Infirmary; and as ordinary GPs, they could be called in by midwives to help in emergencies during delivery. In 1937, 55% of the children in the county were delivered at home by a midwife. In half of these deliveries the GP was called upon, usually to repair a torn perineum. An emergency county-wide obstetric service was also in operation by 1939 to provide home treatment for those women whose removal to hospital was considered too dangerous. Those women deemed in need of hospital confinement for medical reasons were sent to Oxford. Beds were available on social grounds at the Public Assistance Institutions in Woodstock, Banbury and Henley. There were also the county's cottage hospitals (Bicester, Burford, Chipping Norton, Watlington, Thame); and the Elms Maternity home in Banbury (administered by the Banbury Corporation). Other small private maternity homes offered some provision for fee-paying patients, although their number varied over time. Women who lived near hospitals in neighbouring counties (e.g. Wallingford) also made use of those.

The introduction of the NHS in 1948 brought a renewed interest in maternal and infant health. Women and children had gained least from pre-war insurance schemes so were perhaps its greatest beneficiaries. During these middle decades of the century Oxfordshire was often at the forefront of developments in care; for example from the mid 1950s midwives, health visitors and district nurses were attached to GP practices, and health centres were established from the late 1960s. Infant mortality and perinatal mortality rates in the county were generally below the national average. The number of infant welfare clinics dramatically increased. These changes came in part from a forward-looking medical profession, encouraged by the presence of Oxford's teaching hospital, but also because the county attracted influential middle-class intellectuals such as the birth educator Sheila Kitzinger. Kitzinger ran the National Childbirth Trust's first preparation classes for couples from the late 1950s. However Oxfordshire continued to have a more restricted maternal and child welfare service than the city of Oxford. Antenatal classes were not started in Oxfordshire until 1961, and then only two classes were in operation. In Oxford city, mothercraft classes were on offer from 1947.

During the post-war period most Oxfordshire babies were delivered in hospital: by 1958 it was over 70%. Women in need of hospital birth on medical grounds were still sent to Oxford and those on social grounds to the smaller local hospitals. The main difference, of course, was these services were now free. The poor living conditions in some rural areas, with houses without electricity and running water, meant many women were recommended hospital births because their home conditions were deemed unsuitable for domiciliary delivery. After 1966 the number of home births in the county further declined. The opening of the Churchill Hospital's GP Unit in Oxford increased the number of hospital beds available and the policy of discharging patients home early from hospital was introduced to enable as many hospital births as possible. This rapid move to hospital deliveries in Oxfordshire was the result of changes in policy at the national level with the local health department reacting to them. The Cranbrook report in 1959 called for 70% of births to take place in hospital. Then in 1970 the Peel Committee recommended provision for 100% of confinements to take place in hospital. These national debates and developments were reflected in the care on offer to women in Oxfordshire and by the early 1970s over 90% of births took place in hospital.

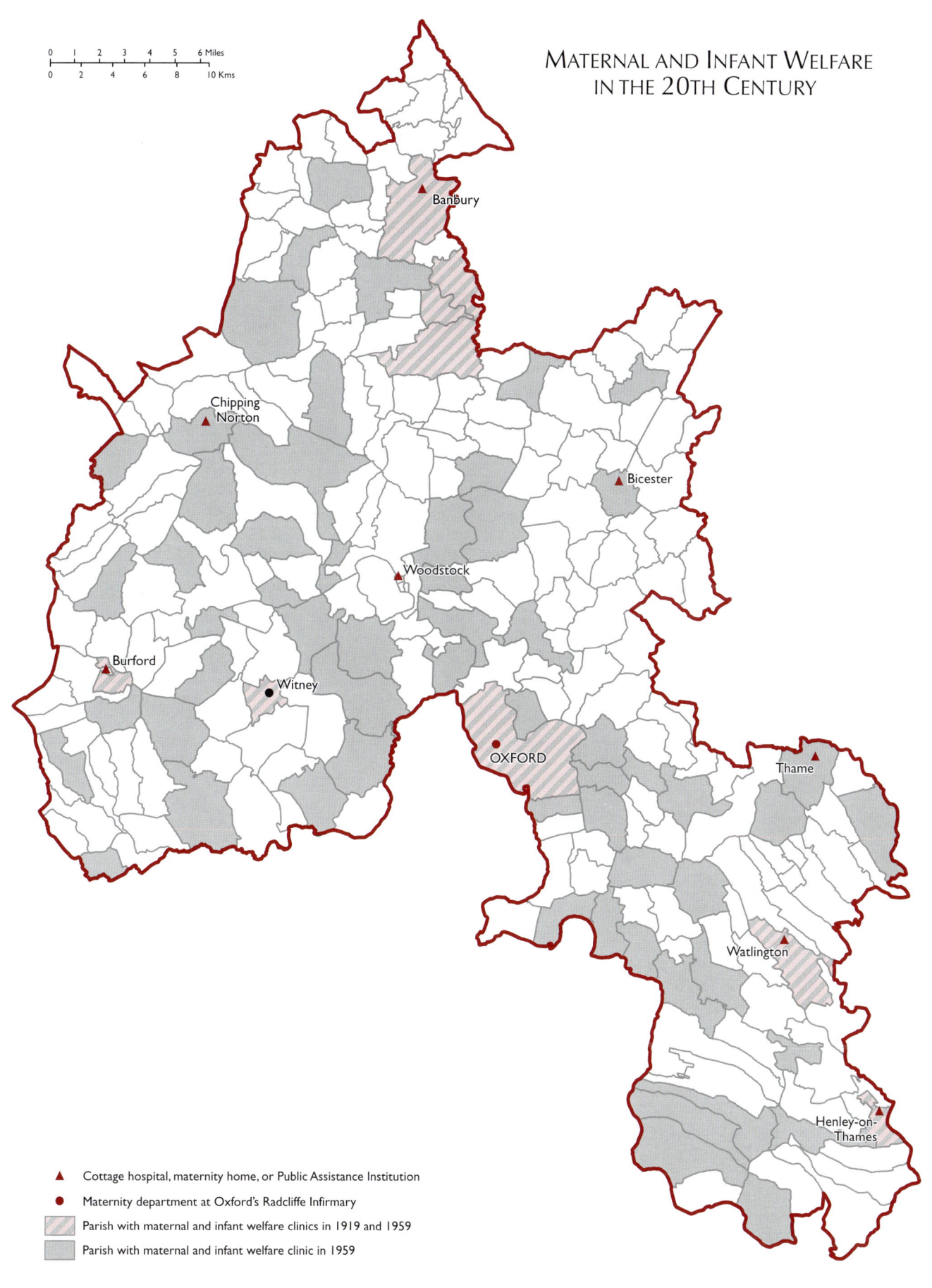

Maternal and Infant Welfare in the 20th Century

- ▲ Cottage hospital, maternity home, or Public Assistance Institution
- ● Maternity department at Oxford's Radcliffe Infirmary
- Parish with maternal and infant welfare clinics in 1919 and 1959
- Parish with maternal and infant welfare clinic in 1959

165

74 · Tourism

Mike Breakell

Tourism is by no means a 20th-century phenomenon. Visitors have been coming to Oxfordshire for many centuries. The county's attractions, from natural landscapes to town and village architecture, from internationally known university to great houses, and from TV locations to shopping opportunities, have matched the tastes and interests of British and international visitors in different periods. The shrines of St Birinus, at Dorchester, and St Frideswide, in Oxford, were places of medieval pilgrimage. In Oxford, the university and its colleges were a focus of visitors from early on. Many of the county's major houses have been open to visitors 'of good social standing' since their construction. The itineraries of travellers, from Leland in the 1530s to Celia Fiennes in the 17th century and on to J. B. Priestley in the 20th century, have frequently described Oxford, the wider county and its rich countryside.

Travellers' destinations were varied but certain places, like Henley, Oxford, Banbury, Thame and Burford, figured repeatedly, reflecting the need to use one of the few major roads passing through the county and to travel via places with river crossings and available accommodation. The development of roads and coaching services in the 18th century further encouraged travel (see entry 43), but it was the arrival of railways from the 1840s (see entry 46) which began the era of mass tourism to Oxfordshire. Railways brought excursionists, into and out of the county. 'Day trippers' came principally to Oxford (for the river as well as the city and university), but also to Blenheim and other attractions. Henley's development as an inland resort was enabled by the opening of a branch line in 1857, and by its proximity to London. Visitors from overseas also began to appear in increasing numbers, recommended by guides such as Baedeker who, in 1877, found that 'Oxford is on the whole more attractive than Cambridge to the ordinary visitor.'

Modern tourism is the result of higher levels of disposable income and ease of travel, especially since 1945, and is now a major part of the county's economy. Although there has been a substantial increase in the number of overseas visitors, by far the majority of visitors are from within the UK. In 2008, there were an estimated 18.2 million day trips to the pre-1974 county, and 2.2 million staying trips.

The most visited place in the county is Oxford. The history and visual appeal of university and college buildings are the major draws, but there is no single dominant visitor attraction. The top, paying attractions are Oxford Castle (Castle Unlocked, opened in 2005), Carfax Tower, a range of walking tours, open-top bus tours and the university's Botanic Garden. Christ Church is the most visited college of the university, enhanced by the popularity of Harry Potter films. The Ashmolean Museum, Museum of Natural History, Pitt Rivers Museum of Ethnology, and Modern Art Oxford are major attractions which do not charge an admission fee.

Although Oxford is the county's principal tourist attraction, it accounts for only 29% of domestic overnight trips to Oxfordshire, and only 25% of the day trips, at about 5.4 million per annum; however some 74% of visits from overseas visitors are to Oxford. Outside the city, the list of the most visited attractions is headed by Blenheim Palace at Woodstock, which in 2009 had 537,000 visitors to the palace itself and, in addition, more than half a million to separate events staged in the house or grounds. The Cotswold Wildlife Park and Gardens at Burford houses a collection of mammals, birds, reptiles and invertebrates from around the world and in 2008 received some 308,000 visitors. Other attractions include an array of museums, country houses and gardens, notable amongst them the River and Rowing Museum at Henley-on-Thames (more than 100,000 visits per year), the Oxfordshire Museum at Woodstock, Broughton Castle, Kelmscott Manor, Chastleton House, Rousham House, Stonor Park, Mapledurham House and watermill, Greys Court and Waterperry Gardens. Hobbs of Henley and Salter Bros of Oxford provide river-boat services, and Hook Norton brewery offers visits to its still-functioning Victorian premises.

Tourism is, however, not all about history. There are numerous annual produce and agricultural shows (e.g. Thame Show) and traditional folk events at Towersey, Cropredy and Bampton. River festivals include Eights Week at Oxford in May and Henley Royal Regatta in July. There are growing, newer festivals like Cornbury Park, as well as literary and cultural festivals in Oxford, Henley, Woodstock and Burford. Oxfordshire's prolific literary, film and TV connections make it even better known, for example as the setting of *Inspector Morse*, *Lewis* and *Midsomer Murders* amongst others.

One of the most visited attractions is now Bicester Village, a retail park of about 130 outlets selling mainly designer fashions. The Village attracts large numbers, the record being over 22,000 in one day. Of its customers 42% are from overseas. The conference trade is now of vital importance to Oxford colleges during vacations, whilst business trips to the county account for 22% of staying trips in Oxford and 22% of expenditure. Language schools (mostly in Oxford) account for 3% of staying trips, but because of the longer stays of students, contribute 18% of the expenditure of staying visitors.

Tourism is worth about £1.4 billion per annum to Oxfordshire, and accounts for around 17,900 full-time equivalent jobs, some 8,200 in Oxford alone. However, such large numbers of visitors can produce problems of management. By far the most popular transport is car or coach, and there are chronic problems of excessive traffic in Oxford, and at some 'honey pots' such as Minster Lovell Hall, Woodstock and Burford at summer weekends and bank holidays. The county's landscape has been protected through the designation of two Areas of Outstanding Natural Beauty and a Green Belt around Oxford (see entry 70). Maintaining and enhancing the county's appeal to visitors without overdevelopment will remain a challenge.

Tourist Destinations

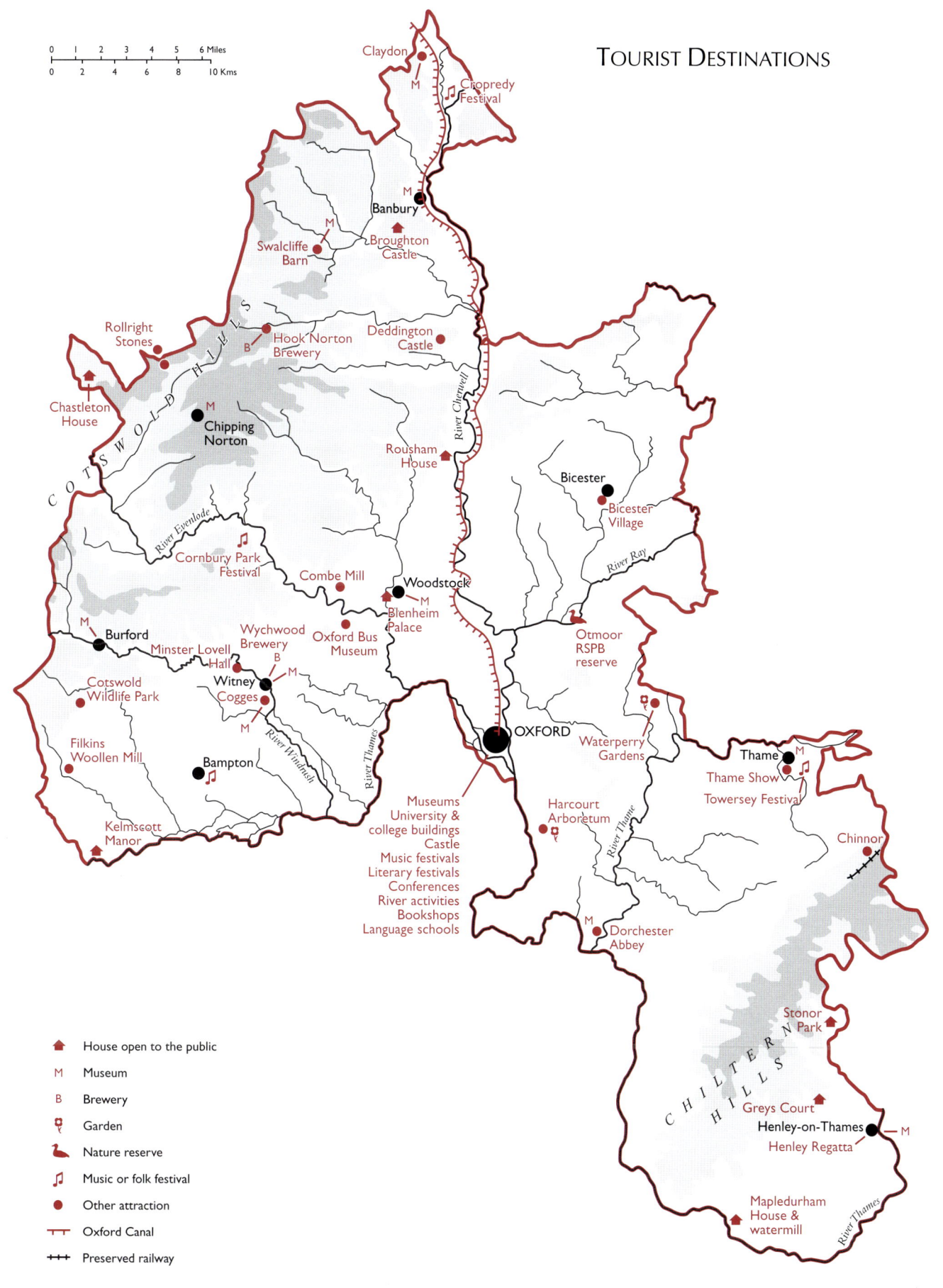

Scale: 0 1 2 3 4 5 6 Miles / 0 2 4 6 8 10 Kms

Locations

- Claydon
- Cropredy Festival
- Banbury
- Swalcliffe Barn
- Broughton Castle
- Rollright Stones
- Hook Norton Brewery
- Deddington Castle
- Chastleton House
- Chipping Norton
- Rousham House
- Bicester
- Bicester Village
- Cornbury Park Festival
- Combe Mill
- Woodstock
- Blenheim Palace
- Burford
- Wychwood Brewery
- Oxford Bus Museum
- Otmoor RSPB reserve
- Minster Lovell Hall
- Witney
- Cogges
- Cotswold Wildlife Park
- Bampton
- Filkins Woollen Mill
- Oxford
- Waterperry Gardens
- Thame
- Thame Show
- Towersey Festival
- Kelmscott Manor
- Harcourt Arboretum
- Chinnor
- Dorchester Abbey
- Stonor Park
- Greys Court
- Henley-on-Thames
- Henley Regatta
- Mapledurham House & watermill

Oxford attractions
- Museums
- University & college buildings
- Castle
- Music festivals
- Literary festivals
- Conferences
- River activities
- Bookshops
- Language schools

Rivers and features
- River Evenlode
- River Cherwell
- River Ray
- River Windrush
- River Thames
- River Thame
- Cotswold Hills
- Chiltern Hills

Legend

- 🏠 House open to the public
- M Museum
- B Brewery
- ⚑ Garden
- Nature reserve
- ♪ Music or folk festival
- ● Other attraction
- ⊢⊢⊢ Oxford Canal
- +++ Preserved railway

167

Notes and Further Reading

This section brings together for each entry any supporting notes relating to the text or maps and selected further reading.

Those wanting to identify a fuller range of reading on Oxfordshire history and archaeology will find OLIS (Oxford Libraries Information System) invaluable. This is a combined catalogue of over eight million items, including the holdings of the Bodleian Library (a copyright library). Access to OLIS is free and the catalogue is searchable by title, author and subject (which includes place). OLIS includes many printed sources from Oxfordshire Studies, the local studies collection of Oxfordshire County Council. See www.lib.ox.ac.uk/olis

It is very clear from this section of the atlas that the Victoria County History of Oxfordshire (VCH, *Oxfordshire*) and *Oxoniensia*, the annual journal of the Oxfordshire Architectural and Historical Society, are key sources across the whole range of periods and subjects. Free, online access to both is now available. See respectively www.british-history.ac.uk and oxoniensia.org

For an introductory guide and overview of printed sources for Oxfordshire history and archaeology see oxfordshirehistory. modhist.ox.ac.uk

REFERENCE MAPS

Ecclesiastical Parishes c.1850
The spelling of names of parishes used on the map of 1850 follows the conventions of VCH, *Oxfordshire*.

Civil Parishes 1933
Names of parishes used on the map of 1933 follow the conventions on the map appearing in part 2 of M. Gelling, *The Place-Names of Oxfordshire*, English Place-Names Society, 2 vols (1953–4).

Many parish, suburb and street names in Oxford are frequently spelt with and without a possessive 's' (e.g. St Ebbe and St Ebbe's). Historically, many names have been spelt both with and without apostrophes (e.g. St Clement's and St Clements; St Giles, St Giles' and St Giles's). The atlas adopts spellings appropriate to the subject and period under discussion.

The editors are grateful to Dr Keith Parry for his invaluable research on parish boundaries and names for these maps.

1 Topography
Emery, F., *The Oxfordshire Landscape* (1974).
Marshall, M. (ed.), *The Land of Britain: Report of the Land Utilisation Survey of Britain*, pt 56, *Oxfordshire* (1943).
Radcliffe Meteorological Station records, www.geog.ox.ac.uk/research/climate/rms/summary.html

2. Geology
Arkell, W. J., 'The Geology of Oxfordshire', in VCH, *Oxfordshire*, vol. 1(1939), pp. 1–26.
Arkell, W. J., *The Geology of Oxford* (1947).
Arkell, W. J., *Oxford Stone* (1947).
Powell, P., *The Geology of Oxfordshire* (2005).

3. Prehistoric Oxfordshire
A note on dating: dates BP (Before Present) are conventionally used for the earlier periods of prehistory, when longer periods of time are involved and dates are less precise. For the later periods it is usual to use dates 'cal BC', which indicates a calibrated radiocarbon date, or 'calendar' date, and, therefore, a higher degree of reliability.

Barclay, A., M. Gray, and G. Lambrick, *Excavations at the Devil's Quoits, Stanton Harcourt, Oxfordshire 1972–3 and 1988*, Oxford Archaeology Thames Valley Landscapes Monograph, vol. 3 (1995).

Barclay, A., G. Lambrick, J. Moore, and M. Robinson, *Lines in the Landscape: Cursus monuments in the Upper Thames Valley. Excavations at the Drayton and Lechlade cursuses*, Oxford: Oxford Archaeology Thames Valley Landscapes Monograph, vol. 15 (2003).
Barton, N., *Ice Age Britain* (2nd edn, 2005).
Benson, D., and D. Miles, *The Upper Thames Valley, an Archaeological Survey of the River Gravels*, Oxford Archaeological Unit Survey no. 2 (1974).
Benson, D., and A. Whittle (eds), *Building Memories: The Neolithic Cotswold Long Barrow at Ascott-under-Wychwood, Oxfordshire* (2006).
Briggs, G., J. Cook and R. T. Rowley (eds), *The Archaeology of the Oxford Region*, Oxford University Department for External Studies (1986), chs 1, 2 and 3.
Conneller, C., *Mesolithic Britain and Ireland: New Approaches* (2006).
Hey, G., P. Garwood, A. Barclay, and P. Bradley, *The Thames through Time. The archaeology of the Upper and Middle Thames: landscape and habitation through the Mesolithic, Neolithic and early Bronze Age*, Thames Valley Landscapes Monograph (forthcoming).
Lambrick, G., *The Rollright Stones: megaliths, monuments and settlement in the prehistoric landscape*, English Heritage Archaeological Report 6 (1988).
Lambrick, G., and M. Robinson, *The Thames through Time: The archaeology of the Gravel Terraces of the Upper and Middle Thames. The Thames Valley in Later Prehistory: 1500 BC–AD 50*, Thames Valley Landscapes Monograph no. 29 (2009).
See also the Solent Thames Research Framework:
Hardaker, T., *The Lower and Middle Palaeolithic of Oxfordshire*.
Hey, G., and A. Roberts, *Oxfordshire in the Mesolithic and Upper Palaeolithic*.
Anon. *Neolithic and Ealy Bronze Age Oxfordshire*.
Allen, T., *Later Bronze Age and Iron Age Oxfordshire*.
(Draft documents are available online at thehumanjourney.net/index.php?option=com_content&task=category&sectionid=8&id=66&Itemid=225 [accessed 26 March 2010])

4. Iron Age Oxfordshire
Allen, T. G., 'The Iron Age Background', in M. Henig and P. Booth (eds), *Roman Oxfordshire* (2000), pp. 1–33.
Cunliffe, B., and D. Miles (eds), *Aspects of the Iron Age in central southern Britain* (1984).
Dodd, A. (ed.), *The Archaeology of the Gravel Terraces of the Upper and Middle Thames: The Thames Valley in Late Prehistory: 1500 BC–AD 50* (2009).
Featherstone, R., and B. Bewley, 'Recent Aerial Reconnaissance in North Oxfordshire', *Oxoniensia*, vol. 65, pp. 13–26.
Lambrick, G., and T. G. Allen, *Gravelly Guy, Stanton Harcourt: the development of a prehistoric and Romano-British community* (2004).
Miles, D., 'Conflict and complexity: The later Prehistory of the Oxford region', *Oxoniensia*, vol. 62, pp.1–19.

5. Roman Oxfordshire
Booth, P., A. Dodd, M. Robinson and A. Smith, *The Thames through time: the archaeology of the gravel terraces of the Upper and Middle Thames. The early historical period: Britons, Romans and the Anglo-Saxons in the Thames Valley AD 1–1000* (2007).
Booth, P., J. Evans, and J. Hiller, *Excavations in the extramural settlement of Roman Alchester, Oxfordshire, 1991*, Oxford Archaeology Monograph 1 (2001).
Brodribb, A. C. C., A. R. Hands and D. R. Walker, *The Roman villa at Shakenoak Farm, Oxfordshire excavations 1960–1976*, British Archaeological Reports (Brit. Ser.) 395 (composite reprint 2005).
Henig, M., and P. Booth, *Roman Oxfordshire* (2000).

Lambrick, G, and T. Allen, *Gravelly Guy, Stanton Harcourt: the development of a prehistoric and Romano-British community*, Thames Valley Landscapes Monograph no. 21 (2004).

Young, C. J., *The Roman pottery industry of the Oxford region*, BAR (Brit. Ser.) 43 (1977).

6. Early Anglo-Saxon Settlement

I am very grateful to Susan Lisk for providing access to data held in the Historic Environment Record for Oxfordshire.

Blair, J., *Anglo-Saxon Oxfordshire* (1994).

Blair, J., 'Anglo-Saxon Bicester: the Minster and the Town', *Oxoniensia*, vol. 67 (2002), pp. 133–40.

Booth, P., A. Dodd, M. Robinson and A. Smith, *The Thames through time: the archaeology of the gravel terraces of the Upper and Middle Thames. The early historical period: Britons, Romans and the Anglo-Saxons in the Thames Valley AD 1–1000* (2007).

Dickinson, T. M., 'The Anglo-Saxon burial sites of the Upper Thames Region and their bearing on the history of Wessex, circa AD 400–700', unpublished DPhil thesis, University of Oxford, 1976.

Hamerow, H., 'Anglo-Saxon Oxfordshire, 400–700', *Oxoniensia*, vol. 64 (1999), pp. 23–38.

7. Yarnton: Late Saxon Rural Settlement

The map has been adapted from material first published in P. Booth, A. Dodd, M. Robinson and A. Smith, *The Thames through time: the archaeology of the gravel terraces of the Upper and Middle Thames. The early historical period: Britons, Romans and the Anglo-Saxons in the Thames Valley AD 1–1000* (2007).

Booth, P., A. Dodd, M. Robinson and A. Smith, ibid.

Hey, G., *Yarnton: Saxon and medieval settlement and landscape* (2004).

8. Place-Name Patterns

Gelling, M., *The Place-Names of Oxfordshire*, 2 vols (1953–4).

Gelling, M., and A. Cole, *The Landscape of Place-Names* (2003).

9. The Anglo-Saxon Minsters

Blair, J., *Anglo-Saxon Oxfordshire* (1994).

Blair, J., *The Church in Anglo-Saxon Society* (2005).

Blair, J., 'The Minsters of the Thames', in J. Blair and B. Golding (eds), *The Cloister and the World* (1996), pp. 5–28.

Boyle, A., 'Excavations in Christ Church Cathedral Graveyard', *Oxoniensia*, vol. 66 (2001), pp. 337–68.

Hardy, A., A. Dodd and G. D. Keevill, *Ælfric's Abbey: Excavations at Eynsham Abbey, Oxfordshire, 1989–92* (2003).

Kelly, S. E., 'An Early Minster at Eynsham, Oxfordshire', in O. J. Padel and D. N. Parsons (eds), *A Commodity of Good Names: Essays in Honour of Margaret Gelling* (2008), pp. 79–85.

10. Communications and Urban Origins before 1066

Blair, J., *Anglo-Saxon Oxfordshire* (1994).

Blair, J., 'Anglo-Saxon Bicester: the Minster and the Town', *Oxoniensia*, vol. 67 (2002), pp. 133–40.

Blair, J., 'Transport and Canal-Building on the Upper Thames, 1000–1300', in J. Blair (ed.), *Waterways and Canal-Building in Medieval England* (2007), pp. 254–94.

Booth, P., A. Dodd, M. Robinson and A. Smith, *The Thames through time: the archaeology of the gravel terraces of the Upper and Middle Thames. The early historical period: Britons, Romans and the Anglo-Saxons in the Thames Valley AD 1–1000* (2007).

Maddicott, J. R., 'London and Droitwich, *c.*650–750', *Anglo-Saxon England*, vol. 34 (2005), pp. 7–58.

Sherratt, A.,'Why Wessex? The Avon Route and River Transport in Later British Prehistory', *Oxford Journal of Archaeology*, vol. 15 (1996), pp. 211–34.

11. Bampton: a Minster-Town

Baxter, S., and J. Blair, 'Land Tenure and Royal Patronage in the Early English Kingdom: a Model and a Case-Study', *Anglo-Norman Studies*, vol. 28 (2006), 19–46.

Blair, J., 'Bampton: an Anglo-Saxon Minster', *Current Archaeology*, 160 (November 1998), pp. 124–30.

Blair, J., *Bampton Folklore* (2001).

Townley, S. C., 'Bampton', in VCH, *Oxfordshire*, vol. 13, *Bampton Hundred (Part One)* (1996), pp. 6–110.

12. Domesday Landholdings and Settlement

Blair, J., 'An Introduction to the Oxfordshire Domesday', in A. Williams and R. W. H. Erskine (eds), *The Oxfordshire Domesday* (1990), pp. 1–19.

Jope, E. M., and I. B. Terrett, 'Oxfordshire', in H. C. Darby and E. M. J. Campbell (eds), *The Domesday Geography of South-East England* (1962), pp. 186–238.

Lennard, R., *Rural England 1086–1135* (1959), ch. 3.

Stenton, F. M., 'Domesday Survey', in VCH, *Oxfordshire*, vol. 1, pp. 373–95.

Individual parish histories in VCH, *Oxfordshire*, vols 5–15 and in preparation.

13. Domesday Landscape and Land Use

Blair, J., 'An Introduction to the Oxfordshire Domesday', in A. Williams and R. W. H. Erskine (eds), *The Oxfordshire Domesday* (1990), pp. 1–19.

Emery, F., *The Oxfordshire Landscape* (1974), ch. 3.

Jope, E. M., and I. B. Terrett, 'Oxfordshire', in H. C. Darby and E. M. J. Campbell (eds), *The Domesday Geography of South-East England* (1962), pp. 186–238.

Individual parish histories in VCH, *Oxfordshire*, vols 5–15 and in preparation.

14. Castles and Moated Sites

Bond, C. J., 'The Oxford region in the middle ages', in G. Briggs, J. Cook & R. T. Rowley (eds), *The Archaeology of the Oxford Region*, Oxford University Department for External Studies (1986), esp. 'Castles and moated sites', pp. 147–51 & map 17, p. 188.

Cathcart King, D. J., *Castellarium Anglicanum: an Index and Bibliography of the Castles in England, Wales and the Islands* (1983), esp. 'Oxfordshire', vol. 2, pp. 384–9.

15. Medieval Towns, Markets and Fairs

Laughton, J., and C. Dyer, 'Small Towns in the East and West Midlands in the Later Middle Ages: A Comparison', *Midland History*, vol. 24 (1999), pp. 24–52.

Letters, S., M. Fernandes, D. Keene, O. Myhill, *Gazetteer of Markets and Fairs in England and Wales to 1516*, List and Index Soc., special series, vols 32–3 (2003).

Peberdy, R. B., 'The Economy, Society, and Government of a Small Town in Late Medieval England: A Study of Henley-on-Thames *c.*1300–*c.*1540', unpublished PhD thesis, University of Leicester, 1994.

Postles, D., 'Markets for Rural Produce in Oxfordshire, 1086–1350', *Midland History*, vol. 12 (1987), pp. 14–26.

Rodwell, K. (ed.), *Historic Towns in Oxfordshire: A Survey of the New County* (1975).

VCH, *Oxfordshire*, vol. 4 (1982), vols 6–14 (1959–2004).

16. Medieval Wool and Cloth Trades

Bridbury, A. R., *Medieval English Clothmaking: An Economic Survey* (1982).

Hurst, D., *Sheep in the Cotswolds: The Medieval Wool Trade* (2005).

Lloyd, T. H., *The English Wool Trade in the Middle Ages* (1977).

Munro, J. H., 'Wool-Price Schedules and the Qualities of English Wools in the Later Middle Ages, c.1270s–1499', *Textile History*, vol. 9 (1978), pp. 118–69.

Peberdy, R. B., 'The Economy, Society, and Government of a Small Town in Late Medieval England: A Study of Henley-on-Thames from c.1300 to c.1540', unpublished PhD thesis, University of Leicester, 1994, ch. 6.

VCH, *Oxfordshire*, vols 2–15 (1907–2006).

17. The Development of Parishes

1. H. E. Salter (ed.), *Cartulary of Oseney Abbey*, 6 vols, Oxford Historical Society, 89, 90, 91, 97, 98, 101 (1929–36), vol. 1, p. 1.
2. *Rotuli Hugonis de Welles, episcopi Lincolniensis, 1209–35*, 3 vols, Canterbury and York Society, 1, 3 and 4 (1907–14), vol. 2, p. 18.
3. H. E. Salter (ed.), *Eynsham Cartulary*, 2 vols, Oxford Historical Society, 49 and 51 (1907–14), vol. 1, p. 43.

Blair, J., *Anglo-Saxon Oxfordshire* (1994).

Blair, J., 'Introduction', *Minsters and parish churches: the local church in transition* (1988).

Pounds, N. J. G., *A history of the English parish: the culture of religion from Augustine to Victoria* (2000).

Taxatio Ecclesiastica Angliae et Walliae Auctoritate P. Nicholai IV, ed. T. Astle, S. Ayscough and J. Caley (Record Commission, 1802) and online version hosted by the Humanities Institute, University of Sheffield: www.hrionline.ac.uk/taxatio

VCH, *Oxfordshire*, in progress, 15 vols (1907–2006).

18. Vicarages and Appropriated Church Livings

Where appropriated rectories changed hands during the Middle Ages (e.g. confiscations from alien religious houses), the appropriator shown is that at the Dissolution. The map excludes vicarages ordained for non-resident rectors, and appropriations by Oxford colleges after the Dissolution. Eton College's acquisitions were mostly confiscated appropriations of alien religious houses.

Cheney, C. R., *From Becket to Langton: English Church Government 1170–1213* (1956), esp. 131–7 and Appendix 2.

Gibbons, A. (ed.), *Liber Antiquus de Ordinationibus Vicariarum tempore Hugonis Wells, Lincolniensis Episcopi, 1209–1235* (1888).

Lincoln bishops' registers, many of them published by the Lincoln Record Society.

Taxatio Ecclesiastica Angliae et Walliae . . . circa AD 1291 (Record Commission, 1802), available online at www.hrionline.ac.uk/taxatio

Valor Ecclesiasticus, tempore Henrici VIII (Record Commission, 1810–34).

VCH, *Oxfordshire*, in progress, 15 vols (1907–2006).

19. Religious Houses

Bond, C. J., 'The Oxford region in the middle ages', in G. Briggs, J. Cook and R. T. Rowley (eds), *The Archaeology of the Oxford Region*, Oxford University Department for External Studies (1986), esp. 'Monastic houses', pp. 143–7 & map 16, p. 187.

Keevill, G., 'Pieces of patterns: archaeological approaches to monastic sites in Oxfordshire', in G. Keevill, M. Aston and T. Hall (eds), *Monastic Archaeology: Papers on the Study of Medieval Monasteries* (2001), pp. 137–9.

Knowles, D., and R. N. Hadcock, *Medieval Religious Houses: England and Wales*, 2nd edn (1971).

20. Medieval Forests and Parks

Bond, J., 'The Oxford Region in the Middle Ages', in G. Briggs, J. Cook and T. Rowley (eds), *The Archaeology of the Oxford Region*, Oxford University Department for External Studies (1986), pp. 151–4.

Bond, J., 'Woodstock Park in the Middle Ages', in J. Bond and K. Tiller (eds), *Blenheim: Landscape for a Palace*, 2nd edn (1997), pp. 22–54.

Broad, J., and R. Hoyle (eds), *Bernwood: The Life and Afterlife of a Forest* (1997).

Schumer, B., *Wychwood: The Evolution of a Wooded Landscape*, 2nd edn (1999).

Schumer, B. (ed.), *Oxfordshire Forests, 1246–1609*, Oxfordshire Record Society, vol. 64 (2004).

Woodward, F., *Oxfordshire Parks* (1982).

21. Late Medieval Communications

Blair, J., 'Transport and Canal-Building on the Upper Thames, 1000–1300' in J. Blair (ed.), *Waterways and Canal-Building in Medieval England* (2007), pp. 254–94.

Grundy, G. B. (ed.), *Saxon Oxfordshire: Charters and Ancient Highways*, Oxfordshire Record Society, vol. 15 (1933).

Harrison, D., *The Bridges of Medieval England: Transport and Society 400–1800* (2004).

Peberdy, R. B., 'Navigation on the River Thames between London and Oxford in the Late Middle Ages: a Reconsideration', *Oxoniensia*, vol. 61 (1996), pp. 313–40.

Preece, P., 'The Tuddingway, an Ancient Road', *Oxfordshire Local History*, vol. 8, no. 1 (summer 2006), pp. 3–10.

VCH, *Oxfordshire*, vols 4–15 (1957–2006).

22. Wealth and Population in 1334 and 1524

Campbell, B. M., and K. Bartley, *England on the Eve of the Black Death: An Atlas of Lay Lordship, Land and Wealth, 1300–49* (2006), esp. pp. 313–49.

Darby, H. C., R. E. Glasscock, J. Sheail and G.R. Versey, 'The changing geographical distribution of wealth in England: 1086–1334–1525', *Journal of Historical Geography*, vol. 5.3 (1979), pp. 247–62.

Glasscock, R. E., (ed.), *The Lay Subsidy of 1334*, British Academy Records of Social and Economic History, new series 2 (1975).

Martin, A. F., and R. W. Steel (eds), *The Oxford Region: A Scientific and Historical Survey* (1954), esp. pp. 106–12, 128, 132–4.

Nightingale, P., 'The lay subsidies and the distribution of wealth in medieval England, 1275–1334', *Economic History Review*, vol. 57 (2004), pp. 1–32.

Sheail, J., ed. R. W. Hoyle, *The Regional Distribution of Wealth in England as indicated in the 1524/5 Lay Subsidy Returns*, List & Index Society Special Series 28–9 (1998).

Whiteman, A., (ed.), *The Compton Census of 1676: a critical edition*, British Academy Records of Social and Economic History, new series 10 (1986).

23. Deserted and Shrunken Settlements

Allison, K. J., M. W. Beresford and J. G. Hurst, *The Deserted Villages of Oxfordshire*, University of Leicester, Department of English Local History Occasional Papers, no. 17 (1965).

Bond, J., 'The Oxford Region in the Middle Ages', in G. Briggs, J. Cook, and T. Rowley (eds), *The Archaeology of the Oxford Region*, Oxford University Department for External Studies (1986), pp. 139–43.

Holden, B., 'The Deserted Medieval Village of Thomley, Oxfordshire', *Oxoniensia*, vol. 50 (1985), pp. 215–38.

Lloyd, T. H., 'Some Documentary Sidelights on the Deserted Oxfordshire Village of Brookend', *Oxoniensia*, vols 29–30 (1966 for 1964–5), pp. 116–28.

Miles, D., and T. Rowley, 'Tusmore Deserted Village', *Oxoniensia*, vol. 41 (1976), pp. 309–15.

Townley, S. (ed.), VCH, *Oxfordshire*, vol. 13, *Henley and Environs* (forthcoming).

24. Medieval Chantries and Hospitals
1. G. Harris, 'The foundation of the College', in L. W. B. Brockliss (ed.), *Magdalen College, Oxford: a History* (2008), p. 16.
2. R. Darwall-Smith, *A History of University College* (2008), p. 11.
3. VCH, *Oxfordshire*, vol. 2, p. 158.
4. S. Sweetinburgh, *The Role of the Hospital in Medieval England: Gift-giving and the Spiritual Economy* (2004), p. 22.

Burgess, C., 'A fond thing vainly invented: an essay on purgatory and pious motive in late medieval England', in S. J. Wright (ed.), *Parish, Church and People: Local Studies in Lay Religion, 1350–750* (1988), pp. 56–84.
Goodall, J. A. A., *God's House at Ewelme: Life, Devotion and Architecture in a Fifteenth-century Almshouse* (2000).
Kreider, A., *English Chantries: the Road to Dissolution* (1979).
Markham, M., *Medieval Hospitals in Oxfordshire*, Oxfordshire Museums Information Sheet, 12 (1979).
Orme, N., and M. Webster, *The English Hospital, 1070–1570* (1995).
Roffey, S., *The Medieval Chantry Chapel: an Archaeology* (2007).
Salter, H. E. (ed.), *A Cartulary of the Hospital of St John the Baptist*, 3 vols, Oxford Historical Society, 66, 68, 69 (1914–17). Vol. 69 has useful introduction.
Sweetinburgh, S., *The Role of the Hospital in Medieval England: Gift-giving and the Spiritual Economy* (2004).
VCH, *Oxfordshire*, vols 1–15.
Wood-Legh, K. L., *Perpetual Chantries in Britain* (1965).

25. University and College Properties before 1500
Catto, J. I., and T. A. R. Evans (eds), *The History of the University of Oxford*, vol. 1, *The Early Oxford Schools* (1984).
Catto, J. I., and T. A. R. Evans (eds), *The History of the University of Oxford*, vol. 2, *Late Medieval Oxford* (1992).
VCH, *Oxfordshire*, vols 1–15 (1907–2006).

26. Pottery and Potters
Blair, J., *Anglo-Saxon Oxfordshire* (1994).
Blinkhorn, P., 'The Pottery' in D. Gilbert, 'Excavations West of St Mary's Church, Black Bourton, Oxfordshire: Early, Middle, and Late Anglo-Saxon Activity', *Oxoniensia*, vol. 73 (2008).
Mellor, M., 'A synthesis of middle and late Saxon, medieval and early post-medieval pottery from the Oxford region', *Oxoniensia* vol. 59, 1994.
Mellor, M., in A. Dodd (ed.), *Oxford Before the University* (2003), Table 6.7: Continental Imported pottery from recent excavations AD 800–1100 & Table 6.8: Regional imported pottery from recent excavations AD 800–1100 .
Mepham, L., and M. J. Heaton, 'A Medieval Pottery Kiln at Ashampstead, Berkshire', *Medieval Ceramics*, vol. 19, 1995).
Newbury By-Pass: Enborne Street and Wheathouse Lane, www.highways.gov.uk/aboutus/1654 – accessed 15.12.2009.

27. Medieval Vernacular Buildings
Alcock, N. W., *Cruck Construction: an introduction and catalogue*, CBA Research Report no. 42 (1981).
Catchpole, A., D. Clark and R. Peberdy, *Burford: buildings and people in a Cotswold town* (2008).
Mercer, E., *English Vernacular Houses* (1975).
Munby, J. T., et al., 'Swalcliffe: a New College Barn in the Fifteenth Century', *Oxoniensia*, vol. 60 (1995).
Pilling, J., *Oxfordshire Houses: a guide to local traditions* (1993).
Townley, S., *Henley-on-Thames: town, trade and river* (2009).
Wood-Jones, R. B., *Traditional Domestic Architecture of the Banbury Region* (1963).

28. Watermills to *c.*1750
The map includes two instances of 'half-mills'. These occur where records show that ownership of a mill was shared but the portions do not add up to a whole number.

Foreman, W., *Oxfordshire Mills* (1983).

29. Oxford before 1800
The map of Oxford in 1279 has been adapted from mapping produced by Julian Munby. The interpretation of Oxford as depicted by Ralph Agas is derived from material produced by John Blair.

Aston, T. H., et al. (eds), *History of the University of Oxford*, vols 1–5 (1984–1997).
Crossley, A. (ed.), VCH, *Oxfordshire*, vol. 4, *City of Oxford* (1979).
Davis, R., *New Map of the County of Oxford, surveyed 1793–4* (1797).
Old Plans of Oxford, Oxford Historical Society, vol. 38 (1899), for maps of Agas (1578) and Loggan (1675).
Dodd, A. (ed.), *Oxford before the University*, Oxford Archaeology Monograph (2003).
Salter, H. E., *Survey of Oxford*, Oxford Historical Society, new series 14, vol 20 (1960, 1969).
Taylor, I., *Plan of the University and City of Oxford* (1751), copy in Bodl. Gough Maps Oxfordshire 12.

30. Agriculture and Farming Regions 1500–1700
Havinden, M. A., 'Agricultural Progress in Open-field Oxfordshire', *Agricultural History Review*, vol. 9 (1961), pp. 73–83.
Havinden, M. A., 'The Rural Economy of Oxfordshire, 1580–1730', unpublished BLitt thesis, University of Oxford, 1961.
Thirsk, J. (ed.), *The Agrarian History of England and Wales*, vol. 4, 1500–1640 (1967).
Wordie, J. R., 'The South: Oxfordshire, Buckinghamshire, Berkshire, Wiltshire, and Hampshire', in J. Thirsk (ed.), *The Agrarian History of England and Wales*, vol. 5, 1640–1750: I. Regional Farming Systems* (1984), 317–57.
Individual parish histories in VCH, *Oxfordshire*, vols 5–15 and in preparation.

31. Early Modern Market Towns
Catchpole, A., D. Clark and R. Peberdy, *Burford: Buildings and People in a Cotswold Town* (2008).
Clark, P. (ed.), *The Cambridge Urban History of Britain*, vol. 2, *1540–1840* (2000).
Eddershaw, D., *Chipping Norton: The Story of a Market Town* (2006).
Rodwell, K., *Historic Towns of Oxfordshire: A Survey of the New County* (1975).
Townley, S., *Henley-on-Thames: Town, Trade and River* (2009).
VCH, *Oxfordshire*, vols 6–8, 10–13 and 15.

32. The Dissolution of the Monasteries
Baskerville, G., 'The Dispossessed Religious of Oxfordshire', *Oxfordshire Archaeological Society Reports and Transactions*, no. 75 (1930).
Bowker, M., *The Henrician Reformation: The Diocese of Lincoln under John Longland 1521–1547* (1981).
English Monastic Archives website: www.ucl.ac.uk/history2/englishmonasticarchives/
Knowles, D., *The Religious Orders in England*, vol. 3 (1959).
VCH, *Oxfordshire*, passim.

33. Tudor Rebellions
Fletcher, A., and D. MacCulloch, *Tudor Rebellions*, 5th revised edn (2008).

NOTES AND FURTHER READING

Halliday, K., 'New light on "the commotion time" of 1549: the Oxfordshire rising', *Historical Research*, vol. 82, no. 218 (November 2009).

Walter, J., 'A "rising of the people"?: the Oxfordshire rising of 1596', *Past and Present*, no. 107 (1985).

Woodman, A. Vere, 'The Buckinghamshire and Oxfordshire rising of 1549', *Oxoniensia*, vol. 22 (1957).

34. Roman Catholic Recusants 1558–1800

Bossy, J., *The English Catholic Community 1570–1850* (1975).

Davidson, A., 'Roman Catholicism in Oxfordshire 1580–1640', unpublished Bristol Univ PhD thesis (1970), in Bodleian Library MS Top Oxon d.602).

Hadland, T., *Thames Valley Papists from Reformation to Emancipation 1534–1829* (1992).

Stapleton, Mrs B., *A History of the Post-Reformation Catholic Missions in Oxfordshire* (1906).

Stonor, R. J., *Stonor – a Catholic sanctuary* (1952).

VCH, *Oxfordshire*. The parish accounts in each volume include details of recusancy. Vol. 2 has a general ecclesiastical history.

35. Early Protestant Nonconformity

Clapinson, M. (ed.), *Bishop Fell and Nonconformity*, Oxfordshire Record Society, vol. 52 (1980).

Lyon Turner, G., *Original Records of Early Nonconformity*, 3 vols (London, 1911–14).

Watts, M., *The Dissenters from the Reformation to the French Revolution* (1978).

Whiteman, A. (ed.), *The Compton Census of 1676: a critical edition*, British Academy Records of Social and Economic History, new series 10 (1986).

36. Elites and Office-Holders: mid 17th Century

Firth, C. H., and R. S. Rait (eds), *Acts and Ordinances of the Interregnum*, 3 vols (1911).

The Names of the Justices of the Peace (1650), pp. 44–5.

VCH, *Oxfordshire, passim*.

www.oxforddnb.com for entries on many men mentioned.

37. Early Modern Shops and Shopkeepers

1. The inventories studied are in the records of the archdeaconry, consistory and peculiar courts for Oxfordshire, the earliest of which date from 1516. For the purpose of analysis records to 1800 have been used, with subdivisions to 1640, 1640–1732, and 1732–1800 used for some comparisons. These reflect both periods commonly used by historians and the arrangement and indexing of the Oxfordshire records.

2. Dannatt, G. H., 'Bicester in the 17th and 18th centuries', *Oxoniensia*, vols 26–27 (1961–2), pp. 252–4.

Cheyne, E., and D. M. Barratt, *Probate Records of the Courts of the Bishop and Archdeacon of Oxford 1516–1732*, vols 1 and 2, British Record Society (1981 and 1985).

Havinden, M. A. (ed.), *Household and Farm Inventories in Oxfordshire, 1550–1590*, Historical Manuscripts Commission, JP10 (1965).

Spufford, M., *The Great Reclothing of Rural England: Petty Chapmen and their Wares in the Seventeenth Century* (1984).

Tiller, K., 'Shopkeeping in Seventeenth-century Oxfordshire: William Brock of Dorchester', *Oxoniensia*, vol. 62 (1997), pp. 270–86.

Vaisey, D. G., 'A Charlbury Mercer's Shop', *Oxoniensia*, vol. 31 (1966), pp. 107–16.

Weatherill, L., *Consumer Behaviour and Material Culture in Britain 1660–1760* (1988).

38. The Great Rebuilding

Airs, M. R., and J. G. Rhodes, 'Wall Paintings from a House in Upper High Street, Thame', *Oxoniensia*, vol. 45 (1980), pp. 235–59.

Buxton, A., 'Domestic Culture in Early Seventeenth-Century Thame, *Oxoniensia*, vol. 67 (2002), pp. 79–115.

Hoskins, W. G., 'The Rebuilding of Rural England 1570–1640', *Past and Present*, no. 4 (1953), pp. 44–59.

Johnson, M. H., 'Rethinking the Great Rebuilding', *Oxford Journal of Archaeology*, vol. 1, no. 1 (1993), pp. 117–25.

Machin, R., 'The Great Rebuilding: a Reassessment', *Past and Present*, no. 77 (1977), pp. 33–56.

Portman, D., 'Little Milton, the Rebuilding of an Oxfordshire Village', *Oxoniensia*, vol. 25 (1960), pp. 49–63.

Portman, D., 'Vernacular Building in the Oxford Region in the Sixteenth and Seventeenth Centuries', in C. W. Chalklin & M. A. Havinden (eds), *Rural Change and Urban Growth 1500–1800* (1974).

Wood-Jones, R., *Traditional Domestic Architecture of the Banbury Region* (1963).

39. Civil War 1642–1649

Bell, J., 'The mortality crisis in Thame and east Oxfordshire 1643', *Oxfordshire Local History*, vol. 3, no. 4 (1990).

Eddershaw, D., *The Civil War in Oxfordshire* (1995).

Phillip, I. G. (ed.), *Journal of Sir Samuel Luke*, Oxfordshire Record Society, vols 29, 31, 33 (1950–3).

Richardson, R. C., *The English Civil Wars: Local Aspects* (1997). [Includes J. A. Dils, 'Epidemics, mortality and the Civil War in Berkshire, 1642–6', which shows how parish registers and other sources can be used to discern the impact of the war locally; and I. Roy, 'The City of Oxford 1640–1660'.]

Roy, I. (ed.), *The Royalist Ordnance Papers*, Oxfordshire Record Society, vols 43, 49 (1964–75)

Sherwood, R., *The Civil War in the Midlands, 1642–1651*, 2nd edn. (1992).

Spalding, R. (ed.), *The Diary of Bulstrode Whitelocke 1605–1675*, British Academy Records of Social and Economic History, new series 13 (1990).

Toynbee, M., *The papers of Captain Henry Stevens, wagon-master to King Charles I*, Oxfordshire Record Society, vol. 42 (1961).

40. Country Houses 1500–1670

Oxfordshire Photographic Archive. The most useful digital resource, accessed via www.oxfordshire.gov.uk/heritagesearch

Sherwood, J., and N. Pevsner, *The Buildings of England : Oxfordshire* (1974).

VCH, *Oxfordshire*, vols 5–15, and further volumes in preparation.

Weinstock, M. M. B. (ed.), *Hearth Tax Returns: Oxfordshire 1665*, Oxfordshire Record Society, vol. 21 (1940).

41. Country Houses 1670–1815

See 40 above

42. Schools in the 18th Century

1. D. McClatchey, *Oxfordshire Clergy, 1777–1869* (1960), p. 33.
2. Bodl. Lib. Theta 662 (43), SPCK list of schools, 1712.

Jones, M. G., *The Charity School Movement* (1938).

Laqueur, T. W., *Religion and Respectability: Sunday Schools and Working Class Culture* (1976).

Lloyd Jukes, H. A. (ed.), B*ishop Secker's Visitation Returns 1738*, Oxfordshire Record Society, vol. 38 (1957).

McClatchey, D., *Oxfordshire Clergy, 1777–1869: A study of the Established Church and the role of its Clergy in local society* (1960).

Oxfordshire Archives (OA), MSS. Oxf. Dioc. pp. d.555–7. Clergy Visitation returns, 1759.
OA, MSS. Oxf. Dioc. pp. d.707. Return of schools, 1808.
O'Day, R., *Education and Society 1500–1800* (1982).
Stephens, W. B., and R. W. Unwin, *Materials for the Local and Regional Study of Schooling, 1700–1900* (British Records Society, Archives and the User 7, 1987).

43. Roads in the 18th and 19th Centuries
The map of the county's roads has been adapted from material first published in M. Jessop, *A History of Oxfordshire* (1975).

Albert, W., *The Turnpike Road System in England 1663–1840* (1972).
Drinkwater, J., *Inheritance: being the first book of an autobiography* (1931);
Gerhold, D., *Carriers & Coachmasters: Trade and Travel before the Turnpikes* (2005).
Pawson, E., *Transport and Economy: the turnpike roads of eighteenth-century Britain* (1977).
Rosevear, A., *Turnpike Roads to Banbury*, Banbury Historical Society, vol. 31 (2010).
Scarfe, N. (ed.), *Innocent Espionage: The La Rochefoucauld Brothers' Tour of England in 1785* (1995).
Webb, S. and B., *The King's Highway* (1913).

44. Rivers and Canals
Compton, H., *The Oxford Canal* (1976).
Hadfield, C., *The Canals of the East Midlands* (1966).
Priestley, J., *An Historical Account of the Navigable Rivers, Canals and Railways of Britain* (1831).
Prior, M., *Fisher Row: Fishermen, Bargemen & Canal Boatmen in Oxford 1500–1900* (1982).
Wenham, S., 'Salters' of Oxford: a History of a Thames Boating Firm over a Century of Evolution (1858–c.1960)', *Oxoniensia*, vol. 71 (2006), pp. 111–43.

45. Towns 1700–1900: Nodality, Growth and Decay
Thiessen polygons. Every point within a polygon is nearer to the market town at the polygon's centre than to any other town. This ignores limiting geographical factors (such as bridging points, the speed and condition of roads and natural topography) and human factors (family or trade links with a locality), which in practice also influenced travel patterns.

Bond, C. J., 'The small towns of Oxfordshire in the nineteenth century', in R. T. Rowley (ed.), in *The Oxford Region*, Oxford University Department for External Studies (1980), pp. 55–79.

46. Railways
Abbreviations:
GWR Great Western Railway
LNWR London and North Western Railway
GCR Great Central Railway
N&BR Northampton and Banbury Railway
SMJR Stratford-upon-Avon and Midland Junction Railway

Christiansen, R. A., *Regional History of the Railways of Great Britain*, vol. 13, *Thames & Severn* (1981).
Hemmings, W., *The Banbury & Cheltenham Railway*, 2 vols (2004).
Jones, H., *The Chiltern Railways Story* (2010).
Lingard, R., *Princes Risborough–Thames–Oxford Railway* (1978).
MacDermot, E. T., *History of the Great Western Railway*, 2 vols (1882), revised edn, ed. C. R. Clinker, 3 vols (1964).
Simpson, B., *Oxford to Cambridge Railway*, vol. 1, *Oxford to Bletchley* (1981).

47. Agriculture 1750–1970

Proportion of total area occupied by estates with following aggregate acreages	All England (%)	Oxfordshire (%)
Great estates (over 10,000 acres)	24	15
Estates of greater gentry (3,000–10,000 acres)	17	25
Estates of squirearchy or lesser gentry (1,000–3,000 acres)	12.4	15
Estates of small landowners:		
Greater yeomen (300–1,000 acres)	14	14
Lesser yeomen (100–300 acres)	12.5	12
Small proprietors (1–100 acres)	12	10

Oxfordshire Land Ownership 1873. Source: J. Bateman, *The Great Landowners of Britain and Ireland* (1883 edn)

Surveys and descriptions of Oxfordshire farming are R. Davis, *General View of the Agriculture of the County of Oxford* (1794); under the same title, A. Young (1809); W. Marshall, Review and *Abstract of the County Reports to the Board of Agriculture*, vol. 4, *The Midlands* (1818); C. S. Read, *On the Farming of Oxfordshire*, Royal Agricultural Society of England Prize Essay (1854); H. Rider Haggard, *Rural England*, vol. 2 (1906); J. Orr, *Agriculture in Oxfordshire: A Survey made on behalf of the Institute for Research in Agricultural Economics, University of Oxford* (1916); Earl of Mayo, S. D. Adshead and P. Abercrombie, *Oxfordshire: A Regional Survey* (1931); M. Marshall (ed.), *The Land of Britain: Report of the Land Utilisation Survey of Britain*, pt 56, *Oxfordshire* (1943); T. W. Gardner, *The Farms and Estates of Oxfordshire*, Department of Agricultural Economics, University of Reading (n.d. [1946?]).

Allen, R. C., *Enclosure and the Yeoman* (1992).
Howkins, A., *The Death of Rural England: A Social History of the English Countryside since 1900* (2003).
Miller, C. (ed.), *Rain and Ruin: The Diary of an Oxfordshire Farmer, John Simpson Calvertt, 1875–1900* (1983).
Ministry of Agriculture and Fisheries, *National Farm Survey of England and Wales: A Summary Report* (1946).
— *Annual Agricultural Statistics*, 1866 to date.
Tiller, K., 'Hook Norton: an Open Village', in J. Thirsk (ed.), *The English Rural Landscape* (2000).

48. Parliamentary Enclosure 1758–1882
Eastwood, D., 'Communities, Protest and Police in early Nineteenth Century Oxfordshire: The Enclosure of Otmoor Reconsidered', *Agricultural History Review*, vol. 44, pt 1 (1996), pp. 35–46.
Mingay, G. E, *Parliamentary Enclosure in England: An introduction to its Causes, Incidence and Impact 1750–1850* (1997).
Oxfordshire County Council, Record Publication No 2, *A Handlist of Inclosure Acts and Awards relating to the County of Oxford*, 2nd edn (1975).
Tate, W. E., 'The cost of Parliamentary Enclosure in England (with special reference to the County of Oxford)', *Economic History Review*, new series 5, 1952/3, pp. 258–62.
Tate, W. E., *Oxfordshire Parliamentary Enclosure 1646–1853*, unpublished B. Litt. dissertation, Oxford, 1947.
Tiller, K., 'Rural Resistance: Custom, Community and Conflict in South Oxfordshire, 1800–1914', in O. Ashton. R. Fyson, R. Stephens (eds), *The Duty of Discontent; essays for Dorothy Thompson* (1995).
VCH, *Oxfordshire*, www.victoriacountyhistory.ac.uk and www.british-

history.ac.uk/subject.aspx?subject=5&gid=26. Details of enclosure are summarised by parish.

Walton, J. R., 'Aspects of Agrarian Change in Oxfordshire 1750–1880', 3 vols, unpublished DPhil thesis, University of Oxford, 1977.

49. Labouring Lives

The map has been adapted from material in J. R. Walton, 'Aspects of Agrarian Change in Oxfordshire 1700–1880', unpublished DPhil thesis, University of Oxford, 1977.

Eastwood, D., 'The Republic in the Village', *Journal of Regional and Local Studies*, vol. 12 (1992), pp. 18–28.

Mills, D., *Lord and Peasant in Nineteenth-century Britain* (1980).

Report of House of Lords Select Committee on Poor Laws, *Parliamentary Papers* (1831), vol. 8.

Rowntree, B. S., and M. Kendall, *How the Labourer Lives Now* (1913).

Second Report of the Royal Commission on the Employment of Children, Young Persons and Women in Agriculture, *Parliamentary Papers* (1868–9), vol. 13.

Song, B. K., 'Parish Typology and the Operation of the Poor Laws in early 19th-century Oxfordshire', *Agricultural History Review*, vol. 50, pt 2 (2000), pp. 203–24.

50. Industrial Oxfordshire: the mid 19th Century

Coleman, D. C., *The British Paper Industry 1495–1860* (1958).

Gourish, T. R., and R G Wilson, *The British Brewing Industry 1830–1980* (1994).

Harman, C. L., *Cheers, Sir! From the Vicarage to the Brewery* (1987).

Mathias, P., *The Brewing Industry in England 1700–1830* (1959).

Shorter, A. H., *Paper-making in the British Isles: a historical & geographical study* (1971).

51. Proto-Industries of 19th-Century Oxfordshire

Plummer, A., and R. Early, *The Blanket Makers 1669–1969: a history of Charles Early & Marriott (Witney) Ltd* (1969).

Early, R. E., *Master Weaver* (1980).

52. Brewing and Malting

Bond, J., and J. Rhodes, *The Oxfordshire Brewer*, Oxfordshire Museums Service (1985).

Gray, J. R., 'Berkshire and Oxfordshire Breweries and Maltings', *CBA Group 9 Industrial Archaeology Bulletin* (January 1971).

Harrison, B., and B. Trinder, 'Drink and sobriety in an Early Victorian Town: Banbury 1830–1860', *English Historical Review* (1969), supplement no. 4.

Mathias, P., *The Brewing Industry in England, 1700–1830* (1959).

Monkton, H. A., *A History of English Ale and Beer* (1966).

Plot, R., *A Natural History of Oxfordshire* (1677).

Sheppard, F., *Brakspear's Brewery, Henley on Thames 1779–1979* (1979).

53. Country Houses 1815–1939

See 40 above

54. Parliamentary Representation

Eastwood, D.,'Toryism, Reform and political culture in Oxfordshire, 1826–1837', *Parliamentary History*, vol. 7 (1988), pp. 98–121.

Fisher, D. (ed.), *The House of Commons, 1820–1832*, History of Parliament (2009).

Robson, R. J., *The Oxfordshire Election of 1754* (1949).

Thorne, R. (ed.), *The House of Commons, 1790–1820*, History of Parliament (1986).

Trinder, B., *A Victorian MP and his Constituents* (1969).

Williams, W., *The Parliamentary History of Oxfordshire* (1899).

55. Education in the 19th Century: Elementary Schools

1. Education Enquiry: Abstract of the Answers and Returns, *Parliamentary Papers* (1835), vol. 42.
2. Report of the Commissioners into the State of Popular Education in England, *Parliamentary Papers* (1861), vol. 21, pt.1.
3. Second Report of the Royal Commission on the Employment of Children, Young Persons and Women in Agriculture, *Parliamentary Papers* (1868–9), vol. 13, p. 351.
4. F. Thompson, *Lark Rise to Candleford* (1945), ch. 11.
5. P. Horn (ed.), *Village Education in 19th-century Oxfordshire*, Oxfordshire Record Society, vol. 51 (1979), p. xxxviii.
6. loc.cit., p. xlv.

56. Education in the 19th Century: the Private Sector

1. K. Tiller, 'A 19th-century Village Boarding School: the Garlick School at Ewelme', *Oxoniensia*, vol. 56 (1992), pp. 331-7.
2. R. Gardener, *History, Gazetteer and Directory of the County of Oxfordshire* (1852); *Kelly's Directory of Oxfordshire* (1883); *Kelly's Directory of Oxfordshire* (1915).

57. The Church of England in 1835

The Ecclesiastical Revenues Commission employed the term 'impropriation', where a tithe was alienated to a layman as opposed to appropriated by an ecclesiastical person or corporation.

Best, G. F. A., *Temporal Pillars: Queen Anne's Bounty, the Ecclesiastical Commissioners, and the Church of England* (1964).

Jacob, W. M., *The Clerical Profession in the Long Eighteenth Century, 1680–1840* (2007).

McClatchey, D., *Oxfordshire Clergy 1777–1869* (1960).

Russell, A., *The Clerical Profession* (1980).

58. Church and Chapel in 1851

Snell, K. D. M., and P. S. Ell, *Rival Jerusalems. The Geography of Victorian Religion* (2000).

Tiller, K., 'The desert begins to blossom': Oxfordshire and Primitive Methodism, 1824–60', *Oxoniensia*, vol. 71 (2007), pp. 85–109.

Tiller, K., 'The Place of Methodism: a Study of Three Counties in 1851', in P. Forsaith and M. Wellings (eds), *Methodism and History: Essays for John Vickers* (2010), pp. 55–89.

Tiller, K. (ed.), *Berkshire Religious Census 1851*, Berkshire Record Society, vol. 14 (2010). See introduction for review of current debates on attendance figures.

Tiller, K. (ed.), *Church and Chapel in Oxfordshire 1851: The returns of the census of religious worship*, Oxfordshire Record Society, vol. 55 (1987).

59. Population Change 1801–1851

Baines, D. E., *Migration in a Mature Economy: emigration and internal migration in England and Wales, 1861–1900* (1985), pp. 230–1.

Eastwood, D.,'Communities, Protest and Police in Early Nineteenth-Century Oxfordshire: the enclosure of Otmoor reconsidered', *Agriculture History Review*, vol. 44, pt 1, pp. 35–46.

Morris, R. J., 'The Friars and Paradise: An Essay in the Building History of Oxford, 1801–61', *Oxoniensia*, vol. 36 (1971), pp. 72–98.

VCH, *Oxfordshire*, vol. 2 (1907), Table of Population, pp. 215–24.

60. Population Change 1851–1901

	England & Wales (000,000)	% growth	Oxfordshire (000)	% growth
1851	17.9		170.4	
1861	20.1	11.9	171.0	0.3
1871	22.7	13.2	178.0	4.1
1881	26.0	14.4	179.6	0.9
1891	29.0	11.7	185.3	3.2
1901	32.5	12.2	181.1	-2.2
1851–1901		81.4		6.3

Population growth: England and Wales compared with Oxfordshire

1. T. Hinchcliffe, *North Oxford* (1992).
2. B. Trinder, *Victorian Banbury* (1982), table 1, p. 194.

Nash, J., 'The New People of East Oxford: the suburbanisation of Cowley, 1851–91', *Oxoniensia*, vol. 63 (1998), pp. 125–45.
Nash, J., 'Aspects of a Town in Decline: a population study of Burford, Oxfordshire, 1851–1901', unpublished DPhil thesis, Oxford, 2006.
Townley, S., *Henley-on-Thames: Town, trade and river* (2009).

61. Migration Patterns 1851–1901
Nash, J., 'Aspects of a Town in Decline: a population study of Burford, Oxfordshire, 1851–1901', unpublished DPhil thesis, Oxford, 2006, ch. 1.
Waller, P. J., *Town, City and Nation: England 1851–1914* (1983), p. 192.

62. Friendly Societies
1. Fourth Report of the Commissioners appointed to inquire into Friendly and Benefit Building Societies, *Parliamentary Papers* (1874), pt 1, p. lxii.
2. Abstract of the Answers and Returns relating to 'An Act for Procuring Returns relative to the Expense and Maintenance of the Poor in England', *Parliamentary Papers* (1804), pp. 398–406.
3. OA, PAR 287/13/F3/1.
4. For example, in the *Chipping Norton Deanery Magazine 1883–1902*, Oxfordshire Studies Library, COS SV.
5. Report of Chief Registrar of Friendly Societies 1891, *Parliamentary Papers* (1893–4, 513–1), and Report of Chief Registrar of Friendly Societies 1886, *Parliamentary Papers* (1889, 113–1).

Bee, M., 'Within the shelter of the old elm tree: Oddfellowship and community in north Oxfordshire, 1871–2002', *Family and Community History*, vol. 6:2 (November 2003), pp. 85–96.
Cordery, S., *British Friendly Societies, 1750–1914* ((2003).
Gosden, P. H. J. H, *The Friendly Societies in England, 1815–1875* (1961).
Howkins, A., *Whitsun in 19th Century Oxfordshire*, History Workshop Pamphlets, no. 8 (1973).

63. Poor Relief 1834–1948
1. Returns showing number of persons relieved in workhouses, *Parliamentary Papers* (1847), vol. 39, p. 107. Figures for Bicester, Thame, Witney and Woodstock Unions.

Eastwood, D., *Governing rural England: Tradition and transformation in local government 1780–1840* (1994).
Englander, D., *Poverty and Poor Law reform in 19th-century Britain 1834–1914* (1998).
Horn, P. (ed.), *Oxfordshire village life: The diaries of George James Dew (1846–1928), Relieving Officer* (1983).

Song, B. K., 'Continuity and change in English rural society: The formation of the Poor Law Unions', *English Historical Review*, vol. 114 (1999), pp. 314–38.
VCH, *Oxfordshire*, vols 4 to 15.
www.workhouses.org.uk

64. The Growth and Impact of Oxford after 1800
Changes to Oxford's boundary progressively incorporated districts into the population figures for the city. The 1841 census included St Clement's; 1871 Cowley St John; 1881 New Hinksey; and 1891 Summertown. The 1931 census included Cowley, Headington, Iffley and Wolvercote; 1961 Blackbird Leys; and 2001 Littlemore and Old Marston.

The map was adapted from material first published in VCH, *Oxfordshire*, vol. 4 (1979), p. 207 by permission of the Director, Victoria County History.

Crossley, A. (ed.), VCH, *Oxfordshire*, vol. 4, *City of Oxford* (1979).
Graham, M., *The Suburbs of Victorian Oxford*, unpublished University of Leicester PhD (1985).
Office for National Statistics – www.neighbourhood.statistics.gov.uk
Oxford City Council, *Oxford Economic Profile* (2009).
Oxford Economic Partnership, *Enterprising Oxfordshire: the Anatomy of the Oxfordshire High-Tech Economy* (2003).
Oxfordshire Strategic Partnership, *Oxford's Sustainable Community Strategy, 2008–2012* (2008).

65. The Motor Industry
Andrews, P. W. S., and Elizabeth Brunner, *The Life of Lord Nuffield* (1954).
Bourdillon, A. F. C. (ed.), *A Survey of the Social Services in the Oxford District*, vol. 1 (1936).
Oxford Economic Partnership, *Enterprising Oxfordshire: the Anatomy of the Oxfordshire High-Tech Economy* (2003).
VCH, *Oxfordshire*, vol. 4 (1979), vol. 10 (1972), vol. 14 (2004).
Wikipedia and firms' websites – motorsport development.

66. Local Government in the 19th and 20th Centuries
1. Municipal boroughs and urban districts (+10000/+20000 respectively) could elect to become LEAs under Part III of the Act: only Banbury MB elected for this status.
2. 1902 Midwives Act, 1907 Education Act, 1911 Tuberculosis Regulations, 1915 Notification of Births Act, 1920 Blind persons Act, 1926 Adoption of Children Act, 1927 Nursing Homes Registration Act.
3. The new boundaries included parts of Cutteslowe, Water Eaton and Wolvercote CPs in Woodstock RD, most of Headington UD (formed only the year before) and parts of Cowley, Marston and Iffley CPs in Headington RD.
4. Bicester, Crowmarsh, Culham, Goring, Headington, Thame and Woodstock RDs.
5. Wheatley UD.
6. Bullingdon and Ploughley RDs.
7. Banbury, Chipping Norton, Henley and Witney RDs.
8. Bicester, Thame and Witney UDs.
9. Banbury, Chipping Norton and Henley MBs.
10. e.g. Henley MB, Witney UD.
11. e.g. Banbury and Chipping Norton MBs.
12. Particularly sewerage and water supplies in rural areas.
13. Cherwell, West Oxfordshire and South Oxfordshire.

67. Housing and Urban Renewal: Oxford 1918–1985
Development of some of the estates shown extended across more than one time period. Dates shown are the start of building work.

Crosby, A. G., *The experience of gradual renewal in the Jericho district of Oxford*, Oxford School of Geography Research Paper 25 (1980).

Crosby, A. G., 'Housing policies and their influence upon the residential development of selected urban areas', unpublished DPhil thesis, University of Oxford, 1982.

Emden, A., et al, *A survey of the social services of the Oxford Region*, vols 1 and 2 (Oxford, 1940)

Loodmer, P. S., 'A geographical investigation of the social justice content of urban planning decisions with special reference to the displacement of the population of St Ebbe's parish, Oxford, 1951–1961', unpublished PhD thesis, University of London, 1977.

Mogey, J., *Family and neighbourhood: two studies in Oxford* (Oxford, 1956).

68. The Second World War
Bowyer, M. J. F., *Action Stations: Military Airfields of Oxfordshire* (1988).

Brooks, R. J., *Oxfordshire Airfields in the Second World War* (2001).

Council of British Archaeology, Defence of Britain database, 2006 – ads.ahds.ac.uk/catalogues/specColl/dob

English Heritage National Monuments Record, Pastscape database – www.pastscape.org.uk

Graham, M., *Oxfordshire at War* (1994).

Oxfordshire County Council, Historic Environment Record.

69. The Cold War
Brooks, R. J., *Oxfordshire Airfields in the Second World War* (2001).

Catford, N., *Cold War Bunkers* (2010).

Cocroft, W. D., and R. J. C. Thomas, *Cold War: Building for Nuclear Confrontation 1946–1989* (2003).

Rowley, T, *The English Landscape in the Twentieth Century* (2006).

www.ringbell.co.uk – website providing overview of UKWMO and its activities.

www.subbrit.org.uk – website containing details and photographs of Cold War sites in Oxfordshire and elsewhere in the UK.

70. Town and Country Planning in the 20th Century
Essays by J. Minett, J. F. Barrow and D. I. Scargill in R. T. Rowley (ed.), *The Oxford Region* (1980).

Mayo, S., D. Adshead and P. Abercrombie, *Regional Report on Oxfordshire* (1931).

Sharp, T., *Oxford Replanned* (1948).

County Development Plans, Town Maps, County Structure and Local Plans, written statements and proposals maps, various dates, available in Oxfordshire Studies library.

71. Education in the 20th Century
Allen, G., *The Story of the Henley College* (2004).

Graham, M., *Oxfordshire at School* (1996).

Pickstock, F. V., 'Adult and Further Education in Oxfordshire', in R. T. Rowley (ed.), *The Oxfordshire Region* (1980), pp. 227–38.

Whiting, R. C., 'University and Locality', in B. Harrison (ed.), *The History of the University of Oxford*, vol. 8, *The Twentieth Century* (1994), pp. 543–76.

72. Religion in the 20th Century
Brown, C. G., *Religion and Society in Twentieth-Century Britain* (2005).

Garnett, J., et al. *Redefining Christian Britain: post-1945 perspectives* (2007).

Royal Commission on the Historical Monuments of England, *An Inventory of Nonconformist Chapels and Meeting-Houses in Central England* (1986).

Sherwood, J., and N. Pevsner, *The Buildings of England: Oxfordshire* (1974).

www.statistics.gov.uk/focuson/religion

73. Maternal and Infant Welfare in the 20th Century
Bourdillon, A. F. C. (ed.), *A Survey of the Social Services in the Oxford District, II*, vol. 2, *Local Administration in a Changing Area* (1940).

Davis, A., 'To What Extent Were Women's Experiences of Maternity Influenced by Locality? Benson, Oxfordshire, c.1945–1970', *Family and Community History*, vol. 8 (2005), pp. 21–34.

Field, K., 'Children of the Nation?: A Study of the Health and Well-Being of Oxfordshire Children, 1891–1939', unpublished DPhil thesis, University of Oxford, 2001.

Parfitt, J., *The Health of a City: Oxford 1770–1974* (1987).

Peretz, E., 'A Maternity Service for England and Wales: Local Authority Maternity Care in the Inter-War Period in Oxfordshire and Tottenham', in J. Garcia, R. Kilpatrick and M. Richards (eds), *The Politics of Maternity Care* (1990).

Peretz, E., 'Infant Welfare between the Wars', in R. C. Whiting (ed.), *Oxford: Studies in the History of a University Town since 1800* (1993).

74. Tourism
Statistics kindly provided by Chris Jackson, West Oxfordshire District Council.

Baedeker, K., *Great Britain* (1887). Route 30 from London to Oxford.

Byng, J., Viscount Torrington, *Rides Round Britain*, ed. D. Anderson (1996)

Haggard, H. Rider, *Rural England*, vol. 2 (1906).

Morris, C. (ed.), *The Journeys of Celia Fiennes* (1947).

Nettel, R. (ed.), *Carl Philip Moritz: Journeys of a German in England in 1782* (1965).

Priestley, J. B., *English Journey* (1934)

Rogers, P. (ed.), *Daniel Defoe. A Tour through the whole island of Great Britain* (1971 edn).

Waters, L., *Rail Centres: Oxford* (1986).

Index

Abercrombie, Sir Patrick, 158
Abingdon, 14, 26, 64, 104, 152
   abbey, 44, 68
   Barton Court estate, 152
   breweries, 122
   industry in, 120, 122
   market, 64
   minster, 46
   monastic cartulary, 42
   motor industry in, 148
   poor law union, 144
   railways in, 108
   role in Civil War, 94
   Roman settlement in, 16
   school, 130
   urban growth of, 106
Acts of Parliament,
   Act of Uniformity (1662), 86
   Agriculture Act (1847), 112
   Catholic Relief Act (1778), 84
   Dissolution of Colleges (1 Edw. VI), 58
   Education Act (1876), 128
   Education Act (1880), 128
   Education Act (1902), 128, 160
   Education Act (1944), 160
   Elementary Education (1870), 128
   General Enclosure Act (1836), 114
   Highways (5 Geo. I), 102
   Housing Act (1930), 152
   Housing and Town Planning Act (1909), 158
   Housing and Town Planning Act (1919), 158
   Housing and Town Planning Act (1932), 158
   Local Government Act (1888), 150
   Local Government Act (1894), 150
   Local Government Act (1929), 144, 150
   Local Government Act (1972), 150
   Maternity and Child Welfare Act (1918), 164
   Municipal Corporations Act (1835), 150
   National Assistance Act (1948), 144
   National Insurance Act (1911), 144
   National Parks and Access to the Countryside Act (1949), 158
   Oxford Extension Act (1928), 150
   Poor Law Amendment Act (1834), 144
   Public Health Act (1872), 150
   Public Health Act (1875), 150
   Redistribution of Seats Act (1885), 126
   Reform Act (1832), 126
   Religious houses (37 Hen. VIII), 58
   Thames Navigation (21 Jas. I), 104
   Thames, The, (3 Jas. I), 104
   Toleration Act (1689), 86
   Town and Country Planning Act (1947), 150, 158
   Town Development Act (1952), 158
Adderbury, 96, 120
   at time of Domesday, 34
   barn, 66
   church, 26
   house, 98
   metal reprocessing plant, 154
   mills, 68
   nonconformists in, 86
   quarry, 118
   rectory, 62
Adoption and adopted children, 150
Adshead, S. D., 158
Advowsons, 42, 62, 80, 132

Adwell, 22
Ælfric, Abbot of Eynsham, 26
Agas, Ralph, 72
Agriculture, farming and landuse, 76, 78, 130, 132, 138
   arable, 32, 34, 38, 40, 52, 76, 82, 110, 112, 136
   as regards forests, 48
   at time of Domesday, 32, 34
   Board of Agriculture, 110
   commercialisation of, 114
   dairying, 40, 76, 112
   depression in, 112, 138
   during Civil War, 94
   during period 1750-1970, 110–12, 114
   during Second World War, 154
   husbandry, 14, 52, 56, 110
   in Anglo-Saxon era, 20
   in Iron Age, 14
   in medieval era, 40
   in Roman era, 16
   livestock farming, 76, 110
   manufacture of implements for, 118
   meadow, 14, 16, 32, 34, 46, 62, 94, 110, 154
   mechanisation in, 110, 112
   of prehistory, 12
   pasture, 8, 12, 14, 24, 32, 34, 38, 40, 48, 52, 76, 82, 112, 114, 136
   rough grazing, 112
   sheep farming, 52, 76, 110
   shows concerning, 166
Airfields, 154
Alchester, 16, 22
Aldridge, Catherine, and Andrew her son, 118
Alfred, an Anglo-Saxon, 32
Alfred the Great, 70
Alkerton, 44
Allen,
   Robert, 110
   William, 84
Allsop, family, 122
Altars and altarages, 44, 58
Alvescot, 24, 136
Alwoldsbury, 32
Ambrosden, 22, 121
   house, 98
   Independent chapel, 134
Andover, Hants, 40
Andover, Viscount, *see* Howard, Charles
Anglo-Saxons, 16, 18, 20, 22, 32, 42
   bishopric of, 46
   bridges of, 28
   buildings of, 28, 36
   impact on Oxford, 70
   king of, 30
   minsters, 26
   pagan cult of, 30
   place-names of, 32
   pottery, 64
   salt-ways of, 50
   towns of, 70
   waterwheel, 68
Animals, birds, etc, 10, 14, 16, 20, 34, 48, 76
   birds, 166
   cattle, 10, 14, 20, 76, 78, 112
   deer, 48, 82, 98
   deer, fallow, 48
   deer, red, 48
   deer, roe, 48
   donkey, 146

   geese, 20
   goats, 10
   hens, 20
   hippopotamus, 10
   horses, 14, 18, 24, 48, 50, 76, 78, 102, 104
   mammals, 166
   mammoth, woolly, 10
   oxen, 24, 34
   packhorses, 50, 102, 106
   pigs, 10, 14, 24, 76, 112
   poultry, 76, 112
   pullets, 112
   rabbits, 48
   reptiles, 166
   sheep, 10, 14, 18, 24, 40, 52, 54, 76, 78, 82, 110, 112
Annesley, Arthur, 98
Annesley, 108
Appletree, Thomas, 88, 89
Apprentices and apprenticeships, 72, 100, 116
Archaeology and archaeological sites, 10
   Anglo-Saxon, 18, 26, 28, 30
   barrows, Bronze Age, 30
   barrows, long, 10, 12
   barrows, prehistoric, 18
   barrows, round, 12
   Beaker burials, 10
   Beaker pottery, 12
   boundary ditches, 14
   burial chambers, 22
   dendrochronology, 66
   Early Bronze Age, 10
   earthworks, 12, 16, 22, 56, 68, 74
   grave goods, 12, 18, 30
   henges, 12
   hillforts, 14, 22
   Iron Age, 8, 12, 14, 16, 22, 28, 30
   Later Bronze Age, 12
   megalithic portal dolmens, 12
   Mesolithic, 10
   Neolithic, 10
   of churches, 42
   Palaeolithic, 10
   radiocarbon dating, 12, 26
   Roman, 16, 30
   sites,
      Big Rings henge monument, 12
      Devil's Quoits, 12
      Gravelly Guy, 10, 12, 14
      Mingies Ditch, 10, 12, 14
      Rollright Stones, 12, 14
      Whispering Knights, 12
   standing stone, 22
   stone circles, 12, 22
   timber circles, 12
   tumulus, 22
Archer, Thomas, 98
Ardley, 121
Areas of Outstanding Natural Beauty, 158, 166
Argyle, Duke of, *see* Campbell, John
Army and military, 36
   55th Border Regiment, 100
   Air Positioning Plotting Unit, 156
   army camps, 154
   foot-soldiers, 82
   garrisons, 94
   Home Guard, 154
   horsemen, 82
   mercenaries, 16
   military service, 32, 100

177

INDEX

ordnance depot, 154
Oxford and Buckinghamshire Light
    Infantry, 156
paratroops, 154
prisoners of war, 154
refugees, 154
Roman, 16
Royal Observer Corps, 156
soldiers, 82, 94
troops, 82, 88, 94
UK Defence Academy, 160
United Kingdom Warning and
    Monitoring Organisation, 156
See also War and warfare
Arncott, 24, 154
Arsic, family, 36
Ascot-under-Wychwood, 10, 12, 120
    castles, 36
Ascott d'Oyley, tower, 36
Ashampstead, 64
Ashurst, Sir Henry, 98
Assendon, 22
Asthall, 16
    barrow, 18
    manor, 124
Aston Rowant, 24, 28, 116, 121
    nonconformists in, 86
Astrop, 24
Atkinson, William, 98
Atomic Energy Research Establishment,
    156
Avonmouth, 154
Aylesbury, 82, 106, 110
Aynho, 108

Babington, family, 84
Bablock Hythe, 24
Baedeker, Karl, 166
Balscott, 24
Bampton, 18, 28, 52, 78
    canal, 28
    castle, 30, 36
    chapel of St Andrew (the Beam), 30
    church, 26, 30, 42, 44
    manor, 32
    market, 30, 32, 38, 106
    medieval development of, 38
    minster, 26, 30
    motor industry in, 148
    nonconformists in, 86
    population of, 136, 138
    poverty in, 116
    railways in, 106
    schools in, 130
    shopkeepers in, 90
    streets and places in, High Street, 130
    urban growth of, 106
    vicarage, 44
    wealth of, 52
    Ham Court; Rushey Weir; and West
        Weald, in, *q.v.*
Bampton, hundred, 136
Banbury, 6, 50, 52, 89, 148, 154
    agriculture in, 76, 112
    air raid in, 154
    Anglo-Saxon settlement in, 18
    archaeology of, 12
    at time of Domesday, 32, 34
    Berwick Motor Company, 148
    borough council, 158
    breweries, 122
    canal, 104

canal community in, 104
castle, 36, 38, 94
cheeses from, 76
church, 26
cloth-making industry in, 40
communications of, 50
corporation, 164
district, 142, 164
Elms Maternity home, 164
fire at, 78
foundries in, 118
geology of, 8
gild, 58, 78
grammar school, 60
hospital of St John the Baptist, 60
industry in, 38, 78, 118, 120, 148
inns in, 78
Iron Age settlements in, 14
manor, 32
market, 78
medieval development of, 38
mosques in, 162
motor industry in, 148
MPs for, 88, 126
nonconformists in, 86, 134
North Oxfordshire Technical College,
    160
people of, 104
poor law union, 144
population of, 38, 106, 136, 138
Public Assistance Institution in, 164
race-meetings, 78
railways in, 106, 108, 109
roads from and to, 102
role in Civil War, 94
Samuelson's Britannia Works, 148
schools in, 128, 160
shopkeepers in, 90
streets and places in,
    Broughton Road, 118
    Hollybush, 102
    Middleton Road, 118
    Mill Lane, 104
suburbs of, 136
tourism in, 166
town hall, 156
Unicorn Inn in, 122
urban growth of, 106, 158
wealth of, 52
Bankruptcy and bankrupts, 118
Baptisms, 84, 116
Barford St John, 24, 120
    air base, 156
Barford St Michael, 24, 120
    Fortnam's Yard in, 118
    vicar of, 82
Barry,
    Sir Charles, 124
    Vincent, 82
Barry, Glam, 108
Barton [Headington], 24, 152
Barton Abbey, 124
Basildon, Lower, bridge, 108
Basingstoke, 156
Baskerville, family, 98
Bassett, Alan, 58
Bateman, C. E., 124
Battersea, 110
Battle, abbey, 46
Baughan, family, 120
Bayeux, Bishop of, *see* Odo, Bishop of
    Bayeux

Bayeux Tapestry, 32
Beaconsfield, 102
Beauforest, Richard, 80
Beaulieu, abbey, 46
Beaumont Castle, Mixbury, 36
Beckley, 6, 8, 24, 40, 138
Beckley Park, 96
    lodge, 36
Bede, Venerable, 18, 26, 46
Bedfordshire, 121
Beehives, 90
Beesley, family, 104
Begbroke, 22
Beggar's Bush Hill, Benson, 118
Bells, 80, 84
Belson,
    family, 84
    Thomas, 84
Benefices, 132
Benson, 18, 32, 102, 120
    air base, 156
    airfield, 154
    Beggar's Bush Hill, 118
    lido, 154
    manor, 32
Berinsfield, 12, 152, 162
    Mount Farm, 154
Berkshire, 20, 24, 28, 36, 64, 66, 68, 76, 84,
    89, 92, 94, 120, 130, 134, 138, 140, 150,
    154
Berkshire, Earl of, *see* Howard, Thomas
Bernwood, forest, 48
Berrick Salome, 24
Bevin, Ernest, 144
Bibles, 84, 118
Bicester, 6, 22, 78, 100, 104, 124, 148, 152,
    154
    agriculture in, 112
    air base, 156
    airfield, 154
    Anglo-Saxon settlement in, 28
    breweries, 122
    Central Ordnance Depot, 156
    cottage hospital, 164
    foundry, 118
    Independent chapel, 134
    industry in, 121
    Iron Age settlements in, 14
    manor, 78
    market, 82
    medieval development of, 38
    minster, 18
    motor industry in, 148
    nonconformists in, 86, 134, 162
    people of, 90
    poor law union, 144
    population of, 38, 136, 138
    priory, 40, 46, 80
        prior of, 58
    shrine of St Edburg in, 80
    race-meetings, 78
    railways in, 106, 108, 109
    retail park, 166
    schools in, 128
    shopkeepers in, 90
    St Edburg's church, 26
    urban growth of, 106, 158, 162
    workhouse, 144
Bignell House, Chesterton, 124
Binfield, 24
Binsey, 22
Birds *see* Animals

178

INDEX

Birinus, Bishop, 46
Birmingham, 102, 108, 109, 122, 124, 158
Bishopland Farm, Dunsden, 118
Bishoprics, 18, 26, 44
   Anglo-Saxon, 46
Bix,
   church, 56
   manors, 32
Bix Brand, 32
Bix Gibwyn, 32
Bixmoor, 24
Black Bourton, 18, 136
   vicar of, 44
Black Country, 104, 118
Blackbird Leys,
   estate, 146, 148, 150, 152
   Holy Family Church, 162
Blackthorn, 108, 121
   Independent chapel, 134
   Windmill Camp near, 154
Bladon, 22, 120, 136
   hillfort, 14
   manor, 64
   pottery, 34, 64
Blandford, Marquess of, 126
Blenheim Palace, 8, 78, 98, 110, 116, 118, 124, 126, 154, 166
Bletchingdon, 18, 50, 82, 94, 96, 118, 144
   park, 98
Bletchley, 108
Bliss,
   Thomas, 120
   William, 120
Blisworth, 108
   tunnel, 104
Blount, family, 84
Bloxham, 24, 28, 120
   church, 26
   Iron Age settlements in, 14
   nonconformists in, 86
   school, 130
Boars Hill, 146, 156
Boarstall, 94
Bodicote, 24
Bodley, G. F., 124
Bolney, 24
Books, 90, 118; *see also* Bibles; Cartularies; Domesday Book
Bordars, 34
Boroughs, 28, 38, 78, 106, 126, 146, 150
Botley, 146
Boudica, rebellion of, 16
Boulter, family, 84
Boulton, Matthew, 124
Bourton, 154
Bowldry, Thomas, 82
Boycott, 144
Brackley, 64, 94
   motor industry in, 148
   poor law union, 144
Bradfield, poor law union, 144
Bradshaw, James, 82
Bradwell Grove, 98, 154
Brailes, 84
Brakspear, Richard, 118
Brassey, Thomas, 124
Braunston, 104
Braziers Park, 98
Breakspear's, brewers, 122
Bribery, 126
Bridges, 28, 50, 72, 74, 78, 94, 108
   stone, 50

Bridgnorth, 104
Brightwell Baldwin, 22
Brill, 6, 64, 94, 121
Bristol, 50, 102, 108
Britwell Salome, 22, 84
   foundry, 118
   house, 98
Brize Norton, 154
   air base, 156
   airfield, 154
   nonconformists in, 86
   RAF Parachute Training School, 156
Broadwell, 22
   manor, 32
   RAF base, 154
   vicarage, 44
Brock, William, 90
Brome, family, 84
Bromsden, 32
Bromsgrove, 118
Brookhampton, 22
Broomhall, priory, 44
Broughton, 22
   castle, 88, 94, 96, 166
   Hazelford Mill, 118
Broughton Poggs, 22
Brown, Capability, 98
Bruern, 22
   abbey, 40, 46, 80, 98, 154
   abbot of, 80
Brunel, Isambard Kingdom, 108
Buckingham, 6, 28, 66
   poor law union, 144
Buckinghamshire, 24, 84, 86, 89, 121, 134, 140
   topography of, 6
Building materials,
   brick, 8, 66, 93, 96, 104, 118
   flint, 93
   stone, 93, 96
   tiles, 8, 66, 118
Buildings *see* Houses
Bullingdon, district, 112, 152
Burcot, 50, 104
Burdrop, 24
Burford, 6, 24, 28, 30, 50, 78, 96
   Anglo-Saxon settlement in, 18
   archaeology of, 12
   at time of Domesday, 32
   brewery, 122
   Bull Cottage in, 66
   coal supplied to, 104
   communications of, 50
   Cotswold Wildlife Park and Gardens, 166
   cottage hospital, 164
   exporters of wool resident in, 40
   festivals in, 166
   geology of, 8
   industry in, 38, 78
   malting in, 78
   market, 78, 106
   nonconformists in, 86
   people of, 94
   population of, 136, 138
   priory, 96
   race-meetings, 78
   railways in, 106
   role in Civil War, 94
   schools in, 128
   shopkeepers in, 90
   stone quarrying in, 66

   streets and places in,
      Calendars, 66
      High Street, 66
      Tolsey, The, 66
   tourism in, 166
   urban growth of, 38, 106
   vicarage, 44
   wealth of, 54
   wool trade in, 40
Burgages, 38, 106
Burials, tombs, etc, 10, 12, 26, 42, 116, 142
   Anglo-Saxon, 16, 18, 20, 30
   cremations, 18, 64
   prehistoric, 22
Burnings *see* Fires
Burton (Burton-on-Trent), 122
Byng, John, Viscount Torrington, 102

Cadogan, William, Earl of Cadogan, 98
Cadwell, 22
Calvertt, J. S., 110
Camberwell, 140
Cambridge, 50, 166
   university and colleges, 44, 62, 72, 84
Cameron, David, 126
Campbell, John, Duke of Argyle, 98
Campion, Edmund, 84
Campsfield, 24
Canals, 28, 74, 104
   Birmingham Canal Navigation, 104
   Coventry Canal, 104
   Grand Junction Canal, 104
   Oxford Canal, 104, 106, 118, 122, 146
   Thames and Severn Canal, 104
   Trent and Mersey Canal, 104
   Warwick and Birmingham Canal, 104
   Warwick and Napton Canal, 104
   Wilts and Berks Canal, 104
Candles, 90
Canterbury, archdiocese, archbishop of, 100; *see also* Chichele, Henry; Laud, William
Cardiff, 108
Cars *see* Transport and Communications
Carterton, 156, 162
Cartularies, 42, 58, 60
Cary,
   Henry, Viscount Falkland, 89
   Lucius, Viscount Falkland, 88
Cassington, 12, 14, 24, 138
   Anglo-Saxon settlement in, 20
   chapel, 42
   tithes, 42
Castle End, Deddington, 92
Castle, Joseph, 118
Castles, 30, 36, 38, 64, 66, 70, 72, 74, 88, 94, 96, 166; *see also* Forts
Catesby, family, 84
Cathedrals and minsters, 38, 42, 44, 46, 80
   chapters of, 42, 44, 80
   prebends of, 44
Caulcot, 24
Cave, Walter, 124
Caversfield, 121, 156
   house, 124
Caversham, 6, 96, 118, 121
   foundry, 118
   park, 98, 124
Cemeteries and churchyards, 14, 26, 30, 38, 94
   Anglo-Saxon, 18, 20, 30
   Roman, 16

179

INDEX

Chadlington, 18, 24, 120
  nonconformists in, 86
Chairs, 120
Chalford, 22
Chalgrove, 22, 64
  American base, 154
  manor, 66
  mills, 68
  Chalgrove Field, battle of, 94
Challow, Faringdon Road in, 108
Chamberlain (Chamberlayne),
  family, 80, 84
  Leonard, steward of Woodstock royal park, 82
Chancels, 66, 80
Chantries, 40, 58
  perpetual, 58
  See also under Chapels
Chapel House, Over Norton, 102
Chapels, 30, 42, 44, 58, 84, 96, 134, 162
  chantry, 58, 60
Charlbury, 26, 28, 32, 154
  industry in, 78, 120
  market, 78
  medieval development of, 38
  nonconformists in, 86
  Old Club, 142
  population of, 136, 138
  railways in, 106
  urban growth of, 106
  vicarage, 44
Charles I, 88, 94, 96
Charles II, 86, 94, 96
Charlton on Otmoor, 22
Chastleton, 96
  church, 42, 44
  hillfort, 14
  house, 166
  rectory, 44
Checkendon, 22
Checkendon Court, 124
Cheltenham, 106
Cheshire, county, 140
Chesterton, 22, 121
  Bignell House, 124
Chichele, Henry, Archbishop of Canterbury, 58
Children and infants,
  adopted, 150
  mortality of, 164
  welfare of, 164
Chilson, 120
Chiltern Hills,
  agriculture in, 40, 76, 110, 132
  Anglo-Saxon settlement in, 18, 32
  arable farming in, 34
  archaeology of, 12
  as an Area of Outstanding Natural Beauty, 158
  at time of Domesday, 34
  benefices in, 132
  enclosure in, 114
  geology of, 8
  hall houses in, 66
  industry in, 120
  meadows in, 34
  mills in, 68
  moated houses in, 36
  nonconformists in, 100
  parks in, 48
  place-names in, 22, 24
  population in, 54, 138

  prehistory of, 10
  roads in, 28
  settlement patterns in, 56
  topography of, 6
  wealth in, 52, 54
Chimney, 22
Chinnor, 8, 18, 24, 38, 102, 118, 121, 138
Chippenham, 50
Chipping Norton, 6, 24, 50, 54, 82
  agriculture in, 112
  brewery, 122
  castle, 36, 38
  church, 82
  cottage hospital, 164
  exporters of wool resident in, 40
  gild, 78
  industry in, 78, 120
  market, 76
  medieval development of, 38
  mill, 148
  nonconformists in, 86, 134
  population of, 38, 136, 138
  race-meetings, 78
  railways in, 106, 108
  Roman Catholics in, 134
  Roman settlement in, 16
  shopkeepers in, 90
  urban growth of, 106, 158
  vicar of, 82
  workhouse, 144
Chippinghurst, 56
  manor, 154
Chislehampton, 22, 98, 120
Church Hanborough, Freeland House, 124
Churches, 8, 20, 26, 30, 32, 38, 42, 44, 46, 56, 58, 60, 70, 74, 82, 94, 130, 132, 134, 162
  abandonment of, 56
  Anglo-Saxon minsters, 26, 30
  appropriated, 44, 62
  attendances at, 162
  Buddhist Temple, 162
  Hindu Temple, 162
  monastic, 80
  mosque, 162
  prebendal, 42
  synagogue, 134, 162
Churchill,
  John, Duke of Marlborough, 98
  Lord Randolph, 126
Churchyards *see* Cemeteries
Cirencester, Glos, 16
Clanfield, 24
  commandery, 46
Clare, 22, 24
Clarence, Duke of, 58
Clarendon, Earl of, *see* Hyde, Edward
Clarke, George Somers, 124
Clattercote, 24
  hospital of St Leonard, 60
  priory, 46, 60, 80, 96
Claydon, 22
Clergy and religious,
  abbess, 80
  abbot, 80, 96
  archbishop, 46, 86
  bishop, 32, 38, 42, 44, 46, 62, 72, 84, 86, 98, 100
  bursar of college, 62
  canon, 26, 30, 44, 46, 80
  chaplain, 42, 44, 58, 84
  curate, 100, 132

  dean, 80
  fellow of college, 62
  friar, 46, 80
  head of college, 62
  missionary, 84
  monk, 26, 46, 80
  nun, 26
  preacher, 86
  priest, 26, 32, 42, 44, 82, 84
  priest, chantry, 58
  rector, 44, 62
  scholar, 70, 72, 128
  student, 62
  treasurer of college, 62
  vicar, 26, 30, 44, 62, 84, 100
  vicar, perpetual, 44
  warden of college, 62
  See also Orders, religious; Religion; Religious houses
Clifton Hampden, 120
Climate and weather, 10
  in Iron Age, 14
  rain, 6
Clinch's, brewers, 122
Clinton, Geoffrey de, 42
Clocks, 148
Cloth and clothing, 38, 40, 70, 116, 120, 142, 146
  blankets, 78, 120, 138
  broadcloth, 40, 78
  burrels, 40
  caps, 90
  fabric, 90
  gloves, 120
  hose, 90
  lace, 90, 120, 121
  ribbon, 90
  russets, 40
  stockings, 90
  tweed, 138
  See also Wool and woollen cloth
Clubs *see* Societies
Cnut, King, 64
Cobb, family, 96
Cockerell,
  C. R., 124
  S. P., 98
Cogges, 36, 120, 136
  alien priory, 46
  manor, 32
  nonconformists in, 86
Coins and coinage, 28, 52
  in Iron Age, 14
  Roman, 16
Coke, Sir Edward, Attorney-General, 82
Cokethorpe, 18, 98
Colchester, 16
Cold Norton, priory, 44, 46, 80
Colleges, 58, 160
  chantries in, 58
  City Technical College, 160
  Lady Spencer-Churchill College of Education, 160
  monastic, 46, 80
  North Oxfordshire Technical College, 160
  of canons, 30
  Royal Military College of Science, 160
  Rycotewood College for Rural Crafts, 160
  secular, 44, 46
  South Oxfordshire Technical College, 160

teacher training colleges, 160
West Oxfordshire Technical College, 160
Westminster College, 160
See also University of Oxford
Collett, Oliver, 148
Combe, 22, 120
    nonconformists in, 86
    vicarage, 44
Committees *see* Companies
Commons, 40, 48
    right of, 82, 114
Commonwealth, 89
Communications *see* Transport
Companies and committees,
    Cottage Benefit Nursing Association, 164
    Council for the Preservation of Rural England, 158
    County War Executive Committee, 112
    Infant Welfare Association, 164
    Interdepartmental Committee on Physical Deterioration, 164
    Joint Regional Advisory Committee, 158
    National Childbirth Trust, 164
    Northern Aluminium Company, 154
    Oxford Preservation Trust, 158
    Oxfordshire Nursing Federation, 164
    Oxfordshire Regional Planning Committee, 158
    Oxfordshire War Agricultural Executive Committee, 154
    Peel Committee, 164
    Pressed Steel Company, 148
Compton Census (1676), 54, 84, 86
Compton Wynyates, 94
Cookham, 140
Cooper, Thomas, 89
Cope,
    family, 80, 98
    William, 96
Cornbury Park, 8, 22, 96, 98, 154
Cornwall, 82, 138
Cornwall, Edmund, Earl of, 58
Cornwell, 22
    manor, 124
Corporations, 38, 78
Cotswold Hills,
    agriculture in, 76, 110
    archaeology of, 12, 16
    as an Area of Outstanding Natural Beauty, 158
    at time of Domesday, 34
    communications of, 50
    enclosure in, 114
    geology of, 6
    mills in, 68
    place-names in, 22, 24
    prehistory of, 10
    railways in, 109
    settlement patterns in, 56
    topography of, 6
    wool from, 38, 40
Cottars, 34
Cottisford, 121, 136
Councils,
    borough, 128, 158, 160
    county, 128, 150, 158, 160, 164
    estates of, 146, 148
    Oxford City Council, 152
    Privy Council, 84
Councils, religious, Second Council of Lyons (1274), 58

Courts,
    borough, 78
    church, 94
    forest, 48
    leet, 78
    manorial, 38, 62, 78
    portmoot, 38
Courtyards, 96, 98
Coventry,, 50
    canal, 104
Cowberry [*unidentified*], 110
Cowley, 8, 40, 52, 126, 136, 138, 146, 152
    airfield, 152, 154
    barracks, 154, 156
    hospital of St Bartholomew, 60
    motor industry in, 148, 158
    Oxford Military College, 148
    Rose Hill, 152
    Temple Cowley, 46, 84
Crawley, 120
Crawshay, family, 124
Cresswell Field, Yarnton, 20
Cricket, 130
Cricklade, 24, 50, 104, 158
Crispin, Miles, 32
Croke,
    family, 80, 89
    John, 96
    Richard, 89
    Unton, 94
    Unton the elder, 89
    Unton the younger, 89
Cromwell,
    Oliver, 89, 94
    Thomas, 80
Cropredy, 18, 166
    at time of Domesday, 34
    church, 26, 44
    Cropredy Bridge, battle of, 94
    mills, 68
    vicarage, 44
Crops, 76, 94, 110, 112
    barley, 10, 14, 24, 76, 110, 122
    beans, 14, 76, 110
    clover, 110
    corn, 16, 40, 68, 76, 104, 114
    damage to, 48
    flax, 14, 76
    fodder, 20, 76, 110
    grain, 38, 50, 52, 56, 68, 70, 76, 82, 102, 112, 118, 154
    hay, 16, 20, 24, 34
    hemp, 76
    hops, 76, 122
    malt, 76, 78, 104, 122
    oats, 76, 110
    peas, 24, 76
    rye, 24, 76
    storage of, 14
    turnips, 110
    watercress, 8, 24
    wheat, 10, 12, 14, 24, 62, 76, 110
Croughton, 156
Crowell, 22
Crowmarsh Gifford, 36
    market, 38
    Queen's Head in, 66
Crowsley, 98
Cubitt, William, 120
Cuddesdon, 18, 22, 54
    bishop's palace, 98
    mill, 68

Culham, 8, 24, 50, 120, 128, 154, 156
    teacher training college, 160
Cumberland, 140
Cumnor Hill, 6
Curacies, 44
Curbridge, 54, 120
Curson, family, 84
Cutslow (Cutteslowe), 22, 146
Cuxham, 24, 34, 62
    manor, 32, 62
    mill, 62
Cynegils, King of Wessex, 46

Dams *see* under Mills
Danby, Earl of, *see* Danvers, Henry
Dancing *see* Music
Danes, 46, 64, 68, 70
Danvers,
    Henry, Earl of Danby, 88, 96
    Sir John, 88
Dashwood,
    family, 124
    Sir James, 98
Davey, family, 84
Dawber, Guy, 124
De Havilland, 154
Dean, 22
Dean, Forest of, 104
Deaneries, 30, 42, 54
Declaration of Breda (1660), 86
Declaration of Indulgence (1672), 86
Deddington, 8, 24, 32, 78, 136
    breweries, 122
    castle, 36, 38, 64
    Castle End, 92
    gild of Holy Trinity, 58
    Leadenporch House, 66, 92
    market, 78, 106
    medieval development of, 38
    metal working in, 118
    mill, 118
    nonconformists in, 86
    population of, 136, 138
    poverty in, 116
    railways in, 106
    shopkeepers in, 90
    urban growth of, 106
    wool trade in, 40
Dedham, 120
Devon, 30, 82
Dew, George, 144
Diamond Light Source, 156
Didcot,108, 158
    motor industry in, 148
Dimmock, John, 118
Disafforestation, 64, 110, 114
Disease, illness, etc, 94, 116, 128, 142, 144, 150
    Black Death, 38, 48, 54, 56, 70
    camp fever, 94
    leprosy, 46, 60
    plague, 56
    tuberculosis, 150
    typhus, 94
Ditches and dykes, 20, 30, 36, 74, 114
    Aves Ditch, 14, 16
    Dike Hills, 22
    Grim's Ditch, 22
    North Oxfordshire Grim's Ditch, 14, 16
    South Oxfordshire Grim's Ditch, 16
    Swift Ditch, 50

INDEX

Ditchley, 22, 82, 89, 96, 98
  park, 98, 124
Domesday Book, 24, 30, 32, 34, 42, 64, 68
Dorchester, 6, 8, 16, 22, 50, 68, 84, 92
  abbey, 44, 46, 66, 80
  Anglo-Saxon settlement in, 18
  archaeology of, 12, 14
  bishopric, 46
  fort, 16
  grammar school, 130
  industry in, 120
  market, 38
  mills, 68
  minster, 26, 42
  monuments at, 10
  nonconformists in, 86
  people of, 80
  shopkeepers in, 90
  shrine of St Birinus, 166
  urban growth of, 38
  vernacular buildings in, 66
Dormer,
  family, 84, 124
  General James, 98
  Sir Robert, 88
Dorset, 138, 140
Douai, Netherlands, 84
Dovecotes, 66
Drainage and drainpipes, 110, 112, 118
Draper, William, 88, 89
Draycot, 24
Drayton [*formerly* Berks], 18
Drayton [in Bloxham hundred], 24
Drayton St Leonard, 24, 120
Drink *see* Food
Droitwich, 28, 50
  salt works, 24
Droving, 50, 78
Druce, family, 130
Drunkeness, 142
Ducklington, 18, 120
  mill-weir, 68
Duke's Cut, 104
Dunch, Edward, 89
Dunsden, 22
Dunstan, Archbishop of Canterbury, 46
Dunthrop, 24
Durham, county, 140
Dyke Hills, 14
Dykes *see* Ditches

Eadwig, King of England, 30
Early, family, 130
East Anglia, 140
  rebellion in, 82
Edgehill, Warw, battle of, 94
Edmunds, William, 122
Education, 146, 150
  adult, 160
  arithmetic, 130
  British & Foreign School Society, 128
  elementary schools, 128
  further, 160
  geography, 128
  geometry, 130
  grammar, 130
  higher, 160
  history, 128
  in 19th century, 128, 130
  in 20th century, 160
  local education authorities, 128, 150, 160

National Society for Promoting the Education of the Poor in the Principles of the Established Church, 128
  needlework, 128
  Oxford Diocesan Education Board, 128
  physical exercise, 128
  private sector, 130
  Revised Code of 1862, 128
  revival of university education, 72
  School Boards, 128
  science parks, 146
  scripture, 128
  secondary, 160
  teacher training, 128, 160
  The Newcastle Commission (1858-61), 128
  Workers' Education Association, 160
  See also Colleges; Schools; University of Oxford and colleges
Edward the Elder, King of England, 70
Edward I, 36
Edward III, 68
Edward VI, 82
Edwards, Ellis, 90
Elmes, John, 40
Elsfield, 24, 100
Emmington, 24, 121
Enclosure, 76, 136
  after 1750, 110, 114
  at time of Domesday, 34
  in 16th century, 82
  in 19th century, 138, 146
  in Anglo-Saxon era, 20, 30
  in Iron Age, 14
  in late medieval era, 54
  of castles, 36
Enslow Hill, 82, 104
Enstone, 22, 28, 112
  Church Farm in, 66
  motor industry in, 148
Environment, 10, 14
Epwell, 22, 128
Erosion, 8
Eton College, 44, 46, 132
Europe, influence of, 28, 64
European Economic Community, 112
Eustace, Thomas, 102
Evelyn, Arthur, 89
Ewelme, 8, 22
  almshouse, 60, 66
  church of St Mary, chantry chapel of St John the Baptist in, 60
  Ewelme Down, 124
  Garlick School in, 130
  grammar school, 60, 66, 100, 130
  Greyhound Inn in, 130
  Mount, The, in, 130
  population of, 138
  Ewelme Down in, *q.v.*
Excommunication, 84
Exeter, 50, 102
  cathedral, 30
  cathedral chapter of, 44
Eynsham, 12, 18, 24, 50, 64, 80, 136
  abbey, 20, 26, 32, 40, 44, 46, 80
    abbot of, 42
  ammunition park, 154
  breweries, 122
  Eynsham Hall Park, hillfort, 14
  hall, 154
  heath, 124
  industry in, 120

  market, 78
  medieval development of, 38
  mill, 118
  minster, 20, 42
  monastic cartulary, 42
  nonconformists in, 162
  park, 124
  people of, 130
  population of, 136, 138
  railways in, 106
  shopkeepers in, 90
  urban growth of, 106
  wharf, 104

Fairfax, Sir Thomas, 94
Fairford, 108
Fairs, 38, 78, 106
Falkland, Viscount, *see* Cary, Henry; Cary, Lucius
Famine, 56
Faringdon, 28, 30, 50
  coal supplied to, 104
  poor law union, 144
  salt-market, 28
Farming *see* Agriculture, farming and land-use
Farms, 24, 36, 46, 54, 56, 62, 66, 76, 80, 90, 110, 112, 118, 154
Fawler, 64, 118, 120
Fazeley, 104
Feasts and festivals, 82
  cultural festivals, 166
  Eights Week, 166
  Henley Royal Regatta, 166
  literary festivals, 166
  river festivals, 166
Fell, John, Bishop of Oxford, 86, 94
Fencott, 22
Fermor,
  Thomas, 40
  William, 98
Fertilisers, 110, 112
Fettiplace, family, 84, 124
Feudalism, 64, 68
Fewcot, 24
Fields and field systems, 40
  animal pens, 20
  at time of Domesday, 34
  of prehistory, 12
  paddocks, 20
Fiennes,
  Celia, 166
  James, 88, 89
  Nathaniel, 88, 89
  William, Baron and Viscount Saye and Sele, 88, 94
Filkins, 32
Finmere, 108, 121
Finstock, 86, 120
Fireplaces *see* Hearths
Fires and burnings, 68, 78, 94, 98, 116, 124
Fish, 50
  eels, 20, 68
  salmon, 20
Fisheries and fishings, 34, 104
FitzAlan, family, 36
Flanders, cloth industry in, 40
Fleetwood,
  Charles, 89
  Miles, 89
  Sir William, 88, 89

INDEX

Floods, floodlands and floodplains, 6, 8, 12, 14, 22, 24, 28, 50, 68, 116, 146
Folklore, 166
  morris-dancing, 30
  mummers's play, 30
Food and drink, 72, 82, 90
  ale, 20, 122
  bacon, 116
  beef, 76
  beer, 76, 116, 122
  bread, 10, 20, 76, 116
  butter, 20, 116
  cheese, 20, 76, 102
  eggs, 112, 116
  honey, 20
  meat, 112, 116
  milk, 112
  oatmeal, 90
  rice, 90
  spices, 90
  spirits, 90
  sugar, 90
  tea, 116
  venison, 48
  wine, 40, 50, 82
Fords, 24, 28, 70
Forest Hill, 8, 44
Forestier, Thomas, 130
Forests, woods, etc,
  chases, 48
  clearance of, 34
  coppiced woodland, 24, 48
  deciduous woodland, 10
  forest, 8, 24, 34, 48, 100
  forest, royal, 48, 94, 96, 110
  woods, 6, 24, 32, 34, 48, 52, 76, 104, 110, 114, 120
  See also Dean, Forest of; Wychwood Forest
Fortescue, family, 84
Forts and fortifications, 16, 36, 94
  Iron Age, 22
  Saxon, 70
  See also Castles
Foundries, 118
Fradley Junction, 104
Framilode, 104
France, 89, 102
  abbeys, 32
  monasteries in, 44
  pottery from, 64
  refugees from, 84
  war with, 58, 98
Fraternities *see* Gilds
Freeland House, Church Hanborough, 124
Freemen, 34, 126
Frere, William, 82
Fringford, 121
Frith, Francis, 104
Fritwell, 22, 120, 121
  manor, 124
Fuel, 48, 64, 104, 116
Fulbrook, 22
Fulham, 104
Fulwell, 22
  church, 44
Furnaces, 118
Furze, 104

Galashiels, 120
Gallows, 84
Gandy, Joseph, 124

Gaols and prisons, 74, 82, 98
Gardens, 34, 36, 96, 98, 124, 130, 166
  market, 136
Garlick, James, 130
Garne, family, 122
Garner, Thomas, 124
Garsington, 8, 22, 24, 54, 152
  manor, 124
Gascoigne, James, 120
Gatehampton Farm, Goring, 10
Gaunt House, Standlake, 94
Gentry, 48, 78, 80, 82, 84, 88, 100, 110, 132
Geology, 6, 8–9
George, Ernest, 124
Germany, 156
Gibbs, James, 98
Gilds and fraternities, 38, 40, 58, 78
Gill Mill, Ducklington, 16
Gladstone, William, 126
Glebes and glebe-lands, 44, 52, 62
Glorious Revolution (1688), 94
Gloucester, 50, 70
Gloucestershire, 28, 34, 120, 134, 140
  topography of, 6
Goddard, Dr Jonathan, 89
Godstow, nunnery, 46, 80
Godwine, 20
Golder, 24
Goring, 6, 28, 121
  Flint House in, 124
  Gatehampton Farm, 10
  Goring Heath, 124
  nunnery, 46, 80
Gosford, 50
Government Evacuation Scheme, 150
Grafton, 24
Graham, Kenneth, 104
Granges, 24, 46
Grantham, family, 104
Grantmesnil, Hugh de, 32
Grasses and grasslands, 12, 14, 24, 34, 76, 110, 112
  clover, 76
  esparto, 118
  lucerne, 76
  reeds, 14
  sainfoin, 76
Gravel and gravel pits, 6, 8, 10, 12, 14, 18, 20, 24, 52, 64, 76, 116
Great Bourton, 118
Great Exhibition (1851), 108
Great Haseley, 8, 24, 82, 84
Great Milton, 8, 18, 120
  church, 44
Great Rollright, 112
Great Tew, 18, 96
  church, 26
  park, 124
Greater Leys, Oxford, 158
  estate, 146
Green Belt, 146, 152, 158, 166
Greenlands House, Hambleden, 94
Grey, William, Lord Grey of Wilton, 82
Greys Court, 36, 66, 96, 166
Grimsbury, 64
Guilford, Earl of, 126

Haggard, Rider, 112
Hailey, 24, 120
Hales,
  John, 118
  Robert, 89

Hall, family, 122, 124
Ham Court, Bampton, 36
Hambleden, Greenlands House, 94
Hampden, John, 94
Hampshire, county, 66, 140, 142
Hampson, Sir Thomas, 89
Hampton Gay, 82
  manor, 96
  mill, 118
Hanwell, castle, 36, 96
Harbours *see* Ports
Harcourt,
  family, 124, 126
  Lord Harcourt, 162
  Simon, Lord Harcourt, 98
Hardwick House, Whitchurch, 96
Hardwick, 121
Hardwick-with-Yelford, 14
Harpsden, 22, 54
  church, 56
  manor, 32
Harris,
  Daniel, keeper of Oxford gaol, 98
  John, 122
Harwell, 92
  Atomic Energy Research Establishment, 156
  Diamond Light Source, 156
  Rutherford Appleton Laboratory, 156
Haseley Court, 84, 98
Hathaway, family, 104
Hayward's, brewers, 122
Hazelford Mill, Broughton, 118
Headington, 8, 70, 118, 146, 148, 152
  Anglo-Saxon settlement in, 18
  Churchill Hospital, 154
  industry in, 118
  nonconformists in, 134
  population of, 136, 138
  Wingfield Morris Hospital, 154
Headington Hill, 146
  hall, 124
Headington, New, 146
Health and welfare, 146, 150, 152
  blind, 144, 150
  deaf, 144
  in 20th century, 164
  Ministry of Health, 158
  National Health Service, 150, 164
  of infants, 164
  of mothers, 164
  poor relief, 144
  social services, 150
Hearths and fireplaces, 92, 96
Heaths, 34, 104
Hedges and hedgerows, 112, 114
Henderson, George, 112
Henley-on-Thames, 6, 24, 28, 38, 50, 68, 74, 76, 164
  at time of Domesday, 32
  breweries, 122
  bridge, 78
  diseases in, 94
  festivals in, 166
  foundry, 118
  Friar Park in, 124
  gild, 38
  industry in, 118, 122
  inns in, 78
  kilns, 64
  malting in, 78
  market, 52

INDEX

merchant gild, 78
nonconformists in, 86, 134, 162
poor law union, 144
population of, 38, 136, 138
Phyllis Court, 94
Public Assistance Institution in, 164
railways in, 106, 108, 109
River and Rowing Museum, 166
river-boat services in, 166
roads from and to, 102
role in Civil War, 94
Royal Regatta, 138, 166
schools in, 128
shopkeepers in, 90
South Oxfordshire Technical College, 160
timber houses in, 66
tourism in, 166
urban growth of, 106, 158
wealth of, 52, 54
wool trade in, 40
workhouse (Townlands Hospital), 144
Henley-on-Thames, deanery, 54
Henry II, 48, 60
Henry V, 58
Henry VI, 46, 58
Henry VII, 96
Henry VIII, 96
Herbert, Philip, Earl of Pembroke, 88
Hereford, 109
Hermon, Edward, 124
Heron, Sir Richard, 96
Hertfordshire, 24, 140
Hervey,
  John, 128
  William, 98
Hethe,
  manor, 34
Heythrop, 24, 98
  house, 124
  Roman Catholics in, 134
High Wycombe, 94, 108, 120
Highcroft, 24
Highways see Roads
Hill, James, 120
Hitchman, family, 122
Hoards, 12, 28
Holidays, 116
Holton, 84
  church, 84
  park, 154
Holwell, 22, 32
Holywell, Oxford, 72, 74, 84
  gardens, 34
  manor, 84
Homer, 22
Hook Norton, 110, 116
  brewery, 122, 166
  church, 26, 42
  Lodge Farm, 110
  market, 38, 78
  nonconformists in, 86
Hooper, George, 118
Horley,
  manor, 32
  nonconformists in, 86
Hornton, 6, 118
Horsepath, 24
Hospitals, 46, 58, 60, 100, 150, 154
  cottage, 164
  leper, 46, 60
  teaching, 164

Houseman, Elizabeth, 84
Houses and buildings, 8, 70, 146, 152, 158, 166; abandonment of, 70; in early 17th century, 92–93; of castles, 36; of prehistory, 10, 12
alehouses see Inns
almshouse, 46, 60, 66, 80
Anglo-Saxon halls, 18, 20, 22
Anglo-Saxon sunken hut, 30
barns, 20, 62, 66, 86
bedrooms, 92, 102
brewery, 118, 122
bunker, 156
butteries, 66
chimneys, 66, 92, 93, 96
clinic, 164
cottage, 130, 134
council houses, 152
country houses, 96, 98, 124, 166
deanery house, 30
dining halls, 66
factories, 120, 154
farmsteads, 16, 20, 36, 56, 66, 92, 110, 114, 124
fowlhouse, 20
granary, 20, 102
halls, 66, 72, 92
kitchens, 66, 92, 93
lodge, 36
lodge, hunting, 96
malthouse, 122
manor, 32, 36, 48, 54, 56, 96
market, 78
medieval, 96
meeting houses, 86, 134, 162
mill, 68
moated, 36
monastic, 26, 80
nursery, 154
outbuildings, 92
pantries, 66
parlours, 66, 92, 93, 102
poorhouse, 80
porches, 96
public houses, 104
refectory, 80
Roman, 16
Roman villas, 16, 18
roofing tiles, 8, 66
roofs, thatched, 14, 66
roundhouses, 12, 14
safe houses for priests, 84
shop, 78, 90, 106, 116
smithy, 20
solars, 66
stable, 102
staircases, 92, 93, 96
stone, 16, 66
storage rooms, 92
supermarket, 162
tannery, 118
temples, 16
timber, 66, 92
tower brewery, 122
town hall, 74, 106
Tudor, 96
vernacular, 66, 90
warehouse, 94
windows, 92, 96
workhouse, 74, 100, 104, 116, 136, 144
workshop, 40, 78
See also Religious houses

Howard,
  Charles, Viscount Andover, 88, 89
  family, 88
  Thomas, Earl of Berkshire, 88
Howbery Park, Crowmarsh Gifford, 124, 154
Hugh of Wells, 44
Hulbert, family, 118
Humprhis, family, 104
Hundreds, 26, 32
Hunt,
  John, 122
  Thomas, 122
Hunt Edmunds, brewers, 122
Hunter, Thomas, 118
Huntercombe, 22
Hunting, 10, 48, 96, 124
Hurstpierpoint, St John's College, 130
Hyde,
  Edward, Earl of Clarendon, 96
  John, 120

Idbury, 22
  hillfort, 14
Iffley, 50, 136, 138, 146, 152
  mill, 62
Ilbury, 22, 62
  hillfort, 14
Illness see Disease
Implements see Tools
Industry and trade, 28, 106, 152
  alum trade, 40
  aluminium factory, 158
  blanket manufacture, 120, 130, 138, 148
  boat-building, 104
  brewing, 72, 76, 118, 122, 146
  brick making, 118
  building trade, 72, 146
  cartridge case making, 154
  cement manufacture, 8, 118
  ceramic industry, 64
  chair making, 120, 121
  cloth-making, 38, 40, 70, 72, 76, 78, 80, 82, 120
  clothing industry, 146
  coach making, 118
  coal mining, 118
  conference trade, 166
  craftwork, 38
  custard making, 158
  during Second World War, 154
  food and drink, 72, 76
  free trade, 112
  fulling cloth, 68, 72
  furniture trade, 121
  glove making, 72, 78, 120
  high-technology businesses, 146
  in 19th century, 118, 120–21
  in Roman era, 16
  lacemaking, 120, 121
  leather glove making, 120
  leather-working, 78
  malt trade, 122
  malting, 78, 118, 122
  manufacture of agricultural implements, 118, 138, 148
  metal reprocessing plant, 154
  metal working, 118
  Morris Motors, 124
  motor industry, 146, 148, 154, 158
  nail making, 118
  paper-making, 118
  parchment making, 118

184

pipe manufacture, 118
pottery making, 16, 48, 64
printing, 146
publishing, 146
retail industry, 146
rope making, 118
sack making, 118
shoemaking, 72, 78
slop tailoring, 120
stone quarrying, 66
stoneware manufacture, 118
superphosphates making, 118
tailoring, 72
tanning, 72, 78, 118
textile manufacturing, 118, 120
tweed manufacture, 138, 148
victualling, 72
weaving, 72, 120
wine trade, 40, 50
wood production, 48
wool-trade, 38, 40, 50, 54, 76, 78, 120
Infants *see* Children
Ingledew, Sir Thomas, 58
Ingoldsby, Richard, 89
Inns, taverns and alehouses, 78, 84, 102, 116, 130, 142
Institutions, to churches, 42
Inventories, 78, 82, 90, 92
Ipsden, 22, 121
Ipswich, pottery from, 64
Ireland, 89
  Catholics from, 134
Ironworks, 124
Islington, 140
Islip, 24, 38, 40, 50, 138, 154
  school, 100
  shopkeepers in, 90
Italy,
  merchants of, 40
  prisoners of war from, 154

James II, 84
Jenkinson, Robert, 88, 89
Jerome, Jerome K., 104
Jersey, Earl of, 98
Jewels and jewellery, 26
Jews, 62, 162
John D'Oyly, 88, 89
Johnson,
  family, 90
  Dr Samuel, 102
  Stephen, 118
Joint European Torus, 156
Jones,
  Horace, 124
  Inigo, 96
  Walter, 96
Jordan, John, 102
Joyce Grove, Nettlebed, 124
Joyes, Henry, Vicar of Chipping Norton, 82

Kelmscott, 6, 24, 32
  manor, 124, 166
Kelsey, Thomas, 89
Kencott, 24, 136
Kennington, 146
  junction, 108
Kent, 88, 89
Kent, William, 98
Kiddington, 24, 84
  hall, 124
  Tomlin's Gate, 14

Kidlington, 24, 108, 136, 146, 152, 154, 156, 158, 162, 166
  adult education centre, 160
  church, 42
  motor industry in, 148
  poverty in, 116
  vicarage, 44
Kidmore, 22
Kilns, 64, 66, 78, 104
King, Robert, Bishop of Oxford, 80
King's Sutton, 108
Kingham, 108
  advowson, 132
  mill, 62
Kingston Blount, 22, 116
  nonconformists in, 86
Kingston upon Hull, 108
Kirtlington, 18, 24, 98, 124
  Iron Age settlements in, 14
Kitzinger, Sheila, 164
Knightcote, 108
Knights, 34, 48
Knightsbridge Lane, Pyrton, 50

La Rochefoucauld, brothers, 102
Lacy, Ilbert de, 32
Lambeth, 140
Lamps, 64
Lancashire, 140
Land Utilisation Survey, 112
Langford, church, and vicarage, 44
Languages and literacy, 100
  English, 26
  French, 84, 100, 130
  Greek, 100
  Hebrew, 100
  illiteracy, 128
  Latin, 100
  schools of, 166
Latchford, 22
Laud, William, Archbishop of Canterbury, 88, 94
Launton, 121
  Independent chapel, 134
Leadbetter, Stiff, 98
Leadenporch House, Deddington, 66, 92
Leafield, 24, 120
  motor industry in, 148
  nonconformists in, 86
Leamington Spa, 108
Lechlade, 28, 50, 104
Ledwell, 22
Lee,
  George Henry, Earl of Lichfield, 98
  Sir Henry, 82, 89
Leicester, 46
Leicestershire, 104
Leland, John, 76, 80, 166
Lenthall,
  family, 84
  William, 88, 89, 94
Lew, 22
Lewis, James, 98
Lewknor, 24, 62, 121
  nonconformists in, 86
Lichfield, Earl of, *see* Lee
Lidstone, 22
Lillingstone Lovell, 89, 144
Lincoln, diocese, 44, 46
  Alexander, Bishop of, 46
  bishop of, 32, 42, 44, 68, 78; *see also* Longland, John

Lincoln, 70
  cathedral, 42
  cathedral chapter of, 44
Lincolnshire, 140
Literacy *see* Languages
Little Haseley, 8
Little Rollright, 56
Littlemore, 18, 152
  nonconformists in, 162
  nunnery, 46, 80
Locks,
  flashlock, 50, 104
  Isis Lock, 104
  poundlock, 50, 104
Loder, Robert, 92
Lodge Farm, Hook Norton, 110
Loggan, David, 72
London, 50, 70, 88, 89, 94
  bankers of, 98
  communications with, 28, 50, 52, 78, 102, 104, 109, 158
  cornmongers from, 38
  firewood exported to, 76
  food exported to, 76
  industry in, 122
  influence of, 18, 30, 38, 40, 64, 70, 114, 118, 122, 144, 166
  markets, 62, 76, 90, 110, 112
  merchants of, 40, 98
  migration to, 140
  people of, 124, 130
  pottery in, 64
  railway stations in,
    Euston, 108
    Marylebone, 108
    Paddington, 108, 140
  roads from and to, 28, 82
  streets and places in, Hambros Wharf, 104
  trade with, 78
  wealth of, 52
Long Hanborough, 50, 118, 120, 136, 154
Long Wittenham, 18, 154
Longford, 104
Longland, John, Bishop of Lincoln, 80
Looms, 120
Lovell, William, 68
Low Countries, pottery from, 64
Lowe, George, 89
Lower Heyford, 18, 144
Lower Heyford *or* Upper Heyford, hillfort, 14
Ludlow, 40
Lundy, Isle of, 89
Lutyens, Sir Edwin, 124
Lyneham, 18
  hillfort, 14
Lyneham, Wilts, air base, 156

Macclesfield, Earl of, 114; *see also* Parker, Thomas
Machines and mechanisation, 122
  sewing-machines, 120
  See also Steam and steam engines
Madmarston, hillfort, 14
Maidenhead, 108
  Warren Row in, *q.v.*
Malmesbury, 80
Malvern College, 154
Manchester, 118
Manley, J. G., 98

INDEX

Manors, 20, 22, 32, 34, 36, 38, 40, 48, 62, 64, 80, 94, 124, 166
Mapledurham, 24, 84, 94, 96, 100, 124
  house, 166
  Mill Farm Cottage in, 66
  water-mill, 166
Marcham, 154
Markets and market places, 16, 26, 30, 38, 50, 52, 64, 70, 72, 74, 76, 78, 82, 90, 100, 106, 112, 138, 144
  cattle-market, 78
  horse-market, 30
  salt-market, 28
  sheep-market, 78
Marlborough, Duke of, 114, 126, 132; see also Churchill, John
Marshall, William, 110
Marston, 22, 89, 94, 152, 162
Mason, Benjamin, Joseph and Samuel, 118
Matilda, Queen, 36
May, Hugh, 96
Mayo, Earl of, 158
Medicines and medical services, 90, 144
  War Emergency Medical Service, 154
Medley, 22
Menmarsh, 22
Mercia, 18, 30, 46, 64, 70
Merseyside, 108
Merton, 24, 46
Middlesex, 140
Middleton Park, Middleton Stoney, 98, 124, 154
Middleton Stoney, 24, 38, 156
  castle, 36, 64
  tower, 36
Midlands, 70, 82, 94, 112, 140
  communications with, 50, 104, 106, 108
  enclosure in, 114
  population of, 138
  settlement patterns in, 56
  topography of, 6
  urban growth of, 38
  wool from, 40
Milcombe, 22
Milham, 24
Miller, Sanderson, 98, 104
Mills, 32, 34, 50, 62, 82, 120
  animal, 16
  corn, 40, 68, 118
  dams of, 50, 68
  fulling, 40, 68, 80
  paper, 118
  sawmill, 118
  stones of, 68
  textile, 118
  water, 16, 68, 80, 118, 166
Milne (Mylne),
  Oswald, 124
  Robert, 98
Milton Park, 156
Minchery Farm, Sandford-on-Thames, 152
Minerals and natural resources,
  alum, 40
  antlers, 10
  bones, 10
  bronze, 12
  coal, 104, 118, 122, 142
  copper, 118
  faggots, 24
  firewood, 48, 76
  glauconite, 8
  iron, 8, 34

iron ore, 8
iron, pig, 118
iron, wrought, 118
ironstone, 108, 118
leather, 38, 64, 72, 78, 118
lime, 76, 104
limestone, 118
manure, 76
metals, 38, 50, 64, 118
oil, 154
potassium, 8
quartzite, 10
salt, 24, 28, 50, 90, 104
softwood, 104
stone, 104, 118
timber, 20, 28, 36, 48, 66, 76, 92, 94
wood, 10, 34, 38, 64
See also Soils
Minety, 64
Minster Lovell, 18, 54, 120
  alien priory, 46
  barn, 66
  churchyard, 26
  dovecote, 66
  hall, 96, 98, 166
  mills, 40, 68
Minsters *see* Cathedrals
Mitchells & Butlers, brewers, 122
Mitford, sisters, 124
Mixbury, 6, 121
Moats, 36
Mollington, 6
Monarchy *see* Royalty
Mongewell, 22, 162
  park, 124
Moors and moorland, 48
Morland, family, 122
Morrell,
  family, 122
  James, 124
  Philip, and Lady Ottoline, his wife, 124
Morris,
  Roger, 98
  William, 124
  William, Lord Nuffield, 146, 148
Morris Radiators, 148
Morse, John, 98
Mount Farm, in Berinsfield, American base, 154
Murcott, 22
Museums, 166
Music and dancing, 142
  brass band, 142
  morris-dancing, 30
Mylles, Dr John, 89
Mylne *see* Milne

Nails, 90
Napper,
  family, 84
  George, 84
Napton-on-the-Hill, 104
National Farm Survey, 112
NATO, 156
Natural regions *see* Soils
Natural resources *see* Minerals
Neanderthals, 10
Needlework, 100, 120
Neithrop, 24, 136
Nettlebed, 8, 154
  ceramic industry in, 64
  industry in, 118, 121

Joyce Grove, 124
  kilns, 66
  people of, 118, 120
  Windmill Hill, 10
New Marston, 146
Newbury, 50, 64, 106
Newcastle upon Tyne, 108
Newington House, 98
Newington, North, mill, 118
Newland, Witney, 120
Newnham Murren, 24, 66
Newspapers and publishers, 116, 138, 142
  Banbury Guardian, 144
  Jackson's Oxford Journal, 100
  Oxford University Press, 84, 118, 146
Newton, Ernest, 124
Nicholas IV, Pope, Taxatio of, 42
Nichols, George, 84
Nixon, John, 88, 89
Noke, 138
Norfolk, 110, 140
Norham, 24
Normandy and the Normans,
  bishops from, 32, 46
  influence of, 36, 38
Norreys (Norris),
  family, 80, 126
  Sir Francis, 88, 89
  Henry, Lord Norreys, 82
North, Frederick, Lord North, Prime Minister, 126
North Hinksey, 146, 152, 154
North Leigh, 16, 18, 24, 34, 120
  nonconformists in, 86
  vicar of, 42
North Stoke, 18
North Weston, 98
Northampton, 50, 102
Northamptonshire, 88, 114, 118, 121, 140, 144
Northmoor, 154
  rectory, 44
  Rectory Farm Barn in, 66
  Watkins Farm, 14
Northumberland, county, 140
Norwich, 70
Nuffield, 24
Nuffield, Lord, 124; *see also* Morris, William
Nuffield Place, 124
Nuneham Courtenay, 8, 24, 98, 124, 162

Occupations *see* Trades
Oddington, 22
Odo, Bishop of Bayeux, 32
Officials, 88
  alderman, 88
  attorney-general, 82
  chancellor of Oxford University, 70, 94
  chancellor of Oxford University, vice, 82, 88
  cofferer to Henry VII, 96
  commissioner of array, 88
  commissioner of the peace, 88
  comptroller of works, 96
  governor of Oxford castle, 88
  justice of the peace (JPs), 88, 89
  keeper of Oxford gaol, 98
  lord lieutenant, 88
  lord lieutenant of Oxfordshire, 82
  major-general, 89
  master of the king's jewels, 80
  mayor, 88

member of Parliament (MP), 88, 89, 94, 126
overseer of the poor, 116
park ranger, 88
paymaster of Charles II, 96
president of St John's College, 94
prime minister, 126
recorder, 88
recorder of Oxford, 89
relieving officer, 144
secretary of state, 88
secretary to the Board of Agriculture, 110
sheriff, 88, 89
speaker of the House of Commons, 88, 94
steward, 84, 88
steward of Oxford, 88
steward of Woodstock royal park, 82
sub-steward of Oxford University, 89
treasurer of the Court of Augmentations, 80
treasurer to Henry VIII, 96
warden of Merton College, 124
Oglander, Mrs, 100
Old age, 116, 144
Orders, religious,
  Augustinian canons, 26, 44, 46, 80
  Augustinian Friars, 72
  Austin Friars, 46
  Benedictines, 20, 26, 44, 46
  Black Friars, 72, 80
  Carmelites, 46, 80
  Cistercians, 44, 46, 98
  Crutched Friars, 46
  Dominicans, 46
  Franciscans, 46
  Friars of the Sack, 46
  Gilbertines, 46, 60, 96
  Grey Friars, 72, 80
  Hospitallers, 44, 46
  Knights Templars, 46
  Mendicant Friars, 46
  Trinitarians, 46
  White Friars, 72
Orphans, 116
Orwin, C. S., 112
Osney, 22
  abbey, 40, 42, 44, 46, 72, 80
  monastic cartulary, 42
Otley, abbey, 46
Otmoor, 6, 8, 22, 34, 110, 114, 136, 158
Over Norton, Chapel House, 102
Owen,
  Dr John, 89
  Nicholas, 84
Oxford, diocese, 44, 80
  bishop of, 100, 132; see also Fell, John; King, Robert; Secker, Thomas; Wilberforce, Samuel
Oxford, archdeaconry, archdeacon of, 86
Oxford, 6, 24
  adult education centre, 160
  advowsons relating to, 132
  Anglo-Saxon settlement in, 18, 70
  archaeology of, 12
  barn, 66
  bombing of, 154
  breweries, 122
  bridges in, 72
    Folly Bridge, 104, 146
    Grandpont, 22, 28, 50, 70, 72, 108

Hythe Bridge, 24, 104
Magdalen Bridge, 74
Pettypont (now Magdalen Bridge), 50
buildings in,
  Ashmolean Museum, 124, 166
  Bocardo prison, 74
  Bodleian Library, 74, 94
  Clarendon Building, 74
  Holywell Music Room, 74
  Modern Art Oxford, 166
  Museum of Natural History, 166
  Old Ashmolean, 74
  Pitt Rivers Museum of Ethnology, 166
  Radcliffe Camera, 74
  Radcliffe Observatory, 74
  Sheldonian Theatre, 74
  United Parishes workhouse, 74
bypass, 158
canal, 28, 74, 104, 106, 118, 122, 146
canal community in, 104
castle, 36, 70, 72, 74, 88, 94, 166
  St George's church in, 46
cathedral chapter of, 132
chantries, 58
churches in, 8, 70, 162
  All Saints, 74
  St Aldate, 70
  St Giles, 44, 66
  St Mary Magdalen, 74
  St Peter in the East, 44
cloth-making industry in, 40
colleges in,
  Cherwell Hall teacher training college, 160
  City Technical College, 160
  College of Further Education, 160
  Felstead House teacher training college, 160
  Oxford School of Art, 160
  Westminster College, 160
communications of, 50
corporation, 78
council houses in, 152
decline of, 70
district, 150
emergency centre, 156
executions in, 82, 84
exporters of wool resident in, 40
festivals in, 166
foundries in, 118
friendly societies in, 142
gaol, 74; keeper of, 98
gates of, 70, 74
geology of, 8
growth of, 72, 146
hospitals in, 154
  Churchill Hospital, 164
  Radcliffe Infirmary, 74, 98, 154, 164
  See also under Oxford, religious houses in
impact of Norman conquest on, 36
industry in, 16, 38, 118, 122
inns [named] in, 84
maps of, 72
markets, 74, 82, 112
mills, 68
minster, 26
monastic colleges, 80
mosques in, 162
motor industry in, 148
MPs for, 88, 89, 126
nonconformists in, 86, 134, 162

Oxford Canal Company, 104
parishes and districts in, 132
  St Aldate, 74, 122
  St Clement, 72, 84, 136, 146
  St Ebbe, 136, 138, 146, 152
  St Giles, 72, 122, 136, 138
  St Thomas, 72, 122, 136, 138, 146, 152
people of, 84, 98, 146
poor law union, 144
population of, 78, 106, 136, 138
pottery in, 64
prehistory of, 10
race-meetings, 78
railway carriage factory, 148
railway stations in, 108
railways in, 106, 108, 109
rebellion in, 82
recorder of, 89
recusants of, 84
religious houses in, 70, 80
  friaries, 46, 72, 80
  hospital of St Clement, 60
  hospital of St John the Baptist, 60, 62
  St Frideswide's priory, 26, 32, 42, 44, 46, 70, 72, 80
  St John's Hospital, 44
river-boat services in, 166
roads, 16, 102
role in Civil War, 94
royal headquarters in, 88
royal palace at, 70
schools in, 58, 130, 154, 160
shopkeepers in, 90
shrine of St Frideswide, 166
streets and places in,
  Bath Street, 162
  Beaumont Street, 22
  Botanic Gardens, 74, 96, 166
  Botley Causeway, 74
  Brewer Street, 122
  Broad Street, 74, 84
  Burford Road, 148
  Carfax, 22, 70, 74, 152
  Carfax Tower, 166
  Catte Street, 70
  Cheney Lane, 50
  Cornmarket, 66, 122
  Cowley Road, 118, 144
  Edmund Road, 148
  Fisher Row, 104
  Gloucester Green, 74
  High Street, 70
  Iffley Road, 74
  Jericho, 152
  Longwall Street, 148
  New Inn Hall Street, 70
  New Road, 74
  New Road wharf, 74
  Oxford Business Park, 148
  Queen Street, 70, 74, 122
  Rewley Road, 108
  St Michael's Street, 74
  Ship Street, 74
  Turl Street, 74
  University Parks, 12
  Wellington Square, 74, 144
  Woodstock Road, 148
suburbs of, 72, 136, 138, 162
surrender of, 88
synagogue, 162
topography of, 6
tourism in, 166

187

INDEX

town hall, 74, 156
Trill Mill Stream in, 68
University of Oxford *see* University of Oxford
university property in, 62
urban growth of, 28, 32, 34, 38, 106, 112, 158
water transport in, 104
wealth of, 52, 54, 70
weavers of, 40
wool trade in, 40
workhouse, 144
Oxford Brookes University, 146, 148, 156, 160
Oxford Polytechnic, 160
Oxford University *see* University of Oxford
Oxford University Press, 84, 118, 146
Oxfordshire Review Order (1932), 150

Paddington, 108, 140
Palaces, 70, 78, 98
Palmer, Henry, 102
Papacy and papists, 42, 84
Parachutes, 156
Pardons, 82
Parishes,
  development of, 42
  population in 19th century, 132
Parker,
  family, 104
  Thomas, Earl of Macclesfield, 98
Parks, 46, 48, 82, 98, 100, 124, 166
  ammunition, 154
  deer, 98
  royal, 82, 98
Parliament, 88, 94, 132
  members of, 126
  See also Acts of Parliament
Paupers *see* Poverty
Peasants and peasantry, 20, 38, 40, 48
Peel, Robert, 126
Peers, Charles, 98
Pembroke, Earl of, *see* Herbert, Philip
Penalties *see* Punishments
Pensions, 42, 44
Pheleley, hermitage, 46
Phillips, family, 122
Phipps, John, 120
Phyllis Court, Henley-on-Thames, 94
Piddington, 24, 121
  salt-market, 28
Pilgrimage, 166
Pillboxes, 154
Pipes, 90
Pishill, 24, 44
Place-names, 22–24
Ploughley, hundred, 112
Ploughs, 34
Plowden, family, 84
Pluralism, 44
Poaching, 48
Pole,
  de la, family, 66
  William de la, Earl of Suffolk, and Alice (Chaucer) his wife, 60
Politics,
  Conservative party, 126
  families prominent in, 80
  importance of university, 70
  in 10th and 11th centuries, 64
  in 16th century, 96
  in mid 17th century, 88

in Middle Ages, 70
local education authorities, 150
local government, 150
local government board, 164
Local Government Boundary Commission, 150
Parliamentary elections, 88
Parliamentary representation, 126
Pollinger, William, 118
Ponds and pools, 22, 36
  fishpond, 36, 48
  millpond, 68
Pope,
  family, 80
  Sir Thomas, 88; as treasurer of the Court of Augmentations, 80
  Sir William, 96
Popish Plot (1678), 84
Population,
  at time of Domesday, 34
  decline in, 18, 38, 54, 56, 72, 74, 106, 138, 146
  depopulation of countryside, 114
  emigration, 56, 114, 116, 136
  growth of, 12, 40, 42, 48, 56, 64, 72, 106, 114, 116, 122, 136, 138, 146, 152
  immigration, 16, 72, 120
  in 19th century, 132, 136, 138
  in Anglo-Saxon era, 18
  in late 17th century, 78
  in late medieval era, 52, 54
  in medieval era, 38
  in Roman era, 16, 18
  migration, 136, 138, 140, 142, 146
  mobility of people, 56
Port Meadow, Oxford, 6, 108
Ports, harbours, etc, 50, 64, 76
Portsmouth, 108
Potterspury, 64
Pottery, 34, 48, 64
  Anglo-Saxon, 18
  coarseware, 64
  cremation pots, 64
  in Iron Age, 14
  in Roman era, 16
  Ipswich wares, 64
  jars, 64
  medieval, 56
  Michelmersh-type vessels, 64
  of prehistory, 10, 12
  pitcher, spouted, 64
  St Neot's-type ware, 64
  Saxon shelly ware, 64
  storage jars, 64
Poverty and paupers, 60, 78, 80, 82, 90, 93, 100, 114
  education of, 100, 128
  of churches, 44
  of minsters, 26
  of religious houses, 44
  poor law, 116, 144, 150
  Poor Law Board, 144
  Poor Law Commission, 144
  poor law unions, 144, 150
  relief of, 116, 144
Powell, family, 80
Power, Francis, 82
Prebends, 44
Prescott, mill, 68
Prichett, William, 120
Priestley, J. B., 166
Princes Risborough, 108

Prisons *see* Gaols
Pritchard, Humphrey, 84
Publishers *see* Newspapers
Punishments and penalties,
  being hanged, drawn and quartered, 82
  execution, 82, 84
  fines, 48, 84, 86
  hanging, 82
  imprisonment, 84, 86
Pye, Sir Robert, 89
Pyrton, 24, 118, 121
  church, 26
  manor, 32
  vicar of, 84

Quainton, Quainton Road railway station, 108
Quarries and quarrying, 8, 10, 12, 18, 66, 96, 118
  ironstone, 118
  limestone, 118
  stone, 22
Quartremain, family, 98
Querns and quernstones, 8, 64

Racing and race-meetings, 78
Radcot, 94
  bridge, 104
  bridge-causeway, 28, 30
  canal, 28
  castle, 36
Radford, 134
Radley, 130
Radway, 118
Railways, 102, 106, 108–9, 110, 112, 124, 136, 140, 146, 148, 166
  Banbury and Cheltenham Direct Railway, 108
  Buckinghamshire Railway, 108
  Chiltern Railways, 109
  Great Central Railway, 108, 109
  Great Western Railway (GWR), 108, 109
  London and Birmingham Railway, 108
  London, Buckinghamshire and West Midland Junction Railway, 108
  Manchester, Sheffield and Lincoln Railway, 108
  Northampton and Banbury Railway, 108
  Oxford and Rugby Railway, 108
  Oxford, Worcester and Wolverhampton Railway (OWW), 108, 109
  Stratford-upon-Avon and Midland Junction Railway, 108
  West Midland Railway, 108
Rainolds, family, 84
Ramparts *see* Walls
Ramsden, 22, 154
Reading, Berks, 8, 50, 108, 112, 138, 140, 158
  abbey, 44
  brewery, 122
  bridge, 158
  role in Civil War, 94
  suburbs of, 162
Rebels and rebellions, 82
  the planned rising of 1596, 82
  the rising of 1549, 82
Rectories, 30, 44, 80
Recusants and recusancy, 84
Redcliffe-Maud, Lord, 150
Redesdale, Lord, 124
Refrigeration, 112, 122

188

Religion,
  atheists, 162
  attendance at services, 134
  Baha'i faith, 162
  Book of Common Prayer, 82, 86
  Buddhism, 162
  Christianity, 26, 30, 64
  church as landholders in Oxfordshire, 32, 82
  Church of England, 54, 62, 84, 100, 128, 132, 134, 160, 162
  Ecclesiastical Revenues Commission, 132
  Hindus, 162
  in 20th century, 162
  Jesuits, 84
  Jewish, 162
  Muslims, 162
  Nonconformists, 54, 86, 94, 100, 116, 128, 132, 134, 160, 162
    Anabaptists, 86
    Baptists, 86, 100, 134, 162
    Christian Science, 162
    Independents (Congregationalists), 86, 134, 162
    Methodists, 134, 162
    Presbyterians, 86, 100
    Primitive Methodists, 134
    Quakers, 86, 100, 130, 134, 162
    Roman Catholics, 162
    Sabbatarians, 86
    Wesleyan Methodists, 100, 134
  paganism, 30
  religious census (1851), 134
  role in education, 100
  Roman Catholics, 80, 84, 88, 100, 128, 132, 134, 162
  Sikhs, 162
  See also Clergy and religious; Orders, religious; Religious houses
Religious houses, 40, 42, 44, 46, 48, 58, 60, 62, 70, 132
  abbeys, 20, 26, 44, 46, 68
  dissolution of, 72, 80
  hermitage, 46
  monasteries, 26, 38, 42, 96, 122
  nunneries, 46, 80
  priories, 46, 80
  priories, alien, 46
Remigius, Bishop, 46
Repton, George Stanley, 124
Return of Owners of Land (1873), 110
Rewley, Oxford, 22
  abbey, 46, 58, 72, 80
  abbot of, 80
Rhineland, pottery from, 64
Riots, 82, 84
Risinghurst, 146
Rivers and waterways, 6, 10, 22, 24, 28, 34, 50, 52, 72, 104, 154
  Avon, 6
  Cherwell, 6, 8, 12, 14, 18, 22, 24, 26, 28, 34, 50, 68, 70, 82, 94, 104, 112, 121, 146, 154
  Chil Brook, 104
  Evenlode, 6, 8, 14, 22, 28
  Glyme, 6, 22, 68
  Great Ouse, 6, 28
  Hazelford Brook, 22
  Humber, 46
  in Iron Age, 14
  Isis, 104
  Kennet, 104
  lakes, 6
  Limb Brook, 104
  Ray, 6, 28, 50, 68, 114
  Severn, 50, 104
  Shill Brook, 30
  Solent, 66
  Sor Brook, 6, 24
  springs, 22
  streams, 6, 22, 34, 68
  Swere, 6, 24
  Thame, 6, 22, 28, 34, 50, 56, 114
  Trill Mill Stream, 68
  Wash, 6, 28, 64, 66
  wetlands, 6
  Windrush, 6, 12, 14, 18, 22, 24, 26, 28, 68, 78, 154
  See also Canals; Thames, River
Roads, highways, etc, 24, 28, 50, 52, 70, 72, 74, 78, 82, 106, 112, 114, 116, 140, 150, 158, 166
  Akeman Street, 16, 28
  causeway, 50, 70
  footpaths, 114
  hollow ways, 56
  Icknield Way, 24, 28, 50, 112
  in 18th century, 102
  in 19th century, 102
  motorway (M40), 158
  Oxford bypass, 158
  ridgeways, 28, 50
  ring road, 152
  Roman roads, 16, 18, 22, 50
  route-ways, 38, 50
  salt-ways, 28, 50
  towpath, 104
  trackways, 12, 20, 24
  turnpikes, 102, 106
Robert, Count of Dreux, 42
Robert, Count of Mortain, 32
Robert d'Oilly, 28, 32, 36, 42, 44, 46, 50, 70
Robert fitz Hamon, 38
Roe, Sir Thomas, 88, 89
Rofford, 22, 24
Roger d'Ivry, 32, 36
Roke, 8
Rollright, 18
  See also Great Rollright; Little Rollright
Romans, influence of, 16, 18, 22
Rose Hill, Cowley, 152
Rotherfield Greys, 24, 96, 121, 136, 138
Rotherfield Peppard, 24, 124
  manor, 32
  mill, 118
Rousham, 24, 94, 96, 98, 124
  house, 166
Routledge, Thomas, 118
Royal Commission (1874), 142
Royalty and monarchy, 94, 96
  as landholders in Oxfordshire, 32
  charters of, 38, 70, 106
  forests of, 48
  influence of, 46, 62
  licence of, 40
  royal residences, 26, 30, 38, 70
Rugby, 108
Rushey Weir, Bampton, 28, 30
Rutherford Appleton Laboratory, 156
Rycote, 24, 82, 96
  deer-park, 82
  park, 154

St Albans (Verulamium), 16

Saints,
  St Augustine of Hippo, 46
  St Beornwald, 30
  St Birinus, 166
  St Diuma, 26
  St Edburg, 80
  St Freomund, 26
  St Frideswide, 166
  St Wulfstan, 28
Salford, 6
Salisbury, 50
  cathedral chapter of, 44
Salmonsbury, 14
Salter, John, 104
Sanderson, John, 98
Sandford-on-Thames, 22, 46, 50, 80
  paper-mill, 118
  vicarage, 44
Sandford St Martin, 22, 136, 154
Sandhurst, 140
Sankey, Jerome, 89
Sansom's Platt, Tackley, 16
Sarsden, 22
  house, 98, 124
Savernake Forest, 64
Saye and Sele, Viscount, see Fiennes, William
Schools, 58, 78, 116, 142, 144, 150, 154
  boarding, 130
  charity, 100, 128, 130
  comprehensive, 160
  dame, 100, 130
  day, 128
  endowed, 100, 128, 130
  evening, 100
  examination, 154
  grammar, 60, 66, 78, 80, 100, 130, 160
  high, 160
  in 18th century, 100
  independent, 160
  industrial, 100
  language, 166
  middle, 160
  national, 130
  preparatory, 160
  primary, 128, 160
  private, 128, 130
  public, 130
  RAF Parachute Training School, 156
  secondary, 128, 160
  secondary modern, 160
  Sunday, 100, 128
  technical, 160
  See also Education
Scotland, 140
  people from, 102
  war with, 88
Scrope,
  Adrian, 89
  Robert, 89
Secker, Thomas, Bishop of Oxford, 86
Selden, John, 88, 89
Settlement and settlement patterns, 22
  abandonment of, 14, 16
  Anglo-Saxon, 18, 20, 26, 28
  at time of Domesday, 32
  deserted, 32, 54, 56, 62, 82
  dispersed, 56
  in Iron Age, 14, 30
  of prehistory, 12
  of towns, 28
  relocation of, 16

INDEX

Roman, 16, 22, 30
shrunken, 56
Shakenoak, 18
Sharp, Thomas, 158
Sheldon, Gilbert, Archbishop of Canterbury, 86
Shelswell, 22, 121
park, 124
Shenlow Hill, Shenington, 6
Shifford, 24, 56
Shillingford, 24
Shilton, farm, 46
Shiplake, 24
mill, 118
Shiplake Court, 124
Shipton-on-Cherwell, 24
church, 32
Shipton-under-Wychwood, 24, 26, 28, 34, 120, 156
church, 44
mills, 68
nonconformists in, 86
Shirburn, 22, 36, 96
castle, 94, 96, 98
hill, 6
Model Farm in, 110
Shorthampton, 120
Chilson in, *q.v.*
Shotover, 8, 24, 34, 48, 50, 124
hill, 6
park, 98
Showell, 22
Shrewsbury, Duke of, *see* Talbot, Charles
Shrewsbury, Earl of, 134
Shrewsbury, 102, 104
Shrines, 30, 80
Shrivenham, Royal Military College of Science, 160
Shutford, 24, 120
Sibford Gower, 46, 120
nonconformists in, 86
Quaker boarding school, 130
Burdrop in, *q.v.*
Sieges and siege-works, 36, 94
Silchester, 16
Simeon, Sir Edward, 98
Simonds' (H&G Simonds), brewers, 122
Slat Mills, 68
Slaves and slavery, 34
Sluices, 68
Smith,
Francis, 98
John, 88, 89
William, 98
Soane, Sir John, 124
Societies and clubs,
Ancient Order of Foresters, 142
Charlbury Old Club, 142
friendly, 142
independent, 142
Independent Order of Odd Fellows Manchester Unity, 142
Oxford Working Women's Benefit Society, 142
Society for the Promotion of Christian Knowledge (SPCK), 100
Standlake Benefit Society, 142
Whitchurch Women's Friendly Society, 142
Soils and natural regions, 76
Banbury ironstone, 8
brick clay, 8

chalk, 6, 10, 22, 76, 114
chalk-with-flints, 52
clay, 6, 8, 10, 20, 22, 34, 36, 52, 56, 64, 76, 110
clay-with-flints, 8, 22, 34, 76
Coombe rock, 8
Cretaceous rocks, 8
flint, 8, 10
freestone, 8
Gault clay, 8, 22
grit, 8
ironstone, 66, 110
Kimmeridge clay, 8, 22
Lias rock, 6
limestone, 6, 8, 10, 22, 34, 52, 54, 76, 92, 114
Lower Greensand rocks, 8
Malmstone, 8
marlstone (Hornton stone), 8, 34, 76
ochre, 8
Oolitic limestone, 6, 66, 110
Oxford Heights, 6
Portland beds, 8
Purbeck beds, 8
purple sandstone, 8
Redlands, 110, 114
sand, 6, 8, 64, 76
sandstone, 8
sarsens, 8
silt, 28
stonebrash, 34, 76
Upper Greensand rocks, 8
white pipe clay, 8
See also Minerals
Somerset, 138, 140
Somerton, 6, 121, 142
Sonning, adult education centre, 160
Souldern, 18, 44, 121
South Leigh, 24, 66, 154
Church Farm, 92
Southampton, 40, 50, 64, 70, 109, 154
Southrop, 24
Soviet Union, 156
Speedometers, 148
Spencer, Sir William, 82
Stadhampton, 22, 24
Stafford, 140
Staines, 158
Standhill, 22
Standlake, 22, 38, 54
Anglo-Saxon settlement in, 18
Benefit Society, 142
cloth-making industry in, 40
manor, 66
Gaunt House in, *q.v.*
Stanley, family, 80, 84
Stanton Harcourt, 10, 22, 98, 138, 154
archaeology of, 12, 14
church, 44, 80
manor, 66, 96
Stanton St John, 22
Steam and steam engines, 118, 120, 122
Steede, Elizabeth, 130
Steeple Aston, 136
Iron Age settlements in, 14
school, 100
Steeple Barton, 92, 120, 136
Steer, Bartholomew, 82
Stephen, King, 36
Stephenson,
George, 108
Robert, 108

Stevens, John, 118
Steventon, 108
Stoke Lyne, 121, 136
Fewcot in, *q.v.*
Stoke Row Farm, Ipsden, 118
Stokenchurch, 102
Stone, Nicholas, 96
Stonesfield, 8, 16, 24, 118, 120, 136, 142
Stonor,
family, 84, 98, 124, 126
Thomas, 78
Stonor, 22, 24, 32, 66, 84, 96, 98, 100, 124
park, 166
Stow, 46
Stowford, 22, 24, 34
Stowood, 22, 24
school, 100
Stratford Bridge, 22
Stratford-upon-Avon, 16
Stratton Audley, 22, 121
Stroud, Glos, 120
Studley, 24
nunnery, 46, 80
priory, 80, 96
Stumpe, William, 80
Subinfeudation, 32
Suburbs, 70, 72, 136, 138, 140, 146, 162
Suffolk, 140
Suffolk, Earl of, *see* Pole, William de la
Summertown, Oxford, 146, 148
farm, 152
Surrey, 89, 140
Sutton Courtenay, [*formerly* Berks], 18, 24
Swalcliffe,
barn, 62, 66
manor, 66
nonconformists in, 86
Swalcliffe Lea, 16
Swerford Park, 124
Swinbrook, 22, 24, 124
Swyncombe, 22, 24, 96
house, 124
Sydenham, 22, 24, 121

Tackley, Sansom's Platt, 16
Tadmarton, 24
hillfort, 14
mill, 68
nonconformists in, 86
Talbot,
Charles, Duke of Shrewsbury, 98
family, 134
Tanfield, Sir Lawrence, 96
Taston, 22
Taunt, Henry, 104, 146
Taverns *see* Inns
Tawney, family, 122
Taxation, taxes and tolls, 48, 56, 72, 84, 94, 116
canal tolls, 104
hearth tax, 92
land tax, 114
lay subsidies, 52, 54
mill tolls, 68
poll tax, 54
Ship Money, 88, 94
tolls, 38, 50
Taynton, 8, 22, 34, 104
quarries, 118
Temple Cowley, 46, 84
Thame, 8, 18, 28, 80, 84
abbey, 40, 68, 80

190

INDEX

agricultural show, 166
agriculture in, 112
at time of Domesday, 32
church, 26
communications of, 50
cottage hospital, 164
deer-park, 82
diseases in, 94
exporters of wool resident in, 40
fairs, 78
grammar school, 80
industry in, 118, 120, 121
inns in, 78
Lord Williams Grammar School, 130
markets, 78
medieval development of, 38
minster, 42
nonconformists in, 86, 134, 162
park, 46, 80, 96, 98
population of, 38, 136, 138
railways in, 106, 108
role in Civil War, 94
Rycotewood College for Rural Crafts, 160
schools in, 128
shopkeepers in, 90
tourism in, 166
Upper High Street, 92
urban growth of, 106, 158
workhouse, 144
Thames, River, 6, 10, 14, 22, 24, 26, 28, 30, 34, 36, 46, 50, 70, 72, 76, 78, 92, 94, 98, 104, 120, 122, 124, 138, 154
archaeology of, 12, 14, 16
bridges over, 108, 158
commissioners of, 104
estuary of, 28
floodplain of, 22, 28, 50, 146
gravel of, 14, 20
meadows by, 34
mills on, 68
navigation of, 50, 104, 106
prehistory of, 10
roads over, 16
valley of, 6, 8, 10, 12, 14, 16, 18, 34, 64, 66, 158
Thatcher, Margaret, 152
Theodore, Archbishop, 46
Thomas, John, 124
Thomley, 56
Thompson,
  Benjamin, 118
  Flora, 128
  James, 118
Thrupp, 24
Tiddington, 22
Tilson, John, 98
Tithes, 42, 44, 52, 62, 80, 94
  appropriation of, 132
  commutation of, 114
Tobacco, 116
Tombs *see* Burials
Tomlin's Gate, Kiddington, 14
Tools and implements (prehistoric),
  burins, 10
  choppers, 10
  cores, 10
  flakes, 10
  handaxes, 10
  microliths, 10
  projectile points, 10
  stone axes, 12
  stone tools, 10

Toot Baldon, 8, 22, 120
Topography, 6–7, 76
Torrington, Viscount, *see* Byng, John
Torture, 82
Tourism and tourists, 74, 166
Towcester, 16, 108
Towers, 84
  of castles, 36
  of churches, 36
  stone, 36
  timber, 36
Towersey, 121, 166
Townesend, William, 98
Towns and urbanisation, 26, 28, 30, 72, 78, 80, 140
  Anglo-Saxon, 70
  at time of Domesday, 32
  decay of, 106
  education in, 100
  growth of, 106, 110, 112, 136, 138, 146
  in 18th century, 106
  in 19th century, 106
  in 20th century, 152, 158
  in later Middle Ages, 56
  market towns, 78
  medieval, 38
Trade *see* Industry
Trades and occupations,
  accountant, 30
  agricultural labourer, 112, 116, 128, 144
  architect, 62, 98, 124, 158
  artisan, 40
  baker, 38, 86, 90
  banker, 98
  blacksmith, 118
  boatbuilder, 104
  boatman, 104
  bodger, 120
  bookkeeper, 118
  bookseller, 84
  brewer, 72, 122, 124
  brick burner, 118
  brick maker, 118
  builder, 148
  butcher, 38, 74, 78, 90, 116, 130
  carpenter, 82, 84
  carrier, 102, 144
  chair framer, 120
  chair maker, 120
  chair turner, 121
  chandler, 90
  chapman, 38, 90
  clerk, 42, 62, 118
  cloth dresser, 120
  cloth finisher, 120
  cloth-maker, 40
  cloth-worker, 72
  clothier, 78, 80
  coach maker, 118
  cooper, 110
  cornmonger, 38
  cotton manufacturer, 124
  craftsman, 38, 70, 72, 74, 78, 120
  draper, 72, 90, 104
  draughtsman, 124
  dressmaker, 90, 120
  drummer, 100
  engineer, 108
  engineer, civil, 158
  farmer, 54, 56, 76, 90, 102, 110, 112, 116, 130, 144, 154
  fisherman, 34

forester, 48, 142
fuller, 38
general practitioner, 164
glove cutter, 120
glove manufacturer, 120
glover, 120
grainer of chairs, 120
grazier, 78, 110
grocer, 90
grounder, 120
haberdasher, 90
hawker, 90
health visitor, 164
hewer of wood, 121
husbandman, 90
innkeeper, 72
jeweller, 148
lacemaker, 121
landscape gardener, 124
lawyer, 88, 94, 96, 98
leather-worker, 72
linen draper, 90
maltster, 78, 122
mason, 62, 96, 98
mercer, 38, 72, 88, 90, 110
merchant, 28, 38, 40, 52, 70, 90, 98, 118
merchant, coal, 104
metal worker, 118
midwife, 150, 164
miller, 82
miner, 118
monitor, 128
nail maker, 118
nurse, 164
pedlar, 90
photographer, 146
pilot, 154
potter, 64
printer, 84
publican, 130
railway contractor, 124
rope maker, 118
sack maker, 118
sawyer, 120
schoolmaster, 112
scourer, 120
servant, 72, 84, 140
sewing machinist, 120
shirt maker, 120
shoemaker, 78
shopkeeper, 74, 90
solicitor, 30
spinner, 78
stainer of chairs, 120
stockbroker, 124
straw-hat maker, 90
tailor, 90
tailoress, 120
tallow chandler, 90
teacher, 128, 160
tradesman, 72, 78
trouser maker, 120
tweed warper, 120
tyer, 120
vest maker, 120
weaver, 40, 82, 120
wharfinger, 104
woodman, 121
wool stapler, 54
woollen draper, 78
woolman, 40
yeoman, 54, 76, 84, 110, 112

191

INDEX

Transport and communications, 28, 30, 50, 72, 110
  aircraft, 154, 156
  barges, 50, 76, 104
  bicycles, 146, 148
  boats, 10, 50, 104
  bus, 112, 146, 148
  by water, 28, 76
  cars, 146, 148, 156, 166
    Aston Martin, 148
    Bampton Voiturette, 148
    BMW, 148
    Bullnose Morris, 148
    Jaguar, 148
    MG sports car, 148
    Mini, 148
    Morris Cowley, 148
    Rover, 148
  carts, 50, 106, 144
  coaches, 74, 102, 166
  coaches, mail, 102
  coaches, stage, 102
  helicopters, 156
  horseback, 50, 90
  motorcycle, 148
  packhorses, 50, 102, 106
  wagons, 102
  See also Canals; Railways; Rivers; Roads
Treacher, family, 122
Trees, 24, 48, 154
  beech, 6
Tribes and tribal regions, 14
  Atrebates, 14, 16
  Catuvellauni, 14, 16
  Dobunni, 14, 16
  Gewisse, 18
Tring, 108
Trowbridge, 120, 122
Turner, Sir Edward, 98
Turville, 24
Tusmore, 56, 84, 98, 100, 121, 124
Tyrrell, James, 98

Unemployment, 82, 128, 144
United States of America,
  air force bases, 156
  bases, 154
  military hospital, 154
University of Oxford, 8, 44, 70, 72, 74, 80, 88, 96, 100, 118, 122, 146, 160
  All Souls College, 58, 62, 74
  attitude to religion, 84
  Balliol College, 62
  Brasenose College, 84
  Canterbury College, 46
  Cardinal College, 80
  Christ Church, 44, 66, 70, 72, 74, 80, 94, 132, 166; Tom Tower in, 74
  Corpus Christi College, 74, 82
  decline of, 74
  development of, 50
  Durham College, 46
  establishment of, 62
  Exeter College, 44, 62
  Gloucester Hall, 46, 72, 84
  graduates of, 84
  King Henry VIII's College, 80
  Lincoln College, 62
  Magdalen College, 58, 60, 62, 74, 82, 84
  Merton College, 44, 62, 70, 94, 124, 132
  MPs for, 126
  New College, 62, 66, 70, 94

Oriel College, 60, 62, 84
Pembroke College, 74
properties before 1500, 62
Queen's College, 62, 74, 122
role in tourism, 166
role of, 132
St Bernard's College, 46
St Hugh's College, 154
St John's College, 44, 72, 84, 94, 132, 138, 146
St Mary's College, 46, 84
teacher training colleges, 128
theology school, 62
Trinity College, 44, 72, 80, 84
University College, 62, 84
university library, 62
Wadham College, 74
Worcester College, 74
Upper Heyford,
  air base, 156
  airfield, 154
  barn, 66
  manor, 32
  wharf, 104
Upper Heyford *or* Lower Heyford, hillfort, 14
Urbanisation *see* Towns
Ushers of Trowbridge, brewers, 122
Uxmore, 22, 24

Vagrants, 144
Vanbrugh, Sir John, 98
Verney Junction, 108
Vestries, 78, 116
Vicarages, 30, 42, 44
  perpetual, 44
Vikings, influence of, 64
Villeins, 34
Violence, 142

Wadard, 32
Wadworth's, brewers, 122
Wales, 50, 70, 78
  border of, 102
  coast of, 108
Wales, north, 102
  conquest of, 36
Wales, south, 104, 108, 124, 148
Wall-painting, 92
Wallingford, 26, 28
  Anglo-Saxon settlement in, 18
  archaeology of, 12
  brewery, 122
  canal, 28
  castle, 8, 36, 66, 94
  industry in, 122
  maltings, 122
  market, 38
  poor law union, 144
  pottery in, 64
  role in Civil War, 94
Walls and ramparts,
  of castles, 36
  of Oxford, 28, 70, 72, 94
  of towns, 16, 36, 70, 72
Walter of Merton, 62
Walter, William, 98
Wantage, 16
War and warfare,
  Admiralty, 154
  against the French, 98
  against the Scots, 88

air raids, 154
Bomber Command, 156
Civil War, 72, 74, 84, 86, 88, 92, 94, 98
Cold War, 156
Falklands campaign, 156
First World War, 108, 112, 148, 164
Gulf Wars, 156
Hundred Years War, 44, 58
in Bosnia, 156
in Kosovo, 156
Korean War, 156
Napoleonic Wars, 114, 120
nuclear threat, 156
Oxford and Buckinghamshire Light Infantry, 154
prisoners of war, 154
Royal Air Force, 154, 156
Second Boer War, 164
Second World War, 104, 122, 124, 148, 150, 154, 156
Strategic Air Command, 156
Warborough, 120
  nonconformists in, 86
  Shillingford in, *q.v.*
Wardington, mill, 68
Wareham, 70
Warfare *see* War
Warpsgrove, 24, 46
Warren Row, Maidenhead, 156
Warrens,
  free, 48
  rabbit, 48
Warwick, 98
Warwickshire, 98, 104, 134, 140, 144
  coalfield in, 104
  topography of, 6
Wastes and wastelands, 34, 36, 48, 72, 110, 114
Watcombe, 22
Water Eaton, 24, 82, 154
  manor, 124
Waterhouse, Alfred, 124
Waterperry, 6, 24, 56, 62, 84
  gardens, 166
  house, 98
Watersheds, 6
Waterstock, 24
  house, 98
  Draycot in, *q.v.*
Waterways *see* Rivers
Waterwheels, 68
Watkins Farm, Northmoor, 14
Watlington, 24, 52, 108
  adult education centre, 160
  breweries, 122
  cottage hospital, 164
  foundry, 118
  grammar school, 78
  industry in, 121
  market house, 78
  nonconformists in, 86
  park, 98
  population of, 136, 138
  railways in, 106
  shopkeepers in, 90
  urban growth of, 106
Watlington Park, 124
Waynflete, William, Bishop of Winchester, 62
Wealth, 52, 70
Weapons, 82
Weather *see* Climate

Webbe, James, Vicar of Barford St Michael, 82
Weedon, 108
Weirs, 28, 50, 68, 104
Welfare *see* Health
Wells, 20
Wells (of Wallingford), brewers, 122
Wendlebury, 121
Wenman,
  family, 80, 84
  Sir Francis, 89
  Philip, Viscount Wenman, 98
  Richard, 54
  Thomas, Viscount Wenman, 88, 89
Wentworth, Sir Peter, 89
Wessex, 46, 64, 70
  king of, 20, 46
West Saxons, 18
  bishopric, 26
West Weald, in Bampton, 130
Westcott Barton, 120
Westminster, 89
Westmorland, 102, 140
Weston-on-the-Green, 24, 121, 154
  air base, 156
  airfield, 154
  church, 42
  manor, 124
Westwell, 12, 100
Wharfs, 50, 74, 104
Wheatfield, 24
Wheatley, 8, 24, 50, 84, 118
  Anglo-Saxon settlement in, 18
  Lady Spencer-Churchill College of Education, 160
Wheatley Bridge, 24
Whistler, John, 88, 89
Whitbread, Samuel, 100
Whitchurch,
  sands, 8
  society, 142
White Horse, Vale of, 110, 150
Whitelocke (Whitelock),
  Sir Bulstrode, 88, 94
  James, 89
Widford, 24
Widows, 116, 118, 130
Wiggington, 22
Wilberforce, Samuel, Bishop of Oxford, 134
Wilcote, 16
  nonconformists in, 86
Wilkinson, William, 124
Willaston, 22
William the Conqueror, 32
Williams,
  Sir John, 82; as master of the king's jewels, 80
  John, Lord Williams, 96
Wiltshire, 88, 89, 134, 136, 138, 140
Winchcombe, abbey, 46
Winchester, diocese, bishop of, 40, 44, 48, 54, 78; *see also* Waynflete, William
Winchester, 50, 64, 70
Windebanke, Sir Francis, 88, 89

Windmill Hill, Nettlebed, 10
Windsor, deanery, dean of, 132
Windsor, 140
  castle, 8
Witney, 22, 50, 52, 64, 78, 148, 154
  aerodrome, 154
  airfield, 148
  at time of Domesday, 32
  blankets from, 40
  borough, 78
  boundaries of, 68
  breweries, 122
  Butter Cross market house, 78
  church, 44
  cloth-making industry in, 40, 82
  clothier from, 80
  coal supplied to, 104
  district, 112
  industry in, 38, 78, 120, 148
  malting in, 78
  manor, 48
  market, 76, 82
  medieval development of, 38
  MP for, 126
  nonconformists in, 86, 134, 162
  people of, 124, 130
  population of, 38, 136, 138
  railways in, 106, 108
  schools in, 128, 160
  shopkeepers in, 90
  timber houses in, 66
  urban growth of, 106, 158
  vicar of, 100
  wealth of, 52, 54
  West Oxfordshire Technical College, 160
  wool trade in, 40
  Newland; and Woodgreen in, *q.v.*
Witney, deanery, 54
Wokingham, 140
Wolseley, Sir Charles, 89
Wolsey, Thomas, cardinal, 80
Wolvercote, 10, 24, 136, 146, 152
  junction, 108
  mill, 118
  Duke's Cut in, *q.v.*
Wolverhampton, 108
Wolverton, 108
Women,
  education of, 130
  role of, 40, 116, 130, 164
Womersley, 89
Woodcote, 24
  RAF depot, 154
Woodeaton, 24
  house, 156
Woodford, 108
Woodgreen, Witney, 156
Woodperry, 24
  house, 98
Woods *see* Forests
Woodstock, 24, 34, 38, 50, 82, 89
  castle, 36
  corporation, 38, 78
  district, 150

festivals in, 166
foundry, 118
gild, 38
industry in, 120
inns in, 78
manor, 94
market, 76
medieval development of, 38
MPs for, 88, 126
nonconformists in, 134
Oxfordshire Museum, 166
park, 48, 98
  mill in, 68
  royal palace in, 78
people of, 90
population of, 136, 138
Public Assistance Institution in, 164
race-meetings, 78
railways in, 106, 108
roads from and to, 102
royal park, 82
shopkeepers in, 90
urban growth of, 106, 158
Blenheim Palace in, *q.v.*
Woodstock, Old, 120
Wool and woollen cloth, 38, 40, 50, 52, 70, 76, 120
Wootton, 18, 120
Wootton, hundred, 136
Worcester, 24, 28, 50, 104, 109
  cathedral archive, 26
Worcestershire, 140
Worminghall, 56
Wornum, R. S., 124
Worsham Mill, Asthall, 120
Worton, 20
  tithes, 42
Wrench, William, 120
Wroxton, 22, 96, 120
  priory, 46, 80, 96, 124
  vicarage, 44
Wychwood Forest, 8, 24, 26, 32, 34, 36, 46, 48, 54, 64, 96, 110, 112, 114
Wychwood Brewery, 122
Wycombe poor law union, 144
Wyfold Court, 124
Wykham Mill, 148
Wykham Park, 154
Wytham Hill, 50

Yarnton, 10, 12, 14, 24, 82, 108
  Anglo-Saxon settlement in, 20
  church, 20
  manor, 20, 124
  Cresswell Field in, *q.v.*
Yaxley, Richard, 84
Yelford, 24, 54
  manor, 66
York, 50, 70, 88
Yorkshire, 140
  cleric from, 58
  people from, 120
Young, Arthur, 102; as secretary to the Board of Agriculture, 110